Secret Cities of Old South America

Secret Cities of Old South America

HAROLD T. WILKINS

NEW YORK

Secret Cities of Old South America
Cover Copyright © 2008 by Cosimo, Inc.

Secret Cities of Old South America was originally published in 1952.

For information, address:
P.O. Box 416, Old Chelsea Station
New York, NY 10011

or visit our website at:
www.cosimobooks.com

Ordering Information:
Cosimo publications are available at online bookstores. They may
also be purchased for educational, business or promotional use:
- *Bulk orders:* special discounts are available on bulk orders for reading
groups, organizations, businesses, and others. For details contact
Cosimo Special Sales at the address above or at info@cosimobooks.com.
- *Custom-label orders:* we can prepare selected books with your cover or
logo of choice. For more information, please contact Cosimo at
info@cosimobooks.com.

Cover Design by www.popshopstudio.com

ISBN: 978-1-60520-321-8

I have, myself, a sketch of a small cross in serpentine form found in an Indian grave in the Canari territory of Ecuador, at Quienjo. Two French archaeologists very dogmatically, after admitting that no object denoting European influence was found in that grave, say: "It is a Christian emblem manufactured in the first years after the Conquest by Indians who continued on the lines of other pagan amulets." So sure, messieurs, are you? Did you fail to note the significance of the fact that this cross was of *green* colour?

—from Chapter Four: "South America's Amazons Existed!"

FOREWORD

ANY MAN or woman who has seen half a century pass over old England from the vanished age of the merry nineties of last century, which, however, were by no means so jocund for many folk outside the country house set, may recognize that the differences between the mental attitudes of the late Victorian, the Edwardian and the Georgian ages might be epitomized as follows: The dogmatic Victorian would say: "It *is* so!" The more urbane Edwardian, with a sceptical lift of a humorous eyebrow, would venture an "*Is* it so?" But our own harder and more austere (?) age would be likely to come out with a Shavian expletive: "It is—well *not* so!"

I am reminded of the above by a letter I have just had which seems to have been posted aboard a liner bound for New York from Southampton, by a young fellow who had read my *Mysteries of Ancient South America*, in, as he says, the intervals of student archæological work on the Clausentum and the Saxon site at Southampton. He is a Harvard student, and he says, *inter alia*: "The entire body of *reputable* scientists have recently come over to the side of believers in ancient giants, with discoveries of early man in Java and China. Professor Blank of Harvard and others now tend to regard the tooth of a giant 'anthropoid' found in a 'Dragon shop' in China, not as that of an ape, but from a primitive type of man. It is calculated that if the proportions of this tooth of Gigantopithecus were similar to that of modern man, the giant would have been twenty feet tall; but there are physiological reasons against that supposition, and, besides, outsize teeth have been found in other gigantic jaws. It does, however, indicate the tremendous size of Gigantopithecus."

My comment on this polite letter is: "But what about the attitude of the other scientists, evolutionary biologists, and palæontologists, say, in Great Britain? Has *their* reputation suffered a slight dimming?"

Gloucester
1950   H. T. W.

Colonel Percy Fawcett.

SECRET CITIES OF OLD SOUTH AMERICA

CONTENTS

ILLUSTRATIONS

Plates

Illustrations in text

and numerous other sketches and diagrams.

CHAPTER ONE

MYSTERIES OF A LOST WORLD

Time like an ever rolling stream
Bears all its sons away.
They fly forgotten as a dream
Dies at the opening day.
                    —ISAAC WATTS—1674–1748.

PROBABLY of no other country are these words of the famous Anglican hymn—words of a poet, not a maker of pious doggerel—truer than of the lands of mysterious South America, cradle of the dim and ancient world's earliest civilization. That mighty continent over which the deep floods of Time have rolled, rolled as with the sound of drums passing out from the despairing land to the boundless, heedless estranging ocean, sinking man and his culture into its depths with "a bubbling groan, without a grave, unknelled, uncoffined and unknown". And ever as the night draws on and the remote and indifferent stars glitter in the vault beyond the Milky Way, old ocean's waters on which Time "writes no wrinkles" return with a sad and ghostly moaning, with the dirge of Victor Hugo's drowned corpses to "*des mères à genoux . . . ces voix désespérées . . . quand vous venez vers nous*".

To those not blinded by preconceived notions and *l'idée fixe* of consecrated fallacies this old continent and North and Central America have their sagas graved in petroglyphs in the weathered rocks of mysterious cañons. They are the still, small voices in desert places which say to those who have eyes to see and ears to hear, not merely that man has existed on this planet thousands of years earlier than encyclopædic historians, archæologists, anthropologists, ethnologists and others of that ilk suppose or theorize; but that civilization itself on this ancient earth is something far more hoary than Menes, Sanconiathon, Berosus, or the kings of Sumer and Akkadia!

Thirty-six years ago—and I am writing in the early autumn of 1947—the expedition of the American savant[1] Dr. Ales Hrdlička, then curator of the Smithsonian Institution at Washington, D.C., went out to the Argentine and Perú to hunt for geological evidence that ancient man lived in South America ages before written history records the fact. In particular, Hrdlička planned to make a collection in Perú that would help anthropologists to enlarge the bounds of our extremely meagre knowledge about the type of prehistoric men in

---

[1] *Vide: Some Results of Recent Anthropological Explorations in Perú:* Ales Hrdlička (Smithsonian Institution, Washington. D.C. [Misc. Collections,] 1911.)

that ancient land. As readers of my book *Mysteries of Ancient South America*[1] may recall, there is good reason for supposing that the traditions and folklore collected from the Peruvian priests and Quichua learned classes by the more thoughtful Spanish historians of the age of the conquest, and especially those fragments that have survived from the lost manuscripts of Blas Valera, embody something much more than myths and fairy tales of an ancient race. These myths, so-called, have been almost entirely held in contempt by the orthodox historians and the academic, or museum archæologist who is too often the most unteachable of all the omniscient fellows who clutter up the way leading to real enlargement of the bounds of knowledge and the attainment of a revivifying spirit of research. These are the gentlemen who, in relation to South American prehistory, are animated by impulses which it would in general be a travesty to call scientific. I feel sure that they will all be deeply appreciative of my remarks and will see fit to undergo the painful process of jettisoning old fallacies and hypotheses rendered obsolete by newer data.

In Perú, the Hrdlička expedition discovered ancient skulls showing compound fractures resulting from the savage hand-to-hand fighting. In prehistoric camps, such as that on Bredon Hill top, in England, or in the Nilotic regions where ancient Egyptians fought with the mysterious shepherd Kings of the Hyksos, or Shasu, similar injuries may be seen in the human remains unearthed from the camp-site, or on the skulls and trunks of some of the Pharaohs. In the case of the Peruvian remains, some of these injuries, or depressions of the crania, had been inflicted by round, or irregularly-shaped stones hurled from a great distance, with immense velocity, by sling-throwers.

These prehistoric men in ancient Perú were armed also with large wooden clubs, extremely hard, and in whose ends splints of copper, or stone had been fastened. (Such weapons seem to be of the sort described as *macanas* in certain old Spanish manuscripts which I have translated and used in this book, and in my preceding work on South America.)

These races also had hatchets both of *copper* and stone. As is known, use and knowledge of certain metals ran side by side with the Stone Age technique of the Neolithic era, in old Europe, and certainly in South America.

Surgical examinations further disclosed a remarkable fact: these ancient races of Western South America had attained advanced medical knowledge in which they made use of a number of things unknown to us to-day. They also well knew of the dangers of a free exposure of wounds to the open air. They also apparently recognized not only that sunlight and rays in the spectrum had the power of asepsis and sterilization, but that if a badly wounded man lay in the sunshine and bathed his injuries in the solar radiation, remarkable cures might

[1] Rider, London, 1946.

be effected. (There are Indian tribes in both Brazil and regions of North-western South America who, to-day, both know and practise this sun-cure technique of healing for terrible wounds.)

Their medicine men also recognized and discriminated between ague, rheumatism, fevers, cerebral disturbances and mental aberration. Fragments of flint sharpened to a point were used for excising and bleeding, and a flint sharpened on the edge played its part in their surgical operations. In their processes of mummification the dead were treated very much as those of old Egypt.

I do not know if any member of the Hrdlička expedition asked himself if these evidences of ancient technique and knowledge indicated the probable, or possible, existence of some extremely ancient and vanished civilization long preceding the age of the remains. It was not till twenty years later that a certain *Señor*,[1] who is the *haciendero* of Esmeraldas, Ecuador, sent down divers off that coast who brought up from a drowned city, off the foreshore of his estate, statuettes of men and women of Asian, Mongolian, Caucasian and Egyptian type, with mirrors, and, one is told, even *lenses*, seals inscribed with hieroglyphs, and pornographic relics. Such finds, in themselves would be evidence of an advanced and extremely ancient and unknown civilization, which had become decadent, and which might or might not be, Mu or Lemuria.

Again, both in North-Central and in South America there is the riddle of the petroglyphs—Odysseys on the rock-walls and cliffs and river-cañons. Among these signs are some that are certainly not Amero-Indian pictographs of some race of nomad hunters. Rather are they signs that someone who passed that lone way, thousands of years ago, either had had contact with ancient civilizations in the Americas, or crystallized in the alien stone ancestral memories of such highly cultured races. It is now believed that the cave-men of prehistoric America, like those in Europe, carved objects in soapstone, or painted figures on walls to help them in working magic in their hunts for animals. Mountain sheep and other animals are recognizable in these early North American pictures and were probably painted[2] for use in rites meant to increase the fertility of the hunted herds, help in their capture or hunting and so plentifully supply food. Other prehistoric pictures marked the sites of water-holes . . . but, as I have pointed out elsewhere in this book, and in my previous volume on the *Mysteries of South America*, there are quite other figures not explicable on these grounds. For example, there are moon-faced, angular figures of human beings scratched as petroglyphs on rocks,

---

[1] He wrote me a letter, sent *via* the British Foreign Office, complaining of "preposterous misrepresentations" by a writer of Russian, or Balkan-Slav origin, but did not reply to my request that he would be so good as to send me a short account of his own investigations.—AUTHOR.

[2] In a cave, near Alpera, Spain, are palæolithic wall paintings, depicting Magdalenian hunters of ibex, with head-dresses remarkably like those of the North American, or Red Indian, of many thousands of years later! (*Vide:* Prof. l'Abbé Breuil, in *L'Anthropologie.* 1912.)

some of which figures seem to represent dancers in ceremonial rites or deities. Some of these deities are garbed in a peculiar dress and suggest men of a very ancient civilized race whose megalithic cities have been found in Central America, in lower southern California, and over the border in Baja California, as well as in South America, down to the altiplanicie of the Argentina.

Again, in Nevada and eastern California, explorers have found elaborately engraved, or drawn figures which *seem* to be "picture puzzles". In some cases, these enigmatic devices have been found deeply buried under old mineral deposits. It is clear that they are extremely ancient pictures, and their meaning has yet to be revealed and interpreted. Their true interpretation will probably result in a drastic recasting of present theories of orthodox archæologists and anthropologists about the age of civilization in the Americas.

Yet another pointer—a living flesh and blood one—to the existence of very ancient highly cultured races in South America are the Tapuyas, a race in the east of Brazil and almost certainly refugees from some long vanished and very remote civilization of white and red people. In the late sixteenth century, the Tapuyas seem to have fallen on evil days and to have become the anthropophagous victims of other Brazilian tribes. Southey, in his *History of Brazil*, tells of an Indian crone to whom a Jesuit missioner had administered extreme unction. The Jesuit asked if he could do anything more for her. Said this old crone: "Ah woe is me! My stomach is so queasy it rebels against everything; but, father, if you could only get me the little hand of a tender Tapuya boy, I think I could pick the little bones. But who is there to go out and shoot one for me?"

(Not extreme unction but a dose of curare would seem to have befitted this old harridan's case. It urgently demanded, and would have had among some of the Brazilian and other South American Indians who prepare this volatile poison, prompt removal, as Cunninghame Graham would have said, to an Indian Trapalanda!)

Colonel Fawcett, who lived among the Tapuyas for some time, said of them: "The Tapuyas are fair as the English. They have hands and feet that are small and delicate. One finds them in the east of Brazil. They are refugees from an older and very great civilization. Their features are of great beauty and they have white, golden and auburn hair. Their skill in the working of gold and the cutting of gems is of high order. They wore diamonds and ornaments of jade".[1]

Allied to the Tapuyas are the Motopaquez who are fair-skinned and *bearded*, in a land where beards are not found among Indians.

About the year 1855 came another revelation of South America's mysterious past when remarkable discoveries were made in the old Spanish province of Nueva Granada, the modern Colombia, of El Liberador, Simon Bolivar. It was in that very region of the upper Rio Magdalena on the wooded-foothills of the Central Cordillera where

[1] A form of jadeite, known as nephrite, is found in Brazil.

Monseñor F. Lunardi, of Bogotá, made his strange finds, of probably the same date and unknown provenance, in 1930–31. (I shall refer to the Lunardi discoveries in a later book.) Close to the town of Neiva, about 150 miles north of the equator, there was discovered, in the course of some excavations on a general's estate, a grotto or cavern the entrance to which was at ground level. The vaults of this grotto were in part natural, formed by the bowels of a mountain, and in part cut out by the chisels of man. Right at the entrance was a colossal tiger carved in very well preserved stone who was the guardian of this vault. The sculptures were in a style and magnitude reminiscent of ancient monuments in old Hindostan; though the reader may understand that one does *not* infer that they were derived from the Orient, but rather that, it may be, antecedently, from some common source, possibly in a long vanished and submerged Pacific island-continent.

This strange grotto was located in a rather narrow ravine between two mountains of the central cordillera of the north-western Andes. The spot is lonely and awesome, to which may be owing its preservation from the hand of the vandal and the destroyer, or militarist.

Now, it seemed evident to the discoverer, General José Hilario Lopez, that in a far-off day, this mysterious and ancient grotto, instead of being located in the recesses of lonely and inaccessible mountains, must originally have lain close to a plain, and that an ancient town had stood close to it. He not unnaturally theorized that it was impossible that such a colossal block of stone, out of which the tiger monument had been graven, could have been transported across high and rugged mountains, over difficult and roadless terrain, such as one sees in our own day. All round about, too, the region was entirely barren and deserted.

Elsewhere in South America, one, to-day, finds that in regions where, in ancient days, vast plains and populated towns existed, there are now only almost unscalable mountains with steep or vertical cliffs and precipice-walls, towering one over the other, set closely together and riven by terrible gorges. They are tokens of the cataclysm that ruined Atlantean Brazil and elevated the proto-Andes.

Going a little way from the grotto and nearer the town of Neiva, Señor Lopez, who was once president of the state of Colombia, started to make considerable excavations in his extensive landed properties. At depths ranging from $6\frac{1}{2}$ to some 16 feet he had taken out colossal statues of great beauty and symmetry. They were statues of *horses*, not, it is usually stated, found in South America, before the Spanish conquistadores brought over their jennets from Castile. There were other great statues of monkeys, toads[1] and men and women.

---

[1] Compare with similar statues of grotesque toads found in prehistoric sites in the ancient island of Haiti, which, by the way, derive from some black "Ierian" cult which is assuredly many thousand years older than the Voodooism imported into that old island of the French creole planters by Congo negroes, brought there as slaves to work the plantations, in the sixteenth, seventeenth and eighteenth centuries A.D.

It was remarked as a singular fact that the colossal statues of the men and women faced *east*, in the direction of the rising sun! That way lay the great island-continent of lost Atlantis.

Close to these excavations there was also found a colossal stone table that fifty men, exerting all their united strength, could barely move an inch. This table was finely polished and set on four feet, like claws, exquisitely fashioned by master craftsmen and springing from a single central shaft. There were other relics, like ancient monuments of the Egyptian Pharaohs. These bore vestiges of inscriptions in characters none could read. They, too, had been cut out of a single block of stone.

Hybrid Mu-an type ancient colonist, Colombia, South American highlands. (Note Atlan-Brazilian letters on headgear.)

In this same region of the upper Magdalena in the provinces of Tolima and Nueva Granada, of Colombia, there have been found remains of giant men—*men*, one repeats, not bones of fossil mastodons, mammoths or elephants — of which I shall have more to say, later, in a subsequent book.

We pass on through the nineteenth century to the third decade, of the twentieth, when the Time Spirit was again moved to raise a corner of the veil from this mystery of ancient South America. In the summer of 1931, an expedition was organized by Monseñor Federico Lunardi of the Apostolic nunciature of Bogotá. I do not know if Monseñor Lunardi is a member of the Society of Jesus; but whatever may be said or thought of this Order, their members are certainly distinguished by centuries of research and out-of-the-way knowledge connected as well with archæology and prehistory in South America, as with the most modern theories and applications of physical science. In particular, speaking as a research worker into this obscure and difficult branch of American prehistory, I would give a great deal to possess photostatic copies of the manuscripts in which Jesuit missioners recorded their discoveries of unknown dead and ancient cities of gold and mystery in Brazil and Paraguay, as well as in western and north-western South America from the late sixteenth to the eighteenth century.

The Monseñor found more remains of some unknown and extremely ancient and highly civilized race once inhabiting this region of ancient South America, of a pre-cataclysmic age. He says that the culture of this unknown race ranks with that of the mysterious races of the Mayas of Yucatan and Guatemala. Their ruins in the upper Magdalena territory lie in the little known and little explored region of San Agustin, deep in forests, jungles, and practically unknown mountains. The empire ruled by the great unknown extended, so far as discoveries up to the present import, some sixty miles along the Upper Rio Magdalena. It may be remembered that from this region of gold and mystery came to old Cartagena much of the gold, laden, into caravels and galleons, for which the buccaneers of Barty Sharp's and Morgan's days lay in wait beyond the barra of Barrameda. I have a fragment of a manuscript of Cromwell's day in which some unknown English buccaneer speaks of the gold of this very region, when it may be expected, and recommending hardy English spirits and cut-throat blades of fortune of that picturesque day to go up river and get some of this gold from the source.

But to return to the ancient unknown race: they built great canals for irrigation purposes, erected colossal statues which they cut from the living rock and transported by some means, *apparently* across high mountains from a great distance. Lunardi appears quite wrongly to suppose that the country in which these ruins are found has always been as one sees it now. It is clear that many of these colossal statues have been carved to depict from the life the great men over whose tombs they were erected.

The people in this remote Colombian village of San Agustin have actually erected some of these colossal statues of ancient men in their Catholic capilla-plaza, and they uphold the marble figure of el Liberador, Simon Bolivar, in a park at San Bogotá. About these megalithic remains there is more than a suggestion of the strange monuments found in Easter Island and other Polynesian and Micronesian islands, such as Ponape, Malden, Pitcairn and the Marquesas. Indeed, the ruins *appear* to antedate even the Andes![1]

Thanks to the courtesy of the British Foreign Office, at a time when Mr. Winston S. Churchill was acting Foreign Secretary, and aided by His Majesty's diplomatic representatives in South America, I got in touch with Monseñor Lunardi, who is *Arzobispo titular de Sede Nuncio Apostólico,* and who had been transferred to Tegucigalpa, in the Republic of Honduras. He wrote me an interesting letter, in

[1] Madame H. P. Blavatsky years ago cited some mysterious secret records of old Hindostan which state that Easter Island, a sort of Valhalla of old Lemuria, emerged with all its statues and volcanoes after long submersion on the bed of the Pacific. Before it arose from the bed of the ocean, she said, a colony of Atlanteans had settled in the island. *Quien sabe?* This may be no more fantastic a theory than the parallel one that Tiahuanacu, now on a paramo of the bleak Andes, some 12,000 feet in the clouds, also arose from the bed of the Pacific, with the ruins which have been so terribly ravaged by piratical conquistadores of Pizarro's day and modern Bolivians of the age of railroads.—AUTHOR.

March 1945, in which he says he believes the San Agustin figures are portrait statues:

> One of the finest statues of the San Agustin race I found—its existence had been unknown—in a tomb, covered with great stone slabs. It had originally been painted red and blue, as are also statues at Copán, of the Mayans, in Honduras. That these statues are idols or gods, as has been theorized by previous investigators, I doubt. I believe they represent the dead, buried in these tombs, to whom were rendered a peculiar worship. There are also statues of various animals that probably represent ancestors that have become animals in the other life, or animals venerated by the people of that place.
> The area in which these statues are found is very large, comprising . . . what, to-day, is the whole region round the Colombian massif, whence take their rise the Rios Magdalena and Cauca. I have found twenty-four more statues than were previously known to exist. Some of those found earlier were unhappily lost by accident.

Lunardi then repeats a story first given currency by a previous German archæologist, Dr. K. Th. Stoepel, director of the Heidelberg Museum (1911), that an alleged British Museum expedition (1899–1902), lost the greater part of a collection of colossal statues and photos when a boat was overturned in rapids on the Rio Patiá, near Tumaco, and that only one of the original statues, transported along the route of the Rio Magdalena, reached the British Museum, to which it was sent by "Vice-Admiral Dowing (*sic*) in 1899". The Keeper of the Department of Ethnography, Mr. H. J. Braunholtz, tells me that no one was sent there by the British Museum, but it is possible that an unofficial expedition may have had financial or moral support from the British Museum. The one statue that the British Museum has was given by Rear-Admiral Dowding, in 1899.

Monseñor Lunardi advances, in this letter, a theory which is probably near the truth, though he admits that *Todavía queda un enigma* (Nevertheless, it remains an enigma). He says:

> Besides these twenty-four statues I also found a fountain and pit-holes, or small bowls, that I believe are not of natural origin, as thought by Dr. Th. Preuss (formerly of the Berlin Ethnographical Museum), but are artificial. Preuss did not find, as I did, carvings of heads, nor the *canals* . . . According to the belief of the ancient inhabitants, death was the continuation of life, somewhat spiritualized, and it was carried on in the tombs, where were interred the race's slaves, women, tools, and seeds for cultivating the land in the other life.

Were these mysterious megalithic men of this region of the ancient South America colonists from the drowned continent of MU?

I shall have much more to say about this and the colossal statues and portrait heads of these enigmatic people, in a subsequent book; but I may here venture to cite from a letter I wrote to Lunardi, and which, if he received it in the spring of 1945, he did not answer:

MONSENOR LUNARDI—

Two glyphs (*simbolos*) appear on two of these San Agustın statues, one of them perhaps a figure of a woman or a goddess(?), and one glyph is the stairway symbol of evolution from a central sun of the universe. Perhaps an exoteric concept of the old people of Lemuria, or Mu, or Rutas. It appears on the neck behind the shoulder, and is on both statues. These signs are found all over North and South America and in ancient ceramics of the pueblo Indians, in the southern states and western states of the U.S.A., and Mexico. Also, it is found on one or more of the monoliths at Tiahuanacu the mysterious. This mystic sun must not be identified with a demi-ourgos, such as Brahma, or Jehovah-Jahveh, but perhaps with the *agnosto Theo* (Unknown God) of the Acts of the Apostles, on Mars Hill, at Athens. This sign also appears on the head of a prehistoric statue of a woman found near Vera Cruz, and now in the Berliner Museum für Völkerkunde.

May be, both these unknown races were heliolithic, older than 15,000 years ago, and dating back to an age when there was a world-wide diffusion of *sun-stone* culture from or to the old Mediterranean and Europe, and to or from America, or the ancient Pacific. The peculiar dentition of the most *farouche* and savage-looking of these strange statues of San Agustin—tusks projecting from the top jaw—is found not only in ancient Mayan and Mexican statues, but on a stone head, of prehistoric date, with similar headgear to that of San Agustin, dug up in the interior of Costa Rica. It is called the culture of the *Guetar*, in that country. *If* the Mayas of the First Empire originated in the Andes of N.W. South America, they have inherited some of these rites and this symbolism from the culture of these San Augustin *megaliticos*; but I, myself, suspect that both derive from a far earlier and exceedingly brutal type of "civilization"—found in ancient Mu, or Lemuria.

I theorize that the San Agustin *megaliticos* hailed from the drowned continent in the Pacific—not *directly* from what is now called Easter Island, but from the land known in the Hindu "myths" as Rutas-Mu, where was spoken Sansar, the tongue of the sun, and the parent of Sanscrit. They may have had later contacts—at a much later phase—with the ancients of Tiahuanacu. Remember what Fray Diego de Alcobaso says of the long-vanished and fine statues of men and women that were once seen standing in a stream on that bleak *paramo* of the Andes. Of course, when the latter statues were executed, the land was about 12,000 feet lower and far warmer. May be, cataclysm caused this ancient race of San Agustin to migrate to what is now the central Cordillera of the Andes, in Colombia. As to your theory of the After Life in the strange tombs of San Agustin, you may have noted that one of these San Agustin statues bears a sort of *moleta de viaje* (travel-hat) and a *baculo* (staff). *Osiris*, of Egypt, *once a man*, before he was deified, also had a staff and hat like these. I believe, not without evidence, that the proto-Egyptians, if they did not originate in, certainly went to South America in a very remote day. In old Egypt lie the clues to the lost continent of Mu . . . As to your Maya labours, let us hope you may carry us forward to the day when we shall be able to read the *non-calendrical glyphs* whose decipherment was stopped by the criminal fanaticism of Bishop Landa and Bishop

Nuñez de Vega of Huehuetan, who both destroyed, or burnt invaluable records and relics of the Quiché-Mayans and the *Votanes*. And, by the way, do not confuse Votan or Odin, or Woden, with Quetzalcoatl, the latter an Atlantean horse of a very different colour. . . .

As you know, we know nothing of the life, culture, and range of secular knowledge of the Mayans, with whom is associated a race of very Caucasian, or non-Cambodian type. They had a glyph denoting a period of 3,200,000 years. Their lost knowledge was probably very extensive. The canals you found in San Augustin rather recall what was found in Ponape . . . The natives of Honduras say, *à propos* of the mysterious *Lolton*, or Cave of Flowers, a Mayan subterranean near the village of Oxcutzcab, Yucatan, that kings, priests and nobles are buried somewhere in recesses of the many and still unexplored, labyrinthine passages of the vast caverns there. They add that *pishans*, or spooks, resent bitterly the intrusion of explorers and will lead them astray. It may be surmised that the subterranean rites of the San Agustin *megaliticos*, deriving as they do from an extremely ancient land lost by cataclysm, were inherited by the Mayans.

It is obvious that, at some date, a Cambodian type of race fused with the men whose features were more like mine or yours than the Buddha-like, slant-eyed priest, or leader, whose stela was removed from old to new Copán of the Second Maya Empire.

Con mis saludos más atentos y el deseo de que su obra tenga un buén exito quedo de V.S. muy atto S.S.

HAROLD T. WILKINS

From a "Bomb Alley" of a blasted region of Kent, in war-year, Spring 1945.

Before closing this passage of the mysteries of an Ancient South America, may I say that I hope, in years to come, that British archæologists and museum experts will *not* continue to be conspicuous by their absence in South America? It is a matter of money, and one hopes that some man with money to leave and a desire to perpetuate his name to future generations—such as, shall we say, Mr. George Bernard Shaw?—will step in and fill the gap left by the late Lord Moyne, assassinated in Cairo by scoundrels of the infamous Stern gang of modern Judæa. In an age like this, we can ill spare such men as Lord Moyne, but very well spare these terrorists.

I may also, in this place, refer to the mystery of the fate of Colonel P. H. Fawcett, D.S.O., F.R.G.S., his son and a young newspaper camera-man, Raleigh Rimell, of British descent and formerly, I am told, domiciled in California. It will be remembered that, in May 1925, they set out on the trail of some of these dead Atlantean cities in the unexplored region of the vast Matto Grosso, and the *terra incognita* of the vast, unknown Rio Roosevelt-Goyaz plateau whose edge only was traversed, years ago, by the late President Theodore Roosevelt. I am not permitted to cite my informant; but may say that a story I was told in late summer of a recent year seems to me a possible solution of their fate. If this story be true, then Colonel Fawcett was killed defending his son from an assault of outraged Indians one of whose vital taboos had been infringed by the son. Somewhere in the jungle there exists, to-day, a shrunken head. It is shrunken in the manner of the technique of the Kaingang, or the Jivaro *Indiós*. Fate has been hard on this paladin of South American exploration. He and his son must have perished, if my story be true, as I fear it *is* true, somewhere between the years 1926 and 1927. What befell Mr. Rimell my informant did not know. But I fear neither this statement, nor any fuller story I could give, were men's lives not at stake in a matter for which the Indians can hardly be blamed, will avail in removing Fawcett from a cloud of sheer legend and mendacity which, as years go by, will certainly place his last quest in the category of legends about the fate of the *Mary Celeste*, the Man in the Iron Mask, or of ex-Archduke Johann Salvator, *alias* Johann Orth.

Great is truth and it shall prevail, when no man cares a bean whether it prevail or not!

My anonymous informant says:

A few years before the Second World War, I was in a liner crossing the Caribbean and bound for the British West Indies island of Trinidad. On a starry evening, a German passenger, whose name, if my memory is correct—and I can't find the passenger list of which I kept a copy for a long time—was Ehrmann, asked me to come down to his cabin. Carefully closing the door and first looking to see that no one was listening, or loitering in the soft-carpeted corridor outside, he said: "There is a dance in the salon to-night, so we can be sure of not being interrupted. You have asked me several times about the fate of Colonel P. H. Fawcett. Well, I am the only white man alive who can tell you what happened to him after he quitted Dead Horse Camp, in the region of the river Xingú, of the Matto Grosso. in May 1925. In 1932, I went by launch, and then by dug-out or piragua (canoe) to the upper reaches of the Xingú, east of which Fawcett vanished. Dead Horse Camp is midway between the Rio Paranatinga and the Xingú. As you know, he sent back a party of Mafuquas Indians, and either struck eastwards into the Brazilian Highlands, or canoed down the Paranatinga. It is likely, however, that he kept to the higher land in between the Paranatinga and the Rio von Steiner, an affluent of the upper Xingú. . . . Under the green arcades, where the sun strikes down, you can see *chispas* of gold gleaming on the bed of the stream. It was days later when I reached the village for which I was bound. It was remote and some miles from the bank of the stream. Here, in past years, I had undergone the ceremony of blood brotherhood with the Indian cacique. All round the Indians are head-hunters. Now I'll read you an extract from my diary, translating as I go, for it is in German:

"Every time I steer the talk round to the mystery of the Fawcett expedition, the old chief glowers and becomes sullen. He won't speak, nor let his Indians speak, and they are sullen enough . . . I feel they know something . . . A week has passed, and this morning, the old man is in a friendly and cheerful mood. He came to my hut and signed to me to follow him. We went to the council house or palaver hut. It is a big hut, in a clearing on the head of the forest. One Indian warrior was on sentry-go at the door. The chief took me into the big hut and touched my lips with his fingers. Then he said quietly: 'My brother, you stay here.

I go into the forest. Seek not to leave this hut. If you do, the sentry has orders to kill you. I shall return by sunset.' He left, and in an hour I heard the sound of marching feet, as a party went into the forest. The chief's guttural voice gave orders, and then all was silent. Food was brought to me, and I was alone in the hut for hours. It must have been about six when the party came back. They had been away for nine hours, so must have gone a good many miles. The door of the hut opened. He carried a torch in one hand. In the other, he had a bag made of some sort of tree bark. He loosened the strings with his mouth. Then he said: 'You, my blood brother, ask me of Colonel Fawcett. *El coronel* was good man. *He*, too, was my blood brother . . . I now show you something, but you must swear on the white man's God to keep silent the name of me and my tribe' . . . I solemnly promised. 'Look!' said the chief. He drew forth from the sack a small and horribly shrunken head. I started back in horror and nausea. *The features were those of Colonel Fawcett!* . . . The old chief told me that his tribe had given Colonel Fawcett and his son shelter and protection; but the son, he said, had broken a *tabu*. It was a *tabu* whose violation no Indian could forgive. The chief could not save the colonel's son, for, as he said, other tribes of Indians around would have heard, and wiped out his own tribe to the last man, woman, and child had the offence been condoned . . . . 'My blood brother, *el coronel* Fawcett, was killed, defending his son, I could not save him, though so brave and good a man.' The chief spoke with great emotion."

My informant could get no word as to the fate of the third member of the Fawcett party, Raleigh Rimell; so *that* part of the mystery remains unsolved![1]

I am often asked about the location of these dead cities of Hy-Brazil, and some of my correspondents seem not so much concerned with pre-history and the riddles of the dark past, as with easy money to be got by walking in and collecting gold, ancient jewels and platinum that may be lying about. But there is no "easy money" on these trails into the unknown of the heart of old South America. Too often the price of solving these mysteries has to be paid for in blood and life. And that may, or may not have been the case in the mystery of Colonel Fawcett. Who can yet positively say? It is sure that the last word has *not* been said!

From my own scanty data I should say that these dead cities of old Brazil range *west* from the unexplored land, far up the Rio Juara on the Andean eastern foothills, in the country of a tribe connected with the well-known Jivaro head-hunters, to the *east*, in the mostly unexplored territory behind the Serra do Cincorá, in the *sertão* of the province of Bahia. On the *north*, more than one of them may be located far up the mysterious River Trombetas, towards the Tumac Humac ranges on the frontiers of the golden Guianas. There is another

[1] Ehrmann, an anthropologist and metallurgist, travelled, on vacation, to Bolivia, *via* the Matto Grosso fringes. In December, 1949, I am told he said he saw the shrivelled heads of Jack Fawcett and Rimell, in the *aldeia* of the violated *tabu* alleged. Also other relics. The whole story seems incredible bathos, quite out of character with the men concerned. However, Clio is not a silent muse!—AUTHOR.

one, with gold and gems transcending the imagination of the old tale-tellers of the Arabian Nights, which lies far up the other mysterious Rio Branco, towards the Sierras de Parima. Both these affluents of the Marañon, or Amazon, are famed as being the last known treks of famous white fighting women, the South American Amazons, in the seventeenth century and early eighteenth century day when the tough *bandeiristas* of São Paulo and the valiant Spanish pioneers were pushing forward into the unknown from the side of Perú and what is now Ecuador and Goyaz.

To the south-east, another of these definitely Atlantean cities, with moats, causeways and megalithic structures, is located in a spot called by the Indians "Guayra", not many leagues from where flows the Rio Pequéry, in São Paulo. Strange remains of megalithic walls and buildings, statuary of men and women, very ancient symbols and unknown letters and glyphs carved in caves, and on cliff walls, lie in remote spots in mountains and on plateaux, and deep in woods, all the way from Ceara and Maranhão to Pernambuco and Rio de Janeiro. They have been seen by Hollanders, in the early sixteenth century, and by Portuguese and Brazilians, and *Indianistas*, in the eighteenth and early nineteenth centuries. Of them I shall speak in a later book.

Here is an account of one in a remote region of Brazilian Guiana, which I take from a travel diary of my own:

I hear of a place where three streams unite and spread out in the waters of a large and deep *lago* (lake). I am told that some of the "rare plucked uns" among the New York Four Hundred, young men and pretty girls, have visited this place. One knows when one is in the neighbourhood, for one hears, coming through the aisles of the deep forests, a roar of thunderous reverberations. It is one of the *catadupas* which frequently figure in the accounts of the travels of the hardy, valiant bandeiristas into the Geraes and the Goyaz and the Matto Grosso, in the eighteenth century . . . Waters vanish over a lip of rock into a great cavity. Here, a great hole yawns in the earth. Close by, many lichened and grey stone steps of a very ancient stairway, "half as old as Time", like the red rose city of Petræa, are cut in rock of black basalt. Reaching the bottom of this stairway, one is startled to find unknown glyphs, or, as they seem to be, ancient and unknown *letters* cut in the rock, which is dank with the spray of the falling waters. One passes into an immense cavern where the air is fresh and cool. Looking up, one sees that the roof is pierced with ancient ventilation shafts, as it might be of a Great Western railroad tunnel in the west of England . . . Inside the great cavern, under an archway, one hears an underground stream roaring into the darkness, which is Stygian. No forest Indian will visit the place. But if one can obtain a canoe, one can paddle in the deep darkness to a point where the walls close in, and the roof comes down as in Edgar Allan Poe's *Pit and Pendulum*, in the dungeons of the old Dominican Inquisition in Toledo. Dangerous eddies appear and white foaming waters roar over the brink of a whirlpool . . . One of the war-time frogmen might try his luck beyond, but he had better be accompanied! . . . Off the main cave a labyrinth of passages branches out. It is anyone's guess what lies beyond the maze. But one passage leads into an eerie mausoleum. Here, in wall-niches around, human *skeletons are walled up*. Above each partition, however, peers a grinning skull! Who are these guardians of this mysterious *huaca*? Why were they walled up, and when? On a frieze, or fresco, over each skeleton strange hieroglyphs are carved deeply in the rock, or they may be signs of some unknown and ancient syllabary. No one knows if this weird *huaca* contains hidden treasures, nor what purpose it served. The forest Indians whisper that, if one follow the right path through the maze of passages, one will finally emerge into the grey ruins of a city of the long dead.

In my previous book, *Mysteries of Ancient South America* (Rider and Co., London, England), I said that the old Jesuit missioners, expelled by the kings of Portugal and Spain, in the late 1770's from their Latin-American dominions, when Pope Ganganelli suppressed the order of San Ignatius Loyola in 1773, knew a lot about these dead cities of old Brazil. Indeed, at this moment, somewhere in the great Vatican Library in Rome, there must be filed manuscripts, written by these missioners giving many details of these strange cities, which the papal authorities may find it best to let lie *perdu*.

About the year 1745, Frey Roch, or Rochus Hundertpfund, native of Bregenz, in south Germany, had charge of one of three Jesuit missions, on the Rio Xingú, in the Matto Grosso. He was only a very short time at this mission, when word came from friendly Indians or converts, that the savage Indians of the forests had determined to murder the father and burn down his mission. They preferred their own wild life to Jesuit ministrations. Indians came by night and took the father down the river in a small boat, and hardly had he gone, when, in the dawn, the wild braves sallied out of the Xingú woods, roared with rage, and put flaming brands to the station. After this, they vanished into the forests.

Way back in faraway Germany, a savant, Christoph Gottlieb von Murr recorded, in the years 1775–1799, many curious matters of ethnographical sort, which he derived from these expelled missioners. He somewhere says that Hundertpfund, in the upper Xingú, heard that, somewhere behind the dense jungles and forests, were prehistoric ruined cities. It was of this mysterious region that Colonel Fawcett spoke, when he said that a tribe of a surprising degree of culture, were ruled by a matriarchate of Amazon women, who were probably direct descendants of the very Amazons whom Psonchis and Psenophis told Solon, the Athenian, formed part of the army of the later Atlantean island of Poseidonis.

There is a Matto Grosso Indian tradition, still extant, about a great and very ancient white ruler of old Brazil, who was a great cacique ruling over ten other chiefs of vassal tribes. This sounds remarkably like an echo of the ten kings who periodically met and held state councils and religious festivals in the great golden temple of Poseidonian Atlantis. (*Vide* Plato's Dialogues of Timæus and Critias.) The same Indians of the Matto Grosso and the Goyaz, as well as down south in the state of São Paulo, have traditions that a great cataclysm forced their ancestors to quit the shores of an ancient Marañon-Amazon basin, where were located great cities of shining white stone ruled over by powerful white chiefs, in a very far day. Even to-day, these Indians have a tradition that, in the western Matto Grosso, as it now is, and on the site of the Gran Chaco of forests and swamps that borders Paraguay, western Brazil and Bolivia—home, by the way, of at least one great monster of an amphibian dinosaur, called the "buey jagua"—there was a prehistoric sea called *O Xarayes*. This name is borne by one Indian tribe in the upper reaches of the Paraguay, contacted, in 1723, by Capitão Antonio Pires de Campos, and called by him "o gentio *Sarayez*". The waters of this prehistoric sea, said to be older than the rise of the Andes, laved the slopes of the old Brazilian Highlands, on which the great megalithic cities were located, and extended a good way southwards to what is now the Argentina.

A correspondent of mine, in São Paulo, tells me that it is known there, by certain people, that, in the 1900's, when Colonel Fawcett was delimiting the frontiers of eastern Perú, Bolivia and Brazil, he reached the country of the formidable Nhambiquaras. These Indians are the subject of jokes among other Indian tribes in Brazil, by reason of the abnormal size of their virile organ! They are powerfully built and dark in hue and may be descendants of the very ancient black aborigines of South America. They are definitely of Stone Age culture.

Fawcett was told by a cacique of the Nhambiquaras that a megalithic ancient city lay east of their country, towards the head-waters of the Rio Xingú. This dead city was hemmed in by a belt of very dense forests, beset with the fierce Suyas, a tribe of very savage Indians. The cacique gave to Fawcett, one is told, a pebble carved in intaglio with a figure of a sandalled man wearing a sort of ancient Roman toga. It was *very* ancient. Other stones were incised with letters like those found in A.D. 1745, by the old bandeiristas who entered another dead Atlantean-Hy Brazilian, considerably to the east of the Xingú country.

These ruins of the Nhambiquara cacique are said to be in a plain encircled with a range of blue mountains, and with dense jungles and forests coming up to the massive walls. There are moats and massive paved stone causeways and streets. It is very reminiscent of the dead city described in my *Mysteries of Ancient South America*. There were also tales of monstrous animals in this region, some of dinosaur type wallowing in reedy lakes, and others oddly like the King Kong ape, of the late Edgar Wallace's fantasy, ten or twelve feet high, with human-like hands instead of opposed thumbs.

Albert de Winton—it is uncertain whether this luckless gentleman was a British or an American citizen, for he lived, at one time, in Hollywood, California—died of poison slipped into his fruit-drink by treacherous Indians of an *aldeia* bordering the land of these very Suyas. De Winton was then (about 1934) searching for a solution of the Fawcett mystery, and he had reached the fringes of the Suyas forests. My São Paulo correspondent says it is believed that poor de Winton left manuscripts that have fallen into private hands in Cuyabá. In one paper, de Winton told of meeting an Indian who had escaped from his savage custodians of Suyas, by whom he had been held captive, and who are guardians of the strange dead city. This Indian spoke of a stone tower of very ancient and massive construction, from which, day and night, there shines an eternal light. It is very bright, and whatever form of physical energy or chemi-luminescence be used in this light, it seems one unknown to modern illuminating engineers.

The Indian said that not even the fierce Suyas will venture within two miles of this light of the tower. They will not even *look* at it; and, when in the neighbourhood, creep through the woods softly and silently as if they were engaged in ambushing intruders. The light and the tower seem to be a sort of pharos of the ruined city which lies quite a considerable way off in the forest. What it suggests is a light tower such as might be erected by a race of sun-worshippers. Towers of this sort, but *not* with "eternal lights" shining from them, were by a very ancient race erected on the site of the *Furetana* of the old Ma-cares, or Karians, worshippers of Melkarth and who, thousands of years ago, put up light pillars on the Highlands of Colombia, also a land of gold, gems and mystery in the days of long ago.

Said my correspondent:

> According to this Indian's story, you had to go up the bank of the Xingutana, an affluent of the upper Xingú, until you came to a vast reed-sown marsh, or *lago*. Looking across the reedy expanse, where are many aquatic birds of brilliant plumage, you saw on an islet in the middle of the great lagoon, a massive and ancient stone wall made of many squared blocks piled one on another. Going out on a canoe, you broke a way over the creeper and liana-shrouded wall and behind it saw the entrance to a tunnel. Through this bore flows a stream and a boat could be rowed along it. At the other end, the tunnel emerges to the side of a massive stone quay, standing in front of a city, grey as Time, of splendid plazas, public buildings, temples and fine streets paved with massive square blocks. There are great houses of stone, all finely masoned and some bearing glyphs, strange letters, and statuary with images of fine men and women of old time. In the far distance rears up a lofty range of blue mountains. The Indians who hold the keys of this dead city are tall, reddish-eyed, and near-white in skin. Physically, they are fine; but mentally, savage and degenerate.

This description suggests all the characteristics of an Atlantean city, with moats, tunnels, causeways, and unending lights. Whether the race now occupying them are descendants of a helot nation, æons ago, ruled over by the ancient white kings and fair gods of old Brazil, or the posterity of the old Hy-Brazilian Atlanteans long gone savage like the late H. G. Wells's Morlocks, must for the time, remain a moot point. It is added that gold and jewels abound in this dead city, and that, around in the countryside, are ancient gold mines. Their caciques wear splendid dresses, gemmed with ritual ornamentation, which may have been taken from the ancient temples there. Their culture is almost Neolithic, and they use stone implements, and like the Atlanteans of old, they enforce labour from badly-treated captives, who are tortured and maltreated in *corvée* fashion. In the region, near *catadupas* and *cachoeiras* (cascades and waterfalls), there are caverns once occupied by the ancients and having carved stones and frescoes with glyphs.

It is suggested that Frey Rochus Hundertpfund heard of this river of the dead city, which was called the Rio Xingutana, and is on the upper courses of the Xingú. He, too, was told that savage and unpacifiable Indians barred the road to it, and as we have seen, he had good reason to believe it!

From all this, it seems clear that the late Dr. Eckener was right when he said that the method of approach to the golden mystery road lay in the use of such aeronautical transport as an airship, filled with helium gas, hydrogen being far too dangerous in the event of tropical thunderstorms. It would be independent of dumps of high octane spirit or gasoline. The road afoot is costly to life and limb and health, though the loathsome pathogenic insects and ticks might be exterminated by bacteriological methods, or use of the insecticides developed in the Second World War.

The Matto Grosso and the adjoining province of Goyaz contain many other strange reminders of the mysterious past of old Brazil. In the upper reaches of the Paraguay, about 200 miles south-west of Cuyabá, are megalithic remains of large squared blocks, piled on one another. On the side of a *serra*, between two rivers, and close to the Lago de Hahaiba, are glyphs of the sun, moon, planets, snakes, imprints of hands and feet and other curious symbols. Such glyphs are found in other regions of central South America. They range from the foothills of the Chilian Andes right up to the Sierra de Santa Marta of modern Colombia, South America. All are very ancient and all cut deeply in hard stone. In this region are miles of strange caves which call for exploration by experienced speleologists; for they have dangers in their recesses.

All the Indians, from the *Coroados* (tonsured tribes) to the *Botocudos* (who wear labrets or *botoques*, shell or bone ornaments speared through their lips), have ancient traditions of a great cataclysm that drowned all people, and left only two persons alive. The Parecis Indians, in particular, have a dim tradition about great stone cities, and of an old and bearded white missioner or culture hero, who ruled them and who was called *Zucutchue*. (It may be noted that the radical of this name is that of the dim *ZU*he, or *ZU*me, whose footprints have been found cut in hard, immemorial rocks, all over Brazil and Paraguay, and who is idiotically linked by R. C. monkish hagiologists with the globe-trotter San Tomas, who never in his dim career came within ten thousand miles of ancient America, North, South or Central! As I have said, these footprints are found as far north as a swamp in *Nova Scotia!*)

Anthony Knivett, a plucky English traveller saw another of these megalithic remains in Brazil, in the year 1597, when he wished to get Indians to war against the Amazons. He had travelled with twelve Portuguese from "the Rio Juwary which riseth in Potosi, Perew", when:

> At Etaoca, Brazil, we came on a great stone house, a great, huge rock with a greate doore for entrance, as fine as any Halle in old England. The Indians say that here St. Thomas did preach to their forefathers. Hard by, standeth a stone as bigge as four great Cannons, and it standeth upon the ground upon four stones little bigger than a man's finger, like stickes. The Indians say that was a miracle which the Saint shewed them, and that that stone had been woode. Likewise, by the sea side, there were great Rockes, upon which I saw great store of the prints of the footing of bare feet, all of one bignesse. The Indians say that the Saint called the fishes of the sea, and they heard him.

There are the famous *Minas dos Martyrios*, fatal bourne of many a hardened land-pirate of a São Paulan bandeirista, and many a tough guy of our day, whose grinning skull is the only memento of him left to adorn some enigmatic forest trail. Such men would have given all the gold and diamonds in the Brazils for a crust of bread or bite of mandioca between their famished teeth, on that lone trail! Here is a word or two of what Capitão Antonio Pires de Campo said of these mines of the Martyrs, in the year A.D. 1750:

> In this hill are flints of crystals that ascend from the middle to the top of the cliff-walls. They show markings like a crown, a lance, and nails of the Passion of Jesus Christ, but all crudely done (*mas tudo tosco*) . . . Looking north and west from the Rio das Mortes, one sees a range of blue mountains that are eight days' journey away, as the *sertanejos* (people of the country) reckon . . . and from here, I arrived at the Tapera (desert place) dos Araes, with my father, whom may God save. We found various wedges and small, thin plates (*folletas*) for the neck and the arms. Of *Gold!* My father ordered them to be used for a glory (*resplandor*) for the image of wood of Our Lady of the Rosary that we have in our house . . . and also a crown of gold that weighed 48 (*missing word in manuscript*) for our Lady of the Hospice of Mount Carmel of the town of Itú. And the Indians told us that these gold plates came from those far blue mountains we saw, the gold being got out after rains.

The same explorer of wildest Brazil tells of the "gentio barbaro" (wild Indians) that are on the route to the gold mines of Cuyabá, in the Matto Grosso. In 1723, he went up the upper Rio Paraguay, reaching a *bahia* (river-creek) called Hiahiba. Here, he saw a "cross of stone", *very* ancient and *not* of Christian origin, though someone had, as usual, affixed to it the name of San Tomas, apostolic globe-trotter. As before, we have here the sign of the ancient Brazilian missioner and culture hero, *Zuhe*. Around, the Indians were nude and cannibals; they tilled land, their women wore *tipoyas* (sleeveless *camisas*, like shifts) made of the bark of a tree. This sort of poncho has two openings and reached from neck to knee. Maybe this is some memory of an ancient matriarchate, for male savages are not wont to go naked while their women are dressed! Among the cannibal tribes of the Ahiquas, and Crucicurus, the men, too, went naked, while the women wore garments of woven straw or sewn bark . . . He met other *clothed* Indians in the unknown wilds:

> Two days away, we came to the mouth of a river-bar called the Yahuri. Here, the men wore *merlotas* (short Moorish cloaks), while their women wore these shifts, or *tipoyas*.

He came on the *Sarayes*, who bear the ancient name of the old sea of prehistoric South America:

> They have a kingdom of many villages, and in one I counted more than nine hundred *chocas* (cabins) . . . peaceful and easy-going folk who are not fond of work, but wage war on none . . . Among the Parecis, on the upper Paraguay, were *aldeias* of thirty houses each. They grow pine-apples and *batatas* and mandioca, and fight only in self-defence. Their swords are made of wood cut in blades from the timber of a very hardwood tree. They have lances and defend their doorways, which, however, are so low that only a cat can enter upright . . . I saw their idol house . . . frightful images bore trumpets made of a gourd . . . but the women dare not even look at these idol houses, where the men meet on feast days and dance in rich dresses. The women have rich featherwork garments of many bright colours. They are handsome and never have I *seen such fair white-skinned women, with shapely hands and feet.* They rear blue macaws and parrots, much as we do cocks and hens . . . These Indians make articles of stone like jasper, in the form of a *Maltese cross*, which their caciques wear dependent from the neck, smooth and polished like marble. They work material as hard as iron, and curious articles they make, but they have no iron or steel tools. Stone axes and other difficult things they make, difficult to credit.

Raymundo José da Cunha Mattos told, in 1874, of ancient hieroglyphs on the faces of cliffs in Brazilian Goyaz. In the Mountain of the Figures (*Monto das Figuras*) are signs shaped like the capital letters "C. E. F. O." Some of them are two palms high. Other figures are crudely fashioned. These figures may be memorials of the old Atlanteans, or some later race; for it is pretty sure that old Carthage and her *Pauchs*, who circumnavigated Africa under Hanno, could hardly have failed, at some time, to contact the shores of South America. Most certainly no bandeiristas would waste their time cutting these glyphs on high and hard rocks. Why should they? Gold—hard, bright, shining and cold—was their objective, not the making of petroglyphs!

Da Cunha Mattos adds:

> I say that near Santa Rita is a stone with a pedestal three palms high, and one-and-a-half palms in diameter. Upon this column, or cylinder, is a stone six palms long and three palms broad, which forms a perfect table (*mesa*) well levelled. The cylinder is cut in the rock, and the table is carved in one piece.

What ancient purpose did this strange platform serve? Echo answers "What?"

In the province of the Geraes is another place with unknown characters like those cut in the Mount of Figures in Goyaz. It, too, is called San Thomé des Letras. At a little village in Goyaz, a man, ploughing, found, on 15th April, 1818: "a skeleton of an amphibian, occupying space of 45 palms, which the country people took for the bones of a giant man and offered alms to it for the repose of the giant's soul! Such remains show that the country around suffered great convulsions in the remote past."

It was in A.D. 1722, that Urbano do Couto, then 22 years old, travelled with soldiers to conquer the wild Goyaz, of Brazil. He wrote in a manuscript, now in Rio de Janeiro:

> By the mercy of God, I found the Mĩnas dos Martyrios. They are up the Rio Araes. I found much gold on the land, and in running water . . . I also came on one of the eight wonders of the world, south-east of the Rio das Mortes . . . The River rises' in a high rock of many colours, like a ship which is dismasted . . . Northwards is another rock of fantastic sort. Lofty as the tower of the famed Babel, it is cut with steps which seem as made by Nature. On its summit is a platform on which twenty or more soldiers could stand. You cannot look down from this stupendous height and not turn giddy . . . Where we found the gold on the wall of a rock by which the river flows, our ship's captain cut a big cross . . .

In another part of the Matto Grosso, in the land of the Bororo Indians, some way from Cuyabá, is a raised earthwork with steps and columns which can hardly be a freak of nature. Frey José Manoel Siqueira speaks of this earthwork, in a manuscript in which he relates the adventures of his father, Capitão Antonio Prado de Siqueira. The Indians called it a "Calvary":

> My father was with a comrade who found gold at Cuyabá. The Indians led them into a deep jungle, and they came on steep mountains. All around is much gold, found near this 'Calvarium' . . . The people of the country took the gold to be yellow balls and played with it as with a hand-ball. Word came to him that ahead many Indians were waiting in ambush to kill them.

So they had to quit this bonanza—a Brazilian Klondyke—in great haste, and never after were they able to find the place!

In the years 1944–1948, the authorities in Rio de Janeiro have at last seriously taken up the problem of attacking the fastnesses between the latitudes of 10 and 15 degrees south, and longitudes 52 and 55 degrees east, where is located the unknown and very dangerous region where the Fawcett expedition vanished in 1926. One of their foremost objects is the exploration of the mysterious Serra do Roncador, or Snorer's Range, where, some folk say, lie some of the Hy-Brazilian Atlantean dead cities which Fawcett was seeking. (However, it should be pointed out that Colonel Fawcett never revealed exactly where these dead cities lay; for he did not want his trail to be dogged by treasure hunters and *garimpeiros* (diamond diggers), and other picturesque and not always very scrupulous or law-abiding adventurers.)

There still remains mystery in the matter of the location of the strange *Serra do Roncador* (Snorer's or Blusterer's Mountain) said to have snow-capped sierras and to be the location of some of the dead cities for which Fawcett was seeking. Some maps I have seen locate this mysterious range between the Rio Paranatinga and the Rio von Steiner, one of the western affluents of the Xingú. On others there appears marked at this location a range called *Serra Azul*, or Blue Mountains. My friend, Senhor Armando Abreu, of São Paulo, wrote me in November 1948, that the Serra do Roncador had been reached on 28th August, 1938, by an expedition called the "Bandeira Piratinga", and one of the first men to climb the range, or its foothills, was Willy Aurelly and newspaper men with "Indianistas"—native-born Brazilians. A book had been written on the Roncador. On the other hand, I am told the Brazilian authorities in London deny that the mysterious range has been found. I have found it impossible to obtain a copy of this book at the time I am writing: March, 1949.

In 1944, the Central Brazilian Foundation in Rio sent out an expedition of 50 men to explore this region of mysteries. It was backed by Senhor Joao Alberto Lins de Barros, Minister of Immigration in Rio de Janeiro, at that time, and the leader was Lieut.-Colonel Flavino de Mattos Vanique. The expedition was called the Roncador-Xingú expedition, and its aim was, and is, to open up the jungles of Central Brazil, just as the ILHA (or Instituto Internacional da Hileia Amazonica), or the International Hylean Institute, under Unesco of the United Nations, aims to open up the forest region of the Amazon.

News of the Roncador—Xingú expedition reached Rio de Janeiro in March, 1948. The expedition was then 1,000 miles to the west and deep in the region of the Chavantes Indiós, a tribe or nation of what, in Brazil, are called *Indiós malos*, or bad Indians. Somewhere west of the territory of the Chavantes, the Fawcett party plunged into the unknown. The Roncador expedition had managed to make a very precarious truce with the Chavantes, whose good will, to say the least of it, cannot be relied on. The Brazilians had to face floods, spreading over the *chapada* from the Rio Araguaya; for there had been heavy rain in the Goyaz plateau. The forests around are full of pathogenic insects—of the type of the *barbeiro* mentioned in my chapter on Monsters—of venomous snakes and even more venomous Indians. All these had to be faced in the course of the expedition's back- and heart-breaking trail towards the unknown headwaters of the Rio Xingú. As they went, they hacked a road through the forests and dense jungle, and, at intervals, laid down strips where small 'planes could land and bring food, fuel and other supplies. De Barros had the ambitious plan to explore some 3,500,000 square miles of what is now unknown forest-jungle.

The expedition is said to have passed along the course of the Kuluene river which is near where Fawcett vanished in 1926. If this is so, it suggests that the mysterious Serra do Roncador does not lie in the region between the Rio das Mortes and the Kuluene. Here, they would enter the territories of other *Indiós malos*, called the Kustenas, many of whom are suspected of being head-hunters. It may be noted that the Roncador-Xingú expedition started out from São Paulo, the southern Brazilian capital and great centre of business, finance and industry.

Along the Kuluene, the expedition forced a way through the jungle into the territory of the Gaiapos Indians, who appeared to have burnt the forests as they retreated from the front of the expedition. By summer, 1948, the expedition were reported to be on the fringe of a "Lost World"—the probable habitat of the King Kong ape whose story I tell in another chapter. They hoped to discover the dead cities which were the quest of Fawcett. It is the unknown Lost World whence adventurers have brought back queer stories of monstrous reptiles of mesozoic type, gigantic anthropoid apes, all of 12 feet high, strange forms of animal life unknown to zoologists, "white Indians" —the descendants of the great white race of "fair gods" who built the ancient Atlantean cities of old Brazil—and the home of Indians alleged to possess remarkable powers of the magical and necromantic sort. If only half the stories of these Brazilian forest Indians' *brujerias* are true, the goetic sciences should receive some remarkable accessions!

The expedition hopes that these riddles of a Lost World may be solved by the year 1950. As to that, one may sound a warning against undue optimism. Not easily will these secrets of the heart of South America be solved, and one fears that the cost will be paid heavily in human blood ere the gods who do not wish the land to be known are forced further into the twilight. The country is a truly terrible one. Already the trail has taken very heavy toll of these pioneers. Half of the expedition starting out from São Paulo, in 1944, have dropped out, and only the toughest men remain. Small 'planes, landing on the jungle air-strips, have flown the casualties back to hospitals. It is with these 'planes that contact has been made with Rio de Janeiro.

The Central Brazilian Institute has wide powers from the Federal Government in Rio, and can make and run railroads, operate air and shipping lines, set up factories and lay out townships. For a world whose food may be threatened with Malthusian restrictions at no far away date, this expedition is of scientific importance. The expedition has built an airport served by small 'planes from Rio and São Paulo, and it is hoped that air liners may later on call there.

It was in dense forests of this sort that Colonel Fawcett, somewhere in eastern Bolivia, shot a 60-foot anaconda. He spoke of fresh-looking tracks in a slimy beach of a swamp lake, which tracks looked like the spoor of a vast reptile of dinosaur proportions. He saw bleached bones of petrified giant saurians on the banks of an affluent of the Rio Madidi, in this region. Called a liar by arm-chair theorists who do their exploration from the smoking-rooms of London West End clubs, Colonel Fawcett shook out the skin of the giant anaconda, in their faces, in London. They said he must have faked it! When someone else, a few months later, shot a 75-foot reptile in the South American jungle, the club warriors tee-hee'd and said the shooter must be just that much bigger liar. Put one of these gallant gentry on such an expedition and you might rely on his falling sick, pronto, if he reached as far as the ports of Rio de Janeiro or Callao. Next thing would be that you would find the gallant sceptic back in his Piccadilly arm-chair, calling for a double whisky and saying he did not know whether to bring in a verdict of suicide or murder against such intrepid old type British explorers and frontiersmen as Colonel Philip Henry Fawcett!

As his distinguished son, Brian Fawcett, a South American railroad engineer and versatile artist who has had strange personal experience in the Andes and the West Indies, wrote me, in December 1948:

> I am perfectly sure, myself, that the heart of South America contains, locked up in its impenetrable privacy, much that has not even been dreamt of. Even on the fringes of the great unknown, there are animals not yet classified. I have that statement in my father's, Colonel Fawcett's, manuscripts, which it is my hope, when time permits, to edit for publication. My father describes one or two of these unknown animals.

My only comment is that the world must await with impatience the appearance of the Fawcett manuscripts, which are certainly calculated to startle even those not totally ignorant of South American mysteries.

Dr. Matthew Stirling of the Ethnological Bureau of the Smithsonian Institution, Washington, D.C., said, about 1935, that he believes that the "missing link" between man and his ape-like progenitor may lie in fossil remains somewhere in the Lost World region of the central cordillera of Colombia, or south in the Andes of Ecuador. About that date an expedition of American archæologists were said to be planning to use airplanes to hunt for such remains and for ruins of pre-Inca cities. True, the fossil remains of the missing link may lie there; but, on the other hand, the Danish scientist, Dr. Lund, who spent most of his life in Brazil, said that the Brazilian Highlands were the first part of America to be thrust up from the archæan sea. Maybe *there*, one should look for the missing link, since it is not altogether unlikely that autochthonous peoples from the Brazilian Highlands wandered into North America and peopled it.

The curious significance of the orientation of those colossal statues of men and women found, about the 1850's, in south-eastern Colombia, was paralleled in a discovery, made in 1642, in the Azores. Here, Dom Alfonso, King of Portugal, sent one Dom Henri to colonize the islands. In Cuervo, his expedition found a colossal equestrian statue whose rider, his left-hand on his bridle, pointed to the *west* with his right! (As I stated in my book on *Mysteries of Ancient South America*, the *bandeiristas* who lit on the dead Atlantean city of Brazil, in A.D. 1750, probably in the interior of the little explored province of modern Bahia, once the eastern side of the Brazilian Highlands, saw the statue of a young man of Greek classic type. [Note, please, young women students of our modern British universities, I am assuredly not, as one of you pityingly hinted to me in Birmingham, in 1939, suggesting that the ancient Hellenes founded these dead cities of Hy-Brazil!] The *bandeiristas* observed with wonder that the man, or youth, standing on a pillar, black with age, extended his right hand to the *north*.)

It has been surmised that this ancient equestrian statue of Cuervo, destroyed in 1643, was sculpted when the Azores were linked to the Mediterranean, then an inland sea of the pre-Ogygian, or Pelasgian cataclysmal era. That would be at a time when the towering pharos, called the Pillars of Hercules, had not come into existence, and when the Azores may have been a continuation of the Atlas range, as we now have it in Mauritanian, or north-west Africa. The statue of Cuervo is said to have borne inscriptions in characters resembling the Phœnician-Carthaginian alphabet: that is, they were, or may have been from the syllabary of the later Atlantean island known as Poseidonis, of whose imperial splendour Solon the Greek was told by the priests of Egyptian Sais and Heliopolis: Sonchis and Psenophis. There is an ancient Hindu tradition which states that the Egyptians are the remnants of the Atlanto-Aryans of the older, or Ruta Atlanteans, whose island continent perished in a cataclysm some thousands of years antecedent to that which overtook Solon's island-continent of Poseidonis; while the Hellenes and the Romans had ancestral connections with Poseidonis-Atlantis. If that were so, the tradition seems to tie up with the statement of Diodorus Siculus, based on records in the temple-archives at old Carthage, that the Phœnician alphabet derived from Atlantis, in a day when the Atlanteans had invented an alphabet; whereas the Egyptian hieroglyphs came from the far earlier civilization of Ruta-Atlantis.

As my book *Mysteries of Ancient South America* has shown, there are to be found in the dead cities and on rocks in the unexplored region of the old Brazilian Highlands, to-day synonymous with the uplands of the unknown Roosevelt-Goyaz plateau of Brazil, and the dense woods and chapadas of the Matto Grosso, both ancient syllabary letters *and* unmistakable hieroglyphs. They are eloquent testimony to the immense antiquity and duration of these white-red-yellow civilizations of old Hy-Brazil.

The shadow of great unknown and extremely ancient civilizations of probable heliolithic type located in Central and South America is seen to be projected over the modern pueblo Indians of Colorado, Utah, New Mexico and Arizona. These pueblo tribes who live in village settlements pay homage to the Sun and look for a Messiah who is to come to them *from the East.* As I have pointed out, in my earlier book, it was from the East that there arrived in ancient Central America the Atlantean-Brazilian sage and culture-bearer in black— great man not deity—who was known as Quetzalcoatl. It was to the east that he vanished, promising one day to return.

Many of the ancient houses of the *Moquis,* as in the cañon of the Mancos, were set to face to the east, so that from there the ancient men might continually watch the eastern horizon. As late as A.D. 1877, the *Moquis* still mounted the roofs of their houses and waited in the crepuscular light of dawn till the sun rose above the skyline.

In A.D. 1540, Capitan Fernando Alarcon, exploring the banks of the Rio Colorado, met Indians who worshipped the sun. The American Lieutenant A. W. Whipple, in Vol. III of Pacific R.R. Reports, says about the pueblo Indians of New Mexico: "They anxiously await the arrival of Montezuma. In San Domingo, one of the nineteen pueblo towns, every morning at sunrise a sentinel climbs to his house-top and looks eastward to watch for Montezuma's coming. The Zuñis (Indians) say that the Montezuma is the son of the unseen deity, and their king."

In the cañon of the Rio Mancos, a northern tributary of the Rio San Juan, in the extreme south-west corner of Colorado, the Indian dwellings are almost invariably found hidden in the cliffs of the western bluffs and, as an American writer picturesquely said in 1880:

From their roofs the people saluted the king of day as he raised himself above the eastern plateau. When faint streaks of red light fall on the low horizon, tall dark figures appear on the parapets of the seven Moquis towns and remain facing the dawn until the sun has risen to view. Then the muffled figures drop, one by one, slowly and sadly away, for the great Messiah, the Montezuma, has not come from the east. Daily life begins again. The subdued hum of household chores floats up, drowning in the sullen and sultry air the sound of the *metates* (hand-mills for grinding corn) coming from the doors and windows of the stone houses like the drone of summer bees. Scores of women now hasten to the verge of the steep bluffs and with *ollas* (water-jars) vanish into the crevices of the rocks below.

This Montezuma, or Moctezuma is the culture-hero of the remarkable myth of the Papagos Indians who, significantly, say he lived in a time when "the earth was warmer and *very much nearer the sun than now*". The Papagos occupied a region between the Santa Cruz river and the Gulf of California. He (Montezuma) was a sort of Prometheus, or friend of man and enemy of gods. It is said that the sun's beams were then so warm that clothing was not needed. The old myth adds that, when Montezuma, a demi-ourgos like Jahveh, or Brahm, or more probably a "giant" who championed man, neglected his duties, the Great Spirit came to earth, remonstrated with him for his pride, and then "pushed back the sun to a remote part of the sky". Which is a very remarkable ancestral memory of some terrifying cosmic cataclysm of world-wide extent . . .

Montezuma, enraged, collected the tribes around him and started to build a house to reach the sky. The builders had finished several apartments, lined with gold and studded with gems and thought their purpose was near accomplishment, when the Great Spirit smote the house to earth amid the crash of thunders . . . Whereupon Montezuma hardened yet his heart and bade the people drag the sacred images through the streets and he desecrated temples amid the derision of the villagers. The Great Spirit then caused an insect to fly towards the east and bring those who would utterly destroy them. . . .

This Great Spirit rather suggests some vindictive hook-nosed Jahveh delighting in burnt sacrifices, clouds of hosannas, and slaughters to the last man, woman and child of some luckless race of Amalekites whom he did not think he liked!

It is odd, however, that no chronicle is said to mention this Montezuma as a culture-hero until after A.D. 1670. The Pecos Valley Indians say he was born at Pecos, wore golden shoes, and left for Mexico, where the people killed him to get the shoes. . . .

Quitting Pecos, he commanded the people that they keep a holy fire burning till he returned. The embers were kept aglow till 1840, and then transferred to Jerrez.

I even venture to dissent from the famous Bandelier who found "nothing even of traditional value" in this myth, which he far too confidently asserts merely referred to the gold-hungry, treasure-hunting Spaniards, called the bearded *Coroados*. However and whenever the myth originated, it has the hall-marks of extreme antiquity. Montezuma, or Mo-tecu-zoma, may have been, if not Quetzalcoatl, another of the same type of ancient culture-heroes, preceding a gigantic cataclysm of the earth. It was probably caused by cometary collision, or the disintegration of a lunar satellite, or one of those asteroids which now represent the place of a missing planet once located between Mars and Jupiter, as Bode's Law lays down.

Surely, none at this time of day will foolishly contend that the Spanish conquistadores, avid for gold and souls, spread among these pueblo Indians the story of the ill-fated Aztec emperor and sun-god

Montezuma? If there are such fools I should refer them to what Montezuma himself, the last Emperor of Aztec Mexico, told our lord, Don Hernando Cortes about the man in black, Quetzalcoatl, who came from the east, the civilized empire of Atlantean Brazil and returned there, promising one day to return and redeem his children. As for the dawn sun-worshipping, on the eastward facing roofs of the pueblo stone houses, what is this ceremonial but a faint reflection of that which took place, many thousands of years ago, on the great sun-towers of the dead cities of Atlantean Brazil and doubtless in Atlantean Central America? The adoration of the sun, regarded in that remote age as the symbol of the unknown and unknowable Central Sun of the Cosmos!

These mysterious megalithic ruins and colossal human statues of North-western and Western South America inevitably raise the question which has still not been finally disposed of by geologists and geophysicists: what is the Age of the Andes? And this is followed by the collateral: did any civilized races of mankind exist in ancient South America in the pre-cataclysmal age before the Andes rose from the bed of the Pacific?

The late English professor, J. W. Gregory, well known as a geologist and South American geographer, lost his life in tragic manner while leading the Gregory Geological Expedition in Perú, in 1932. Its main objective was to make a reconnaissance of the main Andean range in order to determine the age when it rose from the bed of the Pacific. While he was passing through the turbulent waters of the dangerous rapids of the Pongo de Mainique on the upper Rio Urumbambo his canoe overset and he, clinging to the keel, was swept swiftly to his death in the back eddies of two whirlpools. Many valuable geological specimens sank into the stream and the delicate scientific instruments and photographic material were damaged beyond redemption.

As one has pointed out before, the Matto Grosso province of Brazil may hold the key to this riddle. In this vast and mostly unknown region are located the ancient Brazilian Highlands, one of the first lands to emerge from the archæan sea, and some 20,000 years ago the seat of a very ancient white empire of Atlantean type whose civilization and culture, had, in thousands of years before the Great Cataclysm of Solon-Plato-Psenophis, evolved from hieroglyphs to an alphabet and syllabary closely akin to the Phœnician-Greek alphabet. This latter alphabet, in its turn, as Diodorus Siculus hints, came from the motherland of Atlantis. Valuable European, English, and American lives have been lost trying to answer this riddle. It is an answer which the gods of South America have so far willed shall not be given until white explorers pass beyond the dense zone of forests and equatorial swamps and force their way on to what is at present an inaccessible and extremely mysterious plateau. Its approaches are guarded by dwarfish black troglodytes, armed with clubs and about as pleasant to encounter as must have been the dangerous and savage sub-man of the Neanderthal age. These black aboriginals, also found up the unknown headwater reaches of the unexplored Rio Uapes which enters the province of Caqueta, Colombia, from north-western Brazil, must be the world's oldest race, just as they are the earliest inhabitants of old Brazil.

In this unexplored territory of the Brazilian Highlands, ranging between the Rio Roosevelt and the Goyaz Tableland, there is an unknown region of two million square miles where, as geologists will agree, is some of the first land to emerge from the primæval sea. It has probably never been submerged by any cataclysm and has no sedimentary rocks, but only plutonic rocks.

Long ago this mysterious region formed a vast island and it is probably only recently, as geological ages go, that tectonic changes took place, and the shuddering earth laboured in the birth-throes that led to the rise of the Andean cordilleras. From that time, and possibly contemporary with the emergence of the *then* dead city of Tiahuanacu from the bed of the ocean to the bleak, airless paramo where it is now located 12,000 feet above sea level, the Brazilian Isle became separated from the chain of the Andes by vast marshes and swamps whose waters percolated through innumerable channels into the Amazon and thence drained into the Atlantic. To-day, in the southern region of Amazonas, and the eastern and northern Matto Grosso, the land which occupies part of the ancient Brazilian Isle—a high and unexplored tableland—is surrounded by a far-stretching belt of marsh and dense forest-jungle.

It may be that Colonel P. H. Fawcett's friend, the late Dr. George Lynch,[1] was right in his contention that these Brazilian Highlands have a group of massifs, as well as snow-covered peaks, that no white man has ever both seen *and* reported back to civilization. The Indian tribes have traditions of these mountains, which they call *As Serras Brancas* (The White Mountains), and one range of which is known, in the Matto Grosso and Cuyabá, as *A Serra do Roncador* (Snorer's or Roarer's Range). (*Vide supra.*)

However, the birth and rise of the Andes themselves seems to be crystallized, like the fly caught in the Baltic amber, in various traditions of South American Indian tribes. These traditions appear to embody ancestral memories of a far-off age when lands now towering into South American skies, and cold and sterile and so attenuated in atmosphere that the act of breathing is consummated in pain and sickness, and even death may be caused to Europeans unacclimatized

---

[1] Dr. Lynch, was the famous Colonel Lynch, Irish soldier of fortune who championed the South African Boer farmers and burghers against the Imperialist and Rand magnates of the South African War of 1899–1901. He was tried for his life, sentenced to death by a British court, and is said to have been reprieved by influence exerted in his behalf by the late King Edward VII, one of the Liberal-minded actions associated with that King. In later years, Lynch resided in Paris and devoted his life to education and the study of philosophy.

to the region, were lush, warm, low and extremely fruitful. These "myths" of the Indians say that, in the days of their ancestors, luscious fruits ripened in these regions in five days, that birds of glorious plumage flashed through verdant, blossomy woods, and that green meads were carpeted with exquisite flowers burgeoning in the greenest and sweetest of grass.

Dr. Avila, curé of Huarocheri, Perú, who made a collection of these Quechua stories—the Quechuas are the direct descendants of the Peruvians of the Inca—had no doubt of their truth and of the veracity of the Indians who told them. He says that proofs of a former astonishing fertility and traces of ancient cultures may be seen at Puna and on the slopes of the Villcanota mountain, between Huarocheri and Surco.

More than one tribe of Brazilian Indians, besides the Caribs of Guiana and the Orinoco headwaters, met by von Humboldt about A.D.1840, and who swore that their forbears lived in South America "before the moon rode in the skies", have folk lore and traditions about a great cosmic catastrophe associated with the moon's approach to the earth.

Again, in western North America, the *Têtes Droites* Indians assert that the first cycle of ancient civilization had run its course long before the white Europeans landed in America. They go on to say that the second cycle of civilization is now well on its way. In Brazil, the Botocudos, so called from the tribal custom of inserting a botogue or labret in the lip, who live in the territory at the embouchure of the Rio Doce and Belmonte say that the Moon, which occupies the first rank in their cosmogony, is a sinister deity that can prevent, or hinder, the harvesting of certain fruits. From time to time, goes on the tribal "myth", the Moon falls on the Earth and causes the destruction of many men. Farther to the south-west in Paraguay, the Mocobis call the Sun "Gdazou", or the "Consort", the Sun being the "Spouse of the Moon, or Cidiago".[1] The Moon having fallen from the sky, says the myth, a Mocobi picked it up and put it back. But the star of the day, not having been firmly replaced, it fell a second time and burnt all the forests.

This may be rationalized, or euhemerized in several ways. Along the lines of the theory of lunar cataclysms of the Austrian engineer, Hans Hörbiger, one may suppose that a former moon of our earth disintegrated and shattered the crust with its fragments. Or, possibly, a comet, or very large aerolite hit the earth with catastrophic results. Indeed, an impact with a giant meteorite caused loss of life in a remote region of Brazil as recently as 1930. At that time, an eye-witness, the Fray Fidelio, a Jesuit missioner, reported it to his superiors at Loyola and the Vatican.

Some of the ancestors of the Mocobis saved themselves by hiding

---

[1] This myth seems to have some bearing on the Teutonic gender of the Sun: feminine, and of the Moon: masculine.

under waters and submerging themselves in rivers where, says the "myth", they were changed into caimans. Alone, one man and a woman mounted into the crotch of a tall tree to flee the peril, when the flame, in passing, roasted their faces and changed them into monkeys. So much is cited in Guevara's *Historia de la Paraguay*, but we are *not* told that here, in this cataclysm, the human race originated; but merely, as in kindred "legends" among the Quiches and the Aztecs, that men were turned into wood, or monkeys, or became insane.

The "myth" of the Mocobis is on all fours with "legends" of Brazilian tribes, their ancestral contemporaries to the northwards, beyond the Rio Paraguay, that volcanoes opened in the Andes and vomited fire, water and lava and mud, so that all that the deluge had not drowned were destroyed or consumed. They, too, speak of the "Sun" falling from the sky, exactly as the Aztecan codices speak of "Suns" of rain and fire. It burnt up the forests, forced men and women to seek the shelter of deep caves, or take to canoes and rafts on rivers. Steam rose hissing to the skies, while the smoke of burning forests, exhalations of gases, puffs from vent holes in the erupting volcanoes and fire from the rumbling craters blotted out the light of day, caused darkness lasting for months, or, *years*, say some of the Quiché myths. Men cowered on the ground in terror as the nocturnal surroundings were intermittently illumined by lurid flames of a general conflagration. Then down crashed torrents of rain, shot with thunderbolts, and amid the reverberations of appalling thunder. The water hissed on the new-born mountains, turned to steam the hot earth and cut channels in the bare slopes, bursting a way through the detritus and débris, and purifying the air poisoned with mephitic vapours and gases from the volcanoes.

It was in January, 1857, that a very strange event, happening off the shores of Carolina and Florida, drew attention to the existence of a drowned land. An immense welling-up of *sweet* water took place out at sea! Yellow and muddy currents furrowed the ocean, and thousands of dead fish were deposited on the beaches of Uncle Sam's eastern seaboard. Out in the open sea, the salinity was halved, and for a month fishermen drew sweet water every time they dipped their buckets in the sea! At that place there must at one time have existed a submerged land, and it is clear, that periodically, that drowned land is shaken with convulsive tremors. Even to-day, in the Atlantic, and certainly in the Pacific, there are vast stretches where not a sounding has ever been taken. Those areas figure as blank spaces on our charts; for ships keep to well-known tracks, so as to avoid accidents, and vast expanses are never furrowed by a single keel.

A Spanish frigate traversed the Sargasso Sea in 1802, and the captain reported that, at 28° N. lat., 43° 22′ W. long. (from the meridian of Paris) he saw *breakers*, indicating land hardly covered by the sea! The location is in mid-North Atlantic, a long way south-west of the

Azores. Even at great distances from its shores, one finds in the Atlantic *varec* (weed) and other growths, which indicate the existence of an ancient land. However, the Sargasso Sea, of which the U.S. marine biologist, William Beebe, has written so much, is comparatively deep and really does *not* mark the site of ancient Atlantis. Nor, it is likely, can Santa Cruz, or Tenerife, in the *very* deep part off the African mainland.

Professor Hull, looking at the fauna and flora of the Western and Eastern hemispheres, is driven to support the geological theory that there was a common centre in the Atlantic Ocean where life began, and that, during and prior to the ice ages, or glacial epoch, great land-bridges, north and south, spanned the Atlantic Ocean.

"This island-continent of Atlantis was larger than Arabia and Asia (the Near East) put together, and was the way to other islands, and from these you might pass to the whole opposite continent which surrounds the true ocean", so said the aged Egyptian priest Sonchis, of Sais, about the year 540 B.C. In the year A.D. 1923, the engineers of the Western Cable Company investigated the breaking of a cable on the bed of the Atlantic. They found that the bed had been considerably upheaved since the laying of the submarine cable and the soundings taken twenty-five years before. If an elevation can take place in the ocean, in that time, it is reasonable to suppose that a subsidence could take place just as comparatively suddenly in ancient times.

Some 50,000 or more years ago, after the giant cordilleras of the Andes had been thrust up from the bed of the sea of the older Miocene age—for the Andes are recent in the geologic sense—South America consisted of a vast marsh, about 2,000,000 square miles in area which lay between the new Andean cordillera and the Matto Grosso, or what is called the modern Brazilian Highlands. This land of High or Royal Brazil, like the high plateau of Arizona, Nevada and Utah, is one of the oldest which has emerged from the primæval sea. Its first savage inhabitants were black as coal, and their negro kinsmen live in regions round the Orinoco and in parts of Central America. Brazil then formed a great island separated from the Andes by a vast region of flooded lakes and great marshes. The Andes were born of tremendous vulcanism, as was also the southern part of the ancient Brazilian island. Both vast regions were, and are, on an earthquake belt.

I have spoken in my book *Mysteries of Ancient South America*[1] of the giants who once ranged South America, as in the far-off age of the pre-Inca tribes. One tradition in ancient Mexico says that the pyramid of Cholula was built by an antediluvian man, the giant Xelhua, who emerged from the mountain of Tlaloc. He was the Sun-God of the Cross (symbol of coition and creation) of the Atlanteans of old Hy-Brazil, where he and his brothers had sought refuge from the Great Catastrophe that coincided with the ruin of the high and

[1] Rider, London, 1946.

ancient civilization of the old Brazilian Isle and the submersion of the island-continent of Poseidonis-Atlantis, of which Solon, and after him Plato, spoke in Hellenistic echoes of the records of the temples of Sais and Heliopolis.[1]

In old Perú, the Quichuas (Peruvian Inca Indians) say that the *pucaras* (forts and prehistoric strongholds, such as Chanchayillo, and Quellantana, overlooking Lago de Titicaca, near the pueblo of Vilcachico), were *"erected by giants before the sun shone"*, and when savage warrior tribes ranged all over pre-Inca Perú, land of Vira, or the Sun. (Perú, be it noted, is a radical *not* found in Quichua, though in ancient white Brazil of the Atlanteans the name was Vi*ra*, Sun, exactly equivalent to the *Ra* of the Egyptians of the Pharaohs.)

How far the giants ranged in South America we shall see in a moment.

M. Alcide d'Orbigny says that tombs and columns of a colossal type suggesting the sepulchres of giant men have been found not only in the forests of Perú—their remains, as I was told in Ecuador, were actually found at Manta, in modern Ecuador, by railroad constructors—but far north in the once-existing forests of St. Louis, and on the Mississippi, in Missouri. From these remains and the monuments, one may deduce the dimensions of these tomb-temples as some thirty-six yards high, and more than two hundred and ninety-one yards in diameter. These North American giants (?) had forts with walls, made of brick and earth, with an opening to the east, forming a line of defence of some fifty miles in area. These remains of strongholds have been found south of Lake Erie, on the shores of the Ohio, and in New York state. My own observations off the beaten track in the strange province of Nova Scotia suggest that certain somewhat eerie and enigmatic remains in that British Empire territory may be connected with these same prehistoric giants who figure in Algonquin and Osage legends and who appear to have lived in North America in dim ages of which hardly a shadow of a tradition remains. Around these lacustrine shores, on the borders of Canada, these ruins of the age of the giants[2] show that they lived in buildings divided into rooms, similar to others found south in Louisiana. Both idols, or images, and inscriptions were found in the rooms. One has as yet no data in the shape of actual human remains which may enable one definitely to assert that the race unknown building these structures along the Mississippi and Lake Erie were brothers under the skin with those who built these mysterious *pucaras* in pre-Inca Perú. Perhaps, some

---

[1] *Vide:* Rios: Codex Mex. Vaticanus.

[2] Priest, in *American Antiquities*, says that near Braystown, at the headwaters of the Tennessee river there are found, impressed in the solid rock, footprints of immense age. They include *six-toed* feet of giant men, and one print seems to be that of a negro. One among these tracks stands out by its monstrosity. The heel ball is actually 13 *inches wide*! There are also prints of the hoofs of ancient *horses*. One of these horses slipped for several inches and then recovered his footing. The prints suggest that an army of giant men were travelling in the same direction, and that a giant led his horse when passing the mountain with his army! The track of the horse is eight inches by ten inches.

day, a field worker, or museum archæologist of North America, will descend from his perch, where he has too long squatted like Saint Simon Stylites, and probe into these mysteries of the age of the giants in the Americas.

A very curious story of an encounter with giants in North, or it might even be Central, or South America, is told by Adam Bremensis, in his *Historia, Gesta Hammaburgensis Ecclesia Pontificum (ap-Pertz Monumenta)*. Adam was in Bremen in A.D. 1067, a year after the invasion of Saxon England by William the Norman Bastard. He wrote about the middle of the last quarter of the eleventh century, stating that a story was told, by Archbishop Adalbert, of some Frisians who, between A.D. 1033 and 1043, went cruising in the North Atlantic. They reached Iceland, when a storm arose and blew them far south to an island hemmed in by very high cliffs, like city walls.

He proceeds to say:

They found a landing-place and went ashore to see if any folk lived there. Presently, they came on signs of people who, at noonday hid in holes in the earth. At the entrance to these subterraneans lay urns and vases of gold and other metals, that mortals hold for rare and precious. They took as many of the vases as they could carry to their small boats and in great joy rowed back to their ships. Feeling a desire to obtain more of the gold, they returned to the shore, when, on a sudden, they cried out in astonishment to see wonderfully tall men of the sort we call cyclopes, who were with very large dogs of extraordinary fierceness who ran at their heels. These dogs came howling, with the foam slavering at their open jaws, and fell on some of the Frisians whom they tore to pieces and ate. The rest of the seamen at once hastened to the shore to embark, while, behind them on the tall cliffs, the giants shouted in anger as the ships went out to sea. Home in Bremen, the seamen gave Archbishop Aldebrand a full account of their expedition, and to our Lord and St. Willehad hearty thanks for their safe return from their adventures.

"There are," said Antoine Snider-Pellegrini, a forgotten French "Américaniste" of the 1850's, "giants whom we have ourselves seen in America. Among groups of savages, these men were seven feet and the women six feet to six-and-a-half feet tall, but we should not have dared to speak of it for fear that our simple testimony might appear not to have sufficient authority."

However, another Frenchman, not so diffident or modest, one Commodore Byron of the warship *La Patrie*, spoke of what he saw near Port St. Julien, in Patagonia, on 7th March, 1858. There he met a chief of giant stature reminding him "of a Cyclops". Over the chief's shoulder was thrown the skin of a wild beast, in the manner of the braw Hielan'man's Scottish plaid. He showed Byron his body, which was covered with hideous paintings. He was over seven feet tall and the women of the tribe were tall in proportion:

"The band of savages with this chief, also giant men, sang a song that fairly stunned me with its noise (*qui m'abasourdit*). These giants were perfectly built and a lieutenant in my ship who himself was six feet two inches was struck with astonishment at seeing himself made to look like a pygmy by the side of these giants. So much so that I laughed. These Patagonian giants have large shoulders and well developed chests. There were five hundred of them and their height was not bought at the expense of their muscles as might have been the case in Europe."

In the fall of 1929, Dean Byron Cummings of Arizona University and Professor Manuel San Domingo, a Mexican Government scientist of Sonora went to a dangerous spot 160 miles from the international border where the turbulent Yaquis smash excavation work with rifle butts and menace intruders with sudden death. They found three giant skeletons of two men and a woman eight feet tall. The skulls were a foot long and ten inches wide, and there were remains of six children, all six feet tall. In tall ollas were human ashes suggesting either cremation or human sacrifices. The remains were in an ancient burial ground called the "Cyclopes necropolis". Beautiful ceramics were buried with the giants' remains which were also covered with fine jewels. The pottery showed a high degree of skill and the race could hardly be called savage. However, before the expedition could get properly to work, down swooped the Yaquis armed with rifles and knives. They fiercely bade the archæologists quit, or take the consequences. The Mexican professor tried in vain to placate the Indians. His remonstrances were abruptly shattered by a tough Yaqui brave who upraised a heavy rifle butt and battered the giant remains to pieces. The rest followed his example and hacked the finds to pieces. Five children had skeletons showing that they were all over six feet tall in life. Some of the adults were not far short of nine feet tall. The remains of a giant girl were found at the foot of a boy, and an examination suggested that she was buried alive, in truly Mu-an manner! At a conservative estimate, the archæologists say the giants lived at least 2,000 years ago. (The nearest railroad depôt to the spot is Tonichi. It would appear that a battery of machine-guns would be necessary to keep off the wild Yaquis.)

Earlier in the same year (1929) Mr. Paxon Hayes found mummies of a peculiar race of Mongoloid giants in dry caves in the sierras of New Mexico, U.S.A. He got out thirty-four of these mummies, and did four years' hard work in the region. He says the facial angles of these and their burial customs are different from those of Indians. They have slanting eyes and sloping foreheads, and the adults are about seven feet high, though their feet are only seven inches long. Their hair is black, with a peculiarly sunburnt tinge when closely examined. The remains were preserved in asphaltum, or resin, and wrapped in burial clothes bound with fibre. Obviously they were of a much lower order of culture than the Mexican giants, and very few tools or implements were found near the remains.

44

Mr. de Valda, a well-known traveller in South and Central America spoke, in 1938, of astounding remains of giant men and women found in Ecuador, and by himself when he was hunting for a bandit cache in the wilderness of south-western Mexico. In the case of the Mexican remains of both giant men and women of at least eight feet in height, bluish pottery, with them in the grave, bore a Grecian type of meander pattern. The Spanish priest and soldier, Cieza de Leon, spoke of remains of similar giant men—not bones of prehistoric mammoths, elephants or mastodons, or saurians—found, about A.D. 1530, in or near Manta, then located in the northern region of the old empire of Inca Atahualpha. Giants, of course, were not unknown to the ancients of the classic age, or, of course, to the old Irish, or to our ancient forbears, who bequeathed to us the "legends" and folk-lore on which are based such fairy stories as that of Jack the Giant-Killer. Homer, in his *Odyssey*, speaks of the giant Lestrygonians who, when Odysseus, or Ulysses, came on their coasts, sank his ships and ate his companions. Remains found in caves of fjords in Norway incline some to locate these Lestrygonians, to whom Homer did not give a country, as ancient inhabitants of Norway.

By the curious coincidences that mark discoveries of hidden and surprising matters that the too sceptical dismiss as mere moonshine and travellers' or fairy tales, while Commodore Byron was talking with giants in Patagonia, in 1858, in that very year on the other side of the ocean on the site of old Carthage a sarcophagus of giants was found. Tertullianus (J. Septimius Florens) a well-known Christian writer who flourished in this same Carthage, about A.D. 196, said that in *his* day a number of giants were to be found in Carthage. Philostratus, the sophist of Lemnos, who died in A.D. 244, says he himself saw a giant skeleton of a man twenty-two cubits long, and another of twelve cubits on the promontory of Sigeum, which is on the Asian shores of the modern Dardanelles looking out on the Ægean.

Taking the cubit as being equivalent to eighteen or twenty-two modern inches, this *seems* to mean that the giants were from thirty-three to forty feet tall, in the one case, and eighteen to twenty-two feet, in the other! Messecrates of Stira, in Lemnos (opposite the entrance to the modern Dardanelles, westward in the Ægean Sea), found a "giant horrible to behold" (The *Heroica*, page 35).

Pliny, in *Natural History*, speaks of a giant in whom he thought he recognized Orion, a giant born, according to the ancient myth, from the skin of an ox put by a peasant into the earth of Bœotia, at the behest of the (Atlantean) gods Neptune, Mercury, and Jupiter and into which those Atlantean men, or demi-gods, urinated. Orion, it will be recalled, figures in the constellations at the feet of the Bull, an object of worship in the great temples of old Atlantis.

A reference to the Atlantean sun-worshipping of this giant Hercules of Chios, Orion, skilled worker in iron, who fabricated the underground palace of Vulcan, is found in the old myth which tells how he, the blinded giant, recovered his sight, after his eyes had been put out by the perfidious king Œnopion of Chios, by wandering, like Sinbad the sailor, with a workman on his back, to the seashore in the dawn hour when the Sun was rising from the bed of the ancient Mediterranean. Again, Pausanias, the historian and orator who settled at Rome in A.D. 170, asserts that there existed in his day the great tombs of Asterius (the son of King Minos of the mysterious Minoan civilization of Crete); Geryon of Gades, or Tartessus, who kept flocks in a place, not far from Cadiz, at the mouth of the modern Rio Guadalquivir which, recent excavations suggest, was a colony of old Atlantis; and Hillus, son of Hercules. In the Trojan War, Turnus of the Rutuli, or aborigines of Latium, and the Greek heroes hurled stones at their enemies which, said the traditions, four men of the later ages would not have been able to move as much as one inch along the ground. Plutarch tells us that the Roman general Quintus Sertorius, in Spain about 70 B.C., saw the tomb of Antæus, the giant, killed by the mortal Hercules who, it may be recalled, saved the whole Pantheon, refuging from heaven in Egypt, from the wrath of the giants. A myth which *might*, tentatively, be euhemerized by supposing that some insurrection against the ruling castes in old Atlantis had been waged by, or with, the assistance of men of gigantic stature. The skeleton found in this tomb of Antæus, says Plutarch, measured six cubits in length (from nine to eleven feet).

In old Britain we had the Gogmagog, whose statues are, or were before the Nazi bombings of 1940–42, to be seen in London, but not on Plymouth Hoe, and who may not be altogether fairy tales of Geoffrey of Monmouth, or Brut Tysilio of Wales. Oddly enough, the Abbé Pegues, in his *Les Volcans de Grèce*, says that in the neighbourhood of the volcanoes of the isle of Thera (Santorin), in the Ægean, north of Crete, giants with enormous skulls were found laid out under colossal stones, the erection of which in every place must have necessitated the use of titanic powers, and which tradition in all lands associates with ideas about giants, volcanoes and magic.

Time has his revenges: I am told that scientists are now, at least in the U.S.A., coming round to the view that ancient giants existed. One Harvard professor as recently as 1946 gave a course to students and freshmen in which, one is told, he repeatedly mentioned the extraordinary size of a jaw of an anthropoid, early man not giant ape, found at the outbreak of the Second World War in Java. He had been called *Giganto-anthropos*. In a "dragon shop" in China the tooth of such a giant man has recently been found, to which the name of *Giganto-pithecus* (giant ape) had erroneously been given. However, Professor Hooton, and other palæontologists, one is told, now tend to regard the tooth as belonging to a primitive type of man whose proportions, calculated from the size of this tooth, might have been twenty feet tall. Of course, biologists assert that there is a limitation to the size of an organism and, as outsize teeth might sometimes be found in other primitive human and non-human jaws, such a height as twenty feet in the case of a man is not, at present acceptable. Obviously, more than a tooth would be required before such a revolutionary conclusion could be accepted. Nor, of course, I suppose, would any professor, or archæologist agree that such giants co-existed with any degree of civilization or advanced culture. In this, as in other mysteries of the dawn of civilization, hardly a corner of the veil has yet been lifted.[1]

I shall have much more to say in a subsequent book about giant men in the ancient Americas.

My reader may, not without justification, charge me with digressing from my theme, but my purpose is to suggest that there *must* have been land-bridges, long since submerged, across which these giants wandered from the Americas to the old world of Europe and the ancient proto-Mediterranean, in the dim ages of heliolithic culture. Here, again, as so often, evidence, for the undoubted existence of giants, is to be found in South America and old Mexico.

All over Central America and ranging far south of the equatorial line in South America, one finds intimations of cataclysms that have destroyed great civilizations. The ancient traditions crystallized in Indian tribal "myths" and folk lore, in the Aztecan codices, and in the Mayan bible, the *Popul Vuh*, tie with others in the ancient classical literatures of Europe. The myths speak of giants.

Ixtlilxochitl, the native Mexican historian, writing a history of the Chichimecs, speaks of the "Sun", or epoch of water, a cyclic period which was terminated by a cataclysm. He says it was followed by the "Earth Sun", called Tlachitonatuith, which closed in violent earthquakes, when the *Quinames*, or Giants flourished.

In the Mexican frontier province of Chiappas, there lived a priest and vandal, Fray Nuñez de la Vega, local archbishop. This old ass, in an evil hour for archæology, in America got hold of a number of very ancient manuscripts, which seem to be records of an Atlantean, or proto-Phœnician people who pioneered civilization in Central America. He found nothing better to do than to burn all these valuable manuscripts in the market-place of a pueblo in that state, when he made a visitation in the year 1691. These manuscripts tell of an old man who, at the time of the Great Deluge, was saved on a raft with his family. He, the old man, had a great-grandson named Votan, who saw the erection of the Great Tower of Babel. Votan bears a striking resemblance to the old Scandinavian god of war and magic, Woden, of our Wednesday, but it is certainly an anachronism to identify him with the great old man Quetzalcoatl, who came to old Mexico from either the land of Hy-Brazil, or the other lost continent of Antillia, of which the modern Antilles of the West Indians are probably the high spots, above water.

---

[1] Telegrams from Casas Grandes, Mexico, in 1923, announced the discovery of several skeletons of Indians *fifteen feet tall*, buried side by side, with vases of precious stones. The news came from Ciudad Juarez.

The Aztec *Codex Vaticanus* speaks of "vices of men that were the cause of the troubles of the world", and of the goddess Chalchithuitlicul, "who is she who remained, after the deluge, with the man, the tree (or *ark*), and is the mother of the god Tlaloc, whom they have made goddess of water".

Naturally, however, as one has said before, had the pre-Diluvian age man been good, or evil, man of golden age, or a necromancer of a race of demons and devils, he could not have prevented the impact of that planet (or comet, or great aerolite) wandering from outer space into the orbit of our earth! What had to be had to be: for as the Greeks themselves said, not the gods on the high hill of violet-crowned Olympus can deflect by a hair the decision of Fate and destiny.

In ancient Perú there is an Andean tradition speaking symbolically of great earthquakes and hurricanes which changed the face of the earth, erected mountains, and sank and submerged great land-masses in the waters of the ocean; or, on the land of pre-cataclysmic, or proto-South America, depressed great plains. One Andean "myth"[1] says of this period of catastrophe that there was an extraordinary eclipse of the sun. All light vanished for five days! In the Spanish National archives in Madrid there is a manuscript by the old Colonial writer Molina, titled *Relacion de las fabulas y ritos de los Ingas*. (Account of the legends and ceremonies of the Incas.) In it he tells a curious story, which is not altogether legendary, about a Peruvian shepherd who was leading a troop of llamas, when he saw "how sad the animals looked" . . .

And all night they stood watching the march of the stars across the sky. He questioned the llamas, and they bade him observe a group of six stars, ranged one behind the other, which, they said, foretold the end of the world, by water.

Here, again, it is remarkable that ancient Mexican traditions speak of these six stars, which are called the *tzontemocque*: stars falling from the sky at the time of the Great Deluge. But to continue the story from Molina's manuscript:

The llamas advised the shepherd to take his family and flocks on to the mountain tops nearby, and so he would escape the universal disaster. The shepherd obeyed their advice, and when he reached the mountain-top, lo, he found another assembly of animals there! No sooner had he and his family and flocks arrived, than the sea broke her bounds. There was a frightful shaking of the earth, and the great waves of the ocean in awful tumult began to rise over the land from the Pacific. Yet, in proportion as the sea rose over the land, immediately inundating the valleys and the plains, the mountain of Ancasmarca

---

[1] The old Floridans, such as the Seminole Indians, among whom an English sea-surgeon, an ancestor of the writer of this story, lived captive, in the year 1820, say the sun, at the time of the Great Catastrophe, retarded his course by eighty hours, and that the waters of Lake Théom overflowed and covered everything, except a mountain on which took refuge the only men who were saved.

also rose, like a ship borne up on waves. For five days the cataclysm lasted, and all that time the sun ceased to give light, and the earth was in black darkness; but on the fifth day the waters began to roll back and the sun, coming out, shone on a desolated world, that was re-peopled by the posterity of the pastor of llamas.

The mountain of Ancasmarca lies five Spanish leagues, say around eighteen miles, from Cuzco, the old capital of ancient Perú.

Then, listen to the old Spanish writer, Antonio Herrera, who lived in the years A.D. 1549–1625, and who was "Coronista Major" of his Spanish Royal and Catholic Majesty of the Indies and his crown of Castile, and author of the *Historia General de los Hechos de los Castellanos e las Islas i Tierra Firme del Mar Oceano*:

> The Indians have it, by tradition of their ancestors, and it appears in their songs (*cantares*) that, in ancient days, the Sun was not visible for a long time, and that by earnest vows and prayers they made to their gods the Sun came out of Lake Titicaca (on the Andes), and from that island, that is, in it, in the Collao, there presently appeared in the middle of the day, a *white man*, of great body (*hombre blanco de gran cuerpo*), and venerable presence, who was so powerful that he lowered the hills (*sierras*), increased the valleys, and drew fountains from the rocks; whom, for his great powers, they called prince of all created things and father of the Sun; since he gave life to men and animals, and by his great power great benefits came to them, and that, working these marvels, he went a long way towards the North, and, on his way, gave an order of life to nations, when he spoke with much loving kindness, correcting them, that they might be upright (*buenos*), and uniting them one with another, whom, until the last days of the Incas, they called *Ticeuiracocha* or Viracocha[1], and in the Collao, Tupaco, and in other parts Arrauâ, and that they built many temples and many sculptures (*bultos*) they placed in them, in his likeness, to which they sacrificed. The Indians say there also appeared in ancient times another *man* like the foregoing, who healed the sick, and cured the diseased, gave sight to the blind, and that, in the province of los Caños, where the people madly wished to stone him, they saw him kneeling down, upraising his hands to the skies, invoking divine favour, and that there appeared a fire from the skies, that terrified them very much, insomuch that with great cries and shrill screams they prayed that he might deliver them from that danger, since there had come that punishment for their sin. Presently the fire ceased, and the stones were no more burned. They say that to-day the same stones are seen burnt black and so discoloured (*livianos*), and, notwithstanding, they are huge rocks, they ooze (*se le van tan como corcho*) like a cork; and they say that there he stayed by the seas, and entering in it upon his outstretched cloak, he was never more seen; for which they called him *Viracocha*, which meaneth to say: foam of the sea (*espuma de la mar*), a name that afterwards changed its signification, and so that presently they built him a temple in the pueblo of Cacha, and certain Castilians only have said that he must have been an apostle, but the most sensible hold this saying for vanity.

[1] *Vira* in certain remote Brazilian villages means the *Sun*!

Herrera also tells what the Peruvians said of the deluge:

> The oldest Indians said that, by tradition of their elders, many years before the Incas were, all that land was thickly peopled, and there was so great a deluge that the sea overran her bounds, and the land was covered with water, and all the people perished. And after that, say the Guancas, dwellers in the vale of Jauxa, and them of the Chiquito, in the Collao (Titicaca), there were, in the caves and hollows of the highest mountain, some that resolved to return and people the earth anew.

The old Spanish missioner, Cristoval de Molina, priest at Cuzco, Perú, in the mid-sixteenth century, referred to *supra*, tells how, in the house of the Sun called Poquen Cancha, near Cuzco, the Peruvians painted each one of the lives of the Inca Emperors, with the list of their conquests, with figures on certain boards . . . and among these painted fables was the following:

> In the life of Manco Capac, the first Inca, they began to be called Children of the Sun, and from him they had the full story of the Great Deluge. They say that all created things perished in it; for the water rose above all the highest mountains in the world. No living thing survived, except a man and a woman who remained in a box, and when the waters subsided, the winds carried them in the box to Huanacq (the megalithic remains of mysterious Tiahuanaco, in modern Bolivia, and about 230 miles from Cuzco). There are other nations who say that when the deluge came all people were destroyed, except a few who escaped to the hills, in caves, or trees, and that these were very few, but that they began to multiply; and that, in memory of the first of their race, who escaped to such places, they made idols of stone giving the name of him, who had thus escaped, to each *huaca* (monument or burial-place).

It would appear that the influence of the early Incas must at some time have spanned the land-bridge of Panama-Darien, extending its sway from the old Cara-Inca province of Quito, in what is now Ecuador. The Inca civilization must be at least as old as the priestly traditions import, and which survive, in part, in what Montesinos copied from lost manuscripts of Blas Valera, a monk who was the son of a Quichua lady, or *señora*, as early Spanish cronistas assert.

The Inca connection is indicated in the fact that in old Panama was a large tribe, named the Guayana, at the head of which were three chiefs to whom were rendered exactly the same ceremonial obeisances as the Inca emperors received. Yet, there is not to-day even a hoary tradition or a shadow of an ancient myth linking these Guyanas with the Perú of the Incas. (Maybe, both races originated in the lost continent of Mu, or Rutas-Mu.)

One great tribe of Indians—the Guarani of Brazil—say that Monan, the Maker, seeing the ingratitude of men and their contempt for him and his laws that had made them joyous, withdrew from them and sent *tata*, the divine fire, which burned all on the surface of the earth. He swept the fire about; so that, in places, he raised mountains and, in others, deep valleys. Only one man was saved, and he was *Toin Magé*—the man who sees—and after he was carried to Heaven, Monan sent a deluge of rain on the earth, in order to quench the fire; and it flowed from all sides, forming the ocean called *Coll Partana*: the great waters. The tribe has another legend about what happened after the deluge:

> Two brothers, Tupi and Guarani landed on the coast of Brazil, with women and children and built houses and towns. The brothers quarrelled, and dispersed all over a vast region, where they are called Tupi and Guarani.

In the word *Guarani* is a root *car, gar* or *var*, meaning "fighting-men". Guevara, in his *History of Paraguay*, points out that when the old Portuguese landed in Brazil, the Guaranis built no more towns but mere straw huts.

The Panamian Indians, as well as the ancient Mexicans, had also the tradition of the ark and deluge . . . Say the ancient Mexicans:

> Organ survived the great deluge, in a bark. Children were all born dumb, until a dove from a high tree taught them tongues.

The touch about the linguistic dove after the deluge is very curious and apparently unique! Of course, it might easily happen that children who had the ill luck to be born during, or after a cosmic, catastrophe of this sort might easily become idiots, as well as mutes! Mothers in child-birth, or pregnant in such times were hardly likely to transmit happy post-natal influences to their children. As we shall see, humanity which survived in the region of the catastrophe, or escaped from it, lapsed from normality to a condition of insanity from which thousands of years hardly rescued them. The horrible doctrine of the atonement[1] which the old Jews modified, so that an animal—an escaped goat, or scape-goat, instead of a luckless youth or maiden—took the burden of the sins of the community, or pro-pitiated the corn-gods of sowing and the harvest may date from a period of cosmic catastrophe of this kind.

The Tlascalans, a Mexican nation living east of Mexico City, say the men who survived the deluge were turned into *apes*, and recovered speech and reason slowly and by degrees! (*See* Francis Clavijero's *Mexican History*.)

The Mixtecs, a race of civilized Indians in south-west Mexico, speak of a man and a woman who, by magic, raised a great mountain out of the water, and built thereon beautiful palaces for their dwellings. There came a flood and all their sons and daughters were drowned.

In Cuba, the remains of the lost continent of Antillia, which partly submerged about 200 B.C. when the Mayas reached Yucatan,

---

[1] It has also been suggested, in ancient Mexican traditions of very dim and shadowy sort, that the same human sacrifices were carried over to the Americas by migrants from Mu, or Lemuria, parts of which continents were inhabited by a brutal race. More of this may be said, in a later book by myself.—AUTHOR.

were some natives who retorted on a rather too zealous Spanish friar with a hey-nonny-no, and a marry-come-up, when that monastic, name of Fray Gabriel de Cabrera, rebuked an old man for what he deemed shortcomings.

Said the grey-bearded Indian:

> Come, come, *señor* friar, why scold me? Are we not all brothers? Did you not descend from one of the sons of him who built the great ship to save himself from the water, and we from the other?

The tradition had been handed down from generation to generation in Cuba. The friar's reply is not given. One cannot say if the Catholic spiritual panache of his rosary and cassock inspired him to retort in the spirit of the sour-faced Jesuit (?) or Dominican (?) monks in Reade's classic, *The Cloister and the Hearth*, who, when assured by the amiable Burgundian soldier of fortune that they should have: "Courage, mes amis. Le Diable est mort", replied: "God forbid!"

Dark cosmological shadows of the appalling cataclysm that overtook our own planet, and as I tried to show, giving curious evidence, in my previous book, *Mysteries of Ancient South America*, probably drove the rotating globe centrifugally, or eccentrically from a station in our solar system, perhaps as near the Sun-centre as are Venus and Mercury, to its present position and caused a toppling of the gyroscopic spin which made the Pole and Equator change place, are found crystallized both in South American Indian traditions and the sacred lore and codices of the Aztecs. I there drew attention to the significance of the rainbow "myths" of the Gilgamesh story of ancient Assyria and of the parallel rainbow "myths", which must have sprung up independently. They are a hemisphere apart, sundered by a continent and a great ocean. I there suggested that here may lie a cosmogonical and astronomical explanation of the remarkable length of days of the kings of ancient Sumer, as recorded on tablets dug up on their ancient township sites, and of the patriarchs of the Hebrew Genesis: Methuselah, Adam, Seth, Canaan, Enos, and Malaheel, whose days range from 965 to 800 years. Obviously, these "days" must have been years of a mundane rotation when our Earth may have completed its orbital path round the central Sun, not in 365 days, but in 250 or 260 days. At that time, we may have been a neighbour of Venus, spinning not, as now, on an orbit No. 3 from the sun, but far nearer, on No. 2. In that event, our old friend Methuselah, who, in the Hebrew epic, is not quite the oldest patriarch, may have had a span of years each of which was nearer 166 or 172 of our present years.

Perhaps, before some of the clerical gentlemen whose scepticism on this theory is matched by their arrogant, professional holus-bolus acceptance of virgin birth myths and man-god Mediterranean legends superciliously dismiss these unorthodox suggestions, some of my other friends, not so clerical, but more humble, who are not so cock-sure of their cosmogonical and astro-physical infallibility, will cast an eye on these "myths" of a rainbow-less world, existing before an appalling cataclysm. These myths are found in the two ancient Americas. It may be recalled that the *solar* spectrum, or rainbow, the accident of rays of light prismatically intercepted in drops of falling water, cannot exist in the skies of any member of our solar system where rain falls always by night and never by day. And that is the case in Venus,[1] and, according to these cosmological "myths" of Gilgamesh-Genesis, and of ancient Central and South America, was once the case in the "ante-diluvian world" of our own Earth!

Both in the Middle East and in the "New World" of the Americas one has this story of a rainbow, as a sign of a covenant from a demi-ourgos that the Earth should no more be drowned. For example, the old Chibchas of Bogotá, on the high savanas of modern Colombia, say they were civilized by an old man in black, named Bochicha. I, in my book *Mysteries of Ancient South America*, tried to prove that all these "men in black": Quetzalcoatl in the ancient land of the Quiches of Yucatan and Guatemala; Viracocha, the sun (*Vira*) god-man of ancient Perú; and Bochicha were really pioneers, missioners of culture and *men*, not gods or demi-gods. They, perhaps, came to these lands from the old Atlantean empire of the Brazilian Isle (Hy-Brazil) before the Great Cataclysm.

When Bochicha appeared to quell the deluge, says the myth of the Chibchas, *he was seated on a rainbow*. Euhemerism, which explains and rationalizes ancient legends and myths, suggests that Bochicha may have come either before, or after, some calamity which befell one of the dead cities of Brazil, whence he was sent to *find a safer country*.

The Incas of Perú also said, like the ancient Jews, that the rainbow was a sign that the earth would be no more drowned. They connected it with the legend of one Viracocha, or human culture-hero, the sun-god who appeared in Lake Titicaca after a great deluge. But the most startling of all "lights" on the greatest calamity that ever befell our earth, came from places in old Europe and old Mexico with which there could not have been the ghost of a direct *historic* connection. Both "lights", one in Aztec codices, the other in a fragment of a vanished Roman author, are in the form of clear statements about, a revolutionary change in the *apparent course and colour of the planet Venus, as seen from Earth, after the great disaster which overtook Atlantis and parts of Central and South America.*

The first reference to a cosmic catastrophe overtaking our Earth, thousands of years before the birth of Christ, is found in a fragment of a lost book by the "most learned of the Romans", M. Terentius

---

[1] *Venus*, which receives twice as much solar heat as the earth, reflects the light of the sun. It has a thicker atmosphere than the Earth, and is so surrounded with clouds that it is difficult, or impossible, to glimpse the surface. *Mercury* has seven times as much solar heat as Earth. As its annual and diurnal rotations are about equal, one side has perpetual day, the other night, or intense cold. Neither in the case of Mercury nor Venus is there any justification for saying that they are "covered with shoreless icebound oceans". Venus emphatically is *not*; for the thick atmosphere could not co-exist with an ice-bound ocean. *Lunar* rainbows, by the way, are another matter.

Varro. He was lieutenant of Pompey in the piratical wars in the Mediterranean, and died in 28 B.C. St. Augustine quotes the fragment, in *De Civitate Dei*:

Est in Marci Varronis libris quorum inscriptio De gente populi Romani. . . ! In coelo, inquit, mirabile exstitit portentum: nam stellam veneris nobilissiman, quam Plautus Vesperuginam, Homerus appellat, pulcherrimam dicens Castor scribit tantum isse ecstitisse, ut mutaret in colorem, magnitudinem, figuram, cursum, quod factum ita neque antea nec postes sit. Hoc factum Ogygo rege dicebant Adrastos Cyzicenos et Dion Neapolites, mathematici nobiles.

Translation: It is in the book of Marcus Varro, whose title is *Of the Race of the Roman People*, that, in the same place, one reads there, as I myself have set down:

In the heavens (he says) an amazing sign appeared; for the star of Venus, most noble, that Plautus calleth Vesperugu, or the evening star, and Homer, Hesperon (morning star of the west), most beautiful, and of which Castor writes saying that such a portent existed; for it changed in colour, size, form, shape, and course, that neither before, nor after, was the like seen. This event befell in the reign of King Ogyges, saith Adrastos Cyzicenos, and Dion Neapolites, noble mathematicians.

N.B.—Castor was a Greek grammarian, who lived 150 B.C.; Ogyges, son of Neptune, was a man of Atlantean race, who lived in Egypt, or in Phœnicia. Attica, as a result of a deluge in his reign, was waste for nearly 200 years.—AUTHOR.

Obviously, the change of size, colour, form and course in Venus was apparent, and was really caused by the revolutionary change in the earth's orbital position, near Venus, when the impact with the wandering stellar, or planetary, body violently altered the earth's orbit.

In old Mexico, before the Spanish conquistadores under Cortes and Grijaleva came, the Aztecs celebrated a festival *commemorating changes in the condition of several of the constellations*, AFTER THE TIME OF THE CATASTROPHIC DELUGE! One *fiesta* commemorated a change in the planet Venus, called by the Aztecs: Tlahuizcalpan-teuctli, or the lord who lights the house-tops. In the *Codex Telleriano-Remensis* (which came into the hands of a Monsieur Tellier, and is now in the Bibliothèque Nationale of Paris), painted by Aztec scribes, at the request of Spanish *padres*, it is said:

Este Tlahuizcalpan-teuchtli, ò estrella Venus es el Queçavatl . . . Dizen que es aqualla estrella que llamamos Luzero del ava, y asi lo pintan, con una caña, que era su dia.

Translation: This Tlahuizcalpan-teuchtli, or the star Venus, is Quetzalcoatl. They say he is that star we call Light of the day (modern Spanish: *lucero del alba*, or day-star), and so they paint him, with a reed (or cane), and this star was his day.

The Aztecs also had a goddess, called *Itzpapalotl*, or the goddess butterfly with the obsidian knives. She had another name, which means Venus, goddess of lascivious love, or, in Aztec: Ixcuina. In another codex (*Letellier*), it is said:

> She caused death to the world, and is one of the six constellations that fell from the sky at the time of the Deluge.

Another remarkable proto-historic and astronomical-ziggurat-star-tower identity between sacerdotal Babylonia-Assyria and ancient Aztecan Mexico is found in Papantlan. The Babylonian sacerdotal records assert that their own priests received the elements of astronomy and solar science from giants who escaped from an antediluvian world (Atlantis?) and bequeathed to the priests of Baal-Marduk-Vira the knowledge of previous ancient cataclysms that had befallen the ancient world of our own Earth. Outside the walls of modern Iraq's sacred Moslem city of fanatical Samarra may, to-day, be seen an ancient heliacal tower. It stands—this ancient ziggurat—in the desert sands beyond an ancient, quadrilateral walled and now empty, enclosure and is one of the oldest religious buildings in the world. This ziggurat has *seven* tiers dedicated by the ancient Babylonian priests of the sun-god Marduk to the worship of seven planets. Hence, we derive our own week of *seven days*.

Now, at Papantlan, in Mexico, is a very ancient pyramid built of hewn stones of megalithic type. These stones are of extraordinary size and finely-fashioned. Three stairways lead to the top of stepped terraces which were decorated with structures inscribed with hieroglyphs. Small niches are also arranged with exquisite symmetry. Be it noted that in the Papantlan pyramid there are *seven*[1] of these storeys, all tapered! This is certainly no accidental resemblance. It is a sign to our own age of a far-spreading semi-global culture of pre-cataclysmic, antediluvian priest-astronomers of a far day when a land-bridge existed between the civilizations of ancient America and the island-continent of Atlantis, which may be the missing cultural link of the heliolithic age of the ancient world. It is also, probably not without significance that the whole number of the niches in this pyramid of Papantlan contain 318 simple and compound signs denoting the ancient days of the calendar of this unknown heliolithic civilization of ancient Central America.

Whether or no there is a further significance, in that 3.18 is so near the *pi* symbol of the ratio of the circumference of the circle to its diameter (3.14159 . . .), I am not here concerned to demonstrate. I should not be surprised to hear that in the dead cities of the Brazilian Highlands there will one day be found a parallel heliacal, or tapering, tower of *seven* storeys. It will then be interesting to hear, or note, what will be said, or *not* said by modern archæologists and proto-historians on these singular parallelisms.

---

[1] Orientals considered that the planets numbered seven. The Yezidis, or Devil-worshippers of a region near Mosul, Iraq, to-day, say that Satan, or Lucifer, is really the demi-ourgos, one of *seven* spirits, emanating from, or created by, an Unknown First Cause, who is infinitely remote and knows nothing of, nor cares anything for, the Earth.

These strange structures, by the way, have a very curious bearing on the "absurd" statement, as old Ben Jowett, the would-be spouse of Florence Nightingale would certainly have said, of Diogenes Laertius (died A.D. 222). He said that the old priests of Pharaoh had temple records carrying the annals of world history back to 48,863 *years* before Alexander! How many of these same years, by the way, would need to be reckoned as years of the age when our Earth, if the rainbow myth has here been correctly euhemerized, was spinning in an orbit near that of Venus?

To what purpose these ancient Asian towers were put is strangely suggested by Herodotus, a remarkably careful and accurate Greek historian of the ancient world as he knew it. And what he says may also apply to the "supernormal" activities that went on inside the pyramid of Papantlan and those towers which may be found, presently, to exist in the ruins of the dead Brazilian cities. Inside the eighth tower of Belus, the sun-god, in ancient Babylon, were kept stones called *betyli*, or *betylos*. The sacerdotal astrologers of this eighth tower had an upper room, or sanctuary where the vaticinating priestesses, or Pythonesses, slept to receive the message of the god. Beside the woman's couch was a table of stone on which lay various stones. Manetho of old Egypt says these stones, or *betyli*, were, like the stone of the Kaabah at Moslem Mecca in Saudi-Arabistan, ærolites.

It would seem that the woman developed a power of dilating the normal consciousness by pressing the *betylos* against her head and bosom. Similar "psychometrical" experiments took place at the temple of Thebes and at Patara, in Lycia, where the oracle of the sun-god Apollo was. Priests of Cybele wore *betyli* on their bodies (Cybele, the wife of the Atlantean man-god Saturn, was, of course, the ancient goddess of fecundity whose rites went "black" and licentious). Three classic writers, Pliny, Strabo and Helancius even suggested that these ærolites, or *betyli* had "electro-magnetic powers". Whether, however, there be anything in contentions that psychometry is a faculty possessed by certain persons—and I have, in connection with queer relics of Captain William Kidd, the pirate-privateer, vainly desired to put it to the test under proper experimental safeguards—it is the fact that the Babylonians and other ancients derived their knowledge of the planets partly by using these aerolites. If they could be proved to have been put to such use in Asia, then it would be extremely probable that such rites existed in the ancient South and Central American pyramid star-towers.

Investigating field-workers in Colombia have found in certain ancient sites of races unknown indications that these ancient men may have possessed knowledge of some form of illumination very like that of our modern electric current. In the jungle of the Matto Grosso, as an Indian told Colonel P. H. Fawcett in the frontier township of Cuyabá, there are, and have existed for ages, known to and seen by himself—the Indian and his Indian forbears, strange, fixed lights.

This singular light, age by age, untended, shines out of the window openings in tall buildings, shrouded in dense forest, of ancient dead cities of Atlantean Brazil. It seems to be some form of cold light energy, possibly a type of fire-fly luminescence, multiplied by many candle-power, which is unknown to modern physicists.[1]

Even three thousand years ago, by the way, the philosophers of the old world of Asia and Hellenistic Europe anticipated the discovery of Sir William Crookes and Einstein that light has weight, or gravitational force. Crookes, as we know, weighed light in his radiometer, and Einstein showed that a ray of light will experience a curvature of its path when it passes through a gravitational field. The ray will be deflected towards a heavenly body it is passing and such deflection is partly caused by the curvature or geometrical modification of space caused by the sun. That theory was tested and confirmed by expeditions to Brazil and West Africa by the Royal Society and Royal Astronomical Society, at the solar eclipse of 29th May, 1919. *If* a far more ancient world of South America had devised a form of perpetual light, as in cities of the Brazilian Highlands, who knows what may have been the extent of their knowledge and application of physical science?

The followers of Pythagoras held that our sun was not the source of heat, meaning, apparently, that its energy did not reach our upper atmosphere in that form. Indeed, it does not seem very clear how the physicist's "absolute zero" of outer space within the solar system, theoretically, minus 273.7 Centigrade, can co-exist with a direct transmission of heat rays from our sun. One may justifiably theorize, from the probability that the aurora borealis lights may be the phenomenon of electrons from the sun passing through a vacuum in

So-called "perpetual lamps" are said to have been known to the Romans, and Bailey's *Philologos* speaks of them. There was the one found burning in the tomb of Tullia, daughter of Cicero, on the Appian Way, *temp.*, Pope Paul III. It had burnt for 1,550 years, but the opening of the sepulchre caused the light to go out. In Egypt, they are also said to have been known and used in tombs and sepulchres. Kircher's *Œdipi Ægyptiaci Theatrum Hieroglyphicum* also mentions them. Plutarch says he saw one in the temple of Jupiter Ammon where the priests told him it had been alight continuously for years, standing in the open where wind nor water could put it out. Old Memphis's temple is said to have had many such lamps, regarded as the symbol of the immortal spirit, which was distinct from the soul, which was only semi-immortal. Kedrenus says he saw one such lamp at Edessa, Syria, where, hidden on top of a gate, it had burnt for 500 years. Such lamps are said to have been known in Tibet, where the Abbé Huc said he saw one; and at Travancore (Trevandrum), India, by a London missioner. "Oiliness of gold", reduced to a fluid which reasorbs the oily fluid and gives it out again, with a reaction of light, is alleged to "explain" the luminescence, which also seems to have been connected with maintenance of a near-vacuum. Modern science knows of the "cold light" produced by luciferin and a catalyst called luciferase. This system is not "perpetual" and needs reactivation with hydrogen. How the firefly reactivates its own "cold light" none know. But no form of known chemiluminescence will last indefinitely without renewal or attention. The autoluminescence of radioactivity, which, theoretically, should last for one thousand years, means death to human beings exposed to the bombardment of the rays. Also, electroluminescence, such as the neon light, or the sodium vapour lamp, radiates only in one or two particular wave-lengths, such as red or deep yellow, is extremely expensive, and certainly not "perpetual". The ancient world of South America, as also that of old Egypt, possessed some secret we do not know. It would seem that these lights, once started, could never be put out.—AUTHOR.

the upper regions of the stratosphere, that heat may be the reaction of negative particles of electricity, not heat radiation, projected from the sun's photosphere and encountering positive electrical particles in our upper atmosphere. We cannot yet *know* but only speculate what the theocratic astronomers of these ancient South American cities knew of these matters of physical science.[1]

One extremely curious, though, as yet, unsettled or unaccepted piece of evidence of the possible scientific application of aeronautical knowledge in ancient Central America exists in the museum of San Salvador, where a prehistoric earthenware vase bears a burnt-on picture of a clump of tropic palms over which appear what *seem* to be men flying a machine, from which jets smoke, or flame, or incandescent gases. The civilization to which this artifact belongs is unknown, but extremely ancient. (It has been suggested to me that Mu knew of this invention.) If this picture *really* records a conquest of the air in the pre-cataclysmic age of the Americas it may not be altogether fantastic to suppose that such air machines were also operated by the rulers of these Atlantean Brazilian cities in their prime. The San Salvador picture *appears* to present one more bit of evidence of a world-wide diffusion of culture and scientific knowledge extending from some drowned continent in the Pacific across the American landbridge to Atlantis and the old world of Asia, many thousands of years ago.

Keely (*vide*, also, page 79), the forgotten New York inventor of the 1890's, who committed suicide from despair, and to whom the famous Barnato brothers sent a British major to investigate in Keely's laboratory a machine apparently defying the force of gravitation— the major, by the way, was greatly impressed by Keely's discoveries— seems also to have rediscovered some mysterious cosmic force. It was, perhaps akin to that referred to in the ancient Hindu work on magic, known as the *Ashtar Vidya*. One of these forces, said to be a "vibratory form of energy of cosmic origin", was applied to the construction of a flying machine, known as the *Agni-rath*. It supplied the motive force to fly the machine. The other force, according to this ancient Hindu work, was aimed from the air, apparently from a turret of a flying machine, somewhat in the manner of Mr. H. G. Wells's heat-ray projector, focused from *his* Martian machine on a large army embattled on the ground. This unknown force, called, I believe "Mishmak", is said to have incinerated 100,000 men and elephants.

---

[1] I make no comment on the as yet unproved, or unprovable, assertions of mystical quarters in the U.S.A., that, in a far age, beings with a very advanced science and civilization reached the Earth by space ships from another planet. It is also stated, in a vein of what the American editor calls "sci-fantasy", that these "Old Ones" developed scientific machines in great subterraneans, and that, in the manner of the late H. G. Wells's *Men from Mars*, after a great battle with certain peoples or forces, by the poisonous radio activity of the sun they were forced to quit the Earth, leaving behind in these tremendous subterraneans wonderful machines reminiscent of those described in Wells's *Time Machine*. Degenerate beings, such as the Morlocks, or machine-minders and lubricators of Wells's fantasy, are alleged to have these machines in their control. The American mystics call these evil beings "Deros", corresponding to the *Goros* in tunnels in old Tibet.—AUTHOR.

Assuredly, writing as I am doing at this moment in a zone of south-eastern England, on the edge of London, which was exposed by day and night to unheralded Nazi V2 rocket bombs dealing out death, disintegration and destruction on a truly dreadful scale, and from whose detonation over one's head to the final impact and explosion on the ground there is a margin of six seconds in which to take what can hardly be called "shelter", one may rationally say that knowledge of this kind, *if* it were possessed and applied in this antediluvian world of the Americas and Asia, or Atlantis and Mu (Rutas-Lemuria), could not be safely entrusted to beasts using the splendid brains of scientists who, under duress or from motives of nationalist patriotism, prostitute their discoveries. Wars know no law, except that which decrees woe to both victor and vanquished. We, in our cycle, having in the name of the sacred principle of barter *versus* finance plunged a world into the second red hell of barbarism within twenty years, have but little of which to boast. For not even the entreaties of U.S. scientists to President Truman could either induce the War Cabinets to make publicly open the test dropping of the first atomic bomb in the desert of Arizona, or stop atom bombs from being dropped on Nagasaki and Hiroshima. No doubt had the terrible land of Rutas-Mu, or Mu, not been disrupted by cataclysms some, *perhaps* 60,000 years ago, which not even the gods of any high Olympus could avert by an inch or a second, they would, without aid of what-ever gods rule the mysterious cosmos, have in their far distant day infallibly sent to perdition a world not worth the curse of a demi-ourgos.

Is the old saying of this ancient world again to be proved true:

That which has been shall return again?

Or, if *our own* scientists will *not* refuse their co-operation in the annihilation of every cultural and humane value on this crazed planet, called the "Wart" by Jupiterians in Mark Twain's *Captain Stormfield's Visit to Heaven*, are we to be "saved" by a new type of Erewhon rulers who will turn back the age of mechanism to the era of the stage-coach and the windjammer; who will decry death to any inventing new machines, or attempting to revive or recover old scientific and mechanical knowledge? One or the other, gentlemen of science!

As the man in black, Quetzalcoatl of old Brazilian Atlantis, warned the savages or barbarians he came, thousands of years before Columbus's day, to civilize and humanize in old Central America: "Repent, or prepare for the wrath to come! Remember: you, nor we have any continuing city on this planet. Would it not be as well to live as men, not as lunatics, or devils; since you cannot avert the night of unforeseen cataclysm? Be happy, then, and live decently while you can!"

Let the last word be to the old Jacobean English poet of a possibly finer day:

> We have short time to stay, as you,
>   We have as short a Spring;
> As quick a growth to meet decay
>   As you or any thing.
>   We die,
>   As your hours do, and dry
>   Like to the Summer's rain;
>   Or as the pearls of morning's dew
>   *Ne'er to be found again.*

An absurd story that appeared in the London *Daily Express*, on 10th October 1949, purports that Colonel Fawcett "was killed by his own Indian guides who baulked at entering the territory of the Chavantes Indians with him. When he insisted on going on, and knocked down one of the Indians to enforce his point, they preferred to kill him rather than bring on themselves the reprisal raid that would have been the Chavantes' only reply to any trespass".

I note that this "remarkable" dispatch was written at São Domingos, Rio das Mortes, Central Brazil. This *safe* township happens to be at least be 300 miles as the crow flies from the Rio das Mortes. It is safer, in fact, than Piccadilly Circus, London. One is also told by the *Daily Express* writer that the fierce Chavantes *Indiós* bludgeon parcels thrown down from aeroplanes flying over their territory, as warning that they want neither contact nor presents from intruders and adventurers.

In that, I may note, the Chavantes follow the ban imposed on entrance into *their* territories by the San Blas Indians of Darien, Panama State, and for much the same reason: gold, much gold, is in both lands. It attracts the scum and riff-raff of Europe and America. Once an entry is made, the Indians lose their lands, their women are interfered with, and they eventually degenerate from savage but virile men of the wilds into the poor coloured trash that haunts townships sited on land where once they strode the territory as kings.

But just a word about this silly yarn that Fawcett met his death because he knocked down an Indian guide. In the first place, Fawcett is known to have taken a direction contrary to that which would have entered the Chavantes' tribal lands. He, himself, remarked that the Rio das Mortes (River of Death) gave the impression of grave danger, whereas, in fact, it was perfectly safe! Nothing could have been more out of character than for Colonel Fawcett to have raised his hand against an Indian, and it was impossible that he would have knocked down an Indian guide—had he been employing a guide. But, in actual fact, Colonel Fawcett took no guides on *any* of his dangerous trips, which were trips by the way, of a *very* different sort from that undertaken by a young Etonian ridiculously described

60

in this *Daily Express* feature, as "barging through tangled bush, wading up rivers, labouring and starving in his fruitless search for Colonel Fawcett".

The man of whom this nonsense is written himself tells how he and another Etonian turned back *pronto* for the safe river, immediately they sighted, for the first time, smoke from unknown signal fires, miles away. Both young blades were taking no chance of any meeting with really dangerous Indians, or *Indiós malos*. I am pretty sure, too, that Cap'n Peter would be the first to say: "Save me from my friends", when he read this *very* veridical *Daily Express* feature.

Colonel Fawcett needed no guide; for he knew more about where he was going than any one else. Moreover, no Indian would have dared to venture beyond the range of his own particular tribe. *Never* would he (Fawcett) have raised his hand against an Indian. The success of his trip depended on their good will; and in any event, Fawcett was not that sort of vulgar bush-whacker. I make these comments, because I deem them due to the memory of a great Englishman who probably died advancing the frontiers from the edge of the known to the dangerous unknown. Let no jackal bark when the lion roars!

Colonel Fawcett and a companion discover the tracks of a giant reptile on the border of Bolivia and Brazil. Fawcett believed that dinosaurs still lived in the forests.

CHAPTER TWO

IERE-ATLANTIS UNVEILED

We travel not for trafficking alone,
By hotter fires our eager hearts are fanned;
For lust of knowing what should not be known
We take the GOLDEN ROAD to Samarcand.

HASSAN.

IN AUGUST, 1930, the French Academy of Sciences, in a land where, somewhere around 1905, someone left a large sum of money, to endow researches into what is now, in some orthodox quarters, satirically referred to as "Atlantology"[1] solemnly discussed a monograph presented to them by a Russian refugee, living in Algiers. This gentleman, Monsieur Felipoff, rightly pointed out that, not only in the dialogues of Plato, derived from what the ancient Egyptian priests of Sais and Heliopolis told Solon, but in Mexico and South America there are ancient "legends" handed down from generations immemorial telling about the engulfment of Atlantis and Rutas-Mu by the ocean. They tell of a tremendous cosmic cataclysm which brought on vulcanism and a Great Deluge of semi-global extent.

Felipoff emulated a previous scientific congress in pre-1914 Vienna. He said that the ancient Mexican and Egyptian traditions agreed that the island-continent of Atlantis vanished when the Sun was in the zodiacal sign of Cancer. Calculating from data based on the angle made by the spinning Earth and the polar axes with the plane of the ecliptic, or the orbital path of the Earth round the Sun, he reckoned that Atlantis sank into the ocean in the year 7256 B.C. This, of course, is around 3,000 years later than the time alleged by these Egyptian priests, Sonchis and, or Psenophis, to have been recorded in the ancient temple archives of old Egypt.

I have no intention here, of entering into a controversy as old as the days of Herodotus, as to what the ancient Egyptians really meant by a year.[2]

---

[1] Proclus, in his *Dissertions on Timæus* says that *Plato*, when in Egypt, spoke with the Egyptian priest at Sais, named Pateneit; with the priest Ochlapi at Heliopolis, and with the priest Ethimon, at Sebennytus. He says that Pateneit is the priest alluded to in the Timæus.

[2] The French bequest, referred to in *p. supra*, constitutes one of those numerous sardonic commentaries, as the venerable Bernard Shaw should reflect, into the vanity and futility of bequeathing large sums of money to trustees who are directed to lease, lend, or give the said moneys, or income of capital to men of no, or little means, for some definite purpose. As our world wags, such moneys might as well be sunk to the ocean-bed, or blown from the mouth of guns for all purpose they subserve!

But, of course, it is extremely unlikely that they were Hellenes, or classic Greeks who, as the Egyptian priest told Solon, represented old Europe's last hope in repelling the plans for hegemony of the Atlantean invaders. In 1915, Senhor A. Childe, "conservador das antiguidades classicis e orientes no Museo Nacional", Rio de Janeiro, gave a remarkable address at a conference in the Biblioteca Nacional, which is certainly not known to many English readers. Speaking of the consultation of Solon with the learned Sekhenhotep, of the ancient Egyptian college of Memphis, who when younger had been the master of Democritus, Senhor Childe said the migrations of the Greeks, in the *Hellada*, at once dispose of the story that they were the defenders of old Europe. These defenders and worshippers of Neith, the goddess of Sais, were Libyans of North-east Africa.

Senhor Childe is worth citing at some length. The defenders, he said, who confronted the invading Atlantean hosts, were:

People of a white race whose territories reached to the columns of Heracles. They numbered among them numerous tribes, such as the Ausos, worshippers of Poseidon, first lord of Atlantis; the Nasamonos; the Atarantos, and a tribe of Atlanteans in the extreme west, as Herodotos says. They—these faithful Libyans—had had ocular testimony, as they believed, of the Atlantean cataclysm. I find in the 9,000 years interval between the cataclysm and the date when Solon was instructed by Sonchis, the priest of Sais, an argument in favour of the truth of Plato's story. The Egyptians used a decimal system, as we do, and when they sought in the inscriptions to indicate a considerable quantity, they said "one thousand", or "one million". Thus, of the Sun: "ship of a million years", also, on the funerary stelæ, it might be "one thousand fathers", "one thousand vases", "one thousand perfumes", or "one thousand good things", for the double, or *kha* of the dead Osiris, and never 2,000, 6,000, or 9,000. If the number had been emblematic of incalculable duration, Sonchis would have said 10,000 years, not 9,000. Another interesting point is that it was 9,000 years before 593 B.C., when Solon was in Egypt. It leads us to 9,593, and this date occurring before the recent discoveries in the predynastic Egypt does not exceed verisimilitude. . . . Flinders Petrie has found what he calls "sequence dates". Now Menes, according to him, lived *circa* 4750 B.C., and belonged to series 79. To allow 3,000 years for the duration of these dates of Flinders Petrie, which gives a mean of 60 years for each sequence, is not more, according to Foucart, than adopting cyphers commonly accepted in Egyptological biography. And the total obtained gives us 7,550. This conservative computation of the 3,000 years in question is perfectly justified from the archæological point of view. It allows for a difference of 1,843 years, especially as Petrie's series hardly begin with the 30th and, we know not on what of the Egyptian primitive calendars the reckoning was made by the priests. The affirmation of Sonchis to Solon merits more faith than it has so far had.

Precision in the matter of the chronology of these catastrophes —of course, the facts and implications of these catastrophes are either unaccepted, or ignored by orthodox historians and encyclopædic historians, such as the late H. G. Wells—is still impossible in a world-calendar of events. Yet no scientific folklorist can, or should disregard extremely ancient traditions on the Atlantis cataclysm, which exist, to the same tenour, both in Galway, Eire, and at the other end of a long line in the West Indian islands of the Caribbean.

These "myths", naïve as they must be, yet crystallize a magic vision of unknown facts, as one believes them to be, of astonishing character. Strange facts relating to a lost world of which not even some forgotten Greek commentator on the dialogues of Plato-Solon can have dreamt!

In the back country of the British West Indian island of Trinidad, natives of aboriginal stock assert that Trinidad is a very ancient country, and many thousands of years ago formed part "of the largest country in the world". This was at a time "when there was no sea at all". This great, antediluvian country, or continent, the natives call *Iere*, pronounced almost exactly as Eire of Ireland! And old Trinidad, say the natives, prior to a great cataclysm that sank the lost continent, was also known as *Iere*. Gold, goes on the tradition in Trinidad, used to be "brought by donkeys" *overland* from the south, that is, ancient South America, in a day when no Caribbean sea separated Trinidad from this proto-South America. Something happened, say the back-block Trinidadians, which "broke up the land into little bits", and "the sea came in from the north and the south, and the whales". But "new people kept coming and many babies came". In those very ancient days, say the Trinidadian "myths", people "did not walk up or down stairs, or tramp up hill and down. They hit a plate and made a song, which song said where they wanted to go, and they went".[1] . . . "And anybody could dance in the air like leaves blown by the wind. It was a very happy time, and there were no live slaves. All the live people sang and danced and feasted all the time."

The natives add that the only people who worked were "dead peoples who don't feel tired no more and don't feel hungry. But there wasn't much work, because everything was so light." As to what this cryptic phrase about "light" may mean, the native seems unable to explain. But his reference to "dead men" is a singular allusion to what are known in Haïti and on plantations in Dutch Guiana as the "zombies", alleged to be "shells" of resuscitated, dead people acting as slaves, a practice which a queer law in the Haïtian code makes illegal and punishable.

Trinidadian folklore says that, in this golden age of Iere cooked things were not eaten, but plenty of fruit, milk, raw fish and raw

[1] More will be said, later, about this naïve reference to levitation, and of curious evidences of it in ancient South America. "Light", *supra*, may mean anti-gravity force!

meat. They drank plenty of strong drink fermented by the sun from some fruit, or palm juice or sap.[1]

Asked how big was this antediluvian land of Iere, the native says: "I don't know; but it was all the world, and it went on and on towards the East where the sun rose. And the people were very rich and there were buildings like pointed squares". Shown a picture of a pyramid, the native says: "Yes, they were like that". How did the people get to the top of these buildings? The native: "They made the song to the plate; but they didn't want to go there much, because there were secrets up there. There were no fighters, in those days. Nobody ever fought unless they had too much to drink. They did not hunt; but sometimes they caught fish in the rivers, or snared birds, or guana (iguana), or manicu (manatee?). There wasn't anything to hunt in those days."

A native cook named Adela, of Grenada, West Indies, danced a dance which is identical with an Irish jig performed by old women in Galway. She said it was a Fête Dance, performed all over the Great Country of Iere when the harvest was gathered, which maybe, was corn, or might be maize.

"Down in the South," she added—she meant ancient South America—and other natives of other West Indian islands have also this tradition: "there was a Golden Serpent that everyone was afraid of. But I don't know much about that, 'cept that it wore a spiked crown and danced when it was angry. And there was also a god there who threw golden knives when it thundered. My mother told me that the people of Trinidad, who are nearly all dead now, had come from the East, and that they ran away when the land broke up—that was when it all went under the sea."

In Grenada, West Indies, the up-country natives speak of the "leeprawns" and say that when people died, "you had to have a wake for two days, and make a great noise all the time in case you heard the 'bondies' wailing. If you heard them, you died in a year." Here, *and derived from no old Irish settler,*; one has a piece of folklore, suggestive of some long-vanished land-link, which is identical with the wakes of modern Eire-Ireland, the leprechaun, or *lupracan,* or wrinkled old man-goblin of Celtic folklore, and, it would seem, with the banshee. An old man up-country in Trinidad spoke of things he had seen done by the ligaroos, or liggeroos, which, he said, "were evil spirits in some places where folk had done very bad deeds". This must be an

---

[1] Cicero admitted the existence of a second inhabited continent which Macrobius in the fifth century A.D. thought might be some land in the direction of North or South America, though he does not call it by those names. Cicero placed in the mouths of its people these words: "All the land inhabited by you is but a small island compared with this." (*Omnis enim terra quæ colitur a vobis parva quædam insula est.*) But it might equally apply to this mysterious land of *Iere-Atlantis* when ancient "myth" says there was an immense half-moon of land round the Old World, formed of Greenland, Jan Mayen Island—a volcanic island in the Arctic Ocean, 220 miles north-east of Iceland—and Spitzbergen. All these lands had very different climate from to-day, and a sub-tropical flora. (*Vide p.* 70 on the Atlantean letters on a creek-cliff at Hof, Iceland.)—AUTHOR.

undoubted reference to the loup-garou, or werewolf, or lycanthrope of old Teutonic or Anglo-Saxon folklore. It is as reminiscent of unpleasant "black" practices of west and central African native black witch doctors as the making of hubbubs at wakes is of the Tibetan practice of banging drums and blowing horns to frighten ghosts from houses or villages, in the dark hours.

An old black native from up-country in Grenada, West Indies, had also something to say about the ancient gold road overland from South America to the land of Iere. He reiterated a legend about the expulsion of snakes from the proto-Antillia which is strangely reminiscent of St. Patrick and the snakes of old Ireland.[1]

Said the old man: "There are few snakes in the West Indies, because a Great King once cursed them all, as one had bitten him. And them snakes all went to the South, down the Golden Road to the Old Places."

Asked what he meant by "Old Places", he replied: "Don't know. But thousands of years ago, you could walk down the Gold Road from here into South America. Many clever people lived in South America, in those ancient days." He also alleged that in "those ancient days" "folk whose relatives neglected their obsequies"—he used this word!—"did the heavy work in the fields; because they didn't want no food and they kep' on workin' all the time . . . an' they didn't want no money, of course!"

But surely the old man did not really believe that dead men were made to work?

"I old man," said he. "I see a lot o' mighty queer things happen. What you 'spose might be in them old times? Why, anything! I believe, 'cos everyone he tell the same things all for years in these islands. Since I little boy I hear same stories all the time, all over, and what I say is what everyone say must somehow be true. These dead men work all the time for long time till more come. Everyone say they call them all *zombies*. Boss, he pay small money every time for overseer. That's all, for they never get tired and don' want no feedin' . . . An' good mans like me don' have to do no hard work in them days . . . There don' seem to be no *zombies* hereabouts . . ." spoken with great regret . . . "Good mans like me don' have to do no hard work in them days."

The old man then spoke of the Gold Road down which he thought the *zombies* went to "work in mines" when they were no more needed. However, leaving that aside, he said that this Gold Road belonged to a very far-off day, when gold came up from the South and Trinidad, and all other places in the West Indies "was one very big country". His old grandfather, however, had said that Grenada did not belong to the "Big Country", but was post-cataclysmal in origin. Or, to give

[1] An English lady friend of mine points out—she had spent many years in the West Indies—that most of the snakes in the modern West Indies are harmless, the exception being the fer-de-lance.

the old blackie's words: "He says, as other people tell me, that when everything break up, same like volcano, only plenty volcanoes all to once, then Big Country be covered all with water, and Grenada come up from the sea to help people get saved from the waters. Same like the Caribs. That's how they come."

Further questioned, the old blackie said: "I do' know if a new race came up from the sea, or if it was the old ones who escaped being drowned in the waters. But I think them Caribs was the people from the Big Country. No one knows 'zackly how it all happen, but it was *very* long time ago. There's plenty tales in Trinidad."

About the land to the East where the sun rose—this was probably Iere-Atlantis—the old man said: "That were true, too. Plenty land, plenty people, and they all teachers and very wise men, as plenty peoples often tell me." He also added one of those stories of immaculate conception which, of course, far antedate any brand of Christianity, whether Byzantine, Greek, or Roman Catholicism. In fact, later in this book, they will be seen related in ancient Mexican traditions to that wise man in black, the culture hero, Quetzalcoatl, who was either an Atlantean from the motherland, or from her imperial colony in Hy-Brazil, of South America.

Said the old Trinidad native: "Very good man saved my forbears. He was very wise man whose name was Parr. His mother was never with no man for wife. She was the only virgin over the age when men go with women that I ever heard of in the West Indies. And her son was born without a man. Same like Jesus Christ. It could be. The Holy Father says have faith and not ask stupid questions. I am good man and have plenty faith. The Holy Father very pleased with me.[1] My forbears came from the great land to the Far East, where it rains a lot and peoples always feast and have wakes all the time."

Now let us turn to the other end of the line of ancient tradition: in the land of Eire, or Ireland. In Galway there is also a very ancient tradition identical with that of the West Indian back-block natives up-country. It is, however, rather confused; but it is that long, long ago, Galway, on the one side, and Trinidad, on the other, formed

---

[1] I have excellent reasons for saying that none know so much about the mysteries of ancient South America, of the colonies of old Atlantis, and these age-old myths than the men of the order of Ignatius Loyola. But with the wisdom of the serpent, the Roman padre, whether or not a Jesuit, talks little of these things. Nay, with the immemorial subtlety of the College for the Propagation of the Faith, at Rome, he refrains from scouting them as myths. He merely converts them into forerunners of the man-god whose dying body he also eats and drinks in his own Eucharist. Christology and crosses of sacrifice were hoar things long before the time when the propagandists of Rome grafted the bull's blood bath and the cave-resurrection of the dead Mithra, the Roman legionary's god, on to a cultus whose vicar wears a triple tiara which was taken over holus-bolus from the Pontifex Maximus of pagan Rome. I am sure that, in the magnificent library of the Vatican, which contains many a rare volume not to be found either in the splendid library of the British Museum, or in the Bibliothèque Nationale, in Paris, the inheritors of the treasures of the old kings of France, there is also many a rare volume and many a precious manuscript from missioners of orders in South and Central America of the sixteenth–eighteenth centuries. These manuscripts could throw light on these profound mysteries of ancient North, Central and South America.

part of a very large continent that was far from the sea. (I shall have more to say of the Galway end of the "myth" in a few moments.)

An old woman who lived in the Carib settlement in St. Vincent Island, West Indies, told an English lady of my acquaintance this same ancient tradition of a Big Country that disappeared into the sea after a colossal earthquake. It was a story she clearly had heard when she was a young child. "The water came in," she said, "and made the islands; but some of the islands, she had been told, had actually formed part of this ancient Big Country: to wit, modern Trinidad, West Indies, and Barbados. This old woman *insisted* that wakes had *Not* been introduced into the West Indies by modern Irish settlers . . . "No," she said; "wakes were ordered by the Great Serpent, thousands of years ago." They were for the purpose of frightening "off bad spirits who lived in the craters of the dead volcanoes."

The Caribs, she said, were the real owners of the Big Country—Iere—and had a king whose gold crown was in three parts. This reminds one of the triple tiara of the ancient Pontifex Maximus of pagan Rome, and his modern descendant the Holy Father of Vatican Rome of Catholic Christianity. He wore this triple gold crown because,

Old Mexican temple fresco of Atlan Cataclysm (*Teobert Maler*).

said the Carib woman, he had three sons and three daughters and each son married a daughter. As we know, first degree marriages of this type were common in the Egypt of the Pharaohs, the Perú of the Incas, and, some say, in old Atlantis, or some of her continental islands, at a certain epoch. One of the king's sons went to the south, one to the south-west, and the third to the north. Caribs of that far day did not, she said, "have to walk, unless they wanted to. Their wise

68

people could fly quite easily. No; they had no wings. What they did was to clap on gold plates, make music and then they fly."

The old Carib woman then gave a version of the Golden Age and of the Great Deluge-Cataclysm "myth". "Every one feasted, and danced, and sang. No one was ever poor or hungry. So they all got proud and everyone wanted to be king. And some very bad ones stole some sacred fire and destroyed plenty people, because they did not do right."

This story of stealing "sacred fire" I shall refer to later.

She was emphatic that the Big Country was *not* burnt up. "People say it was same like big 'sposion. Everything broke. All the land broke, same like broken ewer. And the water came between all the pieces that was left, and made islands. And there was plenty bloodshed." She could not explain why, or when there was this bloodshed . . . "The king was very angry. He say the sea should cover them all up and no one would know they had ever been alive."

She then gives a variant of the Quetzalcoatl-Viracocha-Bochicha "legends" of the culture-heroes of ancient Central and South America . . . "A very good man came from the East and made all the little islands and saved a lot of good Caribs. But for hundreds and thousands of years there was terrible times. Volcanoes everywhere threw out fire, and it kep' on rainin' an' floodin' everythin', and, soon, the heavens burst one day, and the earth bust all up and the Big Country disappeared, same like the king said. Then there wasn't no king again, and all the people who escaped on the Good Saint's islands had to look after themselves, until they were all killed by the new people who came from the East", except some of her ancestors.

Then she added some curious details which are corroborated in other traditions in classic Greek or Latin writers,[1] about the state of the Atlantic, after Atlantis completely vanished:

[1] Thus, the unknown writer—pseudo-Aristoteles—of *Mirabiles Auscultationes* speaks of Phœnicians of the old port of Gades (Cadiz) navigating beyond the Pillars of Hercules (or columns of Herakles) and blown by an east wind which drove them towards regions of sea grass and weeds, wetted by the sea, the weeds being completely concealed by the overflowing of the water. Herodotus, in the *Melpomena*, mentions one Sataspes, who told the Persian monarch, Xerxes, that he could not go farther navigating the ocean (Atlantic), because his ship was held back in her course, by sea and mud. This may relate to the Sargasso Sea, or it may not! Plutarch, also, in his *Theseus*, comments on the impassibility of the Atlantic in the classic Greek age. The *Periplus* of the Carian geographer, Scylax Caryandenis (*temp.* 550 B.C.), also testifies to unnavigability of the Atlantic, beyond the island of Cernen—just outside the Pillars of Hercules, on the African coast—owing to the "shortness of the sea, and mud and weed." Theophrastus, in his *History of Plants*—he died, aged 107 in 288 B.C.—speaks of weeds and a leek called the scallion, in the remote seas about the Pillars of Hercules, and of a thyme, "transformed to stone (*quæ in lapidem transfigurantur, ut thymum*)" like laurels, and so fibrous that seamen could lash their cables to them. Avienus, the Roman geographer, (*circa* fourth century A.D.), in his *Ora Maritima*, for which he had access to the logs of Phœnician navigators, spoke of weeds which made the Atlantic unnavigable . . . "ships (were) cast among whirlpools, deceptive in appearance, and often with, thick shrubs, the stern of the ship is held back . . . the sheet of water is so shallow that it hardly conceals the underlying sands. Above, there floats a mass of weeds and the wave is constrained by the turmoils of the ocean currents. Monsters swim all these seas, which are filled with mud." Finally, Jornandes, a Gothic secretary, or notary (*circa* A.D. 550), who wrote the *Getica*, on the deeds and origin of the

No one after the terrible time could ever go to the East, and to the land of the Rising Sun, because they had no big boats, only little ones. And they couldn't fly no more and they had to work hard to live.

It is curious that a late thirteenth-century monk, nicknamed "Solitarius", or the recluse—he was a learned scholiast—also mentions the state of the ocean after the sinking of Atlantis. This monk, Honorius Augustodunensis, lived at Autun, about A.D. 1300, and writing about the Atlantis of Plato, he says that where it once stood, the "sea is clotted and curdled" . . . *ubi nunc est Concretum mare*. . . . One might also suppose that Augustodunensis had some reason to believe that Atlantis was famed for a breed of sheep, very white and fleecy, yielding the best wool for dyeing purple, which in Greek myth, he says, was called the Golden Apples of the Hesperides, one of the Atlantean islands. *Melon*, in Greek means either apples or sheep.

The last surviving, post-cataclysmal (?) continental island of Atlantis was called by certain Greek writers Poseidon or Posidonius. It was said by one Marcellus, a geographer, who may have lived some time after the first century of our own era, and who wrote the *Ethiopion history* to have been the last of the Atlantean islands left after the great island was submerged. He cryptically says traditions about Atlantis had been collected by travellers in an inaccessible isle of the ocean:

> The inhabitants of the Atlantic isle of Poseidon, not less than a thousand stadia (say, nearly 115 English miles—AUTHOR), preserved a tradition, handed down to them from their ancestors, of the existence of the Atlantic island of a prodigious magnitude, which had really existed in those seas, and which, during a long period of time, governed all the islands in the Atlantic Ocean.

From this not too clear passage, it seems that Poseidon must not be confused with the greater continent of Atlantis.

Now let us glance back at the story of the long lost and mysterious continent called Iere, which is current among the older folk in Galway. It is of extraordinary interest to those who have reason to suppose that the empire of Atlantis extended far to the north. Indeed, I may here mention, in passing that, in a river-creek called Hof, on the eastern coast of Iceland is a cliff on which are carved a number of *very* ancient symbols, or letters, two of which are identical with letters found in a dead city of Atlantean Brazil, by the old *bandeiristas*, about A.D. 1750.[1]

Goths, says no one is allowed to reach the impassable farther bounds of the Atlantic Ocean, owing to obstructing seaweed and failing winds. "It is plainly inaccessible and unknown." Aristoteles, in his *Meteorologica*, says that the ocean outside the Pillars of Herakles is shallow, with mud, and calm; for it "lies in a hollow". The Egyptian priest—in Plato's dialogue of *Timæus*—rightly told Solon: "The disappearance of the island of Atlantis in the depths of the sea made it, in those parts, impenetrable, because of the shoal of mud in the way caused by the subsidence of the island."

[1] *Vide* chapters two and three of my *Mysteries of Ancient South America*, published by Rider, 1946.

The old folk of Galway, in Western Eire, say that: "The King of Galway in the very old, far-off days was the greatest King in the world. He had three crowns and one crown meant that he owned Africa whence the gold came and the beautiful jewels. He sent one of his sons to Africa to make a great kingdom there, that lasted a million years. And another son lived right away out in the west in the land of the setting sun, where all good men go when they die. There were no ships then, only boats; because there was not any sea at all, but only rivers and lakes. And all this great land was called *Eire*, pronounced *Ay*-ree. In those far-off days, everybody was a fairy or an evil spirit. They danced in the air like leaves blown by the wind, and when the right sort of music was played. It was beautiful sad music, because it was full of wishes, and when people wish they sigh. And the devil was jealous, because everyone was so happy and good and light-hearted. So he sent for a lot of poisonous snakes; but the good St. Patrick came and banished all the snakes for ever, and sent the devil himself away to the west, where he lives to this day, to be sure he does!"

The reader may compare these Irish folklore stories with those told, above, by natives of Grenada and Trinidad. They seem valid evidence of some long past land-link between Galway and the West Indies.

The Galway folklore gives us some remarkable glimpses of this vanished land of Iere-Atlantis. "There was," say the old folk of Galway, "a broad highway, very beautiful, with lights all the way, that led to the Isles of the West, or the Blest(?), and those Isles were many months' journey along the great road. At intervals on the highway were roads that led to other parts of the Great Kingdom of Ayeree, or Iere. One road led to a wonderful land where the people were all black. Further north, the people were all tall and handsome and drove about in golden chariots. They had great buildings, too, the like of which were never seen in Ireland. And those buildings had no stairways, because, in those far-off days, everyone could fly. There was a terrible devil who lived in the west, beyond the Isles of the Blest. He lived on new-born babies and he had a serpent who ate live goats. He was indeed terrible and tried every way he could think of to make men bad.[1]

"But one way to keep him off and render his spells of no avail was to laugh and dance and sing. Then, when everyone was happy, and all the lights shining, he had to hide his face. And if anyone was

[1] This bit of the Galway folklore may have reference to the sadistic practices of the giant men who lived in one of the great continental islands of Mu, or Rutas-Lemuria, about which strange Pacific continent, long sunk by a series of catastrophes, I shall have much to say of a startling character, in a subsequent book. Some of these giants reached ancient North, Central and South America both before and after the terrible catastrophes disrupting a continent which was very far from being a land of a civilized type of ancient man. It was, indeed, a land of Aztecan paranoia, and sanguinary militarism with the correlative of degrading slavery. Pan, the goat-foot god, commemorated, to-day, at Killorglin cattle fair was an old Eire deity.—AUTHOR.

ugly or deformed in the Great Country it was because the devil had struck them. And in the old days such ugly and deformed people were destroyed." (More will be said, later, of this eugenic practice of the Atlanteans, who certainly would never have allowed mental defectives and degenerates to live and propagate their species, as we, in our age, do.)

The Galway folklore has something more to say about St. Patrick who, as one may suspect, has been merged with a Roman Catholic, or Irish Christian-Keltic, hagiological variant of the wise man in black: Quetzalcoatl, the Atlantean missioner and culture-hero of ancient Mexico. He told the Irish folk, says the "myth", of the wise men who lived in the far, far East, where the sun rose, and said that "knowledge, under the rule of the Golden Serpent, was mostly to be found in the West, while Wisdom, an entirely different thing, was to be found under the rule of the Golden Dragon, in the East". This looks like a curious reference to a very ancient China!

One day, says the Galway "myth", the Dragon will eat the Serpent and every one will be wise and good, and "there will be no more babies born". This rather cynical turn to the "myth" might suggest that the attainment of wisdom might induce a desire to exterminate the race of man, or for some form of racial suicide, in a manner likely to earn the sardonic approval of the Venerable George Bernard Shaw, in his more Mephistophelian or Methuselan moods![1]

The "myth" of the Galway folk goes on to say that it "was the devil who caused men to fight; for neither under the rule of the Dragon"—some form of extremely ancient civilization in an ante-diluvian China and Asia?—nor under the rule of the Golden Serpent (Atlantis?) was there any fighting, a great sin being any form of war. But the people of the Serpent became too clever, and would not think of eternity at all. They lived only for the present and to have a good time. So God in his anger sent a great teacher to them, but they laughed at the teacher and called him a bastard and a man of low birth. Then they drove him away and another race of men killed him. So there came a terrible earthquake and it split the Great Country and the water rushed in and the Great Country disappeared to the bottom of the ocean. But it broke off at Galway, because St. Patrick had blessed it; so Galway ever after had a sea coast. (This St. Patrick is clearly not the historical missionary who died about A.D. 463, and who is the subject of Colgan's Latin folios.)

Maybe some light, dim and flickering and doubtful as it is, is thrown on this Galway story of a long lost continent, which became the "Paradise of the Gael", in the singular story told by Plutarch, in his *De facie in orbe lunæ* (The Face in the Orb of the Moon). One,

[1] Modern deep sea soundings show high land existing under water stretching from just off the coasts of Ireland far south to South America. The elevation rises abruptly to 8,000 and 9,000 feet above the ocean-floor, and still slowly rises to the regions of the Azores, St. Paul's rocks. Ascension and Tristan da Cunha. The northern regions of the lost continent of Atlantis-Eire lay very near to the coast of Ireland of to-day.

Sylla, in a dialogue, speaks about a mysterious stranger met in Carthage, and who had skill in astronomy and branches of other philosophy derived from an Atlantean island-continent called Cronus. As A. O. Prickard, M.A., New College, Oxon., pointed out in 1911, when he translated manuscript E of this story, in Paris, the texts are very defective and full of gaps and copyists' errors. One version is that the stranger had a strong desire to see the Great Island, "for so they call our world", and:

> When the thirty years passed and relief parties arrived from home, he said farewell and sailed forth with abundant provisions, golden caskets and complete equipment. He had many adventures and found holy manuscripts, and was initiated into all the mysteries. And he spent a long time in Carthage.

Another version, suggested by Mr. Pickard is that:

> the stranger was a mine owner in the country (of Carthage); a man, also, who once had found certain sacred parchments which had been secretly withdrawn when the Romans destroyed the older city of Carthage. These parchments had lain a long time in the earth unnoticed, and were, he said, oracles of the Phœnician(?) gods. He charged me to pay a special honour to the moon, as being most potent in (or closely connected with) our life.

The gist of part of the queer story is that the visible (to us) side of the moon harbours evil souls reaching there in eclipses, and brass vessels are beaten to reach their ears as they ascend. (*Vide* p. 66 *supra* on the Tibetan custom of banging drums and blowing horns to scare ghosts.) The good souls go through a gulf in the moon till they reach an Elysian plain on the side we never see. But what concerns us here is that the stranger, whether or not a refugee from one of the sunken island-continents of Atlantis, said that:

> Far over the brine lies an Ogygian isle, five days distant from Britain to the west. There are three other islands equidistant from Ogygia and one another, in the direction of the sun's summer setting. One is called the isle of Cronus. To the great continent by which the ocean is fringed is a voyage of about 5,000 stadia[1], made in row boats from Ogygia. It is less distant from the other islands. The sea is slow of passage and full of mud, because of the number of streams which the great mainland discharges, forming alluvial tracks and making the sea heavy like land, whence an opinion prevailed that it is actually frozen. The coasts of the mainland are inhabited by the Greeks, living around a bay as large as the Maeotic (modern Black Sea), with its mouth nearly opposite that of the Caspian . . . These Greeks speak of this as continental, and of

---

[1] The Romans used the Greek stadium for nautical measurements—607 feet a stadium. So this would be about 575 miles. The passage appears to import that this was the distance from an eastern island of Atlantis to ancient America. The term Greek, above, must have the same significance as the term Hellenes used by the Egyptian priest, Sonchis, when he described the final cataclysm that sank the last island of Atlantis, called Poseidonius. That is, it is a "Greece" far anterior to even the archæan Greece of Homer.

those who inhabit our land as islanders, because it is washed all round by the sea. They think that in after-time those who came with Hercules and were left behind by him mingled with the subjects of Cronus (Atlantean king), and rekindled the Hellenic life. Once in every thirty years, the year of the planet Saturn, an expedition is sent out from Carthage to certain islands in the North Atlantic, where Cronus (Saturn) reigns in banishment.

There follows a strange passage which may remind the reader of my statements, *supra*, that Atlantean, and Atlantean Hy-Brazilian letters, or signs, are found on a cliff up a creek, named Hof, on the east shores of Iceland; and that old Atlantis at one time extended up to and, probably, even beyond the Arctic Circle:

> Men are chosen by lot and sent in ships with supplies for the great rowing voyage, before them, and for a long sojourn in a strange land. Those who come safely out of the perils of the sea, land, first, on the outlying islands which are inhabited by the Greeks; and day after day, they, for thirty days, see the sun hidden for less than one hour. This is the night with a darkness which is slight, and of a twilight hue, and has a light over it from the west. There they spend ninety days, and are honourably treated and called holy persons. After this, they pass on, and now with help from the winds. There are no inhabitants except these and those who have been sent before them. . . . The isle of Cronus. . . .

The Atlantean island of Cronus is described by Plutarch, in this curious dialogue, "as a land of plenty, with no pain or trouble, and where life is passed in festivals and sacrifices, or devoted to literature and philosophy, which we may interpret as "science". The god (king?) Cronus was said to manifest himself to men there in shapes and spirit voices, openly seen and heard.

One, Dr. Forrest, is said to have found in the West Indian island of Antigua carved stone work of unknown and ancient date, cut from stone that is quarried *only in Ireland*. No one in Antigua could give him any information about this stone, except that it was very ancient and of origin unknown. Southey, in his *Common Place Book*, says that the folk of Arranmore, the largest of the southern isles of Arran, on the coast of Galway:

> are still persuaded that on a clear day they can see from this coast Hy-Brassail (O'Breasal, the Royal Island) the inchanted island, the paradise of the pagan Irish, of which they relate a number of romantic stories. ("*Conical* buildings are on it", Geo. H. O'Flaherty to the Author.)

Colonel Vallancey, in his *Collectanea de Rebus Hibernicis*, also says:

> The old Irish say that great part of Ireland was swallowed by the sea and that the sunken part often rises and is to be seen on the horizon frequently from the northern coast, or the north-west of the island. This part so appearing is called Tir-Hudi, or the city of the (prophet) Hud . . . It contains a city which once possessed all the riches of the world, the key of which lies buries under some druidical monument.

One might also mention that Buffon, the famous French naturalist, believed that Ireland and the Azores, and America, were once part of the great Atlantean isle of Plato. It is also decidedly curious that, *à propos* of the Galway–West Indian stories of the Great Country of Iere, there is in Ireland a giant rock which an English geologist, who examined it, said probably came from *Africa*. There are also ancient Irish legends which say her circular stones were brought from *Africa* by a sorcerer. An odd circumstance is also connected with Simon Magus, the Firbolg. This ancient priest-magician must not be confused with the Levantine gentleman who so peeved Father Peter, in Rome, by floating gracefully through a window into the outside air. His Petrine rival thaumaturgist unsportingly caused this Simon to crash to the ground and break a leg, with, it is said, Nero somewhere around and no doubt ready for a little excitement. But Simon Magus, the Firbolg, was a member of an ancient race of Neolithic type in Eire, who, in their remote day, were exterminated by the blue-eyed metal workers from Scandinavia, the Tuatha de Danaan, expelled from Greece by Syrian invaders, somewhere between 300 and 150 B.C. According to Gildas, this same Simon the Firbolg was tonsured like *an Egyptian priest*, which, if true, is one more tradition of an ancient connection between Ireland and old Africa.

Another curious vanished land-link between Ireland and the West Indies is the institution of the Bealtine, or Baal feast of the 1st May. Near Gloucester, in the Severn Valley, there is a hill called May Hill, on whose top is a grove of trees. Local tradition says that never more than a hundred trees will grow in this grove on the hill-top, which is anciently associated with the Bealtine of the Sun-god. In another part of the same county, in the Stroud Valley, the custom of the Bealtine, associated with a vanished sun-temple of Silurian origin, has given rise to the name of a very pretty hamlet called Custom Scrubs, and of a hamlet, some seven or more miles away over the Cotswold Hills, in the direction of the River Severn, which is called Custom-mede. In each case, the element *Custom* refers to a very ancient festival: the Bealtine. It is remarkable that this same sun-worshipping custom of a very ancient, world-wide heliolithic race is called, to this day, the *Belton*, by the blacks and Caribs in the West Indies!

An Irish lady I know told me that an old woman in Galway, who had a sinister reputation as a witch, told her that she, the old witch, went each year to the west to keep the Bealtine as the devil's own guest, which presupposes that, in modern times, there is some organization behind this ancient Celtic cultus, and that it has a head-man, or chief, who takes the part of the devil. The old Galway witch said: "It is quite easy to fly, if you know how". In Scotland, the old folk accuse the old Irish of having, long ago, introduced the Beltane, or Bealtine, or Baal dance, and other "infamies" to Scotland.

Now, among the blacks and the Caribs in certain West Indian islands, to-day—and it is evidence of no recent, but of a very ancient connection with *Iere*, rather than Eire—the *Belton* is something about which few natives will talk. It is a rite with which the native police will not interfere, although very ugly rumours of child-sacrifices are whispered about in connection with the *Belton*. In St. Lucia, West Indies, which, among natives has the reputation of being the "home of the devil" or a centre for nefarious rites associated with necromancy or black magic, the *Belton*, or Bealtine, is held yearly, despite the prohibition of the British authorities. An English lady who lived for years in the West Indies told me how she saw a *Belton* procession pass her house on the *morne*, a small, round isolated mountain.

She said to me:

> I was told by the native policeman that they were going up to the top of the Roseau valley, where they did horrible things, even to killing babies as a sacrifice. I asked him why he did not stop them. He said: "I can't, mistress. They are too many for me and have drunk a lot of rum . . . I am a policeman and they don't tell me nothing, but others have seen these things. You can see them in the valley, mistress. And the moon shows it is *Belton* night." He then told me that the devil himself sat in a golden chair and presided over the doings and gave orders. The devil wore three crowns and a serpent was coiled beside him. The serpent ate a live goat. This story I heard, with variations, in Grenada, W.I., where these rites were celebrated at Grand Etang, a lake in the mouth of an extinct crater of a volcano. I was, also, told that the devil had sent for the fer-de-lance—a venomous snake—because he was angry that the good man from the East had expelled the poisonous snakes. (*Vide* page 66 *supra*, on the same story told of the epoch of the vanished continent of Iere.—AUTHOR.) I was also told, added the English lady, that the devil lived most of his time in St. Lucia, and made it unlucky. This statement I could never get clarified. But the Chief of Police told me that criminals in St. Lucia are prone to boast that the devil will see them through. I had first-hand knowledge of a murderer who had a pull somewhere in St. Lucia. How much truth there is in the story of *Belton* orgies is hard to say. The allegation that *zombies* exist is, however, very strong in St. Lucia. . . .

Grenada has a singular tradition that the last king of the Big Country of Iere lies buried in an ancient tomb somewhere in the island of Barbados. But in Barbados itself the tradition is that this ancient king was the last "Emperor of Constantinople". This imparts a singularly Byzantine "twist" to an ancient tradition!

A word may be interjected at this place concerning the alleged power of defying gravitation, or, as it is called, levitation. This power is by ancient tradition attributed to the rulers of Mu, or Lemuria, in relation to ships that could rise above the waves in violent storms. It is also said to have been possessed by the higher castes in old Atlantis. In the Andean highlands of Colombia, along the Rio Magdalena, is the very singular dead civilization of San Agustin, cities or temple-mausolea of a race unknown who left colossal statues, some of them portrait statues, like those in Easter Island. This singular race practised strange after-life cults in underground tombs. A spur of this singular culture of a race unknown runs from Eastern Colombia to the north, whence it extends to the territory around the sea of Valencia, the Indian "Tocarigua" of north Venezuela.

These "underworld" people appear to have had some cultural contact with the Atlanteans of ancient Brazil's Highlands. For on a *gorro* (cap) of a megalithic statue of a "tusked" man (or deity), found in a very ancient tomb in the Andes of Colombia, are to be seen engraved eight letters, of which seven occur in inscriptions copied by the *bandeirista* of Brazil when he and his expedition blundered on the dead city in the little known *sertão* of Bahia province, in A.D. 1750. Mariano Rivero y Ustariz and Tschudi, who reproduce this singular statue in their *Antigüedades Peruanas* (published in Vienna in 1851), did not realize the significance of this inscription. They supposed it had been engraved on the statue by someone in the train of the conquistadores of Jiminez de Quesada, some time during or after the conquest of Nueva Granada (modern Colombia). I have pp. 16 and 95 inset a sketch of this remarkable inscription.

What appear to be branches of this extremely remote and mysterious megalithic race of early South America buried their dead in limestone ranges, and in tombs where the offerings may still be found. They had artisans, very skilled, who fashioned jewellery from gold, and had a system of terrace cultivation. Immense mounds of bones seem to be the débris of ancient *wakes*, lying side by side with many stone tools and ornaments of clay. The funerary urns *sometimes contain remains* of eight skeletons. There are ceramics which seem to indicate that this ancient race dwelt long by a lake; but what I specially wish to point out are fine small pendants with devices of bats and eagles in stone, that are called by the German archæologists, *Klang-Platten.*

No explanation is made as to why these pendants are called *clang-plates,* or sound-discs. Have we, here, anything to do with the alleged power of levitation ascribed in Central and South American folklore to ancient Central and South American races and to the Atlanteans and Hy-Brazilian Atlanteans, whereby, if one struck a disc on the correct pitch or note, the individual striker could rise in the air and fly?

It has been said that these anti-gravity discs were known and used in old Atlantis, where they were part of the normal equipment of every child at birth. They are said to have responded to some sort of unknown vibration, or "wave-length", and one could rise in the air only to sound-waves or vibrations emitted from one's own disc. And, even so, the correct note had to be sounded.

I have some reason for supposing that the ancient Mexicans knew of and used this alleged power of suspending gravity. In this connection a very curious story has reached me from a source I am not allowed, for high political reasons, to name. It is to the effect that among the rich presents made by the last Aztec emperor, Montezuma, or Moctezuma, to Don Hernando Cortes, the Spanish conquistador, and which Cortes subsequently transmitted to the Emperor Carlos V, in old Spain, were two flat discs of pure gold. The discs were shaped rather like a pancake, and had rough edges. One disc was thicker than the other. They were about 10 inches in diameter, one disc being a quarter of an inch thick, the other much thinner.

These discs were regarded as symbols of royalty, and to be worn on the breast, though they are uncomfortably large for such a purpose. Accompanying the discs were cloaks superbly fashioned from the exquisitely coloured feather and plumes of the quetzal, the bird of Quetzalcoatl, and other birds. These cloaks were as light and soft as summer airs; but although people about the court of Montezuma knew for what purpose these gold discs were intended, it is doubtful if Cortes did. And, perhaps, had he been told, one of the holy friars in his train would surely have dubbed them the *brujerias* of a *hechicero*!

Neither of these discs is mentioned in *cartas* and treasure schedules sent aboard the galleons for old Spain, by the *cabildo* of Vera Cruz, on 10th July, 1519. Nor do they appear in the *Manuel del Tesorero of the Contratación of Sevilla*. The Emperor Carlos V, was at Valladolid, when the Aztec gifts arrived during Holy Week. He can never have known for what purpose these discs were meant; or he might have had a rather interesting time among the groves of Estremadura, close to the monastery of Yuste, to which he retired at the peak of his fame.

As is known, Cortes himself went home to Spain to answer the charges of his enemies and did not wait the arrival of the judges sent out from Spain. Gomara says that Cortes took home with him much wrought plate of fine gold, many rich jewels, with bizarre trinkets and ornaments of great value. But no one can say if these discs were among them.

But these discs really did reach old Spain, where they were, as they always have been, regarded as personal treasures of the Crown of Spain and not the property of the Spanish nation. At the abdication of King Alfonso, the discs, with other matters of value, were cached.

What were these discs?

I am told they were *levitation discs*!

Each disc in old Mexico was made to the exact measurement of the person for whom they were meant—in this case, the Emperor Carlos V, and his queen. If the disc were struck, the wearer could rise from the ground, exactly as the ancient West Indian myths import. Some adjustment to "personal vibrations" is said to have been involved. If the vibrations were in a minor key, the disc would be thinner; if in a major key, thicker, but no question of the sex of the wearer had any relevance. My informant says that "every key or intonation in music has its counterpart in the vibrations of the ether, and these in turn affect certain colours, lines and auras". The reader must make of this what he or she can. I can offer no explanation.

78

Nevertheless, before dismissing such stories as pure fantasy or mysticism, I beg again to draw the reader's attention to the fact, that in 1891, Barnato Brothers, hard-headed Jews who made millions in the diamond mines of Kimberley, South Africa, sent from London an engineer, J. Ricardo Seaver, whose commission was to investigate a remarkable motor invented by an American genius named John Worrell Keely of Philadelphia. Keely, investigating the flow of magnetic currents from pole to pole, discovered some unknown cosmic force that he applied to a motor. He said—he was, of course, far in advance of the day of radiology, atom-fission, Röntgen rays and Hertzian waves and television—that the "corpuscles of matter can be divided by certain orders of vibration". In Keely's laboratory in New York, Major Seaver watched him pass a bow across the strings of a violin about 20 feet away from the bench on which the motor was mounted. The machine started and increased its speed till it fairly rocked the bench, to which it was bolted. But the right note had to be struck to start the motor, and to stop it one struck discords on the violin strings, with the bow. Seaver successfully tried this for himself. Unluckily, Keely could not invent an automatic device to strike the correct note, or the discords that would stop the motor. Nor did it occur to him that a gramophone disc might solve that problem. He had also invented a means of overcoming gravity. This device consisted of three glass chambers, or cylinders, about 3½ feet high, set on a glass slab. Each cylinder contained three metal spheres, weighing about 6 ounces each. When a wire of silver and platinum was connected with the glass chambers and linked with a sympathetic transformer, the metal spheres inside the chambers rose or descended, or remained stationary, hovering at any determined point, much as gossamers in an English meadow in autumn. Keely applied this device to the model of an airship, 8 pounds in weight. Then, attaching a differential wire, he caused the model airship to rise, descend, float, or hover stationary, at any height he desired. Keely met the usual fate of the poor inventor in advance of his age. He was neglected, ridiculed, and starved. So, one winter night in 1898, when he was sunk by debts and did not know which way to turn, he burnt all his papers, destroyed his models and apparatus, the fruit of twenty-five years' research, and died, alone in the darkness.

Perhaps this age of all others is less disposed than the cocksure, late nineteenth century to ridicule such claims to discoveries. If it is not, I myself witnessed something quite as wonderful in a house in a field near Doorn, Holland, in 1931, when, by a device using a cosmic ray of a type still unknown to radiologists and laboratory physicists, I saw how cut blooms, raw fruits, pears, apples and plums, plucked with the bloom still on them, raw meat, trussed or untrussed poultry, could be kept perfectly fresh, without odour, or the slightest sign of bacterial decay, for months on end. No decay was possible so long as the ray was projected from the electric transformer. Let it not be thought that, in our cycle alone, have scientific marvels been discovered. Let us remember that few of the invisible octaves of rays in the solar spectrum have yet been explored and that we stand still on the threshold of the unknown in physics, even though we have fissioned the nucleus of isotopes of uranium with neutron ray-wave-atom particles. Nature has yet many secrets hidden from us, and this alleged power of suspending gravitation by the use of discs struck with notes, which tradition ascribes to ancient races in Iere-Atlantis, or in ancient South and Central America, may well be one of them. The heresy of to-day is the dogma of to-morrow, and both are the derision of the day after that! Be not too damnably cocksure, my Scottish friends of the tribe of Pic de la Mirandolle, who spend a few hours in Tiahuanacu and dash on to a train with the sure and certain conviction that you know all that is to be known about those queer ruins and a bit besides!

I have said, in my book *Mysteries of Ancient South America* (Rider and Co.), and I hope not with the dogmatism I am here girding at in others, that, over old South America, lies the shadow of Atlantis.

Now a few words about this ancient land whose very existence as a centre of antediluvian civilization is a joke among many of the archæologists and academicians who sit and pronounce *ex cathedra* from padded library chairs or professorial tribunes. The Atlanteans seem, according to certain traditions, to have been a coldly selfish race, of the pure, dispassionate, cold-blooded, scientific caste-ruling type. The men were very tall, fair, aquiline in nose and very good-looking. Their women were blue-eyed, sometimes reddish-haired, and of great beauty of form and features of the Hellenic type. They were, however, not a cruel or brutal or aggressive race. (We will leave on one side, for the time being, the Solon-Plato-Sonchis story of an invasion, found in the dialogues of Critias and Timæus.) There seems, indeed, at *one* period of the race, to have been about as much passion in their composition as in the late H. G. Wells's Men from Mars.

I may here interpolate a very curious story which has been told me and whose source I am not allowed to site. It purports to tell of the final disruption of Atlantis, but is discrepant with the story of Plato. No documentary, or even traditional verification of the story is possible. It is certainly of the order of "Believe it or not", and, perhaps, of what, in United States journalistic jargon, would be called "sci-fantasy". Something of it, albeit not very much, may find apparent if limited corroboration, in what I said in my former book about the very ancient dead city ruins on the Highlands of Brazil, and behind the dense screen of the Matto Grosso jungle and forests and chapada. Some of it ties up with "myths" of cataclysm and dead lands told in the West Indies and in Mexico.

Especially do some of these details following have relation to the drowned and entirely forgotten continent called *Iere*, in "legends" of the West Indies and Galway. Atlantis had reached a high state of civilization and any sea, in the sense of an environing ocean, was unknown. It will be recalled that, both in Galway and Trinidad, the ancient native folklore says that there was "no sea" in relation to the Great Country of Iere, that stretched from what is now the Caribbean to Ireland.

To the east, where the sun rose, there were very ancient lands. Indeed, Africa, as a continent, was coeval with Atlantis-Iere. In these ancient lands there were centres of greater wisdom, but of less intellectuality and knowledge than in Atlantis. Now and again, great men, or sages came over to Atlantis from these ancient lands to deplore the lack of spirituality, or what we may call mystical religion in Atlantis. But the intellectuals and scientists of that great land treated the visitors as impractical dreamers, or preachers with whom secular scientists and sceptical philosophers had no inclination to argue and who need not be treated seriously.

To the west, where the sun slept were the countries of the "unenlightened races", who "delivered gold and machinery" to the Atlantean ruler-castes. Possibly, they were American colonies with subject races. In Atlantis, the scientists had discovered some form of physical energy recalling what we now call electro-magnetism, or a ray which may one day be found at one of the two ends, beyond the infra-red, or the ultra-violet, of the invisible octaves of the solar spectrum. They were not sun-worshippers for nothing. It was also comparable in its effects to what science may yet discover relating to an advanced form of nuclear energy of the type we have seen at work, in a still inchoate stage in the atom bomb. There is, however, nothing to warrant any theory that the energy was derived from fissioning the isotopes of uranium by blasting atomic nuclei with neutrons and deutrons, producing "chain reactions". Whatever the nature of the force it was under control in the "House of Flame", and this "House" the ordinary Atlantean lower caste citizens were forbidden, on pain of death, to approach. It was, says this singular story, the son of a king of Atlantis, who violated the prohibition and caused a fearful catastrophe.[1]

His motive seems to have been a merely meddlesome inquisitiveness and the human natural desire to violate an edict or veto, just because something had been ordered or forbidden! Merely to make an edict is not enough in any cycle or any age. It is not always even sufficient to use the persuasive powers of sweet reasonableness to explain why, in the name of the common welfare, and for communal well-being, such and such a thing must not be done.

Did not Russel Wallace years ago warn *our own age* and cycle of the terrible dangers attendant on putting atomic forces in the control

[1] Students of mythology and folklore of such old lands as Cornwall, Wales and Brittany, among other lands, will recall the myths in which a woman, or daughter of a king was said to have caused a Great Flood, or catastrophe, by opening flood-gates, etc, in defiance of the commands of a king, or arch-priest. Mr. Lewis Spence has collected many of these myths in his books dealing with Atlantis, as a continent that probably existed.

of men with brains of gods and minds and hearts of demoniac beasts and paranoiac lunatics? Truly, there is little or nothing *new* under the sun!

However, lest gentlewomen be shocked by the wicked words of academicians and scientists, pshawing these revelations, let me proceed!

This ray machine in the "House of Flame" was intended, one is told, to guard the home of pure scientists against the invasion of aggressive militarists, or barbarians, or savages of the type of Hulagu the Tartar, who wrecked the aqueducts of Mesopotamia, in his far later day. Urged by devouring curiosity and the juvenile desire to see what would happen after a *déclenchement* of the controls in the "House of Flame", one is next told that this young prince of Atlantis gained access to the "House of the Flame" and operated the discharge mechanism. The results were catastrophic. Millions of people died, exactly as if some super-atomic bomb had been exploded over them. The wide plains of Atlantis fissured, cracked, and split asunder. Great rivers flowed over the land; the fountains of the deep and the waters of the atmosphere were unleashed and inundated the vast countryside. The waters gathered into great lakes, and the lakes became a vast sea, and the land sank as though "its base were built on stubble and the pillared firmament were rottenness". Men in high stations, which seems to mean in elevated regions, used their powers of defying gravity and rose into the air. They went east above the raging waters to the ancient Africa. They went west, to the old Americas.

The young prince was taken up for judgment. In some high place an Atlantean Sanhedrin of philosophers, rulers, and archons passed judgment on him that he should remain in solitary confinement till he died. It is also said that he did not live long but passed to another plane, where, again, he was judged by some celestial council of very serious and angry beings who condemned him to return to earth, in many reincarnations, until he had served and helped *every* Atlantean who had been destroyed in the catastrophe! This Sisyphean task would occupy a whole cycle of many thousands of years, and his powers of intuition would tell him when he might know whom he should help.

If the indulgent reader choose to consider this a fantasy, or effort of imagination on my part, I can hardly blame him or her. Yet, I may assure any who care that whether this story is taken or left, and I tell it as it was told me, I am *not* akin to the unfortunate gentleman who found the faker's picture of a steamship in a West African, palæolithic painted cavern and was credulous enough to broadcast the surprising news that marine locomotion was known to and used by races coeval with the Old Stone Age!

The teller of this story of Atlantis says that stairs were unknown in Atlantis, and also transport by any form of automobile, railroad train, or steamship. Life is said to have been far easier than any we know in our cycle. Illumination of darkness, by day or night of the sort we use, would have been deemed by Atlanteans, to be both puerile and needless. The Atlantean day, one is told was never gloomy nor dark. Everything was illumined with a soft enduring light or glow, as by some physico-radiological application of a "cold light". Readers of my former book may recall the statement that jungle Indians who have visited Cuyabá, a frontier town in the Brazilian Matto Grosso, have said that such a light burns, untended and age after age in high places where are ruins of the dead Atlantean cities of Hy-Brazil. (I decline to be drawn into a controversy of whether such an assertion conflicts with the law of conservation of energy.)

In old Atlantis, it is said, the night hours were softly and brightly illumined, and, once lit, the source of illumination never waned or could be put out. It burnt on for ages!

Levitation was generally used by the ruling castes of Atlantis, says this story. If so, the ancient West Indian folklore about Iere and the power of defying gravitation may not be destitute of some basis in ancient fact. However, Atlantis, like old Greece of the Hellenes, was a pyramidal state of intellectual aristocrats based on slavery and helotry. It was certainly not a democracy. Great gangs, in a *corvée*, worked on the wide plains of Atlantis, night and day. The ruler castes were not in the least interested in them or their welfare, at this stage of time. The gangs worked in relays and reliefs. It is also strangely asserted that these helots did not seem to need sleep or food. Maybe, here we have the origin of the peculiar West Indian lore about the "zombie". And, equally, maybe not!

Atlantis is said, but not of course in the Plato-Solon dialogues, to have had no enemies, nor was there war anywhere. The "House of the Flame" was regarded as her main defence against external aggression. She is also said to have had no soldiers, according to the tradition given to me, though, again this allegation clashes with what is said to have been recorded in the ancient Egyptian temple archives, in Solon's day, at Sais and Heliopolis, or by Plutarch.

It must be remembered that Atlantis existed for thousands of years. *Greater* Atlantis seems to have stretched from Iceland where, in the Hof creek are ancient Atlantean letters—identical with some in old Brazil—to the region of the Caribbean, as it now is. It may also have included the British Isles, regarded by the Greeks and Romans as the place of ancient mysteries, of Hell, the Styx and Acheron. Part of it included the Apollo sun-god land of old Hyperborei, whose astronomical cycle of 19 years is recorded in the ancient stone circles at Stanton Drew, near Bristol. Hyperborei-Atlan was known to the ancient Frisians. It was a land where mistletoe-bearing virgins danced the solar circle measure, round the golden temple of the sun. From it came the *Papæ*, old men in black carrying crosses, books and bells, and *not* to be confused with their bastard imitators, the Papal missioners from old Rome. It may be that *Lesser* Atlantis, the still great Atlantis, remnant of an earlier great cataclysm is that known as the Seven Islands of Proserpine, which included, in its empire, the old island of Poseidonis, of Solon, Plato, and the old priests of Egypt.

The tradition I have also alleges that there were no wild or dangerous animals in Atlantis. The statuary in the dead city entered by the Brazilian *bandeiristas*, in A.D.1750, appears to bear out the assertions that the Atlanteans were tall, fair, and very good-looking, and the women as beautiful as those in classic Greece. In this present book, I reproduce a typical Atlantean figure which forms one of the pillars, or caryatides, of the Temple of Warriors, in the great Mayan Hall at Chichen-Itza. He may have been carved from a living model in the person of some tall, fair Atlantean who was a refuge in ancient Mexico or Yucatan after one of the cataclysms that fell on Atlantis, in the long ages of her dominion. It was not a case of Sodom and Gomorrah. For had Atlantis been as brutal and sadistic as the giants of some of the continental islands of Mu, or Rutas-Mu, a blind, cosmic catastrophe, caused by a wandering planetoid, or great aerolite, or comet—whatever may have been the cause—is no respecter of persons or nations, good, bad, or indifferent. The Great Disaster would have happened whatever sort of men the Atlanteans were.

So far as one may gather, there were eugenic methods, or euthanasia operated in the case of physically ugly, or deformed people born in Atlantis. It is also alleged that this coldly intellectual race had little of sex or sexual passion in their composition. Like Wells's Men in Mars they had evolved in brain power till at least one of the two desires of the belly, to use the Nietzschean phrase, had been suppressed, inhibited, or eliminated.

But, however, this may be, the Atlanteans are said to have had a *vires viduarium*. Here, selected males were kept on a human stud farm to breed with females marked by fine physical characteristics and superior mental qualities of eugenic value. Such an institution actually exists, at the present day, among the Chamboias Indians of the Rio Araguaya, which river,. by the way, is on the fringe of the former Brazilian Highlands, where old Atlantis erected her splendid stone cities, long since dead, ruined and forgotten.

Something of this seems implicit in the myths of the West Indian aborigines and the old Irish, relating to *Iere*. One has also heard it alleged that insemination was also practised, at one stage in the evolution of Atlantis.

My reader might reasonably retort on me, in the words of Claudus Aelianus:

> This, if any man think the Chian worthy of belief, he may. To me, he seems an egregious Romancer . . . !

The evidence of the strata on the beaches of Spitzbergen, showing fossil flora ranging through the whole gamut of tropical to arctic, seems to indicate violent changes of the position of the north pole in remote ages. There are very ancient traditions in Asia and Egypt that east has not always been east—it was at one time *west*—nor has north always been north—it has been east and west. The earth, these traditions suggest, is constantly, in the slow process of ages, changing the position of her axis. At the present moment, it is being forced on scientists in Australia to note that the Antarctic ice floes seem to be coming nearer Australia. It may be—who can yet say?—that the rotating earth is slowly turning round, sending the southern polar regions nearer the more direct rays of the sun, and breaking up the ice.[1] About 2,400 years ago, the old priests of Egypt told Herodotus that the poles of the earth and the plane of ecliptic coincided —that is, that the spinning gyroscope of the earth sat upright, losing the "normal" of about 23° with the plane of the ecliptic. They said that, even since their first zodiacal records began, the poles had thrice been within the plane of the ecliptic. Also, three times the sun "had risen in the west". The Arctic regions, as North American Indian and old Maya-Toltec myths indicate, were at one time tropical.

The earlier Atlanteans had beautiful bodies and lived harmoniously and in peace. Diseases were non-existent. Cancer and tuberculosis were unknown. Neither was there insanity nor mental aberrations. The men and women were beautiful to the eye, though in later ages, a few folk became ambitious and discontented. Harmony was gradually lost and perfect physical and mental types degenerated. Before any cataclysm came, diseases began to make their appearance. It is said that it was the wiser sort of Atlanteans who built the great ships called "arks" in the old records. For about a century before the Great Cataclysm came, men in black with powers of vatication warned the Atlanteans that a grave change was approaching.

It began with violent volcanic eruptions. All the lands where is now the Gulf of Mexico were swallowed up in the waters. That was the first great inundation. In a few years, several large islands were seen between the shores of primæval America and Africa, and Africa was not known by that name in those far days. The Atlanteans were warned to go east or to Egypt, which, as a centre, was to take the place of Atlantis.

Such a shifting of the axis was taking place, that east seemed to be moving west. There were then hundreds of miles of land between the Sahara Sea and Egypt, but this land became submerged. The migrant Atlanteans arrived in Egypt, and found there a civilized people ready to receive them. Settling among them, the Atlanteans started to build the pyramids. They first of all marked the exact centre of the earth, and a very ancient tradition says that "the most complete angle with the sun is where the Egyptian pyramids now are. A line drawn perpendicularly through the earth from the site of the Great

---

[1] In January 1949, the British Falklands Survey Expedition reached a point 395 miles south of the Antarctic Circle, where they found *mountains completely free of snow*. They saw many melted streams in these mountains, as well as a lake a mile long.

Pyramid will, so it is said, reach the Mayan pyramid at Chichen-Itza— Itza denoted the name of the old Atlantean prince, Azoes. Their mathematical and geo-physical calculations were made with great accuracy in relation to this geophysical "centering".

The Atlanteans, as the Mu-ans, were not ignorant of electricity. There is a story that power used in the erection of the great stones of the pyramid was derived, in some mysterious way, not from water, but from the sands of the Nubian deserts. The stones were cut in the Theban quarries and this sand-derived electrical power was used to erect them into position. Cranes, or derricks, were not used, but there were machines powered by this electrical force and controlling it. From Mu, migrants reached Egypt from India and the Pacific.

As time went on, there was considerable intermarriage between the Atlanteans in Egypt and the Egyptians. Eventually, a sort of racial pride and arrogance developed and what powers they had began to decay and the race degenerated.

Before passing on from this dim reconstruction of the past, a world may be said on the subject of the mysterious *orichalcum* [1] or so-called "mountain brass" of the Atlanteans. No one has ever been able to say just what this metal, or alloy was. I have some reason for suspecting that specimens of this mysterious metal came into the hands of the British War Office, in 1916, year of the First World War, though none of their experts realized what it really was. In India, from the remote past, there have been handed down specimens of a very heavy metal mixed with gold, or gold-fired. Its specific gravity is said to be three times as much as that of any known metal, of modern times. The British War Office wished to use it for some military purpose, but no chemical metallurgist was able to analyse its composition.

With the singular story told above for the first time one may contrast what old Ben Jowett called the "noble lie" of Plato about Atlantis. Nevertheless, it must be said that many classic writers of a later day certainly did not deem it to be a lie or fantasy. Here, the Egyptian priest Sonchis, or Psonchis of the temple of Sais of Pharaoh Amasis, told Solon, who wrote it into a long vanished poem:

> In this island of Atlantis there was a great and wonderful empire which had rule over the whole world and several others and over part of the continent—the "opposite and boundless continent" (of America?— AUTHOR) . . . which surrounds the true ocean . . . (presumably this must be the Pacific ocean!—AUTHOR).

[1] In India, this mysterious metal has been used to make very ancient images in the form of the elephant—an animal which, of course, ranged the forests of old Atlantis. It had also been used to make very ancient incense-burners, inset with gems or crystal, so that the light of the burning shone through the metal. This metal seems to have a large percentage of nickel, and one theory is that it is meteoric iron, which, of course, contains nickel. Prehistoric man seems to have used meteoric iron for his weapons. In some way the mystery metal came into the possession of the monks in Hindu monasteries, but archaic objects, in which it was used by artists, show no precise artistic convention by which they may be dated.—AUTHOR.

In the Platonic dialogue of Timæus, we are told that the Great Island, or one of the great islands of Atlantis, was ruled by aggressive, imperialist kings, or a king, who had *mercenary troops*. This vast power:

gathered into one and endeavoured to subdue at a blow those within the Pillars of Heracles. (That is, Libyan Africa, old Egypt, the lands around a proto-Mediterranean, and old Europe from Iberian Spain to the land of proto- or Pelasgian Greece and the proto-Levant.—AUTHOR.)

Obviously, a necessarily large army for this type of invasion would have needed the transport of a large navy, and Plato says that several thousands ships were used. The story of Psonchis also implies that old Atlantis summoned to her aid and embodied in her armies men from her empire, or other allies in ancient South America. Whether or not these ancient South American cohorts, summoned to Atlantis, included refugees from the rabidly militarist Pacific continent of Mu, or Mu-an colonies in South America, or the powerful tribes on the Andean slopes, known as *Antis*, it is impossible definitely to assert.

It does not, also, at this time, seem possible to reconcile these two versions of Atlantean history preceding the final catastrophe. Yet it must be said that these floating traditions, ranging from Ireland to the Caribbean and down south to the Matto Grosso of the Brazil, of to-day, of a peaceful, unsoldierly, cold, dispassionate, scientific race are, or *seem* consonant with what I have said about applied scientific knowledge revealed in the mysterious Atlantean-Brazilian ruins, which Colonel P. H. Fawcett sought to reach in 1925–26. I refer particularly to the strange light, using a form of energy not yet known to physicists, which the Indians say shines, and has shone for ages, from windows or porticoes of splendid ruined buildings hidden far behind the forests of the Matto Grosso. The floating traditions, too, are consonant with the terrible massacres and exterminations committed on colonies of ancient bearded, white men dwelling near, or in great ancient and ruined sites, by the Colloans, who seem to be descendants of the formidable Cara-Karians.

Says an old Spanish historian, speaking of a strange bearded Amazon race:

The *Mayorumas* of the Amazon are a nation very peculiar in their physical and moral character. They are big men, and numerous, with beards and red hair and skin so white that they resemble the English or the Flemish, rather than the Spaniards. They are the *gitanos* (gypsies) of the Amazon, and cannot be induced to settle in villages. But if they do, they die of melancholy. They eat human flesh . . . of those that fall sick in this nation, and do not give the sick time to grow thin.

This is *not* a case of *albinism*, as is suggested in one London weekly newspaper, with such facility by young, Scottish ploughers of English pasture. It is more probably one of degeneracy from a far higher ancient white race of ancient Hy-Brazil. Or, the *Mayorumas* may have been a helot caste among the ancient white ruling race of Atlantean South America. Or does such a young Scotchman suppose that *all* the members of a numerous race are albinos?

These "White Indians" exist in the hinterland of French Guiana, where they are called the "Oyacoulets", or "Oyaricoulets". Extremely little is known of them, and I have heard of no contact with them since the early 1900's. In December 1846, a remarkable story was published in the *New York Sun* about another mysterious and elusive race of "white Indians", this time in the Mexican state of Sonora:

> They are called the "Munchies" and a work has recently been published in which there is a full account of the race of these "white Indians". They exist, to-day, in a valley among the Sierra de los Mimbros, upon one of the affluents of the Rio Gila in the province of Sonora, Mexico. They number about eight hundred, are of Circassian complexion and have graceful forms. They are peaceable in their habits, honest and virtuous. They live surrounded by inaccessible mountains, where are located their caves and homes. There seems no doubt that the colony exists and what gives form to the opinion are manuscripts of early travellers to America, which are deposited in the Vatican in Rome, describing the large numbers who have for centuries inhabited the valleys of the cordilleras. It is yet to be ascertained whether these people are descendants of Spaniards who landed with Columbus, or descendants of those extraordinary people who built the ancient cities of Mexico, and Yucatan, the ruins of which are spread all over Central America.

I have not been able to trace the work mentioned in the above excerpt, but I draw particular notice to the part about the "manuscripts in the Vatican Library in Rome". Rome knows far more of these mysteries of ancient races in the Americas than she has ever revealed, or, for obvious reasons of policy ever will reveal. Needless to say, again, that the "Munchies" are no more descendants of lost Spaniards than were, or are, the white "aborigines" of Hy-Brazil!

The old *cronista*, Cieza de Leon, was told, about A.D. 1540, of two Cara chiefs, Sapana and Cari who entered one of the larger islands in Lago de Titicaca, where they came across *white, bearded people* whom they fought and exterminated. Antonio de Herrera, *coronista major*, or camp-master of the King of Spain, "in the Indias" (1594–1625), tells the same story of massacre by a Cara-Karian captain Cora, who came to Lago de Titicaca from the vale of Coquimbo, Perú. These same mysterious white-bearded people—Atlantean refugees, or colonists, flying from a great Catastrophe—left great ruins and buildings at Guamanaga, on the great cordillera, well east of Lima. When he asked the Indians who were the builders, the reply was: "A bearded, white people like you Spanish".

As Cieza de Leon comments:

> These ancient men came to these parts many ages before the Incas. . . .
> The buildings do not seem to me Inca; for they are *square*, not long and narrow. Certain letters were found on a tile in these buildings.

There are extremely ancient Chinese myths purporting that the men well inland, in old China, were all of very high stature and belonged to a race that had migrated from a lost continent to avoid a cataclysm. It is said that there are manuscripts in what is called the "Lolo tongue", which are unintelligible to Sinologists, and which relate to this tall race of high intellectual distinction.

As the "Iere myths" have shown, some of the Atlanteans migrated, after a cataclysm, to the shores of Africa, while other dim and misty legends of classic origin say that Atlanteans passed overland to old China. Another singular story said to derive from tribes in the great Gobi desert, speaks of a concealed oasis, somewhere in north-western Tibet, and called Shan-ba-lha, the Shangrila of the recent film, so far as the *name* alone goes. If this place exists it is located in a very blank space on even the most modern maps. The legend is that this oasis was a sacred, or secret, island when a great inland sea extended over middle Asia. After a cataclysm a few tribes took refuge on this island. It cannot be stated whether they were from the drowned Pacific islands-continent of Mu, or Rutas-Mu, or from Atlantis. The story goes that the mystic island can be reached only through tremendous tunnels, radiating from all directions to the island, from very ancient dead cities, caves and temples which abound in India. Some may say that these singular myths may relate to yet another ancient lost world, which preceded by thousands of years the Aryan civilization of old Hindostan. Others will smile in their academic beards.

Curious memories of Atlantis are found all over the vast and mysterious land of Brazil, to-day. Indeed, as the late traveller, A. G. Hales, said in his absorbing autobiography, *Barney O'Hea, Trapper*, nearly every Indian tribe in Brazil has legends of ancient white rulers mixed up with their ancient creeds. These Indians sternly warn off travellers lingering around these ruins. He makes the trapper say: "Some day, perhaps, a man will be born big enough to unravel these mysteries and give the world a real history that will antedate the Jewish story of Adam and Eve and the Creation by a few million years."

To which one may subjoin a curious protest of a travelled and educated native of Borneo. Said he, some years ago (he is said, since, to have gone into perpetual solitude in some Eastern monastery):

You Westerners have only a garbled account of what is called the Great Deluge. Civilization was flourishing in China at that time and I have been told the cataclysm was caused by a pretender who wished to be thought God . . . Now, someone came from a very old land that had been destroyed and he set up an entirely separate country in Central Europe. He gave out that he and his people were the only divinely inspired humans in creation. In fact, he said they were the Lords of Creation. This was a new cult, and it led only to the apotheosis of the whole race of Jews. *Bah*, your Jewish Bible speaks of *one* ark of *one* Noah! Why, there were *hundreds* of such instances of escapes! This Jewish Noah and his ark was merely one of them, and a petty one at that. The Great Flood was world-wide, and everywhere it came where man existed some were saved.

The dead cities of gold and mystery lie, as one has said, round the littoral of the *old* Marañon-Amazon basin, and on the uplands of proto-South America. Many of the expeditions to one region of the unknown—both European and American, and including that of the lost explorer Irwin—have been to the little known territory, watered by the branch of the Amazon tributaries, lying between Obidos and Santarem on the west, and Almereiran on the east, at the embouchure of this mighty waterway. Out of this *terra incognita* will one day come some startling discoveries. In these, an airship or multi-engined aeroplane will play a valiant part, as the Latin-Americans would say.

Somewhere in the north of this region, running from the slopes of mostly unknown and unexplored sierras of the Tumac-Humac and the Parairaima, is a great prehistoric highway known as the Inca Way. It apparently linked this territory of gold, gems and ancient mysteries with what was later the Inca Empire of Quito and Cuzco. Dense bush and far-spreading forests and jungles, beset with fierce Indians who use blow-pipes and poisoned arrows, cover up much of this ancient imperial highway, whose makers may be co-eval with the old Atlantean empire of South America. Deep within this region, at a point where a number of affluents merge, and on the fringes of that mysterious land of Oyapoc where lived the Conoris, or white Amazons of Sir Walter Raleigh's day, is one of a number of dead cities of megalithic date. (Compare this following story with the account of another dead city in Chapter I.)

The jungle Indians, who shun the place as taboo and sacred, say that gold ignots lie in the dust of the dead city. They say it has pillars in naves of ancient temples and great buildings, grey and weathered with extreme age, that blaze with gold and sacerdotal jewels. Around the pillars and the friezes may be seen many hieroglyphic and bizarre letters of no known race. One of these dead cities, far within the forest, and near the slopes of the sierras, is approached by a great stairway of many steps going down, between walls of a towering cliff, to an immense cavern or subterranean. The stairway is cut in the solid rock and is slippery with fungi and dripping with dank moisture. As one nears the bottom of the stairway, which at this point is inscribed with strange glyphs, one hears the roaring of tumultuous waters. A rushing river goes underground through the middle of the subterranean into a tunnel of more than a mile length. The roof comes down, and over the lip of a great crack in the rocks, the waters rush into a *catadupa*—waterfall—at the bottom of which is a maelstrom. None know what lies beyond.

Clearly, the spot is very dangerous. It is probable that, beyond this tunnel lies the dead city, which is said to be about three miles long. The story sounds like a South American version of one of the late Sir Rider Haggard's novels. Attempts have been made by daring explorers to find the way into the dead city, where, as said, is much gold and many rich jewels, but all have been baffled.

Within the subterranean approach there is a hole in the cavern floor at the bottom of which is a quadrate-shaped chamber, clearly of man's make, in which round the walls are numbers of oblong niches. These niches are for four-fifths of their height walled up with stones neatly laid on each other and cut by skilled masons. The explorer, as he casts round his torch in this eerie vault, starts back with an exclamation of horror. Over the top of the walling there grins at him a human skull attached to the skeleton which has been walled up. In some of the niches appear to be mummies.

Just what cult of the underworld was practised here is a riddle. It may be a queer mausoleum, or it may not. Cut into the rock over each niche are lines of strange letters of the type seen by the *bandeiristas* in that dead Atlantean city far south in Bahia. It is useless for explorers to expect any help from the forest Indians, even where one has succeeded in establishing fairly friendly relations. Not a man will venture near this vault of mystery, nor give any hint of the secret and cunningly concealed entrance to the dead city itself. It is likely that herein may lie the solution of the riddle of the disappearance of several American and British adventurers who have been lost in the Amazon jungles in the last thirty years. A man who ventured alone into this strange subterranean and who rafted himself down the underground stream till he was capsized and fell into the whirlpool, roaring far underground, would not leave the least trace to indicate what had happened to him. And the difficulty of locating the spot is very great.

The tradition that gold ingots lie around in the dust of the ancient city is one more of those indications of a great cataclysm, forcing a hurried abandonment of a great centre of culture and high civilization.

What seem to be singular echoes of old Atlantis come from that tributary of the mighty Marañon-Amazon, the Rio Trombetas, along whose banks, some thirty or more years after the Spanish conquest of Nueva Granada (modern Colombia) and Perú there trekked northward a big company of South America's white fighting women, the Amazons. These remarkable women were by no means a figment of the imagination of de Orellana, or the monk Carvajal who wrote the story of that amazing expedition of Castilian soldiers about the year 1535. J. Barbosa Rodrigues, speaking of the "Muyrakytae, e os idolos symbolicos . . . da civilizacao do Amazonas nos tempos prehistoricos" (of the Amazon green stone and symbolical images of the prehistoric civilization of Amazonas) features a protector-idol, which embodies a cithern-shaped frame that has long ears and an expression of suffering and sadness, as of one bearing the woes of the world, like Atlas or Quetzalcoatl.

Rodrigues says: "This idol has a possible cataclysmal significance. It was meant to ensure that the gods would cause the earth to rotate when they had left it . . . and to put them in mind not to forget to turn it. On the plaque of this idol's head-dress are two suspension holes, placed so that if the stone were suspended the central figure of the mournful-looking man with the extended ears, or ear-lobes would be *upside-down."*

It reminds us of the thunderstone, found in certain West Indian islands, a carved and ancient amulet, where a mountain is represented as covering the form of a man, like Enceladus, the giant-titan, blasted by Jupiter, with the Mount Etna laid over his body. It may be, as is the thunderstone, a symbol of some post-cataclysmal race who thus commemorated the overwhelming of great Atlantis by the waters above, on, and under the earth.

A remarkable Atlas figure of this type is found bearing a great mass of stone and earth on his shoulders in the Mayan temple of warriors at Chichen-Itza. Almost side by side with it is that superb profile of a fair, white, handsome Atlantean supporting a massive

1 and 2.—Atlanteans (Chichen-Itza, Mayan caryatides).   3.—Bearded Atlan (later deified as rain god, ancient Mexico).   4.—Woman Atlantean (very ancient Indian glyphs, British Columbia).

stone table-like altar in the sanctuary of the same temple (*vide* page 30 *supra*). These figures were found in 1926 by the expedition of the Carnegie Institution of Washington, D.C. Refugees from Atlantis of just this same classic and handsome type are said traditionally in Mexico to have entered ancient Central America both before and after the Great Cataclysm.

Again, another startling memory of the same Great Cataclysm that disrupted the ancient American empire of Atlantis is found, to-day, among the *Yuracarés*, literally "white men" who live to the number of about 2,000 souls in the region between Santa Cruz de la Sierra on the east, and the longitude of Cochahamba, to the west, in Bolivia. The story is as follows (quoted from a Bolivian historian):

They owe, it is said, to their sojourn in the depths of dank forests that white colour which marks them apart from neighbouring Indians.

They are completely savage and yet have the most intricate mythology. Their myth is that of the destruction of the world by fire, according to which an evil genii, named *Sararumi* sent a fire which burnt up the forests and killed all living people, except one man. He retired with food into a very deep cavern, or subterranean dwelling. To find out when the scourge was nearing its end, he put out a long rod from time to time from the hole of his cave. Twice, he drew it back in flames. The third time it was cold. Four days later, he came forth from the hole and roamed over a devastated country with no food or shelter. As he was mourning his isolation, there appeared *Sararumi* and gave him seeds of grain to sow, and a fine forest sprang up by enchantment.

How far this same "etiolation" is attributable to the possible fact that these Indians are degenerate descendants of some white race who were, perhaps, helots of a ruling Atlantean-Hy-Brazilian caste, is hard to say.

The Chimus of Northern Perú, and the Muyscas or Chibchas of the region of what is now Colombia had also a cataclysm myth of a rainbow. It was adored under the name of *Cuchavira*. "Vira", be it noted is the sun, still worshipped under that name by remote South American Indians in Brazil and the Andes. The myth has also its Atlas!

An old Spanish writer says:

Chibchacum, god of the fields, traders and workers in silver, sent a deluge on the people of Bogotá. They fled to the mountains and implored Bochicha for help. At evening, he appeared in a rainbow. He chastised Chibchacum, after lowering the height of the waters, *and made him bear the burden of the earth*, formerly propped up by pillars of Huayacun wood.

These bearded white men of ancient South America, of whom we have spoken above, are sometimes missioners in a sombre garb of black and were white and blonde, with a ruddy face, as was the old Mu-an Quetzalcoatl, the Atlantean culture-hero. They often dressed in cassocks, open in front, but without the cowls of the far later Roman Catholic monks, the neck of the garment cut in crescent shape and with short sleeves ending at the elbows. They were pacific and avoided and abhorred war and fighting. In one case, as at ancient Panuco, where they landed, they are described as very tall and skilled in the working of gold and silver and jewels. They are also lapidarians, and under Quetzalcoatl they built fine and beautiful homes and magnificent temples and palaces, apparently in an antediluvian day.

But, sometimes, as one has seen, the bearded man are degenerate survivors of a once mighty and highly civilized race of remote antiquity. Even to-day, if one assembles the story of their appearances as late as 1930, in forests on remote eastern Andean slopes, in chapada and jungle, in creek and river generally, far up country towards the headwaters of the Amazon and other rivers flowing into Brazilian selvas from the borders of Colombia, Ecuador, Perú and Venezuela, one would say that they range very far and into regions remote from any airways.[1]

The bearded men were the forerunners of cataclysm and floods that shook half the globe with quakes. They seem, as Burmese myths import, also to have appeared in Asia, dressed in black. "A thousand years before the destruction of the world, a certain *Nat* came from superior abodes, his hair dishevelled, his face sad, his garments black. He went everywhere in the public ways and street, with mournful voice, warning men of what was to come" (*Asiatic Researches: Burma, Vol. VI, p.* 172). And one *Nata* also appeared as a culture-hero and missioner in ancient Mexico, apparently in the far-day before gigantic earthquakes and a great Deluge sank the last fragments of the island-continents of Mu, in the Pacific, and of Atlantis, in the northern and southern regions of what is now the Atlantic Ocean.

If the fate of a prophet is not to be believed when he prophesies evil, it was certainly theirs! And in the case of Quetzalcoatl, man of peace who abhorred human sacrifices, it was borne out in his case in ancient Mexico, as in a far later day in Babylon, that:

> A wonderful and horrible thing is committed in the land; the prophets prophesy falsely and the priests bear rule by their means; and my people love to have it so; and what will ye do in the end thereof?

Quetzalcoatl vanished over seas to the east, whence he came, and the priests in old Mexico, as their like in other parts of the world, in later days, made capital of his fame, created horrible ritual which became a source of monetary profit and, increasing their nefarious power, plunged Mexico into insanity and a paranoia of murder and torture comparable to that in the terrible land of Mu, from which refugees and early colonizers had come. So it was ever. The priest puts his trust in ritual, and his delight in the profit and plunder and power that come from ritual. Has not Dean Inge, formerly of St. Paul's, London, said that he has seen the look in the cold eye of Romanists and ritualists that would bode ill for him and his like had these same sacerdotal gentry the power to turn back the clock and set up once more the bonfires of Smithfield? One may also surmise that something more than an expurgatory index would befall writers

---

[1] I have been amused by the confident statement of a cocksure young Scotsman described as "a well-known writer" by a London Sunday newspaper, who, in a series dealing with missing men, has no hesitation in saying that these stories of lost white races in Brazil are "travellers' tales", because aeroplanes would infallibly detect their presence in Brazil! All I would say is that this young and royal Scot has evidently as much or little knowledge of the *sertão* and the conditions in the Matto Grosso of Brazil, as he has of aeronautics in relation to travel over these vast and still unexplored regions. And that knowledge is in inverse proportion to his cocksureness. It was another debunking, young Scotsman, by the way, who "cleverly" dismissed the Fawcett quest, with the airy statement and truly Etonian lordly comment that one does "not know whether to bring in a verdict of murder or suicide." Well, if he had seen the comment sent to me from Callao, by Mrs. Fawcett, about this old school-tie expedition, as I dubbed it, it would probably as little appeal to his Caledonian guid conceit of himself as my chapter on his expedition in my *Panorama of Treasure Hunting.* (E. P. Dutton and Co., New York City, 1940–41.)—AUTHOR.

of certain books, had the Roman curia and some of the orders the power that vanished, when, as the late Sir Leslie Smith said, a Roman Catholic mob met a Protestant mob.

Where Quetzalcoatl, Bochicha, Viracocha, and other missioners, in the dim past of America, sowed, the sacerdotal priests reaped and perverted. Before the last cataclysm that shook and sank Atlantis,

1 and 2.—Ancient Mexican images of Quetzalcoatl, who was originally a Mu-an, reincarnating in Atlantis. 3.—Hybrid Mu-an type, Central American, ancient ceramic. 4.—Hybrid Mu-an, Colombia Andean highlands.

Quetzalcoatl and his missioners seem to have reached as far north as what is now British Columbia. There are on Indian totem poles in British Columbia the figures of men in ancient costumes identical with those in Atlantean Brazil, carved on rocks. The Thompson Indians say that one *Qoagalal*, a variant of the name Quetzalcoatl, came to what is now British Columbia and with two others worked miracles and transformed things. That is, he gave them laws and civilized institutions.

Another of the riddles of ancient North America—and I shall have much to say of these riddles in a subsequent book—which has never been cleared up is the origin of the singular colossal carved images in cedar wood, found standing outside the doors of cabins in a deserted village of the Hydah Indians, of the Queen Charlotte Islands, British Columbia. They were observed, when Lord Dufferin and Ava visited the place, in his steam yacht, in 1876. The Indians were absent when his party came ashore. The colossal images were, said Molyneux St. John, carved in a way strangely recalling statuary found at excavations around Nineveh and Babylon. They were weird figures standing sentinel before the Indian houses, and their height was 40 feet, and diameter of 2–3 feet. The wood was cedar, taking many ages to decay. The images were of griffins, birds, animals of unknown species, and grotesque human figures, all of huge size, and certainly quite unknown to the Indians. Most of them were very elaborately done and many were coloured. In some of the cabins the cedar had crumbled, which indicates the great age of the wood. All the colossal pillars were old and sound. The Indians knew nothing, or, at least, would say nothing about their origin. They also had carved walking-sticks crowned with small figures of unknown animals. Asked if the Indians would sell some of the pillars, one man replied: "No; and none of us will sell them." If any legends attach to these colossal pillars the Dufferin party had neither time nor opportunity to discover.

Farther east and south, the Algonquins of most of Canada and east of the Mississippi had, among the Ojibway tribes, a legend of one *Keezis* (which sounds rather like Jesus!), who was a giant wrapped in a shining blanket and came from the land of the Whites, or the White Land to the east. This, by the way, does *not* mean Palestine, as Catholic propagandists have sought to make out. It is a variant of the Quetzalcoatl story. The Mojaves, of the lower Colorado river in Arizona and California, spoke of one Matevil who went east, promising to return in later days and live with them. There was, clearly, more than one of these missioners in black, working in ancient North America, thousands of years ago. Crosses and sun-worshippers were found by a puzzled Recollect, Francisco Chrestien Leclercq, in 1675, among the Micmac (branch of the Algonquins) tribes at Miramichi, New Brunswick. (*Vide page* 103 *infra.*)

Quetzalcoatl seems to have wandered over North America, seeking to found a peaceful, agrarian colony for Atlantean refugees and their friends. Probably this was after one of the catastrophes that sank part of Atlantis and presaged a final and greater one. After he had gone, the priests made a very good thing out of introducing human sacrifices in old Mexico. Those marked out for sacrifice in some horrible atonement and propitiation of harvest-gods—certainly no part of Quetzalcoatl's teaching—in Aztec and pre-Aztecan Mexico might "square the priest" and be allowed to substitute a victim who was ill-favoured and otherwise unacceptable. The priests dished the god. Your priest in all ages is a cynic, "off the record". These rascals made a nice little racket out of the business. After the judges had chosen the victims, jewels, or goods, or valuables were paid over to the priest. If a lover had been chosen for immolation in old Mexico, he could get off by handsomely tipping the priest. The like applied to wealthy parents of an only child. The priests, "squared", would "cover" the sacrifice, and themselves substitute an ill-favoured slave, or a fair one whose charms had palled on them, or one who was past labour. The priests would even paint the substitute all over till the substitute was unrecognizable, thus swindling the public, the judges and the chiefs. If the chosen victim were a woman, or fair maiden, your Lothario of a grafting priest in ancient Mexico, having successfully swindled the headman, enjoyed the company of the saved fair one.

Indeed, something of this sort seems to have been perpetrated in the lost Pacific continent of Mu, which was by no means such a bower of bliss and philanthropy as some writers import.

When Sir Lothario, the gay priest of old Mexico, tired of the lady, he might be relied on to find another to suit his jaded palate. In Mu, or Rutas-Mu, the previous fair one, of whom a holy man had tired, was served up for immolation at a banquet where hearts, smoking hot, torn from living bodies, were eaten by broad-bodied, knotted-shouldered, gloating-eyed men of 10 feet or more in stature. They were the Fee-Fi-Fo-Fum of old Mu! I may again asseverate that this happened in Mu, or Rutas-Mu, of which so many dulcet legends have been told. It was done, too, in old Mexico, to which the island-continent of Mu sent colonists, or to which refugees fled to escape cataclysm.[1] This blood-drinking and flesh-eating, too, by the way, is implicit in what the Christian calls the Eucharist, or Last Supper, and not all the fulminations of Roman Catholics between Liverpool, Rome, Ireland, Belgium and Hell, against the unheeding writer of this book will avail to alter the facts one iota!

Nor were Quetzalcoat and his missioners the only culture-heroes wandering over the two Americas (Central and North). There are singular stories of enigmatic and extremely ancient preachers in both South and North America, who, of course, were not of Christian origin. These mysterious men have left strange footprints in grey and ancient rocks in Brazil, Chile, Perú, Ecuador and Paraguay. Such imprints are found in chalky rocks on or near the Mississippi. They are perfectly made, in a block of stone about 8 feet long and 4 feet wide. My old friend, James P. Nolan, gold prospector, has found such a footprint in a rock in the middle of a swamp, where he has gone bumming on the trail in Nova Scotia. Their origin is a complete mystery. They were seen by the first colonists in that region. Whether or no the mound-builders had anything to do with the making is not known. Where the rocks are hard some tools, perhaps of copper, tempered by an art long since lost, may have been used. Such footprints are known in India, as at Nakhaur, in Bihar; and Ibn Batutah, the famous Arabian traveller of Tangier, mentions "Adam's footprint" in Ceylon. Human footprints carved in stone have also been found in ancient Egyptian temples at Karnak and Thebes.

Marc Lescarbot, the late seventeenth-century French traveller to North America, says that one, Dom Emmanuel Nobrega, provincial of the Society of Jesus, in Brazil, saw on the banks of a Brazilian river the footprints of a holy man, who, to escape pursuers, walked across a river—this seems to have reference to *levitation*—and that

---

[1] This tradition is derived from an old Mexican priestess, and not from any Spanish lay, or monastic *cronista*, or historian. (*Sume:* Pelasgian, Karian, *Sum* -erian, Tupi (Brazil), means high priest.)

the Indians say he was *Zome* or *Zuhe*. The Jesuit makes absurd hagiological capital out of the incident and asserts it must have been the globe-trotting St. Thomas the apostle of Christ. *Zuhe*, or *Zome* is probably one of the Atlantean missioners, and so lived thousands of years before Apostle Thomas. John Eusebius Nieremberg, in *Historiæ Naturæ* (*lib.* XIV, cap. cxcvii) makes a statement which may be interpreted very differently from what *he* says:

> East Indians still show a path followed by St. Thomas on his way to the Peruvian kingdoms. . . . [1]

He also says that this mysterious Atlantean (?) missioner is the subject of native traditions along the Rio Iguazi, in Paraguay, and on the Rio Uruguay, at Paraná, where the Indians show a spot where the ancient man sat down to rest. Another ancient tradition is that *Zuhe* foretold the "coming of white men who would announce faith in the true God."

A few more words about this mysterious cenobite, *Zuhe*, may be interesting. This ascetic of a very remote epoch was one of the men in black, white-skinned, and traditional all over South America. He is also called Tsuma, Tume, Sume, Suhe, Zuke, or Chuhe. In Venezuela and Colombia, he is called Suhe. He is depicted in ancient sculpture in South America as clad in a tunic, covered with a hood, or by a *véa*. Sometimes he is grotesquely masked. The *Tecunas Indiós*, in the upper Amazonas, on the frontiers bordering Brazil, still, to-day, hold *fiestas*. They preserve ancient ceremonies of their ancestors in which tunics and horrid masks are used, made from the hairy rind of a *tauri* tree, a species of *couratari*. These are actually representations of the ancient dresses of the proselytes of *Zuhe*, or, as it may be, of Bochicha, also a man in black and bearded and white. The *Tecunas* are indigenous to the cordilleras of Ecuador and Colombia, where these same dresses are used in ceremonies in honour of the culture hero, and ancient teacher, Bochicha.

It is also curious that, in Ceylon, where these footprints exist, the Buddhists say that among the sixty-five figures they profess to see traced on the enormous and ancient footprint (of Adam or Buddha?) is the mystic cross, or *Nandàvartaya*, the symbol of good luck, or the swastika.[2]

---

[1] The capilla at Mylapur, Madras, where is alleged to be an altar with a dove and a cross and enigmatic letters, associated with St. Thomas, is an impudent Jesuit imposture. St. Thomas was never in India, and the altar and inscriptions are of unknown, possibly very early Hindu origin. Even the dove is nothing else than a peacock, a bird of sacred associations in the East.

[2] The same symbol is found on gold bracteates, or ancient coins of Teutonic origin, in *haugs*, or mounds, near Bergen, Norway. It formed a toy, shaped like a maze, used by children of the old Norse, and called the *Troyeborg slot* (castle of Troy). This Troy is associated with old Aasland, land of the Ases, or Asiates, again associated with Odin. Votan, or Woden, whose ancient proto-Sumerian (?) land lay east of the Tanais, or Don, not far from the old home of the Amazon fighting women, who, as to one branch, migrated to South America in some very remote day. Odin, a great chief, lived in Aasgard, of Asaheim (Turkestan). Chinese writers say that ancient shamans, bearing books, which they translated, came from the land of the Ases. Back of it seems to lie some worship of a central sun of the universe, an unknown and unknowable God, Dyaus, or Deus, with which these ancient footprints are in some way associated. Odin and Votan are adored in South America and also in ancient Mexico!—AUTHOR.

A very singular tradition found in Quito, Ecuador, relates to a very remarkable and megalithic monument enshrining some ancient memory of one of these mysterious missioners. It is an immense boulder which stands in the *llanura*, or green plain of Callao, in the Ecuadorian province of Latacunga, a little way off the main road. The Indians say that a man in black ascended this ancient boulder to preach to their ancestors. On the last occasion he left an eternal memorial by stamping the print of his right foot in the rock, which he did by first taking off his sandals, or the *ozhotos*.

Says Fray Juan de Velasco:

> From that time they had the custom of venerating this stone, each day embellishing it with blooms and flowers, as they do to this day. I have seen it with the flowers and have attentively examined the boulder, observing the footprints with wonder. It is enough to see it to know that the footprint is not an artificial thing, but done naturally as in wax.

The same, or another ancient missioner, was known along the Marañon or Amazon. Says an old Spanish writer:

> The celebrated *estrecho*—a dangerous and narrow ravine—called the Pongo de Manceroche is in that part of the cordillera through which breaks that great river, extending the immense sea of its waters to a breadth of 50 *varas* (about 140 feet) for a distance of two leagues.
>
> It appears that to make a channel for its waters, the mighty river cleft one solitary mountain wall, all of living rock, between whose deep and thick parallel walls the waters roar with frightful noises and foaming whirlpools . . . Seen from below, the two highest peaks, or eminences of the steep and craggy mountain are cleft at a spot where no human foot is capable of climbing, no matter what devices it may employ. Notwithstanding, there is seen on the crest, that is, on the western face of the rock a very beautiful orange tree that the Indians assert was sown there by the Holy Man. Its bright globes of fruit can never be gathered, but only when they fall of their own accord on the side where the river foams and dashes. But above the *estrecho* are seen, on the banks, various large stones of whitish colour, some squared, that are called trunks (*petacas*), and others concave, that are called plates, or dishes (*platos*) of St. Bartholomew.

Assuming that the seed of the orange tree was not sown by a bird, there may be here a suggestion implied of that alleged power of defying gravitation, called levitation. This power, as ancient traditions I have cited, *supra*, say, was possessed by the Atlanteans of Iere-Atlantis, and was possibly connected (as suggested *supra*), with the mysterious *klang-platten*, or pendentives, found on the necks of ancient skeletons in what is now Colombia.

These bearded men of South and Central America are also mixed up with legends of Virgins, Virgin births, ritual crosses, crucifixes, Good Fridays, Madonnas, Last Suppers, Eucharists, transubstantiations, resurrections, all of which, of course, are many thousands of years older than Roman Catholicism, or any brand of Christology. They have no more to do with globe-trotting St. Thomases from Mylapur, India, than the Man in the Moon, or Ahashuerus, the Wandering Jew. As we have seen, in the West Indies, these myths are linked with very ancient culture-heroes, such as Quetzalcoatl.

The Chiapas Indians, in Mexico, said that:

> . . . Bocab was killed on a Friday, and we were told by ancient, white-bearded men in very remote times to confess and fast every Friday, in honour of his death. (*Las Casas*.)

It is also added, as a memory of a great cataclysm, that when Quetzalcoatl vanished, the sun and moon were covered in darkness and only a single star remained in the sky. Humboldt, in his *Examen*, says that the Franciscan monk, Mark de Niza, crossed the thirty-seventh parallel, a line linking California with Virginia, seeking a bearded King Tartarax who adored a golden cross and the image of a woman called the Lady of Heaven.[1]

Torquemada, in his *Monarquia Indiana* (Madrid, edn. 1773), relates what the Otomi Indians told Frey Diego de Mercado, in the seventeenth century. Said they to the friar:

> Long, long ago, we Otomis had a book handed down from our fore-fathers and guarded by important persons whose duty was to explain it. Between the columns of this book was painted a picture of a man crucified whose face wore the look of sadness. The many leaves of this book were turned not by hand, but by a tiny stick kept along with the book for that purpose. The Otomis buried this ancient book in the ground as soon as the Spaniards arrived . . .

The book was of extreme antiquity, illuminated and written in two columns. Torquemada also speaks of the Totonacs of Mexico who sacrificed at an annual feast eighteen men and women whose ghosts were sent as messengers "to the Great God to ask him to send his son to renew the physical world . . . when he comes all will grow better and the loaves of bread be much larger".[2]

Again, the Maniacas of Brazil say that a lovely woman, never wedded with a man, gave birth to . . .

> a beautiful child who grew up to be a man and worked many wonders. He raised the dead to life, made the lame walk, the blind to see, and, at last, having one day called the people together in a great crowd he ascended into the sun that lights the earth.

[1] Buddha was said to be born of a virgin named Schakoof in Tibet . . . and the Jesuits were appalled to find that the Virgo Deipara in India was identical with Mary the Virgin, mother of Jesus Christ.
[2] It was said that, in the golden age of Quetzalcoatl, in old Mexico, a head of maize was so large that it needed a man to carry it. The Bannaus, a savage race in the mountains and tablelands of Cochin China, have a myth of a great flood, and say that, in the days before the catastrophe, "one grain of rice sufficed to fill a large saucepan (pot) and feed a whole family.

Here again, seems to be a reference to some man in black from old Atlantis, or Atlantean Brazil. In the Quetzalcoatl myth, his mother is said to have been the virgin Chimalma, who, to cite Mendieta, in his *Historia Ecclesiastica*:

> became pregnant from a small green stone, the *chalchuitl*, which fell in the temple one day when she was sweeping it out.

The Toltecs, said the Tlascaltecs to Bernardino de Sahagun, had a virgin-born god—the birth took place on a mountain—and the curious statement was made by the natives that these myths of immaculate conceptions (and, of course, the Christian is no unique exception) were first given to the Toltecs by Quetzalcoatl. The Chiapas had the same story, even to the assertion that the virgin's son was killed on a Friday, and that the story came from "bearded men, in ancient times, who taught them to fast and confess on every Friday in honour of this god—Bocab's—death".

Again, Torquemada says the part played by the Holy Ghost in the Christian mythology was filled by a white bird's feather which fell from the sky and which a virgin hid in her girdle. She became pregnant of a god whose name meant: "Lord of the Thorn or Wounds in the left side". Which reminds one of the Koran's statement that Jesus Christ was born of a rose smelt by the Virgin! The ancient Mexicans actually built a temple to this Virgin whom they depicted, to the astonishment of Catholic friars, as:

> a fair white woman with rosy cheeks, garments studded with gems, mantle blue as the sky and spangled with fallen stars.

This Isis, of old Mexico, was, however, like Quetzalcoatl appalled by human sacrifices, which she forbade. She spoke through her images to the Sun-God, in intercession for her votaries, and the Totonacs hoped she would send down her son from the skies to free them from human holocausts. Two virgins—male—served her night and day in her temple. Fray Bartoloméo de las Casas[1] tells of an Indian cacique who informed a secular Roman Catholic priest, one Francisco Hernandez:

> Bocab, our god, when he was put to death, was crowned with thorns, and scourged by Eupoca, and hung up with the arms extended from a pole, to which he was not nailed, but tied. There, he died; was dead three days, rose from the dead, ascended to the skies and was now the Sun-God. The Mexican Holy Ghost was one Echnunch, said the cacique, and meant merchant because he brought to the earth all it needed.

Way down in Chile, says Bastian, there came a bearded man who was also shod, and he told the ancient Chilian Indians that he would cure their sick and bring them rain.

---

[1] *Coleccion de Documentos*. No globe-trotting St. Thomas told the Chiapans this Osirian story!—AUTHOR.

Of course, the ancient phallic cross, always a sign of bloody sacrifices in Mu, or Lemuria, and which was "inherited" by Constantine's Christian sacerdotalists, was encountered by the Spanish in America. The Genoese Cristoval de Colonbo (Columbus) found it on one of the Bahamas Islands, on 16th November, 1492. Grijalva lands in Cozumel Island, off Yucatan, in 1518, finds crosses by the dozen, in and outside native temples, and in a plaza of a temple a 9-foot high cross of limestone to which the natives prayed for rain. One man in Cozumel said: "We worship that cross, because a man more resplendent than the sun died on it". It is also to be noted that the ancient Asiatic *Ma*, or *Amma*, or goddess fish sign, taken over by the early Christians and figured on the walls of the catacombs in Rome, was found by Spaniards, in A.D. 1576, on a marble bas-relief in the ancient Temple of the Cross (Mayan) at Palenque. I believe this bas-relief is now at the United States National Museum at Washington, D.C. It is shaped like a Latin cross, surmounting which is a grotesque bird. The cross rests on a base ornamented with the fish symbol, mentioned above. On each side are figures of priests making offerings or praying. At Santa Cruz de Tierra, in Yucatan, the Indians showed the Spaniards a cross chiselled into a rock. Diego Duran, who wrote the *Historia de las Indias de Nueva España*, tells of a Spaniard, at the time of the conquest of Mexico, who said, under oath, that he had seen a very ancient crucifix—*not* done by any friars or Christians—chiselled on the steep walls of a cañon in the country of the old Zapotecs. Another crucifix of the same ancient type was found sculptured on a rock near Tepic, in the province of Jalisco, Mexico. There were also even deerskins, seen, as Bernardino de Sahagun mentions, by Franciscan friars, in the province of Oaxaca, Mexico. Painted on them were pictures which showed two women looking at a wooden cross held by a third, on which was a naked man stretched on the cross—again, extremely ancient and pre-Christian—to which his hands and feet were tied with thongs.

There was an ancient white marble, rosy cross, polished and shining, kept in a huaca, or chapel of one of the Inca's residence, and venerated—why, the Perúvians were not clear. When the "accursed Lutheran corsair", el Draco—Sir Francis Drake—was on the coast of Perú in the *Golden Hind*, he is alleged, by Fray Garcia, to have three times tried to burn such an ancient cross "but each time it came forth from the fire uninjured". Drake tried, also, to break this cross into pieces; but it is said he could not! Allegre, however, in his *Historia de la Compañia de Jesus*, says it was Candish, or Cavendish, who tried to burn this cross, which was of very hard, heavy wood, of a sort not to be found anywhere in old Perú. When the old obispo (bishop) Cervantes took this cross to the city of Guazaca, says de las Casas, the Chiappas told him:

> The cross was erected here by an old, white, venerable bearded man with long, flowing white robes who, with several other long-bearded

men instructed our forefathers and bade them that when a race arrived who venerated that symbol they should accept its religion.

The naïve Roman missioners hastily inferred that these bearded white ancients, some of whom were probably Atlanteans, had had a prophetic vision of the Christian Catholic Spaniards and banditti conquistadores of many thousand of years later. It might just as well be said that they were referring to the sinister gentleman, El Caudillo, Señor Franco, a sort of deputy general of the Order of Jesus of Loyola, one of whose first acts was to restore to that order all its financial and capitalistic interests in the exploitation of Spanish shipping and tin mines!

These crosses are found among the ancient mound-builders in the United States of America. At Zollicoffer Hill, in Tennessee, there was found a copper ornament with a cross surmounting it, and the cross is also found engraved on mound-builders' shells and on copper relics in the same state. In the Cumberland Valley was actually found, under a very ancient mound, a mound-builder's cross with the figure of a man engraved on it. And farther north in New Brunswick, a Recollect friar named Francisco Chrestien Leclercq, was flabbergasted at finding among the Mic-Mac Indians, in 1675, crosses worshipped by the Indians in connection with sun-worshipping rites. They wore the cross on their deerskins, held it up in their hands, put it in their cabins, took it with them on their journeys, and told the friar a legend:

> A beautiful man appeared in a vision to one of our old men and with a cross in his hand told him to go home, make other crosses and give them to their families and their woes and a plague would vanish.

Expectant women and Mic-Mac squaws laid over their stomachs blankets, or shawls adorned with this cross picked out in red porcupine quills. They had cemeteries with these crosses and the tribe met round a nine-foot high cross within a circle, when war or peace was under discussion in the pow-wow. The cross within a circle, as the late Miles Poindexter points out in his *Peruvian Pharaohs*, was in Asia and America the sign of the sun. It was based on an ancient chariot with four spokes, and is enshrined in the tribal place name of Spoke-ane, or Spokane, in the state of Washington: the place of the sun's rays or spoke! When the old Aryans, or proto-Sumerians landed in the Americas they left such heliolithic memorials behind them, and also in Yucatan, where the hot-cross bun sign is identical with that used by the ancient Sumerians.

The early Catholic missioners in Mexico and South America found that last suppers, eucharists and confessionals were no new things to the Indians. In Chiappas, the Indians told the friars that twenty ancient, white-bearded men came to their land, led by one Kukulcan. They wore sandals and were bare-headed, and introduced the confession and penances. Among the Totonacs were aged "pagan" monks making illuminated missals. They were missals of historical matters which the high priest used for the instruction of the Indians.

Nicholas Herborn met a Franciscan who, in 1532, had been sent from Mexico to the General Chapter in Toulouse. What said he?

> Before the Conquest in Tumbez, Perú, were nunneries no man— not even a father or mother—could enter. Two old men directed the nunnery and pure virgins formed the sisterhood. They had a gold statue, five cubits high, depicting a young maid with a babe in her arms. She was called Merca, and the nuns offered her incense. If they had sore feet, they called on her and gave her a hand or foot of gold, when they got well again.[1]

The Zapotecas mention another of these ancient white-skinned and bearded men who came by sea, long ago, with a cross in his hand, and got out of a ship near the coast of Tehuantepec. He was cowled and very venerable, and abjured the men to abstain from the world's delights, fast and do penance. He had a truly mediæval Catholic, monkish, and probably nasty mind, though, of course, he lived long before Christianity was devised. For he bade men abjure female society and would allow no woman to come near him, except for auricular confession. The Indians say he was named Wixepecocha, which sounds very like Viracocha.

Atlantean refugees to the coasts of America, after the Great Cataclysm that sank their motherland, fell on very evil days. If they were peaceful, they would find themselves compelled to take up arms in order to survive among the savage autochthones of South America. The whispers of the forest Indians in North-western South America import that these former ancient white rulers had some form of illumination that singularly recalls our modern electric light. These heirs[2] of a peaceful, coldly scientific race of old Atlantis, as the stories of old Spanish cronistas show, lapsed into degeneracy and were, in their refuges in the forests, and in islands of Lago de Titicaca, exterminated by the savage Colloa-Carians. These Colloas came of ancient ancestors who had known the old island-continent of great Atlantis.

In other cases, helot races of the former Atlantean empire of South America seem to have fallen heirs to the dead cities, wherein, in regions of unexplored Brazilian Guiana, they still survive to-day, as stories in my former book show. One of these dead cities was located in the time of the Spanish conquistadores. It was found on the banks of the Rio Vinaque, in Perú, where Cieza de Leon and Herrera heard of white and bearded ancient men who built very large

---

[1] MS. Cod. No. 1374, Treves City Library. Nicolaus Herborn's *Provincialis Min. Observ. Relatio vera de Novis Insulis.* (Stadtbibliothek Treves, or Trier.)

[2] It must be recalled that the Prussians of the days when, as it was said, France ruled the land, England the seas, and Germany the clouds, numbered among them many great thinkers, scientists, philosophers and mathematicians, such as Kant; or, in a later day, Ernst Haeckel and Friedrich Nietzsche.—AUTHOR.

and ancient buildings, still to be seen in the sixteenth century A.D. Whether or not the Atlanteans had anything to do with the square and very ancient building with three windows in each of four walls, seen by Osery, companion of Castelnau, on top of a mountain near Ollantay-tambo, Perú, and apparently pre-Inca in origin, is not clear. Its possible purpose was astronomical. (Osery was murdered by his guides, on the Marañon, or Rio Amazon.)

In the persons of the "white Indians", who are *not* albinos, these survivors of the old Atlantean races still exist in remote regions along the forests and mountains of the Upper Marañon, and in Brazil, as well as farther north in the mysterious Cundina-Marca province of Colombia, and on the western borders of Venezuela. But they are wary and shy of contact with any save Indians.

The Tupi race of Brazil, with whom is associated the colour yellow in contrast with the Carib red, would appear to have had a very remote contact in a far day with some ancient race. That ancient race may have been either distantly Atlantean or Mu-an, in origin. Southey tells a queer story—which he did not believe—of the relation of "a certain Monsieur de B. who wrote an account" of *Roggevein's Voyage in the Southern Pacific*, when he discovered Easter Island, and another mysterious vanishing island of the dead land of Mu. Monsieur de B. speaks of a curious idol seen by him, or Roggevein (or Rogge-ween), in the island of San Sebastian, São Paulo, off the shores of Brazil. (M. de B. was Carl Friedrich Behrens):[1]

Le père Prieur, named Thomas, showed us an Idol that had been preserved, that the ancients adored. It is a statue half-tiger, half-lion, four feet high and one-and-a-half feet wide. It was made mostly of massive gold. I have difficulty in believing it, and think it was merely gilded. Its feet are rather like the paws of a lion. Its head is ornamented with a double crown bristling with 12 arrows shaped like the darts or javelins the Indian use. One of them on each side was broken in a half. Behind the head, on each side, there was a wing like that of a stork. Inside the statue was a man armed at all points in the manner of the country. He bears on his back a quiver full of arrows. He holds in his left hand a bow, and in his right hand, an arrow. The tail of this monster idol was very long and twines three times round the body of the armed man. Its point, or head, was like that of a dragon. The natives called this idol *Nasil Lichma*. We could not look at it without astonishment. Besides this statue were several antiquities, as much of Europe as America, of which this convent was in possession.

Southey comments that the Indians knew nothing of gilding, and adds that if the image were really gold "it would have been sent to the mint of Brazil, rather than to the museum of a poor convent, in

[1] Behrens, who was an adventurous son of Mecklenburg, was commander of the soldiers in Roggewein's ships. He makes the curious statement that "elephants on account of their teeth, are a source of great profit in Brazil" (1731). Does this mean that fossil elephant ivory had been found there?

this little island". This mystery of the dead past of old Brazil still remains to be cleared up.

From time to time, migratory impulses have seized on Indians in Brazil, who had memories of the golden age of old Atlantis, or Atlantean-Hy-Brazil. For example, after the famous overland trek of de Orellana's soldiers and monks, about 1549, there arrived at Chachapoya, in Perú, three hundred Indians who, ten years before, led by their cacique, Huirahuasu, "the great bird", together with two Portuguese had left the coast of Brazil to seek for a "land of repose where no one died, and rest was eternal". At the start, some 40,000 Indians took part in this movement across the centre of South America. It put quite in the shade any Mosaic wanderings of Hebrews in the peninsula of Sinai!

A similar tale of a mass migration of Brazilian Indians is told in the *"Descripção Estado do Maranhão, Pará, Corupá, e Rio das Amazonas"*, by Mauricio de Heriarte, *ouvidor-geral provedor-mór e auditor*, in the governorship of Dom Pedro de Mello, in the year 1662 . . .[1]

> The beginning of these Tapinambaranas Indians—of the province of Tapajos, of the upper river Amazon, by the rio of the Tapinambaranas —was not as natives of this river. They say that in 1600 their ancestors set out from Brazil in three bands, in search of the terrestrial paradise (a barbarian idea). They broke into and conquered countries, and having journeyed for a long time, reached that place and found abundance and many Indians. And as it was good, they besieged it and conquered it, enslaving the natives, and in time they intermarried with them; but they did not omit to make the natives know that the Tapinambaranas are their superiors. . . . Their rule is barbarous. They worship nothing. Their appetites are their gods. To those they rule, they give their daughters to wive. They have each six or eight wives. Many natives fear them; for they are very vindictive.

One may say, in passing, that there was also no worship of supernatural gods, as such, in the terrible land of Mu, that sunken Pacific island-continent, which sent colonies to ancient South America, and of which I shall have much to say in a subsequent book. There was ancestor worship, as the statues in Easter Island suggest; but gods and a demi-ourgos were unknown.

Other unsolved mysteries flame on the enigmatic walls of cliffs and cañons in South America, and on mesas and tablelands in Argentina. Sir R. F. Burton, the famous Victorian traveller, in his day spoke of the "written rocks" on the lower Rio São Francisco in Brazil, and in other parts of Brazil:

> The people here have stories of *æstrondos* (*Estrondos*: claps like thunderings and loud clangs) and superhumanities which await on these

[1] This valuable manuscript was found in certain royal archives in Vienna, about 1873, and printed at the expense of a Brazilian aristocrat. The edition was published at *Vienna d'Austria, Imprensa do filho de Carlos Gerold, anno* 1874.

indications of buried treasures. At Breja, there is an *olho de agua* (cavity of water) where the clashing of steel rods is heard.

Burton comments that these ancient inscriptions were well known to the older travellers. Koster, indeed, speaks of a stone in the province of Parahyba, or Paraiba, on which human figures, "Indian and woman", and many unknown characters are engraved. One inscribed boulder of great size lay in a nullah, and the natives said that many others were not far off. The Comte de Castelnau copied such inscriptions on rocks along the Araguaya, and speaks of similar stones along the Rio Negro, the Orinoco, and the Essequibo. On the upper Paraguay the huts of the Indians and neighbouring tree trunks were covered with "similar hieroglyphics", *some* of which may be of Phœnician origin. Dom Pedro, the old emperor of Brazil, collected all the current information about these carved rocks and told Burton they were the works of *quilombeiros*, or Marañon negroes, on which Burton rightly comments: "I cannot accept this view, as the African native at home ignores every species of inscription". He adds that the glyphs on the Rio São Francisco, in Brazil, "are much less European in form than those found" by the old *bandeiristas* in A.D. 1750, of which in this and my previous book, I have advanced a theory of Hy-Brazilian-Atlantean origin. Burton cites a Mr. C. H. Williams of Bahia:

who ascended the Panema, an influent of the lower Rio São Francisco, and found, two leagues up the bed, characters traced in red paint upon the underpart of a rough granite slab. It is much to be desired that all these (granite) and ancient inscriptions may be photographed before they are obliterated; at present every *Caipára* (Indian) instinctively digs his knife point into the "letreiro", as if in revenge because it will not betray its secrets. The interpretation will light up a dark place in the prehistoric age of Brazil.

There are other dead cities in ancient South America. In 1922, José Wolf, of the linguistic section of Museo de la Plata, of the Argentina found one of these *cidades encantadas* (enchanted cities) in the region of the Lago de Cardiel, in the territory of Santa Cruz of the Tehuelche Indians. (It may also be here stated that this dead city may be identical with the one up the Rio Baker, in southern Chile, whence, at certain times of the year, it is alleged, come mysterious roars, clashes and clangings and noises, at a time when the river floods cause the frightened *gaucho* to bar his door fast and he crosses himself in his cabin. He calls this, also, "an enchanted city".)
Said Wolf:

In the southern regions of the Argentina are marvellous ruins, fantasies of the *Thousand and One Nights*. In the region of the Lago de Cardiel I found great and splendid ruins, 164 yards long by 13.12 yards high. These ruined sculptures reveal considerably advanced artistic powers. They are remains of an unknown race that reached a high grade of culture. I found, also, to the north of the Rio Santa Cruz, a ravine full of inscriptions, that stretch for about half a league. In these are enshrined the history of a great and vanished race.

He says that what was most curious[1] was that he found very near these mysterious megalithic ruins a race of troglodytes that lived, perhaps, 20,000 or 30,000 years ago. Wolf rightly says that these ancient, black troglodytes must be the vestiges of the first men who lived in the American hemisphere:

> They used a true city of caverns. In the immediate vicinity are ruins of ancient cemeteries, fortifications, etc. This troglodytic city is found on a *campo* (flat field) called Douglas Esperança . . . Also, there are numerous caverns in the zone comprehended between the Lagos San Martin and Cardiel . . . Also I came on remains of the legendary *Cidade Encantada* (Enchanted City). At least, such must be the ruins existing in the Chubut cordillera. In the highest part of this cordillera are remains of an extremely ancient race. Among others, there are ruins of a building of a circular form that the aborigines call *A Casa do Deus Sol* "House of the Sun God".

Traditions of this ancient race are found among the Tehuelches Indians:

> These Indians say that in the old days there was another ancient race they call "keukunk I", that is, "people who were there before", derived from "k. E–U", "before remote times". They say they were a race of high stature and to them they attribute the ancient walls and inscriptions —the Tehuelches never attained to such a culture—and the other mysterious constructions that are found in the region. These last are like enclosures, great and small, of unworked stones and usually met with on the tops of solitary mountains, or in lofty places. It seems they were built for defence. One of these edifices, especially curious, contained the tumulus of a chief, and could also have served for important assemblies. Ameghino, in his immortal work, *The Antiquity of Man in La Plata*, gives a sketch of prehistoric constructions that probably served in such places for assemblies. Who can say if one may not speak of a "Pre-Columbian Congress-Palace"? There are some others that are not so high, in the shape of a semi-circle, and they seem to have been made for merely transitory use, very likely for the chase: since one meets them in places adapted for hunting.

Wolf advances no theory, so far as I know, about this mysterious megalithic race. I have cogent reasons for believing that this mega-lithic race were none others than either colonists from, or refugees of, the terrible lost and disrupted continent of Mu, or Lemuria, about whom I shall say some startling and new things in a subsequent book. If the ancient traditions I have had are not of the nature of complete fantasy they purport that before the final cataclysm that disrupted

[1] The same aboriginal race is found on the approaches to the Atlantean dead cities of Brazil.—AUTHOR.

the four great islands of Mu, *flying machines*, the exclusive property of the terrible ruling castes took selected Mu-an colonists to ancient South America, to regions marked out as suitable for colonization. Great is Allah and the prophet; since this world hath a more mysterious past than is dreamt of in the padded chairs of university libraries, or is found even under glass cases in museum salons!

How many European archæologists, by the way, are even yet aware that, in 1919, there were found along the Lago Cajary, in the valley of the Rio Pindare, in Brazilian Maranhão, vast "staked cities" (*esteirarias*) standing in the middle of the lake? These "staked cities" are visible only in exceptional summers, when the water level lowers and uncovers them. Locally the natives called them *Encantada* (enchanted), a term applied in South America to the mysterious dead cities. But in actual fact, they are *American* lake dwellings of a type unlike those found in Switzerland. In these staked cities there have been found stone axes and the green stone amulets (a symbol of resurrection) famed all the way from old China and ancient Mexico to far down in South America. Such green stones were carried in their great overland treks by the warrior, South American branch of old Europe's and Africa's Amazons—and bits of painted vases, of zoomorphic and other types.

Again, in the region of the Rio Mollar, Argentina, there are *menhirs* such as are found in Cornwall, Wales and Brittany. They are megalithic monuments and examples of world-wide Neolithic diffusion of culture in a very far day. Some of them form a cattlepost on the ranch of one, Francisco Bazin, and about a foot and a half in the ground. One such *menhir* has been erected in the Parque Centenario at Tucúman. They are engraved with symbols, in some cases identical with those found in Europe; but one of them actually bears the living portrait of a man with a beard! Also at Cordoba, in the Argentina, are curious petroglyphs one of which, shaped like a capital B, remarkably evokes the memory of those coloured, inscribed pebbles found in the Azilian culture on the left bank of the Arise, in the famous Mas d'Azil.

Among these pebbles in the Mas d'Azil, by the way, are signs like the capital letters E, the Greek capital Mu, Theta, Iota and Gamma, Upsilon and Omega, and a Neolithic version of the famous backbone, symbol of resurrection, which, in ancient Egypt, was called the tet, or tat of Osiris. This region of the Argentina has not been properly explored by field-workers, yet; so one would not be surprised if symbols identical with these others of the Azilian culture are also some day found, there.

Our last word shall be concerning these black troglodytes of Brazil and other parts of South America, as well as of ancient Mexico and Darien. When Vasco Nuñez de Balboa, leaving his ships and navy at Careta, went with some *compañeros* and Indian guides to see the cacique Torecha, at Cuareca, Darien, he found black slaves, and was told that the Cuarecans warred with blacks "around there" (*cerca de alli*). The blacks came "from remote lands" (Gomara, in his *Historia General de Indias*). There were traditions of these aboriginal American blacks of very ancient date in American *pueblos* and tribes in Darien. They said that when their ancestors first came to that region it was inhabited by blacks of small stature who soon retired to the forests. Certain tribes—the Payas and Tapalisas and the Cuna-cunas—said their race sprang from the union of a woman Indian and a black woman with a man on the borders or banks of the Tatarcura. Skulls with exaggerated prognathism and of a low receding type[1], found in the mountains of Sumapaz by Dr. Juan de Dios Carasquilla, seem connected with this ancient black race. These negroid skulls have a strong suggestion of the ancient Cromagnon man in Europe. But whether the red race of America originated from these ancient American blacks, of which the Otomies of Mexico, the Caracoles of Haiti, the Aravos of the Orinoco, the Porcijis and Matayas of Brazil, the Chuamas of Darien, the Manabis of Quito, and the albinos of Darien are the remains is very doubtful. Carlos Cuervo Marquez holds that the North Red American red race sprang from the aboriginal blacks of South America. Yet, on the evidence of Red Indian folklore, one may theorize that the red races are probably of early Atlantean origin. Their ancestors fled from one of the catastrophes that sank the Old Continent. They reached Egypt in a very early day. Later, ere the time of Pharaoh Psammeticus, after they had sojourned for many centuries in a territory along the Nile, they became a thorn in the sides of the Pharaohs in Thebes. What is more surprising is that they also became a source of irritation to the Asian nomads known as the Shashu, or Hyksos, or Shepherd Kings who overran old Egypt.

There was a revolt *en masse*, and 240,000 of these Red Atlanteans migrated towards Nubia and Abyssinia, and the source of the Nile. They were swallowed up in the heart of Africa.

Ferdinand Ossendowski found the descendants of these Red Men of ancient Egypt, called the *Phut*, united with another branch of the same race and known to-day as the Fulahs of West Africa. When they quitted Egypt, Psammetichus sent after them. To the Pharaoh's emissaries they cavalierly said: "Tell that son of Ra there will be no return! We say to him we will soon find wives and make homes with the good steel of our swords!"

Now, the Red Indians of North America are almost certainly the cousins of these same men of Phut; but the ancestors of the North American Red Indians emigrated, perhaps from old Atlantis westward to the Americas, and not eastward to North Africa, as did the "red soldiers" of old Egypt.

Those autochthonous blacks troubled Perú. An army of them invaded Perú in the time of Inca Yupanqui Pachacuti (A.D. 825?). He

[1] Prognathic statuettes of black men were also found in Tiahuanacu, the mysterious city of the dead, which may be of Lemurian origin.

was killed with a Chimu arrow on his golden litter, as he urged on his army to fight. As the Quechuas were not allowed an armistice to bury the dead, the stink of the carnage brought on a plague, which wiped out victor and vanquished. A ferocious army of the same black men even invaded the mountains and attacked the Inca Pachacuti VI.

The body of a man was found, under a house in Perú, which seemed to have no forehead. A lot of dried herbs had been buried with him, and also little pots and dolls. Naturally, the Perúvian Indians who saw the corpse thought of *brujerias* and they said: "He is a *hechicero* (wizard)". One theory was that the queer corpse was that of one of the Huara *Indiós* of the coast of Perú, who have fine teeth, protruding *negroid* nostrils and small foreheads with the hair growing on each side from the ends of the eyebrows.

It seems a moot point whether these Central and South American, aboriginal blacks stand in the same relation to certain strange dwarfs in the country of the Tupinambas *Indiós*, at or near the mouth of the Rio Negro, Brazil, as do ordinary negroes to the pygmies of the Congo. Castelnau said they were like small children and he saw some on the Rio Juurua, who were the progeny of Indians and monkeys. It must or may have been these oddities who gave rise to the story of de Bry about the men whose feet are all turned backward. The Tupinambas called them "Guayazis", and alleged that their feet were all turned the wrong way, so that a person strange to them would always walk away from them if he trailed their tracks. Another name for them was the Mutayas, and they were slaves to the Tupinambas.

It may be supposed that the great American head, in diorite, at Huayepan, Mexico, and the gigantic axe (Neolithic?) of Veracruz have suggestions of a negroid type.

But the true black aborigine of South America, who is also a troglodyte and who may be of the same race as the mysterious cave-dwellers of the cave-city in the Argentina mountains, is the small, squat, ugly and dangerous negro found in holes and caves of the unexplored, central Brazilian swamp country. It is a lost, mesozoic world which Colonel P. H. Fawcett said lay about a hundred miles from the dead Atlantean city he was seeking when he vanished in 1925–26. They are cannibals, and, as Fawcett said:

Although their only weapon is a club, they are extremely dangerous. Ethnologists know little about these people. I shall attempt to learn something about them, though any intercourse with them will be difficult and dangerous . . . Not only are the Aymores of Brazil negroid, but many of them are black, despite a constant mixture of blood.

Fawcett truly said, as have certain Latin-American travellers and historians, that these same black South American troglodytes are the original inhabitants of the ancient Brazilian Island. That is to say, they were encountered there when the "fair, white gods" of Atlantis first entered this ancient land, say, 60,000 or 80,000 years ago—a time estimate that, of course, will cause the orthodox archæologist to go all "goosey" and to ejaculate some word rather stronger than "Dear me", or "How amazing!"

As I end this chapter, I have a letter from a friend in the island of Tobago, Trinidad, West Indies. She writes:

Dim lore of a great lost continent—probably of Antillia-Atlantis—I find in this island. Negro workers on my husband's estate in the hills have a very vague story about "very, very big men who once lived in this island of Tobago, British West Indies. *But there wasn't no sea then.* Then everything got smashed up . . . the ole moon broke . . . the sea rushed in. After a time Tobago came dry again, but very small, small. How long ago was it? It was long before anybody's grandfather could remember. No, not British white men, these BIG MEN who lived in these days so long, long ago. But *not* black men, either!'

There is a lot of atmosphere in this island. I am intensely interested and shall try to get some more facts, if I can; but it is difficult.

CHAPTER THREE

RED RIDDLES ON THE ROCKS

My purpose holds to sail beyond the western sunset bars,
Until I die —TENNYSON's *King Arthur.*

W AS THE "NEW"—an incredibly ancient civilized—World known to the classic Greeks and Romans?

There are rather obscure passages in both Greek and Roman historians, philosophers and poets which seem to import that these writers had access to lost records, or dim and floating traditions, or myths, which crystallized memories of far past contacts with North, Central and South America. Maybe many of these "myths" came from the temple archives of old Carthage where seem to have been deposited the logs and portolanos of Punic and Carthaginian mariners. Claudus Ælianus, who died in A.D. 140, related in Book III, *c.* 18, of his *Varia Historia*, a curious story borrowed from Theopompus of Chios who flourished in 354 B.C., and was a disciple of Isocrates, the Athenian orator. It is a story of a talk between Midas, the Phrygian, and one Silenus, "son of a nymph and superior to Men and Death" and appears to relate to *America*. Silenus says that Europe, Asia and Africa were islands, surrounded by the ocean, and there "was but one continent only, which was beyond and in magnitude infinite."

In it were bred, besides other very great creatures, men twice as big as ourselves, who lived twice as long as ourselves. They had many great cities and peculiar manners of life, and laws wholly different from ours. In particular, there were two great cities, far bigger than the rest, and quite unlike each other. One was warlike and called *Machimus*; the other was pious, called *Eusebes*. *Machimus*, continually armed and fighting, dominated over many others. The people numbered not fewer than 200 myriads (say, 2 millions). Very rarely, sickness killed them off, but more often they were killed in their wars by stones or wood; for they are invulnerable to steel.[1] Gold and silver were very common and valued less than iron with us. The people planned a voyage to Europe and Africa and sailed upon the ocean, being in number a thousand myriads of men (say 10 millions). But they came to the land of the Hyperboreans, a people leading very happy lives. Contemning the Hyperboreans' inglorious lives, the invaders thought it not worth while going further. . . . What is yet more wonderful is that there are men living amongst them

---

[1] Vasco Nuñez de Balboa, seeking for the "golden temple of Dabaiba", somewhere up the "great Rio Atrato", in Darien, said he reached it, about A.D. 1515; but was attacked by ferocious Indians who wounded him in the face with a *wooden sword*. Here was practised the cult of Dabaiba, mother of the gods, and immense riches were hidden in a temple at the bottom of a tremendous "subterranean" in Darien's wildest mountains.

called *Meropes*, who dwell in many great cities, and at the furthest end of their country is a place they call *Anoston*, whence there is no return, and which is like a gulf, being neither very light nor very dark, the air misty (or dim and dusky) and reddish in hue.

"Myths", floating in the classic age of Greece, import that this Hyperborean continent existed before a great cosmic cataclysm changed a land of sunshine, happiness and smiling Elysian fields into one of darkness, frosts and uninhabitability. It is said that the Earth came into collision with a wandering star, or great comet, or immense aerolite, which deflected the spin of the axis so that the Earth took some 30,000 years to regain her former position in relation to the ecliptic. Another theory is that this collision preceded the asteroids which, according to Bode's Law, take the place of a missing planet once occupying a position between Mars and Jupiter. Still another theory is that the proto-Moon is the nigger in this cosmic woodpile. In this Hyperborean world the Sun was regarded as the Great Benefactor. Whereas in regions such as Western Africa his invisible rays caused him to be deemed something like an evil planet. A matriarchate ruled by Proserpina remained in the land after a great exodus started to the south.

It is once more a case of "Believe it or not!" Yet it is curious that, in ancient Mexico and in Venezuela, native myths speak of the flight of men before the rule of dreadful night and the death of the Sun. These myths say that the sea became frozen over. The Quiché book of the *Popul Vuh* also has a version of this myth, while the Cakchiquel manuscript, or *Memorial of Tecpan Atitlan*, speaks of the arrival of Hyperboreans during an endless night. (Its author is said to have been Prince Ahpatzatziles of Guatemala, son of King Hureq, or Eurig, or Huneq, or Hunig,[1] who ruled before the arrival of the Spanish conquistadores.)

Whatever scientists may say of these theories in relation to the age of man, it is admitted, as in the *Proceedings of the Royal Society*, Vol., 28, that in the Miocene age Greenland and Spitzbergen had an abundance of redwoods, sequoias, planes, willows, oaks, poplars, walnuts, magnolias, beeches and zamia. Hardly trees of arctic growth! Greenland was then a land of eternal sunshine, with a tropical climate, and southern plants not now found in northern lands.

The rest of the story of Silenus tells of trees in *Anoston*, growing on the banks of two rivers. One tree, as big as a plane tree, has fruit causing eternal grief to him who eats it; the other tree on the banks of the river of pleasure has fruit which makes an old man young, and turns back the clock of time till he becomes again an infant, and finally dies.

---

[1] There are versions of the myth in the *Avesta*, where the Aryans are depicted as fleeing from a wave of frosts sent by a prince of darkness who wished to make uninhabitable a land of bliss created by the gods for men.. In the myths, or sagas of Scandinavian races, the gods fly over a cracked bridge into Valhalla, while the man Siegfried battles with the dragon Fafner, or the Satan of fire and darkness.

Ælian, it may be noted in passing, was a townsman of old Rome, who boasted that he never left Italy and never was on a ship, nor ever saw the sea. So one may expect that he would dismiss these stories as an "egregious romance which a man may believe in or not".

As I stated in a footnote, in Chapter II, p. 65, Cicero thought that another unknown continent existed, inhabited by men, and which Marcrobius, in the fifth century A.D., thought might lie in the direction where the Americas were later found by the Spaniards and the Portuguese. Cicero had evidently read the story of Sonchis-Solon-Plato in the well-known Platonic dialogues, which says that beyond the ocean exists the true continent of North and South America. Beyond that continent, again, says the Platonic dialogue, was the Great Sea, or Ocean. This imports that the Pacific Ocean was probably known to both the proto-Egyptians and the far more ancient Atlanteans, to whose fate the dialogues relate.

Again, the Phrygians of Asia Minor, said to have migrated in very ancient times from Thrace, or Macedonia, and looked down on as barbarians by the Hellenes, were a power in the old Levant that old Egypt, in the remotest antiquity, recognized could rival all her claims to dominion in what we now call the Near East.

One other curious point in this story of Silenus about the land of Meropas—A-*mer*-ica is that Theopompus says it was governed by one Queen Merope, daughter of Atlas, king of Libya. She might, or might not have been daughter of a king of an Atlantean colony in Africa set up after the cataclysm that destroyed the whole or great part of Atlantis. Theopompus says she was contemporary with Hercules, Theseus and Laomedonte, son of the king of Troy. Onfroy de Thoron, whose works cite curious evidence of Phœnician maritime and trading contacts with regions in the old Caribbean, theorizes that the radical *Atl-*, which others think denotes *water*, as does *Atl-* in Aztecan Mexico, is an Egypto-Libyan particle, meaning *country*. This, in both ancient Egypt and among the Quichuas, or Quechuas, of South America, was accompanied by a particle meaning the definite article *the*. Atlas, therefore, he urges was an eponymous name, meaning that he was a native of *the* country and descended from the Atlanteans of old Atlantis. And, according to this theory, Atlantis meant "land of the high valleys". De Thoron proceeds to say that the name *Andes*, the giant cordilleras of South America, is derived from the race of the *Antis*, or *Antisis*, a group of South American aborigines dwelling on the eastern slopes of the Andes. There is, of course, an element of risk attached to philological derivations applied to obscure regions in ethnology; since theories resting on such bases are apt to cancel each other out!

However, leaving that aside, de Thoron proceeds to say that part of the tongue of the South American *Antis* is found in the hieroglyphs of ancient Egypt, and also in ancient Greek. He says that the ancient Egyptians, in their painted papyri, depicted themselves as a reddish-skinned, beardless race recalling the reddish, beardless races among the South American Indians. (Herodotos, and other classic writers say that the ancient Egyptians had black skins!) The invasion of old Europe and Africa by militarists from old Atlantis, whose armies were carried in thousands of ships, according to the story of Plato, was, he urged, reinforced by a very large contingent of men drawn from the high valleys of equatorial South America. The South American colonies of old Atlantis were then linked to Atlantis's island of Poseidonis, by land-bridges.

It is indeed affirmed in certain mystic quarters in the Orient that Atlantis had an empire extending to Pelasgian megalithic Greece, proto-Crete, Sicily and Sardinia in a very different, pre-cataclysmic Mediterranean day. It is said, also, that the ancient Æolians, or Akkadians, migrating from regions in Central Asia, eventually reached and settled in a number of islands surrounding the great continental island of Atlantean Poseidonis. It was the last surviving remnant of a far greater continent of Atlantis, which may have been co-extensive with the lost land of *Iere*, mentioned in a previous chapter of this book.

The theory goes on to urge that, in the passage of thousands of years, these Akkadians intermarried with the peoples of the Atlantean islands and were transformed into Atlanteans. When the increasing tremors of the earth and submarine vulcanism betokened a coming cataclysm, these neo-Atlantean Akkadians embarked in a *fleet of arks*, reached the Pillars of Hercules, and landed in various places in Spain, France and Italy, leaving behind them magic arts found in Etruria, Carthage and Syracuse.[1]

Time alone and an immense amount of archæological research, organized, perhaps, by some international body and collating the discoveries of men and women working in widely sundered regions may, some day, resolve these riddles of the ages, and of an ante-diluvian world long sunk below water. Maybe the long forgotten tomb of some priest of old Egypt, as in old *Saḥil* island, at the First Cataract of the Nile, where exists an inscription cut on granite in the days of King Tcheser who built the "stepped tower", or ziggurat preceding the true pyramid, may reveal some ancient history of forgotten Atlantis. *Quien sabe?* Let Cairo excavate!

[1] Some of these "arks" must have been of staggering dimensions! Of course, Noah's "circus" was not the only one. Berosus tells us that ten antediluvian kings of proto-Chaldæa reigned for 120 saris, or 432,000 years, which must have been far shorter "years" than we understand the term. Then came the Great Cataclysm, or Deluge, and King Xisusthrus embarked in an "ark", which was 5 stadia in length, and 2 stadia in breadth. Taking the Asiatic stadium as equivalent to 485·1 feet, his "ark" must have been two-and-a-half times the length of the White-Star liner *Queen Mary*, and seven times her breadth! There may be considerable exaggeration here. But *if* the ancient Irish queen Ceasair, daughter of the Gael named Bitha, was at sea for seven-and-a-half years in an "ark" they built to save themselves from the Great Deluge, then it may be assumed that some of these "arks" were of very large size. A "duan" (poem) in the *Psalter of Cashel* says that Ireland was uninhabited for 200 (or 100) years after the Great Cataclysm. (*Vide:* Chapter IX of this book.)—AUTHOR.

The endlessly shining "cold light" which some Matto Grosso Indians say still shines from openings in great sculptured ruins of incredibly ancient dead cities on the old Brazilian Highlands, or swathed in great forests of the same unknown region, presupposes an Atlantean race whose scientists had discovered some physical or radiant force, or ray-emanation of which we have no knowledge. It certainly appears to conflict with the law of conservation of energy. Such a force may well presuppose that this first, very ancient civilized race of imperial South America were a nation of calm dispassionate scientists of cold, calm intellects, who steadfastly eschewed war, armies and soldiering. *Yet,* unless we suppose that the Atlantean-Hy-Brazilians were, like the Prussians of our day, a race both of militarists and thinkers and philosophers and scientists, it is impossible (I must be forgiven for repeating), to reconcile such a conception with the story of a land-sea invasion of many thousands of belligerent, imperialistic, world-conquering Atlanteans told in the narrative of Plato.

Very ancient statuary sculpted by races unknown and of whom not a scintilla of tradition survives in mysterious South America are found pointing eastwards in Venezuela or Colombia, and westwards in the Canaries. In a previous chapter of this book, I referred to the extremely ancient statues in grottos of Colombia, found many years ago by General José Hilario Lopez. They lay some two or five mètres deep in the ground and included coloured heads of *horses*, monkeys, and men and women, all facing *eastwards*. The counterpart of these extremely ancient hippine heads in grey stone was found in A.D. 1641.. Then Dom Henri, sent out by Alfonso V. of Portugal, found at Cuervo or Curvo, in the Azores, an ancient statue of a cavalier, who, his left hand on the bridle of his horse, pointed to the *west* with his right. Maybe a crevasse had then separated the Azores from the Atlantean Isle. There were inscriptions on the statue, in characters unknown, which reminded some savants of Phœnician letters.

Snider may be right in thinking that this statue and these mysterious letters were not Punic but Atlantean, and that the Guanches are survivors of the ancient Atlanteans, who managed to escape cataclysm.

In my book *Mysteries of Ancient South America* (Rider & Co., London, 1946), I gave a translation of a Portuguese manuscript written about the year A.D. 1755 by some *bandeirista* unknown, who was one of a hardy company of São Paulans and *samboes* and Indians who, in wanderings lasting ten years, blundered by accident on a strange dead city behind a range of volcanic mountains. An ancient paved way, riven and smashed by boulders which had been toppled on to it in some far-gone day from the towering cliffs and precipices environing the road, denoted some terrific catastrophe. I reproduced a number of letters of both unknown character and of proto-Phœnician and Greco-Phœnician form, which had been copied from splendid porticoes façades, archways, obelisks, statues of men and youths, and fountains in plazas, and superb mansions and temples of the dead cities. The place was eerie and most mournful in its desolation. Not a bone of a human being, not a shred of furniture or pottery survived, only bars of silver and great ancient coins of gold, hastily cast to the ground as by men fleeing for their lives from some cataclysm or terrific earthquakes.

A man on a statue-obelisk, with his index finger pointed to the *North* of this dead city of ancient Brazil. Indeed, there is reason to suppose that this ancient forgotten empire extended far beyond America to *Iceland*. For on the river-creek of Hof, on the eastern coast of Iceland, may still be seen, to-day, on the weathered rocks letters and Atlantean glyphs.

Some of these Hof inscriptions are also found in Paradisarhellir, Iceland, as well as on the Assonet rock in the Taunton river of Massachusetts (Narraganset Bay).

One sign seems identical with the *earth-sun* symbol found in mysterious Tiahuanacu.

Here the Indians had a legend, or tradition, that there came to this Massachusetts bay a wooden house and men of another country in it, swimming upon the river Assonet, as this river was then called. They fought the Indians with mighty success.

Others of the Hof inscriptions strangely resemble some of the inscriptions found in the dead, Atlantean-Hy-Brazilian city entered in A.D. 1750, by the *bandeiristas* who set out into the *sertão* from Sao Paulo.

One may ask if this vast lost continent, called in the West Indian island folklore, as in Trinidad, *Iere*, and in the Galway folk-lore, *Eire*, extended far north from Atlantean Antilla to what is now Iceland?

It looks, indeed, as if it did!

But, as to ancient Brazil, the *bandeiristas'* expedition was not the first to discover extremely ancient unknown ruins in Brazil. In

A.D. 1641, when Prince Maurice of Nassau and the Dutch West Indian company aspired to convert all Lusitanian Brazil into a Dutch colony, an expedition led by Elias Herckmann, a Fleming, set out from Recife (Mauritzstadt) into the *sertão*, or Brazilian wilderness. It was hunting for mines of gold and silver. Like the *bandeiristas* of a century later. Herckmann found something he had not expected in the interior of mysterious Brazil. The story is told in Latin, in a book by Caspar Barlæus (van Bærle).[1]

Here, for the first time, I give the English translation. It tells how the expedition guided by a number of Potiguaras Indians, reached a "burning mountain" which they feared to remain by, or climb. The road was so inaccessible and rough that they did not proceed till word came from the Court that the journey was to go on. After ascending the mountain, they cut the marks of the Society on a post, so that the "barbarians of the New World might have a memorial in the manner of Alexander the Great". On they went, meeting denser forests and more toilsome heights:

And so, to avoid the steep mountains they started to attack the lower country where they saw two *millstones* (*duo lapidares molares*) of exact and rounded symmetry and of a stupendous size, whose diameter was 16 feet, and truly so thick that out of the ground hardly could the half part of the stone reach the finger-tips, placed in the erect position. Another (stone) lay upon another, the greater upon the less, and out of the middle a wonderful sight! The trunk of a tree rose over it: *Karawata* (or *Karavvata*). For what purpose the stones were heaped up, the barbarians . . . certainly cannot tell. . . . Herckmann, impatient of the delays, ordered the soldiers to attack the obstacles of the forests and the way beset with swamps that frequently up to the knees embogged the wayfarers, and striving to ascend the mountains they went up with hands and knees, catching hold of rock projections . . . or cutting steps to tread upon. The day passed in fear and labour as they climbed the mountains. Overcome with continual fatigue all cast themselves to the ground in impassable places, seeking rest on the banks of a small stream where they might come at enough sweet water. . . . On many days they had to ascend or descend mountains in long succession. . . . Again, they came on the great millstones heaped up with human labour which in the region of Drent, Belgium, are also to be found[2]. Thou mayest believe that with no transport (carrying) and with no strength of men could stones of that magnitude have been borne hither. . . . Again, the Wirarembucam (Pernambucan) villagers, formerly of Brazil, came to this place to live, where the well-marked steps of men go down to the river Tambahugam, now called the Moschi, on account of the odour of crocodiles, and serpents, akin to the odour of musk. . . .

---

[1] *Rerum per octennium in Brasilia* (Eight years in Brazil). Edition: Clives, ex Officina Tobiæ Silberling, MDCLX (1660).

[2] Colossal Neolithic monuments, called the *Hunebedden*, or giants' stone-beds. They are very large and erratically carved stones found in Drent, Gasterland, Holland, also in Denmark, and the westerly regions of the north German lowlands. In Denmark, they are known as "Deensch Jaetestuer" (Danish Giants' chambers).—AUTHOR.

Similar curious *millwheels* (mos de moinhos) were found by soldiers in the forests along the Rio Pequéry, in March 1773 (state of São Paulo, southern Brazil), close to ruins of a great house, an ancient stone wall, and a very ancient dead city of large size, with a street half a league long, and *moats* girdling the dead city. *Moats*, it may be said, are features of cities of Atlantean origin. More of these enigmatic ruins of mega-lithic cities are to be found in Brazil. In the district of Flores (state of Pernambuco) are two very fine pyramids of granite, each about 110 feet high, and located at Pedra Bonita, six leagues from Belem. These two immense erections are of massive stone of the colour of iron rust, half quadrangular in shape, and rise from the ground opposite one another, rising ever to the same height, and with great similarity to the threads or spirals of a vast screw. Again, at Puiry, on the Amazon, are two very curious figures of a woman, on the north side of a rock, whose head is encircled by a nimbus of rays. Who cut them in the rock none know.

The old *bandeiristas* of A.D. 1745–55, commented on the ancient staircases of many coloured stones which opened into a very wide chamber of a large country mansion in the dead city. It was apparently, somewhere in the interior of the province of Bahia. Causeways of these coloured stones crossed the lake to an ancient temple in old Mexico long ages before the days of the last Aztec emperor, Montezuma. They were, as Plato's dialogues import, probably Atlantean in origin.

Again, the strange region of the Serra de Ereré—a name which has an odd and, perhaps, not altogether fortuitous resemblance to that of the lost western, vanished land of Iere—about 15 miles from the Rio Amazonas, west of Villa de Monte Alegre, east of Obidos, on the Amazon, Brazil, has an 800-foot high ridge. It is about five miles long, with sandstone beds, on which, high up in inaccessible places, remarkable signs have been cut in some enduring, ancient red pigment. Some of the inscriptions look fresher than others and whole cliffs in the rear are covered with enigmatic inscriptions. They can be seen a mile away.

At the western end of the Serra is a curious rayed head ornamented on top with a *queue*, a piscine form suggesting a *comet*! One might be forgiven for wondering if this rupestrian sign had any connection

with memories of some ancient cataclysm in prehistoric South America.

Precisely similar glyphs and figures are found in the cliff-walls of the Rio Tocantins, on the eastern edge of the Matto Grosso. These inscriptions are cut on the hard granite and gneissic walls of the cañons of the mysterious Rio Uapes. This little known river runs on the north-west border of Brazil and Colombia, in a region where dangerous black troglodytes guard the approaches to the Atlantean cities of the dead, full of gold and mysteries. I may, in particular, draw the reader's notice to the two "intrusive (?)" signs, following: "1 7 6 4" and "H S". Both, as one has noted, are drawn in particularly fresh coloured red pigment on lichened and blackened, or whitened surfaces, that obscure the apparently older inscriptions. Both may be ancient.

A singular feature of some of these ancient stone monuments, or monoliths, found as widely apart as in the *sertão* of Brazil and on the Andes in Perú and Chile, is that they ring, when tapped, as sonorously as bells. I shall have something to say about the purpose of these sonorous stones, when treating of the theme in a subsequent book.

With the "1 7 6 4" of the Ereré petroglyphs, and the monogram "H S", which, on the cliffs, are placed in juxtaposition should be compared letters in the dead Brazilian-Atlan cities.

With one glyph in the Ereré signs compare the two Egyptian hieroglyphs, which respectively signified "Life" (*nh*) and *onkh* (to live), the latter glyph being, of course, found as one of three other signs, including the phonogram and determinative, of the Pharaoh. People near London may, in the absence of access to the contents of the Egyptological saloons of the British Museum, see these Pharaonic signs on the breast plaques of the two bronze sphinxes guarding the Cleopatra's Needle-Obelisk on the Victoria Embankment.

There are three more of the inscriptions on the rocks of Serra de Ereré. As to the first, the slant-eyed, stylized face has a queerly proto-Egyptian suggestion. (I shall have something to say, in a subsequent book, about proto-Egyptians in ancient America.)

Two of the petroglyphs (from Ereré), may be compared with a letter found on a façade of a great public building in one of the dead cities of Atlantean Hy-Brazil, and with a pictogram found in Moon (or Koaty) Island. Here in Lake Titicaca, Carian-Colloan savages annihilated an ancient white race of bearded men[1] who were

[1] In my book *Mysteries of Ancient South America* (Rider and Co., London), I cited the accounts of Herrera and also of Cieza de Leon about this extermination of the posterity of the white-bearded Atlanteans. Cieza de Leon tells that: "Before the Incas conquered the country (of old Perú), many of the Indians declare that there were two great lords in the Colloa", which corresponds to modern Bolivia—"one pamed Sapana, the other Cari who conquered many of the *pucares* that are their fortresses, and that one of them entered on

perhaps degenerate descendants of survivors of the global cataclysm that finally overwhelmed ancient Atlantis and her imperial colony in Hy-Brazil.

An enigmatic petroglyph was found in 1900 by Carl Lumholtz, in  "Unknown Mexico". It was cut among other ancient inscriptions on rocks in the Pedras Verdes (Green Stones) River, in the province of North Chihuahua. He also found a striking Egyptian face on a rock, two leagues north of Iztlan, in 1902, among wonderful "monos", as the natives call idols.

Other signs, copied from the cliff-walls of the Serra de Ereré, eastern Rio Amazonas or Marañon, in modern Brazil, seem to be of different dates. One pictograph at the top bears what seem to be three crescent moons, and *may*, accepting the rationalizing of the folklore of the Arcadians of the old pre-Hellenistic Mediterranean, and the Caribs and other races in South America—about a time when, in their ancestors' days, "the moon was not in earth's skies"—date back to the retrogressive era in the earth's history that followed on the cataclysm that sank the last island-continent of Atlantis.

An orient, or rising sun glyph, found on the cliff-walls of the Serra de Ereré in eastern Amazonian Brazil, may be compared with a pictogram found in the island of the Moon (Koaty Indians) in Lake Titicaca, one of the last retreats of the survivors of Atlantean Hy-Brazil ruined by the appalling cataclysm, of some 12,000 years ago. It is the same as that spoken of to Solon the Athenian by the Egyptian priests of Heliopolis and Sais, and which is narrated in the Timæus and Critias dialogues of Plato. The pictogram had the meanings of "Eye", "first", "before, or in front", "Nayra, Nayran, Nayraktahana".

Two glyphs, found cut in a tremendously thick and heavy stone slab enclosing what seemed to be vaults of treasure of talismans close to the dead and extremely ancient city entered by the *bandeiristas* of Brazil in A.D. 1750, may be compared with the glyphs from Ereré. As I may repeat for the sake of clarity, this dead city was of the imperial places of the white race rulers of Atlantean Hy-Brazil.

Two pictures, or pictograms, also found on the cliff-walls of the Serra de Ereré, Amazonian Brazil, are (1) comparable to the

the Lake of Titicaca and that in the greater island that was swampy (*palude*) he came across a white ancient people with whiskers (beards) with whom he fought in such a manner that he was able to kill them all." In the eighteenth century, the Spanish missioner friars found that these Colloan Indians were using a very ancient form of idiographic writing, which is also in use to-day by the Indians of Sampaya, the port of Koaty Island, Titicaca. The Indians told the friars that the writing had been bequeathed to them by their ancestors. In fact it must have been the last heritage of the culture of the luckless white-bearded race of ancient days, which the savage conquerors appropriated. The idiograms, as I have said in my other book, are directly derived from the letters used in Hy-Brazil in the dead cities of Bahia province, etc.

"Eye", or Sun sign found in Moon or Koaty Island, Lago de Titicaca; and (2) *appear* to be a very curious picture of a rostral and very ancient war-galley such as may have been used by the ancient Phœnicians, or other race of ancient Mediterranean sea-rovers and early circumnavigators of the ancient oceans. The upper deck super-structure is unique, as also the "queue" and the prow, or figure-head, like that of a sea serpent of the Loch Ness or plesiosaurus type.

As there is reason to think that these unknown races possessed the Egyptian secret of an indestructible pigment that could defy the tooth of Time and the ravages of the weather, it is risky to suppose, as did the American professor C. Fred Hartt, who saw them about 1872, that both these signs are the work of Jesuit missionaries. It may be noted that the Spanish king, Charles III, expelled this order of intriguers from all his dominions in 1767; but it is known in Rio de Janeiro that Jesuit missioners entered one or more of these dead cities in old Brazil and have left manuscript records of their impressions.

Atlan-Brazilian glyph, found in Brazilian jungles.

Whether or no the sculptures are older than the red paintings on the rock would, perhaps, need for its ascertainment a chemico-physical analysis as well as examination by a competent geologist. The signs "1 7 6 4" appear two rows above the "H S", and the pigment appears to be very fresh and in a lighter red than that of others. As to the "ceriphs" on the "H S" monogram, it may be noted that they are found on letters—*not* hieroglyphs—in inscriptions graved in stone in the dead city of white, imperial Atlantean Hy-Brazil entered by the *bandeiristas* of old Brazil in the year A.D. 1750. Some of the inscriptions in that city of the long dead, of a civilization, possibly in its prime at least 60,000 years ago, include signs which have no ceriphed terminals.

It is probable that this ancient sacred place of the Serra de Ereré was used by unknown races separated in date by perhaps thousands of years and very different degrees of culture. The nature of the signs import as much. These South American *graffiti* remind one of the wave-washed boulder off the strand of rock-bound Chatham Bay, in the notorious pirate treasure island of Cocos, North Pacific, on which some three centuries of skippers and sailing masters inscribed the names of their ships, dates of land-ing and own names or initials.

  S

Dr. Theodor Koch-Grünberg, in his *Sudamerikanische Felszeich-nungen* (South American Petroglyphs), Berlin, 1910, reproduces a figure like that of the second of the Ereré signs.

He says it is found in the Timehru rocks along the Rio Corentyn

(Guiana) and adds: "I found a similar figure close to other rock markings in charcoal on the forefront of a *Maloka*, or big family house that represents a whole village. (An orient sun glyph and a ship with a "sea serpent's head" prow, (Ereré), are also found at Cachoeira and Rio Uaupes, Brazil.)

I may also speculate whether these rock signs in red, or ferruginous earths, carved or painted in rocks, may have been done by ancient cave people or some race, hiding from the pursuit of invaders, and within caves deep in mountain fastnesses or hidden in *barrancas* or gorges. One may wonder what connection, if any, these enigmatic rock signs had with the legend of the Pericues Indians, of Lower California, that:

> Nipanayu, or Niparayu had a son—one of three born of a woman with whom he had cohabited—and who was called Cuajup, or True Man. He lived a long time among men, in order to instruct them, and had many followers brought from the bowels of the earth. They conspired against him, crowned him with thorns and killed him. But his body, extremely beautiful, never decays and he speaks to them through a bird.

Perhaps, the subtle Jesuits were nearer the mark than they would either have appreciated, or desired in affixing their credal marks to the evidence of some mysterious rites of a very ancient American race that anticipated by many thousands of years the Christian dogmas of crucifixion and the Holy Ghost, which Roman Catholics deem so peculiarly their own.

One last word: these signs, or petroglyphs, found in the Amazonas region of Brazil, and at Cachoeira, are remarkably reminiscent of signs in the dead cities of Atlantean Brazil, and of prehistoric glyphs discovered in the wilds of the Sierra de Quintana, in Andalusia, of old Spain. The reader may see this for himself, if he or she glances at prehistoric inscriptions found on the Piedra Escrita, in this sierra of old Spain. This lonely wild region of old Spain, like the Sierra de Ereré in Brazil, is nearly inaccessible and a place of wild beasts and mountain goats. There are two caves, and the ancient inscriptions are in triangular niches polished on the four surfaces. There are some sixty symbols, or hieroglyphs, written in a rustic hand and naïve manner with the forefinger of a rude hand, and in red pigments of bituminous origin. The niches are screened by hard mountain stone, which forms a portico, or *esplanada* in front of the signs. They number a half-moon, the sun, an axe, a bow and arrows, a spike of grain, a heart, a tree, human figures, and a *crowned head*. They were copied in May 1785, by Antonio Lopez y Cardenas, in the presence of the escritor of the town of Montoro, Josef Antonio Diaz y Penez and the alcalde, Alfonso de Bernabe. More of these coloured signs were also found a quarter of a league away in the *Batanera*, a waterfall falling from a great height. A large, live rock, artificially carved, had also once formed a protective façade, but it had failed to save the red hieroglyphs from being partly obliterated by water.

CHAPTER FOUR

SOUTH AMERICA'S AMAZONS EXISTED!

. . . and the Amazons of South America were not necessarily myths.—COLONEL P. H. FAWCETT, in his last message to the English-speaking world, in 1925, from the jungles of Brazil.

WHERE was the strange and elusive country of these amazing white women of South America, telling the naked truth about whom gained for the monk, Father Gaspar Carvajal, the undeserved epithet of *mentirosa* (liar and romancer)?

Are they—*were* they—mere figments of a European imagination nursed on the classical traditions of old Greece and the Mediterranean? Were they merely Indian women fighting by the side of their menfolk in battles with enemy tribes?

Or were they mere travellers' tales invented to soothe the indignation which the old Spanish King and Holy Roman Emperor, Carlos V, might otherwise have shown in royal displeasure against the defaulting Castilian hidalgo, who, with his soldiers, deserted his superior, Spanish officer, in the wilds of eastern Perú, in the year 1542?

The answer the *facts* give, in this chapter, is that the South American Amazons existed in very hard fighting truth and nearly brought about the annihilation of old Europe's finest fighting-men— the Spanish *infanteria* and *hidalgos* of the sixteenth century—in a fierce battle they waged with them, in strange circumstances, in that gorge of the river named after the women. To-day, after and during two world wars, when women figured as auxiliary soldiers, in the British, Russian and American ranks of the United Nations' armies, the world may be less disposed to dismiss these strange women as myths.

Indeed, it is possible that they may yet be found to be still existing in some Lost World of old South America!

Lives of men—famous and the great unrecorded, unknown— soldiers, priests, missioner-monks, gold-hunters, frontiersmen, colonial governors and administrators, adventurers, and even scientists and explorers of the twentieth century, have been lost in South American wilds, seeking the answer to these questions. The quest has now lasted for more than four centuries. The most recent and famous of these lost or missing explorers, Colonel P. H. Fawcett, D.S.O., who tried to establish contact with these remarkable white women—called by the Brazilian-Guiana Indians "the *Aikeambenanas*, or women who live alone"—believed they exist, to-day somewhere in some inaccessible spot on the Andean frontiers of the known territories of mysterious South America.

So does the author of this book! He has examined all the available evidence from Spanish-American, colonial, and even far earlier records, and collated it with what the South American tribes say. He has been driven into the belief that this wonderful republic of women abandoned its *second* motherland, in the headwaters' country behind the range of the Acirai mountains, on the still unknown borders of British Guiana and Northern Brazil, between the Rio Caphú and the Rio Wanamuh, tributaries of the Rio Trombetas, which joins the mighty Amazon, at Obidos, Brazil. And, somewhere about the middle of the eighteenth century they started on another great trek, this time, westwards, towards the still unknown regions of southern Venezuela, or the unexplored Oriente of Ecuador-Perú, or Colombia.

This was (as I shall presently show) their second great overland trek across thousands of miles of equatorial South America. They were motived by probably the same reason, over an interval of about 250 or 300 years: the growing encroachment on their territories of European, Latin-American, white, yellow and black races. They may have felt as did the old frontiersmen and pioneers in Oregon or California, in the days of the Lewis and Clark overland prairie schooner trek from the plains across the Rockies: a sense of overcrowding when the next neighbour had his log cabin on a creek only fifty or a hundred miles away!

But the question mark against this mysterious race of white women warriors is whence did they come, and how is it they so strangely resemble the classic Amazons of Europe, the Near East and Libyan Africa, of three thousand and more years ago? Are they merely a transplantation of a myth to South America by monks and soldiers, of the conquistadorian age who recollected what some of them had read in the European grammar and conventual schools about Theseus and Hercules and their war against the Amazons of Asia and Africa?

The answer to that is: *No!* The South American, Amazon republic of white fighting women, with a queen and cities, was an actual fact of little known history. It was no travellers' tale to impress stay-at-homes, or the staring wonderers who still, to-day, listen to Arabic tale-tellers round the well in the shade of the palm trees of some odorous *souk*, in a Moorish or Berber city of the Atlas. (And the Atlas territory, by the way, is not far from one of the ancient homelands of the African branch of the Amazons. It was from here that their ancient forbears probably crossed the Atlantic to South or Central America.)

For more than three centuries, now, too many of the learned and academic historians who never travel beyond the arm-chairs, or padded thrones of great libraries and museums, have been disposed to adopt without demur the opinions of a man of whom they may never have heard. He was Dom Francisco Xavier Ribeiro de Sampaio, a Portuguese traveller from Lisboa, who, in 1774, published his *Diario da Viagem*, or diary of his travels along the Amazon, in Brazil. Ribeiro thought it was *a priori* improbable that such a republic of women warriors ever existed in South America. He suggested they were a fable of Don Francisco de Orellana, the Spanish conquistador, who with soldiers and priests deserted Gonzalo Pizarro's expedition in the jungles of Eastern Ecuador (then Perú), and, when he reached home in Madrid, rushed to re-establish himself with the Emperor and his court, by tickling their ears with tales of gold and a republic of white, nude, fighting women living without men in a land abounding in precious stones and rare metals.

The Amazons became mixed up with *el Dorado*. But it is the strange fact (not known to Ribeiro, of course), that both, as my own careful investigations show, were strange actualities and, at one period, before the conquistadores pushed their horses over the passes of the cordilleras into old Perú and Nueva Granada (modern Colombia), the Amazon territory was located on the borders of the land of the *Casa del Sol* (the House of the Sun) and the mysterious empire of Gran Paytiti.

Ribeiro urged that the tale-tellers pandered to the tastes for the marvellous of the Spanish Court in old Madrid, and the hidalgoes and grandees of old Castile and Estremadura, by telling them just what they wanted to hear: romantic tales about tons of gold and lovely white women who fought like devils. He even went further and advanced a sexual argument—and, in that he has been followed, without acknowledgment, by numbers of Peruvian and Latin-American historians of to-day and yesterday.

Said Ribeiro: "In a land so torrid and so exceedingly agitating to the soul, as tropical South America, how could men and women live apart and be indifferent to sexual congress?"

No doubt, in South America, to-day, as also in some parts of Italy and modern Mexico, especially on the borders, where no women of attractive appearance dare walk abroad alone, even in the cities of the Argentine, in the dusk, unless she wishes to be greeted with an old Latin-American custom, that argument would carry great weight. (That custom is for some fellow, deeming himself a fine *caballero*, to go up to the woman, and murmuring, *fica, fica!* press the nipples of her breasts between his thumb and forefinger, till she is black and blue! The only defence, apart from fists, nails or "guns", is for the woman to wear a sort of body-armour of reinforced whalebone corset of unusual stature, as some *señoras* I knew really do!)

Well, let us see if that argument is as irresistible as either the old Latin-American custom or the whalebone armour! As I hope to show it does not do away with the weight of historical evidence. But in the days of World War No. 2, the woman warrior has become less of a phenomenon. She is certainly no new thing, either in ancient or modern history, and I speak of the woman *fighting soldier*, not an auxiliary non-combatant.

In 1944–45, Soviet Russia had about 8,000 women soldiers in the Chemical Defence League, and as long back as 1936, 20,000 women were being trained as combatant soldiers, not to speak of fighting aeroplane pilots. In Great War No. 1, as my book *Mysteries of the Great War* (whose translation was banned by the French Fascist bureaucracy and government in Paris in 1937–38), showed, old Imperial Austria, Hohenzollern Germany and Romanoff Czarist, as well as the Republican temporary régime of Kerensky's Russia, had their combatant women soldiers—undisguised, in the case of Russia, and with officers and, sometimes, "Lesbian" type women generals.

Three thousand and more years ago, the woman soldier was a world imperialist power. She was, even then, no new phenomenon in world-history. Figuratively speaking, she is nearly as old as the hills, and was, ages ago, a power in *organized society*, not merely in loose tribal clans and nomadic, shifting communities. Nevertheless she has received precious little than scoffs and jeers from scholars, members of learned societies and even some archæologists. Too many of whom forget that the last word on this subject must be spoken not from inside the walls of dusty libraries and safe and stuffy college and university tutorial class-rooms, but from the world's desert places and the dangerous jungles where savages shoot the curare-tipped arrows first, and see afterwards if the victim is good for the tribal cooking-pot.

Quintus Curtius Rufus, who, in the reign of Vespasian, about A.D. 70, wrote a military history and commentary relating to the world war of Alexander the Great, told of one Thalestris, queen of the Amazons in Asia. She made a journey, with three hundred picked women soldiers, lasting thirty-five days, across deserts and mountains and wild places where jackals picked the bones of dead camels and dromedaries of lost caravans. They passed through unexplored territory in order to meet the Macedonian leader, who was then somewhere on the confines of what is, to-day, modern Persia and Afghanistan. She wished to have a temporary marriage with Alexander, to raise a child by him. It was a case of her beauty and strength and his military genius and uncommon valour. She wanted a girl-child, it is believed; because the Amazons, all over the known world, killed off male children, much in the manner that unwanted female infants are, or used to be, drowned in the waters off Hong Kong and Canton, or in the sacred Ganges and other rivers in old India of the modern Hindus—and surely will be again, now the British raj has withdrawn his "detested" police control.

These Amazons of Asia were doughty women warriors and such good bowmen that both Greek hoplites and Roman legionaries, the world's finest, ancient male warriors, called a good bow and quiver: *Amazonius-a*. In Africa, these women soldiers were also a world-power about 3,000 years before the Christian era. They are said to have crossed the Mediterranean, overrun all the Near East from

Col. P. H. Fawcett, D.S.O. (on log, centre), among Matto Grosso Indians

De Orellana in action with Amazon-led Indians, Brazil (Chap. IV)

Courtesy Royal Ontario Museum

Canadian Flathead squaw and baby: This Atlantean rite
developed the "third eye", or paranormal "sixth sense",
and explains the reason for the occipital deformation

Mesopotamia and Persia to the shores of the Levant and the Ægean, and to have penetrated across the Euxine, or Black Sea, into Thrace and Attica, where their dreams of *Welt-krieg*, World-Empire, and *Drang-nach-Osten* were rudely shattered by the Greek hero, Theseus. And if queer recent discoveries by French archæologists, digging in the unearthly wilderness of the Hoggar and the stony, arid desert country of the veiled Touaregs of France's empire of sand are carefully considered, it will be distinctly unwise to dismiss these stories of imperial women soldiers in the morning of our civilization as mere myths and heroic fables of the dim past.

The Amazons of *Asia*, sisters by race of the African republic of women, had their capital city at Thermidon, in Cappadocia. This town was located in a valley on the southern side of the modern, Pontic mountains, nor far from Erzeroum, in modern Anatolia (Turkey in Asia). These Amazons, too, were a formidable military power, and when they vanished into the mists of ages, it is significant that their successors were a degenerate race of men whose qualities of timidity, sloth and pusillanimity, as well as addiction to unpleasant vices, made them a byword of contempt among the Romans of the Imperial age. Their blood was so foul, said an ancient epigrammatist, that even the viper that bit these male Cappadocians died of the poison *he*, in turn, took from their veins!

One queen of the Asian branch of the Amazons was the celebrated and beautiful Hippolyta, vanquished by Hercules, who took her girdle or baldrick to the Eurystheus who played Jacob to the Esau of Hercules. It was to revenge the expedition of Theseus-Hercules, that the Amazons invaded Attica and crossed the Cimmerian Bosphorus on the ice, as reports Hellanicus, the logographos, or historian of Mytilene, (died 411 B.C.) who wrote a history of the ancient kings of the earth.

The tomb of Hippolyta was shown at Megara, and at Athens there was the Amazoneium and the Horcosmosion, or Oath-House, where the treaty was made between Theseus and Hippolyta. The wars of the archaic age Greeks with the Amazons were, as is well known, depicted on the Metopes, on the north side of the Parthenon.

One does not wish to digress, but since the Amazons have been and still are in many quarters regarded as myths, it may be noted that the blood of the Asian Amazons is mingled with that of the Sarmatians, the ancestors of the modern Poles! The authority for this is the great Herodotos. He tells how the Amazons, after warring with the Greeks and getting the worst of it, invaded the territories of the Scythians, of South Russia, who called them *Oior-pata*, or man-slayers. He says that after gaining the battle of Thermodon, over the Amazons, the Greeks put to sea, taking with them in three ships all the women-warriors they had made prisoner. In the voyage over the Black Sea the Amazons rose, massacred the crews to a man, but found themselves helpless against the winds and tides; "for they knew not how to use rudder, sails or oars". They were carried where the winds listed and at last were thrown ashore under some high cliffs, called the Cremni, and located on the modern sea of Azov.

Going inland into the territory of the free Scythians, the Amazons seized the first wild horses they saw, mounted on their backs and started plundering all around. The Scythians were puzzled by these beardless warriors—not knowing whence they came, or that they were women—and thought they were youths. After a battle, some of the bodies fell into their hands and the secret was out. Hereupon, the Scythians conceived it would be a fine thing to raise children from these women-warriors rather than kill them. So they sent some youths with orders to camp near the Amazons, but evade any assaults. In the end, an Amazon and a Scythian youth met, and the Amazon by signs bade him bring a friend, next day, to a rendezvous where she, too, would bring a friend. This led to nights of love on the free wild Scythian plains, between the handsome youths and the Amazons. The camps joined in one, and the women learned Scythian, though the youths never caught the tongue of the Amazons.

The youths asked the Amazons to give up their mode of life and settle down among the free Scythians as their wives. The Amazons replied: "No, we could not live with your women. Our customs are quite different. We draw the bow, hurl the javelin, bestride the horse. We know naught of womanly employments. Your women stay at home in their wagons. They never go out to hunt. We should never agree."

Eventually, the Amazons got the youths to agree to take a patrimony from their Scythian fathers, and migrate beyond the Tanais, to live with the Amazons as their husbands. They finally settled in the land of the *Sauromatæ* (Sarmatians, or Poles). As says Herodotus:

> The women of the Sauromatæ have continued from that day to this to observe the Amazons' ancient customs, frequently hunting on horseback with their husbands, sometimes even accompanying them into war, taking the field, and wearing the same dress as the men . . . The marriage-law of the Sauromatæ lays it down that no girl shall wed till she have killed a man in battle. Sometimes it happens that a woman dies unmarried at an advanced age, never having been able in her whole lifetime to fulfil the condition.

In entering at some length into these adventures in the ancient lands of Old Russia of the Amazons, my object is for the reader to compare this account with what will be told in this chapter of the amatory and breeding customs of the South American branch of this same race of warrior-women.

Professor Joseph Karst, in his *Grundsteine zu einer Mitteländisch-Asianischen Urgeschichte* (Leipzig, 1928), supposes that the Iberian Amazons—whose remains, as to one chieftainess have been found in a cave near Tartessos, Spain—came originally from the land of Punt, which is, indeed, Babylonian Chaldea. "Punt", it may be noted—not in this place, by Karst—was by the Egyptians applied to the coast of African Somaliland to which in 3000 B.C., the ancient Egyptians sent trading ships for incense and resins. But, in his later book, *Origines Mediterranæ* (Heidelberg, 1931), Karst points out what is nearer the mark: that the root Pun, or Pan, in Punt, identifies it with the old land of Pacific Pan, a name found in the Southern Indian ocean island of Atlantean Panchæa to which Evhemerus undertook a voyage in the days of the Macedonian king, Cassandra—time of Alexander the Great.

Ancient classic traditions say that to this island of Panchæa, the *man* Zeus, the Atlantean, led a band of Atlanteans from the island of Minoan Crete. There is an old Erythræan-Ethiopian tradition mentioned by Arrian, in *Indica*, that the fish-eaters, or Ichthyophagi, were a sort of fishmen descended from a sea-goddess, or Nereid. Pan's weapon, or, as should be said, the characteristic weapon of the men of the Pacific continent of Pan, was the trident, taken over by the western Atlanteans who waged a "Dragon" war for world hegemony and sea and land empire, with the men of the trident. The root Pan is found in Nip-pon, Ypangui—the older name of *Japan*—and is associated with some ancient lost continent ranging from Iran and south-west Arabia southwards into the Indian Ocean. With such a southern Atlantis of a dim Indian Ocean empire of Atlantean migrants in the far, far ago, it would not be surprising to find intimately associated cohorts of Atlantean Amazon fighting women.

Karst recognized three strata of the Amazons. The oldest and lowermost stratum was of a pre-Hamitic Iberian folk of the true Kain'ani or Kain-i stock, linked with the old Basques. We know them as the later Canaanites. Karst is doubtless right in saying that these dim races are one of the oldest civilized races of mankind and closely linked with dolmen-builders of the coasts, who ranged from Atlantis, Europe, and the lands of the early Mediterranean to farther India, Abyssinia, and "Africa-minor". "That is the great primitive nation of the Atlanteans, according to old Egyptian statements." A second layer was found in the Kushite and the Berbero-Hamites and Numidians. The Berber and Touareg name for Amazon was *Amazirgh*. Under the form of *Namazut* it is found as a Libyan and Numidian folk-name.

The ancient homeland of the Berbero-Hamites was farther east, ranging from the Persian Busen (Bu-shire) into Cappadocia, and south-west Asia Minor. What is significant is the peculiar feminine veil and headdress of the formidable Touareg warriors, the veiled horsemen of the Sahara, who, not so many years ago, were known to have had a woman as their ruler. Karst suggests that these Touaregs may have most faithfully preserved the original Amazon type.[1] Their entirely female face-veil so clearly reminds us of the "weaponed women".

---

[1] Military pursuits were common to men and women in the antediluvian days—and in old Atlantis—and the men set up the figure of the goddess in full armour, as a sign of the equality of the sexes in matters of war and peace." *Timæus (Estienne Stephanus.)*

A third stratum is Aryan-Armenoid. Here, we get the name Amazon in the form of *hamazun*, or *hamazeni*, meaning "fellow-countryman". Moreover, the Hittites had the same racial elements and form the north-west group of the Amazon people. He also thinks that the Hyksos shepherd-kings, who overran old Egypt, at one time became in part incorporated with the Amazons in their migrations. Another ancient variation of the name of Amazon is that of *Hapamuni*, or *Hadmoni*, which in old Latium Italy, under the name of *Casamênê* denoted a race settled in south-west Italy, and closely linked with Iberian proto-Hamitic *Sicani*. In pre-Hellenic Greece, the *Kadmians* seem to have been an Amazonian race.

There were ancient Amazons both in the Hebrides and at the mouth of the Loire, Western France! The Amnite women lived in the Nesides islands (close to the "Hebudes" of western Scotland), and performed Bacchic rites. It will be recalled that the fierce Bacchantes acknowledged no master and abandoned themselves to sexual intercourse with strange men who came their way during their frenzied dances and festivals. In the Nesides, these women wore crowns of ivy leaves and berries. Strabo says Amazons lived in a small island off the mouth of the Loire, were Samnites, and worshipped Bacchus in dances and orgies. They allowed no men in the island, and when desire came on them crossed the sea to find a man, afterwards returning to the island. They had a queer custom of unroofing their temple once a year. If a woman dropped a tile off its roof—and the temple had the same day to be re-roofed before sunset—she was torn in pieces, and her limbs carried round the temple, with wild shouts, till their rage was spent. In the old Armorican island of Sena, there were nine virgins who raised winds for mariners, could tell fortunes and predict the future, and cure diseases. They had Circean traits, and could turn themselves into any animals they desired. But they favoured only seamen!

Strabo says that the Amazons formerly dwelt in the mountains of Albania, in the region of the old Caspian Sea. One Theophane, said to have accompanied the Amazon queen, Pompæa on her marches, says that the women lived among the Gelæ and the Leges, Scythian peoples whose country was separated from that of the Amazons by the River Mermedates. Indeed, as late as A.D. 1827, the Leges were still found in these regions and were then called the "Leski, or Legaæ", the name of the river having been changed to that of Mermedik. Strabo adds:

> Other writers, such as Metrodore de Scepsis, and Hypsicrate say that the Amazons were in a land on the borders of the country of the Gargarenses.

These unknown people, too, if one believes Pallas, in his *Nouveaux Voyages*, became the men of the Tscherkesses, who, in or about 1777, lived in the country ascribed to the Gargarenses by Strabo. A learned but forgotten eighteenth-century commentator, Johann Uphagen, of

Dantzig, who wrote, in 1782, the *Parergon*, thinks these Gargarenses were a tribe of the megalithic nation of the Pelasgians, who migrated from Mount Gargara, in the Æolide, to the north of Caspian Albania. This, again, would be a token of the immense antiquity of the Amazons.

Strabo gives an interesting account of these Caspian Amazons:

> The Gargarenses were found dwelling at the northern back of these Caucasian mountains that one calls the Ceraunian ranges. Here, for six months of the year, the Amazons laboured for themselves at husbandry, in plantations, and in the care of cattle, and particularly of horses. The most robust gave themselves much to the chase on horseback, for warlike exercises. In their infancy they burnt off the right teat to have the arm free for lancing the javelin and hurling the lance. They also used the bow and the *sagaris* (a kind of hand-axe), the *pelta* (a shield, or buckler), and they made themselves helmets, breast-plates and girdles of the skins of wild beasts. Every spring they quitted their old haunts, and went to live two months in the mountains separating them from the Gargarenses. These, on their side, followed an old custom, and never failed to come and lie with the Amazons, where, reunited, they offered common sacrifices to the gods. After sexual intercourse, in secret and by night, and for the sole purpose of becoming mothers, the Amazons, as soon as they were pregnant left the Gargarenses. Of the children . . . the Amazons kept only the girls, sending the boys to the fathers to bring up, and none of the Gargarenses ever refused to accept one of these boys in his family, though each might be ignorant whether or no it was his own brat he adopted . . . As to the Gargarenses, if we believe the tradition, it was with the Amazons that they formerly set out from Themiscyra—then, joining in their wanderings with the Thracians and Eubœans, who had penetrated to there, they warred on the Amazons; but after made a treaty with them. Thereafter, they had no more to do with the Amazons, but lived entirely apart from them.

The Asian Amazons are said to have founded some six towns, including Ephesus, to have brought help to Priam, to have fought on the losing side at Troy, and to have made war in Attica. Joining with the Cimmerians of Chersonesus Taurica (the Crimea), they broke into Asia Minor and laid waste with fire the first temple of Ephesus.

The lost history of Trogus Pompeius, epitomized by Justinus, gives a curious story of the origin of the Amazons of Asia. He tells how two young men, named Ylinos and Scopolitus, of the royal family of the Scythians, who claimed to be more ancient than the Egyptians, were chased out of their country by a faction of the nobles, and, with many other young men, came to the borders of Cappadocia, near the River Thermodon. The men's posterity were famed for the dominion of their men—the ancestors of the Parthians and Bactrians—and the virtue, strength and virile qualities in the sense of the Roman *virtus virtutis* of their women, who founded the kingdom of the Amazons. And, comments Trogus, it is uncertain which sex was the more illustrious among them:

> They burned the right breast of their daughters and hunted and were horsewomen, exercising with arms.

Trogus then tells how these women formed their commonwealth:

The descendants of these migrants from Scythia, too unquiet, roused their neighbours against them and were cut in pieces, and the few men left were forced to leave to the women the duty of defending them against the conquerors' insults. The women acquitted themselves with a courage not expected of their sex and became so pleased with themselves that they began to despise men and, soon, to hate them, and they took the cruel resolution of killing all those spared by their enemies' swords. The time of this extraordinary event is not stated. The Amazons elected two queens and cohabited with their neighbours. Their gown, tucked up, did not reach below the knee. These two queens, Martesia and Lampeto, divided their armies in two parts and carried on war in turn. Their conquests ranged far and wide. To enhance their authority, they spread it abroad that Mars was their father. They reigned at Themiscyra at the same time as Egea at Athens, and Adrastos at Argos, and they founded Ephesus and several other Asia Minor towns. They conquered the greater part of Europe. After this, they sent part of their army home with plunder. The rest stayed behind to defend the Amazons' conquests. Then the barbarians rose against them, and in a battle slew their queen Martesia. Her daughter, Orithya, succeeded as queen, and all greatly admired her for keeping her virginity so long, and for her great skill in arms. Now, the king to whom Hercules owed his twelve labours, ordered him, as an impossibility, to bring home the arms of the queen of the Amazons. Hercules went to the land of the Amazons in nine long ships, with the principal youths of Greece, and fell on the Amazons unawares. At that time, two queens shared the rule of the country of the Amazons: Antiope and Orithya, the latter then fighting a war abroad. When Hercules arrived on their coasts there was only a small army with Antiope, who did not anticipate war. So the few of the Amazons that took up arms were easily repulsed. Many of the Amazons were slain and Antiope was taken prisoner, also her two sisters, Menalippe and Hippolyta, captured by Theseus, who took her to wife and had by her Hippolytus. Hercules restored Menalippe and had for ransom the arms of the queen . . . Orithya, finding that the enemy were Athenian princes, harangued her Amazons, telling them they had warred in vain in conquering Pontussinum and Asia, if they were to be at the mercy, not so much of wars as of the Greeks' robberies. She planned to invade all Greece and declared war on Theseus, who speedily marched to the banks of the Thermodon. The Amazon queen then begged help of King Sagulo of the Scythians, telling him that the Amazons, too, were of his nation. She set forth the cutting off of their men and the need to take up arms and the causes of the war. She urged that the Amazons by their courage showed that the women of the Scythians were no less inactive than the men. Moved by her oration, he sent his son Panasglorum to the help of the Amazons with a vast army of horsemen. But a difference arose between the Amazons and their male allies, who deserted them in the face of the Athenians, by whom the Amazons were then conquered. But they took refuge in the *castrum* (armed camp) of their allies, who helped them return to their own land, untouched by any other race.

Herodotus, and others, as we have seen, say, on the other hand, that the Amazons after their defeat were embarked in three ships and in open sea cut the throats of the sailors; but, not being mariners, were driven by the winds on to the shores of the Palus Mæotidus (Sea of Azov). Here, they seized the horses of the natives; but the soldiers, who marched against them, ashamed to fight women so handsome, young and well formed, halted their march.

Trogus proceeds:

> Orithya, after her defeat by Theseus, retreated to her own country, passing many great nations without suffering new losses. After her, Penthesilea became queen and showed great courage by going to the Trojan war, among the strongest men, to carry aid against the Greeks. She was killed in battle and her army cut off, and the few Amazons that remained in the home lands with much difficulty defended themselves against the enemy until the days of Alexander the Great. Thalestris lay with Alexander for thirteen days in order to bear children by him. She returned home, and, in a short time perished, after which the name of the Amazons sunk into oblivion . . . On the borders of the Hyrcanians and Mardians, Thalestris met Alexander the Great, with her 300 women, having marched for 35 days through lands where the nations constantly attacked them. The sight of her and her coming moved all to wonder, both because her dress was so unusual with women and because she wished to lie with the king. Alexander stopped all business for thirteen days, and when her womb, as the queen thought, had been filled, she departed to her own country.

More than one Roman Catholic monk has been greatly taken with the Amazons, as, for example, Dom Bernarde de Montfaucon (of the Benedictine congregation of St. Maur at Paris), who, about 1724, found in Rome a gem cut with the figure of an Amazon, the inscription *athlos* (battle), and showing her with a quiver and a double axe carried over the shoulder. Jean Pierre Bellori, the Italian antiquary (died A.D. 1696), reproduced an ancient engraving of a wounded Amazon aided by a man. He quoted Duris, the Samian historian, who said:

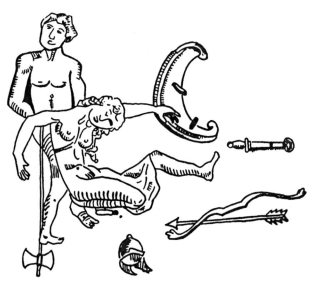

> This picture is of a man named Thermodon — not the river of that name—who carried the wounded Amazon in his arms. Someone dug a hole in the ground to put up a tent and found a statue not very large,

inscribed that this was the statue of Thermodon who carried a wounded Amazon in his arms.

Ancient medallions and cameos show the Amazons wearing a boot that came half-way up the leg and was called the *compagus*, or *ocrea*, or a *greave* (Greek: *knemis*). Their short tunic exposed the teat of one —the right—breast. Tradition, as cited by Hippocrates, said that the Amazons had a law forbidding them to marry (or to cohabit?), till they had killed three male enemies in battle. It was also said that the Amazons warped the legs of their male babies so that they would not grow up too physically strong for them. Which seems to imply that a mother Amazon might find herself fighting her own son in battle! The old commentators on the classics derived the word Amazon from a root *maza*, meaning one teat. It is also alleged that maza, in ancient Georgian, meant Moon, in allusion to the lunar worship of these women. Virgil, in the *Æneid*, speaks of the Amazon queen, Penthesilea and her "golden girdle that bound the breasts". Eustatius said the word meant "without a husband", or came from *amazen*: living in common with no husbands. Someone else said that there was a Greek word *maza*, meaning "with head-dress torn to pieces and brought up with wild beasts". The classic Hellenes do not seem to have liked the Amazons! In fact, they said that if the Amazons begot men they were weak and feeble and could do no deed worthy of strong men.[1]

Their weapons consisted of a half-moon shield, or Scythian girdle, and they wielded *hand-axes*. Claudian speaks of Hippolyta "leading her snow-white, beautiful troops into battle. . . . How often this virago laid waste Arcton and broke Thermodoontiaca Tanais in pieces with the women's battle-axes!" Pliny makes the curious remark that the Indian fig has the breadth of his leaves in the likeness of an Amazon's shield.

Dom Bernarde de Montfaucon, a learned Benedictine, drew a picture of an engraved and ancient stone at Rome, about 1720, which was inscribed with the Greek word *athlos* (*athlesis*) (fight) denoting that the Amazons lived only for war. The Amazon on the stone is shown with the double axe on her shoulder (*Vide* South American Amazon axes, page 177, *Livre de l'Antiquité*), a weapon peculiar to the classic Amazon. Many swords of the remote ages have grips of from 2·4 to 2·8 inches—indicating the hands of women and not men. (*Cf.* Bronze age swords, R. Seine.)

At this point in the story I think I may be pardoned for making public a very singular and little known fact: that descendants of

---

[1] The antipodes of the Amazons were the Essenians, described by Pliny as living on the shores of the Mare Mortuum (Dead Sea). "On its western bank are the race of Essenians who shun all the world marvellously. They live without women, or any libidinousness or money. They do not decrease in numbers, because, from time to time there come to live with them those who, wearied by adverse fortune, wish to follow their customs. Thus, for many centuries, this race has existed among whom none are ever born. Fruitful to them, indeed, is the tedium and fretfulness of others' lives."

these Amazons of Asia must have at some time in the far past have migrated across deserts and mountains to the *Far East*!

A tribe of fighting Amazon women with characteristics strikingly similar to those found in South America, in the days of Fray Carvajal—of whom I shall speak later, in this chapter—*to-day* inhabit the dense forests at the back of the Upper Perak Valley, behind the mountain called Gunond Korbu, in the Federated Malay states. This is within the jurisdiction of the British Empire. Anthropologists know nothing of them. These women are tall in stature, handsome in face, have fine figures and a pale colour of skin recalling that of the classic Amazons. They dance  naked in a glade of the deep woods, when, say the Semang Malays, their nearest neighbours, who are careful to avoid contact with them, offspring are begotten on these women by the evening wind. Men, the women rigorously exclude from their sylvan domains; yet do they manage to bear numerous children, though, of course, the zephyrs are not the putative fathers! These pale-skinned women shoot accurately and with deadly effect, with beautifully carved blow-pipes and well-made arrows.

Ruthlessly do they treat intruders, and the Semangs, as I say, never stray voluntarily or wittingly into the country of the women without husbands. In 1898, Sir Hugh Clifford was told by an aged Semang bearer, over the camp-fire in the Malayan forests, how, as a boy, the bearer had followed his brothers on the trail of a wounded deer. They found the deer lying dead, by a brook, and in its body the shaft of a strange arrow.

The Semangs were bending wonderingly over the arrow, when a threatening cry in a strange tongue came from the trees overhead. They looked up and saw couched in the leaves the "gigantic" form of a pale-skinned woman clad in animal skins. Her big bow whirred and one of the bearer's brothers fell dead, shot through the throat. The Semangs fled, leaving his body untended. The bearer never saw the second brother again. It is stated that these Far Asian women, Amazons of the British Empire, never stray beyond their woodland fastness, and visit sudden death on all male intruders, whether the intrusion be accidental or not.

There seem to have been gynæcocracies also in the South Seas; for a German commission of scientists, in the 1920's, found at Rapa, which may, or may not have been an ancient colony of the people of Lemuria, or Mu, a matriarchate, though a matriarchate is not neces-sarily identical with a commonwealth of fighting Amazon women soldiers. Here, the men, save at certain times, were true drones, while the women worked, governed and administered. They made admirable articles in fine lace, mosaics, or inlaid stuff. In Samoa, the national war-god was a woman.

I have entered rather at length on the story of the Amazons of the so-called Old World of Asia, Africa and Europe, for a reason that will soon appear.

Sir Walter Raleigh, la Condamine, Feijoo, Laet, Cunha, Sarmiento, Herrera, Coronelli, and a host of conquistadorian soldiers, administrators, and Jesuit and Franciscan monks and missioners, in Brazil and Perú, all give the same fundamental facts about the Amazons of South America. Can they *all* have been either liars or self-deceivers who credulously swallowed Indian tales of the marvellous?

The answer, again, is NO! The solution to the riddle lies in much the same strange territory as that of the dead cities in the Highlands of central Brazil and the Matto Grosso, whose walls and porticoes and palace and temple façades have, as I have written, so many letters carved on them that are of obvious Greco-Phœnician form, or Atlantean origin. At some time in the far past, the civilizations of the Amazons of the Old and the New World must have been connected, perhaps by a land-bridge across the Atlantic ocean, that has long ceased to be. Thousands of years ago, there must have been a common centre of diffusion of culture. Ages before the Carthaginians and the men in black, the Phœnicians, who were their kinsmen, started to furrow the waters of the Mediterranean and the outer ocean with the keels of their galleys, and still farther back than the Greece of the Hellenes, or even than the day when the early Aryans defiled through the passes of the Pamirs and pushed down to the Dravidian plains of old India, or Hindostan, there arose a great sea power in the Mediterranean. It was that of the very ancient race of the Carians who preceded the ancient Pelasgians, those mighty builders of megalithic cities and walls in the lands of the Ægean, that recall similar great ruins found, to-day, on the still unexplored cordilleras of the Andes in modern Colombia. For the Carians were in Illyria before the ancient Pelasgians settled there. The Carians probably preceded by some thousands of years the founding of the great city of Cnossos, in Minoan Crete where, also, arose a strangely modern culture and great civilization which suddenly and mysteriously vanished.

Homer knew of the Carians. He calls them *barbaraphonoi*, and says they spoke the ancient tongue of Barbaros, found in ancient Africa and Asia. "It is the oldest tongue in the world," he wrote.

In that, Homer was certainly right!

Bar, *car*, or *var* is a very old word meaning "man". There was in ancient Africa a race called the Varvar. It is the root of the term *Berbers* who are probably the descendants of the ancient people of *Car*-thage, in what is now Tunisia. There are, of course, dangers in pressing philological links too far; but one may be forgiven for pointing out the curious fact, in ancient Africa, that the ancient pyramids of Egypt were called *BrBr*, because of the great men, the Pharaohs, who had them erected.

The Carians were also connected with another very ancient European race: the Basques of the Pyrenees, whom some people believe to have originally come from one of the lost Atlantean island-continents of Plato and the Egyptian priests of the Nile. The Carians, then, were masters of the world and the seas before the age of the Phœnicians and the Aryans; and wherever the Carian race went, there one saw gynæcocracies. For, among them, women had great power, which often degenerated into licentiousness and debauchery.

The Asian branch of the Carians settled in the Ægean countries of Lydia, Caria and Cappadocia (all now located in modern Anatolia, or Turkey-in-Asia of the Ottoman power of Angora). The girls and young women of Caria and Lydia had the nightly habit of going into the groves and quiet places, and by the seashores where they met strangers and foreign merchants to whom they prostituted themselves. There was no shame about it. It was a religious rite; for even matrons and mothers "chaperoned" the girls to the groves of love, the money being used to build funeral monuments and enrich the temples of the god of love, *Makar*. (*Ma* means, of course, love, and *kar* or *car*, fish. Oddly enough in modern French is the word *maquereau* which, too, has the double meaning of fish and pimp of the brothel! The resemblance of terms is no fortuitous thing!)

Makar is the same as the old Phœnician god Melcarth, and, what is to the point, is that in Mexico, in the tongue of the old Quiches is the word *Macar*, which also means whale or fish and the embraces of a prostitute. Melcarth signified the same. Maybe the cult originally came from the memory of a golden age of divine men, or gods of the fortunate isles, such as was once found in the land of the dead Atlantean cities of the Brazilian Highlands. This is suggested in the fact that, on the shores of the Indian Ocean, at Gujerat and Kutch in India, the god Macara was worshipped under the double character of a god of a golden world or age, and an infernal god, to whom human sacrifices were offered. Macara,[1] whose symbol was the whale that conquered the abyss, had a harem of women who hugged and embraced at the same time as they dominated him. The same degeneration and aberration of ideas was, as all know who have read William Hickling Prescott's famous history, seen in Aztec Mexico of the pre-conquest age. (*Vide: Ximinez's Tesoro de las lenguas quiché cakchiquel y zutuhil.*)

We have in the *Codex Chimalpopoca* (*History of the Suns*, or Cosmic epochs) a graphic picture of an Amazonian gynæcocracy of this Carian type. The Codex speaks of a great pre-Aztecan chief on the shores of the *Pacific*. He was called the *Sun*. His nearest relative, a woman,

[1] The radical is found in MU, the Ma-land, or Motherland of the old Pacific. The form of Mu (*cap.*) in the Phœnico-Greek alphabet and our own M. is clearly derived from the *Venus procreatrix*, with her legs indecently akimbo, as shown in one bas-relief of extremely ancient date, and probably derived from some race of Mu-an colonists in proto-South America, which is found at Manabi, in Ecuador.—AUTHOR.

shared the power with him, as at Teotihuacan, Oxomoco and Caïpac-tonal, where the same man-woman, dual sovereignty prevailed. Marriage was a very fluid institution in those remote days of the Carian gynæcocracy. Babylonian type temples with groves and prostitutes were found on the banks of the Mississippi, as on the shores of the Pacific. The supreme pontiff, the *Sun*, ordered that these things be, and his colleague, the woman, queen of the *Maza*, or moon, had her powerful say. At Panuco, the phallus was worshipped, as it must have been in the ancient days of the Marajó Island culture,[1] at the mouth of the Rio Amazon, Brazil. Outside the temple of the phallus at Panuco, and Teo-Colhuacan, stood statues graphically picturing in the round all the pleasures men might enjoy with women; and human figures, nude as they were born, presented, in stone, scenes like those depicted in that ancient *lupanar* in Pompeii's ruins!

So degenerate became some of these ancient American gynæco-cratic races that, as at Panuco, cowardly, born-drunken fellows, when too lazy to swallow their liquor in the ordinary way, lay down and had others pump in, *via* their anal passages, and the medium of a tube, all the liquor they could hold. According to a "gentleman in the train of Cortes", who wrote a *Story of New Spain*, some of these "civilized natives" at Panuco, celebrated a paranoiac rite called *Ixcuirame*. This, supposed to have been brought into old Mexico by tribes from the east who appeared at Tollan centuries before, took the form of a tanner skinning a victim alive and clothing himself in the human skin. (I draw my reader's notice to what the ancients said of the *male Cappadocians*. See page 129 of this chapter.)

The well-known Jesuit monk and traveller, Père Francis Xavier de Charlevoix, who explored the Mississippi about the year 1744, found that traces of the ancient Carian gynæcocracy still existed among the Natchez Indians, now extinct. These Indians in Alabama and Mississippi had a great chief called the *Sun*, and a woman chief—his nearest relative—sharing the power with him.

The *Life of David Zeisberger* has a curious passage about a North American Indian gynæcocracy:

> They steered up the Beaver, and beyond the rapids came to the first town since leaving the fort. It was inhabited, strange to say, by a community of women, all single, and all pledged never to marry.

Monsieur le Vicomte de Châteaubriand, member of the French Academy, who landed in North America about 1791, when he noted that the old religious beliefs of the North American Indians were nearly effaced, spoke of a lunar myth of the Canadian Indians, which is clearly a survival of a dim memory of the matriarchate of the *later* Atlanteans:

> The Great Hare created six men, one of whom mounted to the sky and had sexual relations with a goddess of vengeance called *Athænsie* (the moon). When the Great Hare saw she was pregnant, he kicked her

[1] *Vide:* my book *Mysteries of South America* (Rider & Co).

140

out of heaven and she fell on the back of the tortoise. *N.B.*—The tortoise is a North American symbol of cataclysm and the Great Deluge that sank old Atlantis, while the name of the goddess bears a marked resemblance to that of Athena, or Min-erva of old Atlan, and one of the earth-mothers of ancient Frisia, linked with Atlan-Hyperborei-Æyre. At the little Panathenaia, held on the harbour of the Piræus at old Athens, there was a *peplos*, or robe with a design embroidered in it, showing scenes related to a war of the old Pelasgians of pre-Hellenic Athens with the Atlanteans, in which the latter were beaten. Another saffron-coloured robe showed scenes in the war of the giants with the gods, which may, or may not, denote an insurrection of helots, or lower castes, against the tyranny of the later oligarchs and imperialists of Atlantis. It may be recalled that it was Neptune, striking with his trident, who created the horse—symbol of war—from the earth, while Min-erva-Athena produced the peaceful olive. The Natchez said the Moon—*Athænsic*—was chief of bad spirits, which probably embodies a racial memory of a lunar cataclysm.—AUTHOR.

Châteaubriand goes on to say that another variant of this old Canadian Indian myth was that the moon-goddess had two sons, one of whom killed the other. The fratricide, named Jousekeka, was held to be the *sun*, which may be euhemerized as a dim and garbled memory of a great war or social upheaval in which the moon-matriarchy of *later* Great Atlantis—and this empire lasted thousands of years— was sunk by the sun-patriarchy. It was a war of cults and polities, wherein a man-governed society, linked with Hercules and Theseus— ancient antagonists of the Amazon races—took the place of the older moon-matriarchy.

In the Mississippi region lived the old Natchez race, who, under priests, had anciently migrated from the mountains of a warmer country to the south, where, and on the plains along the "great water" —this was either South or Central America—the "ancients of the old land" had, after many years "forced them to quit". They seem to have been a branch of the race of the old Karians, uprooted from old Europe by the convulsions of the great Trojan War, when these old Karians, who had much of the secret marine lore and sea-routes of their kins- men, by marriage, the Pauchs and Carthaginians, reached old Brazil, and became known as the Karaybas.

The Natchez of the regions of old St. Louis, Mississippi, had *two tongues* just as had the old Karians in Europe, and the Karaybas in old Brazil. Both Karians and Karaybas had wives who would never eat with them, or use their names, and who spoke a different language, from that of their husbands. It has, however, never been explained how the Karians, in their first settlement in old central Brazil, came to lose their ancient alphabet of old Cretan type. Among the Natchez,[1] the nobles spoke one tongue, and the common people another, which was also the custom in Incaic Perú, and probably among the proto- Sumers voyaging from old India to the Pacific and the shores of an

[1] A few survivors of the "Nadches" are found to-day only in reservations in the Indian territory of Oklahoma.

ancient America. Châteaubriand arrived on the Mississippi some eight years before the race died out and their dialect with them. Among this Natchez branch of the ancient American descendants of old Europe's Karians there must, in the dim past, have been a struggle or compromise between the moon or matriarchate, and the sun or patriarchate. Their chief was called the "Sun" and claimed descent from the sun, but kingship descended from the females, so that the son of the dead king's sister might be the new king!

The *femme-chef*—woman co-chief—had, like the Sun-chief, a guard of young folk. . . . She had sway over manners and customs. She took what she wished from lovers and the loved, husbands and affianced. If she fancied, she would have the objects of her caprices strangled . . . If a young sun chief wished when he ascended the throne, he could order his father to be strangled, as not of noble birth. The mantle of corruption of the mother and the heir to the throne fell on other women. The nobles deflowered virgins and even young wives all over the nation. The Sun-king had even gone so far as to order a general prostitution of women as was done in old Babylon. When a *femme-chef* died, her non-noble husband was suffocated. The eldest daughter of the *femme-chef* who succeeded to the dignity, ordered the strangling of twelve children, and their corpses were ranged round the dead bodies of the old woman-chief and her husband. These fourteen corpses were shown on a litter pompously called a bier. C. describes the cortège slowly marching, two by two, young men carrying the bier, the fathers and mothers of the strangled children, slow-marching, two by two, bearing their dead children in their arms. Fourteen other victims to be immolated followed in the rear. They had been forced to spin the hemp of the cord that would strangle them, and carried it in their hands in procession behind the bier. Every ten paces, the fathers and mothers who preceded the bier had to let fall the corpses of their children, on which the bier-bearers stepped, so that when the temple, where a light was perpetually burning, was reached, the flesh of the dead children was in pieces. Here, the fourteen condemned were disrobed and sat on the ground. One of the *allouez* (the young guard) sat on the knees of each victim and another held the victim's hands behind him. They were forced to swallow three pieces of tobacco and drink a cup of water. Then a noose was passed round their necks, and the relations of the *femme-chef* hauled it tight, as they sang songs, and garrotted the unfortunate.

These scenes of sadism and decadence, which recall the last Belsen days of old Mu, were ended by the people withdrawing into the woods and leaving "to it" the Sun-king, and the nobles to cultivate the communal fields. A later and more decent chief abolished the old customs. It is curious that these Natchez, who had a communist system of society and no private property and no wants, had let themselves fall under such a yoke of sadistic despotism. One may shove on one side the vicious screams of female feminists and theorize whether such decadence does not inevitably follow where men decay and gynæcocracies rule? Perhaps Hercules was not so far out when he said that rule by women was not good for the world and that was why he and Theseus stamped out the race of Amazons.

In the highlands of modern Colombia (old Nueva Granada), before the Spaniard conquistadores under Don Jiminez de Quesada conquered the Chibchas, there was a town called Limnés, or Lemma of the Tayronas, where armour of gold was forged and fashioned for the old kings of Mexico and Central America. The god of the town and race was *Macar-Ona*, who also protected the pearl fisheries of the coast. The root is also found in Macaraibo, the famous Venezuelan oil lake. As will be soon seen, these are not accidental resemblances.

On the other side of the world the Carian gynæcocracies, or women's republics of this very ancient race of the Carians spread to the shores of the Black Sea, where they worshipped the moon, which to this day, among the Circassians at the far eastern end of the Black Sea, is called *Maza*. So, the word *Amazon* means a moon-worshipper?

But it is with the considerably older branch of the Carian women race in North Africa that one is here more particularly concerned in relation to South and Central America, and parts of the Mississippi country, United States of America. For, from this long-vanished race in ancient North Africa, almost certainly sprang the Amazons of South America. Their African republic, thousands of years ago, lay on the bounds of the known and inhabited world. Some event or conquest disrupted them. A Carthaginian tradition says these North African Amazons were routed and dispersed to the four winds by the Phœnician Heracles, or Hercules, the strong man who erected the famous light-house pillars of Hercules. Perhaps to commemorate the fact that two lofty mountains, one in Spain called Calpe, the other in Africa called Abyla, once joined together, had been sundered by the breaking-in of the Atlantic, opening the ocean to the closed-in Mediterranean Sea. However and whenever the dispersal happened, the ancestresses of the Amazons of South America probably crossed the ocean from Africa to southern Brazil or the Antilles, by way of some then existing land-bridge, or great islands long "gone west".

R. M. Gatfossé points out that, in the Berber tongue of North Africa, *Am Azon*, or *El Azoun* means people of Azoun in Algiers. *Azoun* was the mother (*moon*) goddess *worshipped after the disappearance of Atlantis*, and known in Ireland, among the oldest branch of the Kelts, as *Ana* or *Danu*. Nations whose lands abutted on the region of the sunken Atlantis were, suggests Monsieur Gatfossé, given to female and not male cults. In this connection it is singular that the Mebengas, a tribe in the South Sea Fiji islands, have a legend that there was a race of all women and some beings with dogs' tails, who rose *after the Flood*.

A glimpse of these African Amazons, who strangely recall those of South America, is given by Diodorus Siculus (of Sicily), who, about 44 to 34 B.C., went to every country of which his histories tell. He tells an interesting story of the Amazon women and their queen, the female president of an early women's republic, located in a land now wholly or partly under sea but which was then in African Libya. Its approximate, modern location would be near Rabat, in Morocco.

Says Diodorus:

> These women lived on the bounds of the inhabited world. Their men spent their days about the house carrying out the orders of their wives, the Amazons, but took no part in military campaigns or office as free citizens. When the babies were born they were turned over to the men, who brought them up on milk and cooked foods suitable for children. The breasts of girls were seared, because they were a hindrance to warfare. Their home was in an island of the west, called Hespera, and it lay in the marsh of Tritonis, near the ocean that surrounds the earth. The Amazons lived in an island of great size and full of fruit trees. They had many flocks and herds of goats and sheep, but no wheat; for wheat was unknown to them. After they had subdued all the cities on their own island they decided on world-conquest, and the first people against whom they advanced were the Atlanteans, the most civilized among the inhabitants of these regions, who dwelt in a prosperous country and possessed great cities. They were kind to strangers and the land was the home of the gods.

Myrina, the queen of the Amazons, collected 30,000 women foot-soldiers, and 3,000 cavalry. They wore large snake skins; for Libya in North Africa contained snakes of immense size. They carried swords and lances. When the enemy pursued them they retreated, shooting backwards with good effect. The Atlanteans were defeated in a pitched battle at Cerne an island without the pillars of Hercules (on the African coast), and the Amazons made their way inside the walls of the city, along with the fleeing enemies, and got the place in their hands

> The men from youth upward were put to the sword, and the women and children fled into captivity. Then the city was razed to the ground. The Atlanteans, struck with terror, capitulated on terms; but Queen Myrina treated them well, and founded a city to bear her name, in place of that razed elsewhere. Here she settled both captives and any native who so desired. Then, at the solicitations of the Atlanteans, the Amazons attacked the Gorgons, and in a mighty battle gained the upper hand. Great numbers were slain and 3,000 taken prisoners, after which the wood into which they had all fled was set on fire. But the timber would not burn, and so Myrina returned to her own country. In the night, the Amazons relaxed their watch, and the captive women rose, got swords, and killed many of the Amazons; but the multitude poured in from every side about them, and the prisoners, fighting bravely, were butchered one and all. Myrina gave a funeral to her foreign comrades, on three pyres, and raised three great heaps of earth, as tombs, called to this day: "The Amazon Mounds" (*Diodorus Siculus*).

He says that, in the end, both the warlike race of women called the Gorgons and the Amazons' race were destroyed by Heracles, when he visited the region to the west, and set up his pillars in Libya. He "felt it would ill accord with his resolve to be a benefactor of the

Lacandone (Mayan) woman with baby, showing "Mongoloid spot" (top of buttock), denoting late fusion of Atlan race with Eastern Asiatic invaders

(*Left*) Old Pekin Seal; (*Right*) Ancient Chinese hieroglyphs. Note Pan-Atlan trident glyph (*top*)

(*Left*) Pre-Sumer statue; (*Right*) Atlantean head-flattened North American mound-builder

whole human race of mankind, if he suffered any nations to be under the rule of women".

He points out that the African Amazons were by far the most ancient of the Amazons, having lived many ages before the Trojan War, whereas the Amazons of Thermodon, located in modern northern Anatolia, in the Black Sea hinterland, lived only a little before it. Diodorus also adds the significant statement that Queen Myrina was the friend of Horus, the son of Isis, who, as one has pointed out, was something more than a mythological god of Egypt, the Nilotic Christ of the Serapeum whose rites have been grafted into Roman Catholicism. Horus, indeed, was a notable of old Atlantis!

Diodorus says that the marsh of Tritonis disappeared from sight when a great earthquake tore asunder those parts of it which lay towards the ocean. Maybe it was before that great cataclysm came and sank the island-continent, or continental islands of the Atlantic Ocean, that the ancestresses of the Amazons crossed from Africa to South America, and the lands lying around the then much larger gulf of Mexico.

How many thousands of years ago these events happened none can say. Since Diodorus drew on traditions and Carthaginian temple-archives it is probably true that there is a real foundation of pre-history behind the seeming legend. We have to grope through a cloud of mythology and racial and ancestral memories and traditions, preserved both in America and old Europe and Africa by Mayan, Peruvian and Aztecan priests and wise men, and Carthaginian and Phœnician or Egyptian temple-record keepers. It is a regular marsh of Tritonis; but, wading through it as best one may, one's feet now and then stumble on to a patch of drier ground in the cloudy swamps of pre-history and tradition.

Piecing together traditions and stories related in fragments of lost works by other Greek and Roman historians, it would seem that the lake of Tritonia, with the island in its centre on which stood the Amazon city of Hespera—and it will be seen that Hespera was a peculiarly Amazonian type of city—was joined to the Atlantic Ocean by a narrow canal, when this sudden inundation took place. These writers say that the catastrophe forced the Amazons to go on trek, wandering in search of a new homeland. Some of them seemed to have turned their wandering and martial footsteps towards what is now called Dahomey where, to-day, live the mounted and armed women called the Amazons of Dahomey, or Abomey, part of the African Equatorial Empire of France. But the main body of emigrants, under Queen Myrina, raided the territory of the Gorgons, said to have been also a society of women warriors, whose land was in modern Algeria (Numidia). After imposing a levy on the Gorgons, Myrina, well furnished with horses, food, clothes and weapons, led her host of women warriors along the shores of Libya into the land of Pharaoh, who received them kindly and gave them food. From Egypt they wandered into Arabia, where they waged war on the Arabians; then to Palestine and Syria, and everywhere fought battles with the races opposing their marches. The Kings of Tyre and Sidon, Phœnicians, made a treaty of peace with Queen Myrina, and the Amazóns stayed in these lands for some years, recovering from the hardships of their long trails from Africa into Asia.

From Phœnicia, the Amazons passed into a territory of the Caucasus, bordered by modern Armenia.[1] Here, Myrina organized a permanent state and remained its head till her death. Once again profound distaste for a settled life seized on these restless warrior-women and they began to invade their neighbours. The Trojan War gave them an outlet for their aggressiveness but when their queen, Penthesilea, was slain by Achilles, the Amazons split into two sections, one section returning to Armenia, where they had an island in the middle of a lake with a temple in which Queen Myrina was buried. This little island-town was *called Faro*. It was clearly modelled on the prototype, submerged Hespera. Another section may have embarked in ships of the Phœnicians and sailed across seas to the West Indies or Brazil. But however this may be, it is odd that in the lower Amazonas, their South American country, there is *also a town called Faro*—it is near modern Obidos—*where exists a lake with an ancient temple concealed in the middle of a little wooded island*. This is *one* theory of their wanderings from the Near or Middle East to old America.

It may be true, but what is certain is that whether across the then existing, but now vanished, land-bridge between Africa and Brazil, or over the Atlantic Ocean, in the ships of the Karian, or old Carian race of soldier-seamen they at last reached the other world, that, as the ancient priests of Egypt said, five or more thousand years ago, surrounded the true ocean. That world was, of course, America. Perhaps, the Amazons were driven there after some war with the more combatant, militarist races of the Atlanteans—some of whom were, also, clearly men of peace and culture. All we know is that both Carian men and Carian women, or Amazons, *were* found in South America thousands of years later, in our own era. That we clearly discern, looming through the mists of the dim, far past.[2]

[1] This version apparently conflicts with that of Trogus in pages 133–135 *supra*.

[2] Thousands of years ago, the Caribbean Islands were considerably larger than they are to-day, and in place of the modern Caribbean Sea there was an extension of the mainland from Central America called "*Car*-aiba". In this great piece of *terra firma*, and in islands around it, lived the seven tribes of the Tupi nations. Maybe here was the origin of the mystic seven cities of Cibola which sent Don Coronados on his fruitless journey into the north of Mexico. These Tupis are variously stated to have been refugees from the submerged Atlantis, and Carians, or Caris, of Mediterranean descent, though they could not be both. Their priests called them sons of *Tupan*. However, bit by bit, this American land of Antillia, or Caraiba, was swallowed up by the sea, until the surviving Tupis got away in small boats and landed about where is now located *Caracas*, modern Venezuela. The Phœnicians of Brazil are said to have transported the Tupis in ships to the north of Brazil. However this may be, when the early Spanish missioners arrived in Venezuela, the Carib-Tupis told the padres that their Tupi ancestors had lost half their people in a cataclysm which overtook a large island in the Caribbean; that the survivors rowed in "little ships" to the mainland of South America, thousands dying on the passage

And we *know*, too, that the Amazons landed in one of the West Indian islands, thousands of years ago.

There now falls a complete blank of more thousands of years. Many empires rose, declined, and vanished in old Europe, around the Mediterranean, in Africa and Asia. It is only in Mexican native traditions that, as I have said in pages 139–140 *supra*, we catch a sudden flash-back of the movie of history. It is a vivid picture of an Amazonian gynæcocracy settled somewhere near the Mississippi, in modern United States of America. Here, women shared power with priests and kings in a land of the Nahuatls, who allied themselves with the old Carians, in America. After a time, as in ancient Lydia and Caria, in the far-away Ægean, licentiousness and lustful debauchery were rampant. Every woman seemed to have a common property in every man, thus reversing the position in the old buccaneering island of Providence, in the Bahamas, in the end of the seventeenth century and early eighteenth century. "Marriage" was very much a matter of convenience and voluptuousness. There were temples around the Mississippi, filled with prostitutes, as in those of Siva, in the India of to-day. These ancient American temples also had pictures and erotic carvings recalling those which the modern Italian guide takes male visitors aside to look at on the ruined walls of what once were bagnios in Roman Pompeii. A faint reflection of the state of affairs in these prehistoric American "all-red light" temples and cities of ortho- and homo-sexuality is to be found in the Bible of the Quiches: *The Popul Vuh*.

The *Annals of Culhuacan* tell of a Toltec king who made an expedition to the province of Huitznahuac where, after many fruitless attempts, he managed to defeat a bold, Amazon princess, Chimalman, who fought stark naked at the head of a body of Amazons. The prince eventually married her—a felicitous marriage of his beauty and her brains!

The Amazons must have arrived in ancient Mexico in a very remote day, for Diego de Camargo, the Mexican historian, quotes an ancient Aztecan source as saying that many hundreds of Amazons invaded the region of Anahuac, in the Mexican Valley. These women came from the eastern coastal region of Huaxtec. Their habit in war was to kill all prisoners, and their weapons were the bow and spear. Their leader in war took the name of Tlazolteotl, who was the ancient Mexican Venus, with another and Hecatean aspect of goddess of witches. (In this chapter, I have noted the existence to-day in a wooded

across; and that "big ships took many others of them away to the south to other great lands". Fray Antonio Vieira, "the apostle of the Brazilian Indians", heard from the Tupinambas, along the Amazon, and the Tabajaras, that their forbears had come to north Brazil from a land across the sea that no more existed; and they were the "most ancient folk of Brazil". However, in that they were greatly mistaken. That distinction belongs to the black troglodytes of the Roosevelt plateau and the Rio Uapes on the still unexplored borders of Colombia, South America, who use clubs as weapons and live on frogs and snakes. This queer race of old Brazil were probably contemporary with the lost white race of bearded men who ruled the great empire of Atlantean Brazil till a great cataclysm swept them and their cities into ruin and oblivion.—AUTHOR.

island in Lago de Titicaca, Perú, of Amazons called the Urus, with a witch-*cacica* at the head.)

There was, also, as stated *supra*, an Amazon state located on the Pacific littoral of ancient Mexico.

Then the veil falls for long ages. We know nothing of the Amazons of Central or South America. But, over the seas, in old Europe, when Britain was split up into seven kingdoms and Dane and Norman pirates looted, raped, and burnt right and left over North and Western England, a band of women warriors, under a queen, Vlasta, rose deep in Bohemia, in the eighth century A.D. They captured and enslaved men in a "Virgins' Castle", which they heavily fortified. Came along a duke who did not take them seriously—at first. But, when they took and slaughtered some of his best fighting-men, he laid siege to this "Virgins' Castle".[1] The women first beheaded twenty-one men prisoners, and then marched out to attack the duke and his army. They fought till all had fallen under the swords and spears of the fighting-men.

In Africa, one of the old homes of the Amazons, but this time, at the opposite end, in old Ethiopia, or Abyssinia, the famous Queen of Sheba of Arabia seems to have set up a race of Amazon warriors.

Dom Francisco Alvarez, a Portuguese monk who went travelling to the land of Prester John, reached, about 1521, the "court of Prete Janni, the great Christian emperor of Ethiopia". He heard a story curiously like that told by Diodorus:

> I was certified that, on the frontiers of Damute and Gorage (modern Guragwe), as you travel south there is a kingdom governed by women, called Amazons, as recorded in the book of Dom Pedro, the Infanta of Portugal. But 6 women have their husbands with them all the year. They have no king, but a queen that hath no certain husband, but suffereth any man to lye with her, to get her with child. The eldest daughter succeeds in the kingdome. They are very valiant women and great warriors, and ride upon certain beasts that are very swift and like unto oxen. They are great archers, and in their youth cause the left breast to be dried up, that it hinder not their shooting. Great store of gold they gather, which is carried into many parts of Ethiopia. The husbands of these women are no warriors, because the women will not suffer them to manage Armes.[2]

Alvarez, in his *Universal History*, says there were Amazons living south of Damote, in Abyssinia, about A.D. 1520, who burnt off the left breast when they were young, and fought with bows and arrows,

[1] This gynæcocracy was set up on the Vidovlé Mountain. For eight years, the women ravaged the plains and constantly rejected peace proposals made them by King Przemislas of Bohemia. They promulgated laws, establishing the absolute predominance of the female sex, and at the last perished valiantly, sword in hand. Ænius Sylvius, later Pope Pius II, was sent on an embassy by King Frederick of Bohemia. In 1450, he saw in Bohemia, a commonwealth exactly like that of the Amazons, set up by the courage of a woman named Valasea. He became Pope in 1458.

[2] Juan de Santos, a grey friar of Portugal, also speaks of a "Government and Nation of women in Africa, who kill all the male children they had by their neighbours."

mounted on bullocks! Such a bright scene out-dazzles anything in fairy-land and would sure have warmed the cockles of the old Yankee heart of the great Barnum! Perhaps they could also have saddled the *African* elephant?

Messer Marco Polo speaks of a kingdom of women ruled by a woman, which was in two islands near Socotra. He calls them "Male and Female Islands". It is possible that here—with another sacred and adjacent "Easter Island"—we have a dim memory of the old Atlantean island of Panchæa, in the Indian Ocean, and from which old India could be seen. Marco adds that these Amazon islands lay 500 miles south of the kingdom of Kesmacoran (province of Mekran, in Baluchistan). The islands are, he says, 30 miles apart, and that men visit the women only in March to May, each year, and return to trade and husbandry in their own island for the rest of the year. Friar Jordanus located these women in what he calls India Tertia (East Africa?). Another writer, Conti, says that those who remain in the island of the others, beyond six months, die.

Dom Juan Burmudez, the patriarch to the emperor of Ethiopia, who went on embassy to the king, Dom João III, of Portugal, in 1565, added that these Amazons of north-eastern equatorial Africa, sent men-children back to the fathers and "burnt their own left paps" for archery . . .

> Their Queen is worshipped among them for a Goddesse. They were set up by the Queene of Saba (Sheba) who went to see king Salomon.

When the veil at last rose on the Amazons in South America, they were already a power behind the eastern cordilleras of the Andes of old Perú. At some date unknown, but long before the conquistadores of Cortes invaded Mexico, or Pizarro's Castilian bandits pushed their horses over the passes into old Cuzco, Perú, a nation of women behind and in the pueblo of Changara, that "is between the country of the Canches, and Collao", built many earthwork fences, great ditches and forts and trenches and fought against a valiant chief named Zapana, who was the Abraham of the Incas. The women were routed and their very name forgotten. The remains of their forts were to be seen in the days of Antonio de Herrera, "coronista major of the king of Spain and Castile, in the Indies", about 1610.

This chapter is not actually a history of the Karians, but the facts are so curious in relation to Central America that it may be pointed out that one of their singular customs, in old Europe and the Levant of an ancient day, was carried across the Atlantic. They seem to have landed in Brazil, where, in some way unexplained, they lost even the elements of their Old World culture as represented by an alphabet. Herodotos and Strabo both point out that the Karian women spoke a different language from the men, and that they never ate at the same table with the men. This custom appears to have originated in a day when the Ionian Greeks committed something approaching a rape of the Sabines on the Karians. The men were all killed and the Karian women, forcibly wedded, swore they would never eat with the husbands, be called by their names, or speak their tongue. The oath was passed on to their daughters.

In Brazil and all over Northern South America, wherever Caribs or Karayba were found, the men spoke, and still to-day speak, a different language from the women and eat alone. The Galibis, another branch of the race, in Northern South America, and at one time, in Darien, not only had one tongue for the women and another for the men, but they also destroyed all male babies, sparing the women. Padre Raymond Bretton, the missioner, who compiled a Carib dictionary, says that, in the late seventeenth century, the Caribs still spoke two different tongues. Some of their words, he pointed out, have distinct affinities with the Phœnician.

The men of the Carian race, being world navigators, at last wandered into the South Pacific, and disembarked at the mouth of the Rio Esmeraldas, on what is now the coast of north-west Ecuador. Ranging inland towards the cordilleras of the Andes, they set up a dynasty of kings, named Scyris. (*Vide:* Velasco's *History of the old kingdom of Quito*, lib. i., i.) Others of their race appeared in more southerly parts of those early seas, off the coast of what is now Chile and Perú. They left ancient tombs in Perú. The Carians were also known as the Colloas. They had probably journeyed all the way from old Mexico, crossing the mountains and launching their ships on the early Pacific. The Colloa-Carians had an idea of their ancestry. They truly said: "We are a very ancient race". They also had a tradition of a great deluge.

A long time before the rise of the Inca power, and the occupation of the country by that imperial race, there suddenly appeared out of the vale of Coquimbo two Carian-Colloan chiefs, Sapani and Cari. Cari passed to Lake Titicaca to attack an island in it, called Chuquito. In this island, which was swampy, he came across *a white bearded race* whom he fought till he exterminated them. The Colloa-Carians took possession of the land around about and settled many colonies. They oppressed the natives all round their frontiers. This white, bearded race must have been the descendants of the lost, highly-civilized white people who built the magnificent, but now dead, Brazilian cities, thousands of years before.

North, where the Andean cordilleras throw a spur into the Darien isthmus, another trail of Carians ended in the highlands of modern Santa Fé de Bogotá and around Lake Macaraibo, the famous oil region of modern Venezuela. The Carians gave their racial name to this lake, and that of their god of love and the sea: *Macara.*

The race of South American Amazon women probably had a contact with their Carian kinsmen of these regions; for, in their great treks across South America from the eastern Andes to the Orinoco they carried with them strange *green stones*, which came from these mysterious mountains of the old Carians and the builders of great dead cities, or from some "lost" country on the Peruvian borders. (More of this in its place.)

The Carians ranged into old Mexico, and allied themselves with

Proto-Crete: Carian (Karian) ruler.

Cara woman, descended from old Karians of Levant. (Ceramic on ancient site, Rio Esmeraldas, Ecuador.)

the Nahuatls, the successors of the Toltecs, who were giants in stature, and skilled workers in gold. They took their gynæcocracies with them, and to-day, 1950, there exists in the isthmus of Tehuantepec, Mexico, a strange race of dancing matriarchs, seldom or never contacted by outsiders, who may be direct descendants of a race of Amazons in old Mexico.

Down in South America, the Amazons are heard of in the time of the ninth Inca emperor, Inti[1] Cussi Huallpa, or Huara Capac.

The Inca was a beautiful youth and he heard, when he was in the country of the Motilone Indians, that east of the cordilleras of the Andes lay a civilized people ruled over by an Amazon queen, Quillago. He had a queer adventure when he marched his army into her country. A river was fortified on both banks by the people, and bridged. The bridge he burnt, and killed many of the Amazon

[1] It may be noted that Inti, in Perúvian Quichua, means *sun*. In India, the Sanscrit meaning of *Indh* is also *sun*. Vira, among certain Brazilian tribes, means *sun*. Vira in the East Indies, means also *sun*. *Indra* (Sanscrit), and *Indh*, mean sun, and to shine.—AUTHOR.

queen's people. The war lasted for two years—it was a *very* modern sort of war, in duration—and none got the upper hand. At last, the queen was captured. The Inca sought to gain her over with rich presents, which she would not accept. Then he ordered her to be liberated. She went back to her city, and then planned to kidnap the Inca. In her palace was an inner apartment with a deep well. She decided to lure the Inca into the inner chamber and then have him drowned; but he got wind of the plot to kill him by water. On the day arranged for his visit to the Amazon queen, the Inca went at a certain hour to her palace, and was received with cordial demonstrations. Hand in hand, Inca and Amazon queen ascended the stairway to the inner chamber where the snare was all set. But, once inside, the Inca caught the lintel of the door, with his left hand, and, bracing his feet strongly against the top of the well, heaved his body against the Amazon queen, and so caused her to stumble and pitch into the well, meeting the fate she had intended for him. A shouting virago of a woman-servant came at him with tooth and nail; but she, too, he seized round the waist, and sent her to join the queen at the bottom of the well.

Another Inca, Tupac Yupanqui, had to wage a fierce war with the Colhuas—a race of white, bearded men said by ancient traditions to have come from the "Seas of the East"—and at the head of 12,000 Quechuas he marched on Huarmi Pucara, which means the "woman fortress". Here he fought with women of the Quillia or *Moon*. The over-confident Quechua army was defeated by the women and only one man escaped to bring the news of the disaster to the Inca. The same Inca led an army of 200,000 men on a new conquest of the Andes, as far as the confines of Huancaville and Caravaya. (The root *Car* clearly denotes a place of the old South American Carians descended from the old Karian migrants from old Europe.) As might be expected, at Caravaya, the Inca found he had entered a province inhabited entirely by women, called the *Huarmi-auca* (women soldiers). From the ancient fortress of Sachsahuaman, at Cuzco, Yupanqui sent out a captain against the revolting Chillis who lived around Tucuman in a land of much fine gold. The Chillis had an army of 20,000 women soldiers and 20,000 men.

The first modern European *known* to have come into contact with the West Indian Amazons was Christopher Columbus, in A.D. 1493, when he landed in Martinique, the old name of which was Matinino. Here, the natives told him traditions of a kingdom of white women of the American Amazonian, or old Carian race, once ruling in old Martinique.

The Caras of the Antilles had "legends", too, of a far-off time, when the sea was not in those regions but all was dry land. It is Peter Martyr, or Peter Martyr of Anghierra, or Angleria, who ran a school for nobles at the court of Queen Isabella of Spain, who, at the court, heard and wrote into his *De Novo Orbo* contemporary stories of the discoveries made by Columbus in the Caribbean. On the first voyage, some of the natives were sent prisoner to old Spain, and they and others, later set free, affirmed that the isle of *Madanino* (Martinique) was inhabited only by women. The Spaniards, at the time of the first voyage heard about these women, and have unfairly been accused, by later historians and critics, of undue credulity and the lending of too ready an ear to native Indian "yarns".

Says Peter Martyr:

> It seems that the cannibals went, at certain times of the year, to visit these women, exactly as the Thracians passed to the isle of Lesbos, where dwelt the Amazons. When the children of this union are weaned they send the boys to the fathers, but keep the girls. It is claimed that the women know of great subterraneans (caverns, vaults, or tunnels) where they hide themselves; so that if men try to visit them before the agreed time and attempt to use force to enter these tunnels, or adopt trickery and ruses, the women defend themselves with arrows, and they know how to shoot them with skill. That at least is what they say. I repeat it to you. (*First Decade: De Orbo Novo.*)

Columbus himself said, on 4th March, 1493, that these women-warriors of old Martinique covered themselves with brazen plates, and used bows and arrows of cane. "These Amazons have many of these plates."

Alfonso Ulloa, a companion of Columbus on the famous voyages, wrote in his *Historia del S. D. Fernando Colombo*, that the Admiral believed that the Indians (Caribs) told him of the Amazons of Matanino (Matrimonio, *sic*), or Martinique, because he "saw the spirit and strength these women displayed." Ulloa also makes a significant comment—not that he appreciated the significance!—of the female cults of lunar worship practised by these West Indian Amazons. (*Vide* p. 143 *supra*):

> Who related that the day was for (by) the Sun, and the night for (by) the Moon: whence these women told the time by the other stars, and when the Great Bear rose, or such a star set.

At Samaña, the rendezvous, on the north-eastern shores of San-Domingo-Hispaniola, of the buccaneers, about 170 years later, Columbus captured some warlike Caribs:

> One of them, coming before the Admiral naked as he was born from his mother's womb, said, in a loud voice, that he and the rest were Caribs, and that the gulf cut off Hispaniola from them. He said that the island of Matanino was peopled only with women to whom the Caribs went on certain days of the year..That the women sent the boys to their fathers to be brought up by them. . . .

Ulloa also says that when the Spaniards of Columbus went ashore in Cuadozupa (Guadalupe), they captured one of these Amazon fighting women who told "them all her history". It is a pity that this unique history does not seem to have been recorded! In the *Journals concerning the First and Last Voyages*, we read:

Enero, el dia 13, *de Domingo:* An Indian of Española told the Admiral that the island of Martinio was entirely peopled by women without men, and had much *twob* (gold or copper). The admiral intended to have taken some of these women home to Ferdinand and Isabella. He wanted to seize five or six of these Amazons—to whom, at a certain time of the year, men came from the island of Carib, some 10–12 leagues away. They kept only the girls of these unions. The men who had sexual intercourse with these Amazons were very fierce and cannibals, but not monsters or malformed. They are naked and wear their hair long as the women of Castile. All the other islands they range, pillaging all they can. They have bows and arrows of cane stems tipped with a small piece of wood. Fierce are they among people who are exceedingly cowardly. They are the men who lie with these women in the island of Martinio, where the women do no feminine work; but use bows and arrows of cane and wear plates of copper of which they have much.

Fernando Colombus says, in another place:

We anchored off the isle of Guadalupe and sent ashore a well-manned boat, but before they came to landing, abundance of women came out of the woods with bows and arrows and feathers, as if they would defend their island. For this, and because the sea ran high and was rough, those in the boat kept aloof, and sent off two Indian women we had taken in Hispaniola. These women went swimming to the beach. The other women, ashore, particularly asked about the Christians, and said if they wanted provisions in exchange for other things, they must go in their ships to the north side, where their husbands were, who would give them what they wanted.

Juan de Grijalva, off the "isle of Yucatan", in March, 1518, saw Cozumel island. Says an old unpublished manuscript, here translated for the first time:

A few days later, we sighted on a point of land a very beautiful tower that we were told by our Indian pilot was lived in by the women who lived without husbands. We thought they were descendants of the Amazons. There are also islands situated on the sides of this Coluacana which only women inhabit. Some think they live after the manner of the Amazons . . . but they that consider the matter more wisely think them to be virgins living in common together, and delighting in solitariness, as in ancient times the virgin vestals, consecrated to *Bona Dea*, used to do. At certain times in the year, men from the bordering islands visit them, not for purpose of procreating, but moved with pity to till their fields and dress their gardens, through which manuring the ground they may better live. Yet report goes that there are other islands, but of corrupt women, who cut the paps of their young girl children, that they may the better practise the art of shooting, and that men resort to them to beget children, and that these women do not keep the boy babies.

Old California, which means Lower, or Baja California, must, in some way as mysterious as the source of Francis Bacon's Atlantean *House of Salomon* in the South Seas, have supplied a Portuguese writer,

Joham or Vasco de Lobeira with a curious story, not altogether unfounded, as much later Lower Californian mountain and cliff discoveries of ancient coloured frescoes and petroglyphs showed, about a race of "Black Amazons". The old writer, drawn on by Garci-Ordoñez de Montalvo who, in 1510, wrote a rare romance, called *Esplandian*, based on Amadis de Gaula's famous epic, said:

> Know ye, that on the right hand of the Indies is an island called California, very near the terrestrial Paradise. It is peopled by black women without any male among them. They live much like the Amazons— valiant in body, fiery in heart. The island has the highest of cliffs and wildest of rocks in all the world. All these women's weapons are of gold. They ride wild beasts they have tamed. They live in caves very well carved for dwelling purposes. They have many ships in which they have sailed to other lands, where the men they captured they carried with them, thereafter putting them to death. . . . Sometimes, in peace, they have carnal relations with neighbouring antagonists and many became pregnant . . . (Follows the usual story of keeping female babies and killing the males). This, so far one knows, was to cow the males so that, few in number, these women could overrun and master their lands, keeping only those needed to save the race from dying out.

The romancer who wrote truer than he knew—for, as I hinted, in queer caves in Lower California are ancient frescoes of clothed men and women, of race unknown, which still await the examination of competent ethnologists—tells how these black Amazons trapped "griffons who abound in the rugged rocks":

> These women went out to take the young griffons, who had very thick hides. They bore them to their caves, reared them, and fed them with men captives and the male children these Black Amazons bore. The women were so cunning that the griffons never killed them! If any man entered this island, the griffons would seize him, bear him aloft flying through the air, and when angered, fail not to let him drop from a height.

Then the "pagans" assembled to go out with great fleets against the emperor of the Christians in Constantinople:

> The queen of California heard. She was great in body and beautiful, and in the flower of her age . . . She knew not what sort of people Christians were; for she had no news of other far lands. Having a desire to do great deeds, she ordered a great fleet to be built, put aboard her women with their gold weapons, and in a lighter barge placed behind network and thick wood cages 500 griffons, reared and fattened on men's flesh and sailed to meet the great men of the pagans. . . . (We are told how, over Turkey, the griffons, released from their cages, flew high in the air, until, far below, they saw from the air, a great army of people, whereon, being very hungry, they flew down and seized the fattest soldier in their talons, bore him off and golloped the long pig and his bacon!)

This yarn was written 25 years before Don Hernando Cortes landed in Aztec Mexico, where Amazons really were to be found. Cortes must have read this romance; for, in 1524, in a report to the emperor,

Charles V, in old Spain, Cortes calls California "an island" and by that name, and adduced native reports about it. And for many years later the old cartographers regarded California as an island or group of islands.

It was from the Aztecan Mexico of Montezuma that the next tidings of the warrior women of the New World reached the Court of the Holy Roman Emperor, and King of Spain, Carlos (Charles) V, in old Madrid. It came in the fourth letter from Hernando Cortes, Conquistador of Aztec Mexico, to the Emperor, and is dated 15th October, 1524:

> We hear of an island of only women, without men, and lying ten days distance from Colima. And many persons have gone there from that province and have seen them. I was also told that they were rich in pearls and gold. From time to time, men go to the island from the mainland, to wive with the women.

Colima[1] is on the western Pacific side of Mexico, which seems to rule out the West Indian islands; but from queer stories still current in Mexico to-day, one may suspect that the location of this "island" of Amazons was not in the isthmus of Tehuantepec.

Six years later, and some years before that mystical Emperor, Don Carlos V (who had wished that his empire be one on which the sun never set), suddenly decided to renounce the world and all its gauds and retire to the oak groves of Yuste, in Estremadura, where, they say, he assisted, one night in the nearby monastery, at the rites of his own funeral, there came to Spain the tidings that a gallant hidalgo was setting out on the trail of the gold, the pearls, and the Amazons. One day there arrived at the bar of San Lucar de Barrameda, near Cadiz, *en route* to Seville, a gallant caballero and hidalgo, who was the emissary of Don Nunno de Guzman. The caballero brought strange and romantic tidings from Don Nunno for the Emperor and King who already dominated most of Europe. It was a letter dated A.D. 1530:

> From Aztatlan (Mexico), thence ten days further, I shall go to find the Amazons, which some say dwell in an arm of the sea, and that they are very rich and reckoned by the people as Goddesses. *They are whiter than other women*. Bows they use, and arrows with targets. They have many and great towns. At a certain time they admit men to go with them, who bring up the males, as those of the female issue. From Omitlan, a Province of Mechuacan (Michoacan) of the Greater Spain, on the eighth day of July, 1530.

It is very significant, in view of what I hinted above, in my remark about modern rumours in Mexico City, that this letter was written on the very frontiers of that Isthmus of Tehuantepec, where, in this year of 1950, *dancing matriarchs* live deep in jungly mountains or wild

[1] Gonzalo de Sandoval told Cortes that he had been told that ten sunrises from Colima, there was a rich island of Amazon women, which, though they searched for it, they could not find. I judge that the name of Cuatlan, as it is called, means "place of women." (*De Herrera: Decada III*. Lib. III.)

recesses, and are seen of none, whether greaser or gringo! Who may say if these dancing matriarchs are not the direct descendants of old Mexico's Amazons of Cortes' day?[1]

The elusive island of Ciguatan of the Amazons seems to have been located in the Gulf of California, near the shores of the modern Mexican states of Sinaloa, or Sonora though Vedia surmised it might be Baja California. Capitán Gonzalo Fernandez de Oviedo y Valdes, "primer cronista del Nuevo Mundo", who wrote of the pacification of the province of Coliman, said to lie near Panuco, said that the Capitán-General Hernando Cortes was told that, at certain times, men went from the mainland to the island to lie with the women to make them pregnant. He added the usual story about the disposal of the children of these unions:

> and they say the island is 10 leagues from that province and that many of the men have seen it, and it is very rich in gold and pearls; but the story of the women no Christian has any faith in, though the Indians testify to its truth. . . . From Sanct Miguel de Neveri, in the Meta province, whose governor is Hieronimo Dortal, is the sea where that cacique lives, and it was where the governor and his people wintered. They reckon it is 150 and more leagues to the south. Here, the Christians came across many pueblos where the women were queens, or *cacicas* and absolute female rulers. They govern, and *not* their husbands. There is one, especially called *Orocomay* who is obeyed in the territory for more than 30 leagues around. She was very friendly to the Christians and was served only by women. And her town and society have no commerce with men, save when they are sent for and ordered to do something, or to go to war. The land of this queen is fertile and healthy with good food and sweet water. The climate is temperate.

In a chapter on the "Conquista of Nuevo Galicia" (north-west Mexico), de Oviedo y Valdes tells how Nuño de Guzman, warring on those coasts had news of women whom he shortly after called Amazons:

> Hearing of this, a *capitán*, Christoval de Oñate begged of the general Nuño de Guzman to allow him to pacify these Amazons and the general sent him to search for them. On the road he was very badly wounded in an Indian pueblo, called *Quinola*, who were aided by another pueblo, a league away, called *Quilla*. Most of his men also being badly hurt, he waited for the arrival of the governor. When the governor arrived, the *capitán maestre de campo*, Gonzalo Lopez, begged to go to the women's pueblo . . . and, by marches, he arrived five leagues from the pueblo of Ciguatan. Here he was overtaken by a message from the governor, who ordered him to wait; for the governor wished to see who were these women and what they were like. Next day, going his rounds of the camp, in sight of the women's town, he met, not far from it, a great number of the female species coming along the road, whom he supposed to be these

[1] As late as 1886, the Tehuantepec women were noted for their fairness and fine carriage. They were tall, and wore petticoats of ankle-length. Their gold and silver *uipils* were richly embroidered with bead-work, and they wore very pretty shoes on dainty feet. They were known to spend as much as £100 on dresses.—AUTHOR.

women. They wore white shifts (chemises) that reached to the feet, and were ruched (plaited) at the wrists and throat. In good order, Capitán Lopez removed to a little distance to make way for these women. But they all took such fright at the horses of the Spaniards, that they decided to come in peace, and they conducted the Spaniards to their pueblo, and gave them many good things to eat. . . .

This pueblo has up to 1,000 houses, well built with streets in very good order. The land is well settled and most fertile and pleasant. The women told the Spaniards that all the young men of the territory came to the town four months in each year to sleep with them, and that the women joined with them in temporary marriage for that time and no more, without the men troubling them to serve or gratify them in any other way. The women ordered the young men to go in the day into the town, or the countryside, to do whatever service the women wanted done, and that at night, they gave up to them their own persons and beds. And in all that time, the men tilled and cultivated the land, and sowed seed in vegetable gardens and cornfields and took and placed the produce in the houses where they were lodged. And when the time was up, these men all went away to their own countries. If the women are pregnant by them, they send the sons to the fathers to rear, or do with them as they please, after they are two-to-three months old; the girls they keep to bring up to increase their republic.

The Spaniards saw among these women turquoises and emeralds, and they told him they had these gems in many numbers and of good quality.

Nunno de Guzman called them Amazons in his report to Cortes, and others told me that the name Ciguatan meant *town of women* . . .

Don Fernando de Oviedo was plainly mystified by this story, and, in the year 1547, when he met de Guzman at the "Court of his Majesty in Madrid", questioned him and was told, as he says:

because he is a good caballero and one ought to believe him, that it was a hoax, and that these women are not Amazons, because, on his return to their village, he met them with their husbands in their houses. I said it might be that the women were husbandless when their husbands were away. So we said and parted.

Don Enrique de Vedia cites the letter that Cortes wrote to the King and Emperor in old Spain. (Carta Quarta de Don Fernando Cortes governador y capitán general por su Majestad en la Nueva, España del Mar Oceano al muy alto y muy potentisimo, invictisimo Señor Don Carlos, Emperador, siempre augusto y Rey de España nuestro Señor.) The *Carta* is dated:

De la gran ciudad de Temixtitlan, desta Nueva España, 15 dias del mes de octubre, de 1524 (three years after the Conquest) . . .

And likewise I had an account of the Lords of the province of Ciguatau, of an island of women without men, to whom men go at certain times from the mainland to have carnal copulation with these women that many of the Spaniards have been there and seen these things. They report to me, also, that it is very rich in pearls and gold. I shall labour in readiness to know the truth and send your Majesty a longer report on it.

Writing about 1750, de Vedia[1] said that the abundance of pearls is obvious, "also, the gold . . . Mines have recently been found of promising richness, of which news has been given me by the most illustrious Señor Don Josef Valdes, who has come from the Peninsula of California at cost of many fatigues . . . and he has sent to our actual excellency, el virrey Marquis de Croix, fine pearls and gems, and ore from a gold mine. The gold is of many carats."

It is Icazbalceta who gives the original narrative of Nunno de Guzman, which narrative—the *Tercera Relación*—is by an anonymous writer who was a partisan and adherent of de Guzman, a *compañero* and not a common soldier. He may have directed the story to the second Audiencia. "I suspect," adds Icazbalceta, "that the *Quarta Relación* had for author Cristobal Flores, Persona Principal y Regidor of Mexico."

This Third *Relación* tells us:

From Piatztla, Nunno de Guzman sent Capitán Christobal de Oñate to find the road. He was sent messengers following up his camp; for he and the (main) army were for eight days, each day, meeting with pueblos and men of war. These pueblos, beyond Piatztla, have houses close together with lofty roofs of straw. At the last of these pueblos, de Oñate came on one that is called Bayla, and from there we went to another, passing one they called Rinconado. (That is, a corner formed by two squares, or streets.—AUTHOR.) Here our army rested four to five days, and we had news we were very near Ciguatan. It came from a cavalier who brought news of a very great thing, though he did not go there. We sent back to the governor and the *maesse de campo* for a reinforcement of 35 horses and to Samaniego for 25 more. There were many Indian pueblos near. Arriving at the Rio de Ciguatan, we came on eight small but fine pueblos; though we ought to call some large, some small. In them were met some men of war and many women, very different from those seen up to then. They were better attired. The men were few, but furnished as warriors with plumes, bows and arrows, and clubs. They had come from neighbouring pueblos to defend the women Amazons. Many of these women were captured . . .

Another of the Spanish caballeros, Garcia del Pilar, tells us that: "We pacified none of the warlike pueblos, and when we arrived at the pueblo de Ciguatan, said to be all women, we had no linguists who understood their tongue well, and it was not to be comprehended if the women lived alone without husbands . . . except that they had very few men and all (*sic*) women".

The anonymous writer of the *Tercera* (Third) *Relación* says, however:

Afterwards, by linguists, we were told that these women had come by sea, and in ancient times kept such a way of life among themselves that they had no husbands, nor permitted marital relations among themselves before a certain time, when there came men from bordering lands to lie

---

[1] De Vedia thought that Ciguatan was a peninsula, not an island, and identified it with Baja California, which is very unlikely.—AUTHOR.

with them and make them pregnant, and if they had girls they remained with them, and if they bore boys they did not kill them, but reared them till ten years, more or less, when they gave them to their fathers. No more could be known of these secrets, because our linguists were not very expert. . . .

The method of disposing of the children conflicts with another version in these documents, which says:

The Amazons buried the boy babies alive and brought up the daughters.

Maybe this apparent conflict of testimony arises from the little knowledge the interpreters had of the women's tongue.

The Third *Relación* adds that the Spaniards came to another pueblo where "they came out to us in peace and told us their chief was a woman whose people were mostly *all blonde* and fair (*era rubia*)." This passage purports that these Mexican Amazons were *white women*.

At this place, a note on the margin of the manuscripts says:

In one of these pueblos, a foot was cut off a servant (or I cut off a foot of a servant), because he gave a knife-thrust to another.

The narrative proceeds:

We were detained in this pueblo for 27 days; because of Passion Week being near and we could find none to give us news of great Indian towns in the middle of the country to the west; but all said the mountains were so craggy and steep they could not pass over them. They also told us that by the coasts of the South Seas (the Pacific: *costa del Sur*), one could go to Ciguatan, and that there were many rich towns, and we determined to cross to the South Sea. . . . Here, in the pueblo of Chiametla, they gave us much news of the Amazons, that they call Ciguatan, and of the much gold and silver and gems near their country.

Don Nuño de Guzman now held a council of war in his tent and proposed to his captains that they march manfully to the north, where he had news were men so warlike that even the women wielded arms with a dexterity equal to that of the men. The captains hesitated, but some of the hardy infanteria, who had seen none of the promised gold on this expedition to conquer Nuevo Galicia, went north to the sierra of Michoacan. All they found were wild highland Indians whose shirt—cutty at that!—if stripped, would have afforded only a horde of starving fleas avid to banquet on new Castilian blood! The captains, frustrated in entering the promised land of Mexican Amazonas, of gold and fair white women, suggested that de Guzman might now talk of the best way to get back to Mexico City . . . And there we must leave the mystery of the Amazons of New Spain!

Fernando Gonzalo de Oviedo, in his *Historia General de las Indias*, tells of the Amazons of old Panama, though they were living with husbands:

These are noblewomen and they bear up their flaccid teats with bars of gold, a span long. For they greatly dispraise loose and hanging teats. The gold is well wrought and some of the bars weigh 200 castellans or

Ducats of gold. Through holes at each end of the gold-bar cords were threaded, and passed over the shoulders and under the armholes . . . Some of these women go to battle with their husbands, and when they themselves are regents in any provinces and execute the office of general captains, they cause themselves to be borne into battle on men's backs, in the manner of caciques.

There were Amazonian women in Nueva Granada (Colombia, South America), and Antonio de Herrera tells how the conquistadores under Don Pedro de Heredia met one, in the year 1532.

He pacified that part of the country, and that behind Cartagena, though with great labour and cunning, and there was a woman that, before they could take her, being about 18 years of age, slew with her bow and arrow eight Spanish soldiers.

Truly, a female more deadly even than ten old Spanish males!

The odd way in which things move in cycles and events are strangely connected, though happening in places remote from each other, is here shown in the fact that, only four years before Don Nunno wrote his letter to Carlos V, a Portuguese monk had brought news to Carlos's neighbour, the King of Portugal, of the existence of a race of Amazons, with much gold, in Abyssinia, the land of Prester Johannes, and the Queen of Sheba. (No, Mr. Sceptic, the one did *not* inspire the other, as we shall soon see!)

Twelve years passed, and then the stamping and neighing of horses and the roar of old cannon resounded in the plazas of old Cuzco, where the bearded Castilians, under Don Francisco Pizarro, the bandit-conquistador, were bringing to ruin the empire of the sun of the Incas of old Perú. Once more contact was made with the South American Amazons, and this time it was war and nearly extermination —for Castilian hidalgos and infanteria and monks, *not* the warrior-women! It came about in this way: Don Marquis Pizarro sent his brother, Gonzalo, from Quito, the northern part of the empire of Perú, in modern Ecuador, to find a region where the precious spice cinnamon grew. This rich region, behind the cordilleras and the eastern montaña, it was hoped, would put in the shade the rich East Indian Islands of spices which the Portuguese were keeping to themselves. It lay beyond the eastern bounds of the empire of Perú.

The expedition was away for three years in a land where, as Colonel P. H. Fawcett, D.S.O., the British explorer found, when he was delimiting the frontiers in 1911, the conditions are appalling, both as to climate and commissariat. Even the hardy and valiant Spanish conquistadores, who accomplished feats of endurance that few or none of our better equipped moderns can equal, let alone surpass, to-day, in our scientific age of mechanism, returned with looks of ghosts risen from a morgue, walking in the daylight, like corpses with earth-spoiled shrouds flapping on their emaciated carcases!

⚓ Don Marquis Francisco Pizarro ordered his brother Gonzalo to conquer this unknown land of the Cinnamon or Canella. Gonzalo started out from Quito with 340 Spanish *infanteria,* about half of them *caballeros* on horse-back, and 4,000 Indians, with arms and supplies, iron, hatchets, knives, ropes, cords of hemp, a herd of 4,000 swine, and a flock of llamas, who carried the baggage over the ranges. They quitted Quito on Christmas Day, 1539, and had soon passed beyond the bounds of the ancient Inca empire. Nor was it long before they met opposition. In the land of the Quijos, the warlike Indians sallied out against them in force; but seeing the multitude of men mounted on strange beasts—horses—the Indians vanished and were seen no more. Then they met their worst foe: rain, rain in torrents crashing on the high *paramos* and the passes. The earth shook with quakes, the ground opened up, and the Spanish infantry endured fifty days of frozen hell and misery as they ascended the high passes over the snowy cordilleras of the Andes.

So cold was the snow, and so thick the drifts, that the lightly-clad Indians were, many of them, frozen to death. The Spaniards grew so sickened of the daily misery that, to get clear of this inhospitable mountain-territory, they rode ahead on their horses and left behind them the swine and provisions. In this they made a serious miscalculation; for this was and is still, to-day, no country on which an army, or sizable expedition may live. They expected to find an Indian village with food; but merely entered a bleak *paramo,* or upland moors, and still thirty leagues from Quito, found themselves on the skirts of a volcano, Zumague or Sumaco. Here, they got some food. Then the rain started again, and for two months it fell, day and night, till their clothes rotted off them. They found cinnamon growing wild in the forests, with plenty of even wilder Indians around, naked as they were born and "savager" than catamounts robbed of their whelps. Out of the rainy season, the land around turned hot, very hot.

Gonzalo cast around to find a road; but here were no old Inca paved roads with the *chasquis* (post-runners) and stone guest-houses of the old Empire. Overburdened with heavy armour and hauberks and morions, the Castilian *infanteria* had to set to and hack a way by main force through the dense wood and undergrowth. Their hatchets were soon badly blunted. They hired or conscripted guides, but these Indians proved treacherous and deliberately led the Spaniards into such inhospitable country that they were driven to gather wild fruits and grub up roots and herbs to stave off the pangs of hunger.

Coming to a wild river-gorge, cleft between walls of towering rock, the Spaniards were almost dazed by the roar of a tremendous cataract. Below this, they attempted to span the *cañon* with a bridge. But the wild Indians who had known no conqueror, sallied out and gave fierce battle, till the conquistadores were forced to use their arquebuses. The flash and roar of the gunpowder startled the savages and they took to their heels with screams of fright, back into the dense forest beyond the gorge and river. With great difficulty, a timber bridge was thrown across the raging torrents, but the height above the river-bed, cluttered with immense boulders, was so great, that the first Spaniard to cross, who glanced down, turned dizzy and plunged to his death in the boiling waters. But, somehow, men and horses passed over the crazy bridge. Once across, Gonzalo's army met with a blank wall of forest—a regular *inferno verde*, or green hell though which no way could be found. All paths seemed to lead right into swamps and lagoons. There was only one thing to do, and none but hardy and valiant Spanish conquistadores would have attempted it, in this wild land between the giant cordilleras.

Gonzalo ordered the men to cut down timber in the woods, while he set to and made a forge for nail-making. Fuel was got with great difficulty, by making charcoal. The plan was to build a barquentine. Having built the keel and hull, they were faced with the problem of caulking the seams to make the ship watertight. All this time the accursèd rain fell in torrents, day and night. The conquistadores stripped themselves to the buff, using the cotton of their shirts to make oakum for caulking. They had gathered gold on the journey, and this, to the amount of 100,000 dollars, they loaded into the ship, along with many fine emeralds, as well as the forge used to make nails for the ship.

Then, down one of the headwater tributaries, which really led into the mighty Amazon, many months away, sailed the conquistadores. In fact they had to row most of the passage, so turbulent was the current. It surprised them that they should have to force a way against a powerful current, so strong that soldiers had to wade ashore, and with hatchets hew out a tow-path along which, by might and main, they hauled the ship. The Spaniards ashore kept pace with the ship when the current eased up, and this lasted for two long months. One day they surprised Indians in the woods. These Indians signed that "*oro, mucho oro*", lay ahead.

The sound of the word *gold* made almost anyone of these land-pirates of Castilian and Estremaduran soldiers willing to cut his mother's throat and rape his nearest female relatives, provided he could but get at the gold! Then, they were told, they would meet the confluence of a larger river, which may have been the Napo, or the Coca.

At this point the trail of one of the leaders of the amazing expedition was destined to lead him straight to the country of the mighty, white woman warriors, the white and beautiful Amazons! He was Don Francisco de Orellana, lieutenant of Gonzalo Pizarro who, seeing how famished the men were, ordered Orellana to go ahead in the barquentine, with fifty soldiers, to the junction with the Napo, and load her with food, and return. The Napo lay eighty leagues away, and when Orellana reached it, he found no food. Now, deciding it was a case of every man to shift for himself, he made the excuse that so strong a current would take him a year to reach back to where he had left the starving soldiers and Gonzalo Pizarro. He said this, though he had taken only three days to descend it, as the monk Carvajal remarked.

Orellana held a perfunctory council with his officers and some monks, though he really paid small heed to their views. Three of the soldiers refused to go on and leave their comrades in the lurch, and a young cavalier-hidalgo, Don Hernan Sanchez de Vargas, of Badajos, in old Spain, and the missioner-monk, Fray Gaspar de Carvajal, opposed the plan. But Orellana talked and coaxed them into a reluctant consent, and, leaving de Vargas and the three loyalist soldiers marooned on the banks of the Rio Napo, sailed down the river on the most extraordinary voyage that was ever undertaken in any age of South American exploration. It is not even matched to-day, in the age of aeroplanes and airships and internal-combustion-engined boats.

Meantime, eighty leagues away, Gonzalo Pizarro made a dozen canoes and *balsas*—the reed boats of old Perú and like that in which Moses was hidden in the bulrushes along the old Nile of Pharaoh's Egypt. Putting his starving and weakened men aboard them, he came down the river, and at the end of two terrible months of hardship and misery and want, reached the junction with the Napo to find that de Orellana had deserted his comrades. On the bank, de Vargas with three soldiers greeted them. They still had eighty horses out of the 150 brought from Quito, and they employed 1,000 Indians to forage around in the dense woods for wild fruits, nuts, herbs, snakes and frogs—anything they could get their famished teeth into and that was not too poisonous!

Four hundred long leagues away lay Quito. And now Gonzalo and the gallant conquistadores began a trek which must be one of the most appalling in even the chequered annals of South American exploration. Gonzalo and his men quitted the river, and hacked a way through the thick and far-spreading woods. They plied axes and bills, and oft-times found themselves bogged to the waists and necks in lagoons and stinking marshes, with dangers of snake-bites, and from reptile's jaws. But they had to eat, and wild fruits and nuts were not sustaining enough for their herculean labours, hacking a path through the forests on the frontiers of modern Ecuador's Oriente. The horses and Spanish greyhounds they had with them, one by one went into the pot. Next, their hunting mastiffs took the same path to the starving belly. They were even *driven to eat their dead comrades*!

Four thousand Indians died of hunger, and two hundred and more Spaniards. At last, eighty of the conquistadores won through to a more open country with game, not far from Quito, where in true, Spanish Catholic fashion, they fell on the earth, kissed it, and praised God, the Saints and the Virgin. When Gonzalo and his eighty comrades, all that were left of a large expedition, at long length staggered into the plaza of Quito, their faces were burnt black as coal from exposure to the sun, their matted locks hung down to their shoulders.

Yea, said an old Spanish chronicler, "so emaciated were their bodies with famine, that, verily, thou mightest have supposed that a charnel-house had given up its dead!"

Meantime, what had been happening to the "traitor-conquistador", Don Francisco de Orellana, he whom Gonzalo and others home in Spain certainly deemed no *caballero*, or "parfait gentle knighte"?

He and his men embarked on a voyage lasting eight months, which would take them right to the south Atlantic, 1,800 old Spanish leagues down the world's longest and mightiest river! They were to find, as I have myself, in South America, that the race of Amazon women warriors were no myth.

I was, not long before World War No. 2, in the old Inca city of Quito, Ecuador, at the foot of the volcanoes of the mighty cordilleras of the Andes. I had gone there, commissioned by a well-known New York magazine publisher to make researches on the spot, into the hidden history of the lost treasures of the last of the Incas, Atahualpha, the murdered emperor, of Perú. Quito is probably the place to which the Inca Peruvians took his body after he had been assassinated by the bandits of the conquistadorian soldiery—for that is what they were. One day, in a colonial Spanish house of a lonely pueblo outside Quito, I came on a very old Spanish manuscript, so brown and mottled with age, and so damaged by the teeth of insects, and perished with neglect, that it is a wonder that it still survives. Even so, pages were missing and mutilated.

The writer must have been a Spanish monk and missioner who lived in the days of the Pizarros and Almagro. About the year 1541, he wrote:

> We were but six leagues from Quito, when we met an *Indió* who told us that Peruvians in that town knew much of the celebrated Amazon woman warriors of the Americas. "Much news, *señores*," he said, "hath come to Quito from the unknown wilds that lie beyond the cordilleras of these mighty Andes. There have been Inca Indians of Quito who have started out, as boys, to reach the country of these terrible women; but whoever hath gone down-stream in his youth, hath never returned from their land, till he be in extreme old age. It is so very far away."

As my inquiries progressed, I was forced to the conclusion that, far from the Amazons being myths—as have been considered Sir Walter Raleigh's land of golden Manoa, and the conquistadores' *ciudad del Gran Paytiti* of gold, where the last of the Incas took refuge in walled cities of stone—the women were living realities. They were certainly no travellers' tales of mendacious, bragging, old Spanish rufflers who tried to magnify the difficulties of the unknown land and explain and justify their own failure to find the tons of gold and jewels. It seemed crystal-clear to me that the Amazons of South America, in whom Sir Walter Raleigh believed, were assuredly in very vigorous and martial existence as late as the end of the seventeenth century of our own era.

The story is unfamiliar, and in fact quite unknown to English-speaking readers, perhaps because the old Spanish manuscripts have not been properly translated into English. I here give extracts from one of the best manuscripts whose narrator was the friar, Fray Gaspar de Carvajal, priest of the Dominican order of Santo Domingo de Guzman. He, in 1541–42, exactly 409 years ago, was eye-witness of the encounter with the valiant women warriors and nearly lost his life, as he certainly lost one eye in the battle. (In my books, I have had reason to say hard things of this Dominican order; so here is the reverse of the arras.)

After de Orellana left Gonzalo Pizarro in the lurch, his company, in the barquentine, sailed down the Napo, till they entered the Rio Orellana, which was the name the Don gave to what was later named the Amazon. About where the Rio Negro joins the main Amazon stream, Orellana captured an Indian who warned them to beware of the Amazons (or *coniapayaras*), fighting-women to whom the land round about belonged. Higher up the river, friendly Indians, who had given the Castilian *expedicionaras* food, had uttered the same warning. Farther down, they saw a large village with Indian men's heads nailed to posts, which Orellana called *Los Picotas* (gibbets). Paved roads issued from this village, with many fruit trees planted on either side. One day, they caught an intelligent Indian woman in the forest who said there were, in the interior, *many white men with beards like the Spaniards.*

These bearded men the Spaniards naturally took to be men of a lost expedition of El Dorado hunters, vanished in the interior, and headed by either Diego de Ordas, or Alonzo de Herreras. Actually, the bearded men were probably descendants of the lost Atlantean white race of old Brazil, or maybe the men of mysterious Gran Paytiti. The Indian woman also spoke of two white women who had been brought down the river by an Indian chief. The Castilians were soon to know what and who were these two white women! They were now approaching the confluence of the Rio Trombetas with the Amazon.

Now, let Father Carvajal take up the strange story which I have for the first time translated from the Spanish:

In the evening of Monday, January 8, 1541, while we were gathering and eating roots and fruits in the forests, our captain, Don Francisco de Orellana, was the first among us to hear the sound of distant drums. On the Monday following, we left there, ever passing through very large villages, and provinces, furnishing us with food, the best we could obtain, when we were in need. This day, we landed in a middling port, where the people expected us. In this pueblo was a very great plaza, and in the middle of it, a great plank (*tablón*[1] or platform) of ten feet square, designed and wrought in relief, a walled city being near by, with a door.

---

[1] This *tablón* was said by the Indians to be a model of one of the pueblos, or towns, of the Amazons.

In the gateway (door) were two very high towers, with lofty summits, and windows. Each tower had a door, one opposite the other, and in each door were two columns. All this work rested on two very ferocious lions, that gazed with their heads turned backwards, as though shy of each other. These lions held up in their arms and joined all this work.

In the middle of this was a spacious plaza, circular, and in.the centre, was a hole (*agujero*), whence they poured out (drank, or offered as a libation) *chicha* to the sun. It is a wine they have, and the sun they hold and worship for God. Indeed, the building was a great spectacle, to look at, and the Captain and all our men were astounded at so great a wonder.

The Spaniards captured an Indian, who was walking on the bank of the river, in the forest.

Said de Orellana: "What doth this raised pueblo mean? To whose memory is it?"

The Indian: "All this land is subject to and taxed by the Amazons. We serve them as vassals, and pay them no other tribute than feathers and plumage of parrots and macaws, for lining the ceilings of their temple-buildings. The pueblos these woman have, have similar edifices, and they worship the memorial as the symbol and insignia of their queen, who is the ruler over all the territory of these women."

In a house in the same plaza, the monk noted vestments of vari-coloured feathers, recalling the gorgeous quetzal-feather cloaks of the Aztecs of Montezuma's day. The Indians wore them when dancing in a *fiesta*, or rejoicing in front of the platform in rites where sacrifices were offered.

They went on down the river and passed another pueblo with a like platform and had to shoot with bows and arquebuses against hostile Indians, standing behind walls.

Now came a Homeric battle wherein the Castilians, hidalgos and soldiers, were to experience the valour of the formidable Amazons. From far and near thousands of Indians had gathered to oppose the advance of the Spaniards.

There was in the middle of that pueblo a very great number of *Indiós*, making a large squadron, and the Captain ordered the bergantines to land and look for food. And as we approached the land the Indians made ready to defend their town. They showered arrows on us in a regular rain. But our arquebusiers and crossbowmen were not idle. They fired and killed many; but still the Indians did not recoil. With all the damage they suffered from us they came at us, some fighting, others dancing, and here, we had nearly all been lost for they had so many arrows that our comrades had enough to do to defend themselves and were not able to continue working the sweeps. We suffered so much damage before we jumped ashore, that the Indians had laid low a fifth of the men in one ship, and they gave me such a blow on the side, that had it not been for my robes (*habitos*) it would have laid me low. Seeing the danger we ran, the Captain began to animate the rowers and hasten the oars that were trying to get ashore. So, although with difficulty and labour, we reached the banks and succeeded in getting ashore, and our comrades stood up in water that reached to their chests: here was a great and dangerous battle, for the Indians were fighting pell-mell in the midst of our Spaniards, who defended themselves with such liveliness that it was a marvellous thing to behold.

The fighting lasted more than an hour, but the Indians did not lose heart before it appeared they were vanquished. Although they saw many of their men lying dead, they rushed to the very front of the fight, and if they retreated, did so only to turn round and come at us again with fury.

It was at this stage of the battle, that the amazed conquistadores who, I again emphasize, were of Europe's finest fighting-stock, actually some of the best infantry in the sixteenth century, rubbed their eyes.

What was the reason for this determined fight, as of a lost legion?

Right in the van of the Indians, and fighting at their very head were *twelve tall, white, handsome nude women*, not a stitch covering even their private parts, their long dark hair plaited and twisted over their heads, robust in figure, a wisp of cloth on their heads (says one manuscript), bows in their hands! They fought like devils, these white women soldiers! Moreover, they had clearly anticipated, four hundred and more years ago in the unknown wilds of South America's forest and rivers, the most modern doctrine of all general staffs and general-issimos in twentieth-century Europe and Asia: the enforcement of the death penalty against any soldier deserting in face of the enemy:

> It is known that the Indians are subject and tributaries of the Amazons, and when they heard of our coming, they sent to seek aid, and there came ten or twelve of the women Amazons, fighting in the van as captains, and with such valour (*animosamente*) that the Indians dared not turn their backs to our soldiers, or the women slew them with clubs (*palos*), and that was the cause that the Indians defended themselves so obstinately.

Carvajal then described the Amazons in the terms given by me above:

> These women go about without any draperies hiding their private parts. They are nude, and white and robust, and with bow and arrows in their hands, they are as good as ten Indians in battle (*haciendo tanta guerra como diez indios*). In truth, one of these women, fighting with her hand shot off by one of the brigantines, and others, appeared to our brigantines like a porcupine. The chief of the Indians, their vassals in this country had sent messengers overland to the queen of the Amazons, Conori, for help against us, which she at once gave.

The conquistadores had dropped right into a hornets' nest, the "queens" being also fighters! The country all round was being roused. Allies were pouring in to the aid of the Amazon-led Indians; so, writes Carvajal:

> Our Lord, for our purpose and the conflict was pleased to give us strength and animation and our *compañeros* killed seven or eight of the Amazons, that we saw, for which reason the Indians were dismayed,

conquered and routed, with great damage to their persons; and as there came from other pueblos many reinforcements, who recoiled, at first, yet, as they came on again, our Captain ordered that in great haste the men re-embark in the ships; for he did not wish to risk the lives of all. And so our men went back to the bergantines (or brigantines), not without great anxiety (*no sin zozobra*); for again the Indians assembled to battle, and more; many canoes in fleets came by the water, and so we went down the river, and forsook the land.

Yes, the Dons, the hidalgos, and *mis compañeros*, with the monks, were decidedly lucky to have got out of so tight a corner as well as they did! Even so, Fray Carvajal was wounded in the eye with an arrow, at a village where the conquistadores were forced to land for food. He, indeed, on this voyage, lost the sight of one eye, poor man.

After they had quitted this land of the vassals of the *coniapayaras*, Orellana, passing down the Amazon, was so harassed by the constant flight of arrows from land and water that he was forced to order his men to make defensive cloths and hang them up on the decks to ward off the missiles. In places where the bergantines passed, embattled Indians were urged on by sorcerers who were accompanied by men playing a sort of jew's harp to encourage the warriors.

Nor were their troubles over:

> We had travelled since we left Gonzalo Pizarro, 1,400 leagues, more or less, and we knew not how far we still were from the sea (that is, the equatorial Atlantic). A few days later, we captured, near the river, an Indian trumpeter, about 30 years old, who was walking in the forest. He had dwelt among the people, and, after his capture, our Captain, who took him along, questioned him and he told us many things about the land in the interior.[1]

Antonio de Herrera, the Spanish historiographer of the Indies, writing in his sixteenth Decade of the *Historia general de las Indias occidentales*, comments, here, that the Indians' stories were always doubtful, and that it seems that de Orellana could hardly have made, in such few days, so correct and copious a vocabulary as to be able to indicate the minute details given by this Indian:

but each reader may believe as much as he likes.

I will again let Father Carvajal take up his own extraordinary story; and I ask to be forgiven by my patient reader for repeating that this is the first time his story has appeared in English.

He says the Indian was a very intelligent man of experience.

> Our captain asked him who were the women that had come to the aid of the Indians and given us battle?
> *The Indian:* "They are women living in the interior seven[1] days journey from the bank of the river. The Indian chief, Quenyuc (Couynco) being

---

[1] The manuscripts of Carvajal's story slightly vary. Some, I have seen, say the distance was 1,004 leagues. Others of the Carvajal manuscripts say four or five days.—AUTHOR.

one of their vassals. The women had come to guard the banks of the river."

Our Captain: "Are these women married?"

The Indian: "No."

Our Captain: "How do they live, then?"

The Indian: "As I say, they live in the interior. I have been to their land many times. I have seen their dwellings, and their way of life. As their vassal, I went to carry to them the tribute when my chief ordered me to go."

Our Captain: "Are these women numerous?"

The Indian: "Yes, I know 70 of their pueblos. I counted them. They were ahead of the place where we then lay. I have been in some of their pueblos."

Our Captain: "Are their towns of straw (*paja*)?"

The Indian: "No; they are of stone, with doors; and from one town (*pueblo*) to another there go roads enclosed (*ceriados*) fenced in one part and another, and, at intervals, guarded; so that none can pass unless he pays dues." (*N.B.*—In the manuscripts of Carvajal's story there are important variations; but the essentials are more or less the same.— AUTHOR.)

Our Captain: "Do these women breed children."

The Indian: "Yes."

Our Captain: "How is this? If they are not married, and men do not live with them, how are they impregnated?"

The Indian: "These *Indias* (*sic*) have intercourse with other Indiós at certain times, when there comes on them the natural desire to have sexual congress. They, then, join in large bands of women soldiers and go to make war on a great chief that holds his land next to theirs, and by force they carry off the men warriors to their own country, and cohabit with them as long as their desire lasts. Afterwards, as soon as they are pregnant, they send the men away back to their own country, doing them no other evil. Later, when they give birth, if the baby is a boy they kill him and send the body to the fathers. If it be a girl, they bring her up with great solemnity, and instruct her in the arts of war. Over all these women is a *señora* (queen), who subjects and holds all the rest under her hand and jurisdiction. This *señora* is called *Conori*.[1] The women have great riches in gold and silver, and all the principal *señoras* have no other table-vessels (*servicio*) than of gold and silver. The rest, the plebeian women, used vessels of wood, except when the vessels are used for cooking, or on the fire, when they are of earthenware. In the beginning, in the principal city in which the queen resides there are five very great houses, that were temples and buildings, dedicated to the Sun, which they call *caranain*. And in these houses, kept within, from above the ground to the middle position, there are, in heavy frames, under ceilinged roofs, paintings of different colours. In these houses are many idols of gold and silver, shaped in the form of women, and many vessels of gold and silver, for the serving of the Sun. The women go clothed in very fine wool, for in that country are many sheep of Perú." (*N.B.*—Either llamas, or vicuñas. The old Spanish chroniclers, called them *ovejes*, and

[1] It is remarkable that Raleigh when in Guiana, called the Amazons *Canuri*! It is possible that a part of the Amazons subsequently migrated to Guiana from where they fought the conquistadores, in 1542.

ovejas, or sheep, in the pre-conquest age of South America, were the property of men of riches or rank, only.—AUTHOR.) "The Amazon women's clothing is" (went on the Indian) "a narrow-waisted, woollen blanket from the breast downwards, put on from above, and other things with mantles clasped, or buckled (*abrochadas*) with cords in front. . . . They wear their hair long, in their own country, and crown it with coronets of gold as wide as two fingers, and enamelled in colours."

Then the Indian described animals he had seen in the Amazons' country, one of which looks very much like an unknown type, and not the llama, as modern South American (Spanish) writers have assumed. The llama, indeed, could hardly (by this forest Indian) have been described to the Spaniards, fresh from Perú, as "otros animales los cuales no supimos entender" (animals of which we had never heard):

> In the women's country there are camels (*camellos*) which carry burdens, and other animals which we have never heard of, that are the size of a horse, and that have their hair as long as the distance between the tip of the thumb and forefinger outstretched, and cleft feet, and that they keep them tied up, as they have so few of them. They have lakes of salt water, and in that country they have salt. He said they have an order at sunset that no male Indian may remain in any of their cities, but must depart outside and go to his own lands; but he said that many provinces of Indians bordering their country are subject to them and pay them tribute and serve them, and they make war on others, and especially with those we have already spoken of, and to fetch them to their town and have sexual intercourse with them. The women are very tall in body and white, and big, and many in number. All that is here said he had seen many times as a man that came and went each day, there.

Carvajal here comments, that, six leagues from Quito, he (the monk) and the Spaniards had heard even more about the Amazons. The women were very well known there by report, and to see them there came many Indians who went down the river, 1,400 leagues, and:

> as they told us, the Indians that had gone to the land of these women went down the river young men (*muchachos*) and returned old men (*viejos*). The country is said to be cold and there is very little firewood (*lena*), but very much of all sorts of food. Also, he said many other things, and each day discovered more; for he is an Indian of much intelligence and considerable understanding, and so are all the rest of that land.

The good monk was clearly not labouring under any illusion, or deluding himself as to the reception his story would obtain from sceptics at home, and the learned whose ideas are bounded by the four walls of a library and who think that, because a thing sounds extraordinary, it must, therefore, be untrue and the narrator an ancestor of Baron von Munchausen, bearded, John (de Mandeville) of Burgundy, or Louis de Rougemont. Here is his *envoi*:

> *Yo, Fray Gaspar de Carvajal, el menor de los religiosos de le orden de nuestro religioso, Padre Santo Domingo* (minor of the order of monks of our

religious house of Santo Domingo) have endeavoured to record in this little work our adventures on land and sea (*camino y navigación*), and to speak and proclaim the truth to all from all; and withal to take away the occasion from many who may endeavour to insinuate that the story of our wanderings is the contrary of what we have suffered and seen: it is the truth in all that I have here written and told; and as over-abundance engenders satiety, so I have here written but briefly and superficially (*superficial y sumariamente*) all that was undergone by the Captain Francisco de Orellana and by the *hidalgos*, and by their company and their *compañeros*, who, with him, went forth from the camp of Gonzalo Pizarro, brother of Don Francisco Pizarro, *Marqués y Gobernador de Peru*.

     Sea Dios loado.
     Amén.

Home in far-away Madrid, old Spain, the Emperor Charles (Carlos) V, and the Court, with the Renaissance spirit moving all souls, were so delighted with the story of these valiant, Castilian and Estremaduran conquistadores who had done an amazing journey of 1,800 leagues in 8 months, right across equatorial and tropical South America, from the South Pacific and the Andean cordilleras to the Atlantic, that de Orellana was made governor of the new land, which he was allowed to join with Nueva Galicia (Venezuela). (That he had deserted his commander, Gonzalo Pizarro was ignored.) He then set to, formed a new expedition and recruited 400 Spaniards, many of them hidalgos, and, in four ships sailed from San Lucar de Barrameda, the sixteenth-century port, 18 miles from Cadiz.

Alas, Fate turned unkind! The brave may *deserve*, but, in our life, he does not necessarily get the fair and fickle, lady Luck. On the voyage to the Canaries, he lost one ship and more than 100 men, and when he arrived at the embouchure of the Marañon, the older native, South American name of the mighty Amazon, he had two ships and less than half the men he had started out with from San Lucar. He managed to force a passage against the current for about 100 leagues; then stopped to build a brigantine, from the remains of his second ship. Here, fifty-seven of the *compañeros* died of a cause—noticed sadly frequently in this book—too well-known to Spain in every age: *hambre*, hunger. Thirty leagues farther on, he lost the last of the ships that had come out from Spain. Others of the valiant *expedicionarias* died, and here, too, died the brave de Orellana, worn out by fatigue and so many calamities. He was buried in the suburbs of Montealioni, Brazil, and his widow and the survivors made back for the sea and the Isla Margarita.

Detractors soon slunk by and yapped at the heels of de Orellana and the monk, Carvajal. They were accused, with some show of plausibility, of spreading stories of the marvellous to cover up the desertion of Gonzalo Pizarro. Lopez de Gomara y Herrera roundly and unjustly called the monk a liar (*mentirosa*). Gomara also took the line that other more modern writers in South American states have taken long since his day: that in so hot a country as equatorial and sub-tropical South America, it was, *a priori*, unlikely that women would or could live without husbands. All knew, he said, that women in South America were so lustful. Antonio de Herrera complained that de Orellana ought *not* to have given the name Amazon to the women; because, said he, in South America ("in the Indias"), it is no new thing for women to fight and shoot arrows, as was seen in some islands of the Barlovento (Windward archipelago), and Cartagena, and their neighbourhood, where they showed as much valour as the men". Another old Spanish-American chronicler, Oviedo, accused the Indian informer "of being (too!) sagacious and very cunning, and completely deceiving the *expediciónaras*. The Indian died, afterwards, in Cubagua" . . . (Yes, but *not* of a broken heart because of the "lies" he had told, *señor!*)

Herrera, however, would have rendered a much better service to posterity if he had taken the trouble to cite, in his history of the Spanish Indies, extracts from a long since vanished *Memoriale* of de Orellana's great expedition, which he got hold of, and also the depositions—equally lost—of two monks accompanying Carvajal. The monks affirmed that things had happened even as Carvajal described them in his narrative.

Antonio de Herrara, in his *Historia general de las Indias occidentales*—he is called the "historiographer of the Indies", and died in A.D. 1625 —significantly locates the scene of the battle between the Amazon-led Indians, and the Orellana *expediciónaras* at the mouth of the Rio Trombetas, a tributary falling into the left, or northern bank of the Amazon, or Marañon, again to give the river its *far* older, native name.

It was in the headwater territory of this Rio Trombetas,[1] on the frontiers of British Guiana and northern Brazil, that Sir Robert Schomburghk, the famous British explorer, was told by Indians to look for the Amazons. In A.D. 1844, Schomburghk explored the region, but found no traces of the women warriors. As was to be expected: since, as I have stated, the women and their queen had, about a century before, migrated from that country, probably west towards a still unknown and unexplored territory behind the Oriente of modern Colombia or Ecuador.

I have, after long study and careful analysis of Spanish-American and British documents, arrived at the careful conclusion that the *original homeland* of these women and their Queen Conori was located *not* in this headwaters territory of the Rio Trombetas and its tributaries, Rios Cephu and Wanamuh (south of the Acirai mountains, bordering British Guiana), but somewhere in that mysterious region of North-east Bolivia, called the Caupolican, and mentioned in this book, as

[1] Heriarte says that this river was, in the sixteenth–seventeenth centuries, peopled by stark naked men and women who blew *trumpets* at their feasts and drunken revels, of which they had many. He says they had little shame—but, of course, they might very well have had a strict, naked code of morality; for did not the ancient Greeks say that morality, or lack of it, is a matter not of the nude, but of the half-clothed? These Indians made beautiful pottery from a fine clay, or *tabatinga*.—AUTHOR.

the site of a "Lost World". The approaches to this region of dense forests, beset by marshes, are guarded by fierce and intractable Indians, who have hardly been pacified by what has come to their ears regarding the nigger-white-yellow men's atrocities in the infamous Putumayo rubber region.

They are called the Guarayos, or, by themselves, the Quinaqui. They are bearded and florid; so that the old chroniclers said they were of the posterity of Spaniards, lost in the forests, when hunting for El Dorado, or el Gran Paytiti. Anyhow, they can fire arrows with such force that they have been known to pin a white man to the deck of a launch on the Rio Paraguay, to which the race extends!

About the year 1570, a Portuguese expedition, led by Dom Martin Carvalho came on the trail of the Amazons, though without being aware of it. He was at the head of a force of 160 Portuguese soldiers, with many Indian carriers, out from Porto Seguro, trying to find a *mountain of green stones*, in a range sparkling like fire with dazzling crystals. The Indians had told him about it and showed him samples of what he took to be emeralds, of no great value. Carvalho had got about 200 leagues into the Brazilian *sertão* when he found gold between two mountains where a foaming river cut through a wild gorge. But hunger drove him and his men out into the wilderness, where they had to chew grass and eat snakes. The Indians told them that the mountain of green stones was 100 leagues farther on, perhaps not very far from Perú. So after eight months, they turned back towards their point of departure, losing all the gold they had won when a canoe over-turned at a rapid.

Fray Cypriano Baraza, missioner of the Company of Jesus, who was martyred at the arrows and spears of the "*barbaros* of the mission to the Moxos tribes in Perú", died in the late seventeenth century. It was said of him:

> Neither is the news of the Amazons to be despised, when confirmed at the time of the discoveries, as P. Cypriano had from the Tapacuras and Guarayos, whose affirmation is, both of them, that they (the Amazons) dwell in the eastern parts to the north (according to the signs that they make) in pueblos of warlike women, and admit as guests, at their own times, men, and kill the boys that are born, keeping the female infants, and that they are three days' journey distant from the Tapacuras, and in this as in other consequences of much importance, the discovery of that Nation is owing to the ardent zeal of Padre Cypriano.
>
> *Relación Sumaria de le Vida y dichosa Muerte del U. P. Cypriano Baraza de la Compania de Jesus, muerto à manos de Barbaros en la Mission de los Moxos de la Provincia del Peru.* (Lima: en la Imprenta Real de Joseph de Cofriras. Ano de 1704.) (A rare black letter, parchment-bound volume in the British Museum.—AUTHOR.)

Both Padre Cypriano Baraza and Ribeira locate the country of the Amazon women somewhere in this very region, to the north-east of Bolivia, roughly between the Rio Mamore and the Rio Heath, or

Sunene, which is where Fawcett heard that the shy, and elusive lost "white Indians" live, to-day.

An Englishman, Anthony Knivett, was in Brazil, in 1597, and went down the "river Javary" (or Juvari), which rises in Potosi, Perú, with twelve Portuguese, "whom the savages eat if they can capture them":

> We travelled north towards the country of the Amazons to avoid the Spaniards (of the Rio de la Plata region?—AUTHOR). The Indians call the Amazon country *Mandiocusyanas*. We took our course southwards again, and would fain have persuaded the Tamoyas to have fought the Amazons, but they durst not, for they said: "We know their country is very populous and we shall all be killed". Then we came to head of the river called Patos. In the country of the Topinaques (Tupinambas?) who are cannibals, we fell in with 30,000 Indians who wanted to go back to the coast; for they had formerly dwelt at Cabo de Frio (east Brazil). We passed hills, deserts, and rivers, finding many precious stones.

Now about the time when Pizarro's bandits, *los conquistadores*, were planning to rape Inca Perú (or shortly after de Orellana's adventure), there would seem to have started a great overland trek of these strange women warriors, and their queen and leaders from this strange land on the borders of Gran Paytiti–el Dorado towards the Amazon, or Marañon. The migration was a mass one; but it is probable from stories told by forest Indians to Spanish explorers, in the seventeenth century, that some of the women remained behind in their old homeland, in the unknown eastern *montaña* and *selvas* of what is now eastern Perú and northern Bolivia. When Sir Walter Raleigh voyaged up the Orinoco in A.D. 1595, he heard that the Amazons were in Guiana. But exactly fifty years before, four years after the death of Pizarro, there had come to Hernando Ribeira, follower of Alvar Nuñez Cabeza de Vaca,[1] conquistador of Paraguay, news of a nation of Amazons living on the western side of a large lake, called *Casa del Sol* (Mansion of the Sun), because that orb sank into it. Once more, we are reminded that this nation of women warriors were moon- and sun-worshippers.

In the very year that Don Francisco de Orellana died, worn out at Montealioni, or Montealeani, in Brazil, Hulderike Schnirdel, voyaging up the Rio de la Plata, heard about the Amazons. His party had come from Cadiz, in fourteen ships, carrying 2,500 Spaniards and 150 High and Low Dutch (Germans and Hollanders of the holy Roman Empire of Charles V). They met an Indian king, or *cacique*, Jeques, of the Sherves, or Scherves. He asked a Spanish *capitán*, Francisco Hernando Riefferl, and ten other Spaniards what they wanted. They, naturally, said: "Gold and silver". What more did any Spaniard, leaving the pleasures of ladies' beds on one side, want in that religious age, but souls to go with it?

---

[1] "Alvaro Nunez Cabeca de Vacca", deposed before the notary, Pero Hernandez, at "Assumpçao" (Assuncion, Paraguay), on 3rd March, 1545: "The Aburuñes Indians say that the Amazon women dwell ten days to the north-west. There are great towns with much white and yellow metal, and there are vases and utensils of the yellow metal. Their chief is a woman much feared by the natives."

Jeques obligingly handed over a "plate of gold about a spanne and halfe long, and half a spanne broade, and other things, cunningly wrought of silver, as well as a crowne of silver of one and a half pounds:

I took this of the Amazons who dwell two months away. They are warlike women who inhabit a very large island reached by canoes. There is no gold and silver in the island; but there is greate treasure on the main land, which the men inhabit. They are very warlike women, continually at war with their neighbours."

Another account says the women lived in an island entirely surrounded by water, "had only one pap, and men came in unto them three or four times a year. The king of the men of the land where the gold came from was called Jeques, or Jegues."

Riefferl: "Wilt lend me porters to carry my baggage into the heart of that country to seek these Amazons?"

Cacique Jeques: "*Si, señor*, I will lend thee twenty men, but be thou warned that this country is under water, and the journey be very difficult and uneasy."

The *cacique* also gave five Indians to each man of the Spanish *expediciónaras*, again warning them: "Though wilt go eight days and meet no other Indians till thou dost reach the country of the Siberis."

A long and toilsome journey followed. The Spaniards were tormented with insects, and for a week, day and night, were up to their knees in water. They made a fire on the top of great blocks of wood on which they stood a pot. It often happened that both pot and wood-fire fell into the water. The Siberis Indian guides swore they had still four days' journey to travel ere they cleared the waters, and then five more days across country to the land of the Orethuisen.

"Your force is not strong enough to force a way," said the Indian guides.

Under humid skies, the waters had been heated and become very hot and the *expediciónaras* were forced to drink it. There were still seven days to travel before reaching the Orethuisen lands. Then down came the rain in torrents, and when they staggered into the village of the Orethuisen, about 10.30 on the ninth day, they had been stricken by plague and famine. Worse: the chief of the Orethuisen said it was one whole month's trail to the land of the Amazons, and all the country around was full of water. The Spaniards now decided to give up the job—and they were tough men, in that age—and turn back on the trail.

Said a leader: "I doubt if the land of the Amazons doth not indeed lie beyond the region of the truth; for warlike wives living in society with men are many."

Whether the *expediciónaras* under Riefferl had gone up the Parana into Paraguay, and got bogged in el Gran Chaco, it is hard to say; but if the rumours about the Amazons related to the House of the Sun of Gran Paytiti and had drifted across 12 or 20 degrees of South latitude to the hinterland of the Rio de la Plata, it may be surmised that they had still a very long way to go. Twelve degrees south would be roughly the location given by Fray Cypriano Baraza and Ribeira, which is a very long way from Paraguay. One thing is clear, that the story cannot relate to the *Canuri* of the hinterland of the Guianan Orinoco, where, said a *cacique* visiting Raleigh, in A.D. 1595, men visited the Amazons in April of each year.

Said Raleigh (in his *Discoveries of Guiana*):

> Upon the river of Caroli are the *Canuri*, which are governed by a woman who is inheritrix of that province, who came farre off to se our nation and asked mee divers questions of her Majesty, our Virgin queen, Elizabeth . . . The kings of the borders assemble, and the Queens of the Amazons, and after the Queens have chosen the rest cast lots for their Valentines. This one moneth they feast, daunce and drinks of their wines in abundance, and the Moone being done, they all depart of their owne Provinces. A present is sent to the Father, if the child bee a girl, but it is not true that the right dug of their breasts be cut off. Prisoners are first used for intercourse by the women, and then killed. They exchanged plates of gold for green stones, called by the Spaniards, *Piedras Hijadas*, or spleen stones.

Two significant points appear in Raleigh's story. The name *Canuri* recalls the name of the Amazon Queen *Conori*, told to Francisco de Orellana by the Indian trumpeter captured on the banks of the Marañon, in June 1541. The green stones, whether emeralds or not, may have been an object of worship, as well as amulets of prophylactic significance. For, on all their long overland trails, the Amazons carried these stones;[1] and, as will be seen, the stones occasionally came into the possession of the Indians through whose countries the warrior women passed on trail.

As I have pointed out the root of the word *Amazon* is a *Caucasian* term *maza*, meaning *Moon*; and, as stated, one of their old European-Asiatic homelands was on the borders of the Caucasus. In South America, as Indian traditions show, the Moon was the object of the Amazons' worship. Their worship was associated with a sacred lake, by which they were said to perform their rites on the nights of a full moon, the lake being called "Mirror of the Moon". From the bed or shores of this lake the Amazons got the green stones which they highly valued as amulets, and which they called *Muiraquitain*, or frog-stones, the frog, as in old Egypt, being the symbol of reproduction and fertility. These green stones, said Indian traditions, were given to "the Women of the Mirror of the Moon by the Mother of the Frogs"—Heqt, the frog-goddess in old Egypt, where their ancestresses had once dwelt!

These green stones, called *chalchuitls*, in old Spanish manuscripts

[1] These "Amazon-stones", green stones, or, as called in old Mexico, *chalchuitls* symbolized, as they do in China, the green of resurrection, or the green of new life. As Miles Poindexter points out in *Peruvian Pharaohs*, "the cult of green in women's dresses has the same idea behind it". (*Vide:* The Chinese ritual work called "Chou Li".)

are worth a little notice. They were associated with the *Karaybas*, just as the old Amazons of Europe and Asia were associated with the Carians (or *Karians*), and von Humboldt in 1804 said that the Karaybas made these green stones and used them as money, selling them at a high price to the Spaniards. H. J. Moke, who wrote a very scarce book, published in Brussels in 1847, says that:

> It is on the banks of the Orinoco that the natives preserve these green stones as amulets, cut in the form of animals and fruits. They have had them from their ancestors, who say they came from the people the Europeans named the Amazons. So hard are they, that one cannot understand how they were cut by men who knew not iron. It is as hard to find their origin. Mineralogists have not found the same substance— *le jade de Saussure*—in any country of the New World.[1]

Heriarte's rare volume tells us that crews of ships of big draught, in the mid-seventeenth century, who came up the Rio Tapajos, Brazil, found that the Tapajos had these green stones, which they called *buraquitas*. (Or, to-day, baraquitas, *muenaquitans, muyrakytas.*—AUTHOR.)

> The men from the North esteem them highly, and, commonly, it is said, these stones are carved in this river from a green clay that is found under water, out of which they make long, rounded beads, drinking vessels, plates, birds, frogs, and the like. Drawing the object made from under the water, it hardens in the air from such clay, and becomes very hard green stone. The Indians seek the stones and much value them.

Among the Nahuas, in old Mexico, the *chalchuitl*, or green stone, was worn round the neck as a badge of nobility, and the Quichés of Yucatan also used them, under the name of *Votanes*, in the worship of Odin. In one small and picturesque town in a remote part of Mexico known to the author of this book, there was a great treasure of gold in tall jars (*tinajas*), hidden in a cellar of an old house, with extremely ancient statues, and these green stones, or *Votanes*, which a Mexican patriot, with clues and a *derrotero* on maguey leaves, urged me to join in seeking, and to finance the hunt. I refused. I had reason to doubt the possibility of being able to leave the pueblo of the treasure without having a shot in the back fired from the revolver of some *revolucionario* lurking in ambush, with patriotic ideas about his own exclusive rights to the use of the ancient gold. There the treasure still remains!

The green stones were said to have been brought into ancient Mexico by the old man Quetzalcoatl, culture-hero, and again as the symbol of a new civilization, re-born from the old. It is also curious that the name *Chalchuitl* was borne by the only woman who is said to have remained alive in ancient Mexico after the Great Deluge.

---

[1] The *chalchuitl* figures in the Codex Vaticanus as a post-deluge demolisher of the Mexican Tower of Babel: the pyramid of Cholula, built by giants, supervising men who passed bricks hand to hand in a long chain. After flattening the tower to the ground, the ancient myth tells us that the *chalchuitl*, which is said to have changed into the form of a *toad*, reprimanded the builders, advising them to look round on the earth before trying to climb the heavens. The Codex says: "At the present day the base of the Tower still remains. It has a circumference of 1,800 feet."

As my footnote, *supra*, states, green nephrite, in the ancient ritual of China symbolizes the green of new leaves and the re-birth of spring.

The great Dragon-god of Mexico and China was green; and in ancient Perú, at Llampallec, the god was carved in green stone. As Miles Poindexter points out in his fine and scholarly work, *Peruvian Pharaohs*, there has been found in the ruins of the great altar of Ollantaytambo, Perú, a green stone intended to have been used as a stone of sacrifice on a high place, in a very far day. In the City of Mexico, there is a teocalli where the priests of the Mu-an blood cult *humped* a green stone, so as to bend upward, handier for the obsidian knife (!), the body of the human victim standing before the altar of the war-god! Roman Catholics may also be interested to learn that the Virgin-Mother of Quetzalcoatl, *Chimalma*, conceived of a small green stone—the *chalchuitl*—as she was one day sweeping out the temple and that she gave birth to one who was called Teo-Huitzlopochtli, which name means: "Lord of the Thorns or *Wounds in the Left Side*". There were, then, crucified Christs many ages before the Petrine priests at Rome developed their ritual and dogmas.

I have, myself, a sketch of a small cross in serpentine form found in an Indian grave in the Canari territory of Ecuador, at Quienjo. Two French archæologists very dogmatically, after admitting that no object denoting European influence was found in that grave, say: "It is a Christian emblem manufactured in the first years after the Conquest by Indians who continued on the lines of other pagan amulets". So sure, *messieurs*, are you? Did you fail to note the significance of the fact that this cross was of *green* colour?

The cacique, Guanajari, who ruled the Tainos of Mayapan, told Columbus, on 21st December, 1492:

> I am descended of kings who were children of the sun and the goddess who lives under water and the waves of the sea in pearly caves. She loved Vagoniana and gives him the sacred Cibas and guaninos (pearls) that girdle my neck.

Dr. José Gullu e Rente says these *Cibas*, black marble or green stones, were the emblem of destruction and royalty. While Camargo tells how Mexican *Amazons* associated with the witches—which Plate 22 of Dupaix's *Monumens* of old Mexico, shows assembled at cross roads in lone places—marched to battle, decked with these green stones of a Virgin-goddess,[1] against a Mexican nation.

So, as the *Ykamiabas*—women who live without husbands—dived to the bottom of a lake to seek the green stones and gave them to the

---

[1] Diego Muñoz de Camargo, a mestizo of Tlaxtecala, and interpreter to the Spaniards, says the Amazons were in great strength and hailed from the Huaxtec region on the east coat of ancient Mexico. They killed all prisoners—in very *modern* European style— and their leader was the Mexican Venus, Tlazoleotl, who, in another aspect was Hecate, goddess of the *hechiceras* (witches) of the *brujerias*. These ancient Mexican Amazons were proficient with the bow.

men who visited them to make them mothers, the Tainos, above, used them, because Vagoniana:

> was taken into the arms of this Venus who gave him these jewels, for the delights of love.

In ancient Mexican Amazon traditions, these *Cibas* were called "shades of night", which may be jadeite or chloromelanite.

Terra-cotta figurines found, in 1872, in the Tapajos country of the green stones, show that the South American Amazon women wore their hair on the top of the head. The green stone has been found as far south as Patagonia, and, in 1882, was found in the Queen Charlotte Islands, off British Columbia, by Commandant Jacobsen. (It may be significant that these same islands are also the enigmatic home of the remarkable colossal prehistoric pillars found by Lord Dufferin in 1876. *Vide* pages 95–6 *supra*.)

In the mostly unpublished Muñoz collection of Spanish-American documents, now in the Academia de Historia in Madrid, there is a report by Don Francisco Ortiz de Vergara to the President of the "Consejo Real de Indias" (Spanish Royal Council of the Indies), who was Don Juan Ovando. Ortiz de Vergara had gone up the Rio de la Plata hoping to reach Perú, and at the old fort of Sancta Cruz de la Sierra had had tidings of the Amazons and el Dorado, which one, Capitán Nuflo de Chaves had hoped to find and conquer.

Old Georgius Horn, an encyclopædic scholar who was professor of geography, history and politics, in the newly-founded university at Harderwijk, in 1648, prefaced his *De Originibus Americanis* (1669) with a woodcut of an Amazon of South America standing on a shore with ships of explorers in harbour and on the horizon. She is naked from the waist up, wears buskins on her calves, and drawers from the waist half-way down the thigh, and has only one teat on the breast. A bow is in her hand and she wears a shield on which is a reptilian figure.

More singular news of the South American women-warriors reached France in the third year of the reign of Louis XIII. A certain Ouyapoc, a South American Indian, on the way to Europe in the ship of a Breton gentleman, was captured by pirates in the English Channel. Later, he managed to reach France where he sought out the *chatelaine* of the Sieur de Rasilly, at a castle in Poitou. The wife's husband, Monsieur de Rasilly, was then in Brazil, and had asked Ouyapoc, who was the son of an Indian cacique, to say he was well and happy, in Brazil. While living at the castle, Ouyapoc chanced one day to be standing by the moat when a pig fell in, and the arrogant *chatelaine* bade him help the servants drag the pig out of the ditch. Ouyapoc, the son of a native king, indignantly refused.

"I may be a savage from a savage land," he said, proudly, "but I have not yet sunk so low as to help drag hogs out of wallows."

The unladylike *chatelaine*, with all that insolence and ill-breeding which produced the later French Revolution, insulted and abused him; but Ouyapoc quietly ignored her and soon quitted the castle. He made his way across France to Paris, where in A.D. 1613, in a great house in the Capucine quarter, he was seen and recognized by one Jean Mocquet, *Garde du Cabinet des singularitez du Roy aux Tuileries.* Ouyapoc, overjoyed, rushed forward and fell on Mocquet's neck, embracing and kissing him. In a day or two, Ouyapoc and other Tupinambi (Brazilian) Indians were introduced to Louis XIII, in the royal court at the Tuileries. The king gave him money, but what became of Ouyapoc afterwards is not known.

Now, this Jean de Mocquet had, on 12th January, 1604, gone out from Havre de Cancale to the West Indies, in the ships of the Sieur de la Rauardière, lieutenant of Monsieur de Rasilly. Mocquet reached the shores of the Amazon, went up country, and met the King of Ouyapoc, or Yapoco, chief of a tribe of the Tupinambi Indians who had had sexual relations with the warrior women.

Says Mocquet:

Thirty or forty miles (*lieues*) up the Rio Amazon there are found other islands where these fighting women dwell. The Amazons wage war with men on the mainland of the coast (river-bank) of Brazil. On the other bank, however, towards Cape Vayanpouc, live Indians, their friends, and allies who go with them into war. These Amazons, for procreation purposes, have relations with the said Indians every year in April. When they desire to lie with the men, the women make a signal that they are ready for the Indians to come to their land and make love to them; all the days and hours of this month of April. But the women see to it that the Indians do not enter their islands in stronger force than they, the women, are. For that purpose, some of the women are appointed to stand to in arms to guard the haven while the other women take their pleasures in the arms of the men. Then these harbour-guards are relieved and enjoy the men's embraces, while other women take their turn on guard-duty. Thus, they pass all the month of April in love, joy and gallantry (*liesse*). At the end of the year, their men friends and allies return to them, and, if the women have borne children the male babies are handed over. The girls are kept and well trained in arms, but the women never retain the males for more than a year. And there are indications that the sons the Amazons have borne to these Indians may afterwards have sexual relations with their sisters and near relatives. For the Amazon women are in the habit of always seeking out the children of those who have had sexual intercourse with them. So these Indians may already be married in their own land on the main, while the Amazons are their sweethearts. They make presents to each other, in token of love and amity. As to these Amazon women some say they have only one teat and burn off the other in the fashion of the ancient Amazons of Thanais and Thermodon. These are fables, however; though it is true the women lose the milk of one breast in order more freely to be able to bend their bows and shoot their arrows.

Mocquet adds some very curious and intimate details about the South American Amazons that are found in no other writer. He says the son of the King Yapoco (Ouyapoc):

> told me that the women let their pubic hairs of their genitals grow very long and comb them like the hair of their head. They are stout women of lofty stature. He said he had been in the women's country with his uncle Ancajoury.[1]

The Frenchmen would like to have sailed their ships farther up the Amazon towards the women's islands; but the currents were too violent and swift, and their ships and even their flyboat (*patache*) drew too much water:

> For the current runs towards the coast, and one cannot go up-stream, except in a boat with oars, or the Indians' canoes which draw only a foot of water. This is what I was told about the Amazons, which does not make me disbelieve what the ancients said of them. They say there are also Amazons in Africa, towards the Cape of Good Hope, in the Kingdom of Monomotapa.

It may be said that the country reached by Mocquet, "was over 120 leagues from the Tupinamba country, lying towards the Rio Amazonas, or Marañon, of Brazil. (I have translated Mocquet's story from the edition published at "Rouen, chez Iacques Caillove, dans le Cour de Palais, *MDCXXXXV*".) In 1655 appeared another edition containing a few more details about the Amazons, which seem to reinforce the verdict of modern anthropologists that in all parts of the world, maternal kinship has existed, or exists side by side with institutions of paternal authority:

> The Amazons of Brazil are assiduous in daily plaiting their heads of hair, and in painting and adorning their persons, and that because they hold it for their whole welfare and spend most of their time thereupon. That was remarked by the young Ouyapoc's uncle, Ancajoury, and his cousins, in the women's country.

How did the Indian's own wives view this annual pilgrimage to the islands of Venus-Amazon?

Says Mocquet:

> Their hot climate inclines these (Tupinamba) Indians to mix their blood and to seek to have to do with a daughter with whose father they are connected. So they become a peculiar set of young people and live comfortably. Then, although these Indians of the continent show themselves foolish, yet their own wives and children have helped the Amazon women out of good neighbourliness, as women friends. They have many times sanctioned this cordial intimacy and nursed the love-present of the man-child. So, when the Indian women's men present them with another's love child, no jealousy arises in the home; but, on the contrary, their men retain their own wives' good will and friendship all the more. Assuredly, out of *our* woman mills in this wise would never any good water flow!

[1] Or, as it runs in Mocquet's own words: "*Le fils du Roy d'Yapoco me disoit entre autres choses que ces femmes portent le poil de leur nature fort long, et le peignent comme des cheveux, et qu'elles sont de fort grande taille . . .*"

Year after year, all through the seventeenth century, reports about the Amazons and their Queen drifted into the old Spanish *audiencias*, at Sante Fé de Bogotá and Quito. Soon a heap of documents had accumulated in the archives of *El Virrey*. They came from Spaniards, or from wandering Indians. The old Spanish governors of Venezuela all agreed that these reports indicated the existence, somewhere in the interior, behind or beyond the Andes and the llanos, of a race of warrior-women living without men, and ruled by a powerful queen.

Among my own papers of Spanish America and the "Indias occidentales" of the colonial age, are transcripts of documents, titled: *Papeles Varios de Indias*. They were sold at the sale of Lord Kingsborough's effects, in March 1893. (I have quoted one of them in a previous chapter.) Some of them tell of the "provinces of Tipuane and the Chunchos and del grade Reyno del Paytite". The land to which they relate is still *terra incognita*, to-day, in 1950. In fact, it seems less known than in Gonzalo Pizarro's time!

Here, again, is what Don Juan Recio de Leon, already mentioned in the chapter on El Dorado and Gran Paytite, was told by Bolivian Indians, about 1620, and whose story he wrote in Madrid, in December 1628: "The Indians told me news that on the north border of the Rio Apurima, boundary of the Gran Paytite, was a province of women who live without men, and when I asked them how the women could perpetuate themselves, living so, they said there were men on the other border of the Paytite, to the east, whom they called the *Marquires*, the Amazons' neighbours."

Don Juan anticipated with a sapient comment the scepticism of his readers:

> The established way of the world is never to credit what, at the moment, has not been seen by one's self. And the second and principal cause why more minute investigations have not been made is because the Indians become angry at being asked many questions, believing as they do, that it is more to our benefit than theirs that we give credit to what they say; and because of that they will not alter their tales, nor discuss more questions.

Beyond the Amazons' country lay their male counterparts:

> a country of *men* without women (*una Provincia de hombres sin mugeres*). These men lived without women, and two months every year, enjoyed women, and went by water from another part to unite with them. They are such valorous women that they fight with their enemies better than if they were men.

Ten years, or more later, there came fresh tidings about the women-warriors. It was in 1637, when a Portuguese expedition, traversing the great route of de Orellana, but from the opposite direction, going to the Andes and Quito, chanced on the trails of the Amazons. Noronha, the Portuguese governor of Para, Brazil, placed the expedition under the leadership of Pedro de Texeira, a man of the *bandeirista* type in valour and endurance. Texeira was almost the last of old, pure Lusitanian stock, whose blood was then becoming corrupted by miscegenation and alliance with *sambos* and blacks. His force consisted of seventy soldiers, and 1,200 Indians in seventy canoes. He quitted Cometa on 28th October, 1637, passed the Rio Negro, which he discovered, and, in January 1638, was in the upper Amazon country. On 3rd July, 1638, he entered the Rio Napo, where he met and joined forces with Dom Pedro de Costa Favilla, with the idea of surveying the country and securing their retreat, if attacked by overwhelming forces of Indians. On 15th August, they entered Quito, where *el Virrey* (the Viceroy) welcomed them. On the return journey, *el Virrey* ordered two monks, Padres Acuña and Artieda to join Texeira. Acuña's job was to write the story of the expedition to be presented to el Rey Don Felipe III, who was then joint King of Portugal and Spain. Acuña, or to give him his full title, Fray Cristoval de Acuña, of the company of Jesus, Censor of the Supreme General Inquisition, had orders from the Viceroy to find out, among other things, about the women-warriors, reports of whom had for years been accumulating in the archives of the *audiencia*, in Quito.

Says Acuña, repeating the story about the Amazons' sexual habits:

They live in villages, and cultivate the land, and, so the reports in the audiencia at Quito say, obtain all they want by the labour of their hands. I do not make particular reference to the stories of the Indians told at Quito, nor to that of the Indian woman, in the city of Pasto (modern Columbia, near the border of Ecuador), who says she had herself been in the country of the Amazons, which was peopled by them, and whose reports agree with all we previously heard. I will dwell only on what I heard with my own ears and carefully investigated from the time we entered the Rio Amazonas, or Marañon. From the time we entered this mighty river, there was no saying more common than that these women inhabit a province on the river, and it is not credible that a lie could be spread throughout so many tongues and nations with such an appearance of truth. If it were not true, then the greatest lie in all the New World would pass more certainly than all the truths of history.

He says his information about the women came from the last village of the *Tupinambas*, where they told him about the route to the Amazon country and its customs. The Indians of the land called the Amazons *Cunuriz*, and said the women's country was about thirty-seven leagues down the Amazon from this village. (This would locate it between the Rio Trombetas and Rio Branco.) It was at about this place that de Orellana encountered the Amazon women-warriors. The tribes of Indians who enjoyed the favours of the Amazons were "*Guacaras*". (The root indicates they were men of *Carian* descent.— AUTHOR.) Acuña adds *new* details about the land of the women:

These man-like women dwell in great forests, on lofty hills, among which is one that rises very high above the rest and is beaten by the winds, for its pride, therefore, with most violence; so that it is bare of vegetation. This mountain is called Yacamiaba, and the cordillera is called the Goyana, and runs along the river. The women have their pueblos on top of these prodigiously high mountains. The Amazons are women of great valour and have always preserved themselves from the ordinary intercourse with men, and even when their neighbours visit them at the times appointed, they receive them with bows and arrows in their hands, which they brandish about them for some time; for they will not be taken by surprise, and must be satisfied that the Indians come with peaceable intentions. The women then drop their arms and go down to the canoes, where each one chooses the hammock of the man nearest her (that being the bed on which he sleeps), and then each woman takes the hammock to her house and hangs it up in a place where the owners will climb into them. Then they confine themselves to their houses and receive the men as guests. At the end of some days, the men go back home, but they never fail to make the return trip at the stated time, each year.

Acuña heard that the daughters so born were brought up to the trade of arms, and to work. "As for the male babies, I know not well what they do with them; but I heard an Indian say, who had found himself in that assembly in the women's country, when he was but a lad, that, in the next year, the Amazons send to the fathers the many sons that they bear. I cannot presume to decide on the common belief that the women kill the male babies . . . Time will discover the truth; but, be it what it may, the Amazons have treasures shut up in their country that would enrich all the world. The bar (mouth) of that river on whose banks the Amazons live is in 2° or more South latitude . . . To deny the existence of these women would be an act against human faith."

Heriarte, whose manuscript remained lost for nearly 200 years in the Imperial Library in old Vienna, where it was found, in 1872, by the Baron de Porto Seguro (de Varnhagen), located the Amazons as at one time living on the banks of lakes in the Brazilian province of Sorimões. Heriarte said, in the year 1662:

Here are thirty lakes (lagunas) in low-lying lands. The villages are peopled by barbarians and they say there are the Amazon women there, and that the Indians who live in these lakes have sexual commerce with them, which seems fabulous. For, entering in them and walking through them, one finds no Amazons, but many Para jaguars. The Indians are very sharpwitted and skilful carvers in wood and bone with tools of stone, but do permit peace with others . . .

Still another monk of a later date in the seventeenth century, one Fray Gili, a *misionero*, contributes a queer item of news about the Amazons, which presents a still unsolved riddle. Gili was told by an Indian of the Quagua tribe that the Amazons were called the "*Aikeambenanos*", or "women who dwell alone". They—the women— live on the banks of the Cuchivero,[1] which falls into the Orinoco."

[1] The Rio Cuchivero is in the modern province of Bolivar, Venezuela. It rises in the lonely Guamapi range, close to Mt. Icutu, and flows through the territory of the Aguaricoto Indians. If Gili were correct, this would locate them a long way from the Rio Trombetas, and shift them from 2 deg. S. lat., to 6·40 deg. N. lat. But, perhaps, this was another colony of the women who attacked the soldiers of Don Francisco de Orellana's expedition, in June 1541.—AUTHOR.

Humboldt calls these women the *Ykamiabas*, or the *Kunhuntan tecoyma*, as also *cougnantain secoima*, which is a French garbling of the Tupi-Brazilian words *Kunhāta-tekoyma*, or young women, who live alone, or without young men. He also calls them *Aikwambenano*, corrupted from the Indian, or ancient verb, *aikambe*: to live, and *nho*: alone. Barbosa Rodrigues, who explored the region between the Rios Trombetas and Yamunda, about 1890, found, as he said, proof that the Amazons wandered about, after leaving their ancient home on the shore (*costa*) of the Rio Para. The Amazons, he says, existed in an island between the mouths of the two rivers, above-mentioned, but the island had, in 1890, partly vanished and was connected with the *vargem* (bank) of the Amazon, named Taukuera of the Amazons:

How do I know that? Because I found many stone axes and pottery and the green stone, or Amazon *muyrakyta* of the historians, used only by the Amazons . . . Why they left this region is not doubtful. They went up the river, as the geological structure shows, and dwelt in an island that was covered by a great inundation, which forced them to fly, as native legend shows. . . . . It was in this island, that existed until 1780, that I picked up the pottery fragments and the green Amazon stones. Why did not the women penetrate into the interior of Brazil? Because all the space between the two rivers formed marshy flats. Naturally, therefore, they sought the high lands that they found in the Parintins, and on the shore of the Amatary, entering above the Rio Negro. The native legends speak of different Amazon exoduses. Those of the Paytunæ and the Yacy-tapere say that the Amazon women vanished in the centre of the territory (the middle of the earth) and in the gulf of Parintins, the tribe of which sought refuge, destroyed by the appearance and sway of a foreign people, The native legends of the *muyrakyta*, or green stone, aver that its (the island's?) destruction was brought about by floods that left perpetual marks on the serra of Velha Pobre. The Uaupes still, to-day, use the Amazon green stones as signs of nobility. Some of the green stones were made of some imitation when nephrite was lacking. The stones are met with in such a way as to show that the Amazons ascended from the Rio Trombetas upwards to the Rio Negro. When Condamine passed, in 1743, over the mountains of Paytuna and Velha Pobre, he was told by the Indians that they were the last refuges of de Orellana's Amazons. There is a mountain called *Iakamaiaba*, or "the mountain of those women that have no breast". I also found a legend of Izy (compare with Egyptian Isis, or Venus, or Virgin Madonna.—*Author of this book*). By this, I judge that part of the tribe crossed also the Amazon, also the belief in Izy extends to the Matto Grosso. The Uaupes have a very feminine appearance and wear their hair in a plait falling down their back. Their young men are easily taken for women and lewd pleasures are reported to pass between them and the old men of the tribe. (*Vide:* the story of male successors of the Amazons, in Asia Minor, page 129 *supra*.)

Colonel P. H. Fawcett has pointed out, that, in Sanscrit, of old Hindostan, there are described the *manusa y'akeneana*, or the "women who are unmarried"! Here, we have another of these very curious, philological links between the old India of the Aryas and South

America. We have similarly sounded words with similar meanings, existing among remote South American tribes and in Asia. No wonder that Fawcett wrote—and there are distinguished North American scholars who agree with him, to-day[1]—that the existence of the republic of Amazon women warriors is not necessarily a myth.

But it was left to a famous French mathematician and geographer of the middle of the eighteenth century to furnish evidence, whose significance he clearly did not recognize, about the exodus of the Amazon women-warriors, either just before or after the Spaniards had started on their conquest of Central and South America. This exodus took them over a trail of more than 2,000 miles of unexplored territories in the equatorial and tropical zone of South America. They appeared to have ended up somewhere on the confines of what is now British Guiana and north-eastern Brazil. Surely this trek was no mean feat when it is recalled that, if Acuña was told the truth, these hardy, white women, of Northern type, habitually dwelt on the tops of mountains in a cold, windy climate.

This mathematician was Charles, Marie de la Condamine, sent out by the Government of Louis XV to measure a degree of the meridian at the equator. La Condamine while in Brazil, in August 1743, met an Indian, José da Costa Punilha, *Sargento Mor de ordenança* (principal orderly sergeant) who said he was a native of Cochiuvera, a southern tributary of the Amazon. Here, it was a received tradition that the Amazons had passed by on their way from south to north, to the Rio Negro.

La Condamine's story is rather long, but interesting:

> An Indian of Sao Joachim dé Omaguas told us that there might be perhaps still found at Coari, an old man whose father had seen the Amazons. At Coari, we heard that this old man was dead, but we spoke with his son, who seems to be 70 years old and was chief of the same village. He said that his grandfather had indeed seen pass those women, at the entry (mouth, or *barra*) of the River Cochiuera; that they came from that of the Cayamé, which debouches into Amazon on the south side, between Tesé and Coari; that he had spoken to four among the women, of whom one had an infant at her breast. He told us the name of each one of the Amazons; and said that in leaving the Rio Cuchiuera, the Amazons traversed the great river (the Marañon, or Amazon), and took the road of the Rio Negro. I obtained certain details, little probable, but which make no difference to the bottom of this affair. Lower down the Cauri, the Indians told us everywhere the same things with some

---

[1] Amazons, called the *Urus*, are rumoured to exist, even *to-day*, in a densely wooded island in Lake Titicaca. Behind the screen of bushes, if one may credit the stories, there is a Queen or *Rimaca*, practising *brujerias* (witchcraft) of a truly negroid Congo, or back-block Haitian sort. At intervals, drums are beaten and dances held in which women only take part—women warriors! Rumours along some parts of the lake-shore are to the effect that these wild mænads practise human sacrifices and drink human blood. What men there are in the island do all the chores and menial work, and are mere chattels. The men's existence is on a lower level than that of an Indian squaw among the Algonquins, or Seminoles, in the eighteenth century. How much the Peruvian authorities know about these savage women one cannot say.—AUTHOR.

variety in the circumstances, but which accorded with what we had been told on the principal points. In particular, those of the Topayos, spoke of certain *green stones*, called *Amazon stones*. They say they inherited these stones from their fathers, who had them from the *Cougnantainsecouima*, or in their tongue, the women who live without husbands, among whom, they added, one found those green stones in great plenty.

An Indian dwelling at the Mortiguera mission near Pará, offered to show me a river up which, according to him, one could go to a little distance from the country, he said, which was actually inhabited by the Amazons. The river is called Urijo, and I passed since by its embouchure between Macapa and the North Cape (Cabo Raso do Norte, at the mouth of the Amazon). According to the report of the same Indian, at the place where this river ceases to be navigable, because of obstacles, it is necessary, in order to penetrate into the country of the Amazons, to march several days through the woods on the western side, and to cross a country of mountains.

An old soldier of the garrison of Cayenne, to-day, dwelling near the waterfalls of the River Oyapoc, assured me that, in a detachment in which he was sent inland to reconnoitre the country in 1726, he reached the *Amicouanes*, a conquered nation, who lived in the land beyond the sources of the Oyapoc, and near another river that betakes itself to the Amazon; and that he had seen hanging at the necks of their women and daughters these same *small, green stones*. They told him that the green stones come from the women who had no husbands, whose lands were 7–8 days' distance further to the west. The *Amicouanes* lived far from the sea, in an elevated country where the rivers are not navigable, thus, they had truly not received this tradition from the Indians of the Amazon, with whom they had no commerce; they knew not the nations contiguous to their lands, amongst whom the French of the Cayenne detachment had taken guides and interpreters.

Again, after an interval of 131 years, we hear of these *green* stones carried by the Amazon women. Condamine says they were cut in the shape of animals, but they resisted the file and were very hard. Their origin (as I have suggested), may, possibly be looked for somewhere in eastern Perú, or in the highlands of modern Colombia, among the ancient craftsmen and jewellers of the ancient Carian race of Tayrona and Antioquia, an ancient province of modern Colombia. One of the early conquistadores, Don Jorge Robledo, explored this mysterious region of Antioquia, and speaks of roads cut at ancient date, in the living rocks. The manuscript is titled:

Relación de lo que sucedio al Magnifico señor Capitan Jorge Robledo en el descubrimiento que hizo de las provincias de Antiochia.

It is exceedingly rare, the only copy known to me being in the Spanish archives of the Royal Academy in Madrid. I have not been able to get hold of a copy of the manuscript, or even to see it, and there is no translation. But here, in old Spain, is where the mystery *may* be cleared up—unless more of Europe's and now the world's endless wars and air-bombings reduce the archives to char and stinks.

La Condamine was in Brazilian territory and French Guiana in A.D. 1743. He says that "Don Diego Portales, living at Madrida a few years ago, and Don Francisco Torralva, his successor as Governor of Venezuela, both agreed on the existence of the Amazon women". Traditions said they were to the east, or the north, or west. Which may very well mean that branches of the strange race were found at that time in several remote parts on the tropical belt of South America. Condamine adds: "But all concur in placing the common centre in the Guiana country, and in the central mountains in a canton in which the Portuguese of Pará, and the French of Cayenne have not yet penetrated."

La Condamine's story reached the eye of a Portuguese traveller, Dom Francisco Xavier Ribeiro de Sampiao and induced him to look up the old *sargento mor*, when, in 1774, Ribeiro de Sampiao was travelling in the Amazonas country, and writing up his diary, the *Diario da Viagem da Capitania do Rio Negro*.

Says he: *sobre a existencia das mulheres Amazonas*:

> I read in the diary of La Condamine the trouble that erudite and luminous academician took to arrive at the true origin of the celebrated Amazons . . . and I found that the *sargento mõr da ordenaña*, José da Costa Pacordilha, whom La C. questioned, was lately deceased; but another Indian of the same place, José Manoel, *alferes da ordenanca*, already over 70 years and of good natural deliberation, in the said ancient *povoaçõ* (village), of Cuchiúuara (that does not exist to-day, having changed its name to the *povoaça̋* of Arvellos), assured me he had many times heard Pacordilha speak of them, who had talked to Monsieur de la Condamine. He also told me there was in that river, among the Indians, an unshakable tradition of the existence of the Amazon women who had withdrawn, penetrating to the lands to the northwards of the mouth of the Rio Negro, from below.

Ribeiro de Sampiao points out that the River Amazon had borne many names. The Indians called it Paranauasu, or the Great River. The Pinções, who were the first that came to its most extensive *barra* (mouth) called it the Smooth, Sweet Sea (*Mar doce*). But Sampiao is wrong in attributing the name Marañon to some early Spanish explorer of the time of Orellana. For, one must repeat, Marañon is the ancient native Brazilian Atlantean name, and, at one time, was the name given to the Mexican Gulf, then much wider than it now is, and extending right to the mouth of the Amazon, of which, indeed in that far day, it formed the southern side! Marañon is almost certainly the name by which the lost white race of the Brazilian Highlands knew the great river. The name is as old as the name Brazil, and that is thousands of years, and not merely dating back to A.D. 1500 and Pedro de Cabral.

Sampiao, who thought the whole affair of the Amazon women a fable, or a marvellous yarn put up by de Orellana to cover up his perfidious desertion of Gonzalo Pizarro, "in which the genius of the age and its liking for novelty concurred in causing the court of Charles V to regard him as a wonderful man and a prodigy", enumerates the Indian tribes of Brazil whose women fight with them in battle:

The Mutucurús for four years in those parts fought against our *povoaçaõs* (pueblos or settlements) of the Rio Tapajos, and they take with them into battle their women, who furnish them with arrows in the fight, as was observed by the commandant of the fort, in 1773, against whom the Indians fought valorously for a long time. The Otomacos, one of the most celebrated of the Orinoco Indians, take their women with them into battle, who pick up the arrows shot by the enemy, which misfire, and redeliver them to their husbands.

Yet, Ribeiro de Sampiao, writing in the year A.D. 1774, had to recognize that in the unexplored interior of Guiana, which the French, Dutch, Portuguese and Spaniards, whose colonies surrounded it, had not entered, "one cannot positively affirm that there is still not there, to-day, the republic of the Amazons, that the fear of Europeans made forsake their native land". He, too, is sceptical about any women in South America, where the "climate so agitates the soul", being able to resist the force of love and remain apart from men.

But who said the Amazons, or any other gynæco-cracies, were as unnaturally chaste as all that?

In August 1889, there was picked up on the banks of the Lago de Jacupa (close to a farm called Boa Vista de Santa Anna), which is near the Rio Trombetas, which itself, was one of the old homes of white fighting women, the Amazons of old Paraguay and Brazil, a horrible but vividly carved stone statue of an anthroposaurian, with the legs and body of a giant man holding round the waist a woman who was nude, and whose arms, thrust back against the monster's giant arms, suggests that she was trying to repel a beast engaged in an act of unnatural coition. Her eyes are agonized and features show clear signs of suffering. The idol is made of rose-coloured sandstone, and holes in the base indicate that, at some time, the statue was used to fasten mooring ropes of a boat or small ship.[1]

The woman's forehead is covered with a veil like that of the Egyptian Isis, while the enveloping monster has a scaly neck, and well-made head, but the tail is unfinished.

Barbosa Rodriguez is probably correct in linking this phalliform idol of the Amazon with the other idols of grotesque and horrid

[1] J. Barbosa Rodriguez, former Director of the Jardim Botanico, in Rio de Janeiro says that a native of Ceara told him that this strange idol had been used as a paper-weight in his office. It had been picked up on the "black lands" of the Lago Yuquerymerim, in Brazilian Amazonas, close to two large stone axes.

form in Nicaragua, and in deeming both connected with lascivious and unnatural sexual rites. It is a moot point, however, whether the hideous Amazon idol, found as it was in the old territory of the Ikamiabas—or women without husbands—who adored the mother of the waters, and carried round with them the chalcuite, or green Amazon stone, which is a symbol of immortality and renewal of life by new births, was linked with these women.

According to the legends of the Uaupes of the upper Amazon, who swore by a goddess, called *Izi*—name singularly akin to that of the ancient Egyptian Isis—women who were barren, or whom the old men could not fecundate, were impregnated by a serpentine monster of the lakes.

Padre Sancho Araujo gives a curious story of some years later than Condamine's expedition, about a gathering of missioners in the pueblo of San Regis de los Yaméos where he was asked about the Amazons of de Orellana. He said he had heard things from different parts, but the subject not being in his line, he had paid no great heed. However, said he:

> I will present to you an old Indian of my pueblo who is rational and a good Christian, and well versed in these stories. The old man was summoned and I made myself his interpreter. He said that there was no person in all the missions that did not take for truth the tradition handed from father to son about the battle of these ancient warrioresses with the first Spaniards. The retreat of the women, he had heard his forefathers say, was towards the North, crossing the Rio Negro, very much into the interior. *It was certain the Amazons still existed,* according to common report, and that certain Indians still went to visit these women each year; but that these did not know the exact country of the women, because they always came from no little distance to the appointed place, where they were entertained, and from which they returned with good presents of gold and with the children that were born male. The women were governed by one they elected and that was the most valorous of all, and ever first in the battles . . . The Indian said that further news of the women could be had from a middle-aged Indian who lived in the pueblo de Santa Ana, of the Portuguese, who every year still visited these women, and perhaps he knew some of their sons. He told the name of this Indian and even some words of the Amazons' language, with the corresponding meanings.
>
> Hitherto (said Araujo), the *misionero*, to whom the Indian told his story and to whom I remarked what Señor Condamine had said of a similar report, had no recollection of what had been told us in such minute detail, either in a summary, or the original of the Travels . . ."

Araujo then recalled a story of a revolt of Portuguese soldiers at the fort of the Rio Negro. He related what had been also told him by a certain Padre, José Baamonté, who had been for forty years in the missions and who gave him, on that occasion, "a story that, had it not been so much later, would have been decisive for Señor Condamine", who was in Brazil, in 1743.

Baamonté's story was as follows:

In the year 1757, there met me in the pueblo of Pevas, some soldier-deserters who had gone up the Amazon, after plundering the royal treasuries, because they had had no pay for long. The soldiers came in small squads. Some stayed in the missions, others plunged into the interior towards Quito. With one of these parties, there arrived an Indian who seemed to be about 60 years of age. He spoke to the Pevas Indiós in their tongue, but was known by none. . . . He came to me in secret and begged me to admit him to the pueblo and make him a Christian. He threw himself at my feet, where others could not hear. He said he had not fallen away, but had lived always as a heathen. He told me the story of his long life; that he was of the Pevas tribe—baptized by Padre Juan Bautista Julian, and he settled in a new pueblo called San Simon de Nahuapo in 1724. But not being able, when young, to submit himself to Christian continency, and having only one wife, he felt a thousand distastes of the *misioneros*, and in order to live as he wished, took himself off, none of his relations knowing where.

After wandering in various parts, the Indian found himself in a Portuguese pueblo, and, from there, he at last landed in a village, where he was on the Rio Tefé.[1] There, through the kindness of a friend, who sheltered him, he entered the room of a dead Indian, who, every year, went to the country of the women who live without husbands.

Having carried on this business for about thirty years, he gained gifts of gold and certain green stones, which he sold at a good price in the fortress of Tefé. There then befell him a rupture of the groin, and it was impossible for him to carry on his employment. Being tormented with remorse, he took the chance to go up the Amazon with soldier-deserters from Tefé and reached my pueblo.

Baamonte said that this Indian died, a few months later, in the odour of sanctity.

Giandomenico Coleti, who, in Venezia, in 1771, published a rare volume, titled *Dizionario storico-geografico dell' America Meridionale*, says that the women of the Omaguas of Brazil, an ancient race dwelling on the banks of the Amazon, are those whom de Orellana fought in his monumental voyage to the mouth of the Amazon-Marañon, and of whom Condamine was told. The Omaguas were converted by the Jesuits in 1686. They were found in the highlands of Orinoco, in Venezuela, and along the Rios Napo and Putumayo, on the borders of Brazil and Colombia and Ecuador. The mission to the Omaguas at the pueblo de San Joachim del Omaguas was lost in 1767. It may be that the Omaguas come of a helot race of the ancient Atlanteans of Hy-Brazil; for they had the Atlantean custom of deforming the heads of their babies with boards. However, this identification of the Omaguas women with the Amazons rests on no basis of good evidence. Coleti says they were a warlike, courteous and tractable race; and, Humboldt, more than forty years later, thought they had the marks of an ancient race of nobility.

[1] The Rio Teffé, or Tefé, is about 500 miles long, and flows into the Rio Solimões, at the embouchure with the Rio Amazon, where there is, to-day, a township called Teffé or Egas.—AUTHOR.

Francis de Castelnau (F. Laporte) who led an expedition into the central regions of South America, under order of the French government, in 1843–1847, rightly said of the Lower Amazon:

I am convinced it will one day offer a vast field to the archæologists. For example, the name of the town of Serpa, in Brazil, which means "graven stone", derives probably from the fact that, among the shingle on the strand of the river, have been found figurines, which, from what I was told, are like some in Perú. . . . *The axes one often meets here are attributed to the Amazon women*, and seem to come from a rude type of felspar. None know whence they originate. I was also given at the Barra bits of jade found in the sands of the Rio Negro. They are little cylinders in the form of beads and exactly like those found in ancient tombs in the Old World. The Indians attribute great medicinal virtues to these *green beads*. We found it impossible to find whence this mineral came. The Indians merely said it was not of the country. At Santarem, I saw a statue from this region. It was very large and rude in workmanship. The head was greatly prolonged to behind, like the skulls found in ancient Peruvian tombs. The people of the country say it *represents an Amazon*; and, indeed, it seems to be hiding its breasts with its hands, and, between its feet, it holds the emblem of the male sex.

He sent this statue of the Amazon to the Musée du Louvre, in Paris. It had been found planted in the ground, by its base, in the middle of a dense forest.

André Thevet, in *Les Singularités de la France Antarctique* (Paris, 1558), gives a picture of the South American Amazons welcoming their water-borne lovers before enjoying nights of love, on couches beneath the hammocks of the men-Indians, strung to the beams of the temporary wife's house.

Thevet tells a story—it may be fiction—of early French explorers landing in a creek off the Guianas. Says Thevet, who was born at Angoulême, in 1502:

We were about to say that our pilgrims had sojourned there only a short while to rest themselves and seek provisions. These women (South American Amazons) were astonished to see them in this ship which was very strange to them. In less than three hours the women and girls, all stark naked, quickly assembled, but with bows and arrows in hands, and began to shout and scream as if they were gazing on their enemies, and this commotion did not end without arrows being fired, to which the others, not wishing to engage in hostilities, at once replied by withdrawing bag and baggage. And raising their anchors, and unbending their sails, it is true that, at their departure, they said adieu by saluting the women with some cannon-shots. The women were in disorder but, nevertheless, it is not likely that they would easily have escaped without feeling something else.

He does not explain—there is no need!—what other weapon the Amazons might have encountered at the hands of these gallant French adventurers, bearded like the pard and swearing worse than Bardolph, who saluted naked South American white-skinned women and girls with cannon-shots!

After all, too, women of this type do not, usually, experience the sexual urge with quite the same force as men; though, of course, there are exceptions to every *approximate* law of nature. Don Juan Recio de Leon was told that these Cyprian nights lasted for two warm months; so that the women seem to have made up pretty well for their abstinence in the other ten months. Sir Walter Raleigh heard that the Guiana branch of the Amazons enjoyed their Valentines during the whole month, with feasting, dancing and plenty of good food and wines. It is true that Fray de Acuña says the nights of love lasted only a few days; but as he was a monk and compulsory virgin, what knowledge could, or ought he to have of such matters, except hearsay? Still, Acuña's narrative partly explains the climatic reason for the comparative continence of the Amazon women in South America.

Shame on these Latin-American and modern Peruvian, Chilian, and Brazilian writers who defame the good name of their own women, calling them "lustful to a degree"—in order to cast doubt on the existence of the white Amazons and their South American republics and gynæcocracies! I say to them *Fica, Fica!* returning them the felonious greeting they themselves—as I pointed out earlier—give, unasked, to young ladies, even of perfectly respectable sort, seen, lost, or walking the streets of South American cities after dusk in tropic nights.

"Enough of the Amazons," said Ribeiro de Sampiao, "let us proceed on our journey."

To whom we retort: "Enough of thee, Dom Francisco, and thy ungallant reflections! Dost thou think, because thou didst write in the eighteenth century of prose and reason, that, therefore, all mystery had vanished from this strange earth?"

Modern folk-lore, and the science of historical origins do not so abruptly dismiss traditions as myths. Often enough those traditions are candles lighting a dark path on which no ray of documentary history shines. At the bottom of the myth and the traveller's story lies a grain of strange truth—even if distorted. In fact, modern American scholars, to-day, are averse from calling the story about South American Amazons a myth transplanted from old world Africa and Asia, by the Spanish conquistadores and Dominican monks of Castile and Estremadura to the so-called new world.

Sir Robert Schomburghk, the famous British explorer of South America, was the last Englishman who set himself to solve this mystery of the South American Amazons. He did it a century ago, in 1844, when, treading in the steps of the luckless Sir Walter Raleigh, he went into the backwater country of the Orinoco, and penetrated into some of the recesses of the still largely unexplored mountain ranges on the borders of Venezuela and British Guiana and Brazil. He talked with the Caribs who told him "gravely", he said, that along the upper part of the Rio Corentyn, in a country called Marrawonne, above two high cataracts, called Pioomoco and Surama, in the land of the Woruisamocos, dwelt women who used blowpipes for arrows, and received and had sexual congress with parties of twenty men each year. These women, said the Caribs, cultivated their own lands.

> These Amazon women were called the *Woruisamocas*, and at a place where two huge rocks called the Pioomoco and Surama rise from each bank of the river and bound it like a portal we might deem ourselves in the land of these women . . . I heard the same thing from the Macusis Indians who live in the savannahs forming the site of Keymiss's supposed El Dorado. On these plains I frequently came on great heaps of broken pottery which the Macusis said had been left by these Amazon women. The Caribs aver that such a woman's republic exists about the head of the Rio Corentyn, where no European has ever been. They say they are the *Woruisamocos*, that they use the *cura* (blow pipe) and bows and arrows, cultivate their own land and grounds, and shun men's company except once a year when the men could see them in parties of twenty (men). Male babies were all killed. (*Schomburghk's Diary*.)

This region is on the borders of Dutch and British Guiana, and some way north of the Rio Trombetas headwater country. So, perhaps, the Caribs were not so far out?

Traditions poured into Schomburghk's camp from all sides. All held that the Amazons were a fact, and still existed. De Orellana, descending the Marañon (or Amazon) had met the Amazon women warriors, fighting at the head of Indians at the Rio Cunuriz (a name, of course, to be compared with that of Conori, or Canuri, their own queen). Several expeditions, at different times before 1840, had tried to explore the Rio Trombetas, but were held up at the cataracts. In some cases, the explorers had been murdered by the savage Indians who live in the upper branches of the Trombetas. Monsieur Montraval, commanding the French warship *La Boulonnaise*, had surveyed the Amazon as high as the Rio Negro, in 1843–44, and heard that Amazon warriors were still to be found in the region of the Rio Trombetas.

Says Schomburghk:

> We have from the south, as well as from the north, the same tradition that the Amazons of the New World inhabit a central district of Guiana. Our route, in 1844, when traversing these very regions, descending the chief branch of the Rio Trombetas, from its source to its junction with the Wanamu, has, unfortunately for the interest attached to this romance, driven the warlike dames from one of their last hiding-places.

But this negative result by no means clears up the mystery. For one thing, the wild country around had not, nay, still *has* not to-day been even partly not to say thoroughly explored. For another, who knows, I repeat, whether the Amazons, seeing their frontiers steadily approached by Dutch, English, Spanish, Portuguese, negroes,

Brazilians and French, had not, long before 1844, in fact perhaps not long after, or before La Condamine's day, begun another long trek? This time westwards towards some still unknown region on the borders of southern Venezuela and Brazil, the headwaters of the Amazon tributaries in Colombia or Ecuador, or even back towards the old homeland, in the mysterious region called the Caupolican?

It might be possible, to-day, to find another remote Indian tribe whose forefathers handed down eye-witnesses' stories of the passing *westwards* of the Amazons. Even as late as 1860, the Macusi Indians of Guiana still related traditions of the existence of the Amazons. This tribe lives in a remote land west of the Rio Branco towards the western borders of British Guiana with Venezuela's province of Amazonas.

All these regions are dangerous to explorers, even to-day. Farther south, around the headwaters of the Rio Branco, Brazil, on the borders of the Trombetas country, the savage Indians and *boticudos* attack all intruders, white, yellow, black or sallow. In January 1941, the government in Rio Janeiro had to rush aeroplanes with troops to the rescue of five members of a Brazilian frontier mission surrounded, near the Venezuelan borders, by a hundred Indians shooting poisoned arrows at them and yelling for blood and murder. The *Indiós malos* all round the wild and mostly unexplored territory had risen *en masse* and beleagured other frontier stations. All the besieged Brazilians would have been exterminated had not one of them chanced to have a radio transmitter on which he flashed an S O S to the nearest town, Belem (Pará). Brazilians of the towns are not at all partial to venturing into the interior, or *sertão*. Of course, there are striking exceptions, such as General Candino Rondon, who is of Indian descent, and the members of the Federal Department of the Indians, in Rio de Janeiro.

If the *Indiós malos*, or *boticudos* are not pacified and the way thrown open to explorers, then, as this book suggests, the unpacifiable Indians, whether of Brazil, eastern Perú, the hinterlands of Venezuela or the Guianas, or of north-western Bolivia will be by-passed by a cruiser land-plane of multi-engines, or a new type of airship, inflated with helium or other non-inflammable gas, not to be ignited by the sudden flashes of tropical lightning in the violent thunderstorms that rage in these wildernesses and dangerous territories.

Science will not, cannot, be halted by savages or Brazilian *boticudos*! Why should it, indeed, seeing that even the threatened disruption of the whole *civilized* (?) globe and the suicide of the ruling white races cannot stay the advance of mechanism and variously ingenious and diabolical systems of atomic, or molecular or radio-magnetic explosions, or cosmic "death rays", any of them enabling man to make the earth almost as great a hell as Nature has it in her own unaided power to make it?

And let us not forget that these lost, white races of ancient South America were also highly evolved in *their* remote day. Of course, man can make earth a near-Paradise and so remove from himself the stigma of the old charge that he is only a splendid beast without a soul, doomed to annihilate himself without the aid of Nature's great cataclysms. But will he? Signs and tokens in Europe alone, in this present year 1950, give little ground for undue optimism.

Such stigmas may be removed by men advancing the bounds of knowledge by re-discovering what these ancient civilized races had discovered in their far day. And this, great men of our later twentieth century may do, so far as mysterious South America is concerned, only by penetrating into places to-day deemed too dangerous for the white explorer and archæologist, or anthropologist.

Perhaps one of the reasons Fawcett's adventures captured the minds of so many was his illustrations.

CHAPTER FIVE

THE MYSTERY OF EL DORADO AND GRAN PAYTITI

Stay thou with me. This day thou shalt have ingots.
BEN JONSON.

Lamentation and an ancient tale of wrong,
Like a tale of little meaning tho' the words be strong,
Chanted from an ill-used race.

EDGAR ALLAN POE, in one of his mystical poems, pictures a dæmon whispering in the ear of a dreamer: "If thou seekest El Dorado thou must ride, boldly ride over the Mountains of the Moon through the Valley of the Shadow" . . .

And that pretty well sums up the prevalent sceptical opinion about the real existence of El Dorado. That it was a South American mirage, or jack o'lanthorn light of the swamps of the foothills of the Andes, which embogged and entrapped many a haughty hidalgo, or cruel German knight of the Holy Roman Empire of Spain and the Rhine to his utter ruin. Or that it was a myth that caused many an adventurer to leave his bones and eyeless skull to rot and grin to the unseeing heedless skies from the depths of some South American *arroyo*, or in the glade of a lone forest where the burnt cabins of a fired Indian village and the scorched earth of native fruit plantations mocked the white survivors who crept back to mourn and starve under the ancient Venezuelan or old Colombian moon.

As for the surviving El Dorado hunters who, century after century, managed to struggle back to Cartagena, or old Quito of the Incas, it must have seemed to their backers and promoters, if not to themselves, with vile tropic diseases gone to the bones and sunk right into the bloodstream, that the more the years processed the more the visionary country of fabulous gold and jewels seemed to retreat beyond the icy summits of the cordilleras, or sink down into the waving line of dense, green tropical South American forests. Its far horizon ever beckoned to old Spanish avarice and ever receded beyond even Castilian reach.

Was El Dorado, then, a mere myth accreted to the dusky figure of an old Colombian cacique condemned to roll his carcase in gold dust and yearly to bathe in the mystic waters of a mountain tarn, wherein had sunk his pretty wife and baby girl, down to the green translucent halls of a Guatavitan Neckan? Was it all based on the lovely and forlorn figure of a queen whose husband had ordered her to be prostituted to any, or the lowest and basest man in the city?

Because, he, the Sultan, had, as he believed, caught her in an intrigue with a young Chibcha gallant about his court, as the native story purported?

Indeed, have we, *to-day*, any reason to suppose that El Dorado, the mysterious country or city of fabulous wealth really existed, and was more than a mystery-myth?

I say, emphatically, that *El Dorado*, or the *Los Dorados*—for there were more than one in South America—really did exist.

Of course, the average, sceptical historian will point out two sources of the "myth": one behind the Rio Orinoco, in the legendary land of golden Manoa and Lago de Parima; the other in the deep, blue, slumbering mountain tarn of Guatavita, high in the mountains behind Santa Fé de Bogotá. And it may *seem* so, after sifting the evidence. But, be it noted, *all* the evidence has not been so examined! One who, in our own day, came nearer than he knew to the true location of the El Dorado of the golden lake and mansion of the sun was the late Sir Arthur Conan Doyle, though his book actually treated of a Lost World of dinosaurs, saurians, monstrous animals, ape-men and trans-Andean Indians. It was in 1912, that Colonel Fawcett, in London, hinted about the monstrous tracks of unknown origin, seen by shuddering Indians, *to-day*, in this mysterious territory. They were in the beach of primæval swamps, old as the uprising of the giant Andes, when the ancient rivers drained into a tremendous swamp covering a million square miles of territory. Doyle was at the lecture and based his *Lost World* novel on what he heard at the lecture.

Behind the swamps, on the edge of the very little explored province of Caupolican of Bolivia, range dense forests not even penetrated by native rubber-gatherers. There are dangerous Indians on the fringes of this forest through which flow the Rios Beni and Heath. Back of this *terra incognita* lies, say the Indians, a lost world of ancient ruined dead cities, wherein is much gold lying in the dust of untold ages. Here is a strange *El Dorado* called by generations of old Spanish explorers, pioneers, gold-seekers, adventurers, mission monks, chroniclers, viceroys, governors, the official of the *audiencias*, and the Jesuits and Dominican friars: *El Gran Paytite*, or *Paytiti*, The Land of the Tiger-King.

It is true that the late Sir Arthur Conan Doyle did not precisely locate his world of Jurassic monsters with large ape-men, later Indians, and lakes and swamps of pterodactyls and mesozoic age saurians, all hemmed in by towering cliffs of basalt and igneous rocks. In actual fact, his "Lost World" was apparently located far up the headwaters of the Amazon, and probably near the region of this same mysterious Caupolican. But doubtless, he would have deemed it an artistic mistake to locate too precisely such a never-never land of terror and fantasy.

But when the careful inquirer raising the curtain of mystery that for centuries on centuries has veiled the South American landscape, peeps round a corner of it, he dimly sees, looming through the mists of long time, a faint picture of stone cities, wherein a strange white race dwell, gold-plated pyramids, and a mystic lake with golden sands which reflect in its wide, pure waters a great temple of the sun, or House of Virgins, called by the conquistadorians, *la Casa del Sol*.

True, the old Spanish explorers and the missionary monks of the early seventeenth century did not distinguish between El Dorado and Gran Paytite. Or, to put the matter in another way, they did not visualize the fact that there was more than one El Dorado, in South America's unknown places. It is a curious fact that the way to one El Dorado lay through the country of the Amazon women-warriors without husbands. And that is the case, both in regard to the never-entered land of gold and the Lake Parime, said to lie in the backwater country of the Rio Orinoco, on the borders of Venezuela, Guiana and north Brazil, and what I believe with a certain old Spanish monk, and Don Juan Recio de Leon, was the homeland of these women in the headwaters territory of the great river named after them. This territory is sundered still by thousands of miles of unknown *campo*, forest, river, *montaña*, swamp and savannah, from the eastern cordilleras of the Andes, behind old Cuzco, in Perú.

The story seems first to have reached European ears in Central America (Aztecan Mexico and Nicaragua), in the first years after the conquest. It was, then, as later, often coupled with the "legend" of Amazon women warriors, on its borders. And it always took the form of a land of glittering and abundant gold and jewels far away in the interior from the Indians who told the story. El Dorado proved, as we know, a mocking mirage to the gold-hungry adventurers, and the stately hidalgos, or hardy Spanish rufflers. All such men were destined to lay their bones in hundreds of unknown swamps, morasses, woodland tracks, wild mountains and weird gorges, or deadly miasmatic savannahs which have actually never been trodden since by the foot of white men, who have lived to return with the story.

The search lasted for three hundred years, and was switched from the edge of western, South America to the unknown hinterland of the north-east of the continent. The hunters were as castaways who watch the smoke of the steamer which is always hull down on the skyline. And the parallel holds good in another way: in both there was, and is, no smoke without fire.

The vision of El Dorado began to flit before the eyes of the conquistadores of South America, in the days of Ximinez de Quesada. It was when his hardy soldiers began to ride over the high passes of the cordilleras of Nueva Granada (modern Colombia), that they came on a curious cultus associated with the ancient, South American worship of the goddess Chia of caves, tunnels and lacustrine *adoratorios*.

But it was the preaching friar, Fray Alonso de Zamora who started in Spanish ears, the story of the El Dorado vision of the mystic lake of Guatavita. I here translate his story for the first time into English. Zamora was "Provincial Qualificador" of the Holy Office. He wrote:

The temples and sanctuaries most celebrated of all the Mosca (Muysca or Chibcha) nation of the province of Nueva Granada, were those of Sogamoso, Bogotá and Chia, the lake of Fuquene, and the lake of Guatavita, that is distant two leagues from that pueblo, between very high hills; with so much beauty and so level a formation has Nature created it, that the water stretches for more than a league around. It is very deep and so crystalline and limpid that a straw that fell into it sent out circles even to the edges of the strand. The Indians report, among their fables, that the Guatavita having taken (*comprehendido*) his principal wife in adultery, ordered that, in his presence and the chief men of the state, certain Indians of the lowest condition in the city should enjoy her. She so keenly felt this public disgrace that, with her only small daughter, she threw herself into the lake.

Remorseful, afterwards, that he had not pardoned her, the Cacique (the Indians are very liberal in piety or compassion [*piedad*]) mourned her so greatly that he went to the banks and filled the waters greatly with his tears, wherein some of his vassals, to gratify their chief, cast themselves; and they all with one voice called on her in lamentation. The demon that set himself to allure the inclinations of everyone that craves, so disposed it that the *Xaques*, or priests who look after the sanctuary, feigned that the *Caciqua* was alive in a beautiful palace under the waters of the lake. And to deceive the people the more, he caused the form of the Caziqua (*sic*) to appear above the waters with her baby daughter in her arms. After these apparitions, sacrifices began to be offered, and as it seemed to the Cacique and his vassals of Guatavita that she was alive, they performed the rites with love, and succoured her wants, making her the richest offerings they could conceive.

The fable is told by all the people of the Muyscas, and also by strangers, who, marvelling at the miracle (*prodigio*) came to make offerings of gifts from various quarters (*por calles diferentes*), of which the tokens are seen to this day. They enter *balsas* of reeds, and, in the middle of the Laguna, cast in their offerings, with ridiculous and vain superstitions. The ordinary people approach the banks of the lake and keep their backs turned as the ceremony proceeds. For they hold it for lack of reverence that any should stare at those waters who might not be of rank qualified. But the tradition is very ancient that here was cast into the water all the gold and emeralds as soon as they heard that the Spaniards sought nothing else.

From this lake, arises the fame of the *Dorado* that has destroyed so many, luring and deceiving them. It is the story that the *Cacique* of Guatavita bathed (*se bañaba*) or dipped himself in turpentine (*trementina*), and placed over that a great quantity of gold and gold dust, and in that shining livery went golden and resplendent to the sacrifice.

Round about this famous lake, General Quesada said the Indians had sanctuaries or idols in temples, and that, asked for the riches that were in it, he gave his brother, Hernan Perez de Quesada the first drainage of the countries, and that he, alone, took out 3,000–4,000 pesos of gold of very fine quality. Not far off the time of the conquest, Antonio de Sepulvada made a second drainage (*desague*), with certain instruments that he had to sound it. He drew out a great sum of gold and an emerald of very great value, of which there is an account in *Los Libros Reales* (The Royal Registers). In those times, they made the greatest and deepest drainage of the lake, but though they fished up something (*han sacado algo*), it did not answer their expectations, or the cost. . . .

The golden dip of the balsamic *Cacique* was followed by a royal banquet when the Indians, now turning their reverential backsides *to the land*, broached whole *balsa* loads of *piwaree* (beer).

Humboldt visited the mystic lake, about 1830. I have already given his impression (in a page, *supra*). Eight years later, Captain Charles Stuart Cochrane, R.N., was there, and he tells a very interesting story:

An old Spaniard, sounding in the centre of the lake, drew up with the lead a small branch of a tree, in the mud round which was a golden image, worth 100 dollars. About the summit of the cone which forms the lagoon is an ancient Indian road, now quite neglected and overgrown with brushwood and trees. On the edge of the cone we saw two of the sepulchres of the *caciques*, hewn out of sandstone rock. And there is said to be a cave connected with the worship of the Lagoon of Guatavita, at the entrance of which is said to have once been standing two golden figures, large as life. A Spanish soldier, who first wandered to the place, cut off one of the fingers, when he was seen and attacked by natives. He was wounded and hardly made his escape. Having told what he had seen to a large body of Spaniards they went well armed to the spot, but found neither figures nor cave. The Indians, hearing that a strong force was on the way, cleverly stopped up the cave and threw the golden statues into the lake.

And, as that lake is 1,000 yards wide and very deep, those gold statues have never been found! People who, in modern times—in the last fifteen years, in fact—have invested money in syndicates started in London, England, by highly coloured and enigmatic folk have reached the conclusion that, if there is not a curse on Guatavita, apart from those too readily vomiting from their own mouths, it is a will o' the wisp luring unwary people's money out of the safety of banks into the marsh and bottomless sands of Suckers' Bay and Mug's Island.

There *ought*-to be a romantic curse on Guatavita, since scoundrel Quesada, the tough Spanish conquistador roasted the Chibcha chief, Sapija, alive, on a hot fire. He perpetrated this atrocity in order to punish him for throwing into the waters of this lake—when he heard that the avaricious Castilians were on the way—two tons of gold and plate, borne on the backs of fifty sweating Indians. As for Antonio de Sepulvada, already mentioned, that luckless Spanish merchant of Bogotá was ruined by his attempt to drain the lake, for the gold he raised, worth 200,000 dollars, and the splendid emerald he fished up from its deep waters, were sequestrated by the *Virrey* for the Crown in Madrid. Romantic, or fancy-free statisticians have said there are

£1,120,000,000 in gold in Guatavita; but nothing like that sum has ever come out in the draught. A British concern, in 1913, spent thirteen years of hard work and £15,000, on the lake, and got out jewels and gold objects worth only £350.

But to hark back to the early days of the conquistadores—though the *cacique* was roasted alive, and the Spanish merchant lost his money and broke his heart over Guatavita, on went the search for mystic gold. Not one of these ruffian bandits, or proud, haughty-eyed and imperious hidalgos of old Spain stopped to ask himself: "Whence came all this gold and those jewels cast into this lake?"

In the not so often high endeavour to resolve this riddle, once for all, Germans of the Holy Roman Empire of Carlos V enlarged the hunting area. These expeditions left the high passes of the Andean cordilleras for the free, hot, insect- and snake-infested, wet llanos of Venezuela. They were headed by daring knights of old Augsburg, in Bavaria, who, sons of merchant princes, as they were, of the old Velser, or Welser family, yet had in their adventurous veins the hot blood of those lansquenets, or German foot-soldiers. The lansquenets' gentle ways, as one has seen in sixteenth-century marble monuments in ancient German or Swiss churches, have caused them to be used as models for the impenitent thieves on crosses, or the soldiers who gave vinegar instead of water to a Saviour, or thieves dying on a cross in ancient Palestine. These Velser knights, with the sword in one hand and pistolet in the other, and their gold pokes and Cordovan leather-bags, for gems and other trifles rifled from *adoratorios,* rattling and bumping at their Spanish jennets' backsides and flanks, started out, about the year A.D. 1530, at the head of 200 Spaniards and Holy Roman, imperial Germans, horse and foot. They had a train of 100 Indians laden with the provisions and equipment for their white lords and masters. The luckless Indians were fettered together with one long chain, their necks none too affectionately clasped with collars, for it was still far from the day when blacks, or red, or pie-bald men were regarded, or affected to be regarded, as brothers in the good Lord with the white and master races. Any man who fell out on the trail, exhausted, had his head struck off to save the gentle Spanish, or German lansquenet the trouble of undoing the chain from his neck and unlocking fetters from his shrunken limbs! The wild beast and the belly of the *uirbiru* then became his sepulchre, and no holy Catholic Spaniard to say a *Paternoster* or *ave Maria* for the poor Indian!

Don Ambrosio de Alfinger was the leader of the first expedition to this other El Dorado. At one place on the banks of the gold river Magdalena, in modern Colombia, the *Indiós* of the villages around were startled by the roaring of matchlocks and the spanging of the arquebuses. They abandoned their villages and fled to some islands in the river. The Spaniards pushed their horses across the whirling waters and killed every Indian, without respect to sex or age. From the *cacique* of another village on the Magdalena, Alfinger and his murdering, raping bandits looted £12,000 worth of gold and jewels. He sent his lieutenant back on the trail with this gold, with orders to buy fresh supplies from Coro, Venezuela. The loyal lieutenant (not a lansquenet for nothing!) left his commander and the men in the lurch, and went out treasure-hunting on his own. A whole year Alfinger waited for the traitor's return, till his men were dying of hunger; in a country which had been scorched and ravaged—the policy of the scorched earth is not new!—till not one stalk of Indian corn or fruit could be found in places from which the Indians had all fled.

At last, the desperate Alfinger, seeing the futility of waiting any longer, ordered the expedition to move. Every village they met on the trail they plundered, burnt and massacred. They dug up the natives' plantations and left the survivors, when they returned from the woods, to die of hunger. The starving Spaniards and Germans were now fain to stay the pangs of their own hungry bellies on wild fruit and any sort of vermin they met in the woods. Fever and want struck them down, and soon they were dying like flies in the fall. The survivors looked like nothing on earth, save ghosts of emaciated corpses, emerging from tombs and charnel-houses with their rags flapping round their gangling limbs and sinking into gulfs round their famished stomachs. Well had the punishment fitted the crime! It made *some* folk, as Clemenceau said, almost believe in Providence.

Presently, they ascended mountains, where their poor starved Indians froze to death, in their nakedness. But the cold and rarefied air of the mountains forced the ruthless Alfinger to turn back again, down to the hot savannahs where avenging Indians, who had aroused the country, lay in wait. The fierce tribes then set on and vanquished the debilitated Spaniards and Germans; but it was the beastly mosquitoes that eventually forced the survivors of the expedition to retreat once more to the *montaña* where cold and wounds killed even the brutal and tough Alfinger. He perished, this Bavarian lansquenet-knight, in the cold, bleak mountains of Cachiri. Only a handful of survivors reached back to Cartagena. They left behind them a memory of cruelty and rapine that made the name of Spaniard stink in Indian nostrils and, across the broad and roaring seas, caused the hardy Elizabethan rovers, and their sons in, and before, Cromwell's day, to style the conquistadores and their posterity a race of "monsters and blood-suckers".

Diego de Ordaz—he was an old conquistador under Cortes, in Mexico—was near the confluence of the Caroni, when, Indians said, that far to the west of the mouth of the Rio Meta (modern Oriente of Colombia) lived great nations who were *clothed*, had much gold, and *rode on animals smaller than stags* (llamas?). But it was in 1535 that the Spaniard, Luis Daza, in the town of Tacunga, near Quito, met an Indian coming from Bogotá, in Nueva Granada, who had been sent by the chief, Zipa, to seek military aid from the Inca Atahualpha who had, as Zipa could not have known, recently been garrotted by Pizarro and his Castilian thugs. The Indian spoke of a priest-king, far away to the east, who powdered his body in greased gold-dust and then plunged into the waters of a mountain tarn.

Georg von Speier, another old German knight, when he was governor of Venezuela, took practical steps to satisfy his yearning for El Dorado and his curiosity about the story. In 1536, undeterred by the fate of Alfinger, his countryman, he headed an expedition of 300 foot-soldiers and 100 cavalry, which started from Coro, on the north-east bank of the gulf of Maracaibo, and struck into the endless llanos of Venezuela. Their trail led them into the mountains of Merida. They reached spots in the South American wilds which have not even been seen by Europeans, or Latin-Americans since their day. Von Speier descended from the mountains into the wet, green plains of the llanos, between the Apure and the Meta. His baggage and horses were futile for penetrating mountains and their recesses eastwards in Guiana. So, south-west into the fires of the sunset, von Speier and his soldiers took the trail for San Juan de los llanos. Clouds of mosquitoes made their life a misery, and when the rains fell the adventurers were reduced to such straits that they had to grub up roots for food. In the dense woods the jaguars jumped on their horses and killed one Spaniard. Going farther into what, to-day, is still unknown territory, they were attacked by savage Indians called the Uapes, who got drunk before battle and painted their bodies black as the devil himself.

At the large native village of La Fragua—Pueblo de Nuestra Señora—Speier said he found the *Temple of the Sun* and a *convent of Virgins*, like those found in Perú and Nueva Granada (modern Colombia). He was away for more than a year, and travelled 1,500 miles from the coast into the unknown. At last, he reached back to the shores of the Caribbean, in Venezuela.

Others took up the search after him. There was Nicolas Fedremann, who was supposed to follow Speier's party with supplies. He wandered off treasure-hunting on his own and was for three years lost in the wilds of the llanos and the still unknown back country of the mountains on the northern Brazilian border. He came back with a budget of strange stories and started others out on the mystic trail. One of them was Philip von Huten, or Hutten—he who is called, in the Spanish colonial archives, Felipe de Urre, or Utre—a former lieutenant of von Speier. In 1541, von Huten, following in the old trail of von Speier, went south across the llanos of Venezuela, with a great expedition. Always these adventurers, like modern German expeditions in Brazil's Matto Grosso, forgot that great expeditions cannot live on *this* country. For a year—a whole year, he and his men wandered in a circle in the wilderness.

They were reduced to such straits that they spread corn-cobs close to the nests of ants in order to capture and eat these insects. They had no idea where they were, or whither going. Somewhere by the Rio Putamene, a tributary, or north of, the Putumayo, in what is even now unknown country, they met an Indian who offered to guide them to a native township, called Macatoa. The guide said it was a rich city, where the people were *clothed*, kept llamas and had vast gold hoards. Surely enough, von Huten came on a place with streets of houses and 800 inhabitants, but it had no gold. He reached the country of the Uapes, who sent him on a trail of from 500–800 miles, in the direction of the sunrise, to Macatoa, in the land of the Omaguas. This pueblo appears to have been somewhere in the vague and misty territory westward and south-westward of the Rio Orinoco's head-water country towards the eastern Andean foothills (and a long way from the Sierra Parime, of southern Venezuela).

The wandering Jesuit missioners—whose records and manuscripts in Brazilian archives tell some queer stories of the mysteries of the ancient land of South America which the members of this order made contact with in the sixteenth and seventeenth centuries, and later— call them, in the words of one Jesuit monk:

> A very noble tribe of *Indiós* of El Dorado. They may be the remains of some ancient monarchy which was in remote times in South America.

Humboldt calls this the "El Dorado of the Omaguas". They were a powerful off-shoot of the once great race of the Caribs, who overran Brazil and spread into the Antilles of the "Caribbean" Sea. Another Latin-American writer suggests that Macatoa lay along the Rio Guiaviare basin towards the Sierra Parima, in southern Venezuela. Wherever the place was, von Huten's hardy men had reached it, in many days. They certainly found a city of 5,000 people, with stone houses, streets and plazas, but it was *not* the city of their golden dreams. The folk, here, sent them on again. El Dorado was still round the corner, or over the skyline. Five days later, von Huten stood on his Pisgah and looked down on the promised land. His wondering men gazed on a city, lying at the foot of the mountain, stretching as far "as the eye could reach", or of "vast size".

"Its limits we could not see, and its many stone houses were built along straight streets. In the centre was a great temple—either a palace of some mighty lord, or the abode of the king-high priest. It was very lofty. Supposing we had reached the very city of El Dorado, where, said the Indians of Uapes, the temple was full of *idolos* of the purest gold, all jewelled, we mounted our horses, as a screen for the foot-soldiers, and charged down the hill into the city. Entering the streets of this wonderful city, we rode our horses into a solid body of these Omaguas, who disputed our passage with great force. Clouds of arrows sang through the air. Our leader was hit and sore wounded. There were, one of our captains estimated, 15,000 of these Omaguas, who were assembling at the beat of drums sounding from afar. At first we drove them back; but so many came on, and so valiantly did they fight, that we were forced to retreat, bearing our leader with us in a *hamac* tied between two horses. The Omaguas followed us, and so sore we were beset, that our men, in the rearguard, had to fight hard as we got out of their country. Only this rearguard battle saved us from extermination."

Von Huten's men at last reached back home to Cartagena, or Maracaibo, and told such stories of the valour of the strong nation of the Omaguas that none ever seem to have braved the dangers of the trail after his day.

Nine years passed, during which even the stream of vast quantities of treasure and jewels, found in Inca Perú, seemed to be running into a desert of sand—in the eyes of the needy crowds of Spanish and other adventurers. *El Virrey*, at Lima, beset by the risings and ructions of hardy, hungry and ruthless men who were not born for farms or monasteries, looked round for some way to rid the land of this picturesque crowd of *bravis* and rufflers and gangsters. What better than to start them out on a new El Dorado trail? If they found treasure, well, the Crown and the *audiencia* would have their lion's share—after the hunters' return. If they did not, then none would return to tell tales out of the belly of a jaguar, or roar defiance at *adelantados y corregidores*, out of the cooking-pots of the anthropophagi, who, everyone knew, dwelt in the far land towards the misty Amazon, behind the cordilleras. It was good riddance to *hijos de las putas*, and might the *Demonio* guard and *keep* his very own fellows!

So that was how Don Pedro de Ursua, was put on the trail of another El Dorado: *El Gran Paytite*.

It was in the year 1560 that this young Navarrese knight passed down the Papamine to the Amazon, on the trail of treasure cities. Although Ursua did not know it, he was really setting out to hunt for the *real* El Dorado: that land of the lost, white race of old and incredibly ancient civilized Hy-Brazil, of cities of gold, pyramids stored with massy statues and images of pure gold and gems, of the *Casa del Sol* (mystic House of the Sun), and of the great golden lake which rivalled the lapidarian vision of that hierophant of the Eastern mysteries who is known as St. John of Patmos, the mystic Evangelist. There were 1,500 men with him, some of them the choicest scoundrels who ever cut throats in old Seville or Toledo. They had got so many *doncellas honradas* with child, or beat up so many reverend friars of orders grey or black—what cared they?—and inquisitive alguazils, that they found it better to run away to sea aboard a lousy, starve-gut galleon than stay to pay the piper, or the padre in the stone-cold *carcel*.

On went the barquentine down the Rio Huallagu, northwards to the mighty Amazon. It was safe to say that if these rufflers ever met the redoubtable, Amazon fighting women and beat them, those would have no need to wait till the following April for any sexual congress dances! The expedition passed the mouth of the Ucayli, when a sudden mutiny—perhaps less sudden than seemed—split the company in two and caused a certain Long John Silver, of old Castile to take steps to suffer no rivals near his new throne. This "Juan Argento" was a land-pirate, named Lopez de Aguirre. No sooner was he elected captain of the new company than he cut the throat of gallant Don Pedro de Ursua and temporarily appointed one Guzman, as commander. Perhaps this step was forced on Aguirre, for, before long, Guzman's throat, too, was cut under a palm tree, and lo, Aguirre was now captain for good and all!

Aguirre's type was singularly like that of pirate Henry Avery, *alias* Every, or Ben Bridgman, of King William III's later day. The monk Pedro Simon paints a lively picture of this picturesque ruffler and land-pirate:

> He was the *Demonio* himself, this Aguirre! About 50 years, short of statue, sparsely built, coarse-featured, of a villainous weasand, which any hangman would have slit with pleasure. His face was small and lean, his neck and cheek pock-marked, his beard black as a coal, and when he looked at you, out of dark eyes piercing as a falcon, his gaze was stern and threatening. But withal, he was a noisy talker and a boaster, if well backed by the *compañeros*, and bold and determined; otherwise, he was an arrant coward. So hardy was his habit of body that he could endure endless fatigue, afoot or on horse-back. Never was he seen without two coats of mail, or a steel breastplate, and he always carried a sword, dagger, arquebus or lance. He slept mostly by day, being careful of his throat, for he was afraid of resting at night lest one steal on him in the dark. Never did he take off his armour altogether, nor hang up his weapons. Turbulent was this *señor* Aguirre, lover of broils and breeder of mutinies, enemy of all good men and deeds.

These land-pirates at last found their barquentine breasting the waters of the young Amazon. Here, it was the villainous Aguirre, after another murder or two, who picked a quarrel with a young and beautiful Spanish widow, Doña Iñez de Altienza who had come with her lover, Don Pedro de Ursua, on this ill-starred and dangerous journey. The Doña must have been a brave woman, fit wife for a gallant Castilian, or Navarrese hidalgo. Aguirre one dusky evening picked on the Doña as did the wolf on the lamb whose ancestors had, according to the wolf, robbed or injured him. On the pretext that her mattress took up too much room in the boat, Aguirre cut her throat! After which he and his gang robbed and murdered a few score of Indians along the banks of the river.

As the poet Castellanos wrote:

Fair Iñez's maids, in grief and sorrow stark,
  Strewed her lone grave with leaves, and flowers red as her gore;
And on a mighty bole they cut in bark
  The name of her old Spain will see no more.

On went Aguirre, the pitiless. He achieved the feat of crossing South America from west to east, though he was not the first to do so.

Arriving on the shores of the Gulf of Paria, he sailed across to the isle of Margarita, where his devils cut Spanish throats, robbed honest men, raped pretty women, and roared defiance at the king in faraway Spain. Aguirre even went so far as to write to the king in old Spain a letter that would have done credit to the most republican-spirited British pirate in one of the Hanoverian Georges' days:

> Listen to me, king of Spain who has been very cruel and ungrateful to me and my *compañeros* for all the good services we have done thee. They who write thee from this land deceive thee, who seest things from too far off. We will obey thee and thy governors no longer. Remember, king Philip, thou hast no right to draw revenues from these provinces. Their conquest hath caused thee no danger. I take it for certain few kings go to hell, only because they are few. If there were many, none would go to heaven. For I believe you are all worse than Lucifer. You hunger and thirst after human blood. I think little of you and despise you all. Your government is no more than an air bubble.

Aguirre then tells of the expedition. How the "Frenchman", de Ursua delayed building ships, and then had them made only in the wet, Motilone country, a year after the *Virrey*, the Marquis de Caneté of Perú, sent him on the expedition to the Amazons:

> Ursua was vain and capricious. The ships were built in the rainy season, and so they came to pieces and we had to build canoes to descend the most powerful river in Perú. It seemed to us we were in a sea of fresh water. For 300 leagues, we went down that river. Ursua was a bad governor, and we killed him. We raised Don Fernando de Guzman to be our king, and because I would not consent to their evil deeds, they wished to murder me. So I killed him, his captain of his guard, lieutenant-general, his major-domo, his chaplain—who said masses—a woman, a knight of the order of Rhodes, an admiral, two ensigns, and five or six of his servants. I named captains and sergeants, but I hanged them for wishing to murder me . . . All the course, evil fortune befell us. In eleven months and a half we reached the mouth of the river, having travelled for more than a hundred days over more than 1,500 leagues. This river had a course of 2,000 leagues of fresh water, and most of the shores are inhabited. God knows how we escaped from that terrible lake! I advise thee, o Philip, send no Spanish fleet up this ill-fortuned river, for if thou sendest 100,000 men not one shall return alive, or dead. We give thanks to our arms for what we may win, denied by thee; but I am rebel against thee till death.

Aguirre and his bandits next transported themselves ashore in Venezuela, where they went into the llanos, sacked farms, ravaged settlements and, generally, turned the country upside-down, till the country was roused and became too hot for them. The governor seduced the bandit's men with a promise of pardon—probably not kept—and, then, at his *hacienda*, one afternoon, Aguirre was warned by his one faithful adherent, Lamoso, that soldiers were on the way to take him. Aguirre rushed into the bedroom of his 14-year old daughter, a "loaded arquebus" (*sic*, but it was probably a matchlock) in his hands. "Commend thee to God, my daughter! I am about to kill thee. It shall be in the power of none to point finger of scorn at thee and call thee daughter of a traitor." A black woman knocked up his arm, and the shot went wide. Aguirre snatched a poniard at his waist, as he heard the clattering of hoofs in the patio, and stabbed his daughter to the heart. "Die as I die!", he screamed, rushing to the door, to find the farm surrounded, and himself seized by soldiers who hanged him, or shot him at once.

The spotlight on the moving picture of El Dorado history then switched from the Amazon country to the Orinoco, where the Carib Indians assured the Spaniards the real "Dorado" lay. In 1536, Pedro de Acosta saw all his men pushed into the cooking-pot of up-country cannibals, when he tried to resolve the riddle of the Orinoco El Dorado. He was followed, a year later, by that Don Diego de Ordaz (referred to *supra*), who met Indians near the confluence of a river with the Caroni. They said it lay to the west of the mouth of the Meta, north of the Sierra Parima. The story took the usual form of great, clothed nations, with tons of gold, riding on animals smaller than stags. The Don himself found nothing; but it was one of his men, a mutineer, Juan Martinez who, years later, told a queer and romantic story, on his death-bed in a convent, about his adventures in the golden city. While de Ordaz's boats were near the mouth of the Caroni, Martinez had an accident with some gunpowder, which exploded all the ammunition of the party. The leader, de Ordaz marooned Martinez. He caused him to be shoved in a canoe with no paddles, or food, and let him drift at the mercy of the stream.

Martinez drifted on the turbid waters into the romance of as fine an autobiographical novel as one might hope to read, in any age, of colour and high emprise!

Many months afterwards, a strange white man, emaciated and burnt black by sun and exposure, staggered out of the jungly forests into an Indian village, where the *cacique* detailed men to take him to the island of Margarita, off the north-eastern coast of Venezuela. He was naked as he was born and sicker than any dog in the hungry town of Cordoba. Yea, he knew what old Spain understands as the national disease: *la hambre*. Here, a good-natured Spanish captain of a ship took pity on him and rescued him off the beach. The strange man was shipped to Porto Rico, where, down and out, and ill and worn, he was charitably taken into a convent of the Dominican friars. He fell sick unto death, and after lapsing in and out of delirium, asked to speak to the prior of the convent, into whose astonished hands, he poured out two gourds of gold beads, praying the black friars to say masses for his poor soul.

He told the prior, between bouts of weakness and delirium, a romantic story:

Your Paternity, behold in me Juan Martinico, called Martinez, I had a misfortune with a flask of powder which caused our captain, Don Diego de Ordaz to ship me into a canoe and set me adrift at the mercy of the stream. The canoe floated down the river, and, in the dusk of the evening, under the golden light of the stars, I, who had no paddles, waved a strip of shirt to some *Indiós*, on the other bank, who paddled out in their canoes and took me off. They were amazed at the sight of my white skin, these Guiana *Indiós*; for never before had they seen or known of white men. So they took me into the forest, to their village, to show me to their cacique, as a strange being found in the river. I was blinded round the eyes with a strip of bark, like cotton-cloth, so that I should not see where I went. On and on we went into forest and across savannahs. For fifteen days we went, sleeping at nights in the dense forests with a fire burning to keep off the prowling *tigres*. Then, one hot day, we climbed a high mountain, and by the sounds of the people around me, I guessed we were in a great city. They removed the bark-bandages, and lo, I saw a wondrous sight! Far before me, as the eye could read, stretched a great city of the plain covered with many houses whose roofs glittered in the blazing sun, as if tiled with gold. There were great and splendid palaces and houses and mansions of great lords. In the middle of the great city lives a great and mighty monarch; but although we travelled the whole of that day, after descending the mountain, we did not reach the royal palace till night had fallen. I was set free, and fed well and treated kindly. I could walk about the great city, but not quit its limits. Here, I stayed 7 months, and one day went down to the shores of this great lake on which this golden city, they call Manoa, stands. They let me take up its golden sands in my own hands. Rich, pure, gold sparkled in the sun! A ransom for a mighty kingdom if so one could take it from the country. But desire to see my countrymen moved me sore, and I asked to be let leave, but was refused. I renewed my petitions many times, and, at last, the king let me go, warning me not to betray the secret of the location to any outside. And the king gave me as much gold as I and the guides could carry. After many days in the forests, and mountains, we reached the banks of the mighty river Orinoco. But one day, the cannibals, who dwell round about here in the wood, fell on our party, stole all the gold we had, except some we had hidden in the gourds under our provisions, and left us only with what we stood up in, to starve and wander on into the country. My guides returned to their own land; but I went on, enduring many hardships, hunger and thirst, and risking life from prowling Indians, till I was taken in an Indian canoe to Margarita. Your Paternity, I am like to die before to-morrow's dawn; so I shall never see again old Spain, where to our Lord the King, I had hoped to tell my story of golden Manoa.

The story fell like a bar of gold, plop and plump into the river of time, and the waves and rings rippled and increased in circumference till they broke far away on the shores of old England. That story was fated to bring about the death at the headman's axe, years later, in the Tower of London, of the gallant Englishman, Sir Walter Raleigh, who liked his pipe and tobacco and was detested by a Scottish pig and pervert and hypocritical barbarian fool, Jamie Stuart who, like his descendant, Queen Victoria, abhorred tobacco and loathed smokers.

It was in the time of the 36th Inca Huira Cocha Capac that the Peruvians decided to investigate the stories of El Dorado. When he was in Quito, the Inca heard of a warlike people who wore decent clothes and lived on the other side of the mountain ranges, which run from Santa Marta to the straits of Magellan. He dispatched six captains with troops and ordered their route to be through the country called *La Canela*, the land of the Cofanes, or Quijos Indians. (Gonzalo Pizarro took that very route "through the country of the Cinnamon", later, in 1539, no doubt having heard in Quito something of the story of this Inca expedition of the recent past.) The Inca expedition saw many peoples living in the dense forest on the eastern slopes of the great Andean cordilleras, and along the banks (barras), and beaches of mighty rivers. Many of the nations wore only their own hair as garments. A great battle took place, and a company of the Inca's soldiers became lost in the forests and had to live on nuts and wild fruits.

Nuñez Cabeza de Vaca, adelantado (provincial governor) of Paraguay, sent Hernando de Ribera up the River Paraguay to visit the Yarayes—a tribe on a land occupied by the great prehistoric South American sea of the Sarayés, somewhere in the region of El Gran Chaco. Ribera reached the middle of the country of the Urtuéses Indians, where he had the first news of the Amazons of Gran Paititi, and of a very rich country located somewhere in the unknown to the north-west. The rainy season came on, and sickness struck down the soldiers. A revolt of the *expedicionarias* forced Ribera to return to Paraguay, in the early part of 1554.

While the Spaniards were in the villages of the Urtuéses, and the Abureñes Indians, Ribera saw many caciques from interior villages, who brought him feathers like those in Inca (Perú) ceremonials, and rudely made plates of metal, called in old Spanish *chefalonias*.[1]

Ribera talked with the caciques about the peoples in the interior. At Valladolid, in 1515, Ribera swore a statement before an *escribano* (public notary), Pedro Hernandez. In this affidavit he said:

> The Urtuése Indians are brave men who till the land . . . I went from this place through an uninhabited country till I reached latitude 14° 20′, following the direction of the setting sun . . . (This would be some way south-west of Cuyabá, in the Brazilian Matto Grosso.—AUTHOR.) Here, the Urtuéses and Aburuñes Indians told me that, ten days' journey away to the north-west, were women who had great towns, with much white and yellow metal, that their chairs and seats (*assientos*) and household utensils were of this yellow metal (gold). Their ruler was a woman of the same nation. They are warriors and much feared by the natives. Before reaching them, there is a nation of very small Indians who war on these women, and on my informant Indians, too. At a certain time of the year, the women unite with their neighbours. If the children are girls they keep them. If they are boys, they feed them until they are weaned,

[1] *Chefalonias:* silver or gold used to make plates, dishes, covers, or objects of gold and silver for the melting pot.

and then send them to the fathers. On the other side of the women's village, are great populations of Indians. I did not have this information about the women, because I had asked for it . . . The Indians told me these women dwelt on the banks of a very large lake, on the side where the sun went down. So they are to the north-west between the flanks of the Mt. Santa Martha and the lake which they call *Casa del Sol* (House of the Sun). Beyond these Indians and the women are very considerable nations of blacks . . . The story these Indians told me is that these blacks have long beards like the Moors (*tenian barbas como aguileñas [hook-noses] a manera de moros*). They knew they were black because their fathers had met them . . . And neighbouring the said land are people who go clothed and who have houses and towns of stone and earth, and are very big people, with much white metal and yellow, in such abundance that they use no other in their houses for their domestic vessels, jars and ollas, which are very large, and they said more besides . . . The Indians signed that these blacks dwelt to the north-west, and if the Spaniards wanted to go there, in 15 days they would reach villages bordering the blacks . . . According to the signs they gave, I judge that the *pueblos* are located in 12° Lat. on the side to the north-west, between the Santa Marta mountains and the Rio Marañon (Amazon). They are warlike and fight with bows and arrows. Also, in the north-west by north, the Indians say, are other great towns of Indians so large that, in a day, one could not cross from one side to the other. All these Indians have much gold and silver, and use it in their houses, and are all clothed. And they can reach there very readily and quickly by land all the way, which is very much populated. And on the side to the west (*ribera*: shore or strand), there is a very large lake of water, so wide that one cannot see the land on the other side. And on the shore of the said lake are great, clothed people who have much metal and stones that shine brilliantly (*relumbraban mucho*), which stones they embroider in their clothes, and they take the stones from that lake. They have very large towns, and are all farmers with abundance of the necessaries of life. They raise many ducks and other birds. These towns lie 15 days from where I spoke with these Indians, my informants. There are good roads there, when the waters are down, but at that time they were swollen with rains.

We should have gone there, but were too few to accept the offer of the Indians to guide us, through wide lands thickly populated . . . The Indians also signed to us that, west by south-west, were large peoples with towns and houses of stone, and that they were very good people (*buena gente:* a decent folk), clothed and very rich, with much silver and gold, and large flocks of sheep, of very large size, which they used in clearing and tilling the ground, as beasts of burden. They said that to reach this country we should pass through thickly populated territory and take little time.

Between the said *poblaciones* were another Christian people, and there were great sandy deserts with no water. The Indians said they knew these were Christian people, because, in past times, the Indians bordering them had heard the natives of the *pueblos* say that, passing through the said deserts, they had seen come many clothed people, white, with beards and with animals, that they signed were horses, and that because there were no waters they had seen the people return, and that many of them had died, and that the Indians of the said *poblaciones* believed the white people had come from the edge of the desert. And also they signed that, on the border of the west, in the southern quarter, were great mountains where none lived, and that they had tried to pass, because of the intelligence they had that people lived on that border; but they had not been able to pass, dying of hunger and thirst . . . These Indians said they knew for a certainty that the other Indians of that country communicated with each other, because they had talked with them and had seen the Christians' horses cross the desert over which they had travelled. Where the sierras fell to the south-west into lower lands there were great towns and nations, very rich in gold. The Indians said they also knew that, on the other side in the salt water, very large ships sailed. And all the nations and towns had only one ruler over them . . . I questioned each of the Indians apart in private, for a day and a night, to see if their stories varied, but after using different methods of inquiries, found their stories never varied or were discrepant . . .

Ribera placed his right hand on a missal and swore by God and St. Mary, and the four evangelists, that all he said was true, and in good faith . . .

The missal was open and held in the hands of Francisco Gonzalez Pan y Agua (Paniagua), and placing his right hand and making the sign of the Cross, Ribera declared he had so been told by the chief and agèd men about the interior of the country, testimony given mainly at Unatabere, a very large village. He also said the Indians assured him that the Rio Areati (Ycareati), above the said mountains that were very high, made a waterfall. By all that he hoped now and hereafter, Don Hernando swore "Amen!" This testimony is signed and witnessed by Padre Pariagua, Sebastian de Valdivieso, *camarero* (chamberlain) of the Governor, Gaspar de Hortigosa, and Juan de Hoces, residents of the city of Cordoba, and the *escribano*, Pedro Hernandez, in the year 1555.

A very remarkable account of this Gran Paititi, of which Hernando de Ribera testified on oath, in 1555, is given in a historical poem by Barco Centenera, which was published at Lisboa, on 10th May, 1601. In it, Centenera seems to have been drawing on lost stories circulated by soldiers in the train of Hernando de Ribera, about 50 years earlier. Gran Paytiti, or Paititi was located, it was supposed, to the north of a swamp in the country of the Xarayes, which, as I have said, is in the region of the Gran Chaco, once the site of a very ancient sea, which was when the Atlantean-Brazilians ruled their empire in old Brazil. It was said to be near the source of the Paraguay, where a king, called *el Gran Moxo* ruled over immense riches.

I, here, for the first time in English, summarize what Centenera says:

The Indian lived in a lagoon. All round were others, in well-built and ordered towns. In the middle of the lake was an island on which were buildings of great beauty and splendour, beyond human understanding. The mansion of the Lord, the Gran Moxo, was built of white stone right to the very roof. It had two very high towers at its entrance, and a stairway in the middle. At a pillar in the middle, on the right, were two live lions. They couched at its sides, in chains, whose links were of gold. On the summit of this pillar, 25 feet high, shone a great moon. It illuminated all the lake, dispelling darkness and shadows by night and day, so that all appeared very bright. Past these towers, you entered a small plaza (square) well squared, and the greater part of its expanse was fresh and cool with shady trees. In the middle of the plaza stood a fine fountain from which water gushed out, in abundance. Its four conduits were of fine and thick gold. The trough of this fountain is more than three feet squared, and seems made by more than mortal man, so great its beauty and perfection. In the utmost degree the silver shines, showing its fineness and loveliness. The water never diminishes in volume and force. Ever it gushes from the basin of the fountain. The gateway of the palace is small, and of copper, but strong and well formed. Its hinges are sunk into the hard stone. Strong buildings are all around. There is an ancient gatekeeper (*portero*). In the middle of the towers and the pillar, his knees prostrated, this old man raises his eyes to the moon, and in a savage voice, proclaims: "Fall down and worship this, that alone is one, The Sun, and there is none other than him." At the top (of the temple?) is an altar of fine silver, with four small lamps that burn at the side, and some never go out. Four priests serve at the shrine. There is a sun more scarlet than a red cardinal's hat. It shines over all. The sun is of fine gold and is adored . . . The Gran Moxo is lord of these riches. He is valorous and noble, and has many strong vassals in his kingdom . . . To our hurt, not long ago, the fieriness of his arrows we experienced . . . To attain these riches, we have to conquer the Chiquitos on the frontiers of the land of the Gran Moxo, lord of the lagoon.[1]

We may comment that there is a very recognizable touch of great Atlantis about these lights of a moon that never goes out, and the moats and towers in this queer city of the Gran Moxo, Lord of the Lagoon. Who knows what of truth and actuality from the secret heart of old South America is crystallized in this story of the Gran Moxo? Just *what* were Hernando de Ribera's soldiers told by the Urtuéses and Aburruñes, Indians, on the upper reaches of the Paraguay, in the year 1554? It is clear that a great deal has not come down to us.

An old Spanish document in Perú tells about a Portuguese effort to find Gran Paititi, in the early seventeenth century:

There has arrived here (in Quito) Padre Acuña of the western Indies. His coming has this purpose and motive: that some Portuguese seek to enter by the Rio Orinoco that flows by many mouths into the northern sea, opposite the shores of Trinidad of the Indies. They have ascended the river for many leagues, infinite in number, until they came near the lake called Patiti. (Is this the Lago de *Parime*?—AUTHOR.) At last, they

---

[1] A monk in the sixteenth century showed in Lima a painted map of the riches of El Dorado, and on it, among other things, were three hills of inestimable value and richness. It was said it was a map of the city of the *Gran Moxo*. At Guatavita, in the old Muysca territory of what is now Colombia, there was also a temple where was a great image of the sun in gold, and the image of the moon was set on top of a pillar, 25 feet high, with a base of a single piece of silver.

reached in sight of Quito, in Perú, a journey never before attempted. The Real Audiencia is startled by this daring attempt, since they were enemies who desired to plunder one of the richest cities in all the Americas. The Audiencia ordered them to return at once, by the same route, and forbade them ever again to navigate it. Padre Acuña adventured to come with them, and he noted the heights, hazards, the latitudes, boundaries, small bays (*calas*), gulfs, islands, and directions of routes, on this journey. He has brought back a detailed itinerary; many strange races, tongues, savage dresses and men never before encountered, or imagined to exist. He says they passed six leagues from the country of the *giants*, where, notwithstanding, their statures were the same as that of the babies they suckled! And that stature is very tall and big . . . They have been ordered to reveal nothing, lest the enemies undertake to prosecute their navigation to a successful end.

Even in these days of fast modern transport, a land journey of close on 2,500 miles over dangerous and nearly unknown territory, right across Venezuela's Parima ranges into the Oriente of Colombia and Ecuador, right to the doors of Quito on the cordilleras of the Andes, would be deemed matter for remark and the news cables. These Portuguese explorers and the "rare plucked 'un'" of a Jesuit padre had in them all the verve and daring of the valiant conquistadores on the El Dorado trail!

About 1575, one Don Toribio de Ortiguera, author of *Noticias y relación de Quito y del Rio de las Amazonas* (manuscript *siglo XVI*), heard that, in December, 1569, here was still living in Quito an old Indian woman, Doña Isabel Guachay who had accompanied the expedition of Inca Huira Capac to the country of the Cofanes.

Says de Ortiguera:

> The Inca troops entered by way of Chapi, in Pamilone, 16 leagues north-east of Quito, and searched the provinces of Iques and Atun-Ique, bordering each other. As the troops went they cut roads through the forests, and in 6 days arrived at a valley of friendly Indians, wearing their hair on the top of the head clipped short, but very long before and behind. These Indians were clothed in mantles, knotted upon the shoulder, after the manner of gypsies, and short, full breeches. Their land is flat, hot and grows maize, cotton, yucas, squashes, sweet potatoes, turkeys, ducks. The men wear great plates of gold like shields, and the women many gold jewels. They shoot missiles with slings. Salt and cutting-axes were all they wanted to barter from Huira Capac. Mines of gold had they, which they dug out with sticks cut from the woods, not having tools. But they got out much gold like squash seeds. In that valley is a river whose banks are thronged with Indians, navigating canoes. Huira Capac erected stone-walled houses, in the valleys, and received the homage of caciques, eight of whom he sent, with thirty Indians, to Cuzco, there to learn the Quichua tongue. When the Spaniards came to the land Inca Huira had died of small-pox, and the conquistadores were never able to see him and speak to him about his discoveries. So they did not visit the region in the forests, nor have they ever been able to find the way to it.

It was Don Antonio de Berreo, fresh from the wars of Europe, who fairly set the "Dorado" ball rolling into the great palace of the Escurial in old Madrid. He wrote a letter to *el Rey*, Don Felipe, who was then in the thick of preparing his grandiose Armada to invade old England, and who, in consequence, was interested in any way of financing his brawls that convulsed all Protestant Europe. Philip of Spain listened with all his avaricious, pious ears to this old soldier of the Holy Roman Emperor, Charles V's wars.

Berreo, born in Segovia, in 1520, had heard in 1584, that:

> beyond the Tunjan, and the cordillera of Santa Fé de Bogotá was a very large laguna, on whose banks, or on the other side of which were great towns, having large populations and king with gold and precious stones.

On 24th May, 1585, he wrote to Philip II, of Spain:

> They say that in the cordillera there is a very large lagoon (*laguna*, or lake) and that on the other side of it are great populations and many large towns, with great riches of gold and gems.

This *may* have been in the Sierra de Mapichi, in Alto Orinoco, a province of southern Venezuela. Round about was one of the famous colonies of the South American fighting women: the Amazons, whose story I told in a previous chapter of this book.

Berreo claimed that, after starting out of Perú, on the Pacific, he reached the mouth of the Rio Orinoco, on the Atlantic, in 1585–88, within four days' journey of the golden "Dorado" city, when hostile Indians forced him to turn away from the promised land. His story appears in the Spanish documents, cited in a British Museum manuscript of A.D. 1593. He tells of "clothed Indians":

> The land of Dorado is eleven days' journey from where the Spaniards arrived. They met Indians who said there is a very large lake in what is called the land of Manoa. Around are a vast number of clothed people, towns, and lords, who arrived there 20 years ago. There are a multitude of people accoutred with small bows, who fought with those of the lake and have been subduing the great part of these nations. I estimate there are there 2,000,000 Indians. The great lake is close to the sierra which is on the right hand, extending through Guiana, away from the cordillera which the Spaniards saw, and faces south. It is a land devoid of forest, a cool land, with pleasant and temperate valleys . . . A multitude of pueblos with great *caciques* is near the river, and all have one great lord whom they obey and revere.

In that very year 1593–4, Captain George Popham captured a galleon at sea, and took off her a letter concerning Berreo's El Dorado, written by Don Domingo de Vera Ibargoyen, *maesse de campo* (camp-major, or adjutant):

Abrill de 1593.

On this fourth of May, we came to a province about five leagues thence, and the *cacique*, one Renato, met us in a friendly and peaceable manner. He entertained us in a very large house, and gave us much gold, and the interpreter asking him whence this gold came, he said: "From a province not a day's journey off, where there are so many Indians as would shadow the sun, and so much gold as all yonder plain will not contain it!" In that country, when they enter into the *Borrachera* they take the gold in dust and anoint themselves all over to make the braver show, and to the end the gold may cover them they anoint their bodies with crushed herbs placed on a glutinous substance. . . .

They promised us they would, if we went with them to this country, give us aid; but they were of such infinite number that if they set about us they would kill us . . . They went to a certain place, or down, and pulled up the grass by the roots, took the earth, putting it into a great bucket which they carried, and washed at the river, and that which they got out in powder of gold, they kept for the *Borracheras*, and that which was in pieces they wrought into Eagles. (*Borrachera*, in Castilian, means a feast with drink, or dancing.—AUTHOR.)

Three days later (7 *de Mayo*), Ibargoyen was in the "valli de Santa Cruz", where "great towns stretched for five leagues on either side". Here, the cacique, Carupano, royally entertained the Spaniards. The cacique said the El Doradans "were Guiana" (*quellos eran Guayana*), and their country was about fifty leagues farther on. They were so many in number "that they veil the light of the sun". Being a fighting people, the El Doradans warred on the many Indian nations around. Carupano then gave Ibargoyen a rather vague route to the land of gold and warriors—past the Rio Marañon (Amazon), through the country of the Piriamy *Indiós*, till you reached a great lagoon, salt, which "they call the sea". "All round are many nations . . . next to the lagoon rises the Rio Caroni . . . To the lagoon from Santa Cruz was eleven to twelve days' journey. . . .

And from it came a great many clothed people and fought them above the lake region, and they conquered and lived among them.

If the story were only half-true, then the strongest expedition of El Dorado hunters might reckon to have the devil of a time on the trail of this Orinoco-Guianan Tom Tiddler's land! They would need all the masses said by Father Francis of the White Friary, together with anticipatory absolution of sins from Fray Dominic of the devilish Black Friars ere ever their tough carcases and assoiled souls entered or prematurely quitted this mystic warriors' country!

Ibargoyen also heard of Indians "as many as be the grasses on ye grounde, whose men have the points of their shoulders higher than their crownes of their heades, and had so many hens, 'twas wonderful! These men wore eagles of gold hanging from their breasts, and pearls in their ears, and they danced, being all covered with gold. An Indian brought us an eagle that weighed 27 pounds of gold!" Which was proof that would, in our day, commend itself to a London or a Bond street jeweller and vassal of the Medici, with the three balls, who advertised for all with gold to haste and exchange it for Bank of England currency paper.

I may, however, interpose a word of comment: Ibargoyen, like de Berreo, writes a very confused story, topographically. It is easy to understand how the old cartographers were misled into locating the mystic Lake Dorade, or Lake Parime—"the great salt Lagoon, they call the sea"—in the Guianas, or what, to-day, would be somewhere on the borders of eastern Venezuela and British Guiana, possibly north of Mount Roraima. Probably, the Serra Parima was much nearer the El Dorado of Berreo and Ibargoyen. It is hard to resist the conclusion that de Berreo and Ibargoyen were unconsciously speaking of two widely separated and different "Dorados". De Berreo's El Dorado is remarkably like that of gunner-bosun Martinez of the Diego de Ordaz expedition, or the El Dorado of the "noble Omaguas". Maybe, the confusion arose, in part, owing to the Spanish, or native Indian confusion of the colonial outpost of the Amazon women, on the borders of Venezuela–Guiana–Brazil with their old original homeland, close, as will be seen in this book, to the mysterious country of El Gran Paytite. As a matter of fact, Raleigh's *Golden Manoa* never did exist in the Guianas of the old Spanish jurisdiction. It lay *far to the west*, somewhere in the foothills of the Rio Amazonas-Marañon, a fact suggested in that a tribe of Indians, associated with ancient writings of unknown origin, and living near the Rio Ucayli, in northern Perú, bore the name of *Manoa! Gold* in plenty was there. (*See page* 211 *supra.*)

The story even impressed those cold-eyed, hard-boiled unimaginative Castilian gentlemen, reverend *señores* who sat on the Sierra de Guadarraman oaken benches of the stone house of the Council of the Indies, far away in old Spain. For, in 1595–96, so I read in the archives at Seville, the council's *señores* even dispatched Flemish fly-boats, with an expedition of tough Castilian gentlemen in them, to seek this El Dorado where gold outshone the sun and pearls transcended the dreams of a Red Sea fisherman. Their destination was the Lake of Parima or Parime—that most elusive sheet of golden water which neither this Flemish fly-boat expedition, nor any of their successors on the trail were destined to attain.

Indeed, how many ill-starred El Dorado expeditions, many of them meeting tragic fates, started out on this heart-break quest to this Orinoco Trapalanda since Berreo's day, none know exactly. Yet I may say I have unearthed at least thirty archival accounts at Sevilla. All nations were lured to this honey-pot, like wasps to ripe plums in summer-time. Many expeditions never returned, not even by one man, from the forests into which they plunged. They left not even a skull with black, or reddish hair adhering, or a gnawed thigh-bone to suggest the grim explanation of the mystery. In the more fortunate cases, nostalgic dons and tough Spanish *infanteria* may have been adopted as mascots, or medicine men by remote tribes who found them wandering, lost in the unknown wilds. Sickness broke them up, and permanently ruined health was often the guerdon of the rudest and most robustious of adventurers.

There was Don Juan Corteso, whom Doña Juana, in old Spain, never saw again in life. He set out for the golden land, but neither he nor his comrades were again heard of in the frontier settlements and Guianan and Venezuelan *pueblos*. Gaspar de Sylva and his two hopeful brothers were inspired to set forth, but they came back to Trinidad, broken, famished, disillusioned, and cursing Berreo and Don Domingo, on their death-beds. Jeronimo Ortao, what luck had he? Great travail and sore famine in the back country of the Orinoco. He saw none of the men of gold whose multitudes did veil the light of the sun at noon-tide, and having spent all his patrimony and others' funds in aid, he returned and, lamenting like his Jewish namesake, died on a sudden in San Domingo. Even a reverend friar, one Fray Francisco Iala, was bitten by the El Dorado bug. He, and a friend, and a few Indian guides were among the lucky ones! Verily, must his influence with the Madonna, or his especial patronal saint have been exceptionally good and strong! For he and they returned to Guiana with gold eagles, idols, and other jewels. But, risking his luck a second time, the father was carved up by Indians on the lone trail. There were cynics in Santa Fé de Bogotá and Cartagena who said that Father Iala had come short in his *ex-voto* promises to Our Lady of El Dorado!

The friar was followed by Don Alonzo de Herrera who suffered great misery and never passed by so much as a league of old Castile into the country of the golden lake. He was slain by waiting Indians on the trail.

Antonio Sedenno, at first, had better luck, finding much gold and many Indian prisoners, whom, in the good, old conquistadorian manner, he fettered and manacled foot and neck, and who, many of them, dropped dead on the way. The camp-following tigers (jaguars) grew satiated with Indian flesh, and, fancying a change of diet, jumped out, one night in the wood, on the Spaniards, who had great difficulty in beating them off. As for Sedenno, did he not die within the bounds of the golden empire of Orinocan El Dorado, was buried, and most of his men with him?

Then came Agostino Delgado to an Indian *cacique* who treated him magnificently, bestowed on him rich jewels and six seemly slaves, and for that Agostino's nights were lonely, gave him, into the bargain, three lovely, lustrous-eyed maidens for his bachelor-bed? To which the generous *cacique* added bounties of six pretty pages and ten young slaves. And the indecent Spanish *señor* requited his kind host by stealing all the gold he could find, manacling all the Indians, and would have taken the *cacique's* golden hat into the bargain had not an enraged Indian, with bow and arrow, sent Delgado with only one eye—the eye he did not shoot out—into purgatory, Satan refusing to admit such an old Spanish swine into the other place.

I remember, in 1934, looking, in the old colonial Spanish cathedral of Cristoval Colon in the Dominican city of Ciudad Trujillo, at a late sixteenth-century tomb, under the flagstones of which, I imagine, must lie the bones of some hidalgo of old Hispaniola, who lived to return from the El Dorado trail. This saddened hidalgo wrote his own epitaph, a melancholy inscription in sonorous Castilian to which no El Doradan, or modern treasure hunter has ever paid, or will pay any heed:

Señores: I have had my days, have ended my course,
Hope and fortune remain and seek others to mock!

Men who returned from the quest with ill-gotten gold won from other rufflers by treacherous point of sword, or dripping poniard, not seldom lived to be hanged on old Castilian gallows in Merida, Caracas, or Santa Fé, as land-pirates and mutineers. As for the Indians, who were carried off as slaves, whose gold ornaments were stolen, provision-grounds and plantations fired and robbed, whose forest-tracks were strewn with corpses of the murdered, with lone mounds in jungle-glades marking the graves of the European murderers, they reacted according to whether they were *Indiós mansos ó bravos* (tame or fighting Indians). The *bravos* shot holes in the hides of the looting rufflers and raping blackguards, and, if they were not too ill-favoured or emaciated, doubled up their sallow carcases and rammed them into cooking-pots. These had otherwise been too narrow in diameter to accommodate the tall meat and Castilian, or old German "long pig". All the *Indiós mansos* could do, was, if warned in time, to burn the plantations and villages and take to the bush; or if taken unawares and lugged off to slavery, to die in their tracks in the evening, and stink the Castilian captors out of tent and thatched-palm shack, before the dawn rose on the Alto Orinoco!

There is a manuscript in the Hans Sloan collection in the British Museum which shows the reaction of Elizabethan Protestant Englishmen to the stories of the cruelties perpetrated on the Indians by the Spanish Papists. The writer is not certainly known, but may be Sir Walter Raleigh.

Says he:

These Spaniards have, in 100 years passed, killed twenty millions of reasonable creatures (Indians), and now the Queen (Elizabeth of England) would not bee persuaded that now at length the great judge of the world hath heard the sighes, grones, lamentations teares and bloud of so many millions of innocent men, women and children, afflicted, robbed, reviled, branded with hot irons, roasted, dismembred, mangled, stabbed, whipped, racked, scalded with hott oyle, suet, and hoggs grease, put to the strappado, ripped alive, beheaded in sport, drowned, dashed against the rocks, famished, deuoured by mastifes, burned and by infinite crueltyes consumed . . . by that accursèd nation . . . in revenge whereof their owne religious men do make accompte that the just God in judgment will one day horribly chasten and peraduenture wholy subuert and root out the Spanish nation from the world.

Theodore de Bry, writing at Frankfurt, in 1596, even cites a tradition sworn to by Don Antonio de Berreo, of all men, that England was destined to turn back the clock and restore the lost glories of the Incas!

He says:

Deum ego testor mihi a Don Antonio de Berreo affirmatum quemadmodum. . . . I take God to witness that Don Antonio de Berreo affirmed to me, and in like manner from another (he has heard) that particularly in (one of) their temples, among other prophecies, which speak of the loss of the kingdom, this truly may be, that it is said that the Incas, or emperors and Kings of Perú may be brought back again into their realm by another people called England (*quo Inclaterra*).

What adds to the mystery of this Inca temple prophecy is another old Inca tradition which, to this day, has never been cleared up. It was that, in the twelfth century A.D., an *English sailor* was wrecked on the coast of Perú, and when he was coming ashore, dripping from the Pacific surf, there met him on the beach an Inca prince, who asked him in the Quichua tongue: "Who are you?"

The sailor, a young and handsome fellow, replied, in English: "I am an Englishman". Thereafter the prince called him *Ingasman-capac* (handsome Englishman), and he became known as Inca-Manco-Capac. (Of course, Manco Capac, in the old Inca tradition, was a member of the ancient *white*, blue-eyed, Atlantean race of Hy-Brazil—fellow countryman with Quetzalcoatl and Bochicha and Virachcocha—who gave civilized customs and the elements of culture to the barbarian or savage ancestors of Inca Peruvians!)

At the beginning of the seventeenth century, as the *Archivo g̃ral de Yndias (Sevilla)* records, an attempt was made to storm El Dorado from the province of Nueva Granada (Colombia). One, Don Fernando de Oruña, reports home to the Council of the Indies, in 1602:

From the city of Arias, I sent Captain Martin Gomez, with more than 100 men and 200 horses (the men armed and equipped to fit out twice their number), to go and enter the provinces nearest the great rocks (*peñoles*), where, according to the accurate information we possessed, he was to enter and discover the land that has given us so much trouble . . . 1,400 leagues away (? 400 *leagues.*—AUTHOR) and 200 leagues from the great rocks, the Spaniards met 5,000–6,000 Indians and fought with them; but afterwards they would not tell the Spaniards how to cross the rocks and ranges (to El Dorado).

Gomez was forced to retreat, and Capitán Don Fernando de Oruña tried hard to find a path on foot across the ranges to El Dorado. He found that the ridges were thickly populated with very warlike Indians to whom the Spaniards gave a good drubbing. Yet, in the end, the Spaniards had to come away, lean, emaciated men with famished horses, and carrying 112–114 wounded . . .

I went from this city of Santo Thomé for 230 leagues, but could find no pass by which to cross the ranges. The riches of the place were all the time very present to my mind; but the land is so barren and uneven that we could not continue, except at the cost of men's lives.

The governor of Nueva Andalucia (the north-west coast of Colombia), Don Diego de Suarez de Amaya, sent a letter to the King of Spain on 10th August, 1602, in which he said:

> It seems the Dorado can never be found. The want of food is the greatest obstacle to the crossing of the ranges. The Indians thereon live on roots. The soldiers are sure beforehand they will meet only with a new disappointment in trying to cross the ranges in order to find El Dorado, which, however, in the coming summer, they intend to do.

The dorse of this document is annotated:

> Examined on 10th March six hundred and four. No action required. File with the papers of the El Dorado.

Follows the King's signature with a regal flourish. It was easy to take it in that nonchalant way, when it was not your royal, or hidalgo carcase whose ribs would knock against your backbone on the road to El Dorado.

But on went the search for El Dorado, no matter how many disillusioned old Castilian hidalgos might carve melancholy, or cynical epitaphs on tombstones in Churriguresque cathedrals of the Spanish Main and Indies. The glowing fires of the sun of Perú passed into the dying west, but the mystic sheen of the gilded man did not wane for two and a half centuries later. By the penultimate and last decades of the eighteenth century, monks—the superior and the brethren of the Capuchin order of Barcelona—became involved in an acrimonious dispute with the colonial military in the *audiencia* of Santa Fé de Bogotá over the upshot of one expedition to the elusive, golden lake of Parimé. The *audiencia* of Nueva Granada (modern Colombia and Venezuela and Guiana), advised the king in old Spain to forbid wandering explorers and adventurers from seeking El Dorado. It had now become an affair of State, on which the grave council of the Indies and attorney-general advised the Crown, in Madrid.

Fray Salvador de Cadiz and other Spanish friars, addressed a memorial to the king of Spain, in 1722, describing the site of the riches of El Dorado, while in 1730, the Capuchin missioners in Venezuela demanded an expedition to prove the truth of the convincing details *they* had added, on the word of Indians, and roaming friars. The demand was backed by the Vice-Prefect of the Capuchin friars, full of zeal for souls and holy gold. Two monks went to old Spain—they were the monk, Salvador, and the friar, Bartolomeo de San Miguel—and asked an audience with the king. He (Fray Salvador) was told that Don José Patiño, President of the Casa de Contratación, would report to the king what the monks had to say. Here is what the monks, fresh from Caracas, said about the El Dorado behind the skyline of the far-rolling forests of the Orinoco. I have for the first time in any English publication, translated these documents from the crabbed and old-fashioned Spanish, in the verdigrised *cajones* of the *Archivos de Indias*, at Sevilla!

> The Indians jointly say to the petitioners that they *know* from the information of their ancestors where, with little error (*diferencia*), the place El Dorado lies, where is to be found much gold, and though the Missioners do not seek gold more than the souls that are there, in so great numbers, nevertheless, your Petitioners do not despise the information that comes from so many well-grounded testimonies in the provinces of Caracas, Itambien, and Casanan, all which may be of consequence to your Majesty.

Indians had come in with their babies for baptism and were questioned by friars. The place they inhabited was most delightful, with a temperate climate, "among middling hills that rose in a very spacious valley which seems to be seen indistinctly from the summit of a mountain and is the Valley between the Rio Apure and the Rio Guarico". The land was fertile, the water abundant, and would make an excellent colony, apart from finding El Dorado—"the Orinoco lands are the best in the Americas". (*Archivo Gral de Indias Secretaria de Nueva España Eclesiastica-Audiencia de Santo Domingo Prov. Caracas. Expedientes* A.D. 1717–1733.)

The project was left to the Spanish *mañana*, failing the money of any independent adventurer who would share with the Crown of old Spain on the very venerable heads-I-win-tails-you-lose principle.

Eight years passed and then another friar, of the Capuchin missions of Caracas, no less than the principal, Fray Marcelino de San Vicente, wrote a long, but interesting, memorial telling the Spanish authorities how to reach El Dorado of the Orinocos. The monk refers to the vain labours of General Felipé de Urre (von Huten) who failed to find the mysterious Mansion of the Sun (*La Casa del Sol*), as the "Indians call the golden city". Yet difficult as was the project, in the monk's judgment the Indians, all spoke the truth about this El Dorado:

> The *derrota* of Felipé de Urre shows the way to El Dorado; but by incapacity, they did not indicate the distance nor the difficulty that would be encountered in so remote and uncultivated a country, and that it will be necessary to conquer the Indians of the Poblaciones (native towns) for those who attempt this task. The discovery cannot be made until the conception of the Dorado is understood, and the idea that it is only imaginary cast away.

The monk piously adds that God must approve the quest, or it must fail. But if he meant the God of the Indians, surely He had hardly been encouraged to smile on the treasure-hunting expeditions of good and bad Catholics of Spain and the Indies . . .

> Since I came to these missions of Venezuela in the year 1699, hearing many times the El Dorado of India (*sic*) spoken of, I questioned the Rev. Padre Fray de Beya, founder of these missions, in the year 1658, and he told me he knew of an Indian that was in the pueblo de Nuestro

·Señor San Francisco whose Indians were converted from heathenism and the Indian was crafty (*era ladino:* sagacious), and told of his hardships (*trabajos*), that he had endured; and he told the padre, Fray de Beya, that the Caribs had captured the Indians and sold them to El Dorado, for gold, and, that after three summers, his kinsmen were ransomed.

Asked what was El Dorado like, the Indian said it was a very wide savannah (level plain), with a great many people, and abundance, and much fertile land, and that they lived in the open air (? *y los echaba al ayre*).

When they went to war, the Indians wore a breastplate. Asked by the Father: "Whence do they get the gold for their *chagualas*" (breast-plates), the Indian said:

Al recrecter (? at the rear?) of the savannah is a *serrania* (ridge of mountains), and when the sun rises, all the range appears like a candle (*Candela*)."

Said the padre: "How is it like a 'candle'?"

The *Indio*: "Look, I place my two fingers and thumb together."

The padre went on to say: "So the gold plate (? *ries:* ingots) comes thence like the thumb and two fingers, and the Indian gets his gold breastplate thence?"

"*Sí, señor.*"

Then the padre said to me: "I believed him, knowing they wear a sort of corselets. . . ." And he went on with the catechism . . . "You reach the El Dorado by way of the Rio Grande" (Orinoco), said the Indian. "And about noon, you come to where another river joins the Orinoco, on the farther bank, and presently, on the bank of the other river, there appear many Indians, and abundance of rich land (*copia preñados de ttierra*). After ascending the river, you come on the great savannah with the *Serrania* that appears like a candle . . . It is two moons away from the mouth of the Rio Grande.[1]

The friar wrote all this down like a good man whose soul had a religious realization that gold was the root of all evil, only if Holy Church, Our Lady Mary the immaculate Virgin, and Father Peter could not get enough of it. "And," he told the other Capuchin monk, "when I returned to Spain, in 1701, I left the account in Seville, in the archives of the missioners, who handed it over to the Rev. Fray Arcadio de Orima, Procurador of the Missions."

Fray Marcelino de San Vicente tells the Council of the Indies that he, himself, had diligently questioned all Indians, coming and going, about this El Dorado, and in affidavit twenty-three of his examinations, had set down what follows:

In 1720, Capitán Ignacio Sanchez and others went to the islands of the Apure (Venezuela) and left us some Acchaqua Indians, bred in the mission of the Rio de Cozede whom we were to bring into contact with their kinsfolk that they might procreate children. These *Achaquara Indiós* are confederates of the Caribs, and have fought with and beaten them

[1]The passage is crabbedly written and obscure in meaning. In one place the meaning seems to be the shape of the ridge; in another, the form of ingots, or nuggets of placer gold.—AUTHOR.

back and settled in Cozede. Their captain (*cacique*), Don Cristobal showèd great kindness to Capitan Ignacio Sanchez, who lodged in the same pueblo, and many times said to him: "I see thou art not well off in this world's goods, friend; bethink thee and come with me and others, my kinsfolk, to the other side of the River Orinoco, and thou must take with thee many glass beads, knives and drinking-vessels, and other things, and thou wilt take back with thee not a little gold; for I have comrades on the other side of the Orinoco, where we and others join together to fetch and carry securely."

This story of bartering, as will be seen, curiously tallies with another story told of another of the South American El Dorados, in this chapter.

Sanchez asked the *cacique*: "But the Indians, will they not know I am white?"

The *cacique*: "Bethink thee, when we go to that land, thou wilt dress as we do and have the colour we have. . . .

> Thou needst not fear. For our Indian comrades and we will sell them the beads and other things and take the gold. They give much gold for the things in our canoes. We have other nations to pass, ere we reach above the Orinoco, that land of the Dorado, but they are all our comrades.

Sanchez found that the *cacique* was resolute and a fighting-man, who had a wife and children in the pueblo. The *cacique*, with a shrewd knock at Spanish avarice, went on:

> When thou fetchest away the gold, thou mayest not say that thou wilt take much, but only a little; thereby they will not take thee as more white than we are . . ."

Fray Marcelino then resumes his own part in the story:

> And so, as the Indian asserted, El Dorado lies on the other bank of the Orinoco, a land of much gold. This past year, A.D. 1726, in January, I, having gone to the other bank of the Orinoco, we caught the Mapoye Indians that had before come to settle in the pueblo de la Santissima Trinidad de Calanzo del Rio Guarico, and they had begotten children who are Christians, and their *cacique* Imayure had a piragua badly damaged at the stern. He told us it was damaged when he was unexpectedly attacked on the other bank of the Orinoco, and he entered the Orinoco, because the current there runs strongly, and rocks are many; and he was not able to hold back the boat from a rock. And they were ill-treated by the Caribs, who eat human flesh. An Indian lad, named Otomaco was trading along that river, and he told me it took two moons to make the return journey to and from El Dorado. He told me the Mapoyes live on the other bank of the Orinoco opposite the Coca, that flows into the Orinoco, by the third arm of the Rio Apure, and from this mouth to the Coca takes a month, and going and returning take quite the fifth part of two months, and the Indian said it took a month to go from the mouth of the Rio Grande to El Dorado.

The monk Marcelino added that, on 3rd March, 1728, an Indian slave, Domingo, who had gone on the trail with the Caribs, was met and told Fray Tómas de Ponte, a Capuchin monk, how Caribs came to be carrying gold up the "Rio Grande that falls into Orinoco, on the other bank":

> There is a great highland (says the *Indió*), and a day's navigation from where the highlands are joined to the mouth of the river, I came to a waterfall that all canoes must ascend with ropes (and that was where the *cacique's* piragua was damaged, adds the friar), and then there was no hindrance, and here were the Macquacme and Penecho Indians that accompany the Caribs from this pueblo, in the year they go to El Dorado. They get the gold, for bartering in exchange, hammocks, knives (*coletta?*) beads, and pins (*pernos?*) for ear-rings. . . .

The Capuchin asked the Indians how much gold came thence. The Indian replied: "*Mucho de oro!*" stretched out his arms more than half a yard, and said a piece of that size—and "the *Indiós* give much" . . . "I (the Capuchin speaking), asked the Indian if he knew where the tribes got the gold. He answered: 'No, *padre*, because they get it out themselves, and we buy it from them . . . It takes more than two moons to go and return. I know the way there from the Rio Grande and from the mouth to the Cerro Grande (Highlands). The Caribs take the gold they get to the *flamencoes* (Dutch) that are located below them. The Indians of the Dorado do not want the Caribs to come there and take the gold to the river.' "

To clinch the matter, the Capuchin friar suggested that an expedition seeking this El Dorado could navigate from the soil of Guiana, or Trinidad right to the Rio Abetta (*Meta*):

> . . . and the soldiers taking the direction to the Meta may encounter the mouth of the Rio de Cazanare that falls into the same Meta, and by the Cazanare the soldiers will reach the missions of the society of Jesus, and thence go by land to Santa Fé de Bogotá . . . But it will not be easy to keep hold of this land of El Dorado, when found, for it will need many king's soldiers to garrison the country and pacify the many Indians that are there, and to prevent the other nations of Europe, after the knowledge of the discovery of El Dorado once gets out, from using their power to possess it.

This would seem to place El Dorado somewhere in the still unknown provinces of Meta, or Cundina-Marcá, or Boyacá, in the Oriente of Colombia, all of which territory is still a blank on the most modern maps of the region.

The friar suggested establishing forts and garrisons on the Isla de Trinidad de barlovento to help subdue the 3,000 and more wild Caribs on the mainland of the Orinoco. "Also the 'Olandeses' (Hollanders), have sold firearms and ammunition to the Caribs, who give them (captured?) negroes for cultivating land, as the news is." Opposition might be looked for from the joint Hollanders of the fort de Castillo, Guiana, and Caribs, because a successful El Dorado expedition would put a stop to the traffic of selling captured Indians as slaves to other islands, as well as the gold, by the Caribs.

The reverend friar again adds that he has set all this down for the honour and advantage of "Our Lord, the King, whom may God guard, and if so many souls may be won, then the settlement of *Iesstibes* (*sic?*) from the Orinoco to Brazil may all live to the glory of God and the salvation of men.—Amen!":

> I have written this in the pueblo of La Santissima Trinidad de Calanazo (*Calaboca, in another letter*) del Rio Guarico, 5th March, 1728. Fray Marcelino, de San Vicente, unworthy *Capuchino Ralincedo Reverendissimo Padre*).

He had a reply, dated 22nd April, 1730, from "his most loving servant and friend, Don Lopez Carillo", governor of Venezuela, writing from Caracas y Herreco. His hand is kissed, his health is drunk, his happiness prayed for by a man who would, doubtless, rather have kicked his reverend backside to Hades. His Majesty, in old Spain, will surely be informed of his reverence's ardent zeal:

> but as the information about the discovery of El Dorado has been so often repeated and is so old . . . It is very remiss of your reverence not to have named to me the persons known to be fit to for this undertaking . . . I cannot decide on such an undertaking . . . but all must rest on the will of God . . .

The reverend Padre replied that he had spent thirty-one years in the province of Caracas, in the missionary vineyard, so that he had travelled all its wildernesses:

> I have been told that the principal nation of the Rio Dorado speaking the Achaqua tongue, are certain *white people*, and warlike populations of traders, that can be no others than the Dutch of Carinama that live in the villages lower down by the mouths of the Orinoco. I excused the captains named from making to verify the information brought by the Indians; because they are much the customs of the Achaquas and Guaiguires we have in our pueblos.

At this point, the author of this book feels impelled to comment that monks, travellers, explorers, officials, and administrators in Spanish South America usually identified these strange white South Americans with lost Spanish adventurers on the El Dorado trail, or with stranded Dutch (Hollanders), or strayed Englishmen. But, as will be seen, later in this chapter, they were more likely descendants of one of the ancient white races of mysterious South America.

The reverend *fraile* advised the Spanish King to send 200 well-armed, single youths from old Spain, who would marry the Indian women of the pueblos that might be pacified on the borders of the El Dorado country:

> Then it may be possible in short time to discover the Dorado. Notwithstanding my age of 74, I would willingly fare forth with the mission to these Indians, with robust courage, on foot, sleeping on the hard ground when necessary.

His reverence, it will be seen, was a man of spirit in the cause of the Lord and His army.

The *Real y Superior Consejo de las Indias* (Royal and Superior Council of the Indies) received the petition, but made no resolution about the affair of *El Dorado*—except the usual one of *mañana*. So, the reverend Padre again petitioned the Crown through the governor of Venezuela, who had probably damned the project with faint praise and cold, Castilian water. He asked the Don (Lopez Carillo y Andrada) to send an expedition into the interior "to solve the truth of the story". He also suggested the names of four Spanish officers to lead it, and pacify the frontier Indians. He even offered to go with it, and sent a royal cedula, of 5th August, 1702, wherein his Spanish Catholic and royal and imperial majesty had, at the cost of the royal exchequer, constructed and fitted out four ships to provide an escort for the *misioneros Capuchinos*.

Home, in faraway Spain, the Attorney-General hummed and hawed, exactly as if he had been legal adviser to the old British Board of Admiralty, pretending to deliberate on sending a King's ship to search an old pirate island. The Council of the Indies gravely yawned in their beards and wrote on the margin of the document: "*El Consejo resolvera Junio* 17 *de* 1731".

Finally, the bored *señores* sent "the monk" his answer, *via* the Governor of Spanish Venezuela:

Consejo, 22 de Nov. de 1731.
Inform the Monk, that his memorial and letters are under consideration, and that certain persons are being asked for information on this subject, which will be communicated to the Council for their better knowledge in this important matter. And send a copy of this letter to the Audiencia de Santa Fé (de Bogotá) (modern Colombia), charging it to procure more reliable and fuller details from the monks of the *compañia* in the missions of the *llanos* de Casanares, and from other persons, that they will be good enough to send better reports, and, in the result, will express their proposals or suggestions in this affair.
Resolvera: (in the margin) *Señores:* Silvia, Zurriga, Machado, Pedrosa, Montemayor, Sopeña, Verdes, Alarçon, Alren.

So that was that! But had Francisco Pizarro deliberated in that way, the English or the Dutch would have added old Perú of the Incas to their Empire! It is clear from this letter of decision that the El Dorado the Capuchin monks had in mind lay *not* in Guiana or Orinoco, but in what is now the *still unexplored Oriente of modern Colombia*.

Yet, deliberate as the Council of the Indies might in old Spain, the El Dorado ghost still walked the llanos of old Venezuela and the Rio Orinoco. The Capuchin monks did not let their Dorado project drop; for another Spanish governor, Don Luis de Unzaga y Amezaga, Governor of Caracas had, in June, 1778, to report to the king in old Spain about an expedition to Lake Parima and El Dorado and the charges against the Capuchin missioners on its failure. Fray Mariano de Sabadel, Prefect of the Capuchin missions at Caracas, and the monks refuted the charges that they hindered the El Dorado expedition.

In the archives at Sevilla, old Spain, is a report from Don Vincente, or Vicente Diaz, lieutenant of infantry, commanding the expedition to El Dorado and Lake Parime. Dated 14th June, 1778, from Caracas, it speaks of the "notorious disaffection and pernicious influences of the Capuchin monks, missioners in Venezuela". The charges and the monks' counter-charges had been remitted to the Viceroy and the *audiencia*, at Santa Fé de Bogotá, in Nueva Granada (Colombia). The monks charged the commandant of the El Dorado expedition, the Don Vicente Diaz (de Fuente), above-mentioned, with taking, without her husband's permission, an Indian's wife, whom he met on the trail, and used to gratify his lusts. It is the usual interference by white men with native women which starts three parts of the trouble in Indian territory. But when did military invaders ever ask permission of the bull to roll the cow over on the common?

The Indian, said the monks, naturally urged his fellow-Indians to kill the invading Spaniards. How could that be the fault of the Capuchin missioners?

Fuente's men had also taken other Indian women and raped, or lain with them. The Spanish commandant replied that the missioners had not furnished the provisions, Indian carriers, and canoes that were necessary and agreed. The reverend Prefect retorted that the monks *had* co-operated, providing Indians with canoes, to go up the Rio Caroni, and cheese and cassava-bread. In fact, one padre at a pueblo had killed all his herds of hogs to feed the hungry Spanish soldiery, and had handed over fodder, rice, cassava, and store of flesh, with or without paternal blessings. Fifty herds of hogs, by Saint Gadarus, had been killed, and Indians lent to porter the baggage to the *poblacion* of Guinor, and yet all this anti-clerical detraction! "It was audacious," added the reverend Capuchin Prefect, "that anyone should say that his monks or the Caribs of the mission reductions had urged other Indians to kill the Spaniards as they went up the rivers towards the Meta. No one with experience of monks would believe it". Indeed the commandant, Don Vicente had even gone so far as to suggest that the monks ought all to be fettered and manacled and shut up in the stone prison of Angostura—missioners who had been the subject of approbation in royal cedulas of past years! "We deserve praise not this blackening deposition of despicable character", ended his rev. Paternity, Fray Mariano de Sabadel.

It also appeared that the Capuchin monks feared that the taking of many Indians from their reductions on an El Dorado expedition would leave them open to attacks from hostile Caribs on the frontiers of the unknown. Moreover, the governor of Guiana had not carried out the orders of the Viceroy at Santa Fé de Bogotá to provide a corporal and 25 soldiers to garrison their mission pueblos.

Don Manuel Centurion, commandant of "Guayna", reported home to the Spanish Secretaria de Guerra, on 20th December, 1776, about a project to found a garrison on the shores of the Lago de Parime, to protect the riches of that El Dorado from foreign interlopers and adventurers, principally Portuguese from Brazil, and Dutch from Guiana.

Centurion made a minute in Guiana, on 28th December, 1771, stating that "a *capitaneje*" had come from Lago de Parime, offering to guide the Spaniards to the shores of the lake and the hill called "Dorado", "saying that, in this Mountain, there are everywhere seen *pyramids of gold* and that the neighbouring Indians carefully guard it from the Caribs and other Indians who traded with the "Olandeses" (Dutch) and the Portuguese. The informant was a cacique of good faith.

Whether or no, the Lago de Parime, like many powerful South American Indian tribes has disappeared into the sands of time, no one appears to know.

After all this meeting of monkish tonsures with ruffling, military moustachios, the ghost of El Dorado and Lake Parime in the backblocks of Guiana and the Orinoco once more sank back into limbo and was laid to rest in the old archives at Santa Fé de Bogotá and Caracas of the Spanish Colonial age. Up to date, it has made no comeback as a *revenant*!

I write this in the year of little peace and no plenty, 1949; but past experience of these matters suggests to me that this book will give such a shaking up to this old and romantic skeleton that postmen and mail-carriers all over Britain, the Empire and the U.S.A. will curse the burden added to their wallets by my fan-mail. Hail, none the less to the spirit of English-speaking youth and adventure. May it never wane as long as the sun shines and blue waters roll!

On the eastern Andean side of mysterious, South America is another El Dorado located in a mysterious region which has not been penetrated since the days of the hardy conquistadores. Humboldt called it the "El Dorado of the Omaguas", and perhaps it is identical with that which the old Capuchin prefect, Fray Vincente de Marcelino, urged the Council of the Indies to seek. The "Omaguas are a very noble tribe of Indians," said an old Jesuit missioner. "They may be the remains of some great monarchy which existed in ancient South America." But Humboldt, the great Prussian traveller and savant— Prussia was great in the world of light and learning in those days— thought the Omaguas were a powerful offshoot of the great Caribs, who overran Brazil and spread into the Antilles.

He does not say so; but more probably these Caribs were themselves a colonial offshoot of Europe's oldest race of colonial navigators the *Cari*ans, who gave their name to the *Cari*bbean! Their El Dorado was located north-west of the Rio Putumayo of the infamous, rubber atrocities of the early twentieth century, towards the foothills of the Andes. They may still exist to-day; for the land is still *terra incognita*.

It is, however, distinct from the most mysterious of all the El Dorados; that called by the old conquistadorians, and the sixteenth to seventeenth century missioners and Spanish chroniclers: "El Gran Paytite". Lured by it, similar ill-starred expeditions of hardy men set out and never returned, or reached back to Quito, Lima, or Cuzco, looking like Haitian *zombies* newly risen from a charnel-house or morgue. Gran Paytite, I believe, also exists to-day. It lies a long way east of Cuzco and the mountains, beyond the great unknown belt of forest and marsh called the Caupolican of north-west Bolivia. As late as 1702, a missioner-monk, Fray Baraza visited the Furnes Indians, by the Rio Itenez. He found that each of their villages was elaborately fortified. They had a long banqueting-hall, and a stone temple stood in the centre of the pueblo. Hereditary rulers, called *Aramas*, governed them, and their women wore clothes. A neighbouring tribe, the *Cayubatabas*, had the same organization, but their civil ruler, who was also the high priest, was called *Paytite* (Tiger, or Father).

In the same mysterious country, a Jesuit missioner, Fray Lucero met Indians, who, in 1681, were camped on the banks of the Rio Huallagu, a tributary of the Amazon-Marañon, in north-eastern Perú. These Indians spoke of a nation called the *Curveros* of Gran Paytite, many leagues behind the forests and mountains eastwards of Cuzco.

Said the Jesuit:

> This empire of Gran Paytite has bearded, white Indians. The nation called the Curveros, these Indians told me, dwell in a place called Yurachuasi, or the "white house". For king, they have a descendant of that Inca Tupac Amaru, who with 40,000 Perúvians, fled far away into the forests, before the face of the conquistadores of Francisco Pizarro's day, in A.D. 1533. He took with him a rich treasure, and the Castilians who pursued him fought each other in the forests, leaving the savage *Chuncho Indiós*, who watched their internecine struggles, to kill off the wounded and shoot the survivors with arrows. I myself have been shown plates of gold and half-moons and ear-rings of gold that have come from this mysterious nation.

Fray Manuel Rodriguez, in his *Amazonas y El Marañon* (lib. VI, cap. IV), says that one of these Castilians was Juan Alvarez Maldonada, a plucky but very fat conquistador, who, at Cuzco, hearing about these 40,000 Inca Peruvians who had fled to the mysterious stone city of gold and silver, far to the eastward of Cuzco, planned to get on their trail and rob the great treasure. After which he proposed to explore the great river Madre de Dios, which rises in these forests. It was the year A.D. 1550, and he heard that another ruffler, one Tordoya was out on the same trail. Both bands fought each other in the great forests of the Carovaya, and when the savage Chunchos finished off the surviving *bandidos*, Maldonada fled through the forests below the snowy range of the Eastern Cordilleras. He carried with him as an amulet a breviary to ward off that evil eye in which even

Italian diplomats of the late nineteenth century have believed. It seems he had worn this amulet beneath his tunic when a bullet struck him full in the chest and knocked him down as he was fighting Gonzalo Pizarro. It, he said, saved his life.

In 1659, a Spanish soldier, Pedro Bohorques, who had served in Chile, went among the Colchaquies Indians. They were a tribe of the Tucumans in the southern region of El Gran Chaco whom the Spaniards could not subdue till 1665. Bohorques said he was an Inca and raised an expedition to search for the mysterious Yurac-huasi, or White House of the Tiger King of Gran Paytite. Bohorques went down the Rio Huallaga, in the Andes of mid-Perú. This river joins the Marañon or Amazon. He lived among the Pelados Indians till 1665, when the Spaniards captured him and hanged him in Lima.

Another contemporary Spanish account says that Bohorques's real name was Chamijo, and that he had been deported from Perú to Chili and jailed at Valdivia, for swindling. He broke gaol and crossed the Cordillera to La Rioja, in the southern Argentine. He had spent years among the Indians of Perú and knew all their customs. He made his concubine *Colla* (queen) and called himself Huallpa-Inca. From the Vale of Catamarca he went to the Aconguija Mountains, and finally to the Valle de Calchaqui, in a triumphant progress with 117 *caciques* in his train. The viceroy, in Lima, ordered Don Alonso de Mercado of y Villacorta, governor of Tucuman, to arrest and send Bohorques in chains. He was captured by a trick, and, in prison, at Lima, organized a new revolt among the Calchaqui Indians. This led to his execution.

A missioner at Santa Maria, Frey Eugenio del Sancho, told Governor Mercado, in a letter that:

> The Indians fêted Bohorques as one of their old Incas.

As the remarkable adventure of "Don" Pedro Bohorques is unknown to most English readers I give the story, here, at some length. Bohorques, who attracted much attention in Perú of his own day, and whose fame in later days partakes of the notoriety that attached to the luckless Louis de Rougemont, was a poor Spanish adventurer, who, soon after quitting old Spain, served in the wars in Chile as a common soldier. He then wandered all over Perú and, about the year 1659 began to call himself *Don Pedro, el Inca*. He represented that in his veins ran the royal blood of the Incas, and among the Colchaquies Indians, in whose huts he lived in a sierra near Tucúman, Argentina, his claims seem to have been accepted.

He entered and left those ranges and in some way his ideas and claims appeared to tickle the humour of these wild and warlike Indians. Not long after, he told them he proposed to assume the royal mantle of the Inca and would engage to restore their lost liberties. The Colchaquies favoured his claims, for obvious reasons. The next thing one hears of him is that Don Pedro bearded the Spanish governor, Don Alfonso de Mercado, in the city of Tucúman and told that high and mighty potentate that he, Don Pedro, had great power over the Indians of the montaña:

> Listen to me, *señor Gobernador*, with no cost to the King in old Spain, I can gain over the Indians to Spain. They love me. I have much influence over them.

Whatever the Governor may have thought, he seems to have assented to Don Pedro's proposition, on the no-cure-no-pay principle, especially as Don Pedro said: "All I seek is only to be declared the Inca Indian."

Back in the ranges, behold Don Pedro assuming the royal purple, or the borla diadem of the Inca, and ruling the Indians from a portable throne! Perhaps those same Colchaquies grinned at the caprice of this madman, but saw a way to profit by it. Don Pedro now began as a treasure hunter. He went out on the gold trail, accompanied by many faithful vassal Indians. But alas, this Don Quixote of the sierra, despite all the Sancho Panzas in his train, found no treasures, though always he was assured that, if he went just a little farther, he would find the place where the rainbow touched the pot of old Inca buried millions!

At this juncture, Bohorques heard about the vast treasure of gold that had been removed from Perú by Manco Ccapac, brother of the Inca Atahualpha, assassinated by the bandit-conquistadores Francisco Pizarro and the Black Monk Vincent de Valleverde. Manco withdrew into the mountains east of Cuzco, followed by 40,000 vassal Quechuas. The Inca's brother went well to the eastwards, so as to secure himself against Spanish pursuit; though it was a sanguinary battle with the Chuncho Indians, after a rival encounter between Spanish bands of treasure hunters, that barred that door! Manco is said to have passed unknown ranges and gone down the Rio Ucayle, tributary of the Marañon-Amazon. Somewhere up the Ucayle gorges he cached a fantastic treasure and it is said that he also subsequently cached an immense treasure of gold carried off by the Indians to this same region, after the death of Tupac Amaru.

The South American Jesuit, the learned Frey Juan de Velasco, author of the still valuable *History of the Royal Kingdom of Quito*, said, in 1789, at Faenza, Italy, after his expulsion, with other members of the order of San Ignatius Loyola, from Spanish America:

> It was said in Lima that the gold land of Paititi, where Inca Manco-Ccapac II, buried treasures, never found after he lost his kingdom, was rendered invisible to the pursuing Spaniard conquistadores. The Incas used magic arts, it is said, to make themselves invisible, as they fled from Cuzco.

The Colchaquies Indians had one doubt—the very marrow of the matter! It was the definite location of the caches; since all the Indians had dispersed, some by the streams of the Ucayle, descending past

Vilcapampa, others by the unknown Rio Huallaga, going by Guaranacu. They had heard some rumour that the richest of these immense caches was in the mystic region of the Paytiti. But other Indians urged that the cache was in the Yurac-Guasi, or the mysterious Palace of the White House, believed to lie somewhere in the unknown region round the Huallaga, a little way before that stream empties itself into the Marañon.

All joyful with these alluring tidings, Bohorques set out on a grand march into the unknown, on the trail of the White House, or Paytiti, or Paititi. Some of the Colchaquies who followed him, he invested as grandees of his court, with full power to rob and kill as many Spaniards as they could. They also might testify, in whatever region the cortège entered, as to the legitimacy of his Inca blood and his right to hunt for the cached gold. He went over a river near Cuzco, crossed the el Jauja and its mountains, and, going southwards, found the Rio Guanaco, the head waters of the Huallaga. He reached the site where his information purported that the cache lay; but, also, he now found he had entered the lands of the unhappy *Peleados*, or *Pelados*, or penniless Indians. They had been given this name by Spaniards who, earlier, had gone there on the trail of El Dorado. Some said the name meant that these Indians used a depilatory of tree juice. Others alleged that it was because these Indians were so poor they did not know what gold was.

These *Pelados* Indians numbered about 10,000. Bohorques received them benevolently, so that his own grandees might have ocular testimony of his royal Inca blood. But gold there was none! However, Bohorques was not dismayed. He believed, on the faith of the Indians' stories, that Paytiti could not be far off. He sent out envoys, and, pending their return, set up a kingdom, and was obeyed and even worshipped by the vassal *Pelados*. He remained among them about two and a half years, from 1665, and built a fine road from the village of the *Pelados* to the banks of the Rio Huallaga. It ran some leagues through the woods which he cut down and made the road broad and adorned it with triumphal arches of flowers and tree branches, in the royal way of the Incas. Over it he was borne in litters, covered with beautiful birds' feathers, on the backs of his vassals. Luckily for them, no Jesuit missioners came up the Marañon, at this time, or they would surely have been sacrificed by his vassals.

A few years later, a monk, one Padre Juan Lorenzo Lucero, saw with his own eyes this royal road of Bohorques, still entire and adorned with the arches, and reported the fact to the Spanish audiencia at Quito. The Indians were now without their King Bohorques, and the monk got them to act as his interpreters. But before that time, the stars had deserted "Inca Bohorques". He could not find the buried gold and returned to the bosom of the Colchaquies, whom he found up in arms and fighting the Spaniards, who had heard about Bohorques' orders to exterminate the Spaniards in that region. He tried to defend the Colchaquies; but was captured and taken to Lima where he was thrown into prison by men who had no sympathy for his claims to royalty. Bohorques was tried and sentenced to death, which he suffered publicly on tall gallows in Lima, in 1667.

He died, indeed, but the wind of avarice had set aflame romantic hearts of grandes caballeros in old Lima. Many might not believe that Don Pedro Bohorques was of Inca blood, but they did believe in the existence of the vast and opulent Court of el Gran Paytiti. None, however, knew where it lay, when, lo, at this fateful juncture, there came over the mountains a friar of the seraphic order in Perú, who wrote a letter, which seems to have reached even unto Madrid. In it, he said he had walked over those mystic mountains, and had even entered the great Court and Kingdom of Gran Paytiti, and marvelled at the grandeur of a country that numbered so many millions of souls —doubtless burning for Catholic salvation—and its great riches, where nothing was more ordinary nor more abundant than gold. Many cynics in Lima cared not a bean about the suffering souls unshriven, but a devil of a lot about this gold! An expedition was arranged, and even the Jesuits, rivals of the Franciscans, enrolled themselves, of course, not for gold, but to save the millions of Indian souls.

Don Benito de Ribera, a gran caballero, and *muy rico*, sold his estates to provide the funds, and, joined by other caballeros of Lima, set out, in 1670, in a veritable land armada for el Gran Paytiti. The Don paid the expenses of the Franciscan monk, and also took another guide, Antonio Lopez de Zarçosa, a resident of Chiquisaca. Two of the Jesuits of the order in the province of Perú begged with great eagerness to be allowed to join the expedition. Time passed, the way was hard, the way was long, and somebody now began to wonder if the seraphic friar had had an ecstatic vision of the night about el Gran Paytiti. It is ill arguing with, or questioning, a mystic in any land or age; and indeed, the old Russians used to say that: "Struggle with a bull as much as you like, you will never get any milk out of him". Some even went so far as to say, with many a *Carajo!* that they did not think the seraphic monk had ever set foot in el Gran Paytiti. They may have been Jesuits! *Quien sabe?*

The painful fact remained that the expedition returned to Lima, having suffered many hardships, deaths and disasters. They had touched no mystic, nor any sort of virgin, nor cached gold, and had met and seen nothing save tribes of poor Indians scattered all over the mountains of the Andes.

Home in old Madrid, in 1682, Padre Manuel Rodriguez, at one time Procurator in Quito, who later wrote a very rare history of el Marañon, met one of the Jesuits who had been in this expedition of 1670, and questioned him. The Jesuit showed him a manuscript in which was the passage following:

The soldiers did not find the gold the monk had promised them, but hardship, illness, and deaths, and we ourselves did not find the millions of souls that he affirmed he had seen in *el Paititi*, although, speaking to the folk of Chuquisaca, that he guided, they said that by enchantment of the Indians he did not find his Court.

Padre Manuel.

Velasco supposed that this mystic Court lay in the *Cerro de la Sal*, or Salt Mountain. But the man who tells most of this queer lost country is the Padre Juan Lorenzo Lucero, in the supplement to Part 2, of an exceedingly rare volume relating to the Missions of Marañon, in 1681. For the first time, I here give the translation into English:

> Thirty days sailing from my pueblo of Santiago de la Laguna . . there are settlements of five small nations, of 10,000 Indians, among whom are the *Pirus* . . . These, not more than a parcel of a very numerous nation, trade with the more numerous nation not very distant, whose leader is a descendant of the Incas, or held to be such. The lands in which they dwell are very rich, and based on information I have from the Manamavovos Indians, I think there are more than 100,000 souls in the pueblo of this Inca. I have seen and had in my hands some *patenas* (thin metal plates), shaped like a half moon, ear-hoops (*orejeras*) and various things of the gold of that nation. Below these nations are the Curibeos, or Curivos, or Curveros, that are about 15,000 and who met me in amity to receive the Gospel. . . .

Padre Manuel Rodriguez supposes that these jewels were those taken with the Indians on their withdrawal from Perú, and naïvely says, "and if there is really gold in some *cerro*, or in the strands of the river where they dwell, they that go to win the souls will not be desirous to keep the gold".

Frey Juan de Velasco speaks of the *Mayorumas* who had a Jesuit *reduccion* (mission) established in their lands. It had been founded at San Miguel, by Padre A. Widman, in 1744. These *Mayorumas*:

> *had well trimmed and bushy beards*, so that they were called *Barbados*. Another Jesuit mission was set up in their territory, earlier, in 1683, by Padre R. de St. Cruz. These Barbudos (or Barbados) *are whiter than Spaniards*, and as white as the Dutch or Flemings. They make holes in their cheeks and lips and stick in them little sticks, which give them a frightful appearance. They have no fixed dwellings and wander in the forests, and so are called *Gitanos* (gypsies) of the Marañon. They eat their sick before they have time to grow thin.

Here, we have a race of the mysterious white Indians found all over central and western South America, from the backwoods of the Guianas, where they are the fierce and solitary *Oyaricoulets*, to the eastern foothills and woods of the Andes in Perú. Shy and elusive and furtive, blue-eyed and white-skinned on the west, to the north-east they are like the Nazis, in that they reach for blow-pipes and bows as soon as they scent the intrusion of modern civilizers who preach culture and religion. The Mayorumas and Barbudos who eat their sick suggest a grim memory of the ancient days when appalling cataclysms forced white and civilized races, in both North and South America, into tunnels to escape the mephitic gases, and the intolerable inundations and endless rains on the surface. Sojourning in these mysterious subterraneans for many months on end—American Indian traditions, both in North and South America, say the old races lived in these tunnels for *years*—it is easy to see that cannibals would subsequently develop. (And the real or alleged motives of the cannibal devouring "long pig", which, some say, is tastier than the best pork, are, if one takes away the sublimation and sacerdotalism, closely related to the symbolism of eating bread and drinking wine in the eucharist of the Roman Catholic High Mass. However, we must not digress.)

These "white Indians" are of the posterity of the ancient Hy-Brazilian Atlanteans, but they differ very greatly in the degrees of decadence and degeneracy to which they have sunk, in many thousands of years, north and south of the old basin of the vast Marañon, and farther north on the shores of the Gulf of Mexico, which was in pre-cataclysmal days, one with the Rio Orinoco basin. Here, in 1840, their posterity were found in lonely sierras, under the name of the "Munchies". (More of this and them in a later book!)

The primitive Indians of the Gran Chaco of Paraguay have stories of visits in the not very remote past from white Indians who came from some mysterious fastness far north-west in the direction of eastern Perú, or the Oriente of Ecuador. These white Indians are said to wear long garments of cotton, or white wool, in which are woven symbolical designs, often found on ancient pottery. They have the powers of *hechiceros*, or medicine men, and use it for the benefit of the forest and swamps Indians, who look on them as a race of superior beings. Now and again they have had encounters with frontier soldiers who have shot at them, much as the old *bandeiristas* did when they met white Indians in old Brazil, in 1745. And like these, the others fled from contact with soldiers.

The way to the land of these elusive white Indians is said to lie through miasmatic swamps and regions of great heat, right into the secret heart of old South America. The fastness of these elusive Indians is said to lie on a high tableland of a range of sierras, with conical peaks. They do not seem to have fire-arms, but fire red arrows with great force.

Velasco, in a manuscript he wrote at Faenza, Italy, in 1792, gives a curious picture of the Paños Indians, who, in 1800, had among them very old painted books of hieroglyphic history. They were found, in 1670, by Frey Juan Lucero, at the Jesuit mission of Santiago de la Laguna:

> They have the queer custom of circumcising their *women*, which one finds nowhere else in the Marañon (Upper Amazon headwaters). They kept this custom for nearly a hundred years after they had been "reduced" (by the Jesuit fathers), and as late as 1660, without any missioner perceiving

it, every year these Indians took into the woods, under various pretexts, young girls of 12 to 14, and a native priestess performed this operation. They regard as infamous all those who marry without undergoing this operation. . . . The province of the Marañon reached from the Pongo de Manseriche to the Rio Negro. Not arms, but the gospel alone could conquer it. Gold is found in the sands of the rivers. The Indians are as many as the leaves on a full-grown tree. From 1646, for 130 years, the Jesuits had 207 *reducciones* (missions) with 260,000 Indians. A revolt of the Indians of the Ucayle—the headwaters of the Amazon—in 1762, lost the Jesuits 40,000 converts . . . Some of these Marañon Indians were almost as white as Europeans, others olive-hued or bronze-coloured. Some were feeble and effeminate, others valiant and robust. They speak different tongues. Some of them have lived on the banks of the Marañon from time immemorial. When Inca Manco-Ccapac II went into the interior from Cuzco, followed by the Peruvians, and abandoned Cuzco to the Spaniards, in the vast regions between the Ucayle and the Apurimac, he set up an empire and built a bridge over the Ucayle whose ruins could be seen in 1780. He was called Inca-Choca . . . The empire of Paititi and that of the Chancha was born when Manco-Ccapac's son, wife and daughter-in-law turned Christian, at Lima, in 1559, where he came with his court . . . In 1569, the Indians proclaimed Tupac Amaru, Inca in the mountains of Urubamba and Villcabamba. He refused to treat with Spain and the Spanish viceroy marched against him in 1571, routed his army, took him prisoner, and beheaded him at Cuzco, despite the prayers of the Spanish nobility there. King Philip II, in Spain, condemned the crime, and all Tupac Amaru's vassals left for the plains of the upper Marañon to join their brothers, left by Manco Ccapac, at Paititi.

The unending Spanish hunt for Gran Paititi, all through the seventeenth and eighteenth centuries, inflamed by the old Castilian and Estremadurian desire for easy money, had a curious sequel in 1710. In the time of the war of the Spanish Succession, the Lusitanian Brazilians made a bid to extend their empire at the expense of Spain. They sent out 1,500 soldiers and 4,000 Indian auxiliaries up the Rio Marañon and surprised all the missions between the Rio Negro and the Rio Napo. The Indians of the missions were sold into slavery in Brazil, and about 40,000 Indians perished. The other Indians saved themselves only by abandoning the missions and fleeing into the dense forests. Later, the Jesuits were expelled, and the Portuguese prepared another expedition and entered into relations with the King of the Chunchos, Bohorques' old subjects, in the province of Tarma. This king claimed to be a descendant of the old Incas.

So long as the Chunchos had kept to their forest and mountain fastnesses, they were not greatly feared by the Spaniards. But as soon as the Portuguese established themselves on the Yavari, near the embouchure of the Ucayle or upper Amazon, they traded with the Chunchos and gave them iron, which they had not formerly had. It was as if, in North America, traders had sold the old Apaches and the Sioux repeater rifles to use against Uncle Sam's settlers and forts. The Portuguese also sent engineers and engineer-officers, who built forts in Chuncho territory and started to train and discipline the Indians. They made them formidable soldiers.

Lima soon heard that the Chunchos were about to declare war on old Spain and the Spanish power in Perú, and the Marques de Villagarcia started to build forts on the confines of the Chuncho territory, in the province of Tarma, into which he put strong garrisons. But the Spaniards were always beaten, and lost much territory to the Chunchos. The next viceroy, the Conde de Superunda, in 1745, arrived in Lima and found the city in a state of consternation. They had no troops to resist a Chuncho invasion. He decided to send an embassy to the King of the Chunchos, as it seemed that the white weapon of diplomacy was a better trick to play than firearms. He chose a Jesuit padre, Carlos Pastoriza and another Limeñan.

Here is the manuscript account of a man in old Lima, translated for the first time into English:

I had what I now tell you from the mouth of Padre Pastoriza, whom I knew well in Europe. I can guarantee its truth. (*Note* by some candid friend of the Jesuits, in this manuscript: 'If there is any truth in this story, it has been terribly exaggerated by the Jesuits to enhance their prestige.') When the ambassadors reached the frontiers of these barbarians, they were advised particularly not to say they were envoys from the viceroy in Lima, and not to enter the Chunchos' territory without getting first that king's permission. They announced themselves as envoys from the Pope in Rome. The king ordered them to be well treated and led to his court. The pomp and éclat with which they were received astonished them. They had never believed they would find these desert towns so well built and fortified. An hour before the monks arrived at the capital, they found two armies of 25–30,000 men drawn up in line along the road. And they saw many African negroes[1] as well as people who seemed as white as Europeans, or were white Europeans. Father Pastoriza told me that the palace of the Chuncho king ·is so magnificent that even those of the viceroy in Lima, and princes in Europe could not stand the comparison. They were led by a great number of officers into a splendid saloon, where they found the king seated on his throne. Sandals were on his feet, but he wore no other clothing than a simple tunic of very fine cloth, according to the custom of the ancient Incas. The Padres bowed thrice and kissed his royal hands, but did not dare speak to him. He spoke to the ambassadors in the Peruvian tongue, for he knew no other.

He asked them who they were and whence they had come. In the same tongue, the Jesuits of Perú answered. They replied that they could tell him that only in private. The king ·then passed with them into another chamber as fine as the first. The fathers then said they were Jesuits and had come from the Pope to propose peace. The king said he was delighted. He especially loved the Jesuits for he knew the good they had done the Indians in their missions. But he did not know why the Pope asked peace of him; for he had no thought of making war on

[1] Were these blacks the posterity of the blacks who invaded the old Inca empire from the southern Andes, ages before the Spanish conquest? And were the white men of the race of the "white Indians"?—AUTHOR.

his Holiness, and that he blamed only the Spaniards who, not content with having kidnapped all Perú, from his ancestors, still wanted to take the little that remained to him.

The Jesuit father replied that the Pope loved peace and wanted him to conclude a peace with the Spaniards.

"And what is the condition of such a peace?" asked the king.

"You must lay down your arms and cease to vex the Spaniards, who, on their side, will agree not to make trouble for your Majesty in the possession of your estates."

"I agree to the treaty," said the king, "on your account, and on condition that the Spaniards give me no new reasons for complaint, otherwise I am determined to reconquer the lands of my ancestors. Go back to your compatriots and tell them what I have said."

The king then withdrew from the room, and next day had the Jesuits taken back to the frontiers with the marks of honour they had had on their arrival. They reported to the viceroy in Lima that they did not think all the forces in Perú were enough to subdue this empire, so well was it fortified; but they did not think the Indians were much to be feared outside their mountains, and, moreover, they did not think the Indians planned new invasions, if they were left alone.

But since this time, the Spaniards, who so anxiously sought for the Empire of Paititi, thought only of keeping clear of it, now they have found it!

Sir Clements Markham, the famous British traveller and explorer of South America heard a story of much the same kind, in 1853, when he was on the banks of the Purus:

My Indian informant, on the banks of the Purus, pointed to the forests which stretched away to the horizon. At the same time, he described a lake on whose banks *Ynti*, the Peruvian sun-deity still finds worshippers. It is a very pleasing reflection that this story may possibly be true.

Markham was not so far out. There *is* truth in the Indian's story!

His informant was one Don Ramon Ordoñez who owned a farm in La Cueva, in the *montaña* of Paucartambo.

In 1740, another man, Juan Santos, native of Guamanga, went into the forests near Tarma, also passing himself off as an Inca. He adopted the name of Atahualpha and started an insurrection among the posterity of those same Chunchos who had finished off the con-quistadorian bandits in the forests, in Maldonada's day, nearly two centuries before. A war of extermination was waged on the Spaniards, the Portuguese, on the west, aiding Santos with arms. He destroyed the Jesuit missions, and frequently defeated Spanish expeditions sent against him.

Antonio de Herrera, in the sixth decade of his *Historia de las Indias*, refers to the voyage of Francisco de Orellana, in 1540-41. This story is told at large, from old Spanish manuscripts, in my chapter of this book relating to the warrior women Amazons of South America. De Herrera had been impressed by the curious discovery by de

Orellana's men, somewhere about the junction of the Rio Putumayo with the Amazon, of a "country house with goblets of glass ornamented with many bright colours, resembling drawings and paintings". The Indians at this place said these goblets came from the interior, along with much gold and silver. The land was about the Rio Negro. A very intelligent Indian woman told de Orellana that, in the interior, were many men like the Spaniards and two white women with a chief who had brought them down the river. "The Spaniards of de Orellana's expedition supposed these white men were part of the expeditions of either Diego de Ordaz or Alonzo de Herrera".

(However, as I have pointed out before, they were men of some ancient white race far, far older than Spaniards, or Germans of the Holy, or Unholy, Roman Empire, or Emperor Carlos V of old Spain and Germany. And the white women were no others than the Amazon warriors of mysterious South America.)

El Gran Paytite oddly resembles the elusive El Dorado back of the beyond in the marches of the dense forests and unexplored mountains of Guiana and the frontiers of northern Brazil, touching on the headwaters of the Rio Orinoco. It, too, had a great lake called *Manoa*, or the *Casa del Sol* (Mansion of the Sun). Who can with certainty say if this were the Manoa vainly sought for by the unfortunate Sir Walter Raleigh?

Amazon fighting-women also dwelt in a country bordering on the great lake of Manoa, of Gran Paytite, exactly as they were said to do around Lake Parima, the mirage which the gold-crazed adventurers of old Spain failed to reach. Hernando de Ribera, follower of the conquistador, Cabeza de Vaca heard of the *Casa del Sol*. He says it was so called, because the great orb of the sun sank into its waters. Obviously, there was a great sun-temple there, which probably was a magnificent structure of Atlantean-Brazilian origin, far older than any Incas of Perú.

El Gran Patite, or *Paytiti*, which almost certainly is still in existence today, in 1949, after a world war which the old Mayan books of gold are said to have foretold, is, I suspect, the mysterious land whence come the furtive white Indians with blue eyes and auburn hair and beards, and features of Grecian type, who barter with the forest Indians of eastern Perú, and vanish as mysteriously as they came. The half-moon, gold objects which Fray Juan Lucero saw, in 1681, remind one of the half-moon figures on the porticoes of the dead city of old Brazil, entered by the *bandeiristas* in A.D. 1750.

No doubt, too, if there are in existence among the Indian tribes in Eastern Perú, or on the foothills of the eastern Andean cordilleras any of those ancient manuscripts of plantain leaves, fastened with agave threads, similar to those seen and taken away—as to one manuscript—by the monk Narcissus Gilbar, in 1840, in the Paños Indian village on the banks of the Rio Ucayli (100 miles east of the Huallagu, a tributary of the Amazon), we may go far towards the discovery of a sort of Rosetta stone in plantain leaves which may partly elucidate these ancient mysteries of South America and Hy-Brazil. As I stated, in a previous chapter the monk dragged out of the reluctant Indians the admission that:

> these bundles of leaves contained the history of a very ancient civilized nation who brought writing with them from the north or east beyond the cañon and the Andean cordilleras.

It is by no means improbable in the view of those knowing something of mysterious South America's ways that these ancient manuscripts still exist. Until we find them we are no farther forward than a man, at this moment, pondering over one of the incised blocks of curious hieroglyphs which the Chilenan museum at Santiago derived from an old original Easter Islander, when that South American state grabbed *that* island of the dead! But to return to Gran Paytite:

A family of Spaniards, probably born in a frontier settlement on the eastern Bolivian confines of the old Viceroyalty of Perú, in a pueblo called Santa Cruz de la Sierra, actually saw, across rolling green plains, miles of forests and shining rivers, the roofs of the mysterious city of Gran Paytiti. The man who told the story was standing on a high, wooded mountain somewhere in north-western Bolivia, bathed in the sunset fires of a year in the first two decades of the seventeenth century. But, like Moses, he and his *hermanos y sobrinos* were never destined to pass beyond that Pisgah into the unpromised, mystic country. For centuries the yellowed parchment of this strange and romantic story has lain mouldering in its *cajon* (box) on an *estante* (shelf), duly filed and lettered (*legajo y letra*) in the *Archivos de Indias*. It is a copy written in a mid-seventeenth century hand. Now the day has come for me to put it into modern English for the first time since the old Spanish vellum was committed to the stone archive rooms of the depository at Simancas.

The autobiographer is a certain Don Alonso Soleto Pernia, in whose veins ran the fierce blood of the hardy, vigorous, stern, undaunted spirits of the conquistadores, of Cortes, Vasco Nuñez de Balboa, Pizarro and Ximinez de Quesada. It coursed like the fierce and heady wine of youth in a day when already the Spanish furore of conquest and the old Castilian courage and invincible spirit were on the wane.

Don Alonso, then still a young man, titles his story:

> *Memoria de lo que han hecho mis padres y yo en busca del Dorado que ansi se llama esta conquista, y dicen que. es* el Paytiti. (Memorial of what my ancestors and I have done in the search for the Dorado, as that quest is called, and that they say is *el Paytiti*.)

He tells us that his father came from Paraguay, in search of the "Dorado", and in the train of a Spanish *gobernador*, with many Indians.

In the land of the Chiquitos[1] they met the Indians, and fourteen Spaniards and many of their own Indian followers were killed. So, the *compañeros* had to turn back on the trail to the safety of the Rio Paraguay. Later on, with women and children, they re-entered the country and founded the pueblo, or settlement of Santa Cruz (de la Sierra). Under a new governor, Don Lorenzo, the pioneers passed farther into the wilderness of old Bolivia, founding another settlement which they called el Pueblo de Santiago de Puerto (St. James of the Haven).

At the head of another expedition, the Governor crossed the mountains and clashed with the intractable Carib Indians, many Spanish soldiers and their Indian allies being killed in battle. The Indians of these wild mountains were fierce fighters, but what discouraged the Spaniards, says Don Alonso, was the total absence of a medicinal plant, the *contra-yerva*, without which the Spaniards could not get on in that land. This plant must be the famous *yerba-maté*, or Paraguayan tea, which, even to-day is all that the Brazilian gaucho or vaquero has with his *carne con ó sin cuero* (beef with, or without the hide, with adherent hair). "They are a people accustomed to yerba," says Don Alonso.

Some time later the Governor, Don Lorenzo, founded and settled the town of San Lorenzo, and sent to Perú, whence came his *mæsse de campo*, Juan de Torres Palomino, with one hundred and eleven Spanish soldiers, who, subsequently, embarked in a shallop, two boats and a barquentine, with pilots, and set sail down one of the tributaries of the Amazon "to old Spain". Don Alonso Soleto Pernia, then a boy, had been sent by his father to help in the ships; but Don Lorenzo, the Governor, died, and Don Gonzales de Solis (Holguin) took charge. The expedition soon broke up, some returning overland to Santa Cruz, others going by the river. Back in Santa Cruz was the Governor of the frontier settlement, Don Beltrán de Guevara by whom members of the expedition expected they would be punished. At that time, however, Don Beltrán was out in the country, hunting wild Indians. On the way across country to Santa Cruz, young Pernia, with the soldiers under the command of the *mæsse de campo*, Hernando de Lomas, entered the Indian territory of the Chiriguanas[2] and the Itatines, where they were attacked and thirteen Spaniards killed.

From the country of the Chiriguanas, the *Gobernador*, Don Gon-

[1] The Chiquitos were a race of gentle and agricultural Indians—at least, in a later day after the conquest. They spoke a peculiar language and, in the seventeenth century, were gathered into missions. Their territory was in north-east Bolivia and the lowlands bordering the affluents of the Rios Madeira and Paraguay. The word Chiquitos (little) alludes to the low doors of their huts, which made the early Spaniards say they must be small men.

[2] The Chiriguanas, or Xiriguanos, or Siriguanos, or Chirihuanos were Bolivian Indian tribes of Tupi stock, inhabiting the lowlands and valleys, south and east of the present site of Santa Cruz de la Sierra. In A.D. 1450, the Incas partly conquered them; but they repulsed the Spaniards of the Viceroy Toledo's invasion, in 1572. The Ititanes, Itanes, Ites, or Itinez were a tribe of north Bolivian Indians on the Rios Guaporé and Mamoré. They were anciently found as far east as Paraguay. Independent but low-grade savages, they spoke a tongue called *Itanoma*, which has never been classified.

zalez sent a company of sixty Spanish soldiers to the north, Pernia going with them on the trail, as it proved to be, of the mystic Gran Paytiti. He tells us:

> We reached some mountains and came on a great road, and arrived at the Rio de Dorado, and met Indians, who gave us news (of el Gran Paytiti), and sought to persuade us (not to venture further into the unknown). These Indians had gone there, their fathers, and they (being but lads), and they could take weapons, and they were met by armed men who came out in such great numbers that the Indians were forced to turn back and escape, which, if they had not done, they knew not what would have become of them, and them that most put them to flight were the leaders. These leaders, they say, appeared in such shining splendour, being clad all over the body in such glistening, silver armour as serves them as a crown on the head, and on the wrists, great bracelets, with, on their necks (throats) very great and beautiful medals (*patenas*) (collars or necklets?) of very rich plate; and this is more than anything else the reason why these Chiriguanas fled and escaped. As they were fleeing, they met, by chance, an Indian woman (*una India*) who came from a small and lonely farm (*chacara?*), with a harnessed (or bridled or haltered) ram, (*carnero de diestro*), and came also an Indian woman spinning wool of the same sheep. And asked if it were a draught animal, they said "No". They had not our animals, but they were beasts with long necks, not like horses or mules. When I knew the language I asked them if they wore clothing of the sheep they sheared. They had a bridge made of *orisneja* (? *a liana*), that passed from one side to the other, and they called that hill (or highland) (*cerro*), "God-Head of Anta" (*la cabeza de Anta*); and they showed us the straight road (*la derechera*) where, almost to the North, the sun sets. It did not seem to the Spaniards that these Indians praised or encouraged them, as they said to us: "Stay, gods, since you have come here. Let us quit going there sooner than I die (*sic*), inasmuch as our fathers went out on the conquest, but did not enjoy it. I counsel you, rejoice at it, sooner than die". . . . Thus said these barbarians, and I enlarge no more, lest one weary of repeating what they said of that quest. . . .

Hence, proceeding farther on their way, the Spaniards became involved in a fierce battle with enemies of the Chiriguanas who had built very queer forts made of uprooted trees (*arrancados*). "The roots have places overhead where their look-outs spy if any other Indians were coming to our help . . ." There were queerer features still about these forts:

> In these uprooted trees were painted faces of demons, charms, wrought with very cunning, wooden tools, and it seemed to me that every time they came here for worship.

The Spanish leader then ordered ten mounted men, armed with lances and carrying leathern shields to advance ahead of the main body, on the road, "and many men said that here was another Montezuma":

> And a captain, Alonso de Solis said it was his duty to capture the lord of that country. . . . . Now ahead of us, we saw a league of ramparts,

as they seemed. . . . And de Solis, who had been in the wars in old Spain, said it seemed to be a rampart-wall, very strongly built, with the sun shining on it, and close to it was an enclosure in the form of an entrenchment, very well defended (*un fuerte muy reforzado*), and there was in the entrenchment six Chiriguanas and Chirivuanos Indians; the fort was made of two hiquerones (large American trees) and cedars, planted one pace in front of another and all round about to surround their city, and these trees, enclosed one within the other, made a gateway so thickly planted with trees that hardly could we enter it, man by man. For it was a trap. . . . So our soldiers, wishing to test it, took axes and cut down a tree of the rampart, and others, and we hurriedly sent forward the horse's to aid the fifteen, brave, hardy and energetic men who entered by this wicket-gate, so great was the multitude of savages that attacked them. But though the help of the horsemen was so brief, yet great was its aiding force. At the end we took fifteen prisoners. The savages fought with bows and arrows and macanas[1] suspended at the wrists for use when they come to hand-grips. There were Indians that scorned to flee, but stayed fighting on foot. They rushed at us with derisive howls and abuse, determined to fight us, and the other Indians, we took for friends, and who had advised us to attack this strong place, presently fled, and without their aid, we saw ourselves in a tight corner, the tightest that could be; but the Spanish race is a race that takes all things, and, presently, we pressed forward and fought in another pueblo, a league distant— and here the roads were so straight and broader than any *calle* that might be, and these roads were so clean and swept that, certes, we had never seen the like. We hurriedly entered this pueblo, not meeting a soul, for we had seen the inhabitants fleeing from our men. In this village, we found in a house in the plaza, no fewer than thirteen sculptured images (*bultos*) all standing up and seeming to be friars; because they had faces of priests, and tonsures like those of monks. And they had hair-shirts (*silicios*) and scourges, hanging from their girdles, and on the scourges was a sort of blood. All these images stood gazing one at the other. And other soldiers entered into another oratorio and they called out: "What is that to gape at yonder? Let all come here, and see something more than that!" . . .

Here, as Pernia tells, there were, in this stockaded village on the border of the unknown, with obvious relics of some vanished civilization of mysterious South America, "all the saints and God the Father, standing together". He added: "The house was like a church, in the name of Jesus, with many images of saints standing so as to show they were subject to the one that covered them with his upraised arms, in the manner of the Father."

At this point, Pernia records, without realizing its significance, that the Indians "signed to us there were others beyond like ourselves. But we did not understand them nor they us."

Here, again, is an undoubted reference to "white Indians", or direct descendants of the white, Atlantean race of old Brazil, existing in the *terra incognita* beyond the eastern Andean cordillera, in the seventeenth century.

[1] *Macanas* were wooden, Indian sabres, studded with flints.—AUTHOR.

He goes on:

From here, we passed to another pueblo, and outside was an image in the shape of a naked man crucified on a sort of cross. It had a countenance like that of our Christ. . . . And we pass on beyond and presently we chance on a resting-place (a sort of park or gardens). Round this place, were trees, as before, with roots standing up; and there were turned, back to front, a sort of devils in figures, because they were so grim and ghastly. It was noted that all we saw inside the houses had good faces, and that no artist's brush could make better, and all that the Christ-like figure was we were externally. The figure has arms, limbs and feet like ours. We left that spectacle, and farther on met a pulpit like an olla (large jar?) and it was of rounded stone and had a mounting-block (*subidero*) for ascending to look around. And I climbed and began to look around, crying aloud above. And an Indian below made signs to me to come down from the pulpit and not annoy his God, and to show what it was and calling louder, the Indian pointed to the sky where the sun was setting, making signs that he had another Lord.

These remarkable images and sculptured figures thus appear to have been associated with the cultus of an ancient sun-worshipping race of South America. A mysterious nation in the line of races from those of Tihuanacu; white, Atlantean Brazil; the Phœnicians, who were really not kinsmen of Semites or Jews, but Aryans from old India; and Incaic Perú and ancient Mexico.

The Spaniards returned home to Santa Cruz where, to son Alonso Pernia, his father, who, evidently, had heard before about what lay behind the mysterious *cerro* of north-west Bolivia, said: "I know those two deep and brimming rivers. They are the Dorado and la Plata. From there, one runs north; the other, south." Young Pernia said that the Indians had wanted him to cross the river and climb the highlands.

Time passed, and the pueblo Santa Cruz became deserted and was left to the bats, the owls, and rodents. The Governor of San Lorenzo, the other Bolivian frontier township now felt a desire to advance the Spanish frontier farther into the wilderness. So he headed an expedition of forty men into the country of the Chiquitos Indians. Young Alonso Pernia's father in whose veins ran the hot fire of the early conquistadores, felt a burning desire that a son of his loins should enter the mysterious land of Gran Paytiti. He enjoined on his son, in that patriarchal age when the command of dead ancestors lay on the bodies and spirits of third and fourth generations of Spaniards as though they had been sons of old China, or German mediatized princes under the rule of Queen Victoria, to join the expedition and seek to pass to the north. There, according to the Indians, Gran Paytiti lay.

The Chiquitos, who, at this time, were by no means the gentle, inoffensive natives they afterwards became when softened by the enervating influences of the Jesuit missioners, opposed the entry of the Spaniards into their country. And, writes Pernia: "The Governor said that if we wished to go to the Mountain in the North, to fetch any Indians (slaves?), or *piezas* (gold or coin?), we might go."

Pernia now bethought himself that, when he and his brothers were at an Indian pueblo called Pocona, in Perú, a boosy *cacique*, by name, Don Pedro, had said to them: "*Sobrinos* (nephews) you have described to me your home in the Chiquitos country, and where north and south lie. Behold, notwithstanding how your fathers may have gone or may go, they have always entered from Perú and have lost themselves! Yourselves, nephews, were close to them already . . ."

"Them" Pernia clearly explains in his manuscript:

> And so the *cacique*, Don Pedro, knew it. He was very old, much more than 100 years of age. And he told us that his ancestors came from that country, and that they were very well off, and *that it was called Paytiti.*

With true, Spanish, pithy sententiousness, Pernia comments: "*Y esto nos dijo el indio, y dicen que los muchachos y los borrachos dicen la verdad*". (And so the Indian told us; for they say that boys and boosers speak the truth.)

So when they entered the Chiquitos country, in the train of the Governor of San Lorenzo, the Pernia brothers joyfully recognized these features of the landscape which Don Pedro, the boosy *cacique* of Pocona, told them indicated the trail to Gran Paytiti. However, between them and the delectable highlands of their Pisgah intervened fierce tribes of cannibal Caribs inhabiting the ridge of high mountains. They were men of the valorous South American native race, whose necks not even the warlike Conquistadores had been able to bend beneath the Castilian yoke:

> They ate human flesh and would and will not submit to the Spaniards, whom their one desire is to kill. Very vile did they prove to us, for they killed eight of our soldiers till our Captain ordered their huts to be burnt down when they were in them; yet they had rather burn to death than give themselves up. So they burnt, enraged and howling and roaring with wrath. . . .

A day or so later, the Pernia brothers travelled abroad in the country, and were passing the burnt-out pueblo, when they saw lying off the trail, in some bushes, an Indian who had been shot with a gun, in the leg. The Spaniards acted as if they had not seen the Indian, and passed on their way; but when they came back, lo the Indian had vanished! When he saw that, one of the Pernia brothers sprang off his horse and said:

> *Hermanos y compañeros*, I will search for that Indian we saw lying here; and starting from a point, we searched the bush for the trail the Indian had made; since he had a broken leg and had to drag it after him to get along. We caught him up, and my brother said: "Here is this barbarian. He is not dead!", and we came on him looking dead, and my brother said he should be taken to our camp, to be questioned, since we had caught no other Indian. . . . And four Indians raised him on their shoulders and brought him along with a *lengua* (interpreter).

The wounded Carib was questioned about what he knew of Gran Paytiti and its strange men.

Soleto: "Why won't you submit to us?"

The Indian: "We know you not, except for enemies . . . *They (the Paytitans) have weapons like yours. The sounds coming from your weapons are like theirs. Their arms fire stones* . . . Round about are persons like yourselves (white Indians!). We will not submit to them; for we wish to be free. . . . We and seven or eight other Indian provinces are vassals of the men of Paytiti."

Follow in the manuscript some curious facts about the white, South American men of this mysterious land!

"They fight cruelly" (said the wounded Carib), "and march many into battle. At their head are so many *galenes* (gallants, or leaders), with many coronets (*coronas*), and medals (*patenas*), and bracelets (*torcs* in the old Celtic fashion, in Gaul and Romano-Britain.—AUTHOR) so that these men appear stars, dazzling, as the sun shines on the glittering devices they wear."

The Indian added that they wore "collars like little flasks. I was left on the field of battle with the dead: because I had been struck with a stone that smashed my ribs. I did not fly, because they would not kill me (among the dead). I stayed till nightfall, and so I escaped, but when we came back to our country, this Lord (of Gran Paytiti) sent a captain to be over us. So we remained in peace and refused to cross the ridge of mountains . . . If you climb the mountain you will see their land from the top of the ridge."

Here, at this point, in this queer story is the only known white, Spanish eye-witness's testimony of the land of Gran Paytiti, and even so, only from the far distance. Don Antonio Sanabria went out from the camp and climbed the mountain. He came back and said he saw nothing. The Indian pointed out that Don Antonio had not climbed the right mountain. "It is from the peak of the other you will see their plains and pueblos":

> And six of us, three Indian Chiquitos, three men from San Lorenzo including myself, went to the top of the mountain the Indian had indicated, and when there we looked from side to side. I said: "*Señores,* we have no needle (*aguja*, compass)." They gave me one, and with it I found the north-south line, and looking north, we saw a *cerro* (hill or highland), running east to west, and all round were mountains (*montañas*) of great height, and where we had come there were also great mountains, and looking towards the sunset, we saw a lake (*laguna*), and towards the north small lakes. And I said to my *compañeros*: "Those three small lakes we see are really one lake, separated by islets", and looking, they agreed. "And there are pueblos round that great lagoon" . . .

The *compañeros*, again staring, said they saw nothing.

Pernia: "Can you not see vapours arising?"

The others: "Yes."

Pernia: "Then follow the smoke as it goes straight up in the air, and does not disperse. There are houses there" . . . . :

> Can you not hear drums? They said: "No, it is the wind in the trees, or blowing through rocks." I said: "Keep your ears open and listen better." They did, and now agreed they heard drums sounding . . . And so we stayed an hour longer, and one of the six said: "If we are six, then we might be the three kings that would conquer the world." And on that we came back, and as we came, I said: "*Hermanos*, let us tell the *compañeros* we've seen nothing. We shall then see how they will wag their feet." When we were back in camp, they asked us what we had seen. I said: "The same as before", whereon, presently, up jumped one of the Spaniards, and we now saw on what foot they hobbled (*y de que pie cojean*). He said: "Let us go home. That savage speaks lies." He who spoke withered my heart to think that such a man had so little courage. And I said to my brother: "What say you of that? Look rather to him who says to his friends that three men alone may resolve to go and conquer the world."

Back in the camp, the rest told the Governor that all was *verdonales* (green, unpeopled wilderness) that could be seen from the top of the mountain ridge. But Pernia, approaching the Governor, who told him what the rest of the *compañeros* had said, gave the true version of the sight of the unpromised land from the Pisgah-like *cerro*:

> The pueblo and the lake stand out clearly, and the compass-needle shows it lies northwards, on the right hand. All is mountain till you reach the *cerro*; while, northwards, all is hillocks and open country. The indications of Gran Paytiti are strong . . . And the Governor said: "I believe the good news you bring."

The sight had set on fire the heart of young Alonso Pernia. "I wished I might take wings of the morning and fly to seek that land."

Alas, the others did not feel that way! (So it looks as if the wings over El Gran Paytiti will have to wait the day after the Second World War, when, from the gondola of a new airship, or the glass front on the nose of a four-engined plane where once sat the forward gunner with the bomb-chute beneath his feet, some observer may see what he will see of the mysterious land of Gran Paytiti . . . And may there be no bombs beneath the moon, when he puts forth above and over that green and rolling sea of unknown South America!)

Their hearts had failed them, if, indeed, the *compañeros* had ever had enough courage and imagination to seek to follow the example of Don Hernando Cortes burning his boats on the shores of the Gulf of Mexico, or gallant Nuñez de Balboa contemplating the unknown Pacific from a peak in Darien. They preferred the fatted beeves and the comfort of their own stone, hidalgo houses back in the safety of the pueblo of San Lorenzo, where, in the society of their own raven-haired *señoras*, they might tell the eagerly questioning *muchachos* that there was *aca nada* to be seen from the *cerro*, looking towards mysterious Gran Paytiti . . . Only an Indian fable whispering like the wind in the green aisles of the northern Bolivian forests . . . No, there had to be no uncertain trails for these Spaniards, even if all the gold of El Dorado lay ahead!

But as we noted, the father, who was then dead, had laid his command upon the Soletos, of whom Alonso Pernia was one, that they were always to strive towards reaching the Golden City of Gran Paytiti, the burning, if not exactly Holy Grail of their ancestral Soletos. And not all the *demonios* that might lie on the lone trail could scare a Soleto from that quest. "Though he be dead," said Antonio Soleto, "we must heed his dying command".

On the next expedition a discussion befell round the camp-fire. When one Soleto cried out, "*Ea; hermanos y sobrinos, siganme todos*" (Come, brothers and nephews, all follow me), only ten men and a padre stepped forward. So the Governor, jumping on his horse, spurred forward, crying out: "*All* follow me!":

> And a few days later (writes Pernia Soleto), we were at the moun-
> tains whence we had seen the pueblo (Gran Paytiti).

They took an *India* (Indian woman?) who led the Spaniards, most of them not too eager for glory and adventure themselves, towards the mountains, and the "army" began to complain that they were quitting the plains and the pampas for the heights. It would appear that the Spaniards had some notion about conscripting the reluctant Indians into accompanying them as allies and guides on the trail towards the unknown. But those Indians, with the fear of God or the more portent Devil-Tiger of Gran Paytiti before their eyes were "not having any". Fights followed. A village was captured and in it was found a palm cross that was borne before one "Ya-ya", some sort of Indian Christ. The Indians, after the fight, were seen howling round camp-fires, and dancing while they committed suttee on the dead. It was found that these Indians also worshipped fishes, but the Spaniards noted their cleanliness—"the kitchen is separate where they cook their food". The Indians had also "kettles" more than six feet high— a tall man could stand upright in them—in which they brewed *chicha*. (N.B.—"Fishes," *supra*: a Pan-Atlan sign.)

Now, the brothers Soleto marched along two roads leading towards the Pisgah *cerro*; but "hinderers were at work". Pernia Soleto sounded a trumpet to rally followers to the trail; but at the sound, the Indians "we took for friends removed themselves afar off". *They* were not crossing any high mountains! Once on top of the *cerro*, the camp pitched below in a *pampichuela*, the Spaniards glimpsed the lake and pueblos of Gran Paytiti, but a captain swore he could see a savage in the distance, by a fire in the plain. "We told him we saw nothing", but their eye of faith and enthusiasm availed naught against the captain's eye of convenient, cold-pausing caution! Several attempts to get the rest to follow on the trail over the mountains were made;

but "hinderers baulked all", saying that the Governor wished them to return to camp below in the *pampichuela:*

Here the Governor said—for we hoped to return and pass beyond the *cerro* another day: "I seek to see no more than I have. There is the Lagoon and in it the stone marking the middle. That is the Paytiti".

A few days later Alonso Pernia Soleto met an unpleasant adventure. Says he:

I took canoes, and joined them with an iron bar (*barrotodas*) so that they be not overset. And when in them I saw the rock (the landmark of the great Lake of Paytiti?). It seemed made by hand, and as I returned to my *compañeros*, one shouted to me: "Look here, on the side!" I looked up, and saw a great cayman and I should not have known he lay in wait for me ahead, but for the warning. The reptile came at me, I fought him off with paddles, while my fellow-oarsman back-watered. The monster came on with open mouth, swimming fast behind us; but we turned and thrashed the water so vigorously with oars and spears, that, in the end, he could not overtake us, and we jumped ashore. As the monster had done at other times, he came where a curve was, and there a soldier, one Juan Lopez, killed him with a gunshot in the head. So fierce and terrible was this monster, that he frightened even the savages.

After the death of the cayman, the Spaniards were followed by an aggressive Indian in a canoe who shot arrows after them in challenge. He came standing up alone, in the canoe. (As do the *Chakoi Indiós,* still, to-day in the Wilds of Darien.) The Governor, importuned, assented to the killing of the Indian, and he was shot in the mouth, all bloody, and later dragged out of the water by the hairs of his head, by "my brother, Diego Soleto":

The others removed themselves in the canoe to a distance, and lay down in it, for love of the rifle-balls.

He speaks of the local clay, hard as the toughest metal, out of which the Indians made a chinaware "that I could not break, in a pitcher, though I gave three hard blows with a *macana*—that wooden Indian sabre studded with sharp flints". (Here is a chance for some modern capitalist to acquire the material for unbreakable china, and, having established his monopoly, to sell out, *por amor de Diós y los hombres,* to the Great World Amalgamated Pottery Combine. Unless some fierce *Indiós,* still left in this "uncivilized" part of old Bolivia break the *entrepreneur's* skull with a *macana,* which may the Good Lord, Manitou, Ya-Ya, the Pope of Rome, and the General of the Jesuits forbid!)

And I was standing by the Governor, when he said to us: "*Hermanos y sobrinos,* we have seen what we came to see, and we have met with the stone of the information . . . Let us return in a year with stores and people . . ." And so we went home, passing a country full of *zapallos* (red pumpkin gourds, as found in Perú.—AUTHOR), luxuriant maize, large farms, but few Indians, save women and children; and we passed by the *Chacaras Indiós* where we met trees blazed with axes made of stones they extract from mines . . . and they plant maize very curiously, the tips of the leaves being below, so that the weevil enter not.

The gallant Soletos begged other Governors to make the trips to the cordilleras as Don Gonzalo de Solis Holguin (accompanied by Padre Jerónimo de Villarno), had done; but all passed in talk when he sent out Antonio Suarez, a *mæsse de campo*. The unpromised land of *El Gran Paytiti* receded farther into the mists of romance and fantasy. For the age of the splendid conquistadores had passed like a "glorious roll of drums", or became as a gorgeous, illuminated bannerol and gonfanon hung in a mouldering, old abbey. Yet, as brother Juan Soleto said when he made the trumpet sound for the trail: "*Animo que Dios es grande*" (Courage, brother, God is great; someone, some day will hear).

A certain Don Juan Recio de Leon, camp-master (*mæsse de campo*) to Governor Pedro de Leaegui Urquiza (ruler of the provinces of Tipuani and the Chunchos, Perú), came within earshot—not eye-shot, like Don Alonso Soleto Pernia and his brothers—of the mysterious kingdom of Gran Paytiti. He, too, left a manuscript in Madrid, which I here translate. It was written in 1625. In it, he writes how the Indians in Bolivia told him El Gran Paytiti lay on the borders of the Rio Apurima, and that on its northern frontier was a "province of Women who live without men . . . but that on the women's own borders to the east, were men called the Marquires, with whom the Amazons periodically had sexual intercourse for procreation". Four other Indians told the Don that you went by land and rivers to a great *Cocha* (lake), in which were many islands with an infinite number of people. These people were very rich and wore amber necklaces. They were fond of perfumes, and wore pearls that were perfumed, which pearls, many in number and irregularly shaped, came from the great lake . . . To the north, many other nations lived on the slopes (*faldas*) of a great, snowy cordillera towering into the skies, close to the Laguna del Paytite, and stretching to the kingdom of Nueva Granada (modern Colombia). They wore clothes and were rich in beasts of burden and silver. When too closely examined about these queer stories, says Don Juan, "I found my Indians became very angry. They said it was more to our benefit to believe than for them to tell." At a great feast of fish, netted in the "famous River Parauri", some "great, roving (Indian) mariners" of these waters told him a story of which he was incredulous:

These *caciques* of Uchipiamo, Inarama and Anamas Indians, say that in the great Laguna del Paytiti, more than eighteen years ago there entered some reddish-skinned *Viracochas*, that they strongly believed were English, or Hollanders, and that every year they brought from the land of Grand Paytiti knives, machetes, coloured glass beads, silks (*tafetanes*) and linen-cloths of the sort these natives want, bartering them for very great riches of gold, silver, pearls, amber and many other things of value. I, having great difficulty in believing this incredible tale, they immediately showed me machetes, knives and some silk stuffs brought from the said Paytiti, a very few days ago. And notwithstanding it is true that I gave things of this kind to the natives' chiefs, when I entered this land, it was fully acknowledged in relation to their story. I observed among them some that they indicated were tools I gave them. And, seeing the great difference that existed between the tools I gave them and those they brought from Paytiti, I believed their story.

All these Indians said that most of them go to Paytiti two or three times a year, to traffic and bargain, which is why they have these tools. And the account certain Indians gave of these reddish Viracochas to certain soldier-interpreters I made to my Governor, and which I have in that chart (*carta*, or *carte*) among my papers.

I said to them that since there were so many wanderers to Gran Paytiti, one of them might be able to show me the form of the great Laguna, and indicate the islands and the rivers that flow out of it. And I put these details in a plate and map of certain kingdoms that is in my possession.

That these strange white men were neither Dutch nor Spanish, Portuguese nor English is made clear by the fact that Don Juan, in A.D. 1625, proceeds to describe that very work of old, Incan military engineering which, as Colonel P. H. Fawcett said, has occasionally been seen by modern Bolivian rubber-gatherers, along with a fine aqueduct, shrouded with vines and bush in the forests of the Caupolican, beyond the eastern cordilleras of the Andes![1]

Don Juan was then visited by four principal Indians from the country of the Marquires, in the border of the Rio Diabeni, which must be the same as the modern Rio Beni of the Bolivian Caupolican borders! Here, writes Don Juan:

> I saw in their province a marvellous fortress that they said the *campo* (army) of the *Hinga* (Inca emperor of old Perú) had made that it might remain a memorial of what the Incas had formerly accomplished in conquering that land . . .

Again, in the country of the Marquires, Don Juan is told of the Amazons, but the Marquires say that they are not their temporary husbands, as reported by other Indians, but that:

> Between these people to the east and the Laguna del Paytiti, they said there was a country of *men without women* (*una Provincia de hombres sin mugeres*). And they said that these men live without women; but for two months in the year they enjoy women from another part, and go by water to unite with them. They are such valorous women that they fight with their enemies better than if they were men.

From two other independent Portuguese sources we again hear of the "strange white Indians" whom Indians and Spaniards, and monks and missioners mistook for lost hunters of El Dorado. One of the witnesses is Capitão Symão Estacio da Sylveira, whose *Relação*

[1] Note also the Indians' use of the name *Viracochas*: derived from the white Atlantean pioneer who came to the ancient, western South American land from Hy-Brazil.

254

Sumaria das Cosas do Maranhão (published *em Lisboa, Anno de* 1624, 7 *de Marzo*), I have, for the first time, translated into English. It is a very rare book and cites an even rarer Portuguese volume by one Peter, or Pero de Magalhães, whose fuller name is Pero Magalhaens de Gandavo. Gandavo was the first to confuse El Dorado with Gran Paytiti, which accounts for the later incredulity and mystification of Don Juan Recio de Leon, and of others long before and after him. Gandavo, in 1575–76, told a story of certain Brazilian Indians, of "gypsy nature", who liked "walking through the world". They started on a long trail across South America, passing some days' journey beyond the Rio Poñete, where a "nation with armour" came out against them and disputed their passage. Overborne, "the gypsies" were obliged to make a détour much farther inland, and encountered many hardships and wars, which killed off large numbers. Those that survived:

> were forced to stay, on arrival (*forão ter à hña terra*) in a country that had very large populations (*pouocãos*), or towns, and many neighbours, among whom were so many riches, and who had streets, very long, with gold-smiths' shops (*ouvriges*). (A sixteenth-century South American Gold-smiths' Row!—AUTHOR.) These artificers were occupied solely with working and fashioning pieces of gold and gems (*pedraria*). Here, the "gypsies" stayed some time, and one day, seeing them (their hosts) bringing iron tools, asked them whence they had them, or how. And their hosts told them that, in a land to the east, in a place by the sea (*ao lago do mar*, or a lake of the sea), there lived a *white race, with beards*, from whom they got iron tools. Then the Indians said these others were of the same sort of people as the Castilians of Perú (*dos Castelhanos do Pirú*), adding, however, that, in another part of *the west* (*outra parte do Ponente*) they heard there was a similar people, with whom they trucked for iron tools, with certain shields plated with gold, and ornaments with emeralds. . . . And (the gypsies) begging their hosts to take them to and show them these people with the iron tools, that they might tell them that those pieces and similar ones they were willing to truck for the (white men's) iron implements (the gypsies) also asked to be put into communication with them so that white men might be prepared to receive them with great good will. . . .
>
> Leaving thence, they trailed to the Rio das Amazonas and navigated its waters for above two years, and they arrived in the Province of Quito, Perú, where immediately they were made known as people of Brazil and told the story of their travels, and offered their round shields which they sold at a great price . . .

It appeared, therefore, that these strange, white, bearded men must be dwellers by a golden lake (*Lago doradou*):

> in which discovery people and Castilian captains have been ruined and come to beggary in our wilderness of the Maranhão (*do nosso Maranhão:* the Amazon) to which they of Perú give the name of *Paytiti* and El Dorado (*Paytiti e Dourado*).

I have seen the very much rarer old Portuguese volume of Gandavo, which is titled: *Historia da provincia Sancta Cruz* (early Portuguese colony in Brazil), in which, in *Capitulo* 14, he speaks of *Das grandes riquezas que se esperam da terra do sertam*. He tells how the wandering, "gypsy" Indians of Brazil, who took two years traversing the continent to Quito, actually entered the goldsmith's row of the very long streets of El Dorado—*not* Gran Paytiti—without realizing where they were! The wanderers commented on the iron tools which the El Doradans had, and were told they came from the Castilians of Perú; but the El Doradans were willing also to barter jewels and gold with the Portuguese for *their* iron tools:

> The Indians said, also, that, on the other side (*banda*) they had news there was a similar people. Then they gave the wanderers certain round shields, all plated with gold (*certas rodellas todas chapadas douro*), and enamelled jewels with emeralds (or emeralds inset in gold: *esmaltadas de esmeraldas*) . . . There is a very general impression among them that a very large lake in the interior of the country has issuing from it the Rio San Francisco, in which are some islands with many towns, with very great suburbs, where, also, is much gold, and more in quantity, it is affirmed, than in any other part of that province.

Probably, Sylveira quoted from an edition of this 1576 volume which has not come down to our own day; for he makes clear that the El Doradans trucked their gold and jewels with the white Gran Paytitans, for the Paytitan's iron tools!

The nineteenth century treated the whole affair as a great golden myth of the Castilian conquistadores; but, in the year 1939, I found out that the tradition is very much an article of faith and firm belief in southern Chile. Here, in a very little explored region of the southern Andean cordillera, and one of vast size, there issues a queer river—queer by reason of its mystery and traditions—called the *Rio Baker*. Its headwater territory has never been explored, not even by aeroplane, and the *peónes* and cattle-men—in whose huts one takes shelter, as the cold mists of night fall down the slopes of the icy cordilleras to the bleak valleys—whisper, as they bend over wood fires and glance nervously around as their shadows lengthen grotesquely on the rafters and walls of the cabins.

They whisper of strange boomings and roarings, which reminded me of the strange *bomba de mar* which one hears as one is rowing in negro-owned boats, off the northern coasts of San Domingo (*Dominicana*) right in the track of the old buccaneers' rendezvous in Samaña Bay. But there the cause is not the same. In southern Chile it may be something more than the breaking up of the waters in the high ranges; whereas, off Dominica, the cause is likely to be that of a water-spout, or the cavern-driving inrush of the Caribbean.

It is perhaps singular that these ear-splitting boomings, crashings and reverberations are heard in this lonely Chilean region only at certain times of the year. The sound comes from the unknown region behind the folds of the cordilleras, which the Rio Baker drains.

I once asked a Chilean *ganadero* what the mysterious noises portended. He made a remarkable reply which I give without comment.

"*Señor mio*, Our fathers have told us that, behind the unknown region from which this river issues, there dwelt, and still dwells a white, blue-eyed, bearded race of men who live in a green valley, where are shining white towers, gilded temples, splendid palaces of lords and kings, stone causeways and bridges and much gold. It is *La Ciudad Encantada* (The Enchanted City), and each year, these men of the blue eyes, open wide the penstocks and flood-gates and sluices and tumultuous water from a great lake goes thundering down the mountains towards *el Pacifico*—the sea!"

Does such a lost and shining city really exist to-day behind these mighty cordilleras, in some valley of Avalon, like the deep valley of the blind, into which *Bogota* of Mr. H. G. Wells's short story fell? There is no smoke without fire, nor are traditions of this kind mere myths.

But, as my Chilean *ganadero* said: "*Quien sabe, Señor?*"

South America is the land of strange secrets, and mysteries old as the earth's early morning of civilization.

It was somewhere back of this mysterious land of unexplored ranges and booming rivers in Southern Chile and the Andean Argentina that lay the strange enchanted city of the Cæsars. But that strange story must be left for a later book. I have no space to tell it here.

One last question may be posed. It is one that is often put to me by readers.

Where were the gold mines from which the Incas derived their wealth? A friend in Australia asks me how it is that, despite the fabulous quantity of gold—placer, found precipitated on the ground, and in lost caches in vast hoards of jewels and ingots—we never see the shares of South American gold mines offered for sale or purchase in the columns of our financial newspapers, nor do we see financial news items about South American gold mines.

I myself dissent from the view that the old Incas—as a race they did not treat their subjects too well—derived the gold by the slow and painful method of collecting *chispas* and dusts from the serfs, washing river-beds and gullies. Much of it came from far older and very ancient races under the shadow of old Brazilian-Atlantis; but the Incas also had gold mines, and these are lost to sight. There is a very old tradition that the Incas mined silver in the Cerro de Famatina and in La Rioja, in what is now the Argentina; but their rich gold mines were in that very country of the Colchaqui Indians (the old Chunchos) where Bohorques made himself Inca and organized revolts against the Spanish crown. The Incas are said to have conscripted thousands of Indians from the neighbouring mountains, to provide the corvées in these gold mines. They held this forced labour down by garrisons in several fortresses. But the Indians kept the secret and no old Spanish conquistador, or later hidalgo, ever penetrated the secret of these lost Inca gold mines.

CHAPTER SIX

MONSTROUS BEASTS OF THE UNEXPLORED SWAMPS AND WILDS

"The first great waters came. They engulfed the seven islands (Atlantis) . . . All the unholy (necromancers and militarists) were annihilated, and with them *most* of the huge animals born of the sweat of the Earth." (*No.* 46 *Stanza of Archaic and Secret Records of old Asia.*)

"There are tracks of strange beasts, huge and unrecognized in the mud of the beaches of these lakes behind the unknown forests of the Bolivian Caupolican." (*Colonel P. H. Fawcett, D.S.O., F.R.G.S., lecturing before the Royal Geographic Society, in London, 1911, when he had among his audience the late Sir Arthur Conan Doyle, who subsequently wrote his novel,* The Lost World.)

THE reader will note that I have italicized the word "most" in the first quotation cited above. It is for a reason applicable both to Africa's dark places and to mysterious South America, which concerns us here, and especially to the blank space on the map, denoting that unknown region ranging from modern north-west Bolivia and the Rio Roosevelt, across the Roosevelt plateau of central Brazil to the Goyaz plateau, located in what are the ancient highlands of Hy-Brazilian Atlantis and modern Brazil.

The Caupolican, to which Fawcett refers above, is a region of dense and unexplored swamps and forests of almost Mesozoic character. Its impenetrable forests, indeed, as I said, *supra*, are perhaps less known, to-day, than they were in the days of Inca Topo Yupanqui, who sent an army into its fringes in A.D. 1491. It is a lost world shunned by the fiercest and most unpacifiable Indians, and is made the more inaccessible by what the Indians remember, to-day, of the Putumayo rubber atrocities, whose lessons they have applied in a way not encouraging to modern explorers. Let us give a glance at this strange region of the Earth.

The Caupolican is located east of the Andean cordilleras, in north-west Bolivia. (I referred to it in my book, *Mysteries of Ancient South America*, Rider and Co., London, in relation to the lost white race of ancient South America, whose memory is enshrined in tribal traditions current all over Amazonian Brazil.) The Indians, however, *malos* they may be, shun any penetration of this region of the unknown and bar off white explorers from it. It is bounded by the Rio Madeira and Rio Beni, draining a triangle of around 35,000 square miles in area. When the Andes were born in the gigantic throes of tellurian

258

and cataclysmic disturbances, it was into this region that there drained waters which turned it into a vast swamp.

The Inca emperor, Yupanqui, of the pre-conquest age, crossed the Andes with 40,000 fighting men of the Orejones type. His plan was to subdue the warlike Chunchos in a day, when, in faraway England, Henry VI, the monkish king, was founding "the college of Eton-by-Windsore" for those poor and needy scholars who have never been seen there from that day to this.

The Inca built two fortresses in enduring stone, but the forests have long since covered them up; and, to this mid-twentieth-century day, A.D., they cannot be traced. He linked them with a fine military road, as good as anything the Roman legionaries built in Britain, or any part of their Empire; but the road, and vestiges of an aqueduct lie also shrouded in immense forests, somewhere on the trail to San José.

On the fringe of this Lost World lie rubber concessions connected with the infamous Putumayo atrocities; but the dangerous Guaraya *Indiós* do not encourage either Europeans or Latin-Americans to venture beyond the fringe of forest villages well outside the Guaraya territory.

Somewhere, where no white man or roaming adventurer has ever been and returned alive to tell the tale, and far behind a screen of forest and swamp that lines the still unexplored rivers, is the home of mysterious beings of whom vague, but strange, rumours have drifted into the rubber-collecting outposts of north-west Bolivia. The forest Indians fervently believe in the existence of these mysterious beings; but they hold them in such fear and awe that no Indian will venture into the forest beyond the riverine belt, or agree to act as guide to a white expedition. No bribe that can be offered will tempt one Indian to break what amounts to a *tabu*. The old gods of the South American shades have spoken, and no Indian or *Indianista* will dare to invade the *Inferno Verde*, which is the ante-room to the *Lost World*.

Maybe, some day, in a saner age, a post-war type of airship or long-range cruiser-aeroplane may cruise over this vast and dangerous territory. But there is no safe landing-ground should the aircraft be forced down in the attempt to roll up the veil which hides these mysteries of thousands of years. The future may see!

Fawcett, when he was delimiting the boundaries of this unknown territory as far back as 1910, called it "an abominable forest, dripping with moisture, the home of malaria and deadly diseases of an obscure South American type", unknown to institutes of tropical medicine. No organized expedition has got beyond the fringes, since the Inca's day. Fawcett was head of the Bolivian Boundary Commission and had navigated rivers closed to explorers for at least five centuries. He was accompanied by three British citizens: James Murray, scientist of Sir Ernest Shackleton's Antarctic expeditions; Corporal Costin, of the Rifle Brigade; and a Mr. Manley.

The two last men were stricken down with grave illness at the time when Fawcett, as valiant and hardy as one of the old Spanish conquistadores or a roaming *bandeirista* of old São Paulo, was trying to penetrate farther into these vast, dank regions, where beastly insects beset the traveller. One of these insects—a species of maggot, called the *sututus*—infected James Murray, the scientist, and he had to be hurried out of the forest to save his life. For many weeks he lay hovering between life and death, in a small Indian village, where was located one of the food depôts of the Boundary Commission. (And it be noted, of all the lands that are most difficult or impossible to "live on", this is probably the world's worst, save the Antarctic!)

Even Fawcett found it hard to endure the hardships; and, at last, was forced to abandon his project. It is plain, therefore, that this part of South America is no land for "old school tie" expeditions, of the type whose members "potter about" the civilized regions at a safe distance from the edge of the dangerous unknown, and babble a lot of nonsense about the "exaggerated dangers" of the South American wilderness. If Fawcett found the going hard, much more so would the gilded amateur, or any writer of Baron Munchausen tales. At the first sight of the smoke fires of *Indiós malos*, such heroes are pretty sure to make tracks for the *avenidas* of Rio Janeiro, or Buenos Aires and tell the world that they cannot tell whether to bring in a verdict of murder or suicide, in the case of the pukka explorers, who *have* ventured into the unknown. I name no names here lest an old Etonian be peeved.

While Fawcett was trying to get beyond the dangerous swamps which fringe the rivers, threading their mostly unknown way through the immense forests, Indians told him they had seen strange footsteps of unknown animals of prehistoric size and stature in the mud and silt on the "beaches" of these marshes. They seemed to be animals of ante-diluvian type. There were also strange flora and strange, elusive men whom none could contact:

> I have hinted at the romances which await the explorer if he will leave the rivers and get away from the rubber districts into the more remote forests. They are not exaggerated. There are strange beasts and weird insects for the naturalists, and reason, at any rate, for not condemning as a myth the existence of mysterious, white Indians. There are rumours of forest pygmies and old ruins. Nearer civilization there are lost mines . . . tracks of strange beasts, huge and unrecognized . . . Nothing whatever is known of the country a few hundred yards from the river-banks . . . I could tickle the appetite of the romantic with more; but it is not definite enough to warrant courting a reputation for traveller's tales from the incredulous folk who sit at home and think they know all that is to be known about the world.

Listening to this lecture of Colonel Fawcett, delivered before the Royal Geographical Society, in London in 1911, as I must be forgiven for reiterating, was the late Sir Arthur Conan Doyle. It inspired him to write his *Lost World* novel, of the adventures of Professor Challenger, which are set in this very region.

Here, seems the place to interject a natural query which the reader may make: Was *homo sapiens* a contemporary of these monsters of the antediluvian, slime, hot swamps and wildernesses?

The orthodox ethnologist, biologist and encyclopædic historian of the type of H. G. Wells is, perhaps, a little too confident and dogmatic in affirming that he was *not*! But curious antiquities in South America and ancient traditions in China and India suggest that, perhaps, one may have to revise one's ideas of the age of man on the earth. That he may even have existed in the later Tertiary Age. A variety of extremely ancient myths and traditions of races, both known and unknown, may be euhemerized as implying that antediluvian man, a giant in stature, may have, in some cases, fought with, and even tamed, some of these monsters. In various parts of South America of the Megalithic Age, some of these memories of strange animals and monstrous extinct species seem to have been recorded and crystallized in weathered stone. In page 91 of my *Mysteries of Ancient South America* (Rider and Co.), I reproduced a picture of an unknown and extinct animal whose image was found hidden in a cavern or catacomb, in that strange mausoleum whose ancient name has not survived in a garbled form of primitive myth: Easter Island, probably an outpost of the gigantic and brutal race of Mu, or Moo-Ah, that drowned, Pacific continent known as Rutas in the ancient legends of Hindostan. This same animal is pictured on very ancient ceramics dug up at Trujillo, in Northern Perú, to which the empire of Mu may have extended, in some day more than 60,000 years ago. It has a cat-like face, long body, arms and legs. It looks like a strange marine animal. At Manabi, in Ecuador, the seat of another unknown race of the Megalithic Age, the same, or a similar monster is found engraved on a bas-relief, and is complete with eight octopoid arms emerging from its cat-like head. Not far from Manabi, is another place called Manta, where, some years back, bones of giant men and women (*not* dinosaurs or saurians!), were dug up, or found in caves of immense age, judged by the stalagmites and stalactites in them. The finders were making a railroad track. Also, in the patio of some business premises in the same pueblo of Manta, are two very singular sculptures of monstrous, extinct animals, of unknown species, with long necks and parts of a body. These sculptures were taken from ruins of immense age of some megalithic race unknown, who are a standing puzzle to archæol-ogists, and about whom I shall have something to say presently, in this chapter and in a later book. They are people of the "Manabi culture".

Old medals in cabinets of collectors of classic antiquities, in the sixteenth, or seventeenth, or eighteenth centuries in Europe, depict the Titans, who stormed the gods on Olympus, in the Greek myths, as half-men, half-reptiles. Northern mythologies also suppose that the giants were half-men, half-reptile, semi-saurians who struggled against the gods, or men of a higher intellectual stature. It may be recalled that the Gorgons, ruled by the Medusa, sight of whose face turned men to stone, were also ruled by a matriarchate of coarse and sensual women who used for weapons the skins of enormous reptiles, swarming and pullulating in the hot, proto-African swamps.

Chinese mythology tells us that in the ten ages of the *Ki*, after the creation, men lived in caves and climbed trees while struggling with monsters who had the face of men and bodies of serpents, and who rode dragons, which sounds like a tamed dinosaur used as a horse! Fairy stories, no doubt, calculated to make the scientific historian smile in his beard? Other ancient myths imply that the seas swarmed with saurians who emerged on the beaches and attacked from the swamps, fens and reedy lakes, of enormous expanse, all steamy with heat. They attacked "anthroposaurians" who had taken refuge in the mountains. A frightful battle raged between monsters of the land and the sea.

The gods of cataclysm intervened. Vulcanism was unchained and changed the face of the Earth. A collision with some celestial body caused the axis of the Earth to topple, and catastrophically altered the lush, warm conditions to an ice age. Bode's theory formulated into a law, at the end of the eighteenth century, might suggest that some planetoid, formed from one of the asteroids that are the remains of a missing planet disrupted by some cosmic body interposing itself between Mars and Jupiter, came near the Earth, and, swerved from its orbit by our own planet's gravitational pull, grazed our Earth, and turned away from it. Or our Moon may have done the mischief. Another theory is that the animal species were evolved—the cave-bear, cave-lion, reindeer, wolf, dog and bison, and man half-spiritually and half-mentally developed—at the time of a collision of a comet with the Earth. This, if it did not fall on our planet, deflected its axial spin, so that pole and equator gradually changed places, and glaciation set in for a cycle of some 30,000 years, till the spinning earth regained its former position in relation to the angle made by the polar axis with the plane of the ecliptic. Our Earth then "sat upright" again, like a spinning top, or gyroscope whose axial rotation has been deflected. "My guess is almost as good as yours", one may say to the sceptical astro-physicist. The heresy of to-day becomes the orthodox canon of the day after, and *both* become the derision of the day after that!

The old Hindus had records which seem based on ancient ancestral memories of what happened on the Earth at the time of the Great Cataclysm. They say it was "at the end of the second age of two million years". Whether the cataclysm was caused by impact with a great comet, or vast ærolite such as may have been thrown off when the missing planet disrupted, that Bode's law says once moved in an orbit between Mars and the Earth, and was anciently named Lucifer, no one may say. One theory is almost as good as another in relation to the causation. These Oriental myths say that the early Earth was covered with clay, water and mud, and islets in warm seas, pullulating with great saurians and enormous reptiles. These myths say that when the Earth froze at the poles, it formed, in contraposition with the equatorial swamps, mountains that, sheltered by their situation, emitted a dense and cloudy atmosphere. There, the enormous reptiles degenerated, losing strength and ferocity, while, on the other hand, the mammals progressed.

The ancient lands under the archaic seas were alive and swarming with monstrous saurians and reptiles, while, according to these ancient myths, the summits and slopes and valleys of the mountains were alive with mammals! On the one side, the anthroposaurians, from the wide plains, bordering the early lakes and shallow seas, arrayed themselves in battle, and, mounted on tamed dinosaurs, confronted a higher and more intelligent race of men who made up for lack of girth and muscle in brain power and intellect. Then came tremendous battles! The saurians remained masters of the ancient seas and swamps and of the enormous lakes. In the meantime, the anthroposaurians— occurring in the Greek and Roman myths as hydras, chimæras, men-dragons, tritons, and so forth—ascended to the mountains where again terrible battles raged. In the old myths, we are told that these Titanic monsters were struck with thunderbolts, which perhaps, may mean that the god-men of the uplands had command of weapons using some ray or electrical force; for it must not be too hastily supposed that only our own era has devised mechanism and applied scientific laws to the end of using natural forces. Then, while below on the plains and in the warm seas, the plesiosaurus and the icthyosaurus paddled the waters and mounted the rocks, aloft monster men and god-men were locked in titanic conflict in the mountains.

In the middle of the combat, the Earth heaved to its foundations, the summits of the mountains split and vomited fire and gases, and all the pent-up forces of vulcanism and flood conspired together to change the face of our world.

The fair Hyperborean land of Proserpina, said in the old world myths to be the first place on the Earth with viable conditions had, before the Great Cataclysm radically altered warm temperate con-ditions in the far north to their present arctic climate, a very genial climate, with two crops a year, fertile land, and many luscious fruits that needed no cultivation by man. Its climate was temperate in relation to the torrid conditions elsewhere on the globe.

The ancient giant men of America, shown on petroglyphs as attacking, or attacked by monster animals, are graphically described in ancient Asian documents, as of gigantic stature, between 12 and 15 feet tall. Their skin was dark of an almond colour and tawny, their lower jaw bones prominent, their countenances oddly flattened, their eyes small but penetrating, and very widely apart. They had no fore-head, but an extraordinary mass of flesh bulged out, and the head was of a very much retreating slant, while round and about it was a reptilian skin with extraordinary reflections as the light shone on it

The legs and arms above all were proportionately very long, much longer than those of the modern man. Their hands, and feet and heels were very pronounced. From the back and on the shoulders hung a skin like that of a rhinoceros, but very scaly, like the hide of a saurian. This race lived with the dinosaurs and saurians and appear to have ruled over and enslaved them. In the right hand, these monster men carried a war club, and in the left, held in leash by a cord made of strong vegetable fibre, was an enormous and repulsive reptile that rendered them the services of a falcon in the chase. (The reader may recall that I said that a strange and ancient statue of Vira-cocha, seen by the old Spanish conquistadores in old Perú, depicted this very tall culture hero and holding a monster animal by a leash.)

A dim memory of such a Great Cataclysm was symbolized by the head of an unknown and very sinister-looking, evil monster which was given to the former god-man, or king of old Hyperborea, who was called Set. This Set, our own Satan, or the Egyptian Thoth, and the *Tahitian* Toth, or Tah, or Tath, retreated into the twilight world of damned men or man-gods, becoming Typhun of old Egypt, or the same Typhoon of the old Mexican pantheon, a god of cataclysm, hurricanes and typhoons and raging waters. Just the same, in the ancient Mexican pantheon the god Tezcatlipoca

Ancient Babylonian image of dinosaur.

was represented by the head of an unknown monster.

The monstrous fauna of old Mu, the great Pacific four-island continent which had colonies in North, South and Central America, presents a weird world of life "red in tooth and claw" and wallowing in the slime of beaches, or prowling and preying in the antediluvian forests and deep jungles of that strange land.

Ancient lore says that old Mu had huge hunting dogs somewhat like a heavily-built Saluki, the old Arabian gazelle-hound. But these dogs were as large as horses and used for hunting and for tracking captive escapees, often horridly tortured and skinned alive by obsidian knives wielded by the gorilla Mu-ans, who were wardens of one of the prison islands of this queer continent. The cats of Mu were as large as pumas, but not tame, and were used to kill vermin by very tall, dark-skinned and low-browed, and heavy-featured Lemurians. They (the men of Mu) were from 10 to 15 feet tall, had large fleshy noses, square jowls, and huge knotted shoulders, like a Congo gorilla.

264

In the great forests of old Mu there lived another huge monster that was never seen, and heard crashing through the dense jungles only occasionally. The head-men often ordered that girl-children—not valued in old Mu—be taken to the forest and left there on great stones, that were rounded and like very large drums. There, the abandoned girls were to be eaten by the unseen monster, which seems to purport that he was deemed to be worth placating with human sacrifices. A small type of mastodon was also used for hunting in Mu. Ancient and very curious myths, current in the North Pacific, say that old Mu had queer quadrupeds that possessed bat-like wings and could fly! These queer animals were about the size of a large sheep, but more or less harmless, and lived in the trees. There were also flying serpents around four feet long and they had three pairs of wings on their back-ridges.

The trees of the great forests of Mu harboured giant serpents and were festooned with a beautiful white and red creeper that oozed a sap the colour of blood, when cut. The dinosaurs and mastodons of Mu fed on a species of mimosa. The dinosaurs were amphibious and resembled a distorted, huge crocodile with longer legs, and had their habitat in great marshes, or on land bordered by sedgy lakes.

When in the course of ages, old Mu, which its folk held to be the motherland of the world, albeit in old Asia, there also existed older civilizations still, began to be disturbed by eruptions and increasing vulcanism, the seas around became sulphur-coloured and, for many months at a time, the killed fish exhaled a horrible stench. Immense squids and monstrous cephalopods of devilish ferocity would come ashore on the beaches of Mu's great islands, and even carried off adult folk of 10 to 15 feet high, but they usually preferred as food the huge dogs and cats of Mu. Now and again, terrific combats raged between sea monsters and devil fishes who came on to the beaches and disputed each other's conquests!

There was also a saurian or dinosaur that resembled the plesiosaurus, but they were not usually aggressive, though, when enraged, they exhibited enormous power. It was not a healthy pastime for any 10-foot Mu-an boy to tease one of these monsters! The myths say that these plesiosauri bred in mountain caves on the Mu-an islands.

A monstrous orchid grew in the forests of Mu, and its ways resembled those of a devil tree said to be found in out of the way paths deep in the forests of the Amazon, and in the Chaco wilderness in the Northern Argentine of to-day. The orchid was very poisonous, and if a Lemurian ventured near it, its tentacles would catch him by leg or arm, and sear the flesh. So virulent was its poison that death was certain, for the Mu-ans never found an antidote for its poison. Old Mu was, in many ways, not an idyllic land, as these glances at it show, and more than one cataclysm shook and disrupted it in the course of its very long history.

Whether or no the ice ages and glaciation spelt the doom of

monstrous saurians and animals *all over the globe*—and this chapter suggests that, probably some escaped in the deeps of the sea, or in southern swamps and recesses of the land where neither ice glaciated, nor over which the waters of the Deluge rolled—curious memorials of these monsters of the antediluvian age are found in South America. Bæssler dug up a piece of statuary in Chimbote, Northern Perú, which depicts a flying dragon. Two other monsters, pictured in extremely ancient ceramics of an unknown prehistoric race, in the same region of Chimbote, are one of a sea serpent of exactly the same sort as has been described by skippers of sailing ships in the nineteenth century, and commanders of submarines in this! (*Vide* page 309 *infra.*) That is, a sea monster of unknown marine biological species, with camel-like head, toothed jaws, scaly colubrine body, and great length. The other is of a roaring, flying dragon, with mailed body and human legs and arms, holding up by the hair a human head, which the monster clutches in his right hand. A third flying dragon of Chimbote has a hippine head, mailed body, armoured tail, and human legs, and grasps shield and weapons in his right hand. Maybe, this is not *totally* a fantasy of a pre-Inca artist of Chimbote, but embodied some far-off ancestral memory. *Quien sabe?*

The earliest story of the encounter of a European with a strange unknown monster of the South American wilderness occurs in the travels of John Lerius, or de Léry. "A Frenchman who lived in Brazil, with Mons. Villagagon. Ann. 1557–58."[1] Lerius was wandering in a wood, with two Frenchmen. They were somewhere in the country of the Tupinamba Indians . . . "Wee had with us no hand gunne, but onely our Swords. Wee had not Barbarians to guide us . . . and therefore wandred in the Woods and passed through a deepe Valley, hearing the noise of a certain beast comming towards us, supposing it to be some timerous and harmelesse wilde beast, notwithstanding,

[1] Honorius Augustodunensis, the learned monk and *scholasticus*, nicknamed the "Solitary", who lived at Autun, about A.D. 1300, may be the man ultimately responsible for the yarns about monsters met in America by veracious mariners, at the time of the first voyages. De Bry put them into his finely illustrated *American History* and gave them further currency. In *Summam historiarum seu chronicon de ætatibus mundi*, Augustodunensis tells—but does not locate them—of monsters with soles turned backwards—sixteen toes to the two feet. He mentioned others who have talons and dog-like heads, with hides like cattle and voices like barking dogs. "Of certain mothers who gave birth to dog-like progeny which in old age grew black and lived longer than our own." But it is in the story of the Cyclopes and one-eyed Arismaspi and the Schinopodæ, that someone seems to have spoofed de Bry into recording that they were inhabitants of South or Central America. He—Augustodunensis—gave a fine fancy range when he spoke of Schinopodæ, or Scinopodæ, with one very large foot propped up as they flew in the air; but, when not in flight, they lay on the ground with the sole of the foot erected to make shade! "There are others without heads, but which have eyes in the shoulders, and for nose and mouth two openings in the chest, just as they have bristles like wild animals." The other spoofer, who wrote the mythical travels of Sir John de Maundeville, illustrated these monsters, adding one of his own. Perhaps, Pliny and his "ape", Solinus of the Polyhistor, first started these stories. Augustodunensis also spoke of serpents so great in size that they can eat stags, and they also swim in the ocean. He called them *Ceucocrocæ* and says they had body of an ass, buttocks of a stag, breast and legs of a lion, feet of a horse, with immense cloven horn, vast mouth stretching when open to the ears, solid bone in place of teeth, and almost the voice of a man.

proceeding on our intended Journey, wee were secure and quiet in minde; but presently, thirtie paces distant almost from us, on the right hand, wee saw a Lizard on an hill, bigger than the body of a man and five or sixe foot long. Hee, being spread all over with white and rough scales like oyster-shells, holding up one of his forefeet with his head aloft and shining eyes, began to behold us. Wherefore, being astonished . . . wee had onelie our Swords att our sides and Bowes and Arrowes which weapons could not greatly hurt that Monster, armed with such hard scales; neverthelesse, fearing lest if wee shifted for ourselves by flight, being swifter then wee, hee would dispatch us altogether, when one fearefully beheld the other, wee stood still in the same places. But after that prodigious, fearefull Lizard had beheld us a quarter of an houre, with open mouth, and because it was exceedingly hot weather (for it was a cleere day, almost at noone), fetching a deepe groane, that wee might easily heare it, upon a sodaine, hee went unto the top of a Mountaine with so greate noise of the crashing and breaking of twigs and boughs, as a Deere running through a wood would scarce have made, wee[1], therefore, who were very much affrighted, not being very careful to pursue him, gave thanks unto God and pursued our intended Journey, and embracing their opinion who affirme that the Lizard is delighted with the sight of a man, it seemed to me that the beholding of us pleased that Monster so much as wee were tormented through his presence."

Some might smile and suggest that the Monster was a *jacaré*, or cayman; but the description of de Léry does not fit with that theory. Moreover, caymans do not climb mountain tops and break a way through forests in the manner of some saurian of the ages of Mesozoic coal-swamps. To-day, one is less inclined than one would have been in the days of the cocksure Ben. Jowett, Master of Balliol, to dismiss this story with an indulgent smile and a reference to poor Louis de Rougemont. Men who have been into the unknown *sertão* of the Brazilian wilderness, or have ventured into the sinister Matto Grosso *catinga* are not so sure on these points as, say, a fellow sitting in a padded chair in a Piccadilly club who jeeringly demands to know why such a Monster cannot be found in a Tier-garten, or the London Zoological Gardens. Even professors of zoology and fellows of zoological societies have not plumbed *every* mystery of the wilds, and less so of South America than any other continent. To all such sceptics we would say: Remember the Komodo dragon! It was only the accident of a complaint poured into the ears of a Dutch official, by natives

---

[1] Durand de Villegaignon, native of Provence, and a naval officer, had command of this expedition, and took possession of an island in the bay of Rio de Janeiro, in order to found a settlement for persecuted Huguenots. Villegaignon, however, was a scoundrelly and secret adherent of the Guises, Catholics; and so Jean de Léry had to flee home from Brazil to France in a ship rotten as touchwood, with no food save for the rats and mice on which his comrades fed, after catching them. They were reduced, like old buccaneers of a later day, to boil the leather of their boots and trunks for food. Even so, Villegaignon had given them a letter which would have ensured their execution in any French port controlled by the party of the Guises.

imprisoned on that queer, prehistoric lumber room of an East Indian island, not many years back, that revealed to European and American zoologists the existence of *that* great saurian-lizard. And one knows of an equally strange "haunted" island, lying north of the Philippines, in the Bashee channel, which fishermen shun, partly by reason of the unpleasant habits of a flying reptile, unknown to modern herpetologists, which is blood-brother to the pterodactyl.

Native legends in Colombia, the old Nueva Granada of the Spanish colonial age, say that the old wise man in black, Bochicha, the Quetzal-coatl of that land of the ancient Moscas or Muyscas, was accompanied by certain strange, unknown and bulky animals when he came to that country *from the east*, across the great Andean cordillera, bringing the arts of civilization and teaching laws to savages.

Who knows what animals these were? The early Spanish padres thought they were *mastodons*!

The double-headed eagle, found on ancient stones in both old Mexico and in Chile, was actually something more veridical and factual in the zoological and teratological sense than, say, a heraldic wyvern or griffon. In the days when the Marqués de Vallero was viceroy of Nueva España, or Mexico, he found in some ancient tomb near Mexico City, *two embalmed heads of double-headed* eagles, which he gave to the Monasterio del Escorial, in old Spain, with a statement that he had found these eagles in old Mexico! There is another enigmatic figure on an ancient stone monument found at Quauhquelchuli, near Atlixco, Mexico. It carries on the back a coat of arms and has two curved claws like hooks. It may have been merely a heraldic animal, say, like the old English wyvern of armorial bearings, but it also vividly suggests a species of unknown marine monster, being cut in a hard-veined stone of various colours, while, close by, an ancient figure on a boulder looks towards the town, with some suggestion of having served a purpose like that of the ancient Roman terminus, or boundary stone.

At Atitlan, in Guatemala, is another monstrosity carved on a big boulder. It takes the form of a cat with a sort of ruff at his throat, which points to the east. On the top of the boulder is a basin, but what purpose this cavity served, unless to hold a human victim's sacrificial blood, is unknown.

The American traveller, J. Lloyd Stephens, when in Central America in 1838, noted the ancient ruins of a mysterious race called the Mams, located close to Huehuetenango, in Guatemala. At a point where a river runs through a wild ravine, he saw where the banks had been washed away at high water, and here had been found the skeleton of some mysterious animal of extraordinary size. Stephens saw one on the bank, and the imprints were from 25 to 30 feet long. Others were still larger.

But even more amazing evidence of the connection and contemporaneity of Tertiary man in U.S.A. with dinosaurs is found in the states of California and Arizona. The high plateaux of Utah, Nevada and Arizona, are, along with the Roosevelt-Goyaz plateau, in Central Brazil, and their Asiatic counterparts in the Siberian provinces of Yakutsk and Irkutsk, the oldest parts of the Earth, and parts, too, that have not been under sea this side of an æon of more than 50,000,000 years. On one rock in Nevada is a petroglyph made by a very early Mongolian race, or type of Central Asiatic invader, thousands of years ago; for on it are cut glyphs identical with idiograms used in ancient China at least 1,000 years before Confucius. (I have a copy of these petroglyphs, collated with identical signs in ancient China.)

Yet are these ancient glyphs merely modern in comparison with the astounding figure, of most realistic character, of the fearsome dinosaur Tyrannosaurus carved in the rock by an extremely ancient man of a very early American race, who must have been an eye witness of this horrid reptile! He was also of a race of giants—or, as the Indians say, "a big feller"—who cut through the patina of iron scale on to the red sandstone face of the gorge of Supai, in north Arizona. This terrible monster is shown standing erect as he must have been seen by the artist—how many years ago? Why, more than 1,000,000 years ago! And this pictograph is emphatically no modern fake! It was first brought to public notice by the Doheny Scientific Expedition to the Havai Supai cañon, in 1924.

That the artist was a giant seems evident in the fact that another startling petroglyph in this cañon, shows a *giant* man in actual combat with a mammoth! Over his head, which reaches just under the mammoth's trunk, the mammoth is shown extending his trunk.

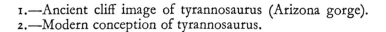

1.—Ancient cliff image of tyrannosaurus (Arizona gorge).
2.—Modern conception of tyrannosaurus.

Then we have the amazing find by a man named Jordan, near Granby, Colorado, when he was excavating a garage. He uncovered at a depth of 12 feet an idol carved out of very hard green material quite unlike anything known in the region. Other remains found suggest that here had been an extremely ancient settlement. The green stone of the idol seems to have come from some distance. On it, carved in high relief, is the figure of a dinosaur and an elephant. Both monsters are carved on the back of the idol. The elephant has a long, curved trunk. In this connection, Professor E. L. Hewitt, of Las Vegas University, tells us he has found in the homes of ancient people fossil remains of mastodons, and sabre-toothed tigers, also utensils made out of *live*, as distinct from fossil, ivory. It may be again added that both in North and South America artifacts have been found in conditions clearly associating them with the bones of mammoths and mastodons found with them.

The Supai dinosaur petroglyphs were made by a *giant* man who used a sharp flint tool, with which he scratched through a black over-surface of iron scale on to the sandstone—

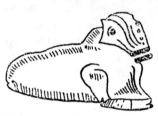

Unknown Monster (image found in ancient N. American mound).

as I stated—and this scale renders the glyphs practically indestructible, for it would take ages to weather off. About 100 miles away dinosaur tracks were found by Charles W. Gilmour, palæontologist of the United States National Museum. Cut on the same wall as the petroglyph of tyrannosaurus were images of goat-like creatures and serpents and curious signs, one of which is identical with the ancient Greek sign of Mars, and showing shield and spear.

Iron, which tends in time to form on the surface of the sand-stone, had *begun* to form in the furrows of the petroglyphs, which must indicate incredible antiquity. This raises the question: Did ancient man live in America in the Triassic period, millions of years ago, or did the age of the dinosaurs last into that of the mammoths?

Some attempt to answer this question will be made below; but it may be said that it has been theorized that the elephant and mammoth glyphs are not as old as that of the dinosaur.

Much of Grand Cañon, Arizona, has never been explored by white men. In three places in this cañon, the Doheny expedition found ibex pictured on the walls, and there are pictographs of prehistoric hunters driving seven ibex and two deer into a trap. It is odd that up to date no ibex and not even fossil ibex have been found in America.[1]

Half a mile down the main Supai cañon, from these wall pictures, is the strange figure of a *giant woman* in limestone. The Supai Indians call the figure "Conda-pavich", or "very big woman, long time dead". The Indians say her body was turned into stone by the action of

[1] I have sketches of rock paintings, or pictographs, found in 1910 by Senor Paschale Serrano Gomes, in hilly country, north of Alpera, Spain, not far from Alicante on the Mediterranean littoral. They are of Magdalenians said to have lived in the last phases of the ice age. They had playing grounds on terraces, and their women danced. This race wore a headdress *remarkably like that of North American Indians*, had hunting dogs with bushy tails, and looking like jackals, and also had half-tamed wolves. The rock-drawings show *the men hunting ibex and stags*. If, as some believe, these Magdalenians were of Atlantean race, then, here, in Arizona, we seem to have some evidence of the land-bridge that existed between old America and lost Atlantis.—AUTHOR.

lime and water. Beside her is a baby wrapped in skins, also petrified. The body lies some 60 feet up from the floor of the gorge, and is very difficult to reach as it lies in rock-crevice. It is bedded into the red sandstone and shows no sign of a joint that might indicate carving.

In the region known as "the Bad Lands of Wyoming", Charles Sternberg, a palæontologist, found a *mummy of a dinosaur*—the trachodon, or duck-billed genus. The "Bad Lands", or as the earlier French explorers called them, *"Les Terres Mauvaises"*, extend through south-west Dakota and north-west Nebraska, and are noted for their fossil deposits. Sternberg describes this discovery and shows a picture of it in his *Life of a Fossil-Hunter*. The American Museum of New York acquired this specimen which has dried-up flesh and skin- texture.

Another remarkable artifact was found in an old clearing close to the Sandy River, around 15 miles east of Portland, Oregon. It is a carving in volcanic tufa of an armoured type of saurian which resembles the stegosaurus. The artist is of a race unknown, but must have been a man of an extremely ancient nation, which, in a far day, lived in the region where now flows the River Colombia. The image is 3 feet long and 7 inches thick, but the legs and tail seem to be missing, though a formidable array of teeth are in the jaws and its back is ridged, sides armoured. The artifact was found on the site of an old encampment of Red Indians, and the stone in  which it is carved is very hard. Again, the question is raised: how old is man, and is it the fact that *all* the dinosaurs perished, as many palæontologists theorize, before the first appearance of the mammoth, the mammals, and mastodon, on the earth?

If the dinosaur became extinct 12,000,000 years ago, how can the mummy found by Sternberg have lasted all that immense time, in *any* conditions, and not have fallen into dust? Also, if the skulls found by le Baron, in that queer vault on the "Hill of a Thousand Tombs" in the Nevada desert, had turned into dust in an almost hermetically sealed tomb in very dry atmospheric conditions, how comes it that a dinosaur mummy, exposed to wind, rain, snow and frost, still remained intact?

Some scientists contend that the dinosaurs throve in an atmosphere consisting largely of carbonic acid gas, and that the dense flora of the Mesozoic Age absorbed the carbon, releasing the oxygen, and so making conditions suitable for the mammal.

"I am beginning to believe," said Doheny, "that a flood swept away dinosaurs that persisted into the age of mammals, and that some forms, such as the aquatic dinosaurs, were here long after man appeared. I have found the tracks of a wolf on the stone edge of an area, out in the Painted Desert, where are seen dinosaur tracks."

Dr. R. L. Lull, professor of Vertebrate Palæontology at Yale University, pointed out, as long ago as 1917, that not a single trace of a dinosaur, or its remains, has, or have been found in America in rocks of the Tertiary Age. The elevation of the land and the draining of the great inland Cretaceous rocks along the low-lying shores, where the dinosaurs had their homes[1] spelled their doom. The career of the dinosaurs, contrary to some folk's notions, was *not* brief; for the duration of their recorded evolution is thrice that of the entire mammalian age. The dinosaur does *not* represent a futile attempt on the part of Nature to people the world with creatures of insignificant moment, but the genus is comparable in majestic rise, slow culmination and dramatic fall to the great nations of antiquity.

These artifacts, then, suggest that, as in the old continent of Mu, the dinosaur was contemporary in ancient America with the existence of a race of *giant* men.

From another source, one learns that in South America—in Brazil and the Andean region south of and round Lago de Titicaca— all marine formations end with the carboniferous age, and in Brazil later-marine formations are found only in sublittoral areas. Marine beds of the Tertiary age are entirely absent. In south Brazil, the marine beds, in general, are little developed. Cretaceous marls, here and there containing remains of dinosaurs, and fresh water shells are recorded at heights of 13,123 feet, in the pre-Cordilleras. Nowhere between 14° and 35° South latitude, in the whole region of the Andes between east of Lago de Titicaca and the volcano of Tinguirica, is there a Mesozoic completion of the marine series. In the Argentina, the geologic series correspond very closely with those in Brazil: from the Carboniferous to the upper Cretaceous no marine beds make their appearance. Through long periods no sea existed here. *A priori*, then, we have possible conditions favouring the existence of monsters and dinosaurs extinct elsewhere in most parts of the Earth.

Before I go on to discuss evidence for the concurrent existence of antediluvian man in America and the dinosaur, I may draw attention to the other remarkable discoveries in North America. In Arizona, a monster like the pterodactyl, or an unknown species of giant flying lizard, has been found cut in a very ancient food bowl. Another nondescript unknown monster, with a duck-like bill, is found cut in a natural sandstone concretion and fastened on a thin plate of light-

[1] It was reported in Calcutta in May 1948, that tribesmen on the southern side of the Himalayas, on the Assam borders, had been badly scared by the appearance of an enormous monster, resembling the dinotherium. The tribesmen said it was a veritable "moving mountain of flesh", and they quitted their villages in the region. The Calcutta story said that this monster was around 90 feet long and 20 feet tall. Palæontologists say that dinotherium belonged to an extinct genus of proboscidean mammals, larger than an elephant; and living in the Miocene Age. It was noted for a pair of tusks directed downwards from the decurved apex of the lower jaw. Although this region, like the headwaters of the Salween, is very imperfectly known, one can but say that while, when the British raj controlled India, the authorities at Delhi might have made efforts to investigate this story; as things are in anarchic Hindostan, at the time of writing, it is unlikely that much will be done to investigate this story.—AUTHOR.

brown flint. The eyes are of quartz glass fastened on with some kind of cement. They give a fierce look to the monster. This image was found by a farmer ploughing into a mound at Davenport, Iowa, on the Mississippi. A prehistoric figure of an elephant was picked up by a German, named Mare, in a cornfield on his Iowa farm. In 1850, there was found on a cliff at Pend d'Oreille lake, in Idaho and Montana, brightly-coloured pictographs of strange beasts, of men and other images of unknown import. The Indians regarded them with great dread, as the work of the race that preceded their own.

Had ancient North and South America, like old China, traditions of *dragons*?

I mentioned above the strange resemblances of the fiery dragon whose head is found carved on the so-called Toltec pyramid at Xochicalco, Mexico (and on the stairway and balustrade of the temple of Quetzalcoatl at Teotihuacan), with a living monster said to exist, to-day, in the Gran Chaco wilderness of marsh and brake in Paraguay. In both Central and North America (United States of America) there have been found, as in mounds in Florida and Georgia, shell gorgets and painted rocks with objects much like stylized dragons. They appear also in the Cortesian Codex of old Mexico, which shows the first man and woman sitting under a tree with a serpent's head near the woman. (Needless to say these ancient Mexican glyphs were assuredly not "borrowed" from Genesis!)[1]

But no country in the world has, or rather *had*, so amazing a pictorial representation of the dragon as was found on a water-washed rock high up on a bluff at Alton, Mississippi. As Marquette, the old French traveller, said of this dragon:

No painter in old France excelled this representation on the bluff at Alton.

Nothing is known of the mysterious race who made this glyph, which is also found on ancient pottery, red in colour and highly

[1] The dragons of the Mexican codices are furnished with claws, and often a back with spines which bristle when the monster is enraged. It has a calendrical significance. With its thirteen appendages, the dragon represents the thirteen days of the old Mexican week, twenty of which weeks made up the sacred Mexican year. Four dragons represent an astronomical cycle of fifty-two years. The dragon's divisions are multiplied by the number of bundles, with knots, in the glyphs. In old China, the dragon was a symbol of death and cataclysm. The tree symbolizes life. Did this symbol come from the submerged continent of Mu?

glazed. Schoolcraft describes monsters like this dragon, or pictographic saurian called the "Piassa dragon", as common among the Indians of the north.

Père Marquette's description of the Piassa dragon is worth giving fully. He says:

> As we were coasting along rocks frightful from their height and length, we saw on one of them two painted Monsters which at first frightened us, and near which the most hardened and valiant savages dare not linger for long. The monsters have eyes as big as a cow, and horns on the head like those of a roe-deer. Their eyes are red. The monsters have a frightful look and a beard like a tiger's. Their faces have something of the appearance of a man. The body is covered with scales, and the tail is so long that it goes twice round the body, passing above the head, and entering between the legs, where it terminates in a fish's tail. The colours are green, red and blackish. Moreover, these two monsters are so well painted that one cannot believe that any savages can have been the artists, for the best painters in old France would have been hard put to it to draw them so well. Besides, they are so high up on the rocks that it would be very difficult to reach there easily to paint them. (He gives a sketch of them.)
>
> (From the manuscript formerly at Les Religieuses de l'Hôtel de Dieu, de Quebec. *Vide:* Père Marquette's "Récit des Voyages et des Découvertes du R. Père Jacques Marquette, de la Compagnie de Jesus, en l'année 1673".)

The Dakota Indians had ancestral memories of the Piassa dragon, or a similar sort type of monster. They told Marquette that a "demon" haunted the river at this spot, and roared so that he could be heard at a great distance. He would engulf them in the abyss where he dwells. They also said the waters at this weird spot had, in ancient days, been filled with saurians who would devour men. It is also curious that a picture of a horned man appears on the rocks at Alton, and it does not give the impression that it is a man merely wearing a mask.

Alas, the great American Piassa dragon has become as extinct as the æpyornis or moa of old Madagascar, or New Zealand. During the War of the North and South, in the 1860's, an idiot who commanded a gunboat fired at the rocks and destroyed the splendid pictograph. War, of course, spells senseless destruction, as old Europe too well knows.

It is also curious that a granite boulder, found in 1880, at Green Lake, split in two, has an inscription with circles like a colander, and between the circles are engravings of canoes, with Indians in them. Between the canoes are curious monsters with bony spines and long tails, with dragon-like heads.

In a prehistoric mound at Cincinnati, there was found, in 1796, a carving of a monster in the shape of an enormous bird with a long beak, and of unknown species. The mastodon appears in a pictograph found in a cave at West Salem. Also, an unknown type of prehistoric animal with the head of a horse, but a skull larger than that of an elephant, was said by the *Chicago Record*, in 1895, to have been found in California, along with *gigantic remains of men and women*, the men 9 feet tall and the women a foot less. In the same year, ancient ruins of a city were found on the Gila, and there were signs that it had been shaken by a great earthquake. Nine feet under the surface, diggers unearthed an immense quantity of bone dust, lying in a 70-foot long trench. No clues to the mystery of this unknown race came to light. Another mastodon picture was found on high hills at Fort Ancient, near the Miami River, Ohio, close to very ancient pavements and stone altars. The pavement, 6 feet below ground was around 4 feet wide and 400 yards long and running directly south. Near it was a huge boulder on the face of which the mastodon was cut.

A mammoth is depicted attacking a man, and the lively and extremely ancient glyph appears on the Lenape stone, found on a farm near Doyleston, Buck county, Pennsylvania. One part of the stone was found in 1872, the other part in 1882. Savages are shown attacking a hairy mammoth on the edge of a forest. The monster, with tail erect and in a great rage, is shown approaching the forest, in which can be seen wigwams standing between the trees. One of the plates of the famous Davenport prehistoric tablet, found in Ohio, attracted the notice of Professor G. Seyforth, Ph.D., who, in the Journal of the "Davenport Academy of Natural Science" (1876), said that, besides a patriarch with a sceptre in his hand, and a sitting woman, this plate (II), showed an ancient elephant, and *animals in cages*. It looked as if the animals had been encaged to be preserved for a future time. Another plate represented a Great Deluge reminding one, as Pojano says in *Della universalita del Diluvio* (Poligrapho di Verona, Vol. XI., p. 145), of a carving on an ancient Mexican temple façade, of the image of an immense ocean in which there appears only one boat occupied by a man and a woman. Plate I of the pictures of this Davenport tablet suggests the immense antiquity of the glyphs; for it shows an ancient American sacrifice offered to the sun and the moon, and 12-foot tall gods in stony heavens, with stars in between the sun and moon, and zodiacal signs in scrolls. This ancient American mystery race worshipped the seven planets (which are symbolized by the seven stages of the famous ancient Babylonian Babel tower, still to be seen to-day in the deserts of Iraq) and the twelve signs of the Zodiac. Not only did it know monstrous animals, but it also knew that the Earth was round and had the idea of the ancient Mexicans, of an astronomical cycle of 52 years. For there is, in the glyph, between the belt of the Zodiac and the Earth, a girdle divided into four quadrants, each containing 13 signs.

It is also exceedingly curious that on this same tablet there appear a number of letters of an unknown alphabet. There are thirteen of these strange letters in one line, and nineteen in a second line. Folk in 1874, when this tablet was found, seemed very eager to pass it off as a hoax of the Latter Day Saints or Mormons, in and for which assertion there is not a spark of truth, nor any evidence. Inasmuch as one of the curious human figures has a rimless hat, while besides unidentifiable animals there is a figure of a mastodon without a trunk, one can only wonder that no gentleman has come forward to assert that both the Davenport tablet and the Easter Island colossi and glyphs must be the work of the same "hoaxer"!

Indeed, the American elephant must have attained a size far beyond that of the Asian and African elephant of modern times. In 1891, Professor Williston reported that an immense fossil elephant had been found in an arid region among sandhills in the western part of Kansas, which was larger than any remains of any mammoth found in America. From the sole of the foot to the shoulder, the fossil had a height of 16 feet, and his length was proportionately great.

North American Indian traditions are not silent on the subject of monsters of an antediluvian world, nor of giants. Of the latter, they say that old America was once peopled by giants who "could with ease stride over wide rivers and out-topped the tallest pine trees". However much there may be of hyperbole in these ancient myths, the giants found carved in stone in Easter Island certainly suggest that, in those days in the old land of Mu, of which this queer Valhalla formed the southern termination, giants of incredible stature existed.[1]

⅏ The ancient traditions of the Six Nations of the Oneida and Tuscarora Indians, told to David Cusick, the trapper, about the year 1820, have cryptic references to a mysterious foreign people who sailed in ships from a port unknown to the "Great Island" (North America) and were wrecked on the southern part of the Great Island. A few men got ashore with implements. They were "covered in leathern bags", or wore a dress of leather or hides, and "big hawks" carried them to the summit of a high mountain. Does this mean some form of airship, or the power of levitation defying gravity, which ancient myths say the Atlantean higher castes possessed? It is added that the "hawks seemed to threaten them", and that the men were forced to quit the mountain and come down to the plain, where they had to set to and build a small fort, as a protection against a *furious monster*. It is said that the monster later overran the country and destroyed them.

---

[1] It is curious that Swift in *Gulliver's Travels,* located his giant Brobdingnags in *North America*! But it can hardly be supposed, by any hardened sceptic, that any North American Indian nation had ever heard of, or read the passage in the Greek historian, Herodotos, in which he tells how a Greek smith, at Tegea, told Lichas, the Lacedæmonian, that he was digging a well in his forge, when he came on a coffin, 7 cubits long (say 140 inches, or 12 feet), in which was a body of the same length. The smith measured the skeleton and re-buried it. It was supposed to be the body of Orestes, of which an oracle had said, he would be found buried in a plain of Arcadian Tegea, where two winds blew (that is, a bellows) and stroke answered stroke, and evil lies on evil (that is, iron on iron).—Author.

The myths also say that a dragon, or some form of great horned saurian appeared in Lake Ontario about 2,200 years before Columbus and caused many diseases, from which many folk died. "But with the aid of thunderbolts, the monster was compelled to retire." An aerolite, or blazing comet fell on a fort of the Indians on the St. Lawrence and destroyed them. Not long after, they—the northern nations—went to war till they had utterly destroyed themselves.

It may be said that very "modern wars" of this sort were by no means unknown among the ancient Toltecs in ancient Mexico. . . . "The Great Island then became once more in the possession of fierce animals." (Of course, it is not necessary to take too literally the chronology given in the myths.)

The myths then speak of the appearance of a culture-hero called the "Heaven-Holder". The name has a curious and probably significant suggestion of Atlas, the king of old Atlantis. This culture hero, who has all the appearance of having come from some great land sunken by cataclysm, gave the Indians of the Great Island corn, beans, squashes, potatoes and tobacco, and taught them the elements of civilization and morality. While this Atlas was absent from North America, there was an invasion of monsters of dragon-form who are called "Ko-nea-rau-neh-neh", or Flying Heads. They came in the night and ate people:

> But the people foiled them by quitting their huts and hiding in other huts prepared for the purpose. But there was an old woman, who lived at Onondaga, and who was left alone in the hut, one evening, after the others deserted. She sat near the fire, parching acorns, and when the Monstrous Head looked in at the door, it looked at the woman and was amazed to see her eat the coals of the fire. They were by this put to flight, and ever after the Heads disappeared, and were supposed to have been concealed in the earth.

A short time after, "a monster of the deep" overran the country and "forced the Five Families to take refuge in forts, in their towns, from the devouring monster". Atlas (Heaven-Holder) then re-appeared, and the monster retreated into the deep places of the lake. This monster of the deep was followed by a snake with the shape of a human head that opposed the passage between the Onondaga and the Goyo-gouh (Cayugo), cutting off all intercourse. "The serpent sat in the principal path that led through the settlements. Finally, the best warriors of Onondaga attacked and killed him after a severe conflict." "The Lake serpent was often seen by the people, but a thunderbolt destroyed the serpent and forced the serpents to return to the deep."

It is not easy to say whether by "serpents" is meant some invading nation who had for symbol or totem a snake. The myth may, or may not import that the monster was routed by some electrical, or ray weapon used by Atlas, or Heaven-Holder.

"In the reign of Atoharho XI, probably about 150 years before Columbus. Heaven-Holder ceased to appear in bodily forms, but came as a prophet", and exactly as Montezuma had warned the Indians of the Pecos region, and Quetzalcoatl had warned the ancient Mexicans, Heaven-Holder, in a dream, warned the Five Nations that the whites would cross the Big Waters, bring liquors and buy up the red people's land.

Further details in the Five Nations epic say the monster that invaded Lake Onondaga "flew about with a long sticker and sucked people's blood":

> The warriors failed to expel the monster, but Heaven-Holder attacked him as he flew about the fort Onondaga. The monster flew so rapidly that he could hardly keep sight of it; but, after a few days, the monster began to fail, and on the borders of the Great Lakes towards the sun-setting and round the great country, he overtook it and killed it near the salt lake, Onondaga, and from its blood came small mosquitoes.

Until around 1885, the monster's tracks and those of this Atlas were shown near Brighton, south of Syracuse, New York. It is added that the tracks were often renewed by Indians. The tracks were bird-like, 20 inches long, and extended for 20 rods. He was slain at Center-ville, north-east of Syracuse. The Tuscaroras used to point out a curious stone on their reservations where, they said, Holder of the Heavens rested and smoked in the chase. They showed a depression where he reclined and a hollow made by his arm in rising, also a hole burnt where he emptied his pipe!

Another Onondaga story tells of two of these monsters, one on the Seneca river above Cross Lake, and another at Montezuma where the combined forces of the Onondagas and Cayugos destroyed them. The name Montezuma is curious in this connection.

On the banks of the Ohio River, in the days of Ototarho VI, "perhaps 650 years before Columbus came" (this date, too, must not be taken literally) the Indians had another contact with a giant saurian:

> A small party of Indians left the fort Keadanyeek, or Tontawanta plains, on the war path, and camped on the Ohio's banks. They ran out of food and sought game. A certain warrior found a hollow tree where he supposed was a bear. One man climbed the tree and put fire to it, when out came a furious Lizard, grasped the man and jumped into the tree hollow. There was a grumbling noise, and the young ones devoured the man. The terrified warriors retired, but one warrior stayed by the tree. The monster chased and killed all the warriors. Then he came back and chased the man who had stayed by the tree. The man fled along the trail till he met Holder of the Heavens, who told him to make fire and collect sticks. Holder of the Heavens changed into a lion and fought the great monster, and the warrior hooked up the severed flesh bitten off the Lizard and threw it into the fire so that it might not unite. The Protector vanished from sight.

278

The chronology is all haywire, but, making all allowance for the naïveté and the mythopoeic tendencies of primitive races, it seems that we may say that the remote ancestors of the North American Indians had their fierce encounters with monstrous animals and saurians in antediluvian and postdiluvian America.

The mammoth appears in American myth, as well as upon the petroglyphs and pictographs of the caves and rocks. Cusick tells a curious story of the Oneida Indians about an encounter their ancestors had with a mammoth called "Big Quisquiss". This monster invaded settlements south of Lake Ontario and in a fury pushed down houses and made a general hell-raising. The people were forced to flee the monster. Warriors tried to stop him, but failed. Then a certain chief warrior collected men from several towns and fought a severe battle, till at last the monster retired. But the people were not left long in peace; for Big Elk (probably a mammoth) came in a fury and invaded the town, killed many folk, till more men assembled and after a furious battle killed the monster.

On the evidence given in a collection of Indian tales by Miss A. E. Smith, it would seem that a race of pigmies hunted these giant mammals. We hear that a sick warrior, left by a salt lick beyond the Alleghany saw three pigmies come and lie in ambush for these great animals "which came out of the ground". They killed two buffaloes and fed the warrior, who told the story round the camp fire when he returned. It is the fact that round this lick have been found by Indians many large animals killed by the pigmies, who may, or may not be identical with the Esquimaux who, in the Miocene Age, or before the Ice Age, came as far south as Nevada, where the "men of the South" drove them back.

The Tungusks and Ostiaks, Siberian tribes, seem to share with these North American Indian tribes the notion that the mammoth and mastodon *lived underground*. Isbrand Ides, who travelled from Moscow to China, in 1692, started this myth of the mammoth that by reason of severe climate lives continually underground. He tells us that:

> The heathen of Takuti, Tungusi and Ostiakia say that these monsters continually go back and forward, under the earth. If the monster comes so near the surface as to smell or see the air, he at once dies. This, they say, is the reason why so many of them are found on the high banks, where they come out of the ground. The infidels (heathen Siberians) never see these beasts. . . . The Russians told me that they thought the mammoths were elephants drowned in the Flood and akin to Job's behemoth "who is caught with his own eyes".

In old China, one humorous sage even said that earthquake need no longer be an insoluble problem, for they were caused by the mammoth burrowing underground!

If we can accept the evidence of some curious brass tablets found at Kinterbrook, Pike County, Illinois, the mastodon was domesticated and milked as a cow till the third century A.D.![1]

President Jefferson, in his *Notes on Virginia*, written at the end of the eighteenth century, mentions a Mr. Stanley captured by the Indians at the mouth of the Tennessee, and carried westwards beyond the Missouri, as saying that the Indians asserted that both mammoth and mastodon still lived in the north of America. They described them so that they seemed like elephants. Père Charlevoix, Jesuit missioner in La Nouvelle France (Canada), in 1744, says he was told by the Indians a tradition of "a great elk beside whom others seem like ants. He has legs so high that eight feet of snow do not embarrass him. His skin is proof against all sorts of weapons and he has a sort of arm that comes out of his shoulder and which he uses as we do ours." This seems to fit the appearance of the mammoth, or of the mastodon. Ohio Indians told Mather that mastodons were at one time abundant.[2] They fed on the boughs of a kind of lime tree and leant against it to doze or sleep, as they did not lie down! The Indians of Louisiana called a creek Carrion Crow creek, because they said that in the time of their fathers, a mastodon died in one of these creeks and a great number of crows flocked to feed on his carcase. A mastodon's skeleton was found in the spot indicated by the Indians.

Tribes in the north-west territory of Canada actually said that their

Mastodon (Palæolithic cave, Pyrénées).

ancestors built lake dwellings on piles, like those in Switzerland, to protect themselves against mastodons or mammoths which ravaged the country in the long ago. The Peace River Indians, like the Suogolami, have traditions of the mastodon, and they are very widely separated Indians. Captain C. Croghon took down from bands of Iroquois and Wyandotte Indians traditions about a monster called the "Great Buffalo", which seems the same as the "Father of Oxen", of William Walker, Indian agent, and identical with either mammoth or mastodon.

Ohio, like the extremely ancient stone avenues of Avebury, in Wiltshire, England, shows remains of very ancient enclosures associated with water cults. These ancient water cults, both in England and America, beyond any doubt enshrine memories of a Great Deluge. No animal might drink of the ancient springs and streams that ran

---

[1] These tablets are said to contain the history of the Algewas. It is also said that the same story is told about cow-mastodons in "Solomon Spaulding's Roman manuscripts", found in a cave in Ohio, and written in Latin which fell into decay before they could be deciphered. I can find no details about "Solomon Spaulding's Latin manuscripts", so can offer no comment on its authenticity, or the reverse.—AUTHOR.

[2] Evidence of Stickney, many years Indian agent for the United States in north-west Ohio. (*Vide: Nat. Hist. of N. Y.* pt. IV., Geolog. *by* W. W. Mather, p. 44.)

near these queer works in Ohio. And it is very significant that images of the tortoise or turtle, which North American Indian lore always associates with a Great Deluge, was carved on very ancient vessels kept in a crevice or alcove of the wall of the spring close to these ancient works. I theorize that these Wabash glyphs were associated with the Great Cataclysm that wiped out ancient American civilizations, say, around 12,000 B.C. Refugees who took shelter in this strange cave may have felt the urge to perpetuate themselves, their way of life, their dress and their ideas, so that posterity, in a far later age, might see them as they were in the days before the Great Cataclysm, and wonder at what had been! How else shall we explain the ancient coins with unknown hieroglyphs, not infrequently found at the bottom, or in the bore of American wells hundreds of feet deep?

Again, there sounds the words of the old hymn:

> Time like an ever-rolling stream
> Bears all its sons away.
> They fly, forgotten, as a dream
> Dies at the opening day.

In North America, there have been one famous American, some French explorers and one old English roamer, who have contended that the so-called fabulous Unicorn, whose figure appears in the royal coat of arms of the Kings of England and Empire have actually existed in quite modern times in what is now the United States of America! This, perhaps, *not* so fabulous animal has a very long and distinguished history, for 2,394 years ago, the great Greek historian and geographer, Herodotos, called him the "horned ass of Asia". Ctesias, a century or so later, says he is the wild ass of Hindostan, with a cubit-long (about 22 inches) straight horn, on the forehead, the tip red, and the middle, back, and end of the horn, white. Drinking cups made of this horn were supposed to be an antidote to poisoned drinks. Ctesias says the unicorn is fleet of foot, untameable and that it is almost impossible to capture him. Which may explain why no Roman emperor, in the most palmy days of the gladiatorial arena in old Roman Latium ever loosed one on the captives of the triumph.

Julius Cæsar, in *de Bello Gallico*, which, in the author's far-off days at grammar school, used to bore him excessively, says there was a great animal, large as an ox, in the dense forests of Hyrcania (southeast end of the Caspian Sea) which had a single straight horn in the middle of the forehead, which horn was straighter than any horn he knew. Plinius Secundus says he is a ferocious beast with the body of a horse, a deer's head, elephant-like feet, tail of a wild boar, and a single black horn two cubits (three feet eight inches long) in his forehead.

The British Museum of Natural History, London, England, has a horn from Africa, which is unlike the horn of the rhinoceros, which is narrow at the base and very long and heavy. This strange horn is flexible. Is it that of a unicorn?

Now, the story of the first real or alleged contact with the *unicorn of North America* was told by David Ingram, an English sailor, who, in the years 1568 to 1569, travelled from the "Rio das Minas, on the Gulph of Mexico", right up the coast of what is now eastern United States, to Cape Breton, in Accadia, modern Nova Scotia. His *Relacion* of the journey is exceedingly rare, and does not figure even in the unrivalled Library of the British Museum. It was reprinted in an also very rare book by Colonel Charles Jennett Weston, as a document concerned with the history of South Carolina.

Ingram, who travelled with two other English sailors, either castaways from a wreck, or men fleeing the tortures of the Spanish Inquisition of the Black or Dominican monks, in Mexico, says:

> The Expedition did alsoe see in those Countrys a Monstruous Beaste twyse as bigge as a Horse, bothe in mayne, hoofe, hears (hair) and neighinge, savynge it was towards the hinder part like a greyhounde. These Beasts have twoe teeth, or hornes, of a foote longe, growing straight furthe of there nostrells; they are naturall Enimyes to the Horse . . . He did also see in that Countrye both Elephantes and Uunces . . . and one other Straunge Beaste, bigger than a Beare; yt had nether (*sic*) head nor necke, his eyes and mouthe weare in his breaste; this beaste is verye ouglie to beholde and Cowardlie of kynde; yt beareth very fine Skynne like a Ratte, full of sylver heare . . .

Ingram and his pals undertook an exceedingly dangerous and adventurous trip at a time when almost nothing was known of the vast stretch of territory from the Gulf Mexico, past Florida up to what are now Maine and Nova Scotia. Far north, probably beyond New York state, he entered an elusive country marked on the spouting dolphin and amorous mermaid maps of the cosmographers' of the late sixteenth century, as "Norimbega", which may be a garbling of Norway, and is located about the region of Massachusetts, Maine, Vermont and New Hampshire.

But we hear again of the North American Unicorn, in 1719, as found round the middle course of the Red River of Louisiana, by the expedition of the French explorer, Bénard de la Harpe. The Frenchmen joined a party of Nawdishe Indians who, near the confluence of the Washita (probably the False Washita, in the old Indian Territory) were *roasting unicorns*. La Harpe says that the unicorns were the size of a common horse, with reddish hair as long as the hair of a goat (*il a la poil rouge*), legs rather thin, and a single horn in the middle of the forehead, which does not branch out into prongs or tines, and its meat is very palatable. He adds: "This discovery agrees very well with what Monsieur de Bienville heard from the savages, that on the Upper Washita River, unicorns were to be found."

It will be noted that la Harpe's description fits in with what Pliny and Aristotle said of the unicorn, and does not agree with the shape and appearance of the buffalo or North American bison.

But an even more mysterious North American beast, of gigantic size and unexampled ferocity is the *Megalonyx,* of which thrilling stories were told in the eighteenth century. The spotlight was thrown on this monster by no less a personage than President Thomas Jefferson. In 1799, in the *Transactions of the American Philosophical Society,* Jefferson said that, in the west part of Virginia, in a cave, in 1797, labourers dug up, at a depth of 2 to 3 feet, the bones of an unknown clawed animal. The earth was "nitrous", and the bones those of an unguiculated (clawed) quadruped, the lion being his nearest in size, but the monster was around three times the size of the African *leo felis* (lion).

Jefferson gave some interesting comparative measurement:

Megalonyx	*Lion* (African)
Claw; 7.5 inches long.	1.45 inches.
Diameter of Middle Femur:	
4.25 inches.	1.15 inches.

There were traditions that the early adventurers in the county of Greenbriar, Virginia, were alarmed in the night, at their camp, by the appalling roaring of some beast unknown to them. The monster went round and round their camp and they saw his eyes shine like two balls of fire in the light of the camp blaze. They piled on the logs to make a blaze that would keep him off. So terrified were their horses, that they crouched down on the earth, and their dogs crept in among the scared men, not daring even to bark. So frightened were the men that next day they packed up and quitted the territory. This adventure seems to have happened around the year 1765. In the same year, 1765, George Wilson and John Davies went on a hunting trip to the Cheat River, a branch of the Monongahela, in western Virginia. One night, they heard, some way off their camp, a tremendous roar, which became louder, till it reverberated among the rocks and in the aisles of the forest, like thunder.

The very earth seemed to tremble! Their dogs prowled round their camp, though at other times they were very fierce. But, now, they crept close to the men's feet and would neither quit the camp nor bark. About the same time, the hunters heard the same roars repeated from the top of a mountain, a mile off, and within a minute the roar was answered by a similar roar coming from a neighbouring height. It would seem that these hunters deemed discretion the better part of valour; for they did not try to trail one of the monsters and add his pelt to cover their bedroom floors, wayback in the old home township. Wilson told the story to a Colonel John Stewart, in 1769, who was later a lieutenant-colonel in a Penna regiment, fighting in the War of Revolution against that unrivalled idiot and demented imbecile, German Hanoverian George III, of England. Some years later, the other hunter, Davies, who was alive in Kentucky, as late as 1799, also spilled the beans about the fearsome night in old Virginia.

In South Africa, dogs are said to behave in this way when lions are about in the night hours.

A third hunter, named Draper, had also a personal contact with this monster, when, in 1790, he went hunting on the Kanhawa, or Great Kanawha River, 650 miles long, which runs from North Carolina and Virginia, past the Blue Ridge of North Carolina, to the Ohio, and is known in Virginia and North Carolina, as the New River. Draper turned his horse loose in the wilds and put a bell on his neck, so that he could be heard if he strayed far. Hardly had the horse left the camp, before Draper heard the bell ringing rapidly and furiously. Thinking the Indians might be around, Draper went to the scene, but before he arrived the horse had been half eaten. His dog scented the trail of some animal, and led Draper farther into the forest. Before long, they came in sight of an animal of such monstrous size that, though Draper was a regular Hawkeye of a marksmen and a most daring hunter, he at once checked and brought off his dog, and beat a hasty and silent retreat. He recalled no more of the monster than that he was in general outline of the cat tribe and had a terrible bulk. It was not a panther or any animal he knew.

It is probable that the monstrous megalonyx of Virginia, and North Carolina, died out in the early nineteenth century. Sure, he would have offered rare sport to the railroad engineers pushing the iron road over the Alleghanies, in the 40's and 50's of last century! A megalonyx in the caboose, or astride the coal bunkers of a locomotive puffing up the grades, could hardly have been evicted as easily as a bum riding the rods to avoid paying his fare!

It may be added that, around the year 1850, Dr. Dickson of Natchez found the pelvic bone of an ancient man alongside the remains of both a megalonyx and a mastodon. (*Vide Journal of the Philadelphia Academy of Science*).

To sum up, I think my reader will agree that I have given, in this chapter, enough data to shake any preconceived notions that *all* we know of the mysterious past of the world, in general, and North America, in particular, has been put within the pages of the latest book on zoology or biology. There must still be within the secret places on the earth, below the earth, and in the waters under the earth, many things of which science has yet to take cognizance. We do not know the half of it yet! Remember the Komodo Dragon, for example! His existence in the islands of Flores and Sumbawi was ridiculed as a jest and hoax till, one day, an American came along, captured some of the young dragons and shipped them on board a liner bound for New York City, where they were placed in the Zoo Park! The moral is: Be not too cocksure of anything in this mysterious world of ours.

Now, it is a curious fact that certain Red Indian tribes, of North America, asserted, as late as the early years of the nineteenth century, that the mammoth, a species of extinct elephant closely akin to the mastodon (the structure of whose teeth differs from those of the mammoth), still exists in certain remote mountain country in northern, or western America. Whether or not this is ancestral memory cannot now be affirmed. (See President Jefferson's *Notes on the State of Virginia.*)

Mammoth meat, thousands of years old, has been quite recently eaten at Soviet banquets in Moscow! Russian chefs have found that the meat was firm and fresh, even after thousands of years immurement in frozen mud. The Russian journal *Isvestia*, and the U.S.S.R. Academy of Science said that steaks from the mammoth were served at a banquet, and with the characteristic Soviet Russian exploitation of old Russian proletarian and mujik superstition, rings were made from the thick dark fur of the mammoth and sold as good luck amulets and charms, in aid of the funds of scientific bodies! One man, at one of these Moscow banquets, even suggested that the Arctic could be used to store surplus grain, also meats, fats and carbo-hydrates, while grain could be kept there for 50 years, and re-sown or eaten. But that is another story more concerned, perhaps, with the next war to end war, than with the subject of this book.

In North America, the mastodon and the mammoth occur in strata much more recent in date than in Europe or Asia, and very well preserved. In California, human bones and ancient stone tools have been found in gold-bearing strata along with mastodon and other ancient mammalian remains. Near Silver Lake, Oregon, mastodon bones were found mixed with flint arrow-heads and spear-heads, while in Mexico City, in 1884, a human skeleton was found embedded in calcareous deposits along with elephants' bones. The beds in California where these mastodon bones were found must be extremely ancient, since great beds of lava cover the gold, and water has cut cañons through these lava-beds, denoting the onrush of a great cataclysm that fell on ancient America thousands of years back.

President Thomas Jefferson, wrote, in 1797, that "the mammoth may still exist in the unexplored regions of the northern and western parts of America, now, as formerly he did, where we find his bones". Jefferson's opinion is also held by modern trappers in the Yukon and Alaska, and in the Canadian North West Territory who say that both mammoths and mastodons are alive, at this day, in the remote recesses of the Rockies.

The mammoth was certainly not unknown to the ancient artists and sculptors in Maya Yucatan and Nahua-Aztecan Mexico, ages before the conquest by Cortes. Waldeck gives a picture of a bas-relief in the ancient palace of Palenque, which depicts a "proboscidian". It is "part of a head-dress and contains a trunk and a tusk, with a horn above the tusk". Also, the savant, Baron Wilhelm von Humboldt describes a trunk of an elephant in an ancient head-dress at Aztalan, "which shows that their traditions reach back to the time of the American elephant".[1]

1 *Vide:* Humboldt's *Vue des Cordillères*, plate XV.

Dr. Adam Clarke weighed a presumed grinder of a mammoth, found in a cave in Kentucky, around 1830, and its weight was 4 pounds 8 ounces. He weighed a modern elephant's grinder and it was only 2 pounds. He computed the size of a mammoth as equal to those of two and a quarter Asiatic modern elephants. Josiah Priest, about that time, visualized a herd of mammoths nibbling a forest of trees and says that the whole western continent would prove a small enough pasture ground for a moderate herd of mammoths! The prodigious size of the old American mammoth was demonstrated when one of nine skeletons was dug out of the ground, near Shongum Mountain, Ulster County, New York, and put in Peale's Museum. Spafford's *Gazetteer of New York* says the other eight were sent to New York City. It was computed that these mammoths were all of 25 feet high, and 60 feet long, the bones of one toe alone being more than 3 feet long.

Near May's Lick, or Salt Spring, Kentucky, are mammoth wallows close to which are banks rubbed semi-circularly by mammoths who carried off tons of earth plastered on their hides to shield them from flies. The reader can imagine how hastily he would look round for a tall tree when one of these monsters, maddened by pestiferous stinging and tickling and tormenting flies, came charging down the trail towards him! The wicked *flea* when no man pursueth would sure have roused the worst passions in any old American mammoth, especially if the ever-wicked one nipped his testicles or his backside! Indeed, one of these scooped-out banks, done by the old mammoth bulldozer, looks like the side of a hill from which 100,000 loads of soil have been rubbed away. Hard by the wallows and the hill, bones and whole skeletons of mammoths, bemired in marsh and old swamps, have been found.

Authors of the Victorian nineteenth century, in the far days before the sceptics and cynics of the twentieth century had retorted on old spade-beards, who pompously pronounced that such a thing *was* so, with "it damned well is *not* so!", were very apt to talk as though the mammoth and the mastodon were *carnivorous*. In point of fact, these monsters, like the modern elephant and the horse, are herbivorous and would not give a thank-ye for the primest cut from the stern-end of Ten-Ton Buster Bella of any old English circus! Professor Winchell of Michigan found bones of mastodons and mammoths, as well as those of the ancient American "elephas primigenius", or woolly and hairy mammoth, embedded in peat-bogs so shallow that he felt certain the ancient North American men were their contemporaries. This, too, is suggested by such ancient American artifacts as tobacco pipes carved on bowl or stem with the image of the elephant, or mammoth. A mass of leaves, branches, sedges, and rush, common in Virginia, has been found in the stomach of a mammoth dug up six feet below ground in Pennsylvania. Indeed, bog-cutters excavating the bed of a modern canal, near Covington, Fountain County,

Indiana, found a mastodon skeleton embedded in peat, and they split open the large bones and *greased their boots with his ancient marrow*.[1]

That the mastodon, as well as the mammoth, was attacked by ancient Americans was shown by a discovery made, in 1846, by Dr. Koch, of St. Louis, in the "bottom land" of the Bourbouse River, Missouri. He found remains of a mastodon, sunk under its own weight in the bed of ancient marsh—the Gasconnade swamp. It had fallen on its side, as it struggled to regain its feet when ancient men, who had brought from a long way off rocks, weighing 25 pounds, hurled the boulders upon it. There was no stone nearer than the river, 400 yards away, and one hundred and fifty pieces of limestone rock, from 3 to 25 pounds in weight, lay around the spot, in ashes of old fires lit in a ring round the bemired monster, by the ancient hunters. The heaps of ancient cinders reached 6 feet high. Koch said he found the fore and hind legs standing in a perpendicular position; suggesting that the monster had been bemired.

In Brinton County, Missouri, Koch also found under the thigh bone of a mastodon an ancient arrow of pink quartz, and a little farther away were other arrows that had been shot at the mastodon. He also found a mummy mastodon in a swamp in Missouri, and said that the monster was capable of feeding itself with its fore-feet, in the manner of the beaver. He was laughed at, but the *Scientific American*, for January, 1892, recorded the find of a mastodon at Newberg, New York, with fore-legs that could be thrown over low foliage or brushwood, and a crushing effected by the somewhat expanded *manus* (distal segment of the fore limb). No such movement is possible to the *elephas*. The Newberg monster was just beneath the soil in a pool of water.

Stephen D. Peet found, in Ohio, around 1888, mastodon bones mixed with ashes of fires, arrow-heads, and stone weapons. The monster had also been bemired in peat-beds and attacked by prehistoric men. Davenport Academy, Iowa, has two pipes, shaped like a mastodon, or an elephant, which were found by a German parson, Blumer, in the depths of a mound in Louisa County, Iowa. A second, finely carved elephant pipe was found in a corn-field by an Iowa farmer named Myers, who lived near Davenport. Other folk have found human artifacts mixed with mastodon bones, as Dr. Holmes, who, in 1859, told the Philadelphia Academy of Natural Science, that he found pottery fragments, on the Ashley River, South Carolina, lying by the bones of an extinct megatherium and a mastodon. Implements and weapons found on such sites, sometimes go back as E. C. Berthoud suggested in 1891, to the Tertiary age, for they are totally unlike those of the Red Indians or the more ancient mound-builders. Peet thought the mammoth and the mastodon were in North America

[1] *Vide:* Fourteenth Ann. Rep. *Geology and Nat. Hist. of Ind.* pp. 32–33. In the article by Prof. Dr. John Collett it is said that, in summer 1880, a nearly complete skeleton of a mastodon was found in Iroquois Co., Illinois, which was 11 feet high, and had a crushed mass of herbs and grass in its stomach.

long before the glacial period, and in a cave at Dordogne, France, mastodon images are found carved on bones, by prehistoric artists.

It has been supposed that the apparently inexhaustible quantity of huge bones near a spring in the ravine of a forest in Boone County, Kentucky, and called the "Bone Lick", denotes that, in a far day, these huge monsters were caught when a Great Cataclysm opened up the earth and engulfed them all. How old these remains may be and the extreme antiquity of the ancient men who lived at those times was suggested by the remarkable discovery made by folk exploring the famous Mammoth Cave, Kentucky, in 1815. In a recess of the labyrinthine cavern there was found a female mummy with features delicately chiselled and all the signs of youth. One story was the body was petrified with nitre drippings and that she must have been lost in the great caves, wandering in the terrifying darkness, till she fell down and died. (I believe the mummy is now in the Cincinnati Museum.)

The last find, so far as one knows, was made by a miner. C. W. Boehler, hunting for silica near Kimmswick, Missouri, in 1891, when he lit on many mastodon bones mixed with pottery.

The *woolly* mammoth possesses a long curved tusk not found in the mastodon, and that both were known to very ancient man in Europe, as in Asia, is shown by the vivid and spirited drawing of a mammoth, done by a Palæolithic artist, many thousands of years ago, in Magdalenian times, on a cave wall at Combarelles, near Les Eyzies, in Pyrenean France. Also, the long extinct woolly rhinoceros, with two horns, appears in another spirited drawing, by a Magdalenian artist, perhaps as long back as 80,000 years ago, high up on the wall of a rock-fissure, at Font-de-Goume, near the same Eyzies.

I have dealt at some length with mammoth and mastodon, because of the many people who assert these animals died out in North America long before the days of the ancestors of the Red Indians. Now we must pass on to other queer monsters of the great American wilderness.

Farther north at Nanaimo, British Columbia, near the river mouth, is a horizontal rock carved by prehistoric man with figures of various monsters like lizards and wolves, but with numerous appendages on the vertebral ridges that are unknown in any living animals of these species. (These curious images were photographed and reproduced in plaster casts, by the Harlan I. Smith expedition, of the American Museum of Natural History, New York, and published in the annual report of that institution, in 1898.)

Among them is a petroglyph of a sea serpent called the "Haietlik", or lightning snake. He is something more than a merely symbolical picture. The same monster also appears entwined round a totem pole, at Clayoquot, on the west coast, near Vancouver, British Columbia. The head of this striking totem pole is that of a very handsome and regal sort of man wearing a coronet, and of the same type of features as one *finds associated with Atlantean figures*, in some of the Mayan statuary and caryatides. Here, it is probably intended as an emblem of the Great Cataclysm that sank old Atlantis and brought hell on earth to ancient American races, as one has shown elsewhere in this book. But, as I have hinted the "Haietlik" actually swam and was seen in modern times in the North American seas! The unpublished journal of supercargo of the ship *Columbia*, written in 1791, in winter quarters at Clayoquot tells us that, on a hunting expedition:

> An Indian saw a frightful monster near the shore. He was shaped like an alligator. The Indians said it was a sea serpent and very scarce. It was a long creature with a huge mouth. They offered twenty sea-otter skins for a specimen. For if they should have but the least piece of this monster in their boat, they were sure to kill a whale, as it ensures success at all times.

To-day, saurians of veritable sea serpent type, but quite unknown to marine biologists, are said to exist in the region of the mysterious Monashee Mountains, known also as the Gold Range, where, in eastern British Columbia, the River Columbia takes its rise. As the poet Bryant said of the River Oregon, or Columbia, this monster in the "Barcan wilderness, rolls and hears no sound save his own dashings, come from the umbrageous woods". On the west of the Monashee Range, even now but little explored, is Lake Okanagan, where is the home of the Inakmeep tribe of the Okanagan Indians. Only a few months ago, I had a letter from a man who had read a book of mine on "Mysterious South America", and who assured me he had seen something queer in the waters of this lake. He says that the Indians have age-old traditions about the existence in Lake Okanagan and on the Monashee Mountains of giant prehistoric reptiles, and they are still very much alive to-day! The Indians know nothing about geological theories of the life of the Mesozoic Age and the monstrous beasts of the Cretaceous seas, but they describe monstrous reptiles that are singularly like dinosaurs and prehistoric marine saurians.

One of these Indians not long ago drew on a bit of wood a picture of one of these saurians. But in August 1933, the Great Okanagan monster got into the headlines of newspapers far away in

Ottawa and Toronto, and even in old London, England. The Indians believed he had died, because he had not been seen for a long time. Then, lo, one morning, he suddenly appeared all a-foaming and a-blowing in the waters of Lake Okanagan! These waters are very deep. He was said to have the head of a sheep and body of prodigious size and girth. The Indians further said he appears but once a year, and when he does he signalizes his appearance with a noise like the explosions of the engine of a motor launch. The stories import that the monster is a unique specimen of a fresh-water saurian of the sea-serpent type; for he is said to have snout of canine appearance, and very large head appendages like the flapping ears of an African elephant. Three people said they saw the monster, and that they guessed he was more than 30 feet long. They further said he rose to the surface close to the shore, nodded his flappers, and then submerged. He rose again, and then was no more seen. A white hunter was told by the Indians that the monster was called the "Ogopo", and had been the theme of numerous stories told round the camp fire and in the wigwams.

A venerable Inakmeep Indian said:

I am 90 years old. I heard my grandfather tell of this monster when I was a little boy. He is called the *Auck*. I remember that when I was 10 years old, I saw a bone 18 inches long and 12 inches wide that had come from the Ogopo's back. Years ago, a splendid deer was hunted into the lake, and was suddenly dragged down by something unseen. The waters boiled like a cauldron. A white man and an Indian were surrounded in their canoe by a school of these monsters at play. I saw one of them shoot a fountain of water into the air, and it jetted more than 50 feet into the air above the lake.

Clearly, here we have the very rare case in these annals of monsters' supposed by many to be extinct, which import that they have fathers and mothers, sisters and brothers, and do not live alone *in vacuo*. It seems that folk at Peachland, British Columbia, say they caught a glimpse of the Ogopo, one day in 1932. One can but suggest that marine biologists, who must be found in Canada as in other lands, should do something more than the old shellback of Hull, England, who one summer morning in 1928, peered over the bulwarks and drew back quickly, and with a violent seafaring oath, swore that if he saw any more of them "bleedin' sea sarpins in the North Sea" he would give up the sea and go on a farm. They should make tracks for Lake Okanagan and try to net one of these monsters. The cause of science demands it, gentlemen!

But one of the most amazing testimonies of the existence of unknown monsters in North America occurs in the cavern of the Glyphs in Ohio, 20 miles below the mouth of the Wabash. It is a cave in a rock just above the river at floodwater. In the days of the early settlements in Ohio, this remarkable cave was the rendezvous of a notorious gang of outlawed Kentuckians called Wilson's gang. Wilson, the chieftain, brought his family to the cave and fitted it up as a dwelling. He set up a sign on the waterside, which read: "Wilson's Liquor Vault and House of Entertainment". Then he organized a band of robbers and hi-jackers, and planned to waylay and assassinate crews of boats stopping at this tavern.

In due time, Nemesis overtook the gang. They were rounded up and the strange cave was entered and found to be 12 rods long and 5 wide; but what more concerns us here, was that this cave was found to have been the former home and religious centre of a very ancient and unknown race. The floor was as flat as that of a mediæval cathedral in old England, and its sides rose in stony grades, much in the manner of seats in a theatre pit. On the walls were well-drawn figures of *unknown animals* and hieroglyphs.

Beyond and above this main cavern lay another even more gloomy one, joined from the main cavern by a passage with an opening of around 14 feet, ascending which was like passing up a chimney. Far above rose a mountain. Some time after the robbers had been routed and dispersed, searchers in the upper cavern came on sixty skeletons, supposed to be those of men murdered by Wilson's gang, though they might have been the remains of prehistoric men. Nothing, at any rate, in the data available, conflicts with this latter theory.

On the walls of the lower, or main cave, were remarkable images. The sun was depicted in various phases of rising and setting; the moon was shown in its lunations and phases; there were ancient pictures of a viper and a vulture; buzzards were shown tearing out the heart of a prostrate man, recalling the ways of a paranoiac old Aztec priest; a panther was held by the ears by a child; there also appeared a crocodile, trees, shrubs, a fox, a curious hydra-headed serpent, two doves, bears, two scorpions, an eagle, an owl, quails, and pictures of *animals of species unknown*. Three of these eight animals were said to be like elephants, except that either the tusk and tail were different, or were missing. It is thus difficult to say whether or not they were mammoths, or mastodons. Two others were like tigers, one was like a wild boar, another was like a sloth, and the last looked like a curious sort of *quadrumane* rather than a quadruped, the claws being alike before and behind, and it was shown in the act of conveying something to the mouth, located in the centre of the monster!

There were also fine representations of men and women, clothed, and not naked, and *quite* unlike North American Indians. They were, in strange fact, *dressed in the manner of classic Greece and Rome*. There was also a glyph of a snake biting its tail in an orb or circle. This glyph is also found in ancient Mexico, being the ancient cosmic symbol of the rotation of the Earth and planets, the evolution of creatures and of matter, and implying that the world feeds on itself and receives from itself renewal, refreshment and renovation. The ancient Greeks so symbolized the revolving year, and it was known also in ancient Egypt.

The hydra-headed serpents suggest the Gorgons, or a type of Amazon fighting women of the ancient world, and it is probably linked with the lost continent of Hyperborea, or Aeyre-Atlantis, referred to in an earlier chapter of this book. The old myths of Echidna, the monster, born of Chrysaor, son of Medusa by Neptune, and of Callirhoe, the daughter of the Atlantean Oceanidus; of the Hydra, of Chimæra, and the Sphinx, monsters born of Echidna and Typhon, the Atlantean giant Typhun, who is identical with the old Mexican god of winds and water-deluge, Typhoon, all link up with the drowned land of Hyperborean Atlantis. The hydra-headed monster probably symbolizes the great snakes and reptiles whose skins were worn by the fighting women called the Gorgonian Amazons, in whose ancient land such monsters pullulated in the woods and great marshes of a very lush and warm day in the northern hemisphere.

The kinship of these American ancients, who left these amazing glyphs in this amazing cavern of the Wabash, in Ohio, with old Aeyre-Atlantis, whose American colonies may have extended to this region of the Ohio and the Mississippi, is further suggested by the details of the dress of the men of these people, as depicted in the cavern. They wear a rich antique cloak, like the old Roman *carbasus*; have a *subucula*, or waistcoat; breeches open at the knees, like those in old Rome called the *supparum*; are shod in sandals or soles, tied across the toes and heels; and have the head encircled by a bandeau tied with feathers.

The women in these Wabash cave-glyphs, are depicted with a Hellenic cast of face, the hair girdled by a coronet and confined with a bodkin. The rest of the costume is in a Roman-like style, with stola or *toga pura* flounced from the shoulders to the ground. These flounces singularly recall the dress of the mysterious Minoan race, seen on frescoes at Knossos in Crete. Underneath the toga peeps an *inclusium*, or petticoat, while an *indusium*, or kind of camisole, is confined under the breasts by a *cestus*, or zone. The women are shown wearing sandals.

The monstrous *quadrumanes* of these glyphs recalls the queer fact that, in 1892, relics, called Palæolithic, were found in Ohio. These extremely ancient relics represented two species of *quadrumana*, or four-handed monsters, *elephas primigenius*, *ursus* (the bear's ancestor), bison, *opossums*, and a great cat, all of them apparently found in ancient antediluvian America. Many of these ancient artifacts were found on the surface where the gravel crops out, and in the boulder clay, in the river gravel, and in the glacial drift. Near these relics was also found, in the boulder clay, a broken tusk perhaps belonging to some monstrous animal hurled to the ground by falling rocks thrown forth by Ignatius Donnelly's disintegrating comet! One theory was that the tusk belonged to Foster's *Castoroides Ohioensis*, or giant beaver. Also, a molar of *Elephas Americana* (ancient American elephant) came from the river gravel, and may have been washed out of glacial drift. These remarkable relics showed no signs that they had had any utilitarian purpose, and even flint nodules found there had been flaked into animal forms!

The Wabash cavern glyphs should be compared with a remarkable discovery made in a cavern in a coal mine, in the Pas de Calais, France, about January, 1884. Here, six fossilized human bodies were found, with remains of arms and utensils, in petrified wood and stone. In a second cave were eleven ·giant *human bodies*, animals, and even precious stones. The walls of this cave were decorated with pictures of combat *between giant men and beasts of gigantic size.*

The evidence of these remarkable petroglyphs, and the stories in American myth and folklore concerning giant men, and strange monsters who appear half-men and half-reptile—as depicted in ancient statues and artifacts in Central and South America—as also the queer horned man pictograph on the rock at Alton, near Cahokia, Mississippi —he does not at all look as if he were wearing a mask—seem to have some light thrown on them, so far as light can penetrate so dark a place in the past, by the ancient lore of East Africa, the strange life of the submerged Pacific continent of old Mu, and by ancient classic myths of old Greece and Rome.

A *most* ancient colossal figure of a bearded head of a man of heroic size, his hair and beard painted blue and face red, was, in 1887, found on the top of the Acropolis, in old Athens. The rest of the body was formed like that of a serpent, and the termination was a fish's tail. Some said he was a triton. Triton, it will be remembered, in the ancient mythology, was the son of Atlantean Neptune or Poseidon, and as the white horse, or Leucippe, was one of the symbols of old Atlantis, ancient sculptors sometimes represented him as having the fore part of a horse, with half the body of a man. But, here again, as in the case of old American relics, I may venture to ask if, in a far day, there were beings of this hybridized type on this queer planet of ours?

It is also very singular that, in 1820, mastodons were reported to have been seen grazing near the snow line of some still unexplored peaks in the Andean cordilleras, in modern Colombia, South America. In these wild regions are gigantic ruins, great paved roads fissured by long-past earthquakes, and hidden treasures of ancient gold and emeralds, showing signs of fine craftsmanship. There are also Indians who live in the rarefied air regions where no white man, European or Latin-American, could exist. These Indians are not affected by the *socorroche*, or mountain sickness, which troubles most travellers on any of the mountain railroads in Ecuador, or across the cordilleras from the Andes to the plains of the Argentine. But the Colombian Indians keep their secrets.

In this region Captain Charles Stewart Cochrane, R.N., reported that, in 1820, someone saw through a telescope, a herd of these great mastodons grazing on the edge of a snow-field. Perhaps, from fear of acquiring a reputation for travellers' tales, he did not say it was himself. He was, one day, passing near the small and remote village of Ubaté, which is very close to the Pamochia de la Mesa, with its great cave-caches of gold and emeralds—made by a long-dead and very ancient unknown race.

Says Cochrane:

> We were told by Señor Flores that, during the heavy rains, a stream of water passes through the *Suta*, yielding particularly fine emeralds, some larger than a pigeon's egg, brought down from the interior by the mountain torrent . . . We commenced preparations for my departure from Choco . . . In the evening I rode on an excursion with the *juez politico*, Señor Zereso, Don Luis and Mons. de la Roche, to a small hill commanding the town, when, the evening being fine, we had a fine view of a ridge of mountains which divides this valley from the Pacific Ocean. The summit was entirely covered with snow. From a small chain of highlands close to this range of mountains, with a good glass has been seen numbers of carnivorous elephants feeding on the plains which skirt these frozen regions. Their enormous teeth have been occasionally seen, but no one has yet succeeded in killing one of these animals, or, indeed, in getting near them. There are great quantities of wild cattle in these plains, to kill which the Indians sometimes make excursions. This chain of mountains runs north-east and south-west.

Cochrane, it may be noted, was not the only British writer who, at about this date, spoke of the existence of *mastodons* in the recesses of the Andean cordilleras. John Ranking, who, in 1827, published his *Historical Researches concerning the Conquest of Peru*, says, categorically, that *mastodons* are still living in the Andes, and teeth shed by them have been found! It may be that future explorations of these lost worlds of South America may provide scientists with those zoological, as well as archæological and mineralogical surprises, which were not actually found in summer 1937, on the top of the "lost world plateau" along the Rio Colorado, in United States of America. If we live, we may see.

If we do not, it may be noted that geologists and evolutionists have recently been confronted with a mystery of a lost world 12,000 feet up on the giant cordilleras of the eastern Andes.

The scene of the mystery is close to the remote township of Tarija, in Bolivia. Here is a valley of dry bones and arid death, located close to ridges of mountains, on the other side of which lies this strange, vast valley, strewn with rocks, covered with coarse grass and stunted shrubs, and fissured with ravines which traverse high bluffs. The place looks like the workshop of a nascent world. Nothing lives in this great valley, which is a geologist's and palæontologist's paradise. They called it the "Valley of Giants", and they have reason for it. Around 15,000,000 years ago, when South America was a large island, with sea-bed newly risen to form a land-bridge with North America, monstrous animals and dinosaurs such as the shell-backed glyptodon, colossal ground-sloths, a 90-foot long dinosaur, the macrauchenia (a camel-like creature with enormous, tapering snout); a phororachus (a vast, bird-like carnivore with a head the size of a horse); a borhyæna (carnivore as large as a big bear); and toxodons (like hippopotami with huge tusks), began to migrate north, across the land-bridge from South America, at the same time as a similar stream of monsters were seized with the urge to migrate southwards.

The North American stream of monsters appears to have taken the trail first, and when the north-bound, South American monsters reached what is now Tarija, Bolivia, they passed down over what is *now* a 12,000-foot mountain into an immense valley. In this tremendous amphitheatre, which, even to-day, has more the appearance of some lost, dead world on Mars, or the Moon than our Earth—there happened what has never been explained.

Both hordes died and left their bones in vast numbers. Scientists of the Field Museum of Natural History of Chicago do *not* believe that these monsters fought each other in a titanic, pitched battle, disputing the right of way. No; the fossilized bones of both trains of monsters mingle over a vast area, and they are in a condition which appears to indicate that both sets of monsters died at the same time, and from some unknown catastrophe of Nature. (One gargantuan dinosaur, whose bones were dug out of the hillside, had to be raised with derrick and hawser.) Nevertheless, with due respect to Professor Elmer S. Riggs, I venture to suggest the question, having in mind Fawcett's story of the huge, recent tracks in a lake in that very region of South America, whether in fact, *all* these monsters did die at that time?

In modern Colombia, on the Andean highlands not far from Santa Fé de Bogotá, is a strange and vast plain called the "Giants' Field", already mentioned in another connection, in this book. It is covered with petrified bones of mastodons, who must have been overtaken by a cataclysmic elevation of the shores and littoral of western South America, which created the Andes. Or, perhaps, more accurately, raised the mountains to their present immense height, in rarefied air, of the giant cordilleras. Before this catastrophe took place these mastodons were feeding in a lush, warm plain near the Pacific. Their feeding-grounds were raised to the clouds, their pastures withered, so that they died of starvation in rarefied heights where to draw breath is a pain and almost a torture to those unused to them. It is computed that this sudden elevation of the land took place about 60,000 years ago, and as the "Giants' Field" is at the same height as the mysterious dead city of Tihuanacu, that city may be contemporary with the raising of the mighty Andes! In any case, a breath-taking glimpse into a world of incredibly ancient civilization, far transcending those of old Africa or Europe, but, perhaps, not those of *older* Asia of the pre-Himalayan age, is here tantalizingly given.

In Ceara, state of Brazil, bones of mastodons of colossal girth have been found, one fossil tusk being more than a yard long.

A likely region for the abode of a *King Kong*, the great ape of the fantasy of the late Edgar Wallace—and, as we shall see, presently, South America has a *King Kong!*—and other interesting monsters, lasting over from the Mesozoic or Pleistocene Ages, lies on the edge of British Empire territory in South America.

It is a Lost World located in an unexplored enclave round the mysterious Mount Auyantepuy, on the frontiers of Venezuela and northern Brazil, with British Guiana looming in the distance. Mount Auyantepuy will be found on no chorographical map of South America, since it was not discovered till 1936. It is 8,000 feet high, and topped by a tableland. Thick jungle and reedy marsh and swampy lakes cut off the approaches, even as the terrible jungles of Guatemala and Yucatan bar off the path to many dead cities of ages long preceding even the Mayan culture. The only approach is by aeroplane, and, in December 1937, the United States Museum of Natural History sponsored such an expedition under the leadership of Dr. Tate. He reached Ciudad Bolivar on the Orinoco River in spring 1938, and planned to strike off from there into this mysterious region which, ages ago, was eroded from an ancient plateau of mesozoic times. True, Dr. Tate did not expect to find any great apes, or prehistoric saurians, or dinosaurs; but he thought it likely that he would reap a great harvest of fossils, bones and other palæontological remains. Unfortunately the German and Italian dictators and international financiers arranged a general European *bouleversement* about that time, so that I never found out what befell this expedition to the Lost World of Auyantepuy.

Strange anthropoid apes[1] are reported to have been discovered in the Peruvian Oriente and Montaña, by Dr. de Loys, in 1929, and were the subject of a learned article by Dr. Montandan, in a scientific society's journal, in Paris. If a story told me in Balboa, in the Panama canal zone, in 1927, has any truth in it, then explorers of the still unknown region of south-western Darien, less than 100 miles across the land-bridge separating Colombia from Panama state, may, some time, spring another surprise on the world. This region is closed against explorers and prospectors—closed by the Darien Indians, who will not even allow the President of Panama State into their territories. Death is the penalty for adventuring into Darien mountains from the Caribbean or Colombian side. The goal of many adventurers, in modern days, as in the days of the Spanish conquistadores is a strange city of the dead called Dabaiba, or Dahabya, a golden temple: 30 leagues southwards of Antigua, up the great river of Atrato, in Darien mountains. The city was said, in an old British lower-deck buccaneer's manuscript I have, to be lined with gold, and governed

---

[1] Apes of this unknown species have also been found in a remote corner of Costa Rica. Found around the late 1920's!—AUTHOR.

by a theocratic company of strangely garbed priests who offered human sacrifices.

The conquistador of Perú, Don Francisco Pizarro, and the unfortunate Vasco Nuñez de Balboa, who was beheaded by the cold-hearted, formal and sadistic Pedrarias, first Spanish governor of Panama, a complete scoundrel, headed an expedition of mailed Castilians into these wild mountains. The Darien Indians took to the tree-tops, in the rainy season, and rained down stones on the heads of the hardy and valiant Spanish *infanteria*, whose shields bent under their force. The mailed-coated Castilians thereupon cut down the trees. Three Spanish expeditions attempted to reach this city of gold, in 1515; but natives dived into the river and overturned their boats and great floods roared down the stream-beds from the mountains and put paid to the Castilian account. Even Pizarro refused to go any farther, or to take command. So Balboa went on alone, manfully sweating up the wooded mountains and forcing his intrepid way over the swollen streams, as the old English and French buccaneers and filibusters were to do a century after his date. Balboa said he actually reached the strange, white stone city, but was forced to turn back, having been wounded in the face, with a *wooden sword* and pierced with an arrow in his arm. Other Spanish historians say that no Spaniard has ever reached the dead city in these wild mountains.

Now, Dababya is, or was the seat of the cult of Chia: the moon-goddess who, said legend in Bogotá of the Muyscas of Colombia, the Nueva Granada of the old Spanish conquistadores, was the beautiful wife of Bochicha, the man in black, who, as we have seen, bearded, and wearing long garments came over the mountains from the east from Atlantean Hy-Brazil, to the highlands of Bogotá.[1] The temple was said to be hidden at the bottom of a cavern in the wild mountains of Darien and concealed immense riches which the Spaniards were never able to find. *Quien sabe?* Some day, some sun-dried, leather-skinned adventurer may get out of the land of south-western Darien with rude sketches of those mysterious ruins on plàteaux behind la Serrania del Sapo, whereon, says rumour in Panama City, are picture-writings. They are somewhere in the Tule country of south-western Panama.

There are also, it was whispered to me, in Balboa, Panama Canal zone, terraced pyramids in the jungles, a dead city of unknown age, where a great, reedy moat is haunted by great saurians, or monster lizards, who *skate upright*, as they skim the surface of the duck-thronged backwaters and, in behind the Sambú ranges, a stone city in which strange men of a "lost world" live.

The land of the monster saurians of unknown Darien resembles strangely that of the lost Brazilian Highland cities of Hy-Brazil; for it, too, is a country of unseen elusive "white Indians, with blue eyes and auburn hair".

[1] See my book *Mysteries of South America* (Rider and Co., London).

It was behind the Sambú ranges that one Thaddeus O'Shea, an Irish-American adventurer and gold-prospector, had an adventure with a remarkable and unknown type of anthropoid ape. The story of his adventure was told to me in Balboa by an Englishman who keeps a *pulperia* on whose walls hangs a seventeenth-century canvas-portrait of the celebrated buccaneer, Sir Henry (then Captain) Morgan. There is very good reason to suspect that that same giant ape may be found in recesses of the Oriente of Ecuador, to-day.

O'Shea had spent some time in the Darien mountains among a tribe of Indians said to use arts of very black necromancy. There were old women, and younger, who were said to have a power of Circe over captured white men, and a story ran round that, some-where in the wooded hills, were two deserters from the United States Army, in the Panama Canal zone, whom these women could make go round on hands and knees, barking like dogs and chattering like monkeys. (*Vide* page 59, of my *Mysteries of Ancient South America*, Rider and Co., London.)

Getting out of the country where, no doubt, Thaddeus had exhausted his welcome, he and a pal hired or stole a passage on a banana-carrying lugger sailing across the Bahia de San Miguel to Puerto Pinas. It was just after the end of the rainy season of 1920 that Thaddeus O'Shea and friend found themselves paddling up the Rio Sambú considerably beyond the banana plantations.

They had great difficulty in reaching the headwaters of this river, where they separated. The other man was never afterwards heard of, and must be presumed one of the numerous victims to this strange land's gods. O'Shea got overset in his canoe, and lost all his gear and food. Nothing for it, but to turn back on his trail and make for the nearest settlement on the wooded coast of the Bahia de San Miguel!

Thaddeus broke a way through thick woods and staggered along the banks of rushing streams, which led him gradually downwards from the saddle-back ridge of the Serrania del Sapo, which is drained by the Rio Sambú. There is much virgin gold in this unknown country, if only a man might live to get it out. One day, worn down with hunger and fatigue, he reached the top of the divide, where he stumbled around till he lit on a half-rotten, Indian dug-out canoe. Breaking sticks off some overhanging trees, he fashioned two paddles and then went down the lonely stream till he fetched up in the Rio de Las Dos Bocas, which runs southwards to Puerto Pinas, on the Pacific Coast of Panama-Darien.

One night, in a ravine on the top of a rugged, wooded cleft in the range, he went to sleep in a hut he had fashioned from leaves and boughs. All round in the far-spreading forest, howler monkeys screamed and the cicadas whistled like the siren of a small steam-boat. About midnight, he started out of a troubled sleep and sat up on his elbow, in his heap of dried leaves. He listened hard. There was only the night wind eerily falling on the trees of the lonely forest like waves on a sleeping islet's shore in mid-Pacific.

"Must have fancied something, or dreamt it," he grumbled, and was settling back in his bed of leaves when, outside the hut, there came the sound of some large creature lumbering around and snuffing and wheezing like a heavy, railroad freight engine ascending a gradient in mountains. Thaddeus reached for his *lignum vitæ* club, but having no gun (that is, rifle), decided to lie still and make no sound. Minutes passed and the sound, whatever it was caused by, passed away. Thaddeus fell asleep, and in the morning had a good look round in the wooded glen. He found no tracks, but big bushes had been trampled down and boughs of trees torn up and cast on the ground. He climbed a ridge, crowned by bushes, and was reaching a clump of wild bananas when he started back. . . . A big bush was shoved aside and to use his own terms, the "very Divill himself peered out, and no holy water to sprinkle him with".

A monstrous "black man", *all of ten feet in height*, standing erect, covered with thick, black hair, glared and gibbered at him in rage. It raised hairy arms and seemed about starting a charge down on Thaddeus, when he remembered that he had in his belt a revolver with one cartridge, saved for just such an emergency. He slipped it from his holster, drew a bead on the monster and toppled him over just as he was about to make a rush. The monster screamed and fell over, dead. It was a lucky shot, and, surely, Thaddeus must have had his patron saint well on the look-out that previous night and the next morning to be able to drop such a monster with a single revolver shot.

As soon as he recovered from his fright, Thaddeus took a piece of string from his poke and measured that "ould, black divill". He had the chest of a Congo gorilla, and the fangs of a sacred, red baboon of Arabia and Abyssinia; but what made Thaddeus start back and cross himself with an invocation of the "Blessed Vargin and all the saints in glory" were the monster's feet . . . they were *human, big toes like those of a man*, and not opposed thumbs, like those of an ape! He was a missing link. Thaddeus reached Pinas Bay, many weeks later, and got aboard a coast steamer which landed him at Balboa, where he was sent to hospital.

Before dismissing this story as a traveller's tale, let us look back.

It is known that, about the year 1640, a Spanish gold-hunting expedition in the region of this very Pinas Bay, off the south-west coast of Darien, reported shooting fourteen of these monstrous anthropoids. Indeed, Indians, all the way from Nicaragua to Ecuador, swear that great apes of this sort live on the slopes of jungle-covered mountains, into which no Indian will venture alone, even in the broad, hot sunshine of day.

When the Spanish conquistadores started to explore Perú and the Andes, in the first half of the sixteenth century they heard queer stories of large anthropoid apes in Perú. Cieza de Leon, the old soldier-monk, tells what he heard, in his *Crónica del Perú* (capitulo XCV). But, as even writers in the none too fastidious eighteenth century never translated this curious passage about "the bad customs of the Indians who live in the interior of the *montaña*" of the Andes of Perú, I here, for the first time, in English, give the translation for its curious and scientific interest:

They also say, for I have not seen them, that very large female apes walk and run in the trees, where, by temptation of the devil, who at all times lies in wait, men may commit great and deadly sins and use the apes as women. And they affirm that these apes sometimes give birth to monsters with the heads and private parts (*miembros deshonestos*) of men, with the hands and feet of apes. Also, they have little bodies of monstrous shape and hairy. Indeed, if they speak the truth, they resemble the devil, their father. They tell more: that the monsters have no speech, save a dreadful howl or moan. . . . It pains me greatly that such things may be possible. In 1549, I went to Los Charcos to see the provinces and cities they have there, and begged the president Gasca to give me letters of introduction to all the *corregidores* (provincial mayors) that they might aid me to explore the most notable of the provinces. One night I chanced to sleep in a tent with a nobleman (*hidalgo*), resident in Malaga, by name Don Inigo López de Nuncilba, who mentioned that a Spaniard, who there lived, had with his own eyes seen in the *montaña* one of these monsters lying dead, of the shape already mentioned. And Juan de Vargas, who dwelt in the city of La Paz, told me that, in Guanuco, Indians told him they had heard the howling of these devils, or apes; so is the repute of the sin committed by these evil-fortuned people. I have heard that Francisco de Almendras, who resided in La Plata, caught an Indian woman and a dog, in the act of committing this sin, and commanded the Indian woman to be burnt. And, besides all this, I was told by López de Mendieta and Juan de Ortiz o Zárete, and other residents of the town of La Plata, that, in the province of Aulaga, an Indian woman, by a dog, conceived and gave birth to three or four monsters who lived only a few days. Let us pray to our Lord he will not suffer sins so hideous and enormous.

The passage reminds one of the warning in the Pentateuchal book of *Leviticus* xviii, 24: "For in all these things the nations are defiled which I cast out before you". Old races have passed away from this very ancient world we call the *New* World.

Dr. Montandan notes that, in Yucatan, to-day, are statues resembling gorillas. They were found at Tekax and are now in the Archæological and Historical Museum in Merida. The statues depict anthropoids of powerful physique, and one of them seems to be bi-sexual, recalling the peculiarities of the sexual organs of an ape shot, in 1929, by Dr. de Loys in South America. It may be that, in the days of ancient and decadent civilizations in Central and South America, as in the times of the welter of Semitic and non-Semitic races who peopled the land of the prediluvian (and postdiluvian)

Mediterranean and the shores and land of Canaan, and what we call the Levant, there are periods when Nature, or the unknown power behind the universe, which the old Brahmins called *Dyaus*, tired of the human race as it seems to be evoluting, turns against mankind and seems blindly to grope to put something else in his place. Ancient myths say there *have* been such periods in the remote past. However, I do not wish to vex or bore the reader with Shavian warnings. Let us pass on to another curious phase of this subject.

I have been told that the Peruvian authorities have had to pass a law compelling *arrieros* (muleteers) to take their women with them, owing to the syphilis derived from the llama, who seems to be a carrier of it! It is not known, generally, that the Inca Peruvians were dying out as a race, from the ravages of this disease, when the Spanish conquistadores arrived.

A singular and attested case of comparatively modern sexual relations between Brazilian Indian women and monkeys is recorded by the Brazilian historian Noronha, who says he believed it. It relates to the Indians of the Coatátapiia nation of the Rio Jurua, Amazonas, who are said to have a tail like that of an ape or large monkey, of the *coatas* species. The story is told in a certificate attested by Frei (Padre) José de Santa Theresa Ribeira, missioner of Castro de Avelões, on 15th October, 1768, concerning a strange Indian that had a tail and came down the Rio Japuró:

Frei José de Sante Thereza Ribeira, missionario, da ordem de Nossa Senhor do Monte do Carmo de antigo observancia: Certifico e juro in verbo sacerdoti e aos Santos Evangelhos: that being a missioner of the ancient aldeia of Parauari, afterwards called, as to-day, de Nagueira, there arrived in the said aldeia, in the year 1751, or 1752, an Indian called Manuel da Silva, native of Pernambuco, or of Bahia, who came from the Rio Japurá, with certain redeemed Indians, among which was brought a savage infidel Indian, of 30 years more or less, of whom the said Manuel da Silva certified me that he had a tail, and for that I gave no credit to so extraordinary a novelty, he ordered the Indian to be summoned and made him take off his clothing under pretext of taking some tortoises from a stream where I kept them, whereby in this way I could examine into the truth of what he said, without being able to have any deceit put on me. The said Indian had a tail of the thickness of a thumb, or great toe, and of the length of half a palm of the hand, covered with a shell (or husk: *cairo lesó*) without hairs . . . And the same Manuel da Silva assured me that the Indian told him that every month he cut the tail so that it should not grow too long; after which it grew again . . . I did not inquire the nation of the Indian, nor the region where he lived; nor if any other, or most of the Indians of his nation had a tail; however, four years ago, more or less, there came to me news that the Rio Jurúa has a nation of Indians with tails.

And for that all this is true, I have here set my signature and seal. From Castro de Avelöes, 15 de Outubro, de 1768. *Frei* José de Santa Theresa Ribeira.

The wild gauchos who herd wilder cattle on the edge of the Matto Grosso in the province of Goyaz, Brazil, know more about the region of the Brazilian Highlands and the vast wilderness of the Great Forest—which is the English of Matto Grosso—than any other folk. I remember a chat I had with a Goyaz gaucho in that town called Bahia for short, but to which the old Portuguese founders gave the sonorous name of Bahia de São Salvador de todos òs Santos (Bahia or Bay of our Holy Saviour of all the Saints).

This one-time dreaded "yellow-jack" city, the nightmare of the old windjammer sailor and of the later day of the British screw and propeller steamers of the 1890's and 1900's, is, to-day, a curious mixture of the modern and the Churriguresque. Church and monastery bells, by the hundred, ring and tang from dawn till dusk and, in *fiesta* times, all night long. Ketelby and the late King George V would have been at home here. It is a town of the most Christian Catholic sort, with many old convents dating from the far-off day of the old Franciscan and Jesuit missioner, of the age when a Borgia pope grandiosely ruled a line across a map—*cis*: the dominions of the most Christian king, Dom Emanuel of Lisboa; *trans*: the lands of the most Christian and Catholic king, our Lord Don Felipe, in the palace of the old Escurial in Madrid. Cutting into the sound of the Catholic bells is the clank of the electric tram and the honk-honk of the American automobile. The picturesque and unhealthy lower town of narrow streets, just as they were in the sixteenth century, is a huddle of houses with worm-eaten rafters, rotting and rotten beams, and places with open sewers, no sanitation and open drains. *Samboes* with glistening skins and gaudy cotton clothes stroll past bronzed mulattresses with fine torsos and graceful figures that many a European woman would envy. Their snowy head-dresses and brilliant cotton skirts make a fine splash of colour where the sun strikes down; though, at night, the frowsy streets of the lower town are lit with dim and dirty oil lamps. However, the city fathers are, bit by bit, cleaning up their town. They plan to bring health and sanitation to its port where the harbours and docks are being enlarged and modernized. The lower faubourgs of Bahia are joined to the upper town with electric elevators and the dawn of a newer age is on the old city.

I met the gaucho in the bar of a hotel which, like many South American places of entertainment off the tourist track of the capital cities, both on the east and west coasts, is perhaps fitter for bazaar ladies, as they say in India, than for European ladies of the most strait-laced and respectable sort.

The gaucho, after drinking a tall glass of the potent *cana*, showed his teeth in a smile and assured me that only the gauchos knew this region and how to take good care of themselves in it.

"*Senhor*," said he, "too many Englishmen have gone into the wilderness on the trail of lost gold mines, mines of platinum, and diamond-rivers and have left their bones there. I found, at death's door, out there, one day, when I was hunting for a lost cow, an Englishman who had stepped off a cattle-boat in São Paulo and tramped his way up-country to Goyaz. He had a map on dirty sheep's skin, made by some monk about 250 years ago, which was said to show where there was a lost platinum mine, worked in the days of the Jesuit missioners, and abandoned by those fathers when they had to quit the country in a hurry.

"*Indiós bravos* track down men for days and keep themselves out of sight, as they move noiselessly through the *chapada*. The *whing* of a poisoned arrow is the first token you get of their presence. It is also the last, *por Deus*! The Matto Grosso has an evil lure for *o forasteiro*. Some demon seems to be always drawing him on to destruction. The gold and platinum mines are often in caves thousands of years old, it seems. I've never entered one. Vampire bats that suck the life out of men and horses are there, and quicksands that embog even the wild horses. There is a devil tree, there, as big as a willow. It hides its branches deep in the earth; but if you go near it, the branches creep up from the soil, the tendrils curl over and catch you in their grip. If you are alone, you will never free yourself, till it has sucked the life out of your body. It will capture even a wild steer in this way. Even bees in this land of southern Brazil forsake their habits of storing up honey in hives. I knew a fellow who started a bee-farm in Goyaz, and imported bees from Italy. In two years, they stopped storing honey, because they could get all the nectar they wanted from the ever-blooming flowers . . . and in sugar regions, *senhor*, the bees won't be at the trouble of sucking flowers, where cane is being refined."

In these central Brazilian jungles lives a queer, "lost world" bird, called the *hoactzin*, or, by ornithologists: *opisthocomus cristatus*. It, too, is an ancient world denizen of the Matto Grosso. This queer bird, barred with an olive-white plumage and tipped with yellow on the tail-feathers, would fit in well with a forest composed of monkey-tree puzzles (*araucaria*). It haunts low bushes near lakes, where it builds bulky nests. So eerie is its ancient-world appearance, that one is not surprised to find that the hoactzin is a direct descendant of an extinct bird-reptile—*Archæopterix lythopatica*—of which a fossil specimen was, a few years back, dug out of a quarry in Germany. Hardly any wonder that explorers, who see this weird bird in the *catinga* of the Matto Grosso, are disposed to agree that there may be other mysteries of lost worlds behind the screen of the jungle and beyond the belt of wild savages, when such a "mesozoic" bird hovers on its fringes.

Nor are prehistoric portents of this kind confined to modern Brazil. Years ago, Charles Darwin, in the voyage of the *Beagle*, came on traces of a prehistoric animal of great size which may have been used as a beast of burden by the original inhabitants of what is now Patagonia. The present natives are a miserable dirty and starved race of stunted folk; but, so large were these beasts, that only giants could have handled them. It was in a cave in the fjord of Ultima Speranza that he came on the bones of these giant beasts—mylodons. The cave had been used as a stable; for there was cut grass—dried—along with balls of dung containing part-digested grass ejected by monsters kept for haulage or store-stock.

Señor Julio de Moura, writing a doctoral thesis on American man, advanced the theory, in 1889, that in Argentina and Patagonia, where ancient habitations had been found (by Ameghino, in 1868–72), made of the breast and dorsal bones of the Glyptodontes, these dwellings, at the latest, cannot be of post-Neolithic times.

But what is the hoactzin compared with the unknown monsters of the Rio Araguaya, in the still unexplored territory of the Matto Grosso woods and unfriendly *chapada?*

In March and April, 1937, strange stories came over the telegraph wire to Rio and São Paulo. An immense, ape-like monster had come out of the unknown and started a real reign of terror round the country bordering the Rio Araguaya. The monster had all the marks of Edgar Wallace's *King Kong.* Swooping down on cattle ranches and *fazendas,* and lone villages, long after sundown, this mysterious monster roared in the blackness of the tropic night like the father of ten thousand demons come out of hell for a lively holiday. In the light of broad day, terrified people, who, all the long night had remained indoors, barring and bolting themselves securely, and barricading themselves against the Evil One from without, crept out, shaking, to find dozens of yellow cattle of old Spanish origin, lying dead on the pampas, their tongues torn out! As these cattle and steers charge a man at sight, if he is not mounted, and will toss him dead to the moon, if no tree is handy for him to climb, it may be supposed that something very unusual must have happened to them, that night. But more was to come. . . .

The *peónes* walked a few yards across the pampas, after tiptoeing round the dead cows and steers, as if someone on the watch might hear and come roaring out at them. Then they started back with many a *Deus* and *Maria Santissima,* and invocations to every saint in the Roman calendar. Round the carcases of several wild cattle which would charge a jaguar at sight, even if he would face them, there were great, man-like footprints, *some eighteen inches long.* Gauchos, all of a shudder at this irruption from some diabolical, lost world of the Matto Grosso, swore that "he", or "it" that left these prints in the dust must be more than *twelve feet high!* But what was so odd was that none of the fierce cattle, lying dead, showed any signs of a struggle with what had leapt on them out of the darkness of Matto Grosso night.

In the *fazendas* and the cabins and huts of the gauchos and *peónes* these terrifying matters were discussed all that day, and little or no work done; nor would a man venture out of sight of the hitching-post of the *fazenda patio*. Night fell, and again came the horrible roaring from the dark. No nerves could stand it, and as soon after dawn as was judged safe, a great trek of panic-stricken Brazilians headed for the nearest outpost of civilization. A few men of sterner mould remained behind, prepared to sell their lives dearly if, so be, they might wing the monstrous, roaring *King Kong*, or catch him off his guard. Three weeks passed, and then came the news to Rio, that the monstrous beast had been captured—by whom was not stated; nor how, nor how he was disposed of; nor anything about his identity, or morphology, or histology, or biology, nor even if he had been taken dead or alive. But it was said that a horse he had killed bore the imprint of a monstrous, human-like hand, more than twice as large as that of any human being. Should this fall on the eyes of any of my old friends in the Geraes, the Goyaz, or Matto Grosso, or even in Rio de Janeiro, will they tell me what became of the monster, living or dead?

Let the reader glance at a really good map of Brazil, such, as with characteristic *durchgehendener* attention to detail, the German publishers of Steiner's Atlas issued before the war that the half-caste Jew, Hitler and his thugs and paranoiacs sprang on a world that, as regards the *common folk* of all nations, certainly wanted no war. Let him or her glance at such a map and note where this Rio Araguaya lies and bear in mind that it was into this mysterious territory, the approach and portals to the "Lost World" of the Roosevelt-Goyaz tableland of the Brazilian Highlands—the old world of the white Atlantean empire-builders of ancient Hy-Brazil—that Colonel P. H. Fawcett, his son and Mr. Raleigh Rimmel vanished. (*Vide* my book: *Mysteries of South America*, Rider and Co., London, England.)

From what lost world came this monster of the Rio Araguaya? I think it is probable that he came from that unknown world located in what is called the Roosevelt Plateau. It was in 1913 that the late President Theodore Roosevelt, guided by the famous *Indianista*, General Candino Rondon, explored the course of the unknown river he afterwards called the River of Doubt, and which, still later, was called the Rio Roosevelt. This river journeys on the fringe of a vast unknown wilderness. It has a turbulent course, interrupted with foaming cataracts and rapids. West of the long. of 60°, the Rio Roosevelt has an embouchure with the Rio Madeira, and it is from about here to the long. of 50°, and between 5° and 12° South lat., that is located this plateau. Even on the most detailed military map of the German *Grosse-General Stab*—a characteristically thorough piece of work—the space is a blank. One side of it, the east, is bounded by the Rio Araguaya; and it is cut into by the Rios Tapajos and Xingú.

It is in this region that the dead cities of the Hy-Brazilian Atlantean race lie. Here, the lost race had their seat of ancient Empire, in a day before the shores of South America were thrust up some 12,000 feet. Persistent rumours at outlying settlements in Amazonas and the Matto

Grosso allege that this vast unknown plateau, the least known of its great size in the wide world, has great swamps which are the home of giant saurians, extinct elsewhere on earth millions of years ago. In the spreading forests range great monstrous mammals of the mammoth and King Kong type. The saurians and great lizards haunt the green swamps and swollen rivers bathing the ruins of great and splendid stone cities which are swathed in high grasses, their temple columns twined with lianas attached to great trees, and their grey and weathered mansions and majestic plazas burgeoning with gorgeous orchids shining in the green darkness of forests and deep bush. All these jungles, in the passing of thousands of years since the cataclysm, have swept like the waves of Time over these very ancient haunts of advanced civilization. It is this race I have called the Atlantean Hy-Brazilians, in a previous book, who perhaps left the strange rock-pictures, letters and hieroglyphs cut in rocks overhanging the torrents and the *cachoeiras* and *catadupas* (rapids and cataracts). When violent earthquakes, and, it may be, the approach to this planet of the wandering star that was to become our Moon, erased the men and the life in these ancient cities, the words of the prophet-poet Isaiah about a far-later culture in a far-away eastern world became true. Civilized men maddened by the cataclysm, fled far away, and giant monsters and saurians moved in, *and still live there*, so say Amazonas Indians.

The reader may dismiss this as fantasy. Let him or her, however, remember that South America is a strange continent. That unknown, vast region of the Roosevelt Plateau happens to be the oldest land in the world. It has never been submerged. It felt no slow, death-dealing oncoming of an Ice Age. Its climate has always been torrid and sultry in its lower levels; but, like Kenya colony uplands, healthy for white men who might reach its higher levels. And these ancients were *white* and bearded men! Geologists point out that this ancient Brazilian tableland has its ancient counterpart in the Siberian provinces of Yakutsk and Irkutsk, which, too, have never been submerged. In both are found the most ancient insect in the world: *Brazilophis Bondari*, a plant louse called after its discoverer, Professor G. G. Bondar, now of Brazil, but formerly of Russia. This insect lives on the lower parts of plants, and any inundation would at once have killed it. Moreover, the strata is plutonic, as older strata often is, and *not* alluvial, indicating past floods. Here, the Indians locate traditions of the lost white race of old Brazil which once ruled a great empire. So we see that the lost world of Hy-Brazil has, possibly, become the last home of monsters and dinosaurs where climate and conditions provide the right habitat.

This King Kong of old Brazil is on a level with the fierce and gigantic lizard, a veritable dinosaur, known to Australian prospectors in the central deserts, as the "Kaditcha", or prenty. In September, 1932, Big Jim, an old fossicker, met up with one on the slopes of the Stuart Range, when he was looking for opals.

Said he:

I hears a peculiar sound, and looking up, begad, there was looking towards me, as if he challenged me to move a step his way, an enormous reptile. I snatched up a rock and was going to chuck it at the horrible divil, when he lashed his scaly tail and undulating his back, came springin' towards me! He lets out a roar as could be heard 20 miles away, between the bark of a big dog and roar of a lion. I beat it fer me life, you bet! Went back next day with pals well armed, and measured the bleedin' varmint's tracks. From one outside claw to the other was 6 feet 3 inches, and he must ha' been 15 feet long!

Australia, too, may at one far day, have been a southern extension of the old continent of Lemuria, or Mu.

In the Llanganati Highlands in Ecuador, where lies an old Inca gold cache, an American traveller, Richard Doylly, says that he encountered a dinosaur, a few years ago, but unfortunately one has no details.

In the strange island, Marajó, at the mouth of the Rio Amazonas, which has a mausoleum of remarkable and very artistic ceramics, denoting ancient contact of this prehistoric race with a vanished . nation who themselves took over idiograms and symbols and hieroglyphs which are identical with many in old Egypt and ancient China, there are ancient funerary urns on which are found, *inter alia*, figures of man-headed saurians. In one case the monster has a tail that, at the extremity, and contrary to nature, swells out into the form of a shovel. Again, at Sangay, in Brazil, there stands a curious, prehistoric black stone on which is seen an unknown monster devouring its prey. The Indians around this Amazonian region say that travellers and explorers who tamper with, or closely examine this figure of a monster on a stone will suffer death or serious bodily injury. Anyone who lingers around it with a camera, or near any ancient ruin of the ancient white race of Brazil, runs serious risk of having his camera smashed and himself being painfully and forcibly expelled.

Prehistoric Perú has strange monsters carved on very ancient bas-reliefs in immemorial stone. Paymaster Thomson, of the U.S.S. *Mohican,* found on very ancient pottery he dug out of huacas on the shores of southern Perú, an unknown monster with a cat's head and the curved form of a man, with bent back and long thin arms, which is identical with figures of a monster on frescoes found in that Valhalla of ancient Mu, called Easter Island. Palæontologists know no such animal. Lasso de la Vega, el Inca, tells of a statue of the white Hy-Brazilian Vira-cocha (Sun of the Sea) who came from the east to civilize old Perú. At Puerto Viejo, Vira-cocha's disciples and the master went on the sea and walked on it, having neither ships nor boats. The culture-hero was shown on this statue, holding in one hand, by a chain attached to its neck, a great unknown animal with lion's claws. And it may be also noted that farther north in the land of the old Muyscas, whose ancient civilization had its habitat in what is now the Andean territory of modern Colombia, South America, another ancient white culture-hero, Bochicha, was accompanied by a strange animal of great bulk and size, which the old Spanish padres of the conquest supposed was a mastodon.

There are prehistoric bas-reliefs in granite, which were the work of unknown sculptors, at Cabaña, Pashash, Perú, who must have had some powerful motive in commemorating in so hard a stone a monster

 like a double-headed snake, with the ridged back of a sea serpent, and a broad snout and lupine teeth.[1]

A dinosaur of mesozoic, but unknown type, figures on an ancient stone at Sina, Perú, left there by a race unknown. And a monster, in the shape of half-cat, half-reptile, with eight arms springing from its feline head, buttocks like those of a human being, curved legs ending in five long flipper-paws, and arms with similar terminations, is found on a bas-relief at Manabi, in Ecuador. This monster does not seem to be either an allegorical or mythic representation, nor a symbol, for his belly has been slit open by the ancient sculptor to show his vertebral column. Close by is a bas-relief of "mother" Mu, or Venus, the origin of the Phœnician-Greek letter Mu, and of our M. It shows her in indecent posture with legs akimbo, and the inference is that both the monster and the *Venus procreatrix* hail from one of the aberrant sex-mad islands of old Mu.

[1] In old Cuzco, there was a special quarter called *Amaryicancha*, where condemned criminals were sacrificed to great snakes, which, of course, denotes an atavistic cult of human sacrifice. In the old Inca provinces of the Antis and Tumbez, great boas, thicker than the thigh of a full-grown man, were adored. They were 30 feet long, and as recently as 1928 the Mojos Indians of Bolivia had and even the rancheros have in their houses tamed boa constrictors considered *"como amigo de la casa"* (friends of the house!) Pachacuti tells of how, when the old Inca Yupanqui invaded the western region of the empire, called the Cunti-suyos, at the head of an army of twelve thousand men, they were attacked by two huge snakes, one of which an eagle killed, and the other burst in pieces as he was climbing a tree to attack and destroy the bastard-brother of the Inca, the captain Ttopas Ccapac. At the end, the Inca, in memory of the miracle, ordered that there be placed on a terrace of the Andes (*andenes*) a snake carved in stone, afterwards called *Vati-pirca*. The Piutes of Nevada kept a great monster of a saurian, said to be still living in the waters of Lake Pegrand, as late as 1880, and fed it with human victims. It made the waters of the lake boil like a storm on these occasions.—AUTHOR.

Again, at Chimbote, Perú, where are other remains of unknown antiquity, there are prehistoric depictions of other curious monsters. In one case, a dragon-headed monster holds a human head in human-like hands, and at his posteriors is a lively representation of a *veritable sea serpent*, one of the types often described as seen on the high seas by sailing and steamships in the nineteenth and twentieth centuries of our own day. A second monster is shaped like a sort of "mammalian lizard" with long, slender body and tail, and a long tongue, also with three-toed flippers like paddles. A third monster is depicted in black and white like an armoured horse of some mediæval knight, breathing fire. He has human legs, one of which carries what appears to be an armoury of weapons, shields, lances and spears.

Moving northwards to Central America, we have more strange monsters carved in immemorial stone and apparently much more than

mere composite symbols. Old Panama has the statue of a monster of a scaly animal which is almost identical with that carved on the bas-relief at Manabi (referred to above). By its side is the statue, on a pillar, of an archaic type of nude man with a necklace and the cross of torture on his chest. He looks like a type of ancient colonist from old Mu. This statue is at least 12,000 years old, say the archæologists. This scaly monster of old Panama, standing on a pillar, seems to be of the same species as another monster, covered with scales, and with a "quiff" on his head, which figures in Lord Kingsborough's famous collection of ancient Mexican monuments.

Some of the ancient Panama statues face east, which may suggest an Atlantean connection, and there are others in the forms of elephants.

In Nicaragua, there are monsters carved in stone that suggest a connection with men of the *Tertiary Age*, since they have been found in quarries near Lake Managua, where are also footprints in lava made by very ancient men. It was these same ancient men who made inscriptions of *sea monsters* with uncommon accuracy and in high relief. Says Dr. Flint, their discoverer, "I was unable to copy these glyphs of sea monsters correctly without the aid of instruments. Yet these ancient men of the Tertiary Age, lying face upwards, chiselled them in solid rock."

He adds:

> These ancient men saw the first eruption of the volcanoes when they were close to their feet, and on opposite sides. They, with the animals, passed over the lava immediately, when it was moistened with rain, and left imprints in the plastic mass which soon hardened and preserved them. Four subsequent eruptions soon followed, as shown by four barely perceptible seams. A repose of long duration followed, when vegetation crept slowly over the volcanic débris. Forests sprang up . . . We pass over the hills . . . to a strip of land unmoved by the convulsions, and find a cave filled with sandstone, not suddenly like its neighbours, but soon after by the wash from their graves. We remove the rock, and copy the records on the inner roof made by these ancient men of Tertiary times. They are faithful delineations of *animal monsters*, and other objects or signs. Some are cut with sharp angles with great skill, indicating a people capable of protecting their feet as they walked over the tufa. No skeletons of these great monsters were found. One vertebra was all that we could add to the shells. Its diameter is about 10 inches . . . Nicaragua is too far removed to awaken scientific attention. . . . Here, we wander alone among the hills and vainly try to impress our convictions on others.

This was written at Rivas, Nicaragua, on 4th April, 1888, and one American scientific editor then appealed to archæologists and geologists to put their heads together and unravel these riddles. We know no more of these remarkable petroglyphs, even now, sixty years afterwards, which suggests that it would be just as futile to put together the heads of two archæologists, bang them good and hard, and expect sense to emerge. Dr. Earl Flint also discovered, in another Nicaraguan region of fossil leaves and shells and the erupted lava of a now entirely extinct volcano where Tertiary men had left more footprints, more remarkable petroglyphs carved, and not without difficulty, on the roofs of sandstone caverns. As he sardonically said: " I have no fear of their being described by the closet writers. Man was here long before the upheaval of the coast ranges."

Tomas Lopez Medel said, in his *Relacion* of 1612—a very rare book I here for the first time translate into English:

> Some old Indians of Yucatan affirmed to me that at the time of human sacrifices in the *cenote* (great and deep well) at Chichen Itza, they sometimes saw a fierce and frightful dragon which they took for a monstrous sort of crocodile, and who came out from these deep waters to receive what had been given him. And certainly considering the

nature of the place no dragon or crocodile could live there, the nature of the water opposing it. I suppose it might be a demon, though no such thing has been seen in other *cenotes* . . ."[1]

Now, in the Gran Chaco, on the edge of Paraguay, which was the scene of sanguinary fighting—League of Nations or not—between Bolivia and Paraguay, in the 1930's, we have a vast tract of marsh and forest over which three South American states claim territorial rights. It is roamed over by the wild Chaco Indians, who are degenerate but show traces of a very ancient culture. These Indians symbolize the First Cause by a beetle. Just as did the ancient Egyptians, these Indians believe that the beetle sent forth forms of life from its hole in the ground. The ancient Egyptians said that life issued from the mud of the Nile, and that, the scarabæus, or beetle, was the chief type.[2] The Gran Chaco Indians also have traditions of a very ancient race of superior beings before man's advent, which may be euhemerized as a contact, with the old white and highly-civilized race of the dead cities of the central Brazilian Highlands, whose culture extended, in a far day, well into the interior from the shores of mightier Marañon. or Amazon.

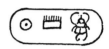

Ancient Egyptian cartouche of scarabæus.

Somewhere north of the township of Concepción, where the Rio Paraguay flows along the border of the Gran Chaco, a region most unhealthy for white men, there was whispered a story that eventually drifted into the capital of Asunción, in 1930. It was about a mysterious amphibious monster called *el buey jagua*, which is a name implying that it is a lacustrine or "palustrine" (marsh or lake) monster, big enough to drag down one of the formidable yellow steers that are the descendants of the old Spanish cattle that roam the pampas, and selvas. It was said by the Indians and the *vaqueros* (cow-hands) to have the head of a dog and alligator combined, great tusked jaws, and a canine bark. Its formidable tail ends in a sort of prong. The Indians swear that the *buey jagua* has its home in "el pantano del diablo" (the devil swamp), located around 200 miles north-west of Concepción, and between the Rios Paraguay and Pilcomayo. The *buey jagua*[3] is

[1] The Licenciado (lawyer) Palacio spoke, in an unpublished manuscript, of the year 1576, which was sent to the king in old Spain, about, *inter alia*, a lake close to the town of San Salvador, then in old Guatemala. He says it was at Long. 13° 13' 36", N., about five leagues in extent, and is of very little use, for few fish are in it. "The old Indians tell that there is in the lake a great serpent of prodigious size, and the cacique of a village called Atempamacegua says he saw one, which, by his account, must be at least 50 feet long. I know not if the fact be well authenticated, for no one says he has seen it, except this cacique; but it is an idea spread long ago in this country."
[2] The vanished and mysterious connection, here, may be that the proto-Egyptians who came from the western regions of the ancient Earth to the Nile, and were, perhaps originally, a race of one of the Atlantean islands, had contact with ancient South America *via* a landbridge from the submerged Atlantis, in the South Atlantic.—AUTHOR.
[3] *Buey*, in the Argentine, means a bullock, while *jagua*, in Colombia, South America, denotes the colour of the ferruginous sands left in the pan after washing auriferous gravel.—AUTHOR.

unknown to modern zoologists, or herpetologists. It reminds me of the strange lizard that has been seen *skating* over the reedy and sedgy waters of a lake close to a dead city in the wild mountains of unexplored south-western Darien. The Chaco Indians also say that the *buey jagua* has the girth of a giant man, and that when it uprears its tail it shows an underside of dirty white covered with scales; from all of which one might conclude that here we have a type of dinosaur of a carnivorous species. Its adult length is further said to be more than 18 feet, and that in its amphibious prowlings it preys upon cattle and large animals. It will lie in wait near the swamp at a spot, in the forest, and if it can surprise a man coming down to water his horse, or slake his own thirst, the monster leaps out on him, stuns him with a terrific blow, and lances the spiked end of its tail deep into his body.

But what amazed the author of this book and his friend, Major C. Hardy, former intelligence officer of the British Army in World War II, and himself, a former resident and hacendero in Paraguay, was that the description of this formidable dinosaur makes it possess a very marked and remarkable resemblance to the monstrous reptilian animalian heads on certain statues in the mausoleum of Zapataro, Nicaragua, and to the so-called feathered serpent figuring in ancient statues in both Mayan and old Toltec temples! I do not think the resemblance is accidental, but that the *buey jagua* had ancestors in both ancient South and Central America.

The late A. G. Hales who travelled over remote regions of South America, as he did Asia, tells a story of a monstrous saurian which he heard from the Indians while he was far up the Rio Amazon in Brazil. It will be found in his absorbing story of *Barney O'Hara, Trapper*. This monster inhabits recesses of lush and steamy marshes and lagoons. One night, an Indian, fearing to sleep ashore, anchored his canoe in mid-stream. In the middle of the night he woke up and gazed ashore to the woods. There, his eyes were caught and fixed by two queer moons that seemed gently to sway in the tree-tops. They had a hypnotic force that made him take up his paddles and row ashore. The moons continued gently and rhythmically swaying, and turned golden green. The Indian, as one mesmerized, heard unearthly music and drums beat. Time seemed no more. He was nearing the shore and death, when, on a sudden, came a great wave of water under the bow of his canoe, and the moon, emerging from a break in the dense trees of the forest, lit up a scene from the Mesozoic Age. An immense reptile of species unknown rose from the waters and clashed his immense, tusked jaws on the neck of a giant anaconda. A frightful struggle followed and the tremendous coils of the snake were dragged from the tree down into the waters of the river. Mr. Hales makes the significant comment that snakes with these mesmeric powers are seen near ancient temples in the forests of Brazil, luring parrots, with hypnotic eyes that rapidly change their lights from green to crimson.[1]

One race of ancient South American giants appears to have tamed a monstrous race of mylodons. Darwin, as one noted above, entered a great cave where he found dung-balls of chewed grass, close to the gigantic bones of these mylodons. He thought that only giants could have tamed such monsters and used them as beasts of burden. And that giants invaded ancient Perú from the south, there is plenty of evidence in ancient stone-lined wells, artifacts, and even skeletons of giant men and women, in places as far apart as Trujillo and Manta, in Ecuador. It is probable that it was the rarefied air of the great heights that beat these giants, used to warm lowlands. They attacked one old Cara (Karian) city to obtain women. The lost manuscript of Blas Valera has a surviving extract, recording, from ancient sources, that these giants built a sumptuous temple, with iron tools, at Pachacamac, in the time of the Inca Ayatarcó Cuso, around 500 B.C.

That giant animals were contemporary with ancient man in South America, is again proved by the discoveries of the naturalist, Lund, in a limestone cave on the borders of a lake in Minas Geraes, Brazil. Lund found in six caves forty-four extinct species, including a peccary, twice the modern size; a megatherium, a cat bigger than a jaguar, a smilodon, a large animal akin to the sabre-toothed tiger, and a species of horse, like our own. Lund claims that man existed in South America —and the like certainly applies to what are now the United States of America!—at a time far more remote than in Europe; for he found that several species of animals had disappeared from the fauna *after early man's advent.*

A wounded megatherium's head was found in a deposit of the Rio de la Plata, seven leagues from the north of Buenos Aires. The monster had been wounded by a prehistoric hunter. Burmeister says that the bones of great animals found in the Argentina, are mixed with those of ancient man and his artifacts. Dr. Holmes, in 1859, told the Philadelphia Museum of Natural Science, that he found megatherium and mastodon bones at the bottom of banks of the Ashley River, South Carolina, mixed with ancient pottery.

In the Argentina, Ameghino, as long ago as 1868–77, found that ancient men had actually made their dwellings out of dorsal bones of the giant glyptodon, at a date that cannot be later than Neolithic times! Ameghino and Keidel found, at Miramar, four silex arrow points close to the vertebral column of the toxodon, which was the size of the East Indian rhinoceros, and quartzite arrow-

---

[1] The Bahia de Caldera, Chile, has a fish that emits musical sounds. Gilliss, in his *U.S. Naval Astronomical Expedition to Chile* (1849–52), writes: "I knew of a man who went out in a boat and lay with his ear to the bottom, when he heard well defined musical sounds. These sounds, heard from January to March, were reported in 1852." A singing fish is said to be found in Ceylon and a musical snail at Corfu. In the Victoria river, south of Arnhem Land, Northern Territory, Australia, is a catfish said to make a trumpet sound in the water, and after landing. Bollaert says he heard similar sounds when cat-fishing in Texas rivers, about 1822.

heads were there found buried in the vertebræ of extinct animals, and are now to be seen in the Museo de la Plata, of Buenos Aires. An Argentinian Government Commission found that the arrow-heads had been made by men of the Tertiary age, and of the Miocene and lower Pliocene ages. Again, 600 miles north-west of this place, Ameghino found the femur of a toxodon in the same pebbly bed in which was embedded a quartzite arrow, or lance-head of a Tertiary age man. The arrow had been shot into the bone of the animal *while it was still alive*! On the banks of the little stream of the Frias, twenty leagues from Buenos Aires, he found human fossils with pottery, charcoal, burnt bones, arrow-heads, chisels, stone knives, and bones of extinct animals which ancient man had chopped. Yet the bigoted and purblind Argentina "Scientific" Society refused even to *hear* his memoir read! What these asses would have said of Lund's findings, in the Minas Geraes, we may leave to the reader's imagination. Eyes they have and do not see, and "brains" stuffed with hoary fallacies and obsolete theories.

Fray Pedro Simon, author of a rare book on Latin America[1] tells a story of a strange saurian type of monster, met with on the El Dorado trail, in the year 1534, when Nicolas Fedremann was second in command of Georg von Speier's expedition of 500 Spaniards (300 *infanteria* and 200 *caballeros*, or cavalry). It started inland from Coro, in 1534, and Fedremann had orders to follow up von Speier with supplies. The latter got into the interior some 1,500 miles, encountering incredible hardships. Jaguars carried off their horses, and attacked and killed some of their Indian bearers and one Spaniard. Sickness and starvation on the long trail more than decimated them. Fedremann had orders which he did not carry out; for he avoided contact with the leader, and wandered at the head of 200 soldiers, seeking glory and gold. He emerged from the mountain passes on to the plains of Bogotá, in April, 1539. Before that, high up in the *montaña*, they had crossed a rather narrow river, where they found signs of very ancient populations. Sickness had overtaken them, and they were very short of food:

> They had to halt and send out men to search for food in that wild region. And some soldiers had not gone far into the country when they came across some villages with people and food, and taking from them one and the other, they quickly returned to the camp, where Fedremann resolved to find out the cause of the ruins of those small settlements. And inquiring of the Indians brought into the camp, they said there had been a fierce and savage animal *with many heads*, bred in that river, and so fearless and valiant that little by little he had destroyed the people of the villages, which occasioned them to withdraw from the neighbourhood of those waters, where he had his customary haunt. And some went where the soldiers had found them, and others to other parts. The soldiers

[1] *Las Noticias Historiales de las Conquistas de Tierra Firme en las Indias Occidentales, por Fray Pedro Simon, Cuenza, anno* 1625. This is the first time this passage has been given in English, as it is here.—AUTHOR.

found no difficulty in believing this, since some amongst them had heard the valiant and horrible roarings of this monster within the same ranchos. Others affirmed they had seen him with their own eyes and judged him to have several heads (*varias cabeças*), and certified that he was a fierce and frightful monster. Some said he was a snake, others that he was a dragon.

They seem to have made no attempt to capture this monster, but packed up, on the orders of Fedremann, who determined to make his way back to the mountains, as he was afraid of missing the chief of the expedition.

Fray Pedro also speaks of another queer monster, found only in the province of Cumana, Venezuela, that comes out of the jungle, in the dark hours and at no other time, to the edge of the Indians' villages. "Here it weeps like a child very loudly to cozen the people, and if any come to see who is weeping, and gets within arms' length, he is devoured. It is of the shape and size of a full-grown greyhound (*galgo*). And for dread of it, the Indians, when night comes on their cabins, carry flaming brands. Another monster growing almost to the same size, but with a very ugly head and countenance, often defecates (*shits: se ensocia*) small snakes, that afterwards plunge into the craggy brambles, but die soon after."[1]

Another old Spanish-American writer—who, too, is for the first time, here translated into English (he is Don Diego de Avalos y Figueroa) tells a truly astonishing story of weird animals of the South American *selvas* (woods), which had been encountered in the late sixteenth century. His book, *La Miscellanea Austral* was published at Lima, in 1602, and dedicated to "Don Luys de Velasco, Cavallero de la Orden de Santiago y Visorey y Capitan-general de los Reynos del Piru, Chile, y Tierra Firme, the dedication being written at La Paz (Bolivia), "6 de Septembro 1601 años".

These astounding animals were called "Sacharunas", meaning "persons of the selvas, or mountains":

Sometimes I have heard them discussed, although not at the length that might be wished. As the Indians relate, these animals are like apes, very big and their statures are almost equal to that of a lad of 12 years. They walk almost always on two feet, and their face is more like that of humans than apes or monkeys. They have hair all over the body and none on the face, and are so slender (*delicado*) that their feet are like those of human beings, the only difference being that they flex them like the hand. The Indians attribute to them a rare and special instinct, because they say they have them *to throw lances* at the deer and to catch the *parasu* for livelihood. And others go farther, saying they have *pelotas* (balls) and *that they play with them!* And there lack not those who even say they make tabours to play them. Some affirm that some of these species have horns, which I have not seen, but I have heard their voices afar off, and, these, of the ordinary sort, are very like the human voices. I have

---

[1] One is reminded of the tears of the Nile crocodile, said to lure sympathetic victims to his jaws, and also of the habit of the English viper which, when sunning herself on a bank of a quiet brook, will swallow into her belly, should anyone approach, her small fry of new-born snakes!—AUTHOR.

seen one dead, because it wandered in the cold country (*tierra fria*), while I observed the peculiarities to which I have already referred, and he who brought it assured me that at the place where he saw it close at hand, it was so melancholy that it lost the desire to eat and died, and the great store he had of its usual diet did not suffice to save it. That diet consists of almonds of the Andes, with other forest fruits and some flesh-meat.

I had heard the like of them many other times and had never given entire credit to the account, as I have here given it; for I judged it to be some animal like the satyr, faun, or sylvanus, that the poets call gods of the woods. According to its extraordinary instincts, this description fitted them and no less because the Indians say these creatures will not speak lest services or tributes be demanded of them.

De Avalos refers us to the old story of Jerome, that St. Anthony, on a visit to St. Paul, saw one of these animals in the desert. He describes the food of these Andean *Sacharunas*:

> The nuts of this almond tree are not bad in taste, but they soon sour. The tree is very tall, upright and smooth, right to its top, where the branches grow out like the Spanish cypress. It is so lofty that one can scarce see the fruit, which are a sort of balls as large as *crescidas toronjas* (large grape fruit, or shaddocks), of a hard wood, and inside are the almonds, appearing like the quarters of an orange, and in the same way, covered with another shell, not the less strong, though thinner. Since this tree is so lofty, how do these animals manage to gather the almonds? I am told they do not climb up to them, for that is impossible; but wait till the nuts are ripe and fall, just as we gather ours. So when they pick the nuts up they have not had much time to get rancid. But it must be that these animals cannot all the time find these nuts, nor always hunt, as the Indians say, the deer . . .

Had this story appeared in "our excellent and indispensable eighteenth century of prose and reason", say, about the time when the Dutch, or Hollander N. D. Foersch wrote about the Bohun-Upas tree of Java and the human sacrifices offered to it, in the shape of the vile bodies of the condemned crooks of the year 1783, and not in 1601 at La Paz, Bolivia, one can guess the reception it would have had!

From time to time, the monstrous saurians or lizards travel from the interior to the edge of the unknown. In 1926, on a bend of this same Rio Araguaya, in a roaring confusion of waters of a *cañon*, a monstrous reptile poked up his snout, like some kraken, and crushed to pieces the timbers of a boat laden with *garimpeiros* (tough, hardy, Brazilian diamond-diggers), whom he ate, one by one!

King Kong of the Araguaya of the Matto Grosso has his exact counterpart in the jungles of Honduras, part of the old Empire of the Mayas of Yucatan. It was in 1927, that the late Dr. Thomas Gann, exploring the tree-shrouded and creeper-covered remains of ancient cities of the 1,500 years-old Mayan Old Empire, was approached by shuddering natives who warned him to quit the forests if he wanted to live.

316

"*Señor*," said one sallow-skinned and sloe-eyed Indian, "there is in this region of the forest a strange monster of a terrible beast which leaps on men from behind, claws them to pieces and dashes away. A *sambo* (half-caste negro) in the next village, was torn to pieces by it. I saw the body with these eyes."

It so happened that the negro had been a carrier in the party of Mr. Frank Blaucaneaux, who has studied the zoology of Central and South America. Accompanied by Blaucaneaux, Gann trailed the strange monster's footsteps to a cave deep in the forest. Close to the mouth of the cave both men were brought up, all standing. Sunk deeply in soft clay and mud were footprints almost exactly like the thumb and first fingers of a *gigantic human hand*. Each digit was armed with a great claw. Persistent efforts have been made to capture the beast, but with no success. Think what a draw he would be to the London Zoological Garden or the New York Zoological Park!

Blaucaneaux's story, as told to the late Dr. Gann and to a Honduran one met in Mexico City in 1939, raises, as always in these cases, the question that marks in a scarlet note all adventures of this sort. And I ask none to remind me of Louis de Rougemont; for that luckless gentleman, in his day, or soon after it, was proved to have been by no means a romantic liar, *in toto*! That question is: Who are the fathers, mothers, brothers and sisters and wives of these monsters? Where are they now living? If they are extinct, then how old are their posterity? It is on a footing with the natural query about the Loch Ness Monster: Where, in between his appearances in that loch, does he live?

Mr. Blaucaneaux is an experienced Central American bushman, planter and naturalist. He is the author of *Biologica Americana Centrale*. He was hunting around the headwaters of the Rio Mopan, north-west of Arenal, which is dense jungle where not a soul lives. It is much as it may have been when the mastodon and the mammoth roved the grassy plains, and the sabre-toothed tiger made many a tasty morsel of our eocene ancestors. One noon-day, in the virgin bush, Mr. Blaucaneaux and his negro attendant, looking for shelter from the fierce sun rays, lit on a circular dell whose floor was covered with a very coarse, wiry grass. The day was sultry in the extreme, not a breath of wind stirred. As they lay down in the shadow of a tall cottonwood, they noted that, in the centre of this circular glade, there uprose a tall palm (found in Honduras, and tropical South America) of the cohune species. Its trunk was very smooth and straight. (The large, hard nuts yield oil and material for fancy articles.) Only lizards stirred in the enervating heat, where the rays of the sun shimmered in reverberating waves. Blaucaneaux and his black friend were sinking to sleep, when the negro suddenly jerked up with a cry of astonishment.

"Golly massa, what dat dere, *eh*?" he asked, pointing with shaking finger.

Blaucaneaux's eyes fell on the cohune palm. Twenty feet and more upraised in the air it was shaking as if a gale were bustling among the branches. Yet not a breath of air stirred. Clearly, something was shaking the tree. Blaucaneaux sent the reluctant black to find what it was.

"Obeah, massa! The debil-debil foh shuah! I'se feared to ma very bones."

Indeed, the poor black was shaking with fear and his face was as near a dirty white as it could approach. However, he reluctantly picked up his traps and shuffled through the bush towards the agitated palm. He carried a gun, firing duck-shot. Slowly he crept through the bush towards the tree. Blaucaneaux marked his progress by the moving of the undergrowth. A few minutes passed, and then Blaucaneaux was electrified. A series of appalling shrieks came from the circular glade. The negro was only too obviously in agony, mental and physical. Grabbing his rifle, Blaucaneaux made for the cohune palm, no longer shaking. As he forced his way into the scrub, he was struck by the tracks made by some very heavy animal which had trampled its way through, previously. He reached the spot below the palm, where was a large open space. Here lay the poor black, a sight for a military surgeon in the first Great War! His shirt was ripped from his body exposing his belly, which was gouged to some inches deep with four great furrows, from which the entrails protruded. From chin to forehead, his face was a mass of bloody pulp and shredded flesh. What, in the name of zoology, was this monster who had disembowelled the unfortunate negro?

Blaucaneaux had a flask of rum and, raising the poor black's head, he poured some into his mouth; but it was clear the sufferer had not long to live. He just managed to whisper to Blaucaneaux, "De ole debbil rip me up, den he run foh de bush, massa!"

Staying just long enough to bury his poor black under the cohune palm, Blaucaneaux followed on the trail through the bush. Wherever the monster had gone, he had torn and broken branches and left a trail of torn-off leaves and twigs. Straight through the bush went his trail, till Blaucaneaux debouched into a savannah of coarse grass, which led to more dense primæval jungle, rising steadily, in three miles or more, to a ridge of whitish hills—riddled with limestone caverns, such as one finds in Yucatan, or round Palenque, in western Guatemala's jungles, of the Maya cities of the dead. Approaching the range, the monster had turned into a donga, or dried bed of a big brook running east-west in the line of the hills. The bed was cluttered with big fallen boulders, with only coarse tussocks of grass, here and there. As the monster went, he had turned over great boulders, and torn away the dense lianas, tough as a man-o'-war's hawser. Blaucaneaux had some trouble in following up the trail in this dry ground: but, at last, he found himself standing listening, and peering at the mouth of a dark cave. Night was coming on. Overhead towered steep cliffs, like the bastions of Sir Arthur Conan Doyle's *Lost World* of

Professor Challenger—which, by the way, I may again remind my reader is not altogether a work of absorbing *fiction*.

Blaucaneaux ventured into the cave, in the failing light; and he managed to see prints on the soft, wettish floor of the cavern, which stretched a long way into darkness. Bending down, he made out the monstrous imprints of a great human sort of thumb with two giant fingers armoured with claws. But it was not the place to linger around in the growing darkness of oncoming night—not with prehistoric monsters of this sort somewhere in the rear behind the blackness of the cavern. Suppose that hairy black monster had comrades? A harem of female demons with smaller fiends of like taste and capabilities in the line of disembowelment? Maybe even an express bullet might not stop him, or them?

Blaucaneaux set off while the going was still good. Right through the bush he trailed the monstrous tracks in reverse till he reached the glade of the cohune palm. Sunset, at last; darkness came over the whistling, eerie forest, and Blaucaneaux lost his way—even he, an experienced Central American roamer was bushed! He would have to sleep out for the night in the forest, hoping that no other similar monsters had nocturnal habits. In the morning light, he followed a pocket-compass course to the nearest river and settlement, where he planned to hire a band of fifty Indians and attack the monster in his den, after well and truly stifling him with smoke.

In two days' hard travel, he reached a village; but no natives would accompany him on the hunt of the "hairy, black devil!" Also, he had lost his bearings and failed to relocate the glade of the cohune palm and the cave. The natives of the bush village had heard before about this monster. Its habit had been to steal up from behind on women in the bush, raise them in the air, tear off their clothes—the demon had an aversion to clothes—and throw them to earth again. The women were too terrified to take notice of the monster. All they remembered was that the beast was large, very large, clutched them in great arms, armed with terrible claws, scratched their skins and tore off their clothes. Then lumbering into the bush some way, it cast them into the scrub and went off, alone. They remembered that it was covered with very long, stiff, black hairs.

Just before he died, Dr. Gann heard another report about the monster. It came from an archæological friend at Arenal:

> Indians here have found on the trunk of a large tree, deep marks scratched in the bark. At five or six feet above the ground, it looks as if some large animal had rubbed his hide against the rough bark. Where he has rubbed himself, the bark has, adhering to it, some long, very stiff, black hairs, marked with some whitish, soft mud and dust, which may come from a limestone cavern.

Dr. Thomas Gann, who was a member of a British Museum expedition, to Honduras and Yucatan, died in a London nursing home in February, 1938. Some years before his death, he came across the tracks of what he thought was a gigantic iguanodon, extinct at least 2,000 years ago. In the Mesozoic Age, these saurians reached 40 feet in length, and lived on grass and vegetation. Gann found the tracks near one of the ancient jungle cities in Mayan Yucatan, while he was endeavouring to solve the mystery of the hairy monster of British Honduran jungles, who is reputed to carry off men and women.

Another beast of unknown type was seen by Gann as he and his expedition were riding, in 1932, through the *acaiché*, or marshy territory close to the Rio Hondo border of British Honduras. He says it had a large body covered with black, shaggy hair, and a head with a white mane that covered the face. It trotted like a large ape, on all fours and calmly vanished into the forest without taking any notice of the expedition—men or horses. At Sac Xan, in old Mayan territory, he also saw a horrid reptile that "seemed to be a cross between a snake and eel. A most uncanny creature, like a reptile from some earlier age."

Those monsters who leave footsteps in the mud on the edge of swamps, in the unknown Caupolican in Bolivia's "abominable forests", inhabit a type of Mesozoic world which must be, or would have been congenial to the monster sea-serpent reported to have been seen in the year 1925, swept out on a spate of floodwaters, after heavy rains, or a freshet, from the Serra do Pacaraima, injected into the great Rio Orinoco of Venezuela. It was believed to have reached the River Ortoire, on the eastern side of British Trinidad. If it be not this saurian, then the monster called, in Trinidad, the "Huillia" is closely related to the Orinoco beast. In January, 1934, just before I went to Rio de Janeiro, the folk of the Port of Spain were all agog about this monstrous reptile. An expedition was on the point of setting out for the Rio Ortoire to try and snare him. They took with them a Hindu snake-charmer with pipes to lull the monster into slumber; whereas, one supposes, a Svend-Foyn harpoon gun of a modern whaler, or a mammoth electric derrick would have wilted under the strain.

The "Huillia" appeared to have made his last appearance in the year 1840, evidence of which is published by E. L. Joseph, in his rare *History of Trinidad*. Mr. Joseph says the monster haunts the region up-river in British Trinidad, and was, at that date, forty years old. (So, to-day, he must be 150 years old?) The "Huillia" is 50 feet long, as thick round the waist as a man's body, and has a pleasant old, Norwegian kraken's habit of creeping swiftly and slyly over-land, across country from the river, after swimming the water with steamboat speed. He creeps up on cattle, or unwary sheep browsing in the riverine meadows and swallows a few for breakfast. It may be noted, by the way, that sea serpents are believed to appear and vanish at intervals of years. What they are doing in the long intervals, or where and how they spend their time, no one can say, and one either rejects *in toto* the evidence offered, or keeps an open mind about it.

(*Top*) Spaniards garrotting Inca Atahualpa. (*Bottom*) Pizarro
attacks old Cuzco, Perú

16th century engravings

(*Top*) Inca Indian treasure for Pizarro. (*Bottom*) Llama gold train for old Cuzco

Ingeneiro Antonio Pauly, in his *Ensayo Etnografia ·Americana*, tells of his experience among the Mojos *Indiós* of Bolivia. Says he:

> One day, I lay down on some matting in a hut, smoking and dreaming, when I was startled by the sudden apparition of a boa constrictor (*boa ó choza*) which glided through the door of the hut and came in my direction. Leaping off the lounge, I grasped my. machete, the one weapon in reach. The hand of the owner of the ranch was laid on my arm. He said the snake was inoffensive and killed rats and toads. Furthermore, it was looked on as a friend of the house. A traveller later on told me that he had lived in the same pueblo and that the custom of taming snakes was common among the Indians.

The Pecos Indians of Arizona who have a legend of Montezuma—which despite what Bandelier says strangely recalls the cataclysmic elements in the life of the man in black, Quetzalcoatl, who came from Atlantis, or her colony, Hy-Brazil—are rumoured to have a hidden subterranean in the mountains. Here, they adore a monstrous snake: *la vivora grande*. Mariano Ruiz, who got on the trail of this story, about 1883, credited it, and said the cult is practised by the Tacos and Jerrez tribes. It is an enormous rattlesnake kept alive in a carefully hidden mountain recess and there is a whisper that what keeps it alive are sacrifices of human beings. The Indians, who are reticent about their aboriginal beliefs, deny the story; but Ruiz, in 1883, assured Bandelier that it was true as far as the Pecos Indians went. Ruiz said: "I can never get to see this monster, but it is a *cascabel* (rattlesnake)."

Anyone wishing to visualize what these strange and unrecognized monsters and dinosaurs of the South American "lost worlds" may be like at close quarters might study this picture of a fearsome reptilian monster, who figured in a singular story published about summer, or late autumn, of 1908, in a journal in Paris, France. This immense beast may have wandered across the land-bridge connecting South and North America (See pages 194-5 *supra*), and eventually found his way far north, in latitude 62°, 136° West longitude. I doubt not that scientists may smile and zoologists and palæontologists dismiss the stories as legends—material for psychologists—after they have asked us where are the mothers and fathers of these monsters? Where are their progeny? Do they live in *vacuo* eternally? How did they escape the fate that befell their ancestors, millions of years ago, when the oncoming of the ice ages spelled *their* doom, as the lush, steaming marshes vanished along with the day when Earth was like Venus? It was then that the sun shone hot and ever bright in a cobalt sky, and rain, as in Venus, fell only in warm showers at night and never by day—to *produce rainbows?*

Well, sirs, as a Scotsman would do, one may ask, in one's turn, the question whether the monkey-puzzle tree (*araucaria*) and the Welwitchia (*tumboa*) of the South African desert are the *only* survivors from the hot, steaming life of the swamps and vaporous plains of the

Mesozoic Age? If prehistoric reptiles left bird survivors and the saurians left Komodo dragons, now living on a plateau of an island well above the sea called Flores, may there not be other lost enclaves where other monsters survive, such as in the equatorial tropics, the far northern Arctic barrens, or the great deeps of the ocean?

As old Aloysius Horn said of Africa: "Aye—I believe there's beasts still living in the dark places and lakes that no white man's ever seen", so it may be true, or found to be true, some day, of South, Central and North America.

In 1908, one Monsieur Georges Dupuy told, in a long defunct journal of Paris, this strange story of a terrestrial monster he and other men saw in the lonely region of Partridge Creek, in the Yukon Territory.

This adventure purports to have happened some years earlier when Dupuy, a man named Buttler, said to have been a banker in San Francisco, the Rev. Padre Pierre Lavagneux, a French-Canadian missioner stationed, at the time, in the Indian village of Armstrong Creek (close to the McQuesten river in the Yukon Territory), and Indians were actually hunting the monster. Mr. Buttler had come to Dawson City in order to buy gold-mining concessions, after which he planned a hunting trip with Dupuy. Dupuy was waiting the arrival of Buttler, when one morning, he saw him rowing up the river in a canoe, paddled by Indians, who set him down at the door of Father Lavagneux's log cabin, in the wilderness. Buttler seemed very excited. He said a prospector and he had been hunting three enormous moose round the mouth of Clear Creek. They spent some time watching the moose feed on moss and lichen.

Suddenly, the three animals, which had been so quietly browsing, gave three simultaneous leaps. The male moose uttered a loud bellow— never emitted unless the moose be mortally wounded or hunted—and the animals went off at a mad gallop across country to the north. The men approached cautiously and around the moose "lick" saw, in the mud, the fresh imprints of the body of some monstrous animal whose belly had left a mark 2 feet deep in the slime. His body, judging by the prints, was 30 feet long, and 12 feet wide! There were marks of four gigantic paws deeply impressed in the slushy mud. The marks measured 5 feet long by 2 feet wide, the imprints of the claws alone being 1 foot in depth. The sharp points had embedded themselves deeply in the mud. The men followed the tracks of this monster down the valley, and noted that it had a tail 10 feet long by some 16 inches wide. The trail led them about 6 miles across country, till in the gulch of Partridge Creek, the marks ceased suddenly and the trail unaccountably vanished.

Some argument and scoffing followed, and then the padre, Dupuy, Buttler, and a miner and five Alaskan Indians went out on the trail and all day searched the valley around the little River McQuesten and along the flats of Partridge Creek. They went even farther afield, tried the country between Barlow and the lofty snow-covered mountains. They drew blank. A sergeant of the Royal Canadian Mounted Police jeered sceptically at the story and would not join them, nor would a mail-carrier (postman). By evening, the hunters were jaded. They had waded all over an extensive marsh. So they halted at the top of a grade in a rocky ravine and lit a fire of pine logs. As the flames flared up and the aromatic smell of burning pine resin perfumed the evening air, the great red ball of the sun glowed level with the tops of the snowy peak. It made the snow blush red, as with blood or fire.

Lying by the fire, the men let their eyes roam over the expanse of marsh they had just traversed. It glittered as the fires of the dying sun struck the facets of the crystals of hoar frost and ice . . . A peaceful evening of a day in the Far North-West! The hunters were hungry and the tea was on the boil. Each man was about to dip his pannikin in the steaming bucket, when, on a sudden, the noise of rolling stones, followed by a strange, harsh and frightful roar, came over the hill. The men jumped to their feet and grabbed their rifles. One man's eyes almost jumped out of his head.

He pointed, with shaking fingers, to the opposite side of the ravine, where the great boulders were rolling and plunging into the gulch. A gigantic, black animal was slowly and heavily climbing the grade. The men watched in terror. The corners of the horrible monster's mouth were dripping with blood and slime. His immense jaws crushed and crumbled something. The padre, the miner and Dupuy unconsciously clasped each other's hands and tried to speak but could not utter a word.[1] The five Indians crouched to earth, hiding their faces against a big stone. They trembled and quivered like leaves of aspentrees. Then Buttler, for some reason he could never explain, jumped up and rushed down the hill as if to fetch help.

The tongue-tied, almost paralysed men gazed fascinatedly as the monster stopped about two hundred paces away. He did not seem to have noticed them, and, luckily, they were on the down windward side of him. As they watched, the horrible beast rested on his huge belly, staring motionless into the eye of the red sun which was bathing the landscape in weird and lurid light. It was a scene which must have been familiar to those giants who lived, as the Hebrew epic tells us, in the morning of the world's long day. The monster stood for ten minutes while the men were riveted to the spot and even stifled the sound of their breathing. Then he turned his neck, but still did not seem to see the men. His body was, they reckoned, quite 50 feet long. On his jaw was a rhinoceros type of horn. His hide resembled that of a huge wild boar's, thick with greyish-black bristles. Mud was plastered all over his belly. Buttler now came creeping up the grade

[1] It is likely that when giants roamed this antediluvian earth—as to which see Chapter I in this book—such encounters were not uncommon with monstrous animals or dinosaurs of this type.

and whispered in Dupuy's ear: "God, the thing must weigh around 40 tons!"

As he whispered, the dinosaur moved his jaws and emitted a sound like the crunching of bones. Then he raised himself on his hind legs, emitted another frightful, hollow roar, and, wheeling round with the agility of a kangaroo, gave a prodigious bound and vanished into the ravine.

The watchers not being equipped with a howitzer, or machine-gun, wisely forbore following on his trail. They concluded they had all had enough excitement for one day, and ought not rashly to attempt to capture or exterminate a doubtless unique and valuable animal. Back in Dawson City, Dupuy asked the Canadian governor for mules and fifty armed men—though, surely a detachment of artillery would not have been out of place!

The governor refused, angrily, giving the impression that he believed a foolish attempt was being made to hoax authority.

The *Dawson City Nugget*, very much read among the old diggers and sourdoughs of that day of, or very near to the mushing over Chilkaat Pass, heard about the story and, quite unlike any modern United States and Canadian newspaper or feature magazine of the sort divided into partitions for ten or fifteen minutes' reading, said, in the fall of 1903, that poor Dupuy was the son of Baron de Munchausen, and friend of Edgar Allen Poe and Louis de Rougemont. Hence, all concerned were forced to follow the example—or perhaps I should have said anticipate it—of those naval gentlemen who look for promotion, and, when they see sea serpents on their cruises in foreign or home waters, carefully refrain from logging the encounters, lest it be seen by their Lordships of the Admiralty, and tell against promotion.

Dupuy went home to France, and in January 1908, had a letter from Père Lavagneux:

North-West Territories, Canada,
Armstrong Creek, Christmas Day, 1907.

Mon cher Fils,

Will you believe me when I tell you that ten of my Indians and myself saw again, on Christmas Eve, that horrible beast of Partridge Creek? He passed like a whirlwind over the frozen surface of the river, breaking off with his hind feet enormous blocks of ice from the rough surface.

His fur was covered with hoar frost crystals and his little eyes gleamed like fire in the twilight. He held in his jaws something which seemed to me like a caribou. He was moving at the rate of more than ten miles an hour. That day, the temperature was 45° below zero. At the corner of the cut-off, it disappeared. It is undoubtedly the same animal we saw when you were here. Accompanied by the chief Stineshane and two of his sons, I followed the trail, and the marks were exactly like those we—you and the rest of us—saw in the mud of the moose lick. Six times in the snow we were able to measure the impressions of his enormous body. It was the same size we measured before, almost to the twentieth of an inch. We followed the tracks to Stewart, fully two miles, when the snow began to fall slightly and blotted out the traces.[1]

Palæontologists tell us that one of the principal reasons for the disappearance of dinosaurs and the monstrous reptilia of the great swamps and warm mosses of the hot Mesozoic Age—life's long summer on the earth—was the oncoming of the Ice Age. After recurring periods of cold and less warmth, they say, the monsters died out, leaving no descendants. Yes, doubtless that was so; but who may say whether or not a peculiar type of dinosaur, existing in the Mesozoic Age, was able to adapt himself to changing climates and survive? Of course, the problem is exactly that we have in the case of sea serpents and other monsters of the great deep: are we to suppose that the monster of Partridge Creek has lived for countless ages—like a god—without father, mother, brother, sister, or child? Does he hibernate—no, *estivate* for long periods—emerging to the life above ground when the great herds of caribou, or the moose are migrating after fresh pasture and mosses? How does he compare with the monsters in the Caupolican, or on the slopes of the unknown mountains of the Brazilian Matto Grosso, the headwaters country of the Orinoco, the swamps of Trinidad, or of the jungles of Honduras?

The existence to-day of such land monsters, equally as those of the marine depths, such as the so-called sea serpent—a poor and very inaccurate description for mysterious monsters often described as having manes, humps, cow-like heads and scaly bodies and tails—obviously presupposes that, unlike Long John Silver's parrot, they cannot "live mostly for ever", nor can they exist *in vacuo* without relation to others of their elusive species. I, for one refuse to dismiss *all* stories of encounters with marine monsters as hoaxes and projections of the over ruddy and whiskified imaginations of veracious shell-backs. *Some* of the evidence emanates from reliable observers. For example, in the war year of 1917, the British warship *H.M.S. Hilary*, was off the coast of Iceland, some 70 miles to the south-east, sea flat and calm, barometer set fair, when the officer of

Sea serpent! ancient ceramic.   Chimbote, Perú.

[1] Mr. H. von Beyer, an engineer, of Washington, D.C., was at Port Townsend, Puget Sound, in December, 1887, when mysterious rumours were current about similar strange monsters seen in the interior of Alaska. White trappers had been in contact with Indians who had ascended the Yukon river, to a great distance from the coast, when they found monstrous tracks in the ground. They followed these tracks for miles and finally came in sight of immense hairy animals they took for mammoths. The creatures were of such enormous size that the Indians made haste to escape. The monsters were said to make tracks in circles. It may be said that the Iroquois Indians have traditions of a huge animal making tracks in circles.—Author.

the watch reported to Captain F. W. Dean, R.N., the appearance of a creature, with a neck around 20 feet long, a whitish head with a cow's nostrils, and a dorsal fin rising above the water for 4 feet.

As Dean entered in his statement to the British Admiralty:

> We fired shells from our six-pounders at it at 1,200 yards range, and must have scored a direct hit, for it submerged and was seen no more. A few days later, our ship was torpedoed and our logs and journals went down with her.

Herr Kapitän Baron von Forstner, of *Unterseeboot* (submarine) 28, was patrolling the Atlantic, on 30th July, 1915, when he torpedoed the British freighter *Iberian*. After the shot had gone home, he wrote in his log:

> There was a violent explosion, 25 seconds after the *Iberian* had gone under, and a few seconds later, a gigantic sea monster was hurled, writhing and struggling, around 30 yards into the air. The monster was around 60 feet long, shaped like a crocodile. His head was long and pointed, and he had four legs terminating in big fins. He remained above water only around 15 seconds, so there was no time to photograph him. Three other officers saw him.

Two other German submarine commanders also reported encounters with marine monsters unknown to marine biology. Kapitän Werner-Löwisch said he saw a marine monster when he was officer of the first watch in *Unterseeboot* 20, in 1915. The night was clear and the moon shone. He made a note in his diary:

> Saw a sea serpent at 10 p.m., without possibility of doubt. The creature had a longish head, scales like a crocodile's, and legs with proper feet. The mate saw him, but when the captain came up from below, the monster had vanished. The monster was about 90 feet long.

The late Sir Arthur Conan Doyle wrote, in 1929, that he was on the bridge of a liner off the coast of Ægina, with the famous Temple of Neptune on the port bow when:

> I saw, swimming parallel to the ship, under water, a curious creature around four feet long with a long neck and large flippers. I believe, as did my wife who also saw it, that it was a young plesiosaurus. A Queensland correspondent wrote me that a young plesiosaurus was taken in a net off Mudgee Beach, Australia. He sent me a sketch which is like the one I myself saw off the coast of Greece.

Again, in 1935, Professor Selim Hassan, when excavating round the pyramid of Chephren, found some ancient boats in one of which was the head of a gigantic animal with huge teeth, whose identity no one could establish. In September, 1938, a skeleton of an extinct type of monstrous mammal which was contemporary with the dinosaur and on the borderline between the mammal and the saurian, was found by the Danish Arctic expedition, led by Dr. Lauge Koch, in the mountains west of Jameson Land, near Scoresby Sound. It is now in the museum at Kjobenhaven, Denmark. In August, 1932, there appeared in a South African newspaper a photograph of a huge lizard-like creature feeding on the carcase of a dead hippopotamus, in a swamp in the Dilolo region of the Congo, Central Africa. It (the picture) was said to have been taken by a German scientist of the Schomburgk expedition, which went to the swamp in the hope of filming this monster, called by the negroes "the chepekwe". Another man, J. C. Johanson, a Swedish overseer of a plantation in the Kasai district, reported that he had seen this same monster on 16th February, 1932. He took a photograph of it, and he said:

> Suddenly I saw two elephants and behind them a monster around 16 yards long. He had a lizard head and tail. I made three snaps with my camera, but only one picture came out well. The monster moved with astonishing rapidity. I was very scared, and started back home. On the way I had to cross a big swamp and again I saw the huge head of this monster. It looked like a great lizard and this time it was covered in ooze, and devouring a dead rhinoceros. I took more pictures, and remained hiding till the monster vanished.

If this story be true, and the photos are, or seem, genuine it reminds one of the saying of old Trader Aloysius Horn: "Ma'am, Africa's a strange place. I believe there's beasts still living in the dark places no white man's ever seen."

I myself have a photograph of a weird monster, of marine but unknown biological type, which was found cast up on a beach in California. It has a beak and jointed backbone, and reminds me of the strange skeleton of another weird marine monster with a square head and similar beak and tail that was found on 17th January, 1948, in the mud flats off Brightlingsea, Essex, England. Experts who examined it were baffled to say what it was. There was even a case reported in North Wales, in October, 1805, in which a queer marine monster was alleged to have come aboard a coast ship, the *Robert Ellis*. The report is very rare and curious:

> This small ship of the Traeth was sailing slowly on the Menai, the strait in North Wales, in calm weather, when the people on board saw a strange beast like an immense worm swimming on the water after them. He overtook them and climbed aboard through the tiller-hole, and coiled himself on the deck under the mast. The people, at first frightened, took courage and attacked him with an oar, and they drove him overboard. He followed the ship for some miles, but a breeze came and the ship left him in the rear.

My old friend Roger Pocock, of the Legion of Frontiersmen— he died in a Wiltshire village, England, in World War II—and who earned fame in the West in the 1880's, when he rode a horse from Mexico right up the western shores of the United States, told me, some years before he died, that some Norse fisherman, some years ago, had an eerie adventure off the nightmare waters surrounding the Lofoten Islands, in north-west Norway. This region has tidal overfalls, invisible islands, the awful world-famed maelstrom, and weird and dreadful folk tales. Its waters are also the home of the far-famed giant squid known as the Kraken, and, said Roger Pocock, "he is more than a legend to the line-fishers." I heard a story, through an interpreter, of an adventure of an ancestor of Herr Nicolaissen:

"After bad day's fishing, the skipper said: 'We'll try the Ramstakken ground. . . .' Here, they caught one big fish after another, as fast as they could haul. But, all the time, though the boat's position was the same in reference to the nearby mountains, the water kept on shoaling. The bottom ought to have been at 80 fathoms, but it went down to 20. Then the skipper said: 'Haul in. Let's row as if we'd stolen the boat and oars.' They had rowed a rifle shot away, when on the very spot where they had been, rose arms with suckers, long as a boat's mast and thick as timber stocks, which clashed together with a report like a gun shot. All round them the sea boiled and foamed in tumult. The kraken, seen in 1522 is not so often seen as the sea serpent."[1]

The little-known writer—except to bibliophiles and Oriental scholars—Evilya or Evluja Effendi, a Turkish or Ottoman diplomat and traveller of the Near East, in the seventeenth century, who died in 1680, says that the Caspian Sea of his day had marine monsters of the sort which, even in the last few years, have startled Russian Soviet sailors and even police, in the Black Sea. He tells us:

A "whale" had been driven ashore. It was 100 yards long (*sic*), had two heads, one at the tail end, of the size of a cupola. In the upper jaw it had 150 teeth, each a yard long (*sic*), ears like an elephant, and eyes the size of a round table, and was covered with a beaver's hair. The inhabitants of Derbend and Shamáki flocked to see it. Khoka Sarúkham, a voyager in the Caspian Sea, told me that this kind of "whale" was common in that sea; there are certainly many strange creatures and animals in that sea which are not found elsewhere; the shore is covered with bones and carcases of monsters, which have strange kinds of square and pentagonal heads, and there are an immense number of extraordinary fish. Sailors say that the circumference of the Caspian is 24,000 miles; it has no islands like the Black Sea and the White Sea, wherein 2,040 islands are reckoned. Its depth is 3,000 cubits (around 916 fathoms, (*sic*)).

I have also a copy of an old Spanish manuscript, which was written round 1650, in Mexico. It has never, so far as I know,

[1] In summer 1927, a British steamer bound from Hamburg to Hull, England, ran into thick fog in the North Sea. When the fog lifted, the look-out shouted "Derelict dead ahead!" The captain on the bridge saw what looked like *a mast some 12 feet high* standing out of the water. He rang down to the engine-room ordering the ship to go astern. While the telegraph bells were yet ringing the "mast" moved and swam round to the port side. Here it reappeared, and a second "mast" curved round like an elephant's trunk of astounding girth. This weird object rose a little higher, and passengers who had rushed up on deck saw what looked like a black body. Then the thing submerged and once more the fog shut down on the scene. It looks as if the old kraken of the Lofotens has some nephews who go wandering round the North Sea. And that the great deeps and the middle deeps hold astounding surprises for the marine biologists of a future day seems obvious.

appeared before in English, and is curious enough to be worth giving here:

In the year 1648, there appeared on the *playa* (beach) of Santa Maria del Mar, Oaxaca, a dreadful monster which, on the flood tide of the sea, was thrown up on the waves. Its bulk was great and appeared to the eye like a reef. The folk of the pueblo, 200 paces away from where it was, saw it at break of day, and were so terrified that they were on the point of quitting their houses. It moved and swayed slowly on the sands, and on the second day the motion was less. On the third day it was motionless. In eight days a bad smell arose from the huge carcase, and the folk saw birds swoop down from the sky and dogs began to eat the putrefying flesh. Convinced thereby that the monster was dead, the people plucked up courage to approach it. They found it to be 15 varas long (41·70 feet), and upon the sands, it exceeded two varas (5·56 feet) high. Its pelt was remarkable, of a red colour, like that of a cow. Its ears lacked folds (*cangilones*). It had two fore-feet, and its tail was like a pillar, being so oily and greasy, and stinking so much that not even the dogs could eat it. A shoulder-blade, shaped like a fan, was jointed, and a third of a vara in diameter (around eight and a half inches). Its rib was the width of an eighth (of a vara?) and two varas long (5·56 feet). The tail, or caudal extremity, reached to the shoulder blade and formed very singular buttocks.

Don Juan Nepomuceno, a physician, verified these curious details, and a bone of this "sea serpent" was, at one time, suspended from one of the windows of the library of the convent of Santo Domingo, "facing east".

In an earlier day, the ship of the Spanish viceroy, Don Juan de Velasco de Varre, which was transporting to old Spain from the Philippines the body of a giant man, saw in the latitude of Bermudas, a monster of the sea who showed himself thrice to the ship. The "General ordered one of the ship's clerks to put it in writing to certifye the King of Spain". (*Manuscript narrative of an English sailor, Job Hartop of the ship of Master John Hawkins of Devon.*)

One may give two more stories of encounters with these marine monsters not, at least officially, recognized by marine biological stations! The first marine teratological encounter was told of by fishermen of Lowestoft, England. It would not be accepted as evidence, for the tale is one of what was seen by three mates, of Banff, Scotland, one evening in October, 1896, off the coast:

The lugger *Conquest* of Banff was a few miles off the shore and all the crew were on deck at six p.m. There were eight of them. They heard on their lee quarter a noise like a big steamer cutting her way through the water. Looking in that direction, they saw a huge sea serpent only 20 yards away. They say the monster was fully 300 feet long, and moved at about eight miles an hour. It resembled three enormous half circles in line, each circle being 50 feet long and 10 feet high, and there was room enough between each of them for the lugger to have passed. Still making the same noise, it passed close under the lugger's stern. All the crew watched it for fully a quarter of an hour. They describe it as like a fishing boat turned upside down and equally large in girth.

In November 1948, the New York press carried stories about a commotion among the folk of the Suwanee River country, in Georgia and Florida. Three-toed tracks had been found in soft land on the edge of a swamp. The tracks were 14 inches wide and 15 inches long, and the middle toe was longer than the other two, with terminal impressions of nails. An Australian editor dismissed them as hoaxes. A few years before, there were found, after dawn, close to a groyne on a beach of a Floridan sea resort, great imprints in the sand that looked as if some marine saurian, in the dark hours, had come ashore for a breather and returned to his native element before longshoremen were up and about. Earlier, in January 1948, the Grace Steamship Company's liner *Santa Clare* saw a huge snake-like head rear itself from the sea. Three witnesses said its head was 3 feet across, 2 feet thick and 5 feet long. Its body was 3 feet thick and neck close on 2 feet in diameter. The visible part of the body was about 35 feet long. As the monster came abeam of the bridge, the officers saw that the sea was stained with blood. Astern, the monster was seen thrashing the sea in agony. It looked as if the ship's stem had cut it in two. Another hoax? The monster did not think so!

Nevertheless, those who dismiss *all* such stories of strange monsters on a scientific, or biological, *a priori* principle, should recollect that the log of H.M.S. *Hilary*, mentioned, *supra,* attested, in May 1917, during World War No. I, the fact that a sea-serpent was used as a target by the warship's guns, when she was cruising off the coast of Iceland. A German submarine commander, who torpedoed a freighter, in mid-Atlantic, in U-boat 108, entered in the log that he saw on a moonlit night:

A sea serpent . . . with longish head, scales like a crocodile, and legs with proper feet.

The log of the Latvian motor schooner, *Elsa Croy* of Riga, said (19th July, 1934, 12.15 p.m.):

"Off Tiree island, Hebrides, weather calm, we saw in sea unknown monster, like large lizard (*not* basking shark). He was 50 feet long, neck immensely long, mouth vast, and had long tail with fins on top and underneath. Body of drayhorse. Ship put on his course. He saw us following, and turned and charged us at great speed. Gunner fired harpoon, but monster escaped with part of ship's rail."

Remember, too, again, that it was simply the accident of a complaint by Javanese convicts to a Dutch travelling inspector that revealed to the world outside the existence of the giant Komodo dragons, on that island, many feet above the sea, off the western end of Flores. These dragon-lizards, of which only very small immature specimens, reached zoos in London and New York, are when full-grown, easily able to leap on and kill a water-buffalo, or caribou, found living with them on the Komodo plateau. Nor is that the only island in the Java Sea where monsters, unknown to science, exist. At Sumbawa, for example, in a queer little island, there is an enormous saurian called by the natives *cheekchuk bezar*. It has a body said to reach more than 30 feet long—as long as a coconut tree. It lives in caves and holes in dry places—little grows on the island—and attacks men at sight. Jumping on all four scaly feet, with forked tongue playing and writhing, it stabs its victim and engulfs him in its jaws, which are snagged with a battery of ivory crushers. A small one is about 8 feet, and might be killed by the natives or their dogs; but the natives steer very clear indeed of the jungly scrub where these monsters are known to live.

Only a few years back, the author of this book was urged by an ex-American police commandant of Manila, to join him in a hunt up a wild, craggy gorge of a "haunted" island, for rich treasures piled into Ming jars by old Celestial pirates, who crowned each of the jars with a man's skull. The island lay somewhere in the Bashee channel. Exactly where, for the sake of thwarting the rascality of Japanese yellow thieves and spies, I may not specify. But, said my America commandant:

No fisherman will go near the place. Not only do they swear it's haunted; but there are queer flying lizards to be met there.

Why, then, should Asia, and not ancient South America, have hairy dragons and monstrous animals? Is Loch Ness to be their only derided habitat in this mysterious earth?

As the old monk of Lydgate's day said:

"Straunge thynges ther be in land and sea."

CHAPTER SEVEN

WEIRD DENIZENS OF ANTEDILUVIAN FORESTS

SOUTH AMERICA, the mysterious, lives up to its reputation in the strange specimens of often amazing plants and trees, some of them of really uncanny types, to be found in its unexplored or little known regions and recesses. That they are sometimes plants, trees and shrubs not catalogued in the *Index Kewensis* need surprise none who recall Colonel P. H. Fawcett's statement in his lecture to the London Royal Geographical Society, in 1911, that this continent, as regards explorers and exploration, is not in the fashion.

Some of them, as well as strange and fearsome types of insects[1] and *arachnida*, are found in that *terra incognita* of the Matto Grosso, located between the Roosevelt Tableland and the embouchure of the Rio Madeira and Rio Roosevelt and the Goyaz plateau, where is a veritable Lost World of the sort which fascinated the late Sir Arthur Conan Doyle. They are also, as known to the Indian tribes and wandering *gauchos* in the Occidental plains and llanos of Venezuela, in the mysterious provinces of Cundina-Marca and Meta (National Territory of Colombia), and on the highlands of Colombia, or deep in the little known forest and Orinoco headwater lands of the Guianas and northern Brazil.

Such a thing, of course, might be expected of so ancient a land. One must again remember that the unknown regions of the Brazilian Highlands were never ground under the glaciers of the Ice Age. We have already noticed remarkable evidence of the archaic survivals of this strange world in the discovery of the Brazilian entomologist, the Russian-born savant, Professor G. G. Bondar. He there found a plant louse, called *Brazilaphis Bondari*, the most ancient surviving species of insect in the Earth, which lives on the lowest parts of a plant growing in the stunted wilderness of the Central Brazilian *chapada* and *campo cerrado*. This lowly form of organism could never have survived a flood.

Here will be found strange plants and trees possessing valuable and dangerous properties, which will add immensely to the knowledge of the modern physician and his materia medica and confer on the pharmacologist secrets now known only to and used by savage

---

[1] Bees, in Brazil, are very *dangerous* non-domesticated insects, with the exception of one stingless variety. Even their honey is often dangerous to eat. The imported bee from Europe learns to abandon making honey in northern and central Brazil. She has abundant nectar from wild flowers, or sugar in the refining regions; so why should she take the trouble to store up honey, or even suck the cups of flowers when sugar cane exists? *N.B.* I must not be misunderstood as implying that honey is not produced in Brazil. It *is*, in the south, as in the Rio Grande do Sul.—AUTHOR.

medicine men and witch-doctors of primitive Indian tribes and aboriginal South Americans.

These potentialities of plant science and toxicological medicine, now secrets of primitive or savage men of the forests and wooded foothills, were brought personally home to me in what I have heard of the adventures of an early nineteenth-century ancestor of mine who was a ship's surgeon, having in his youth been the wild boy and scapegrace of a Warwickshire family, the Hintons, who were domiciled in that county, in the days of wild William Shakespeare and the Lucy family of squires of Charlecote manor.

In the days of Wellington and Waterloo, this man sowed so many wild oats that he was shipped off to the high seas before he had qualified as a doctor. He lived to fight against Barbary pirates in the days of Lord Exmouth and was shipwrecked about a dozen times in the South Pacific, the Caribbean and the Indian Ocean. At last he was thrown ashore on the wild and then little-known coast of Florida, about the year 1820, where, in a Red Indian encampment, he supplanted the medicine man among a tribe of the Seminoles. Always he had an eye to the collection of medicinal secrets, rare herbs and strange simples in use among savage and primitive peoples among whom, by the hand of Fate, he fell, or was cast by the hungry sea. Seventy years ago, this old chap, with his eagle eye and bearded face came over the south Cotswold Hills from the port of Bristol, pushing before him a barrow on which was a heavy sea-chest filled with queer charts of pirate islands, and many dried and exotic herbs, fishes, barks, and native ointments. He quartered himself in a lonely and pretty upland village in the house of a pious Primitive Methodist local preacher. Having survived the fratricidal war of the Union in which he fought on the side of the Federals, he had such a budget of wild tales to spin that, in the blustering autumn nights, when the sou'-westers bowed the great oaks and moaned in the churchyard elms and bustled the immemorial yews, the boys of that house were too scared to go alone to the jakes in the bottom of the long garden.

You could see the mulatto pirates grinning with knives in their teeth, as he spun his yarn, and hear the sound of the jaws of a tiger-shark clashing on the limbs of some unhappy castaway sailor trying to make the shallows of a coral island in the South Pacific, but too weak to make the final spurt to save his life. . . .

"Yes, lads, I owe the knowledge I gained to the wild Indians and savages in Central and South America and the Pacific islands," he said. "It is knowledge of the power of certain herbs and ointments of which doctors know nothing. By their power, I saved my life among the Seminoles of Florida, when I was able to cure the son of the Red Indian chief of a disease that had made him skin and bone. But it roused the medicine men among the tribes, and I saved my life from their jealous plots only by hiding in the forests till, one dawn, I saw a long boat of a whaler from New Bedford come ashore to wood and water at a spring close to the beach.''

Well, the old ship's surgeon has now been dead many a year and his recipes and exotic simples form the stock-in-trade of a druggist in the city of Gloucester who is reputed to have made a good thing out of them. Yet I doubt if that old shellback of a surgeon-sawbones of my family tree ever in all his long and adventurous life came across stranger plants and more amazing insects than are found in unknown South America to-day. Be it said, too, that they are, in the main, plants and insects of which the European botanists and entomologists know *nothing*. Indeed, even the authorities of Kew know not many of them!

They are plants and forms of life that drive home, once again, on the imagination how very ancient and antediluvian a country is South America, home of mysteries unparalleled except in drowned continents ages and ages sunk under ocean, or disrupted in terrific vulcanism and earthquakes. It may yet be many years before a tithe of these secrets of Nature at her strangest will be revealed to the world of science, struggling so hard to free herself from the annihilators. Many of the mysteries are locked up in the green hell of Brazil, deep in the far-stretching woods and immense marshes and forests of Amazonas. Or they are hiddden in the *terra incognita* of the headwaters country of the mighty Amazon and her great tributaries. But this is not formally a book about South American botany. It is a suggestive sketch of the shape of things to come, one day, out of the still unknown secret places of the immense territory lying between the bleak, hungry lands of Patagonia and round Cape Horn, and the yet unexplored neck of Darien.

Most people have heard of *maté*. It is the tea of South America, native of Paraguay, which is sucked through a silver tube called the *bombilla*, from the *cuia*, or gourd, in which it is brewed. The gaucho on the pampas, that sea of grass which he steers through without a compass, lives, or used to live, on *maté* and beef, often without bread. The dried leaf comes from a tree about 20 feet high which grows like a holly under the shadow of the stately Araucaria, or southern pine which towers into the blue sky of the southern temperate zone of South America. I have seen the Brazilian in the Geraes place dried leaves of *maté* in the gourd, put in a bit of red-hot charcoal, shake them till they are browned and roasted and then pour boiling water over them. He does this twice, and the second brew is even stronger than the first! None but a stingy Victorian type of landlady would try that way with tea—and not with *women* lodgers! The liquor is madder in colour, tinged with green. In the wars of the mongrel dictator Lopez, the miscegenated butcher of Paraguay, the docile Guarani troops fought in the immense woods and beastly swamps with only *maté* to sustain them. In World War No. I, the Croix Rouge Française heard of *maté* and imported it to Havre for use in the war-hospitals. But how many sufferers from diabetes know, as I recently told a war-working friend of mine, that *maté* is a sovereign remedy for this distressing disease?

A pity it is not better known in Britain!

In the First World War, we may add in passing, Brazil's mines and forests were put to curious uses by the British, French and Germans. In the limestone ranges of Jacuperanga, lying miles from the railroad is found a mineral known as Brazilite. In 1905, German military chemists heard of it, and imported it to Berlin, so that Krupps' chemists and metallurgists could use it as an alloy in the secret metal of the famous *Pariser Geschütz*, which the French called the "Big Bertha Gun", used to bombard Paris in 1918. They also heard of a tree growing on the slopes of the mountains back of Bahia. This tree, the *andiroba*, or crab-wood tree, is a combined soap and candle-factory and also, a police and military arsenal. The nuts, producing stearine, are useful to butcher, baker and candlestick-maker, in places on the edge of the *campo cerrado*—wilderness of stunted bush and trees— and in other parts of the *sertão* where electric power stations or lighting-plant are still only a dream.

But it has a queerer natural by-product still: each year the tree grows, its annual concentric layers and central nucleus accumulate a yellow powder. They call it *pó de Bahia*, Bahia powder. Some ingenious German military chemist found that this yellow dust can be made to furnish *tear-gas* for lachrymatory shells, such as were used to fill gas-shells in the First World War, as police-weapons against Uncle Sam's formidable strikers and mutineers in his "big houses" and Alcatraz type prisons; and for bull-dozing British citizens into carrying respirators and gas-masks around with them in World War II, as the Americans called it. Indeed, so pungent are the exhalations from *o pó de Bahia* that no flea will stay in any house in which it is found.

In the Amazon forests of Brazil there is found a species of euphorbia called the manchineel or mancinella. Known as *o arvore de morte* (the death tree) it is said to have the power of killing any who sleep in its shade. One is, of course, well aware that scientists and botanists deny this "legend of the manchineel". The tree is mentioned in various learned compilations and monographs on tropical flora, as in John Kerner's *Illustrated Plates* (1825), and *Fl. Antill.* (Vol. III, 1824). Here, it is called *Mancinella*, or *venenata tussac*. John Lindley, Ph.D., F.R.S. gives an account of it in his *Natural System of Botany*, of 1836; but the tree is not mentioned in the *Index Kewensis*.

Most modern scientific encyclopædias—whose compilers often resemble those who "bundle" together medical cyclopædias, in that each copies from his predecessor, repeating all his errors, "certainties", hypotheses and fallacies and shows little or no original research—the manchineel is usually dismissed, as follows:

Manchineel, or *Hippomane Mancinella*: tree, of moderate size with very white, milky sap, caustic and poisonous and of exaggerated virulence. Is especially deleterious to the eyes . . . This famous tree is said to be so poisonous that persons have died merely from sleeping in its shade.

Lindley, in his *Natural System of Botany*, gets nearer the truth about the manchineel. He says the juice of "Excæcaria Agollocha, and even its smoke (Euphorbia) when burnt, affect the eyes with intolerable pain, as has been experienced occasionally by sailors sent ashore to cut wood for fuel, who, according to Rumphius (2. 238), having accidentally rubbed their eyes with the juice became blinded and ran about like distracted men. They, some of them, finally lose their sight". Yet, he, too, doubts, on the authority of another brother (Dutch) botanist, Baron Nicolas Joseph Jacquin, who died in Vienna in 1817, whether Hippomane Mancinella has the power of killing people who sleep in its shade, "but it is by no means improbable that the story has some foundation, in truth, particularly as, if Antoine de Jussieu (died in Paris, 1853), truly remarks, the volatile nature of the poisonous properties of these plants is considered. The juice of *Hura crepitans* is said to be of the same fatal nature, and its seeds were administered to negro slaves as purgatives in number not exceeding one or two, with fatal consequences".

Meyerbeer, the nineteenth century composer, mentioned this tree in his opera *L'Africaine*, where it is called *manzanillo*, the Spanish name. Explorers in other (West Indian) jungles, such as those of Haïti, or adjacent San Domingo, say that if one slashes the leaves of the manchineel with the machete, as one forces a way through the undergrowth, it sprays the sap around. This sap is as acrid as sulphuric acid, and falling on the skin, burns minute holes; so that, even with alkali treatment, the burns are exceedingly painful and take a long time to heal.

In Haïti, by the way, another part of the old empire of Atlantis-Antilla as remains and statuettes of *extremely ancient* black necromantic, as well as *prehistoric* white type show, the manchineel has the appearance of a dwarfed crab apple tree, bearing small red fruit. The juice of these "apples" is virulently dangerous; so that even a small piece no bigger than a pea, can cause, if eaten, an agonizing death. (Naturally, having toxic properties of this kind, it no doubt possesses also great medicinal powers). From the tree exudes a resin which is also extremely poisonous. In the days of the old creole French planters, before the revolution of the blacks in Haïti, the tree was well known to black and revolting slaves at a time when it was far more abundant than to-day. In fact the white planters used to destroy every mancinella tree they could find, in order to put it beyond the reach of blacks avenging themselves on white slave-masters.

I have been told, in some parts of the island, as at Port-au-Prince, that modern Haitian botanists say the tree is exceedingly rare, and can be found only in isolated parts of the mountain jungles. Probably hardly twenty of these stunted trees can be found to-day in Haïti.

Magdalenian cave-drawing, woolly rhino. (Fr. Pyrénées)

Courtesy Cracow Museum

Female rhino, petrified in ice-age bog

Courtesy F. Neil Mackay, Esq., MacFisheries

Mammoth tusks (*circa* 50,000 B.C.) dredged from sea-bed, Shetlands

Mexican temple serpent modelled from monster like living "buey jagua"
(Gran Chaco swamp)

Unknown marine monster (Californian beach)

Their whereabouts may be known, however, to some of the blacks of the hinterland regions who secretly practise the rites of Voodoo— which rites, by the way, are thousands of years older, in Haïti, as queer and grotesque prehistoric artifacts show which were reproduced in a very well got-up brochure published at the time of the holding of the recent Carib Congress of Pre-Columbian art, held at Port-au-Prince.

Cornelis de Pauw gave a curious description of this devil plant in a rather rare French book, titled, *Recherches Philosophiques sur les Américains* (Berlin, 1770). He says that the first European who bent down to pick up gold on the beaches of America died instantly, poisoned by an arrow tipped with manchineel venom, shot at him from the woods by a wild Carib. This gentleman was the Spanish Conte de Fogeda. Pauw died at Cleves, in the western Rhineland, in 1790, where he spent his time on recondite researches.

Says he:

> Of the shrub and two trees used in America for poison, the Man-canillier, or Mancelinier, is the most dangerous. The name is derived from two native Carib words, *Manc-anill*. Père Pumier, in his *Nova Plantarium Americanarum genera*, calls it Mancanilla, or the hippomane vegetal of Brown. In height and look the Manchineel is like our apple trees, and the place where it grows and which is most to its liking is the island of San Juan de Porto Rico. It is found less abundantly in the Antilles and on some American beaches, but is never seen far inland.

As to that Pauw was wrong. The manchineel is to-day found in the northern woods of tropical Brazil. He gives us further details.

> The trunk is about two feet in circumference, and the bark glossy and soft. The flowers are red and set on a single stalk. The fruit is a round berry, fleshy and succulent, and has a peach-like bloom on its skin. Under the pulp is a rugged and knotty nut, with six to twelve compart-ments, and a kernel in each when the fruit is perfect, which is rare. The leaves, like those of a pear tree, transpire a milky juice when the sun's rays fall on them. In full sunshine these leaves breathe out poisons so freely that no one dare handle the branches. But when the sun's rays are not darted on them, one may pick and handle the fruit at one's ease. But, especially, when they flower, it is dangerous to lie down under the manchineels. This is because a prolific dust falls abundantly from the stamens of the flowers; also, the dew wetting the leaves, trickles down with dangerous poisons. It corrodes all it touches. When the wild Indians cut the trunk of this tree to get arrow-poison, they take extreme care to cover their faces, lest the spurting sap blind them, or, with great suddenness, strike them dead.

These wild Indians drain the liquid into shells set at the top of the trunk. They wait till the fluid coagulates, and then dip their arrow-points in it. A man or beast hit with one of these poisoned arrows dies as if struck with a thunderbolt. Even a slight scratch or light wound is fatal. Darts poisoned with manchineel were taken to old France, and it was found that, 150 years afterwards, the venom was scarcely less virulent. Philip II, of Spain—the "Armada" king—was told by Spaniards, who were trying to conquer the fierce Caribs in the West Indies and South America, that some of the soldiers had been killed with arrows tipped with manchineel venom. They said that crushed tobacco leaves was an antidote; but when the king tried it on some hunting dogs he found that, bathing their wounds poisoned with manchineel juice, the tobacco juice was useless.

Pauw advises as an antidote for this terrible poison that the patient drink four goblets of salt sea water, or swallow pinches of salt. The secret of the antidote was got by "grilling" a Carib boy who said that in his own village they used salt to cure manchineel wounds. "But viper salt is better," adds Pauw.

A woman friend of mine who has spent many years of her life in the West Indies tells me some interesting facts about this deadly poison plant:

> I know a great deal about it. The manchineel grows abundantly near the sea in the Windward Islands. All along Vigie Bay in Santa Lucia the shore is fringed with them. The definite cure, for *a small quantity* of the poison is, as your Dutchman says, salt water. All the West Indian doctors know this. On one occasion an ex-R.N. captain was made harbour master in Santa Lucia. We'll call him X. He was rather unpopular, because of his unwillingness to spend money. He had a wife and little boy of 10. One day the family decided to have an outing and picnic on the beautiful Vigie Bay. They had not been long in the island. Innocently, they sat down under the manch trees, as we called them and had their tucker. Suddenly, Captain X spotted the fruit of the manch. He was thrilled. "Look at that lovely fruit, Mary! There's tons of it, and all free for the picking. Why buy fruit, when you can get it for nothing?" They picked it and tasted it. Their little son watched them with wide eyes. Very soon, they began to foam at the mouth and had awful pains. They lay down and were violently sick. Captain X feebly told the little boy to run quickly and fetch a doctor. He ran and came back with Dr. Leonard Slinger, who was then visiting the quarantine station. He ran both of them into the sea and made them swallow as much salt water as they could. The doctor asked the little boy if he had eaten any of the fruit. The child solemnly shook his head. "Oh no! My mammy has always told me *never* to pick and eat stuff off the bushes and trees, if I don't know what it is!" Of course, the story ran all round Santa Lucia, *via* the men's club, and the whole island laughed. From that day to when they left, everybody in the island always referred to them as Captain and Mrs. Manchineel! As Dr. Slinger told us the story, he said: "If ever you happen to get a drop of the sap on your skins, at once run to the sea and drink salt water. It is *the* cure". Odd, isn't it, how the antidote grows so near the poison? The *Grenada Handbook* for 1926 cites manchineel as a valuable timber, but difficult to work on account of its blistering properties.

In its volatile toxic properties the manchineel strongly reminds one of another plant found in Central America, and, I believe, in certain species, in South America. My old friend, James P. Nolan, gold prospector and diviner of Nova Scotia, was attacked by this other plant when in the back ranges of Southern California. He and another roamer were ill for weeks, when they reached back to Los Angeles, and cured themselves after, on the advice of another bear-hunter, they fired their doctor, and took a solution of baking-powder. The same volatile poison was at work in the Stroud Valley, Gloucestershire, in December 1937, when cottagers were attacked by a mysterious illness and bad blisters on their hands. Doctors were puzzled about the cause. Then someone noticed the nights had been damp, and that some foolish person had planted in his garden poison ivy of the sumach group, which affects the body—even many yards away and not in contact—by exuding poison, with damp air as a medium of transmission.

South America, like Madagascar, has a legend of a devil-tree. It is called the "Octopod", and is said to be located somewhere in Amazonas, in the jungle along one of that mighty river's tributaries. Captain Thomas W. H. Sarll, who, when at home, has or had before the war a private menagerie in the grounds of a country house on the River Ash estate, in Middlesex, England, has determined to try and capture it (or "him"!). Captain Sarll, set off for the Amazon, in summer 1932, and his principal plan was to find and bring back the mysterious octopod, in whose existence he had faith.

He said:

It is like the octopus: an uncanny tree of the Amazonas[1] jungle, which puts forth its tentacular limbs in the darkness or subdued light of the jungle, and waits for passing animals or men. Native Indians and greasers have fallen victim to it. You can't see the limbs, for they hide in the bush and undergrowth. They are massive and gigantic, and when the animal trips up over them, its days are numbered. I know cases in which white men have been clutched by the limbs, drawn in towards the monster's body and held tightly till they died of starvation or fear. Then, the monster of the swamp devours them . . . I have bought a small lugger from Lowestoft, and, once in the Amazonas territory, I shall not return to England till I have caught an octopod.

Captain Sarll does not explain how he proposes to drag a big tree —if it be a tree—to the banks of the Amazon, and when, or if he got it there, whether his little ketch would be able to accommodate such unwieldly freight. He went, but the silence of the great Brazilian jungle is over all. Down at the herbarium at Kew, London, England, they have not heard of the arrival of the octopod—or, even the Devil tree of the Malagassies! For a showman, or a short film producer, either monster would be a fortune in itself.

The famous Devil Tree of Madagascar, another lumber room island of the vanished "wicked continent" of Mu, Moo-Ah, or Rutas-

[1] In the jungles of Brazil is another type of octopus tree. Its whereabouts are signalled, so it is said, by a smell like a rotting carcase. Birds are lured by sweet berries. As the bird perches to peck the berries, a tentacle of the tree catches a wing, and unless the bird can tear itself from the other tentacles, it is drawn to the trunk, caught up in thick, viscous suckers and crushed to tissue. The blood is absorbed and the feathers, like the cast of the prey of a hawk, rejected.

Mu, is matched by a climbing plant, known to the Indians of the great Chaco forest, on the borders of Bolivia and Argentina, as *el iuy-juy*. The plant is one of great beauty and seductiveness and is said to exhale a soporific perfume which sends to sleep men or large animals unlucky enough to seek its shade, in the noonday and siesta hours when the denizens of the forest are silent. Once the victim has sunk into a drugged sleep, the floral canopy overhead sends down masses of lovely blossoms, each flower of which is armed with a powerful sucker, which draws from the body all its blood and juices, leaving not even a fragment to tempt the vulture to shoot down from the skies to gorge on a bare skeleton.

One wonders how many dental surgeons, in either Britain or the United States of America have ever heard of another remarkable Brazilian plant? Probably not a man or woman on the register. It is called the tooth plant, and grows in the jungles and forests of the province of Amazonas, and when the Indians are troubled with their teeth, they crush the leaves and tender stems of this plant, and rub the concoction on their aching gums. The pain at once ceases. If the tooth be hollow, the stems of the tooth plant are packed into the cavity, and, in a few days, the tooth disintegrates and can be painlessly removed! In fact, the anæsthetic power of the plant is so great that if one even touched the skin of one's face, or the tip of one's tongue with it, the numbing effect lasts for an hour afterwards. How the victim of the drill in the dental parlour must long for the Brazilian tooth plant!

An even more amazing plant still grows in the headwaters region of the upper Amazon. Its name is the *peyotl* and it yields the wonderful drug called *yage*, in Brazil. The *peyotl* grows deep within the loneliest forests and one may suppose, may or must have been known to the witch doctors of the South American Tupi and Carib tribes. It may have been the wizard's best familiar. Dr. Bayon of Rio told me about the strange experience with *yage*, of Colonel C. Morales, who was commanding a detachment in one of the provincial forest areas of Brazil.

"Colonel Morales took *yage*, in an experiment to see how this powerful drug would affect him. He became immediately conscious of the death of his own father, and the illness of a loved sister, both of whom were then living in Colombia, separated from that part of Amazonas, by many hundreds of miles of dense forests, jungles, and high and impassable mountain ranges. A month after Morales' waking vision there arrived at the post a courier who bore news of the death of Morales' father. I have named the precipitates of peyotl: *telepatina*.

It is known in Brazil that Indians who have taken this drug and reduced themselves to a cataleptic state have seen European sights, and heard music and other sounds utterly strange or incomprehensible to them. They have not been able to explain them in their meagre vocabulary, but have tried to elucidate them with rude drawings.

Yage, or yague "séances" are also held in Colombia and in remote Indian pueblos on the borders of Perú and Brazil. Whether or no it is identical with a plant called "Baresteria Caapi Spruce", the method of distilling reminds one of the preparation of the dreadful poison *curare*. The brew is boiled and re-boiled for days, and the distillation is done by some ancient crone or witch of the tribe.

Strange plants of this antediluvian world type must be, or may have been among those which were used by the Quichua wizards of old Inca Perú, and may have been the secret medium through which they accomplished those *brujerias* which fill so many pages of old and rare histories, like those Fray Bernabé de Cobo, who in the early seventeenth century, so carefully examined and described the ruins of Tiahuanacu. Fray de Cobo spoke very much at large of the secret life of the native underworld of his day and of the place held in it by the native *hechicero*, or witch-doctor. In one aspect of the *hechiceros'* work, they are like the witch-doctors and aged crones of the equatorial African forests powerful herbalists whose peculiar knowledge, handed down from the generations, would, if they could be induced to impart it, make some amazing additions to the pharmacopœia and materia medica. The Peruvian *hechiceros* seek in the forests, on the slopes of the Andes, rare plants that enhance or produce supernormal powers. One plant, known in Quichua, as *vilica*, poisons or intoxicates some region of the cerebral cortex, so that the victim believes he sees ghosts and is haunted. The same witch man is said to go into the depths of the forests, remove all his clothes and plant his naked feet against the earth in order to set in force "psychic currents", or some form of hypnotism, directed against man or woman who has incurred his ill-will. The local wizards are alleged even to have a hierarchy of mahatmas who dwell in remote Andean mountain caves, to which secret roads lead, and where "elemental spooks" are invoked to keep watch while the wizards within the cave are engaged in unholy rites of some mysterious character. Whether true or not, these things are an article of faith with the *peónes* and even the half-caste mestizos.

The highlands and wooded foothills of modern Colombia, in regions seldom visited since the time of Jiminez de Quesada and his conquistadores, and of which old archbishop Piedrahita wrote, have also weird plants and trees of which one will find no mention in manuals of tropical botany. Splendid orchids are found in these forests, and one orchid of giant size is worshipped by a native Indian tribe who say that the parasite grows on the limbs of an enormous oak. Like the celebrated devil tree of Madagascar, this orchid is found only in one region. There is a native story about a spirit haunting the trunk, which cried out oracles and imprecations supposed to be uttered by the orchid —which may or may not be so. In 1929, I heard of an orchid collector, present at an exhibition in Chelsea, London, who said he had been warned that if he attempted to add this orchid to his collection, the *montaña* Indians would kill him, which was probably no idle threat.

Another plant found in the wilds of Colombia, South America, is used by a remote Indian tribe to preserve their teeth. An American scientist met this tribe, in 1932, and reported to the Smithsonian Institution at Washington, D.C., that he found that the skulls of ancestors of these Indians had also almost perfect teeth. The plant is of the coffee family, and when chewed deposits a black film over the teeth. The adults of the tribe chew the leaves twice each year and children fairly regularly use the plant.

The *campesinos* of Colombia, and especially that section of them who tend cattle in the llanos and steaming plains of the Oriente of this land, once known as Nueva Granada, whisper of the secrets carefully hidden, by the reticent Meta *Indiós*, from white, sallow, gringo or greaser. One of them is about a low shrub from which subtle toxins are prepared for their blow-guns, which toxins seem to be as deadly as curare. This shrub of the Meta, west of the Rio Orinoco, is boiled for two weeks in water, and the resulting distillation tested on some old crone of the tribe whose room is preferred to her presence. Applied to a cut, the powerful poison kills instantaneously.

No doubt many of these South American vegetable alkaloids must possess styptic and other surgical-medical properties that would make them of great value to western science. Who knows how many old Spanish roamers on the El Dorado trail, through the woods and jungly swamps of this very Meta region, had the efficacy of this virulent poison tested on their carcases? Never again would they see Caracas, or listen to the campaniles and tolling bells in the mountain city of Santa Fé de Bogotá where black-robed and cowled Jesuit priests and Capuchin monks summoned and still summon descendants of old Spanish Christians to prayers.

Colombia's dense green forests, where magnificent orchids bloom and rare butterflies of astounding beauty soar up from rotting carrion, has another peculiar tree, which is also found in the Sierra de Merida, in the wild hinterland south of the Laguna de Maracaibo of Venezuela. It is significantly called *el Palo Tigre*: the Tiger Wood. So appalling are said to be its effects that the most hardened and bloodthirsty brigand of these wild mountains who would cut his maiden aunt's throat for less than a peso will turn back on the trail sooner than pass under, near, or anywhere within 200 yards of it. Here is what a Venezuelan orchid-spotter told me of this tree. Its diabolical properties must be well calculated to sober up the reddest-eyed *automobilista* who ever took *panela* with his *aguardiente* at the tiendero's *pulperia*, before he nearly dashed your carcase to the bottom of a precipice on the new one-track international motor-highway into Venezuela from Pamplona!

He said:

This devil tree is found also south in the Rio Caqueta's forests of my country, La Gran Colombia; but I have seen it in the sierras of Venezuela. You will see a tree with greyish-silver leaves and it looks as harmless as a doncella whose leg being broken, she had to stay at home and mind grandmamma. But *carajo*, señor, beware! If you but touch this tree, not to say cut it with knife or machete, the saints and *Nostra Señora de Guadalupe* have you in their care! Walk under it, and the skin of your whole body is soon covered with the most terrible of rashes. Your whole *cuero* will become puffed up like a rotten fungus in the forests, and I have known many people die of it.

Similarly amazing trees and shrubs are also to be found in the wild llanos of Venezuela, and along the hot and swampy banks of the great Rio Orinoco and her affluents, in the country of Paez, that chivalrous *revolucionario* of the age of Simon Bolivar. Such strange flora are found in recesses of those savage and romantic plains beloved of *el gran caballero*, the late Don Roberto, R. B. Cunninghame Graham. These trees and plants, too, have many species which are not found in the great catalogue: the *Index Kewensis*.

Among these trees is the *flamboyante*, with its startling red leaves and a bark which shines like fire in the sun, and lights up the forest of the night where *el tigre* "burns so bright". It is sworn to both by *los llaneros* and *los Indiós*, that birds, or insects alighting on the dangerous leaves of the *flamboyante* fall instantly dead. In the same region, too, is the tree named *la sombra que mate* (the shadow that kills). It is shaped like an umbrella. If a tired wanderer lies down beneath its shade, the evaporation rising from the sweat of his body touches the fruit of the tree, and causes the acidic pulp to burst. It sprays down on the sleeping man and poisons him with severe burns. Its brother in the South American plant world is the celebrated *Chloroform* tree. At a distance the *Chloroform* tree looks like the pacoba, or Brazilian wild banana. Two hundred yards away, if you are down wind, you will smell the sweet and sickly scent it exudes. But beware of going nearer; for, at 20 yards, you will fall to the ground unconscious.

Then there is the charming *ague* tree, a light touch with whose leaves makes the unwary traveller shake as with a quartan fever. Here, the cure is the hair of the dog that bites you: take a leaf from the tree, cut it across the middle, and rub yourself with the juice. It will take the shakes away from you more surely than Jemaco rum did the tremors of the ague from suffering buccaneers in Morgan's hectic day, in the Caribbean.

The jungles of the "tierra caliente" (hot lowlands) of Mexico and other parts of Central America, run Haïti closely in the unpleasant properties of certain devil plants and trees. There is the "jimba", a bamboo, with long, sharp spines, which have a pathogenic effect if they pierce the skin. The *peónes* dread the jimba for its spines badly infect the skin of a human being, much in the manner of its counterpart in the insect world of Brazil, the horrible "barbeiro" (barber surgeon), or Triatoma megista. (This terrible insect issues out of a cranny in a wooden shack, at night time, in the regions of Minas and Parana, and with batteries of prickers and probes injects a deadly germ, the trypanosome, in the leg or arm of any human or animal sleeping in the shack.) The plant called *chechen* is also dreaded by the Mexicans on account of its latex, or sap, which will cause paralysis.

But we enter the realm of psycho-pathology when we meet with a remarkable desert cactus which, as long ago as the 1930's, proved a headache to the police of Paris, France, and other large cities, who were perturbed by its frequent use among drug addicts, mainly women. This plant grows in the hot deserts of Central America and was known to the old Aztecs as "The Flesh of the Gods", and to their descendants, the modern *peónes* of Mexico, as "Sacred Mushroom of the Aztecs", or the "Devil's Root". The name of the powerful and dangerous drug extracted from the "Aztecs' Sacred Mushroom" is *mescal*. In the 1930's, a neurologist, Dr. Macdonald Critchley, of King's College Hospital, London, and some friends carried out on themselves—always the best method of psycho-pathological experimentation, though one is afraid few vivisectors would be prepared to adopt it!—experiments with this drug. Crritchley gave some remarkable reports of what the effects of mescal were on him:

> I took one-fifth of a gram of mescaline sulphate, and in 25 minutes the visual phenomena began. At first, the hallucinatory images were simple in pattern and colour, and were visible when I shut my eyes. Then came the stage when the patterns became more complicated. They no longer comprised simple geometrical designs, but became three-dimensional, and were most brilliantly illuminated and coloured. I could see the hallucination with my eyes opened, but not the same in extent as when they were shut. This bewildering state reached the maximum in 90 minutes and lasted at this intensity for some hours . . . One of my collaborators made some notes or dictated them while under the influence of mescal. One of the notes read:
>
> "A very picturesque scene . . . an old-fashioned one-span bridge across the upper reaches of a river, boulders by the side of the stream, and a navigable channel in the middle. Now there comes a close-up of the bridge, which is of the old-fashioned type, made of large blocks of stone. A pillar has appeared in the centre, and transformed it to a double-span bridge. Now, the water dries up and a rocky bed becomes visible. The bed is gradually transformed into a stone road in a scene on lonely moors. Later, it becomes a green meadow with yellow and white flowers. Again, it changes into a band stand in a park, with chairs, each chair whirling swiftly on its axis."

One pays for these hallucinations. For a long time after, the patient suffers insomnia, vertigo and severe headaches.

Nicaragua has a queer acacia called the "bull's horn", from the shape of its huge spines which grow in pairs. Its scientific name is *acacia spadicigera*. These horns are hollow and are the home of a species of ant with a poisonous bite of hellish virulence. The least touch on the branches brings these ants down in a shower of vicious fury. Honey is secreted by the plant host for the benefit of its guests, who thus protect it from the attack of man and animals. If an animal tried to climb this tree he would infallibly be bitten to death. It reminds one of another Asian plant, a yam, which has tubers much liked by wild pigs. The pig starts to burrow to get at the succulent tubers, but he runs his snout against the hedge of the most ferocious thorns which the plant grows underground to safeguard its roots. Yet, if this plant is cultivated, it does not grow these thorns.

Just one word about another Mexico devil plant that is very well known to the police of California and to certain degenerates on the fringes of Hollywood, California. It is the *Marihuana*, and is banned under the criminal code of California. This Mexican herb is akin to hashish. It fills the gaols with negroes and depraved whites, who use it in exotic orgies and fantastic cults known to Los Angeles. Used in quantity, it drives the victim to seek raw blood for human sacrifice cults, by no means unknown in the "black" underworld of North America. If mingled with incense in small amounts, it slightly affects the brain and the powers of imagination.

Even when these exotic plants of peculiar and eerie properties have been added to European botanical institutions, they present standing riddles to scientists. Take the telegraph plant—so called. A specimen of it was, before the Second World War, to be found in the old Physic Garden established by Sir Hans Sloane, in 1721, at Chelsea. The small leaves of this plant jerk up and down at regular intervals, like the arm of a semaphore. Botanists know *how* the plant mechanism works; but not *why*! For that, prolonged study and observation in its native South American jungle habitat would be needed.

There are American plants and trees wherein Nature imitates art. The lace-tree or lace-bark (*Layetta lintearia*), a West Indian and South American hymelæceous shrub, has interlacing fibres of bast. This inner bark, or bast is woven by nature into excellent cloth, laid criss-cross to form weft and woof. The Spaniards of the late sixteenth century sent to the King in old Spain a splendid collar of lace made of this tree-bark, soaked in water and split into layers.

Everyone has heard of the cinchona which an Indian cacique of Malacotos revealed to a corregidor (Magistrate) of Loxa, Perú, who was taken ill with an intermittent fever. When the Countess of Chinchon, wife of *el virrey* of Perú, fell ill, a packet of the bark was sent to her. But by no means every South American knows that the wild tobacco, like the wild banana is a native of old Brazil. It is likely that it was the antediluvian people of Hy-Brazil who cultivated and improved the wild banana of Hy-Brazil, and subsequently introduced it into the mother land of Atlantis, whence was derived the Canary banana which is the most luscious of the bananas.

There is also a plant resembling pig-weed and known to the Aztecs as "haauhtli". It filled their granaries when Cortes arrived, and, in a later day, the colonial Spanish made cakes from its flour. It will grow in arid regions where corn will not. One may surmise that the species of pig-weeds were well known in ancient South

America, in a far warmer age, and that they spread northward, modifying their habits of growth. The mysterious thing about this plant, native of the tropics, is that it springs up on the ploughed land of the Canadian prairie, though its seeds are neither wind- nor bird-borne. No one has seen it growing on the *natural* prairie and no one can explain its origin.

The one plant that remains to be discovered in the wilds of South America is the relation of that which was found, in 1912, in the forests of India, or so it was alleged in that year. It has amazing electric power and magnetic sensitivity. If one breaks off a leaf one has a shock like that from the conductor of an electric coil. Even at a distance of eighteen yards this Indian plant will affect a magnetic needle. And what is remarkable is that its electric power has most force when the sun is hottest, and that, when storms approach, the plant increases the intensity of its electric energy-emission in striking proportion. No bird or insect is said to alight on or hover round this plant. In the continent whose riverine waters are famed for the gymnotus or electric eel, it would seem, *a priori*, that one day a plant may be found akin to this Indian "shocker".

I am also inclined to theorize that the remarkable rain tree of Ferro (Hierro) in the Canaries, may have been ultimately derived from the dry regions of ancient Hy-Brazil and exported to old Atlantis. This tree was a solitary specimen and is not found, to-day, in Hierro, where, indeed, no springs exist. When the Spaniards discovered this island the tree was said to be found near Valverde. It was called *El Garoe*, or El Árbol Santo (the Holy Tree), and the "legend" was that it distilled enough water from its leaves to supply the aborigines of the island with water. These aborigines, the Bimbachos, or Ben-Bachers of this island or Hierro (called by them Ombrios), were friendly to the Spaniards. But they covered the tree with dried grasses; so that the Castilians were not able to find it. A Bimbacha girl who fell in love with a caballero revealed the secret. The woman was put to death; but the tree vanished, though one may still find part of the tank into which the waters drained. Fray Juan de Abreu Galindo wrote about this tree, which he piously supposed had been given to the natives as a reward for their faith which, he said,[1] resembled the Roman Catholic faith. It was evidently not a native of the island, when the Spaniards saw the island. Whether or no my theory may be subsequently borne out by a discovery in the forests of Amazonas or the Matto Grosso one may one day see.

The well-known Brazilian botanist, Dr. Roquette Pinto of the Museo Nacional of Rio Janeiro refers in his pamphlets, published by the Sociedade Nacional Agricola, to a plant found in the jungles

---

[1] The whole ritual of Madonnas, monks, nuns, crucified saviours, trinity of Gods, and so on, existed in ancient Mexico *long* before the Spanish conquest and the coming of Spanish Catholic friars. Nor did the Apostle Thomas introduce such ritual there, or anywhere in ancient Central or South America!

of Pará, Amazons and Maranhão (North East Brazil). It is called *diamba* and is used by the jungle Indians for the same purpose as the Quichua Indians of Perú use *coca* or *cuca* (*Erythroxylum coca*): to stay hunger and stimulate (or over-stimulate) physical endurance. *Coca* is a pick-me-up of lands where what the old Spaniards knew as *la hambre* (malnutrition verging on actual starvation) prevails, precisely as it did in old Spain after the expulsion of the Moriscos and in the days when into old war-making Spain there poured the plundered millions of Aztec and Inca gold. But *diamba* does more: it paralyses the action of the gastric nerves of the stomach, when inhaled like snuff.

Other virulently toxic plants growing wild in the *sertão* of Brazil are nux vomica, canabi (causing convulsions), black solanum (acting on the heart and stupefying), *strichnos gardnerii* (dilating the vascular system), and croton.

The magnificent victoria regia (or giant water-lily) grows in the Upper Amazon and Rio Negro backwaters, with 16-inch-wide rosy blossoms and stalks, back of the leaves of which is an armoury of spines to hinder plant-collectors wishing to grub up the roots. One might also wonder if the proto-Egyptians, whom some Brazilian archæologists say hailed from old Brazil, exported to the Nile from these far lands the papyrus (*piri-piri* in Tupi, or Brazilian Indian tongue) which grows so luxuriantly in the great swamps round Rio as to be a nuisance. A German agronomist some years back invented a process by which this plant can be turned into fuel-briquettes.

I have never heard whether South America possesses a "jumping bean"[1] such as is found in Mexico; but in British Guiana's woods, there is a nut called the monkeys' dinner-bell. Nature expels these nuts to a distance of some 16 yards from the parent tree, in whose proximity they could not germinate. The explosion sounds like a revolver shot. If the nut be placed under a glass case, the force of explosion will shatter the case. In the forests, it scares the monkeys into flight from the tree.

Another curious fact is that the runner bean, which originated in the southern hemisphere, will always climb in only one way round sticks. Probably the rotation of the earth dictates this peculiarity; but in the northern hemisphere, where even the winds obey the law of deviation of Ferrel—towards the right in the northern hemisphere, and the left in the southern—directed by the earth's rotation, the runner bean keeps the same direction of climb as it had in the south. (Which, one may suppose, may suggest that plants have a memory, as in the case of the African mesenbryanthema at Kew, which, in England, uncloses its leaves only at the hour when the sun rises in Africa!)

---

[1] The larva of a moth makes the bean jump. It cannot endure the heat of the Mexican sun and, gripping the silk strands of a cocoon it spins, inside the bean, hits the walls with its tail and jerks the bean over.

One could not conclude a chapter on the weird plants of Brazil without referring to the famous *curare*[1]. In Venezuelan forest-jungles and in the *sertão* of Brazil one is on the confines of the wild jungle where the savage *Indiós* still to-day brew this terrible poison. Some may recall that, in 1917, a woman and her daughter, living in Derby, England, were alleged to have sought to bring about the death of Prime Minister David Lloyd George by somehow injecting curare into his veins. It might, as the Americans say, have been a "bright idea", though many people in saner times may have doubted if it had really been intended to put it into practice, despite the special pleading of the supercilious, million-horse-power-brained egotist: the first Lord Birkenhead (F. E. Smith of Liverpool), at the trial. The whole business so much reminded some folk of the advice of the celebrated Mrs. Glasse about jugged hares: first catch your wild Welsh hare, rather a hard job in war-time!

Southey, in his *Brazil*, gives an account of the making of *curare* in his day. It was used not only to shoot your enemy off the face of this green hell called *Earth*, but to cure a nagging battle-axe of a wife, or get rid of some old beldame of the tribe who had whiskers on her wrinkled chin and a tongue clacking like a mill-race in full career. He tells how it was prepared by the Caverres of the Rio Orinoco. It was made from the tree, of the same name, which has neither leaves nor stem, and grew only in the stinking mud of the water of a stagnant swamp. The hell brew was prepared by washing the root, cutting it in pieces, and boiling it in a cauldron or gourd over a slow fire. The most useless and ill-favoured women of the tribe were made to take on this job of witch-brewing. Each old woman stooped over the pot till the vapours killed her. Then her place was taken by another. As the mass coalesced the danger increased; for the old woman had to press the leaves till the juice was all extracted. When she could stand no more, another old crone came to boil the liquor, and this went on in relays, till its bulk was reduced by two-thirds. Then the surviving crone called the chief of the tribe to examine and prove the distillation.

A boy would cut his arm or leg, just touch the tip of a sharpened stone in the *curare* and place the poisoned point near the flowing blood. If the blood drew back, the poison was good. If it only stood still, and ceased to flow, the brew needed more boiling. An arrow dipped in the concentrated poison kept its virulence for many years, and needed only to be wetted in the mouth before use. There were few antidotes, and those doubtful. Gumilla said that a bit of common salt in a person's mouth was an antidote to the injection. (As I said in the footnote *infra*, this is not so.) Ulloa suggested sugar-cane water. Pauw says that *curare* poison on arrow-tips was tried in Europe, 150

[1] Common salt is said to be an antidote; but experiments have not borne out its alleged efficacy. The strongest curare is made by the Brazilian tribes of the Rio Papura, and much of it is made along the Rio Tocantins.

years after the poison had been made, and the toxins proved still virulent, much to the amazement of the experimenters. Hardly any of its dreadful Borgia potency was lost in the passing of a century and more.

Southey, the old English poet who wrote the above, has, however, misquoted Cornelius de Pauw, the Hollander miscellanist, who was in this case speaking of the terrible toxin of the manchineel or mancinella, and *not* curare. He wrote, in his *Recherches Philosophiques sur les Américains*, published at Berlin, Germany, in 1770:

At Leyden, Holland, in 1744, arrows poisoned with curare were brought from South America by the famous traveller, Monsieur Condamine, by him the points were used to prick two chickens, in the presence (of three Hollanders mentioned). The bird that had not been made to swallow sugar (an alleged antidote) died in six minutes. The bird that swallowed sugar died only some minutes later.

Pauw theorized that perhaps it was the cold climate of Holland, in an icy January, that prevented sugar from being an antidote:

As had happened at Cayenne, in French Guiana, where men and animals wounded with curare-tipped darts had had their lives saved from the action of the venom. The sugar acts on the blood the instant one swallows it, because the vivacity of the curare does not give the stomach time to digest the sugar.

However, whatever saved the lives of the men and animals at Cayenne, about 1760, it could *not* have been sugar. Pauw gives a curious account about curare which he says he took from "old manuscript memoirs":

The source of curare is a Liana, or *Bejuque*, which grows in the swamps or inundated lands. (Bejuque is a French variant of the Indian-Antillean word *Batuco*, meaning a creeping, or twining old plant.) The manuscripts I have seen say it has four-petal flowers, with fruit shaped like small beans inside a pear-shaped capsule. The root of this liana is dug up in the autumn, cut up in round slices, and slowly cooked in great *marabous*, or Indian cauldrons, until the juice thickens to a syrup. The effluvia and vapours are fatal, during the brewing, to any who receive them in the mouth, or nose, and that is why the Indians use decrepit and useless old women, who will not be missed if they are killed by them.

He says that the Ticuanas—naked tribes of savages who live by hunting in Brazil and western Amazonas, even to-day—use over thirty kinds of pounded herbs to increase the virulence of the curare, whereas the Caverre Indians of the Orinoco use only the liana itself. The concentrate of curare is tested by dipping an arrow-point in fresh blood. If instantaneous coagulation of the blood does not follow, the brew is returned for further distillation, and over the fire is stirred with a wooden spoon. The Ticunas and the Caverres are said to have used this fearful poison only for hunting wild animals, such as monkeys for the pot, and never on human beings; but the formidable Caribs used it to kill humans in their wars and even private quarrels.

Curare was either shot from bows, or blown with the mouth from a *sarbacane*, or native blow-pipe made from a reed hollowed out by ants who feed on the pith. He adds:

> When blowing it from a *sarbacane*, the savage takes care to wet the dart with spittle, when he puts the blow-pipe in his mouth. For the poison acts only when mixed with blood, which it coagulates on the instant. It acts on blood as does milk mixed with a little vinegar. Monkeys, hit by the curare-tipped darts, die as they fall from the boughs of trees. I have been told that when the game is eaten, the tip of the poisoned dart is found under their teeth, just as one finds small shot in the mouths of shot hares and partridges."

Curare poison was first brought to England from the forests of Guiana by the famous English traveller and Rationalist, Sir Walter Raleigh, in the reign of the royal pervert and boorish Scottish pietist, James I, Stuart king of Great Britain. There is reason to suppose that either curare, or the deadly venom of the West Indian *manchineel* tree, of which we spoke, *supra*, was used by the infamous Italian Renaissance Borgia family some years after the discovery and conquest of Brazil and the Spanish Indies. Tradition has it that one of these diabolical tree poisons was used in a ring, called the "anello della morte" (ring of death), which played an infamous part in the campaign of political murder, by the Borgia Pope of Rome, Alexander VI, and by his daughter, the beautiful poisoner, Lucrezia Borgia. (Of course, Popes are *deemed* celibates!) This ring was elaborately ornamented, and worked in gold, and at the back of the bezel was hidden a sharp needle point. When the murderer shook hands with his victim, he pressed a certain part of his ring, which operated a spring connecting the needle with a cavity behind—on the principle of the serpent's fang and poison bag. The needle point slightly scratched the skin of the victim, and injected a dose of poison, but so imperceptibly that the victim did not know what had happened. These ancient Venetian rings are rare, to-day, and need the most careful handling, since, in the case of manchineel, whose venom is potent for a century or more, the poison is found adhering to the rusty needle, or is still within the hollow of the ring. A person in poor health who unconsciously caused the spring to work when he put on the ring of death, would die in a short time. (Curare venom lasts many years, but it is not known if the viability of the poison extends over 150 years, as in the case of the poison of the terrible manchineel.)

The Borgias hailed from Spain, and were in touch with all "novelties" of this sort, imported from the "Spanish Indies". In London, in 1935, a newspaper advertised for sale to curio collectors, a splendidly decorated "poison" cabinet which had been a present from Cardinal Cesare Borgia, son of the Borgia Pope, to his sister, the beautiful Lucrezia, infamous, as I said, as a poisoner. The cabinet was of ivory decorated with bronze, crowned with a handsome clock which ticked away the victim's numbered hours. Hidden in the lock of this rare period piece was a poison receptacle, which, said the advertisement, "still functions to-day". Marks drawn on the wood with a dagger point contained the secret of the subtle poison used to remove "undesirable" folk. As a mark of gratitude, the cabinet had been given to Tsar Nicholas I of Russia, by Cardinal Ferdinand de Medici, for "the Tsar's protection of Roman Catholics in Russia". It remained in the Tsarskoe Seloe palace till 1917, when, in that year of the Russian Revolution, it was smugggled out in a haycart by some old Russian grandee who conveyed it to Finland, and then to Berlin and London.

If this subtle poison were curare, the reader will have noted what I have said about the passing of many years in no wise lessening its lethal potency. Curare was probably among the virulent toxins imported from Italy into France in the reign of the "Sun King", the degenerate sybarite, Louis XIV. When his own life was threatened by the machinations of a "Chemical Society", whose members were debauched women, Jesuit and Franciscan monks, and high society ladies and nobles, the police of Paris were prodded into action and found that this society made many thousands of gold livres making and selling poisons to fashionable folk and socialites of that day in France. Arsenic and, probably, also curare, figured among the "removers".

Curare has one devil plant congener (in the Transvaal, South Africa) that matches it. It came into notice in March, 1931, when a South African newspaper cabled to London:

> The deadliest poison known to science has been found by Dr. H. H. Green of the Onderstepoort Laboratory. One drop of it is so deadly that it can kill no fewer than 10,000 men! It is 5,000 times deadlier than strychnine, for one-thousandth part of a grain is enough to kill an adult. The scientific name of it is *adenia*, and it comes from a bulbous plant, or herb, growing in the Transvaal. A gang of white railroad workers, making a railroad along the Pienaars River, found the herb and tested the bulbs to quench their thirst. One who swallowed the juice started to foam at the mouth. He was rushed to hospital and died almost immediately. All the rest became violently ill. Dr. Green ordered two natives to cut up the bulbs under his supervision. The fumes from the leaves made them unconscious and their lives were saved with great difficulty. The poison is so subtle that it leaves no trace in the organs of its victims, and another doctor says it would be untraceable after death. The South African Government has ordered that the process of manufacture shall be kept a secret.

Baron Alexander von Humbolt tells of his experiences with *curare*:

> The Otomacs (of a savage clay-eating tribe of Central Venezuela) often poison the thumb-nail with curare. A mere scratch of the nail is deadly if the curare mixes with the blood. We obtained a specimen of the climbing plant[1] from the juice of which curare is prepared, at Esmeralda in the upper Orinoco; but, unfortunately, we did not find it in blossom.

[1] It is evident that more than one method and plant is used in brewing curare.—AUTHOR.

Schomburg found it among the Caribs of Guiana, but they do not know how to make it. Curare seems to have the effect of paralysing voluntary muscular movement, while the heart and intestines continue to act. Boussingault, a chemist, asserts there is strychnine in it, contrary to the popular belief.

And strychnine is found, be it noted, in *strichnos gardnerii*, a plant growing naturally in tropical Brazil, where, also, curare is manu-factured in a peculiar way. Like most powerful poisons, curare is probably also a powerful medicine. Its styptic or blood-stopping, properties might render it a valuable treatment for hæmorrhage, or the rare blood disease called hæmophilia, which has afflicted various royal familes of old Europe whose inbred stock has run down to degeneracy, such as the Romanoff's of old Imperial Russia, or the Bourbon family of the late Alfonso, ex-King of Spain.

Dr. Bach, in *Revista do Museo Paulista* (of São Paulo) tells how the Amazonian Indians, the Guiacas of tropical Brazil make curare. They use two jungle plants: the *uirari* and *icu*. Strychnine is the principle of *uirari* (*Strychnas castelmæi*). When the time comes to prepare the poison, three men are chosen by lot, the medicine man presiding over rites of a religious sort. A slow fire is made and two big gourds, one large and one small, are filled with a chocolate-coloured brew. The smaller gourd, half-full, is stirred for three hours, till the whole of the brew has been used up, and the poison distilled. The man who stirs the pot over the fire eventually falls unconscious, his place being taken by No. 2 man, who endures the ordeal for a shorter time of one and a half hours, since the poison grows more concentrated. The third man takes over and stirs the brew for one hour, till he, too, goes out—stupefied. By this time, the brew is the colour of bog oak. All this time the tribes carefully remain to windward, so that the deadly fumes can blow away into the forest. They squat on a slope over-looking the wizard's cauldron. So potent is the infernal essence that, says Bach, two boatmen who were wounded in the legs by arrows shot from ambush by the river Tapajos, died in five minutes. Artificial respiration may cure the victim, if taken in time; but so deadly is the poison that Indians on the war-path in the Brazilian jungle take great care to carry the curare-tipped arrows in special sheaths, while the brewed essence itself is borne in specially-shaped jars, by special warriors, who take great care to watch out for obstacles on the jungle-paths. If one tripped and cracked a pot and the leaking liquor came in contact with a lesion in the skin, the jungle apothecary would have one fewer customer for his salves.

Brazil's dreadful poison plants are well matched by her terrible insects and snakes. It was aptly conceived by H. G. Wells to make the protagonists of one of his lurid short stories: the *saubas*, or traveller ants of Brazil, who in Well's "sci-fantasy", as the United States "pulps" call it, under the leadership of intelligent and deadly ants with brains, overran and depopulated all west Brazil, annihilated her armies and "ironclads", and prepared to invade Europe from the parts of Para and Rio. Indeed, every insect in Brazil stings and lances like the old-fashioned medical saw-bones of Dickens's early day, who had to get in his hand somehow, and acquire his fearful and wonderful technique recorded on both his own and other people's tombstones! The difference is that some of the fearful insects of Brazil and other regions of South America do *their* blood-letting with far greater skill than the old English surgeon of a country infirmary who ordered the porter-dresser to hold down the roaring patient by force while the surgeon slit open the patient's gizzard on the operating table and bathed his "scientific" hands, in almost old Aztecan fashion, in the patient's very heart blood! Why, you never feel the vampire bat at *his* blood-letting till you wake up in the chilly South American dawn! Nor has the vampire bat ever been known to tell the patient that it hurt the operator more in his moral feelings than it did the sufferer, who would scarcely be consoled by the fine mural tablet later put up in the back aisles of the local cathedral, to the memory of the said surgeon, and his mortal "triumphs" of technique.

However, let not my shuddering reader be too much harrowed. I shall mention only three insects and an arachnid, and make a passing reference to a queer type of fire-fly who plays, in regard to a jungle lizard, a part similar to that played by the pilot fish in regard to the shark. This fire-fly emits, from an organ in the middle of the head, red and green lights signalling to the lizard the approach of a man on the jungle trail!

No homeless wanderer, or travelling Syrian pedlar, or other sort of horsed packman in the woods of the cattle states of Goyaz, or the remote *sertão* of the Geraes, ever stays a night in any old wooden shack he may chance on in a clearing of the forest. Not if he knows the country and is wise!

Comes the topaz night of brilliant Brazilian stars, and out of a cranny in the hut, or from under the rotten flooring creep a hideous army of really appalling insects called *os Barbeiros* (the barbers). They are brown and black in hue, and pilled with red bands on the thorax and head. Moreover, they are the barber-surgeons of the Brazilian entomological world, equipped with borers and drillers, probes and lancets, pinchers and pliers which, too, are poisoned with a deadly *bacterium*. A dog or man is all game to them. At first, the bite produces no pain. The bite, too, leaves no great mark, but, afterwards, when the deadly pathogenic germ—a trypanosome, which the barber carrier bears as host—gets to work, one may wish that one could die immediately. Death surely comes to children who are bitten, and sleeping sickness to adults. Anyway, the affects are extremely serious.

O Barbeiro has a cousin in the llanos of the province of Cundina-Marca, Colombia. He is called the *Cicada of Death* (La Cigarra de la Muerte), and a nightmare vision is he! Even the hardened and acclimatized Meta Indians, not to speak of the fierce *llaneros* who, as Don Roberto said of the gauchos of the Argentina of his day, hold it merit of a man not to be mean of his throat when the conquering soldier comes to cut it after the losing of the battle, are scared to death of this demon of Satan, lord of flies! About 5 inches long, the *Cicada of Death* is a large moth with grey and mottled wings, which wings are laid *parallel* to the thorax. But it is the diabolic head, huge and loathsome and out of all proportion to the body that makes *gringos* from London or New York, and caballeros from Caracas and Antioquia, and also the wild Indians of the Orinoco plains, think of their sins and ultimate destination. One man who met, but was not seen by this horrid antediluvian world denizen likened his skull to the head of a Mesozoic Age saurian!

Said the Colombian: "Behind this devilish head, *señor*, is a long spear or probe. *Por diablo*, this demon out of hell flies heavily, bobbing up and down like a cork or bottle on the sea, and if it sees a man, who sees it not, it lights on his skin and lances him. Men die insane in a day and night of his bite . . . and, *señor*, if an Indian sees it in the paths of swampy woods, he at once casts himself on the ground in terror, hoping by all his tribal gods that the demon *Cigarra* will not see him."

Anyone stung by *La Cigarra de la Muerte* will, say the Indians, die insane in less than 24 hours.

The second is a grub, found only in very remote parts of the forests of Amazonas, which is said to have the property, when eaten, of renewing the youth and vitality of the most worn-out and jaded Indian. It is soft and fat, and far from appetizing, being very oily and saponaceous in taste. It clings to a tree which is of a similar species to the famous Australian iron-wood, or jarrah. The eyes are extremely minute and the head is equipped with a hooked beak. It bores round holes into the extremely hard wood and not, it is said by the Indians, by using its beak[1]

The third is in the species of Brazilian ant called the *sauva*. But I speak of an uncommon and terrible species and not of the *sauva*, and his cousins, the *Cuyabanas*, marching in armies of billions across the Matto Grosso territories to be halted by none, while great snakes, poisonous reptiles, and the fierce jaguar—*el tigre*—fly before them like the wind. Hosts of birds bring up the rear and gobble up the ants in millions. No, it is of a terrible *red ant* found in the *sertão* of the Matto Grosso!

These ants sense the coming of a man on horseback, or of a yellow steer, across the wilderness of scrub and jungle, shimmering in the

[1] Brazil, in the immense Amazon woods of *el Infierno Verde*, has a gorgeous bird of which no zoo has a specimen, with plumage like that of the Birds of Paradise of New Guinea. At times of the year, the birds vanish—where, no Indian knows, or can find out. But the lore of the Indian has it that the birds dig up colouring matter of mineral origin which they eat to enrich their blood and form the magnificent plumage. Even the *morpho rhetinor*, that gloriously blue butterfly found in deep woods in both central and northern South America, renews its energies by feeding on foul carrion. Morpho is caught by Indians using very long poles from the tops of the tallest trees.

heat-waves of the blazing sun. Grouping themselves on boulders near their nests, these terrible red ants form up in fighter squadrons, and, flying in arrow-head formations, give chase to the appalled *gaucho* on horseback. The horses of the Brazilian pampas know their deadly peril. They need no whip or spur, but, with nostrils distended and eyes glaring in terror, they rush towards the nearest water. On come the ants, foam flecks from the jaws of the terrified horse, his eye-balls glare. The rider crouches low on his mane and withers. The hoofs drum the earth, while the gaucho prays that his horse's feet may not stumble into a burrow. Faster than Mazeppa's horse, he tears across the wastes. Unhappy horse and rider, if he catch his fetlock in a hole and throw his rider! The terrible red ants, behind, can eat a carcase to the bone, in 20 minutes! The horse rushes for a river flowing through a gorge which cleaves the *campo cerrado*. His breath now comes in pants. Even as he plunges into the stream an advance battalion of the red demons are on his back. He takes the water, and his rider slides off his back and swims and ducks, holding the horse by the crupper. Overhead fly the ants. They sting like demons from hell, but the man dives under, remaining submerged till the red demons give up the chase. Running water is not to be overcome by any—even antediluvian—insects!

I have no space to enlarge on the ways of the terrible praying mantis of the green wood whose "dame" attracts him, then bites his head in two and feasts only on the brain; nor on the fire-caterpillars —called tataranas—whose hairs, for hours afterwards, burn the body touching them; and I have only a few words for the tarantula whose habit is to lie doggo in one's boots, all the chilly night. His sting is diabolically poisonous and he is as hairy and ugly as the very Devil! Yet, I must not pass unsung the memory of the red demon ants' great ally in the *catinga* and *campo cerrado* of the Matto Grosso. I speak of a strange, fearsome, horned boa constrictor who lies hidden in the foliage of a great forest tree watching for an unwary Spanish steer to wander his way. Be that steer as fierce as the yellow bull of the Venezuelan *llanos*, descendant of the old Spanish cattle, who charges at sight any unhorsed, or unmounted man, forcing them for their lives to climb trees, the boa will yet catch him, coil rapidly round his chest and throttle his throat till his bones crack and his eyes stand out of his head as he gasps his life away. Slowly he dies and the red ants will eat all that is left.

One other part of the strange Matto Grosso, on the approaches to the Highlands of the old Hy-Brazilian-Atlantean race, demands wariness of any caught out in its waste after the dark hours. Such a roamer need take care to keep well within the circle of the heat and rays of the camp fire. Soon after night has fallen, hairy monsters, nearly as big as a small bantam cock, sidle out of the darkness of the scrub and, with crab-like gait, side-step towards the camp fire. As the dancing light of the flames falls on these unearthly beings, their eyes gleam like Burma rubies. They halt. Then they begin to advance boldly. Your eyes have now pierced the darkness. As you realize what these things are you shudder violently and wonder if the man was right who speculated that these creatures are not native and indigenous to our planet, but were borne here from far in space.

They advance boldly, then they halt, and scuttle backwards, and, as they do, their colour seems to change. When one's eyes have pierced the shadows, one sees what these horrible things are. One's hackles rise and one's flesh shudders. They are *huge spiders* of a type as unknown to science as the black troglodytes of the approaches to the dead Hy-Brazilian-Atlantean cities are to ethnologists. They have armoured shells like land crabs on some desert Pacific island where, as Masefield said, the pirates "had a thoughtful way with mutineers of makin' 'em maroons" and the land crabs were left to repel any who came to anchor in Los Muertos bays. True, these monstrous Matto Grosso spiders have no power to harm while the camp fire burns; but if they got near enough to sting a sleeping adventurer— well, the tough gaucho who has spent all his days on the edge of this weird Mesozoic wilderness and many a time has gone cattle rustling into the scrub has known men to die of their venom in fewer than twelve hours by the clock.

Yes, there are dreadful forms of life hidden in these unknown recesses of old Brazil, despite what the writers, or old public school amateurs may say who took care not to get more than a mile or two, or, at the most, half a day's march from the safety of the navigable rivers of the *sertão*. The ogre spider and the demon red ant would prove their valour well enough. Maybe they would cause such fellows to suspect that these ancient lands are not all they seem where camp fires burn a few yards from where the waters of known and well-used rivers flow down to the sea, and boats are handy, if urgent need suggest the wisdom of not standing on the order of one's going, but of pushing on, *pronto*!

El Liberador, Simon Bolivar's legions scrambling up terrible precipices and going along appalling paths through gorges, in Gran Colombia, which swallowed up man and beast, met horrible tarantulas and spiders of huge size, squat and purple, whose bite killed a horse, and a soldier snail whose bite was also fatal. All these monstrosities of Nature were encountered, in an earlier day, by the Spanish and German conquistadores on the El Dorado trail with Velser.

In the forests of Brazilian Guiana are insects that act as living semaphores to a lizard. These queer insects emit red and green phosphorescent lights from chemi-luminescent organs in the middle of their heads. These lights they use to signal to the lizard when enemies are about. What reward the lizard gives them in return one does not know.

CHAPTER EIGHT

NEW LIGHT ON ATLANTIS FROM THE WORLD'S OLDEST BOOK

"Science schooner, *Meta* (Husum), with diving bell, is searching sea bed,
off Frisian Islands, for Atlantis." (*Press cable*, July 1950.)

IN THE first chapter of this book I have drawn up a corner of
the veil of mystery that, for thousands of years, has hidden the strange
fate of drowned Atlantis-Aere, or that great northern extension of
Greater Atlantis which the Greeks knew as Hyperborea, the fair land
beyond Pliny's "Aquilonian" glacier, which included what is the
Iceland of our own day. As the reader will have seen I have tapped
the virginal sources of West Indian folklore. In these stories, still,
to-day, told by negro and Carib women, are crystallized the traditions
and memories of their very remote ancestors who were eye-witnesses
and endured the tortures of Hades when the Great Cataclysm disrupted
and sank to the bed of the ocean that great continent ranging from
modern Trinidad, of the British West Indies, to and probably far
beyond the land of modern Eire. The fair gods of white Atlantis
retreated to the twilight world of dead deities, and the god Set,
Saturn, Thoth, or the Tauth of Tahiti—he was known by all these
names—became lord of the flaming hell and underworld where he
ruled the demons and the damned souls, under the name of Satan or
Lucifer of the Hebraic-Christian mythology. In the old Egyptian
Pantheon, he became the Soutekh of the Hyksos divinities, being
given the head of a sinister and unknown monster.

I have now to present the reader with certain remarkable revelations contained in what must certainly be the oldest book in the
world, far older than the frequently re-edited and codified Hebrew
Bible, and probably contemporary with the more archaic parts of
the bible of the Quichés of old Yucatan and Guatemala, known as
the Popul Vuh. It is a book of which the scholars of our own
day are completely ignorant. Moreover, it carries the implication
that the ancient British Isles became the home of the refugees who
fled on rafts, in ships and even by air, in ages when the higher caster
of Atlantis knew the secrets of what is called levitation. (Among
modern North American or Red Indian tribes, to-day, there are
traditions recording the landing on American shores of both men
and women who appeared *flying* into their American skies from the
east, over the western ocean, or Atlantic.)

In Britain, to-day, as on the hills and downs of Wiltshire, and
at Stanton Drew, near Bristol, these Atlantean refugees' descendants
left those circles and white horses carved in the chalky turf, and
those avenues of stones connected with post-cataclysmal cults of

water; and, on the hills of north Gloucestershire, with human sacrifices of atonement and fertility rites. All of them, here, as on the plains of the Mississippi, or the Ohio, or in the sierras of the western states of the United States of America, betoken degradation and degeneration and the paranoia which reached a revolting climax in the land of the Nahuas and the Aztecs. At their best, these ancient remains, as at Avebury, Stonehenge and Stanton Drew embody astronomical cults commemorating the life of the fair gods in that genial Hyperborean land of choric dances to the strains of the cithara and lutes, in and around the round temple, blazing with gold and jewels dedicated to the worship of *Vira*, the sun, or, as the Greeks call him Hyperion, or the Latin Apollo. At their worst, murder and madness. Life and reason had reeled under whatever cosmic bodies caused our earth to oscillate violently through an angle of about 90 degrees, so that pole and equator changed places till the earth began the gyroscopic precession back again to its approximate former position. Or it may have been a collision with a tremendous comet as Ignatius Donnelly and Comyns Beaumont contend, or the fall of a lunar body.

Whatever the cause or the time in which the Great Disaster befell our earth, we have, from the ancient men and women of a white European race closely allied to the Angles and the Saxons— our own English race—an eye-witness's and intensely moving and dramatic story of the horror of the skies and the dreadful night into which the Northern hemisphere and some part of ancient South America were plunged to perdition.

Our story of these revelations, goes back to the year 1869, when there was living at Den Helder, in Northern Holland, facing the ancient Frisian island of Texel, a certain Cornelis Over de Linden, *rijkshelling-baas* ("boss", or master shipwright of the Royal Netherlands Dockyards). In his family, for generations beyond memory, there had been handed down to the eldest sons a very old manuscript—an ancient family heirloom which none could read or understand. Cornelis Over de Linden knew just as much of the origin of the curious document as he did of what it contained. And that was nothing!

Its uncial-like, or old Gothic sort of script seemed as mysterious as its subject. He knew one thing, however: that, for many generations in the Over de Linden family, there had been strict injunctions that the manuscript be kept carefully preserved and free from harm or damage. This ancestral trust had descended from father to eldest son for many centuries.

Cornelis's grandfather, *Dee Heer* Andries Over de Linden, died at Entkuisen, aged 61, in April, 1820, before Cornelis came of age. So the manuscript was taken care of, till Cornelis's majority, by his aunt, Mrs. Aafjie Meylhof. However, it was not till August 1848, that Cornelis had the manuscript from his aunt, who, for twenty-eight years, kept it in her house. She had been given it by her father, Andries Over de Linden, on 15th April, 1820, just before he died.

Nearly twenty years passed by, till, in 1867, Cornelis Over de Linden was for some reason impelled to hand either some part or the whole of the manuscript to Dr. Eelco Verwijs, librarian of the Provincial Library at Leeuwarden in Friesland. Verwijs was struck with the archaic script and formed the impression that it was an old Frisian family chronicle. He thought that the language of the manuscript was very old Frisian, while the lettering suggested runes, or some form of lapidarian and archaic Greek. It had thirty-four letters, with three forms of *a*, and *u*; two forms for *e*, *i*, *y*, *o*; and four pairs of double consonants: *ng*, *th*, *ks*, *rgs*.

Verwijs got Over de Linden to permit him to make a copy of the whole manuscript, and the Frisian Society—for the study of Frisian philology, history and antiquities—showed itself unwilling to risk any money on the translation, editing, production and publication of a document, which it clearly suspected might be a hoax or forgery. It had nothing to say when a *Gedeputeende* (a kind of deputy states alderman) of Friesland commissioned Verwijs to edit a complete copy of the old manuscript. The Dutch are, to some extent, a canny and often far from open-handed race, being in that respect like the Caledonians of the kingdom o' auld Scotelan'; so nothing was said about who was to foot the bill for the job.

The whole affair would have fallen to the ground and the old manuscript been left to parch in the weltering winds of auld Friesland, had not Dr. J. G. Ottema come forward and, being convinced of the genuineness of the old manuscript, put his hand in his pocket and had the manuscript published. He titled it: *Thet Oera Linda Bok*.[1]

How was the discovery received in Holland?

The answer is that, here, as in other lands, the historians and the archæologists and antiquarians showed all that eager haste and great joy to rush to welcome a new discovery which the tribe customarily evince in the exalted academic and august learned societies and circles of other lands, on both sides of the Atlantic. Without troubling to examine the document, many of the whiskery gentlemen—it was, of course, the age of "whiskers all down to here", as a certain Titty Fal-lal announced on the London music-hall stage—roundly called it a hoax. Some of them advanced a queer theory that the perpetrator must have been living around the year 1775. This remarkable pronouncement was made, apparently because a thirteenth-century copyist of the *Oera Linda Boek* had warned his posterity to keep the book

[1] *Thet Oera Linda Bok*, naar een handschrift uit de 13 de eeuw bewerkt (Leeuwarden), vertaald, en uitgegeven bij Dr. J. G. Ottema, mit vergunning van den eigenaar den Heer C. Over de Linden, aan den Helder. *Idem:* Geschiedkundige anteekeningen en ophelderungen bij Thet Oera Linda Bok. " (Leeuwarden, 1872.) (*The Oera Linda Book* compiled from a manuscript of the thirteenth century and translated and published by Dr. J. G. Ottema, by permission of the owner, C. Over de Linden. With the elucidation of a historian's annotations.) J. F. Overwijn, in 1941, published a new edition, with a 57-page introduction, and in Dutch and old Frisian.

from the eyes of *påppekappe*—the old Norse and Frisian word for Roman Catholic monks—who, with sweet words, would endeavour to nobble the manuscript, destroy it, and doubtless for the good of the copyist's suffering soul condemn him in a yellow jacket to purge his sins in a place where he could sizzle like a hot potato. Clearly, then, the gentleman who faked the *Oera Linda Boek* must have been an anti-clericalist associated, as everyone knew, with the free-thinking school of the French Encyclopædists and all those Gallic philosophers of the eighteenth century of prose and reason, tinctured with that hatred of monasticism and Roman Catholicism which culminated in Voltaire's famous: *Ecrasez l'infâme.*

Among the Dutch sceptics was Professor Vitringa who, in the *Devanter Courant*, wrote twelve letters about the *Oera Linda Boek*. He started out by disbelieving in its authenticity; but he was candid enough to admit that: "I cannot find but that the facts related in the *Oera Linda Boek*, so far as they can be controlled by regular history, are not untruthful."

But leaving on one side, for the moment, the questions of literary controversy revolving around the *Oera Linda Boek*, let us see what it contains. As both the older Dutch and Frisian versions are long out of print, and William R. Sandbach's English translation made in London, in 1876, is to be got neither for love nor money to-day, I think it worth while to give pretty full extracts from the *Oera Linda Boek*, with an adequate summary of contents.

The book was written, in different ages, widely sundered, by more than one author, and, in the long passages of time, re-copied. The first part of the book is headed by a letter written by Liko, surnamed Ovira Linda, in A.D. 803, which would be about the time when the Anglo-Saxon king, Egbert, was at the court of Charlemagne. The Frankish emperor was then planning to evoke the ghost of the Roman empire, with the aid of the Roman pontiff, Leo III, who had thrown off the Eastern Empire of Byzantium, because it was then held by a woman, the Empress Irene. In A.D. 804, Charlemagne had ended a war of thirty years against the Saxons, drafting many thousands of them out of their own country into Flanders and Northern France.

Liko introduces the first part of the book with a "warning":

> Beloved posterity, for the sake of our dead forefathers, and of our sweet freedom, I implore you a thousand times never to let the eye of a monk (*papekappe*) look on these words and writings. They speak sweet words (*Hja sprêkath swêta wirda*) and with cunning will destroy in an underhand manner all that belongs to us Frisians. They do so in order to obtain rich prebends (*rika prebende*), for which they plot with foreign kings who know we are their bitterest foes, because we dare speak to their peoples of liberty, rights, and the duties of princes. Therefore, do they seek to destroy all that we have from our forefathers, and all that is left of our old customs. Ah, my dear boys, I have seen them in their courts

(et hove wêst). If Wralda allow it, and we show not ourselves strong to resist, they will altogether wipe us out *(us algádur vridilig ja)*.

Written at Ljudwerd, in the year 803 of the Christian reckoning, LIKO, surnamed ovira Linda *(Liko, tonomath ovira Linda)*.

This letter is followed by another, written 453 years later, with the natural change in the language, considerable between the ninth and the thirteenth centuries. The writer is Hiddo oera Linda, and the year is A.D. 1256. Hiddo had re-copied the old manuscript on, as he says, "foreign paper", which he may have got from traders dealing with Arab paper factories in old Spain. In the thirteenth century the Moors, or Arabs, had paper factories at Valencia and Toledo, the secret of which, *via* China, had been discovered by the Arabs when they, under the Caliph Walid, conquered Samarcand, in A.D. 704. In Damascus, such paper was called "Charta Damascena". The Greeks in old Byzantium made this paper, and there were also paper factories in the march of Ancona. Such paper, by the thirteenth century, had began to supersede vellum, and we find that rag paper is mentioned, as early as A.D. 1148, by Peter of Cluny, in old Burgundy.

The ink used by Hiddo appears to be black and the letters are written between fine lines carefully drawn with lead. I have not been able to obtain a specimen of the manuscript of Hiddo, but I hope, at the time of writing this, to secure a photostat of some part of the manuscript, and, indeed, the original is still in existence. Here, clearly, is scope for the use of modern methods applied to the examination of old documents, and involving the use of micro-chemical or optical and radiological technique, such as used by scientists attached to museums or art galleries. It was stated, as long ago as 1875, that the ink used by Hiddo contains no iron, whereas after 1276, ink often contained iron so that the colour later faded to grey or yellow. That is advanced as a probability of the date of the re-copying by Hiddo. However, my purpose here is not to deal with technical matters in the manner of an American police examiner of questioned documents, but to examine the *contents* of the old manuscript.

The Frisian used is the very oldest and purer and more archaic than even that of the code of laws, called the *Fries Rjuchtboek*, said to have been drawn up by Charlemagne, prior to A.D. 814. It is a distinct dialect of Fries or Frisian, being that spoken, at one time, between the Vlie and the Scheldt. Very considerable changes of structure and pronunciation are shown between the older and later parts of the *Oera Linda Boek*. So much is understood when it is stated that the last part of the book was copied 500 years after the first.

The original writer of the earliest part of the *Oera Linda Boek* was Adela, wife of Apol, chief of the Linda land. Her son and daughter continue the chronicle. The third book of the Oera Linda chronicle was written 250 years after the first. Adela is said to have been 7 feet tall; so that these ancient white Frisians must have been among the giants of the ancient world.

Hiddo introduces, as I have said, the story of Adela, which he re-copied in A.D.1256, with a warning, ended significantly with the word *Wâk* (Watch!):

Okke, my son,

You must keep these books with body and soul. In them are the histories of all our people, and of our forefathers. Last year, I saved them in the flood, as well as your mother, and you. But they got wet and so began to perish. In order not to lose them I copied them on foreign paper. When you inherit them you must likewise copy them, and your children must do so too. They may, therefore, never be lost.

> Written at Liuwert (*Ljuwert*) in the 3,449th year after Atland (*Atlantis*) sank, or 1256, the year of the Christian reckoning.
> HIDDO, surnamed oera Linda. *WATCH!*
> (*Skrêven to Ljuwert, Nêi âtland svnken is thât thria thû sond ffvwer hvndred ând njugon ând fjvwertigoste jêr. HIDDO tobinomath oera Linda. Wâk!*)

Queen Adela shows that the old Frisians were ruled by a matriarchate, the suzeraine being the *Eeremoeder* (Earth-mother) under whom were old maidens, or priestesses, whose immediate chieftainess was the *Burgtmaad* (borough-maid), superior of the college of vestal virgins. At one time, the superior of the vestals was *Min-erva*. There were male kings, but they could do nothing without the sanction of the *Eeremoeder*. Their ancient religion was monotheistic, the First Cause being *Wralda*, the supreme ruler of the *wrald*, or world.[1] Frya, the first *Eeremoeder*, their culture heroine, was the mother of the white races; Finda, daughter of the Earth, was mother of the yellow peoples; and Lyda of the black races. The old Frisian *foddik* (vestals) kept a lamp perpetually burning in a temple.

Frya, the Earth-mother, is described as white like snow, her hair the sheen of gold as the sun shining on a midsummer morning, her eyes blue as a sleeping tarn in the mountains. Beautiful and strong was the Great Mother. She taught her children to respect themselves, and never to enslave others, for he who enslaved others would eventually be enslaved himself. Her second command was love of the brothers and sisters. Her third, freedom; without that all was deception and misery. She was equalitarian and social-minded. Frya lived and ruled the old Frisians in a holy island situated towards the setting sun. It was the paradise of the Gael and may have been some island off old Atlan-Hyperborei-Aeyre. Above the Mother was only Wralda, He who ruled the w-rald, or w-orld, the unknown central

[1] Frya's sign of the sickle with dots (and the dot in a circle or triangle with re-entrant base, with human foot attached, is also a very ancient sign of sex) appears on large rings of gold and gold trinkets and bracteates hidden in bogs, and linked with Northern European hidden treasures of the Stone and Bronze ages. The gold was intended for use in the other world! It was buried deep in the earth by the Old Vikings, or sunk in a spring where neither the cacher nor his kin could come at it. The thralls who cached it were all killed to a man, to act as *hogboys*, or spook-guardians of the hoards. The old pirates and buccaneers inherited this tradition. Frya's sign is also on a golden horn found on a road in Schleswig, in 1734.—AUTHOR.

Sun of the Universe, above all gods and demi-urges, and who is found symbolized in the sign of the stairway on glyphs and artifacts all over South America, and in most ancient Tiahuanacu, and whose name was never pronounced by the old Aztecs. The island of Frya was called Textla, or Texel.

The Earth-mother had much gold, but used it only for social purposes and to bring happiness. When Frya thought her end was near, she called her kinsfolk together in her castle high in Flyland, or Vlieland, which means "a refuge or asylum". Here, she gave them the Law or *Tex*, and when she had done this, says the ancient record, "the Earth trembled, the bottom of the isle of Textla sank, the heavens grew dark, and there were heavy explosions and reverberation of thunder. So she went up to her star, after giving her last injunction to her people: 'Make no war on your neighbours, unless they first attack you. Seek ever to bridge the gap between nations and that which religions cause among the peoples.'"

Ancient Roman statue of Nyhellena, Rhineland.

Adela says that, in her day, there were extant other ancient Frisian writings of Nyhellenia, or Min-erva.

Atland (or Atlan) which is Atlantis, she says, was the old or Ald-land, and in her day it stretched far out to the west of Jutland, and included Heligoland (Holy Land) and the north Frisian islands. The first *Eeremoeder* appointed by Frya—the Friga of our Friday—was called Fasta. (It will be remembered that in ancient Rome the *dies fastus* was that on which the prætor, or chief officer of the state, could pronounce the words: "I give, I say, I pronounce (*do dico addico*)". It was a day of judgment, and the *fasti* were calendars or records of events.)

An ancient king of old Frisia was Minno, the sea-king. His name bears a remarkable and by no means fortuitous resemblance to that of Minos, the law-giver of Crete and Cnossos, founder of the line of Pharaohs of this strange civilization, who were all called Minos. Minno, of the ancient Frisians, was a seer and a philosopher, just as Minos was in ancient Crete. Minno was born at Lindaard, wandered the world and sailed its seas, and died happily, in his bed, at Lindahem.

The *Oera Linda Boek* describes the invention of writing, which was based on the *Jol*,[1] or wheel, or apparent rotation of the sun. It, says the old book, had to be written round like the sun. Both a set—lapidarian and inscription form—and a cursive or running (writing) form were invented. I here attach, copied from the *Oera Linda Boek* the ancient forms of the *Jol* or *Juul* writing whose inventor is said to have been Frya. She called it the *TEX*[2] and based it on solar "wheel".

The "Witkoning", or Godfried the Old, the sea king, made separate numbers, says the chronicle, for the *set* (*stand*) hand and for the runic (or *run*) hand. Finda made a mode of writing "so high flown and flourished, that her descendants lost the meaning of it". (I thought at first that by Finda might be meant old Egypt and her hieroglyphs, but my friend, Comyns Beaumont, who has spent years of his life researching in the obscure byways of ancient pre-history, makes the interesting suggestion that the element *Fin* may be related to *finis*, and so denote a land at the end of the world. I suggest that, here, *Finland* is meant, a race allied to the Atlantean island helot race the Basques, and one of the oldest in Europe. Sometimes, however, the context of the *Oera Linda Boek* makes it doubtful whether by "Finda's people" any race between Central Asia and the Nile, may be understood.)[3]

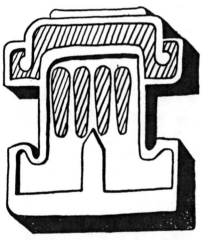

Glyphic ancient American plaque. (*Vide* footnote 1.)

We are told that the *stands*, or set writing, was a lapidarian type of writing. Exactly as was the Pauch or Phœnician, and devoted not to books or ordinary writing or literature but to inscriptions on stone. For, says the *Oera Linda Boek*: "The *stands* are engraved upon all the citadels (*Burgam*)".

---

[1] The Juul wheel of Frya had four quarters, or points. Both in old Ezekiel's fiery wheel, and in North American prehistoric mounds, the sign of four figures. In the North American mounds it is found with other solar glyphs on gold plaques, left by a curious people with aquiline noses and high caste.

[2] Tex in Texel, and our own "text". *Vide* illustation, facing page 375.

[3] Both Egypt and India are called, in the *Oera Linda Boek*, "Finda's lands".

Woden, says the book, was a chief of the Frisians. He may be progenitor of the Votans of old Central America, who, says the Central American myths, were kings of the snake people—that is, a people of the Great Cataclysm, who, through tremendous and very ancient—not to say mysterious—Atlantean tunnels, journeyed to Central America in a very remote day. But the reader will understand that what I say about Votan of the Quichés is derived *not* from the *Oera Linda Boek*, but from my own researches in American pre-history. It is a thousand pities that the other ancient Frisian writings mentioned by Adela are no longer extant; for they would have thrown light on many dark mysteries of the past.

The *Oera Linda Boek* goes on to say that the old Frisians traded with the Phœnicians (whether or not around 1600 B.C.), and it calls them

Nude priestesses, Bronze Age (*left top*), weighing souls of the dead (?).

Kadheimar, or coast men, a name which may be compared with Kadmus said to have introduced into Greece an alphabet of sixteen letters different from that previously in use by the Pelasgian races of early or proto-Greece and the Levant.

A priestess of the old Frisians, who dwelt in a castle in the island of Walcheren, on which stands modern Flushing, or Vlissingen, was she whom the *Oera Linda Boek* calls Min-erva, or Nyhellenia. It was she who settled with a colony of old Frisians at ancient Athens where a castle was founded. We are told the Greeks got their letters, *via* the Finns, from Frya, the culture heroine of the Frisians. But the writings of the Finns, as shown in the "ancient accounts written on the walls of Waraburch", show that the Greeks retained the names of the Finn letters, though the Greeks used the forms found actually in ancient Frisian writing.

Later, the *Oera Linda Boek* tells us of a Frisian colony that came from India—the Punjaub—with the fleet of Nearchus, the general of Alexander the Great, in his Indian expedition. The book adds: "But these Frisians were *not* Indians. They were descended from a Frisian colony which, after the death of Nyhellenia, or Min-erva, settled in the east of the Punjaub under the guidance of a priestess, named Geert. They were hence called *Geertmen*."

It may be here noted that Strabo speaks of *Germanes* in ancient India, who, he makes clear, were entirely distinct from the *Bruchmanes*, or Brahmins, in manners, language and religion. Alexander's expedition found in India a race of Scytho-Indians, or Indo-Scythians— white men—of European origin.

An old Frisian, Lindgert, remarks that in summer, in India, the sun stood right above the Frisian heads. As Kilpert shows, the map of Ptolemy shows two places called Minnagara, at 24° North latitude, on the western side of the Indus, near modern Karachi, and at 22° North, located somewhere in what is to-day Rajputana. The place name embodies, as we have seen, that of the Frisian *Eeremoeder*, or culture-heroine, Minna.

We get a remarkable passage in which we see that when the old Frisians voyaged from old Greece to the Red Sea, they left the Mediterranean by an ancient, pre-cataclysmal strait which still ran directly into the Red Sea! But when, after long ages, their descendants returned, as navigators in the fleet of Nearchus, to the Mediterranean from old India, *the strait no longer existed!* Nearchus used ships built by the Geertmen in India, along the Indus, and enlisted the sailors of the Frisian Geertmen to work the ships. One of these Frisian sailors was named *Friso*.

By Nearchus's orders the fleet had to be taken through the Red Sea from the Persian Gulf, and when they reached near what is now Suez, man-power of workers and sailors, reinforced by two hundred elephants, one thousand camels, and an apparatus of timber and ropes were used to haul the fleet overland to the Mediterranean. This prodigious haulage took three months to accomplish.

We also hear of one *Neef-tunis*, a Frisian sea king of Alderga, near modern Alkmaar, on the North Holland peninsula. His real name was Teunis, but he was called Neef Teunis, because he was *neef*, or cousin Teunis of the Mediterranean. Naturally, the name recalls that of Neptune, the Nethunus of the mysterious race of Etruscans, probably one of the old race of the Atlantean islanders who migrated to escape the cataclysm. The strong libertarian feeling of the ancient white Frisians is vividly shown in their ordinance, strictly enjoined on them by Frya, that prisoners taken in battle be either set free or killed. None should be slaves; "for", said Frya, "they who rob others of their freedom and enslave shall inevitably lose their own."

What other races in the ancient world reached such a lofty humanitarian altitude? Most assuredly not the much-vaunted nation of the Hellenes! One can name, indeed, no other race whose laws reached such a degree of civilization, in a very remote day.

Now we come to the vivid part of the Oera Linda chronicle in which Adela describes the antediluvian world as she saw and knew it.

Says she:

> Before the bad time came—*arge tim* (or time of the Great Cataclysm that disrupted old Atlantis, or part of that ancient land)—our country was the most beautiful in the world. *The sun rose higher* and there was seldom frost.[1] The trees and shrubs produced fruits of various sorts we no longer know and that are lost. In the fields we had not only barley, oats and rye, but wheat which shone like gold and could be baked in the sun's rays. The years were not counted, for one was as happy as another. On one side we were bounded by Wralda's sea, on which no one but us might sail. On the other side, we were hedged in by the broad Twisklând (Deutschland, or Germany), (Brede Tusscheland), through which Finda's people (probably the Finns of Finland, or the land at the edge of the world), dared not come by reason of the dense forests and the dangerous wild animals. To the east, our boundary went to the extremity of the East (*Aster-sê*)[2] Sea, and westward to the Middle Sea (*middelsê:* Mediterranean as it was before the Great Deluge over-whelmed ancient, antediluvian lands and created the Mediterranean as we now see it). So, besides the small rivers, we had 12 large rivers of Wralda to keep our land moist and to show our seafaring folk the way to His sea. Opposite to us there lay to the west Britain (*Britanja*), or the Westland, with her tin mines . . .[3]

Here, the story of Adela raises a veil and gives us a very unsuspected glance at what the Westland, or Britain of her very far day, was:

> *Britanja* was the land of exiles to which, with the help of their *Burgtmaad* (chief priestess) they had gone away to save their lives; but in order that the exiles might not come back they were tattooed with a *B* on the forehead. Those who had been banished had the brand done in a red dye, the other criminals were branded in blue.

[1] Surely a most vivid glance at our Earth in a day when she was either nearer the sun like Venus, or had a very different axial angle in relation to the ecliptic, made by the poles in relation to her ante-diluvian orbit round the sun!

[2] This seems to relate to an ancient sea that may have lain, as ancient Hindu traditions say, in Central Asia, and was the seat of a very advanced civilization linked by tremendous tunnels with old India.

[3] Procopius, (mid sixth century A.D.) speaks of war between the Varni and the soldiers of the island *Brittia*. The Varni dwelt beyond the Ister, and as far north as the Rhine and the northern ocean. The Rhine separated the Varni from the Franks. *Brittia* lay 200 stadia (about 28 miles) away, right opposite the old Rhine mouth, but *Britannia* (sic) lay towards the setting sun, at the extreme of the Spaniards' land, and 4,000 stadia (about 860 miles) from the continent. *Brittia* lay at the hindermost extreme of Gaul, where it bordered the ocean . . . Angli, Phriscones (Frisians) and Britones possessed Brittia. This curious passage either links *Britannia* with old Ierne, or Eire, or crystallizes some ancient connection of Britonland with the old land of Atlan-Hyperborei-Aeyre.—AUTHOR.

Adela proceeds:

Our sailors and merchants had many factories in Lydia (perhaps, this was N. African Libya), where the men are black, and among the distant *Krekelanders* (people of a land of creeks of locality unknown). As our country was great and extensive we had many different names.

Now comes one of the most dramatic stories that have ever been told of a doomed Earth! It is headed: "*Ho Arge tid Kem!*" How the Bad Days came:

During the whole summer the sun had been hidden behind the clouds, as though it would not look on the earth. There was a perpetual calm, and the damp mist hung like a wet sail over the houses and marshes. The air was heavy and oppressive, and men were neither cheerful nor joyful. In the midst of this stillness, the earth began to tremble as if she were dying. The mountains vomited fire and flames. Some sank into the bosom of the earth, and in other places mountains rose out of the plain. *Aldland truch the stjurar Atland heten svnk ând thât wilde hef stâpton alsa nâka wr berg ând dêlon, that ella vndere se bid vliven wêre . . . Thrju jêr was irtha also to lydande. Men the hju betên wêre macht mân hira vvnda sja. Felo landa wêron vrsunken ôra uta se resen and thât Twiskland to fâra-n halfdel vntwalt.* Aldland, (Atlantis), called by the seafaring people Atland, disappeared and the wild water rose so high over hill and valley that everything was buried under sea. Many people were swallowed up by the earth and others who had escaped death by fire perished in the waters. It was not only in Finda's land that the earth vomited fire, but also in Tusscheland (Germany). Whole forests were burnt one after the other, and when the wind blew from that quarter our land was covered with ashes. Rivers changed their course, and at their mouths new islands were formed of sand and drift. For three years this continued, but at length it ceased, and the forests became visible. Many countries were sunk under the waters, and in other places the land rose above the sea, and the woods were destroyed through half Tusscheland. Bands of Finda's people came and settled in the empty lands. Our dispersed people were exterminated or made slaves. Then watchfulness was doubly impressed on us and time taught us that union is strength.

The ancient land of the Finda, or the Finns, had a custom akin to that of the old Hy-Brazilians, or Brazilian Atlanteans in the dead cities of still unknown central Brazil. Those who have read my previous book: *Mysteries of Ancient South America* (published by Rider and Co., London, in 1946), will recall that the *bandeiristas* of São Paulo, in 1745, found on the walls and porticoes and temple friezes of one of those dead cities, ruined by a tremendous cataclysm and vulcanism that may have happened about this very time described by Adela, strange inscriptions in letters of Greco-Phoenician type, as well as in others of unknown and bizarre character, which probably record great events for the information of posterity. In the case of Finda's land, Adela tells us that the story of the Great Cataclysm was inscribed upon the walls of *Waraburch* by one, *Aldega Muga*. She adds:

Warabuch is not a maiden's city (that is, not one of those ruled by the matriarchate or gynæcocracy of Frya's, Adela's own white Frisian people), but the place where all the foreign articles brought by our sailors were stored. It lies three hours south from *Medeasblik*.[1]

Adela now relates a story of the chaotic state of old Europe one hundred and one years after the sinking of Atlantis:

. . . One hundred and one years after Aldland sank, there came out of the east a people who were driven by another. Behind us in Tusscheland they fell into quarrels, and each after disputes went his own way. Of the one people no account has come to us; of the other, we know they came into the back of *Skenland* (Scandinavia) which, particularly in the upper part, was thinly peopled. They were, therefore, able to take the country without fighting; but, as they did no other harm, we would not make war about it. Now we have learned to know them we will describe their customs. They were not wild or savage people, but, like most of Finda's race, and like the Egyptians they had priests and statues in their temples. They call themselves Magyars, and Magy is their high priest and king in one. Their priests are their rulers. The rest of the people are of no account, and are vassals to them. This people had no name, even, and we will call them Finns. Their festivals are melancholy and bloody, and so formal that we are inferior to them in that respect. But they are not to be envied; for they are slaves to their priests and still more to their creeds. They believe evil spirits are everywhere and take possession of man and beast. But of the spirit of Wralda they know nothing. They have weapons of stone. They say they can summon evil spirits, and this so frightens the people that you never there see a cheerful face. When they were well established the Magyars sought to be friends with us. They praised our language and customs and our cattle and *iron* weapons . . .

Here, we have a very early reference to the iron age; but it may be pointed out that one has found evidence deep in ancient mines in California, as well as in tumuli or prehistoric mounds in the Middle West of United States of America, which strongly suggests, whatever the conventional, dunderheaded archæologist may say, that a race, unknown, in ancient America may have used iron even in the *Tertiary Age*.

Adela goes on:

They would gladly have bartered their gold and silver ornaments for our cattle and iron. These people always kept within their own boundaries and that outwitted our vigilance. Eight years later, at the time of the *Juulfeast* (the Yule tide of the ancient white race before the early Christian monastics and missioners took it over lock, stock, and barrel and emasculated it), they overran our land like snowflakes driven

[1] Medea, born at Colchis, north of Armenia, and west of Iberia, which may be modern Georgia, was a king's daughter. She was famed as magician and rejuvenator. From her country came those Argonauts who sought the Golden Fleece, and as the *Oera Linda Boek* suggests, the gold of the Golden Fleece was washed out of the waters of the Rhine by fossickers using wool much in the same way as the sourdoughs of the Klondyke and Alaska, and the 'forty-niners in old California won gold from auriferous creeks and rivers. It is extremely curious, in view of what the *Oera Linda Boek* says of Woden, the son of the sea king, Sterik, having been enchanted with the magic herbs of the Magy and Magyars, that Medea and the people of Colchis, or Iolchos, were renowned, or notorious, for their machinations with poisonous herbs, or magical medicaments. Pharaoh Sesostris is said to have settled a colony of ancient Egyptians in Colchis, and they were sometimes called, by the ancients, the original people of Colchis—AUTHOR.

by the wind. All who could not flee were killed. In Texland, Minna, the *Eeremoeder*, called all the sailors and young men from Oost Eyland and Denmark. The Burgtmaad, Kat, of Godasburgt, being too haughty to seek aid or counsel from the Mother . . .

Now comes on the scene, Woden, eldest son of the sea king, of the white Frisians, who was named Sterik, and lived at *Aldergamude*. Woden had lived, with his parents, at Lumkamakia, near the Eeremoeder at Ostflyland:

> He had once commanded soldiers. Teunis and Inka were naval chiefs. The young warriors chose Woden for king and leader, and Teunis for sea chief or admiral. The navy sailed to Denmark, where they took on board Woden and his valiant troops. They drove back the Finns and Magyars as though they had been children. But Woden became king of the Magy and was enchanted by the magic herbs of the Magy. He disavowed Frya and Wralda, and after seven years *vanished*.[1]

We hear from the story of Adela that it was during a storm that the high priestess Kat, aboard a ship as prisoner of the Magyars, uttered a prophecy, and then committed suicide by jumping overboard. Hence, the narrow strait between Jutland and Sweden "got its name as the Kattegat".

Some time passed, and Neef-Tunis planned to sail through the straits to the Middle Sea, or Mediterranean. He wished to become a mercenary of the rich King of Egypt, as he had been before and Inka, his cousin, said: "I have had enough of all these Finda's people. I think that perhaps I might find some high land still above water—that is, some high-lying part of old Atland. If there be such an island in the ocean, I and my people may live on it in peace."

They reached a town in Spain, called Kadik (probably Cadiz, or near the location of the Atlantean port of Tartessos), "where there is a stone wharf, and here they fell into disagreement. Teunis planted a red flag on the shore, and Inka a blue flag. Every man of the companies could chose which he liked, and to the astonishment of all, the greater part of the Finns and Magyars followed Inka, who had said he objected to serve Finda's people. (The procedure is not unlike that adopted by Francisco Pizarro in 1526, on the small island of Gallo, off the coast of Ecuador, the slight difference being that Pizarro used a sword to draw a line in the sand, while *Inka*, who must have

---

[1] Woden, under the name of Votan, subsequently appeared in ancient Yucatan and the land of the Quichés and Tzendals where he and his descendants founded a great empire. The bible of the Quichés, the *Popul Vuh*, calls him "Heart of the Ocean", and his symbol was a heart. *Tan*, in Mayan, means breast, or heart. The old Quiché myths say Votan came from the east over the great waters. Where the Roman fanatic monks and the Dominicans of the Inquisition overran old Central America and tortured the natives in public plazas and autos-da-fé, the *Votan codex*, with a history of the very ancient world, vanished underground. But truth cannot *always* be hidden deep in the earth, or burnt in the flames of the Roman Catholic hell, no matter how much the Papas and the ultramontanists of the Vatican, or the subtle order of San Ignatius de Loyola may have wished and plotted to kill it. Often like the devil come to prayers it unexpectedly appears. *Magna est veritas et prevalebit*, even though, as it has been said, when no one cares a bean whether it prevail or not.—AUTHOR.

given his name to the *Inca* of Peru, used a blue flag! Here is assuredly a case where Nature and history lived up to art!

When Neef-Tunis, or Neptune, had counted the people, they divided the ships, and one sailed east, the other west, and nothing more did Adela know of the fate of Inka.

Neef-Tunis entered the Mediterranean through the straits, and, as Adela says:

> When Atland sank there was on the shores of the Middle Sea much suffering, on which account many of Finda's people, the Krekelanders (maybe they were Ionians or proto-Greeks, or Pelasgians) and people from Lyda's land (Libya) came to us. On the other hand, many of our people went to Lyda's land. So the Krekelanders, far and wide, were lost to the control of the mother. Teunis arrived on the coast of the Phœnicians, but the people there seeing their fleet looked so shattered took them for pirates and drove them off. Teunis reached the shores of the Phœnicians and landed there 193 years after Atland had been submerged. He built three cities, one of them being in an island on the coast. He walled it. Then the Punic merchants of Sidon—their god was Thyr—loaded 200 of the ships of Teunis with wine, honey and tanned leather and saddles, with bridles mounted with gold, and lent him rowers. The ships sailed to Westflyland with all this treasure and this started a regular trade, between factories (emporia) at the mouth of the Flymeer, called Almanaland (*Allemands* of the French language), and Sidon. The Phœnicians bought iron weapons which the Eeremoeder had advised the Frisians not to sell. At last, the Frisians decided to allow only seven Tyrian ships (*Thyr jar skêpa*) a year.

The story of the *Oera Linda Boek* calls the land of the Phœnicians "Palm Land", and it may be noted that some Greek historians say that they were called Phœnicians owing to the great number of palm trees—in the Greek, *Phoinikes*—in their neighbourhood. The *Oera Linda Boek* also says their priests were called *Golen*:

> The *Golen* heard there were plenty of men but few women in *Britanja*. So the Phœnicians carried off girls from everywhere and gave them to the Britons for nothing.

A curious suggestion of early Phœnician contacts with Wales is the fact that I myself possess a copy of a Welsh "wiseman's" charm or recipe for curing disease in sheep, and in the cabbalistic characters of the charm there actually occur more than one character from the *palæographic* Phœnician alphabet![1]

---

[1] The ancient Pauch or Philistine migrations may have begun, as Waddell says, in old India. They were Aryans. But it is also likely that one branch of the Pauchs, called the Kaphtorims, migrated from old Crete, or Kaphtor. Phœnician *Joppa, or Jope* in Palestine, was declared by the ancients to be antediluvian. Pliny says Phœnician Palestine was older than the Great Deluge, or the Flood that covered the earth. "Jope is on a hill, girdled by a rock, in which the fetters of Andromeda are seen. The legend is attached to the whale." (The whale is both a sign of cataclysm and of a great world war between the Dragon power of old Atlantis and a mysterious Pacific sea and land empire, associated with the trident, found in Californian graves as a symbol, and with Pan of the pan pipes, found in old Peruvian *huacas*. We may here dimly discern why the old Caledonians, linked with Atlan-Hyperborei, would not eat fish, an aversion also found among South American Indians far up the Amazon.)—AUTHOR.

The south Frisian countries had plenty of iron, says the *Oera Linda Boek*, for which the Phœnicians merchants exchanged beautiful copper weapons and all sorts of jewels. It was they who bought from the Frisians the Island on which modern Marseilles stands.

Then, by another Frisian chronicler, we are told of the coming of *Ulysus*, king of the Jonischen clans. He is identical with the Odysseus of Homer, and the story of his coming, says the *Oera Linda Boek*, has been inscribed on the eastern wall of *Fryasburt*:

> Three ships finer than any one had ever before seen came to Alamanland, and in the largest was Ulysus, king of the Jonischen clans. He had been told by a priestess that he would become king of all Italy if he could get a lamp lit at the lamp burning in Texland. He brought treasures and jewels and women more beautiful than had ever been seen before. They were taken from *Troja* (Troy), a town which the Greeks had taken. The Mother would have nothing to do with his treasures. So he went to Walcheren, and there saw the Burgtmaad, who was called *Kalip* because her lower lip stuck out like a mast-head. The maidens say he obtained a lamp from her, but it did him no good, for when he got to sea his ship was lost and he was taken up naked and destitute by another ship.

This Ulysus left behind a writer, of pure Frya's blood, who had been born in the harbour of Athens. The *Oera Linda Boek* says this man was the enlightened Cecrops, said to be son of a Frisian girl by an Egyptian priest:

> Cecrops had blue eyes, for many of our girls had been stolen and sold to Egypt. The Greeks speak badly of him, but he showed us more friendship than all the other priests put together. He was a foe of oppression and, unlike other priests, virtuous, and he valued the wisdom of distant nations. When he died, his successors soon tore up our charters, and made so many bad and unsuitable laws that at last nothing remained to us, in Attica, of liberty except a shadow of what had been.

The *Oera Linda Boek* gives a vivid picture of that homo-sexualism that is known to students of psychological aberrations as "Greek love". We get an unpleasant picture of the shameful amours of vicious and nasty-minded Hellenic priests—depraved celibates—and princes wallowing in luxuries derived from foreign trade. Old Greece was the land, be it remembered, where some men justified incest because, it was held, unnatural relations between father and daughter and brother and sister evolved the highest type of physical beauty even if it led to intellectual and moral and physical degeneration:

> They wished for boys rather than girls. One sometimes saw boys dressed in splendid, flowing robes to the disgrace of their parents and maidens, and to the shame of their own sex. If our simple parents came to a general assembly in Athens and made complaints, a cry was raised: "Hear, hear, there is a sea monster going to speak". Athens became like a morass in a tropical land—a place in which no man of decent habits could set his foot.

Here follows in the *Oera Linda Boek* the first of several curious prophecies, on which I shall make a brief comment, later. We hear that:

Frana, the Mother of Texland and the ever-burning lamp, prophesied that 2,000 years after Atland sank, there will be a great war. All shall fall by murder, and the sons will testify against the fathers, but what they have proclaimed shall endure. The spoke of the *Juul* (wheel) of the sun stood at the top when Atland sank, but after that our freedom went with it. Three thousand years after the sinking the wheel had gone deeper into the darkness and in the bloodshed over you, by the wickedness of princes and priests. But the dawn will glow and the false priests and princes will wrestle against freedom, love and unity . . . All the stories in praise of princes and priests shall be cast into the flames, and, henceforth your children shall be in peace.

Wiljo, "the maiden who came with Frethorik from Saxenmarken —both of Adela and the Frisian race"—now takes up the mantle of the ancient chronicler. She says:

Sixteen hundred years (ago) is Atland sunken and at that time something appeared that none had reckoned on. In the heart of Finda's land, upon a mountain, there lies a plain called Kasamyr (Kashmir) that is *sjeldsum* (extraordinary). There was a child born whose mother was a king's daughter and the father a high priest. To hide their shame they were forced to renounce their own blood. So the child was removed from the town to the care of poor people. As the child grew up nothing was hidden from him and in all he did he tried to acquire wisdom. His intellect was such that he understood everything he saw or heard. The people looked on him with respect, but the priests feared his questions. When he came of age, he went to his parents. They had to listen to some hard things, and to get rid of him, gave him jewels, but dared not openly to acknowledge him. Overcome with sorrow at the false shame of his parents he wandered abroad and met a Frisian sailor who was a slave and taught him manners and customs. He bought the freedom of the Frisian and they were friends till death. Wherever he went he taught people not to tolerate rich men or priests, and that they should ward themselves against false shame, which in all places warred against charity. Earth, said he, gives her goods to those who scratch her skin. All must dig, plough, sow or reap; but none are forced to do anything for another, save out of good will. Men should not seek in the bowels of the earth for gold, silver or gems, for they cause envy and destroy love. To embellish your wives and daughters there is the pure stream of the river. No man can make everybody rich, but all men ought to make each other as equally rich and happy as they can. Men should not despise any knowledge, but justice is the greatest knowledge time can teach. For she wards offences and promotes love.[1]

[1] This account of the teachings of Jes-os of Kasamyr recalls what the chiefs of the Brahmans are alleged, in one version of the pseudo-Kallisthenes' memoirs to have told Alexander the Great, in India. Mas'udi says these Brahmans took their name from Brahma, who reigned 365 years. They were vegetarians and wore a yellow thread round their necks and seven of them in the founder's days, assembled to debate that insoluble riddle that has beaten all philosophers: the riddle of man's existence, the why and wherefore of

His first name was *Jes-os*, but the priests who detested him, called him *Fo* (false, or *falx*), while the common folk called him *Kris-en*, or herder. (This is, of course, Krishna, *a man* who, like Quetzalcoatl, the old culture-hero and *man* of Central America, became transformed into a divinity; for there have been many Christs before the Jew who is alleged to have been born in Bethlehem. *e.g.*, Issa of Ladakh, Tibet.

The Oera Linda chronicle tells us that Jes-os was called by his Frisian sailor-friend *Bûda umbe* (purse), because he "was a purse of wisdom and his heart a treasure of love":

At last, he had to flee the venom of the priests, but wherever he went his teaching had gone before him, while his enemies followed him like his shadow. When *Jes-os* had travelled twelve years in this way he died, but his teaching had gone abroad. His friends preserved it and spread it to any who would hear.

Wiljo warns the Frisians to beware the tricks of priests. She said that the priests went to the land of his birth to make known the death of Jes-os, or *Jes-vs*. With guile they posed as his friends and tore their clothes and shaved their heads in pretended sorrow. We all know what happened to the teacher of the Aryan way, Buddha Guatama, when the Hindu monastics and Tibetan shamans took over his way, built monasteries, and waxed fat on the riches of the land. We, some of us, also know the parallel case of what happened when the murderer Constantine, mis-named the Great, became patron of Christianity, did a deal with the priests in old Byzantium and Rome, and ennobled the Bishop of Rome with the dignities and riches of the old pagan Pontifex Maximus, whose triple tiara, the Pope of Rome to-day wears under the dome of the Vatican and the Duomo de San Pietro.

She (Wiljo) adds:

The priests went to live in caves in the mountains, where they had hidden their treasures. They made images of *Jes-vs* which they gave to simple folk, and said he was a god, had declared himself to them, and that all who followed him should enter his kingdom hereafter, where all was joy and bliss. These cunning priests announced that poverty, suffering and humility was the door to the kingdom of *Jes-vs*, and that all who suffered the most on earth should enjoy the greatest happiness there. *Jes-vs* had taught men to control their passions, but the priests taught men to stifle them, and to become perfect by being as unfeeling as the cold stones. The priests pretended outward poverty, said they had no sexual feelings, and so took no wives. But, if any young girl had made a false step they quickly forgave her. (This reminds us of the

the world, why He who created them brought death on them, and why man was created. Their chiefs are alleged by the pseudo-Kallisthenes to have told Alexander (*Vide* the Coptic version held at Magdala, Abyssinia, by Theodore, until the British Army came on the scene, in 1868): "When evening cometh, we go to the forest near and sit down under the trees and eat all the fruit we want, with our wives. And we drink the water of the river till we have had enough," They ate one meal a day and held that the Earth was spherical.—AUTHOR.

374

satire of Chaucer against the abbey-lubber of his own day who went from town to town in mediæval England, confessing women and girls and enjoying their sexual favours, so that, as was said, a nunnery was on one hill, a monastery on another, and a foundling hospital in the valley below.)

All the way from Kashmir and the plains of the Ganges to the hills and quiet villages of old England, we found, as Wiljo says of the priests of her story: "that they told all men that to be saved they must give goods to the church". The priests so managed affairs that they enjoyed all the fun and pleasure of the married state without its responsibility. "They were rich without working":

> But the people grew ever poorer and more miserable. This doctrine that requires priests to possess no further knowledge than to speak with deceit and pretend to be pious, while acting unjustly, will come to our country also, as it spreads from east to west.

Then comes another curious prophecy:

> But when the priests fancy that they have entirely put out the light of Frya and Jes-vs then shall all classes of men rise up who have carefully preserved the truth among themselves and hidden it from the priests. The false priests shall be swept away from the earth, and there shall be neither priests nor rulers, save those chosen by the general voice of the people. Then Frya shall rejoice and the earth bestow her goods only on those who work. All this shall begin 4,000 years after the sinking of Atland and 1,000 years later there shall no longer exist either priest or oppressor.

The later part of the *Oera Linda Boek* speaks of Adela's followers and what they did. We get a curious glance at the citadel and tower of *Liudgaarde*. The tower had six sides and was 90 feet high:

> It has a flat roof with a small house on top from which they look at the stars. On either side of the tower is a house 300 feet long, and 21 feet broad, and 21 feet high, besides the roof which is round. All is of hard-baked brick, and there is nothing else. The citadel is surrounded by a dyke with a moat.

As Atlantean students know, these moats in old Atlantis, as in dead cities found in the woods of the state of São Paulo, Brazil, were features of their cities:

> The moat is 36 feet broad and 21 feet deep. If you look down from the tower, you see the form of the *Juul* (wheel of the·sun). In the ground among the houses on the south side are all sorts of native and foreign herbs, which the maidens must study as to their healing and medicinal qualities. Among the houses on the north side there are only fields. The three houses on the north are full of corn and other necessaries. In the two houses on the south, the maidens live and keep school. The most southerly house is where lives the Burgtmaad. In the tower hangs the lamp. Its walls are decorated with precious stones. On the south wall is the *Tex*." (I have given a reproduction of the Tex, of old Frisian script, facing page 416.—AUTHOR.)

On the right side of the wall were the "form-lere," on the left the code of laws, and on the three other sides were others—probably historical records. Outside the city was "a fort an hour of the sun long, and inside is a plain 5 feet below the top". These features of the city recall those described as being in Old Atlantis, in the city described in the Solon-Plato story, and by some called "Chekhon, or the Sardegon of the seven hills" (not, of course, mentioned in the *Oera Linda Boek*). (*N.B.* "Form-lere": ancient lore).

We also get an explanation of very singular sort as to what the old Greeks' story of Jason meant as the Golden Fleece:

About the Rhine, there are everywhere folks who dig holes. They get out the sand and put it into fleeces over which water is poured. That is to get the gold. *But the people are poor. Their girls wear no golden crowns!* At one time they were more numerous, but since we lost Schoonland (Scandinavia) they have gone up to the mountains. There they dig ore and make iron.

A visit to the ancient Swiss lake dwellings is described:

The Burgtmaad with three grey-headed Burgtheere (male aldermen) and three old maidens went above the Rhine and among the mountains I saw the *Marsata*. They live on the lake-sides and their houses are built on piles. This is to protect them against wild beasts and wicked people. Here are wolves, bears and horrible lions. There come the Swiss, the nearest to the frontiers of the distant Italians, the followers of *Kalta*, and the savage Twiskars, avid for robbery and booty. The *Marsata* live by fishing and hunting. Their women sew skins together, prepared with birch bark. The small skins are soft as the breasts of a woman. The Burgtmaad at Fryasburg (Freiburg?) told us they were good people and simple, but if I had not heard her speak of them first I should have thought they were not people of Frya. They looked so impudent. Their wool and herbs are bought by the Rhine people, and taken to foreign lands by the ships' captains. Along the other side of the Rhine was a great river or lake, and on this lake were also people living in houses on piles. But they were not Frya's people. They were black and brown men, who had been employed as rowers to bring home men from foreign voyages. And they have to stay there till the fleet goes back.[1]

Now before I make a running commentary on the *Oera Linda Boek*, we may give a glance at the later reception this old chronicle got in Holland. The critics and the sceptics started a hue and cry to find the nigger in the woodpile, or, in plain Dutch, or English, the man who had "perpetrated the forgery". Not a man stopped to ask himself what, in the singular circumstances of the preservation of the book, could have been the motive of the alleged forger. No;

[1] Moncius says that "in the time of Yao, the waters strayed from their courses and spread over China. Trees and plants covered the earth with a thick forest. The land was full of snakes and dragons . . . In the lowlands, men built huts on piles against the monsters. In the highlands they hollowed out caverns." In the north-west territory of Canada, the Indians say their ancient forbears built lake-dwellings on piles, like those in Switzerland, to protect themselves against mammoths and mastodons, ravaging and roaming the country long ago. (Yao deluge 2,297 B.C.?)

the savants and the clever sceptics did not waste time on any little thing like that! It was "forgery" of obvious character, and the only thing to be settled was "who dunnit?"

J. Beckering Vinckers wrote a book published at Haarlem in 1877. In it he said the *Oera Linda Boek* was written in a *waartaal* (jargon), and that the forger must have been Cornelis Over de Linden. He was joined by many of the learned, and a regular Bilstumpsismark controversy raged, of which the echoes have not even yet died away in Germany, Holland and Poland. The lack of motive on the part of the old copyist in 1256 occurred to no one. None, either, wasted one moment in bethinking themselves that he would be a damnably clever man who could have faked an old chronicle in an archaic language, vary it from age to age to suit the changes in the language, and have at his command a most recondite knowledge of the byways of ancient history, which few specialists in any age could, or can possess. None stopped to ask: "Does this ancient chronicle add knowledge where we did not possess it before?"

The controversy died down, the echoes were stilled, until, fifty years later, in 1927, M. de Jong (*Hzn*), wrote a book on the *Secret of the Oera Linda Boek*, in which he proved to his own satisfaction that the faker must have been Dr. Eelco Verwijs the librarian who, in 1869, at Leeuwarden, was the first to be shown by Over de Linden a part of the manuscript. De Jong nailed poor Verwijs' hand to the table in the manner of legionaries in the French foreign barracks at Sidi bel Abbes, who catch a comrade cheating at cards, and fix his hand to the table by impaling it with a bayonet. Verwijs, swore de Jong, must have been a visionary, a Frisiomaniac and a dilettante. In 1933, came forward P. C. J. A. Boeles, who, in a book published at Leeuwarden, swore that the forger must have been Cornelis Over de Linden. But J. J. Hof, in his book: *Verwijs en het Oera Linda Boek*, published at Leeuwarden, 1928, cocked a snook at both controversialists, and asserted that Verwijs and Over de Linden had collaborated in "putting over a fast one". Hof also dragged in a mysterious gentleman named F. Haverschmidt, of whom one has never heard, as a third collaborator in a forgery. Since then, Polish academicians have joined the fray, and Herman Wirth, who, in *Die Ura Linda Kronik* (Berlin, and Leipzig, 1934) defends the *Oera Linda Boek* from a middle point of view. He contends that it is:

> that last codification of a primitive Arian monotheism (*Arian-Oer*) whose tradition, handed down in Friesland, appears to be the oldest as to a custodian ... This family chronicle is not a forgery, but contains a kernel that is of the greatest significance for the study of Germanic antiquity.

In England, in the 1870's, the *Oera Linda Boek* had a mixed reception. An excellent translation was published by Wm. R. Sandbach (London, 1876); but the book has long been out of print, and the collector will find it extremely difficult to-day to find a copy outside a great library. A Dutch correspondent, Jules Andrieu, in the Athenæum, August, 1876, anticipates the method of a modern examiner of questioned documents, but in days with no modern scientific technique to help him. He said:

> F. Muller, a bibliographer of Amsterdam, was allowed by Over de Linden to see a part of the manuscript of the *Oera Linda Boek* which, hitherto, he had shown only to Frisians . . . He thought that the paper and ink showed that it had been written not much earlier than 1800. A papermaker, Van Gelder, of Wormerveer, N. Holland, thought the paper could not be earlier than about 1840 . . . I have found a romance by a Flemish councillor, published in 1806, which tries to prove that the Elysian Fields and Hades were in islands in the Lower Rhine, and that Ulysses left his name in the form of Flushing . . . This councillor made great use of Olaf Rudbeck and of Lipsius. Rudbeck talks of Minerva and Atlan . . .

But Andrieu fails to show how on earth such a romancer, who he clearly thinks is the forger of the *Oera Linda Boek*, could have done the job in the most archaic form of old Frisic! It is not here a question of founding a cult in the manner of the angel who is said to have delivered to Joseph Smith, of the church of Latter Day Saints, the golden plates of the book of the ancient American prophet Moroni, hidden in the hill of Cumorah, New York.

Then came an anonymous writer in the *Cornhill Magazine* of 1876. He notes the "obscurity of the book", but does not stop to consider whether a "hoaxer" could afford to indulge in obscurity and expect to "get away with it". He thought the forger had seen a re-issue of the old Frisian code of laws, published in Leeuwarden in 1782, but is forced to note that this ancient code makes no mention of Frya, or Wralda, but only of the Virgin Mary and the God, Jesus. He has a smart crack at the name *Inka*, which, omitting to see that many a true word may be spoken in jest, he said must be that of the Inca of Peru. The anonymous writer, who was probably a young Anglican parson just down from Oxford, has heard from Andrieu of the old Swedish savant, Olaf Rudbeck.[1] The forger, says the anonymous gentleman, whose Anglicanism has evidently been revolted by what he deems the "anti-clericalism and atheism" of the *Oera Linda Boek*, arrives at the ingenious conclusion that the nigger in this woodpile must have been "a man of talent and learning but no genius, who must have written the book just after the days of the Terror and the Jacobins in Paris!" But why, again, in *old Frisian*, so that the book remained lost to sight for more than a century in the bosom of a private family in the out-of-the-way spot in Friesland?

[1] Olaf Rudbeck planned a canal and was the first to discover, or at least describe the lymphatic glands. In 1675–98, Rudbeck, at Upsal, Sweden, published three prodigiously erudite volumes in Latin and Swedish, trying to prove, *inter alia*, that Sweden is really the Biblical Paradise and the Atlantis of Plato, and that "Atland eller Mannheim" (Atlantica or Manheim), was the Paradise of old Atlantis, the "nursery of the god, and the first home of the civilization of the ancients".

It reminds one of the cartoon in *Punch*, prior to 1914, before the journal turned *Scottish*, or, as we may say, *Scotch*. Two Oxford University, or Civil Service Commissions examiners are seen standing in a wood in springtime. One guy uplifts his lily-white hand. Says he: "O cuckoo, art thou but a bird, or art a wandering voice?" To him replies the other guy: "State the alternative preferred. Give reasons for thy choice."

The one man, at that time in England, whose scholarship and specialized knowledge in this field qualified him to pass judgment on the *Oera Linda Boek*, was the Rev. William Barnes, the Dorset dialect poet and authority on Anglo-Saxon philology and antiquities. (And it must be remembered that old Frisian is very closely akin to the East Anglian dialect of old England.) Barnes wrote an article in the London *Macmillan's Magazine*, long ago defunct, maybe as in so many other cases owing to a succession of poor editors. Barnes noted the name "Wr-alda", the "infinitely old", not occurring, so far as I know, elsewhere. He pointed out:

Tacitus says in *Germania*, *c.* 9, 8, that the old Germans thought there was something prophetic in women, so gladly heeded their counsels. Also, the Romans said that the Teutons had no national king at home. The *Oera Linda Boek* says that Friday (*Fryasday*) was always kept as a Sabbath: hence the notion that to go to sea on a Friday was unlucky. The Book says that business begun on Frya's hallowed day shall always end badly. The word *Stjurar*, meaning steerers or sailors, in the Book, may be compared with the Latin *sturii*, and the term *Sicambri* (Latin) with the Frisic *Seekampar*, sea-fighters. As to exiles from Europe working as slaves in *Westland*, or Britain, in the tin mines, and Britain being the refuge of outlaws who fled there, we find that the Saxon St. Guthlac, hermit of Crowland, Northamptonshire (on the border of East Anglia), had a vision in which he heard accursed spirits speak British, which he understood; because, in his wild youth, Guthlac had been exiled among the outlaws: "*mid him waes on wraec* (exile)". The tin mine slaves fled to Scotland where were other banished men, Frisians and Britons.

Barnes notes that Solinus, the Second century author of the *Polyhistor*, heard, in A.D. 150, a tradition that Britain knew that Ulysses (Ulysus) had landed in Caledonia; but he (Barnes) thought it odd that he was not given his Greek name of Odysseus, in the *Oera Linda Boek*. As to the story of Athens founded by the Frisian Min-erva, the walls of the Piræus, which the *Oera Linda Boek* says "were two horns (long walls), all the way down to the sea", those walls were built after the Peloponnesian war of 431 B.C.[1] In the *Oera Linda Boek*, it is complained that a mongrel race with Greek blood spoke bad Frisic, saying *had* for *hald*, *wra* for *wrald*, *ma* for *man*. Barnes pointed out that for two hundred years, down to the day of Japix, the Frisian poet (born A.D. 1603), the *l*, *r*, and *m*, were suppressed in West Frisic. "This, in the *Oera Linda Boek* is clear evidence of *very old Frisic. If this* Oera Linda

---

[1] The *Cambridge Ancient History* says the massive walls uniting and surrounding Athens and the Piræus were built and maintained in the fifth century B.C.

Boek *were a forgery, where did the forger take his model in the last sixty or two hundred years?"* Again, says Barnes: "In one passage of the *Oera Linda Boek* we read: 'I cannot alone cast up a *therp*'. *Therp* (thorp) was a hard-heaped mound cast up on the marshland as site for a village." He thinks that the Frisic of the *Oera Linda Boek* "is not so old as the Moeso-Gothic of Ulphilus, but older than the Frisic of Japix" (born 1603). (Ulfilas, or. Wulfia, bishop of the Goths, was author of the Moeso-Gothic Bible, the oldest specimen known of the Teutonic languages, and lived between A.D. 311 and 381.) Barnes also refers to the *Juul*, the *Oera Linda Boek's* "wheel of the sun, or Yule . . . *Yule-tid*, the night of the year's end". He also comments on the curious word *naka*, in the *Oera Linda Boek*, meaning "nighest to the skin, Saxon *nacod*, and occurring in the Northern England verb, *nake* to make naked".

Professor Albert Hermann, a savant of Berlin Universität, who wrote *Unsere Ahnen und Atlantis*, in 1934, says that the *Oera Linda Boek*, as handed down in the family of the Over de Lindens, consisted of two hundred quarto pages, of whose "very different fragments the concluding parts do not seem to be extant". He says that a member of the Frisian *Genootshaft* (society), got up at a meeting of the society, on 24th November, 1870, and said:

> The contents of the *Oera Linda Boek* are in the highest degree strange, part mythological, part historical. The language is in part very old, but there are also expressions that seem of very recent date.

Hermann alleges that the Dutch philologist, J. Beckering Vinckers, found out from pumping the members of the Over de Linden family that, in 1854–60, Cornelis Over de Linden had spent his leisure hours researching in old Frisian and ancient literature, and that Vinckers unearthed memoranda, in Cornelis's handwriting, of a list of books Cornelis had obtained. Says Hermann:

> This all appears to confirm the suspicion that between this date of the literature and the manuscript, various textual associations subsist . . . Certain passages in Volney's *Ruins of Empires*, referring to the birth of Buddha, his home and names, almost word for word repeat themselves in the *Oera Linda Boek* Chronicle . . . It seems to be proved that the whole book is the wretched bungling of the master-shipwright, Cornelis Over de Linden. But the most awkward was the sequel to the examination of the paper used for the *Oera Linda Boek* manuscript. It gave the impression of very great antiquity, and the editor, Ottema was convinced it derived from A.D. 1256 . . . . But now it turned out that, to the general surprise, the paper had apparently been artfully made old in a chimney (*Rauchsang*), and in truth was of wholly modern making, by machine, probably in a factory at Maastricht. In three pages examined, expert opinion certified, on 5 August 1876, that this paper could not be older than 25 years. That signifies, therefore, that the manuscript, cannot have been written before the year 1851, and that, therefore, the author is this same Cornelis.

Hermann goes on:

On 7 March 1876, four signatories attested on Cornelis's behalf that, particularly between 1848 and 1850, the manuscript of the *Oera Linda Boek* was known to be in existence. It had been later translated by J. G. Ottema, who edited it. Finally, there came forward a Lieut.-Commander, W. M. Visser, as witness that, on 23 December 1854, Cornelis Over de Linden had told him that he had an old *Family Chronicle*, a remarkable book preserved by him at the present time. It was not only in a foreign tongue, but written in such strange characters that, despite all his pains, he, Cornelis, could read only a few words of it. Visser recommended Cornelis to have recourse to a philologist in regard to the manuscript, and gave him some addresses for an appointment to examine it. But it did not come about, and Visser was officially hindered at that time and soon after went on furlough.

Now Hermann administers the knock-out blow:

So, for all this time, the paper of the *Oera Linda Boek* manuscript was produced before 1851 at the earliest, and a corresponding Chronicle existed? It must then have been the text of this Chronicle. But why had not Cornelis made accessible the text that has caused the publicity? Why did he produce only a transcript of it, at first? Why, soon after the meeting with Lieut.-Commander Visser, did he not resort to the philologist but withdrew himself to his writing-desk, there to busy himself with Old Frisian and other literature? The existing memoranda and the borrowings from the French Book—(Hermann here refers to *Ruines ou Méditations sur les révolutions des empires*, written by the *érudit français, le Comte de Constantin-François de Chasseboeuf*, who took the alias of "Volney" (born 1757, died 1820—AUTHOR), could certainly, in part at least, attest that and answer all these questions . . . The translation Cornelis must have made between 1855–1860 is no literal transcript, but a revision or compilation (*Bearbeitung*), or an amplification of the older *Oera Linda Boek* Chronicle. In this altered form, then, Cornelis must have offered the document. One reflects that he kept the manuscript hidden for over 50 years, in order first, in the year 1860, to lay it before headmaster Sipkins in Den Helder. It was this same (revision) that 12 years later in book form, came out from Ottema. The Philologist (presumably, this is Vinckers) stated that the *Oera Linda Boek* was therefore a pure forgery, and so the book soon fell into oblivion.

I have referred Professor Hermann's rather downright assertions and allegations to a Dutch gentleman, whom I know, who is a native of the Nederlanden Province of Frisia, knows the *Oera Linda* Manuscript and translations very well, and who happens to be connected with the family of the Lieut.-Commander J. M. Visser above-mentioned.

My correspondent wrote me, on 9th March, 1949, from den Haag, the Hague:

Dear Mr. Wilkins,

A German professor of the following of Hermann Wirth, I believe it was Kosinna, brought forth a theory; but owing to the German manner of turning everything in the (mostly wrong) direction of their *Blut und Boden* theory, we do not believe he had any proofs. To answer your queries:

(1) It is not sure if Cornelis Over de Linden ever made a copy of the *Oera Linda manuscript*, with the probable errors coming from copying a manuscript as this is; so it is not to be said if there is any truth in that allegation of Herr Professor (Hermann).

(2) We come of a family of very old Frisian stock, and many of our branch of our family, of the Vissers, were seafarers. We are the oldest branch and are not quite sure if Lieut.-Commander J. M. Visser was of our family. The "M" would stand for "Meinard" as my father and my eldest son was, and is, named. In our family papers, as they still exist, is nothing about the *Oera Linda Boek*. The "M" points to J. M. Visser as being of our mutual roots. Den Helder is a marine station.

(3) In the Frisian Library at Leeuwarden is now again the original manuscript of Cornelis Over de Linden. There is also a copy made which fell into the hands of the Germans, but which is now also back again.

(4) Mr. F. J. Overwijn has made a recent translation into Dutch, from the original. (*N.B.*—By courtesy of my correspondent I have a copy of it. It is a valuable work of research.—AUTHOR.)

(5) Somebody alleged that the paper on which the *Oera Linda Boek* was written was a fake, of modern make, originally manufactured in Maastricht, Holland, but there was never any definite proof if the specimen of this paper which was sent to the "Laboratorium" was really taken from the original. *For do not forget* that the Roman Catholics were against it, and that Maastricht all around is Roman Catholic territory, where anyone would swear to or declare anything so long as it favoured the propaganda of the Roman Church. Besides that, other persons involved, even Protestants, were hostile to the *Oera Linda Boek*, and not over scrupulous in what they said, or did, either. In Maastricht, the paper factory concerned was a very old family business in the line of paper, so that even if the paper *had* been derived from Maastricht, it may very well be that the paper had been made for centuries from the same material and by the same methods.

(6) As to alleging that Over de Linden hid *the original*: *this is impossible*: for it is known that Cornelis Over de Linden himself could not read the old script and was no great scholar either. In any case, he was somewhat "limited" in the gentle arts of writing and reading. In no case could he have read Volney, as he did not read English or French. J. Beckering Vinckers was an antagonist, *and a forger* at that! He was a freemason of high degree. My own opinion is that the *Oera Linda Boek* was and is no forgery. At that time nobody could have forged this manuscript, and especially not its story, as many things were not yet known—things recorded in the manuscript—as they are nowadays.

Professor Albert Hermann, author of *Unsere Ahnen und Atlantis* (Berlin, 1934), contends that the Thyrisburg, of the *Oera Linda Boek*, where Neftunis's men settled is not the Phœnician Tyre on the Palestinian coast, but the site of the modern Tunis, in North Africa. Here, says he, the fellow-traveller-Finns, begged that the new settlement be called Thyr, named after their god, Thyr, the northern deity we know as Thor. It was on the anniversary of this day that they disembarked.

Says Hermann:

> It was something quite different from what the *Valscher* (forger) has read into the *Oera Linda Boek*. The forger naturally believed that this Tyrus was on the coast of Palestine.

If so, can Herr Professor explain why this ancient Tyrus of Tunisia comes to bear *not* the name of Thyr, but that of Tunis, the name of the old Frisian seafarer, Neftunis? Why on earth should any alleged forger have concocted the name Neftunis, as Herr Professor hints, from that of the old, old Roman-Etruscan-Hyperborei god of the sea, Neptune of the trident?

Hermann dogmatically adds, with characteristic German arrogance:

> The *Valscher* could not have known that at that time *no* such place as the Tyrus on the Palestinian coast existed.

So, Herr Professor?

Then will you, as the wartime British Tommy said in Germany, take a "dekko" at the following?

The old Phœnician priests in the time of Herodotos claimed that the Phœnicians had an antiquity of 30,000 years. Herodotos went to this Palestinian Tyre and talked with the priests. He asked them when *this* Tyre, of the old Levant, was founded. They said 2,300 years before the day of Herodotos, that is 2576 B.C. Here is what Herodotos says:

> I made a voyage to Tyre, hearing there was a temple of Hercules at that place. I found the temple richly adorned . . . and two pillars, one of pure gold, the other of emerald, shining with great brilliancy at night. In a talk I had with the priests, I asked them how long the temple had been built . . . They said at the same time as the city was founded, and that Tyre was founded 2,300 years ago . . . I saw another temple in Tyre. It was built by the Phœnicians when they colonized an island of gold mines, which was when they sailed in search of Europe. (*N.B.* Europe in the Semitic tongue, meant land of the sunset, or *Ereb.* Arab: *Gharb.*)

Perhaps Herr Professor can produce this very clever forger out of his top hat, with conjurer-like facility? No one else, since 1870 has been able to do it!

Professor Hermann refers to the ancient Chinese Bamboo tablets, found by robbers opening a very ancient royal grave in the province of Honan, in A.D. 279. These tablets are written in the very ancient Chinese seal character, which, by the way, has been found on curious porcelain and other objects taken out of the bed of an Irish river, and denoting a very ancient Chinese trading contact with this land of immemorial western antiquity. One of these Honan grave tablets records a cosmic catastrophe:

> XVII. The Emperor Kwei. In his tenth year, and in *shin*, 29th of the cycle (1688 B.C. *circa*), the five planets went out of their courses, in the night the stars fell like rain. The earth shook, the J. and Loh (rivers in Honan) became dry.

Hermann seems to suggest that this Chinese-recorded cataclysm happened at the same time as that recorded in the *Oera Linda Boek*, and dated 2193 B.C. It is identical he says, with the sinking of Atlan. (I will venture to splinter a lance of contradiction against the jerkin of Herr Professor, in a moment). Hermann refers to a colleague named Professor Walther Penck, who was in Constantinople, now Istanbul, in 1916, year of the First World War. Penck indicated that in the old Stone Age the Black Sea was an inland sea, but that, when Aldland sank, the theatre of the catastrophe must be looked for *not* in the western world and ocean, and in the region of old Hyperborei–Atlan that lay bounded in the northern ocean, by Iceland on the north, the British Isles to the south, Old Frya's land to the east, and Scandinavia, or Skene- or Schoon-land to the south-east. No, the theatre was in the eastern Mediterranean and the Black Sea and Bosphorus, and Hellespont–Dardanelles. A catastrophe tilted the land, caused the waters of the Black Sea to flow in colossal volume and force over the lip where now is the Golden Horn and Bosphorus, and roar into the Greek Sea, where frightful scenes of devastation ensued.

He cites a Greek legend preserved by Diodorus Siculus:

> Not far from the Dardanelles lies the island of Samothrace whose people speak of a great inundation. The estuary of the Kyaneen (Bosphorus) was pierced, and after that the Hellespont (Dardanelles). Till then, the Pontus had been a sea (Black Sea), but after, by rushing waters swollen so high a mighty piercing of the Hellespont was forced. Thereby, a great part of Asia Minor, so much as lies on the sea, was flooded and a considerable part, even to Samothrace, turned into a sea. Thus we see, how, in later ages, fishermen brought up in their nets the' capitals and marble columns . . . Whole cities had been swallowed up by the sea.

But the professor talks as if there was only *one* Great Catastrophe; whereas, there were *many*, in the thousands of years, in which both Lesser and *Greater* Atlantis, section by section, were sent to perdition and the hell of old Satan-Thoth-Seth, old-time king of Greater Atlan, *and a man*, not a deity, infernal or divine! It is clearly impossible that the old *Oera Linda Boek* chroniclers did not know the difference between the western ocean and the lands of Little Asia. Not even Hermann's *Valscher* was so naïve!

It is extremely unlikely that either the catastrophe of the Bamboo annals, or that described by Diodorus was identical with that of the Aldland or Atlan of the *Oera Linda Boek*. It is very curious, however, that the late Sir Norman Lockyer, the well-known astronomer, using data derived from the secular phenomena of the precession of the

384

equinoxes, and the gyroscopic shift of the spinning axis of the earth, in relation to the plane of the ecliptic, calculated that the date of 1768 B.C., recorded in the Bamboo tablets of old China, is probably that of the erection of Stonehenge. He allowed a margin of two hundred years, before or after, for any error of calculation. Lockyer calculated that the *much* more ancient avenues and megalithic images and obelisks of Avebury were constructed about 3500 B.C., those of Challacombe, North Devon, in 3600 B.C., and those of Carnac, in Brittany, in 2900 B.C. Glass beads of Pharaoh Thotmes have been found at Stonehenge, and in other parts of Wiltshire, and their possible date may be about 1400 B.C., say, if Lockyer were approximately right, about two hundred years later than the presumed date of erection of Stonehenge, which Hermann seems to consider synchronous with the *Oera Linda Boek* cataclysm of Aldland.

My own running commentary on the *Oera Linda Boek* may interest the reader.

The *Juul* recalls the fact that, in 1891, there was found in the great bog of Jutland a remarkable and ancient hammered-out series of silver plates, on one of which is an ancient god with a wheel, and another *with an elephant*. The Danish National Museum expedition theorized that these plates were the work of a Gallic artist about 100 B.C., as the wheel was in old Gaul the sun-god's symbol; but no note is taken of the *Oera Linda Boek* story of Atlan's submersion when the cataclysm poured the turbulent waters of the North Seas over the ancient Rhine mouth, and probably severed the old land-bridge uniting ancient Britain with the European mainland. The effigy of the elephant is also ignored; and, of course, the story in Plato's dialogues that elephants existed in Atlantis. In ancient caves in France there are evidences that a cataclysm tumbled the bones of mastodons, mammoths and elephants among those of prehistoric, antediluvian men.

Evidence of the frightful consequences of the impact of the pole of our earth, whether with a great comet, as Ignatius Donnelly and Comyns Beaumont suggest, or with a lunar satellite, as the Austrian engineer Hans Hörbiger has it, is seen vividly in polar Spitzbergen where one has the whole gamut, in the strata, of tropic, sub-tropic, down to arctic zones. The succession of such strata in Spitzbergen suggest that the pole and equator changed places, as the collision started a gyroscopic precession or spin through an angle of 90 degrees, and, very slowly, an oscillation back to the present angle of the spinning pole of our Earth with the plane of the ecliptic.

Was the cataclysm of the *Oera Linda Boek* that called Deucalion's Deluge?

The date given by Adela would be either 2193 B.C. or 2214 B.C. If so, unless we take the Egyptian year to be a month, Adela's date can in no wise relate to the cataclysm described in Plato's dialogue as happening 9,000 years before the day of Sonchis and Psenophis, priests of Sais and Heliopolis, in ancient Egypt. Indeed, the *Timæus* of Plato says that three other cataclysms preceded that of Deucalion, with many centuries intervening. No. 3 cataclysm, in this series, or that preceding Deucalion's Deluge, is that described in Plato's *Timæus*.

> Many great deluges took place in the 9,000 years. The soil of the earth all round the coasts of old Greece fell away all round and sank into the sea, out of sight, leaving marine troughs of great depths. Only the skeleton of the old land was left. All the richer and softer parts have gone, where, formerly, the high hills were covered with soil and well wooded, and the plains full of rich earth . . . A single night of excessive rain washed away all the rich antediluvian soil of old (Pelasgian) Greece, and laid bare the rock. At the same time, there were earthquakes and then occurred the extraordinary inundation, which was the third before the great destruction of Deucalion (*Timæus*).[1]

It is to say the least, highly improbable that Hiddo ovira Linda took this date of A.D. 2193 from any learned monk, such as the Venerable Bede, or that, in A.D. 1256, he knew of any fragments of Varro (Roman historian, died about 28 B.C.), said to give a date of around 2200 B.C. as that of Deucalion's Deluge. Only two of Varro's writings survive, and that Hiddo, who warns all and sundry to keep the *Oera Linda Boek* from the sight of treacherous Roman Catholic monks—*pappekâppe*—would have paid any heed to quotations of Varro given in the books of the *Christian* bishop of Hippo, Augustine —even had he known of their existence in his far day—is again, *most* unlikely. But that natural errors may have been made in the copying and re-copying of a very ancient Frisian manuscript, in the course of thousands of years, is not improbable. The point is moot, and not to be solved at this time. It may, or may not be, that an error in dating this cataclysm has been made in the *Oera Linda Boek*.

Augustine, bishop of Hippo, cites Varro as saying that when Cranaus, successor of Cecrops, reigned in Athens, there befell the Deucalion Deluge. (On the other hand, Jerome and Eusebius say it happened when Cecrops himself was ruler in Athens.)

Says Augustine, citing Varro's lost book, *De gente populi Romani*:

> It was called Great, because it was the most extreme in his kingdom, but it did not touch, or come near Egypt, or its confines . . . There was a great deluge in Ogyges' time, not so great as that of the Ark of Noah, not mentioned in Latin or Greek authors. But of the Ogygean flood the writers have no certainty as to time; for where Varro begins his book, as I showed before, he made the Romans' origin go no farther back than the deluge of Ogyges; whereas Eusebius and Jerome, following more ancient authors, say the Ogygean deluge happened in the time of Phoroneus, second king of Argos, 300 years after the time aforesaid. But this, however, is certain: that in Cecrop's time, who was either the builder or restorer of Athens, Minerva was there adored with divine honours.

[1] An oceanographical expedition of 1947–48 reports a depth of 100 feet of thick mud at every hundred miles on the bed of the Atlantic between region of the Azores—the old land named after Azaes, the Atlantean king—and Trinidad. The Atlantean island-continent ranged across a great deal of this vast expanse of ocean.

Cecrops, mentioned in the *Oera Linda Boek* as being white Frisian, is, in the Hellenic myths, said to be a culture hero with half a dragon's or snake's body denoting that he was contemporary with a cataclysm. He was first king of Athens, and in one story is said to have come to Attica from Sais, in Egypt. He introduced to the aborigines of proto-Greece the laws of civilization, marriage, property and religion. When Poseidon (the Atlantean king) and Athens contended for the possession of the land of proto-Greece, Poseidon struck the rock of the Acropolis with his trident and a *horse* came forth. Atlantis was the old home of horse-racing, and it is curious that the mother-in-law of the "fair god", Poseidon of Atlantis was the aboriginal Leucippe, a name in Greek meaning "white horse". Maybe, we have here the obscure explanation of why the White Horse appears cut as a symbol, by some post-cataclysmal race, in the turf of the Wiltshire downs at some four spots.[1]

What is remarkable is that an extremely ancient Irish chronicle speaks of:

> Gathelas, son of Cecrops, of Argos, who, having married the daughter of the King of Egypt sailed with her from Egypt to Spain, and there inhabited.

The *Oera Linda Boek* says that there were three Earth-Mothers: Frya, of the white races; Lyda, of the blacks; and Finda, of the yellow men.

The ancient Americans had also their Earth-Mothers. The South Alaskan tribes of Indians, who have also a tradition of a Great Deluge, oddly enough, like that of Deucalion and Pyrrha, recording that the earth was re-peopled by a god-man who collected stones and threw them backwards over his shoulder. Each stone, touching the ground, became a man or woman. The South Alaskans' story of the Great Deluge is remarkably like that of the *Oera Linda Boek*:

> In the days of the old folks, long ago, there came a time of terrible thundering and lightning, with rain in torrents. With all this there came long-continued shocks of earthquakes which rent the earth, broke down the old mountains and raised new. Besides the torrent of rain which fell, water rushed up from the rents in the earth and the sea came surging over the land, caused by its constant heavings. The people fled in terror. They had canoes, but few reached a place of safety. Many were swamped

---

[1] The old Angli, the Reudigni, and the Varni, or Varini, adored an Earth-Mother, called Herthum, who lived in an island in the ocean and benevolently concerned herself with men's affairs. She must have been head of some Hyperborean-Atlan matriarchate. In the ocean-island, she lived in a grove of holy character, and had a holy car covered with golden tapestry. Only one priest could approach it, and he saw the goddess borne by *female* owls. After converse with the goddess in the temple, he quitted the place, and the goddess, car and tapestry were all washed by slaves in a lake, and the lake swallowed them all up. In old Naharvali, East Germania, the grove of this ancient matricharchal religion had a priest in *female* attire. Here, the gods were the Alci, or Castor and Pollux, who, on *white* horses, headed the Roman armies in battle. Here is a dim hint of a link with the Atlantean white horse, found cut in the turf at four places on the Wiltshire Downs, and in Belgium. In old Germania, the white horses were deemed in touch with unseen powers and able to divinate.

in the surging waters, and hit by floating wreckage. Others were struck and upset by logs and trees whose roots, loosened by the rending earth and borne onwards by the rising waters, struck their canoes from underneath. After a time of fearful perils, a few gained a mountain whose top towered high above the waste of waters. Here, they lived till the waters went down, and then they returned to the lower and badly torn lands.

The white Toltecs of old Mexico had also an earth-mother, or common mother of all men. She is shown in one pictorial codex carrying a serpent, the serpent or dragon being a symbol of a water deluge, exactly as Cecrops had half a dragon's body, and as the Babylonian culture-hero, Joannes, the dragon of the waters of the Old Testament, had a fish-tail. The Toltecan earth-mother was Ciacacoatl and the myth says she—like Eve—was the one by whom sin came to the world.

Again, in North America, the Sia Indians, allied to the Tusayans of Arizona, said that the spider—also symbol of a great deluge—was the only one in the beginning, and that after a time two earth-mothers appeared in *Ha-art*, the earth.[1] They were Ut-Set and Now-ut. They remade the earth at a second creation at the same time as the *rainbow* appeared. (Readers of my *Mysteries of Ancient South America*, Rider and Co., 1947), will recall how I associated the rainbow with an earth much nearer the sun, when the years were shorter, and when, as in Venus, rain fell in the night hours, and so there was no "accident of prismatic light from the sun in drops of falling water" since no rain fell in the pre-cataclysmal earth in the day. Myths in North, South and Central America all make a great point that rainbows *were* not seen in our skies before the time of the Great Flood.

Adela's Frisians were globe-trotters. They had ancient colonies in lands all the way from the old Levant and North Africa to the Punjaub. It is remarkable that a stone age people with white skin and blue eyes, very skilful in making tools, dishes and ornaments out of flint and obsidian, invaded Egypt in the days before Menes, the first historic king who turned the course of the Nile. Either these white Libyans, or the old Frisians who are chronicled as peopling old Ireland in the dim days before written history, may have been identical with the Firbolgs, a tall, fair-skinned race, with golden or reddish hair and blue or blue-grey eyes. Some of the stories call them pirates of the Mediterranean. The same old Irish myths say that Eire remained an unpeopled wilderness for two hundred years after the Great Deluge.

The Geertmen of the Punjaub and Rajputana recall what Pliny says of a fellow named Annius Plocamus, a Red Sea tax-farmer, who, in the reign of Claudius, sent a freedman to double the coast of

[1] The ancient Egyptians called the Sphinx *Ha* or *Habar*, or *Ahar*. In the Maya of Yucatan, the names mean water or swamp. Does this mean that the King represented by the mysterious Sphinx dwelt in lands surrounded by water, or came from over the sea? In Egypt the Sphinx faces east with his—or her—back to the west, as if to indicate that the Sphinx came to Africa from the west. The proto-*Egyptians certainly knew South America!*

Arabia and drop anchor in the port of Hippuros, in Taprobane (Ceylon). He learnt the tongue of Taprobane, and among other things told him:

> of a race called the *Seras* who lived beyond Taprobane and the mountains of Emados. An ambassador had been sent to the Seras to open up trade. The Seras appeared before the Taprobanians. They passed the ordinary height of men, had red hair and blue eyes, and a rough voice, and no tongue to communicate their thoughts. What the Taprobanians said of the Seras was like the information of our own merchants . . . Goods were brought to the river-bank on the side of the Seras, who took them away, leaving the money if the goods suited them.[1]

Had these Seras any of the blood of Frya in their veins?

Strabo speaks of Tiryns, who seems to have been a king of the great megalithic city of that name, which may have been eponymous. He is said to have walled up the Piræus with the help of the Cyclopes, giants with one eye, or wearing a sort of face-mask that had a hole in the middle of the forehead. These giants worshipped the sun— as did some of the mound-builders of ancient North America, who also had giants as neighbours, under the sign of the serpent. Both in old North and South America and Europe the name *Vira* is found, in each case associated with man as born of flame and the sun. *Vira*, in ancient Brazil, is still worshipped by the Indians under that name, each dawn, when they turn to the sun, invoking him as *Vira*.[2] The Cyclopes, like the old Frisians of Adela's day and before, kept a lamp perpetually burning on the tops of their temples.

The *Oera Linda Boek*, speaks of *Skenland*, later of *Schoonland* (Scandinavia), as having been part of their empire in old Europe, and before and after the day when Min-erva, their Eeremoeder, founded the city of Athens.

In 1887, there was dug up at Haggarstalund, in Sweden, a weathered stone cut with ancient *Futhorc*, or runes, which commemorated two men who died in Greece.

The *Marsata*, or Swiss pile-dwellers: We are told by the *Oera Linda Boek* that these people lived on houses built on piles by the lake-side, as a safeguard against wicked men and *lions*. Lions in Europe?

Herodotos says that lions came down from their lairs, by night,

---

[1] The Seras or Seres have always puzzled the commentators, such as Bruzen la Martinière, not to speak of the writers of the classic age. Lucan located them towards the sources of the Nile. Heliodorus reckoned them with the mythical Blemyes, people of Africa, with "eyes and mouth in the middle of the chest, but no heads". Pausanias says they spun silk from silkworms, on an island in the most remote part of the Red Sea. They were also said to be linked with the Abasas, or old Abyssinian-Ethiopians. Pomponius Mela puts them between the "Indos", or Hindus, and the Scythians, and says they had somehow got mixed with the Indians, Ptolemy seems near the mark. He says they lived beyond the "Imaus" (Himalayas). He names towns of theirs. They may have come into remote and intimate contact with the old Frisians and Geertmen in the Punjaub; for Ptolemy says *Serum Regia* had contacts with the Indus, the land beyond the Ganges, and reached even over as far as ports of old Cathay, or China, Hence, the silkworm story.—AUTHOR.

[2] The Cymmry said that men and fire were identical. *Irish: fear* (man); Hindu-Sanscrit, *Vira* strong man and sun; Latin *vir*; Turkish *er*; Hebrew *ur*; Dutch *vuur*; Welsh *gwr*.

and attacked the baggage camels of Xerxes' train, while that Persian invader was marching through the modern Balkans, as it now is, to attack the Greeks. The lions ignored the men. He says: "The whole region between the River Nestus" (located in the Rhodope Mountains, of what to-day is Bulgaria), "and the Achelon, but not in all parts of Europe—is full of lions and wild bulls with gigantic horns that are brought to Greece." Aristotle, a native of Macedonia, says that lions were found in the Balkans, in his day; but by A.D. 120, Dion Chrysostom says lions had disappeared from Europe.

Now those who decried the *Oera Linda Boek* as a forgery never stopped to ask themselves how it was that Hiddo ovira Linda, in A.D. 1256, or a forger in the eighteenth century, or even Cornelis Over de Linden, in 1820, could have known about the past existence of the prehistoric pile-dwellers in Switzerland. Moreover, when a document adds knowledge we did not before possess, or that can be found nowhere else—as the name *Marsata*—what then, Mr. Sceptic?

It was not till the winter of 1853–54, when an abnormal drought and long-continued cold caused the Alpine rivers to shrink and the level of the water in the lakes to fall at Obermeilen that the first of the Swiss lake-dwellings on piles was found. Comyns Beaumont tells me he saw more of these ancient pile-dwellings when he was living on the shores of Lake Luzern. These ancient houses are of the age of polished stone, say the archæologists, and also reach to that of bronze and iron—which is borne out by the story of the *Oera Linda Boek*. In some of the Swiss dwellings beads of glass and nephrite of Egypt, Phœnicia and Asia have been found—again bearing out the story of the *Oera Linda Boek* of foreign traders in ships dealing with the *Marsata*. Again, in 1879, the finger-prints of a woman were found on a bit of pottery left on the shores near prehistoric lake-dwellings at Courcelettes, on Lake Neuchatel. Dr. Kollman of Basel took a cast of the prints and deduced that their owner had been a woman with narrow hands and, by correlation, a long narrow face with the bodily form of the people of a fine and cultivated race. (The *Oera Linda Boek*, tells us that the *Marsata* were the people of the white Frya, their own Earth-mother.)

I may here, in passing, say that pile dwellings of this prehistoric lacustrine type are also found in North and South America: in old Brazil, close to the Amazon, and in the north-west Territory of Canada, where the Indians say their remote ancestors built lake-dwellings on piles "to protect themselves against monsters, such as mammoths and saurians who ranged the country in the long ago".

We now come to the extremely difficult question of chronology. In ages where lapidarian inscriptions and word of mouth are the sole guides, there can be no criteria for the scientific historian. He stands on a base of shifting sand and must do the best he can. In one place, Hiddo says Atlan sank in 2193 B.C. Then Adela says Ulysus came to Texland, in the region of the modern Zuyder Zee, 1,005 years after

Atlan sank and that his visit was after the fall of Troja, or Troy. The Parian Chronicle, now among the Arundelian marbles at Oxford University, England, says Troy was taken in 1209 B.C. (But Plutarch, Josephus and others discredit the Parian Chronicle, and Herodotos and Thucydides say Troy fell in or about 1260 B.C., while Duris of Samos plumps for 1335 B.C., and Clemens of Alexandria for 1149 B.C. If the data of the *Oera Linda Boek* be approximately correct the Atlan cataclysm took place between 2240 B.C. and 2145 B.C. (Hiddo ovira Linda says 2193 B.C.)

The ancient scribe Ellit-Aya, of Sippara, in old Babylon, copied a very ancient Deluge story from an even more ancient source than was used in the Gilgamesh Tablets. He used a terra-cotta tablet found by Père V. Scheil at Sippara. In this tablet, now in the Ottoman Museum at Istanbul, the scribe says he made his copy about 2140 B.C., when King Ammizaduga reigned and built the fort at Sippara. It tells of a safety ship riding out the Great Flood, and the ruin of city and land, but the scribe copied from a source already then so ancient that he inserted in his copy the word "Hibis" (illegible). Also, this terra-cotta tablet is merely the tenth chapter of a story of *While the Men Rested*. The story was compiled from twelve books, one for each month. On the other hand, the Nineveh tablets of Assurbanipal go back only to 600 B.C. So, it appears, that, in the Orient, the traditions of a Great Deluge were already ancient in 2140 B.C.

It, therefore, seems that the Deluge described in Ellit-Aya's copy was long anterior to that described in the *Oera Linda Boek*. The Parian Chronicle, drawn up by tables in 265 B.C., says that the Great Flood of Deucalion happened about 1530 B.C. Apollodorus says that Zeus wished to destroy the men of the Bronze Age and that Deucalion built an ark or chest in which he floated for nine days and nights. Men fled to the mountain tops and all others were drowned. Suidas tells us of one Nannakos, an antediluvian king of the old Phrygians, who, suggests Comyns Beaumont, were identical with the old Frisians. Nannakos, foreseeing the cataclysm, gathered his people into sanctuaries to watch and pray. Nannakos is said to have lived for three hundred years, and when his friends, tired of the old man, asked the oracle when he would die, the oracle replied: "When he dies, all men will die with him."[1]

[1] Lucian, in *dea Syria*, tells a curious story. At the north gate of the great temple of Olympian Zeus at Athens, as late as A.D. 180, there stood two tall obelisks, 360 feet high, up which twice a year men climbed to remain seven days. That was to commemorate how men climbed mountains and tall trees to escape the waters of the Great Deluge. Down a cleft in the precincts, where the waters of the deluge had poured away, cakes and water were thrown to feed the souls who died in the catastrophe. Here, Deucalion had built a rain temple. Ogyges' deluge, which Varro said happened in 2136 B.C., after Ogyges founded Thebes, saw even the snowy waters wash over the top of Parnassus. Eusebius, no impartial guide, puts the Noachian deluge as 2,200 years before that of Ogyges, said to be founder of Eleusis. *All over the region of Bœotia are dead ruined cities, race unknown.* Here, perhaps, lived Ogyges before he fled to higher and drier sites at the day of his Great Deluge. As Sir James Frazer said: "These mysterious cities of the dead seem to have been created at a blow and perished at a blow."

All said and done, therefore, it seems inadvisable to take *au pied de la lettre* the date of the cataclysm given in the *Oera Linda Boek*. We must make allowance for the immense period of time during which the ancient Frisian chronicle had been copied and re-copied. Who can say whether some of the copyists had not, like Ellit-Aya of Sippara, in 2140 B.C., to deplore the fact that parts of the original manuscript had become illegible—*Hibis*—in the lapse of time, and under catastrophes of fire, flood, ruin, war, rapine, invasion, slavery, and dispersion? But this does not alter the general truth of this amazing story.

Inca: the white Frisian who, with his Argonauts of Finns and Magyars took the voyage over the Western Ocean and was never more heard of by his kinsmen in the old European land of Frya, what of him?

I incline to believe that the name *Inca* which is not Quechuan, comes from that of *Inka*! In old Perú, as Miles Poindexter points out in his great work *Peruvian Pharaohs*, much of the labour of building the pre-Incan megalithic cities was done by black men under the supervision of high caste white rulers and engineers. In fact, the Quechua word, in Perú, for servants, was *yanas*, or blacks. Neither the word Vira—as in Viracocha—nor Inca, is, as I say, Quechuan, the tongue of the common folk of old Perú; for the nobles and the Inca emperor *spoke a secret language of their own*. And there is strange evidence that, in a very remote day, *white Frisians actually reached Chile*.

A certain Spanish knight of the order of "San Jacobus de Carolo Casari à Cubiculis", whose name was Dom Alonso, or Alfonso de Ercilla wrote, in the late sixteenth century, a poem called *La Araucana*. It tells of the adventures of a beautiful virgin of the redoubtable Araucanians of Chile whom even the valiant conquistador, Pedro de Valdivia, in his wars, was never able to conquer. Her name was Glaura, and when she was questioned by Ercilla about her ancestry, she said:

> My name is Glaura. I was born in a propitious hour. The daughter I am of a good cacique, *Quilacura*, of the noble blood of the old Frisians. I derive my name, my land and my house from *Fresolano*—an old Frisian leader or chieftain. I bear in my face and form the look of *Fresolano*. The daughter am I of the good cacique, *Quilacura*, of the noble blood of the Frisians. My land and my house I derive from *Fresolano*.

This *Fresolano* was an ancient chief or ruler of the old Araucanians, and his name strongly suggests Frisian affinities.

Glaura, one notes, told de Ercilla that she "bore in her face and form the look of Fresolano".

Gregorio Garcia, the Dominican monk whose book, *Historia Ecclesiastica y seglar de la Yndia Oriental y Occidental*, was printed "at Baeca, in 1620", tells us: "The name *Fresolano*, borne and used by Glaura, daughter of an Araucanian cacique, appears to be derived from Frisian."

If, therefore, the ancient Frisians reached the coasts of western South America, in a very remote age, it may well be that Inka founded an early dynasty in pre-Inca Perú, which, later, included Chile, at a time when white and high caste rulers governed an alien race which carried out, under the supervision of architects and engineers, works based on slave labour, on which, contrary to the law of Frya, the city-states of the Hellenes, were based. That the Araucanians, or Chile Indians, had a remote past in which they were in contact with a much more cultivated race than the Spaniards encountered in the sixteenth century, was suggested as long ago as 1550, by a learned Spanish historian and priest, Cristobal de Molina, *capellan* (chaplain) of the Spanish hospital at Cuzco, and author of the *Cronica de la Conquista y poblacion del Perú*.

Molina noted that the Araucanian tongue had abstract terms that the Indians of his day did not understand. "Its language", he says, "has a harmonious structure, and its very richness radiates the learnings of a far more civilized past. It may be that the Araucanians are the residuum of a once great and illustrious people."

When Inka and his Magyars reached the coasts of ancient South America—of which we have as yet no *documentary* proof—some centuries had passed since the Great Cataclysm had rent and shook ancient South America, to the roar of flames above and on the land beneath, just as in ancient Europe it killed off monstrous animals, mammoths and *elephas primegenius* and deposited their bones and skulls in caves with their contemporaries, prehistoric man. Inka and his men may have passed along the shores of the Amazon, or on the ancient highlands that fringed those shores of a mightier Marañon, and have seen the ruins of some of those amazing dead cities of Atlantean Hy-Brazil, on the façades and porticoes of whose splendid mansions and temples the Brazilian land-pirates and gold-hunters of A.D. 1745, noted the strange and bizarre inscriptions which one of them copied. They must have observed that this ancient race of South America shared with their own European race the custom of inscribing on the walls of cities historical records.

It is a curious fact that both in China and old Perú some ancient white race of pioneers have left on the landscape the name "Chili", or chilly, as in Pechili. The late Miles Poindexter, distinguished author of the *Ayars of the Incas*, and *Peruvian Pharaohs*, comments on the suggestion in the sound of the word *Chile*; but nearly three hundred years ago, both Garcia Gregorio, the Spanish monk in Perú, and Petrus Suffridus, the Frisian of Leeuwarden, who, in 1698, wrote *De Frisionum Antiquitate et Origini*, as well as Martin Hamconius, author of the Latin work on the *Men and Illustrious Deeds of Frisia* (published at "Frankekaræ", in 1620), all enjoy this philological and patriotic tit-bit. Garcia cites Lasso de la Vega (Garcilasso, el Inca), as saying that:

> The name *Chile*, originally that of a valley, was by synecdoche extended to the whole land, and that it means *cold* or *chilly*, the same as

in Frisian, where "Killing", or "Kildinghe" is the cold of the Flamencos (Flemings or Frisians). Also, double-headed eagles, found in Santiago de Chile, were common figures in Frisland.

Against this, it may be said that in Quechua, the tongue of the common folk of Perú, *not* the secret language spoken by the higher castes, and the emperor, and the Orejones, or his bodyguard, the word Chile meant a province. Tschudi, in his *Der Kechua Sprache*, gives the word, but with neither the spelling "Chile" or "Tchili". He says that in Quechua it means "the best of a thing".

This is exceedingly unconvincing, however the dunderheaded archæologists may regard it. They seem to forget the fact that off this western coast of South America runs the *cold* and *chilly* Humboldt current from the Antarctic. The word of Miles Poindexter is alone worth credence on this matter.

As to the escutcheons of the double-headed eagles found in the Vale of Cautem[1] and in Santiago de Chile, it is not necessary to drag in old Frisians, for these eagles are found in old Mexico, as at "the place of the eagle", cut with life-like clearness on a boulder at Cuernavaca, where it might have served as a terminus, like the old Roman boundary stone. On this ancient Mexican boulder, the eagle bears on his shoulder or breast a bâton or pastoral. In old Egypt, the eagle, as in ancient Mexico, was the symbol of the sun—of Osiris in Egypt, and placed on his altar at the winter solstice, and at Thebes, the stone eagle bore a bâton just as he did in Mexico. The eagle, like the Peruvian and Chilian bird of high altitude, the condor of the Andes, was believed to be able to gaze unflinchingly on the sun, in full noontide glory.

But what is amazing is that the *licenciado* (lawyer) Don Francisco Ramirez de Valenzuela, writing in 1775, tells a story of a former viceroy of Mexico, the Marqués de Valero, later el Duque de Arion, who found the embalmed body of a double-headed eagle in Mexico, which he gave to the Monastery of the Escorial in old Spain, stating that *such eagles were once bred in Mexico*.[2]

George Hornius, the old German encyclopædic scholar and historian (died at Leyden, Holland, in 1670) is, therefore, justified when, in his black letter book, *De Originibus Americanis*, he remarks:

> That double-headed eagles are met with in America ought not to excite wonder when it is considered that in Mexico and Perú they greatly venerate the bird and depict it in pictures with gold and silver.

[1] See *Justis Lipsius*, Dict., Lib. 2., cap. 19.

[2] This would not be the first case in which an actual and living monster was used either as a heraldic symbol or placed in an ancient Mexican temple. For example, in the Toltec temple in the ancient citadel at Teotihuacan, in the archæological zone of Mexico, is a monstrous figure of a dog-headed dragon, with a crest—oddly called a feathered serpent—which singularly recalls a horrid saurian, with a similar head of a canine—a fearsome dinosaur—which in recent years, prior to the recent Gran Chaco war, was found, or seen, in a swamp in the densely wooded forest-jungle of the Gran Chaco, on the eastern borders of Paraguay! I cannot, here, enter in this teratological theme of South America, which I must leave for a later book. *Vide* Chapters 6 and 7 . . . *supra*—AUTHOR.

The old Frisians no more left the eagle symbol in South America than they did the cross; for the cross is, as a symbol of torture, æons older than any brand of Petrine or Byzantine Christianity, dating back, as it does, to the sadists of Mu. You will find it in many an ancient site all over South and Central America, and among the mysterious mound-builders' remains on the plains of North America —*and* the sun-sign of the eagle! The old Frisian writer and Latin versifier—pretty bad verses, too!—Martinius Hamconius, who wrote *Frisia seu de viris rebusque Frisiæ* (*Franekaræ*, 1620), says that: "And so laughing Mexico, even more supplied with gold . . . and with the riches of America, the Frisian race heaped up treasures in Europe, and at the beginning in the empty spaces they have borne colonists to Chile, to set up the refulgent mysteries of the faith and the Cross." Hamconius was right in one way, but wrong in another. None of Frya's monotheistic faith could ever have set up the Christian or any other savage rite of the cross in ancient America, whether or not associated with phallicism of the lustful *Venus procreatrix*, and other hideous priestly and predatory ritual associated with this vicious emblem of a vile doctrine of atonement and blood baths of Mithra.

Where he and others went wrong was in associating with Hispaniola and Cuba a queer voyage made by old Frisian nobles and *Zee-kampers*, or roamers, about the year 1060, time of Harald Hardrada of Norway, when they reached some mysterious land far north in the Arctic, where giants with great mastiffs lived in subterranean caves outside which were gold and silver vessels, which the Frisians took. On their retreat to their ships in a creek, the roaring giants came from the caves, at noon, caught and tore one Frisian thief to pieces, and, lining the cliffs, discharged great rocks on to the ships as the thieves went out to sea. The story is told in the Hamburg chronicle by an old Saxon monk who was master in the cathedral school of Bremen, and got access to certain lost letters of one called the Pontifex Alibrandus, and also talked with folk who had visited strange lands and with traders and missioners passing through Bremen. But it was *not* the West Indian island of Cuba or of Hispaniola where they met the giants, but very likely off Greenland where was the last retreat of the mysterious Skrellings, or giants of the North of America. Columbus, who was *not* the first white European to land in America, made this mistake, also.

That the old Frisians roamed the seas both before and long after the fall of Atlantis is certainly true, whether or no, as Scherer maintains, they bequeathed to the Araucanians the use of the bow and arrow, operating that weapon in the peculiar way characterizing the Frisians, in days when Greater Frisia comprised seven united provinces between what we now call the Low Countries and Germany.

My last word is of the curious prophecies in the *Oera Linda Boek*. They remind me of the old saying: you cannot argue with a prophet, you can only disbelieve him.

No. 1 vaticination is that there would be a "great war 2,000 years after the sinking of Atlan". If we take the date of this cataclysm, or the date of Hiddo ovira Linda, to be about 2193 B.C., this great war would have occurred about 220 B.C.; or, on the date alleged for the visit of Ulysus to Tex-land, Frisia, about 214 B.C. In or about 220 B.C. the great wall of China was built by an emperor of China to keep out the barbarians. The only war one can find to square with the war of the lower classes against priests and rulers, as predicted in the *Oera Linda Boek's* first prophecy is that of Spartacus the gladiator, who between 73 and 71 B.C., with 10,000 men in the woods of Campania, later rising to around ten times that number of discontented men and revolting slaves, very nearly put paid to old Rome. Even the great general Crassus at first despaired of success, and the valiant Spartacus died upon a heap of Roman slain, and accompanied to the Elysian Fields—no doubt the startled well-to-do of old Rome would have said Hades—by 40,000 rebel ghosts. One is really afraid that something went wrong with that prediction, or, any rate that, unlike the London Sunday newspaper dope astrologers, the vaticinator could not blame it on to the fickleness of the stars. It was not till A.D. 164 that great plagues devastated Asia and lasted until the death of Marcus Aurelius, when a long period of war and disorder ushered in the death of the Roman Empire, already rendered rotten by the corrosive sublimate of a new creed from the hills of Judæa.

No. 2 Vaticination: A revolution to down false priests, corrupt rulers and oppressors, "none after to hold rule save by the general voice of the people, to start 4,000 years after the sinking of Atlan, and 1,000 years after, then shall be neither priest nor oppressor".

That would take us to about the year 1807 or 1828. In 1807, England was at war with the Corsican dictator, Napoleon Bonaparte. In Seville, the French soldier-liberators put paid to the foul dungeons of the Holy Dominican Roman Catholic Inquisition, and prevented the Spanish inquisitor from burning the records of some horrible cases of lust and sadism in which these black Inquisitors, blasphemously invoking the name of their Prince of Peace and Charity to all men, had horribly tortured men, women and young children. It was late in the eighteenth century when a Bourbon king of Spain, Charles III, one of the ablest of the Spanish kings in that century, expelled from all his dominions all members of the subtle, sinister, and dangerous order of the Society of Jesus of Loyola, who left quite a lot of treasure behind them cached in South and Central America, which has been dug up since by their myrmidons.

As to the tail-piece of the final *Oera Linda Boek* prediction, all one need say that it very much seems, at the time of writing, that we and our posterity may not need to wait till A.D. 2807 or 2828 for the ushering in of the Third World War, which will leave precious few of us, now alive and now rotting in Western Europe, to see the consummation of the final *Oera Linda* prediction. It will be what the late cynical clericalist—Lord Balfour—called "a very interesting situation".

396

CHAPTER NINE

THE MYSTERY OF OLD MAN NOAH AND THE ARKS

Des mythes d'ancienne limite occidentale du monde connu peuvent, donc, avoir eu quelque fondement historique.
BARON WILHELM VON HUMBOLDT, in A.D. 1839

A MAN well known to the writer of this book, who has travelled widely in Persia, Egypt and the Near East, and is a former attaché of the British Embassy in Teheran, in 1949, planned to raise some £5,000 for what may be regarded, according to views, as a fantastic quest, or a romantic adventure in the spirit of a Don Quixote of an austere and a disillusioned age. And it is, oddly enough, a quest that has some very queer but none the less veridical South and North American repercussions.

He lives in a house in a prosaic and matter-of-fact square in the artists' quarter of Chelsea, London, though he is not a professional artist. Oddly enough, however, he was, temporarily, an official of the British Ministry of Labour, and of the suave and diplomatic type which would by many folk be deemed the least likely to embark on such a quest. It is also a quest which at any time would not lack the element of personal danger and hardship in a disturbed and rugged quarter of the earth, close to the Russian Soviet frontiers of Armenia with Anatolian Turkey. His name is Egerton Sykes.

I am writing in the spring of 1949, some five months in advance of the time of this project. This man planned, in company with his wife, widely travelled in the Near East, and a camera-man, an archæologist and geologist, to cross the little known Pontic mountains and other more or less trackless ranges, from the shores of the Black Sea to a very remote corner of Eastern Turkey, about 30 miles from the Soviet border. Their patrols in Russian-dominated Armenia would have very mistaken notions about the object of this unusual quest, which is in not the remotest sense concerned with high or other politics. The region is "right off the map", remote from railroads and any airways that would serve his purpose. As the crow flies, the region for which he was bound is 250 miles from the shores of the Black Sea; but many more on foot or horseback. For political-geographical reasons, his route is compulsorily circuitous. He made a previous attempt to reach his objective in the 1930's, but the Russian authorities barred his way, so one is told. Luckily, in 1949, he had not to depend on a permit from the U.S.S.R. authorities, which would undoubtedly not have been granted. Even if he had told those hard-boiled cynics at the Kremlin what his objective was, they would not have been impressed in the way he would have desired. He planned to *reach and photograph, and film Noah's Ark.*

Political geography and the inalienable suspicion of the Western powers cherished by the Soviet power, forced him to plan the probably worst route to the Ark. Railways and air lines would very considerably shorten a trail of this sort if it had been possible to travel over U.S.S.R. territory. And as his base was the old nut and tobacco port of Trebizond, it might not be probable that the Turkish authorities would or could allow the use of a three-engined 'plane boosted and supercharged for high altitude flights over one of the "roofs of the world". The turbulent and shifting currents of power politics do not make plain or easy the path of scientists or explorers engaged in entirely disinterested and non-political investigations and research.

A man, to-day, faced by these difficulties is little better, perhaps much worse off than was the famous Kinglake, of the fine travelling-book thriller *Eothen*, in the 1830's or 1850's. What may be hours by air become weeks on foot. Planted in such a picturesque, out-of-the-world harbour as Trebizond, he may find himself reduced to sitting on the veranda of his hotel and sadly reflecting, as he watches the blue smoke of his Turkish cigarette wisp upwards under an Arabian Night's moon, while the muezzin calls to prayers from the top of the Prophet's minaret across the flat-topped, white houses. These cigarettes should be cheap, if nothing else is, and aid him to reflect philosophically on the vast mass of conglomerated mountains and massifs that lie between him and the Ark.

But let no archæologist smile into his beard, or *tchah* into his coffee cup! An expedition of this sort is not the fantasy it seems. It is not an affair out of Sir John de Mandeville's Travels or the Adventures of Baron von Munchausen. Old Noah's Ark is not merely a pretty and naïve fable told by a Sunday School marm to keep restless children quiet on a warm summer Sunday afternoon. *That ark existed.* It still exists. It has been the subject of investigations by the Turkish Commission of the 1880's, and as late as the First World War it was actually measured and photographed by order of the last Tsar of the Romanoff dynasty. In fact, these photographs are actually, at this moment, pigeon-holed in some labyrinthine offices of some Soviet commissary, either at Leningrad, or the Kremlin in Moscow. The ark has been known to be in existence, not merely for a century past, but way back to the days of the Roman emperor, Augustus Cæsar, and even long before his day, if we take the testimony of classic writers. (Augustus was born in 63 B.C., and died in A.D. 14.) But the first *modern* reference to the ark appeared in the *Chicago Tribune* on 10th August, 1883, whose correspondent had cabled it from London. It read:

A paper at Constantinople announces the discovery of Noah's Ark. It appears that some Turkish commissioners appointed to investigate the avalanches on Mount Ararat, suddenly came upon a gigantic structure of very dark wood protruding from a glacier. They made inquiries of the local folk. These had seen it for six years, but had been afraid to approach it, because a spirit of fierce aspect had been seen looking out of the upper window. The Turkish Commissioners, however, are bold men, not deterred by such trifles, and they determined to reach it. Situated as it was among the fastnesses of one of the glens of Mount Ararat, it was a work of enormous difficulty, and it was only after incredible hardships that they succeeded. The Ark was in a good state of preservation, although the angles—observe, not the bow, or the stern—had· been a good deal broken in its descent. They recognized it at once. There was an English-speaking man among them, who had presumably read his Bible, and he saw it was made of the ancient gopher wood of scripture, which, as everyone knows, grows only on the plains of the Euphrates. Effecting an entrance into the structure, which was painted brown, they found that the Admiralty requirements for the conveyance of horses had been carried out, and the interior was divided into partitions fifteen feet high. Into three of these only could they get, the others being full of ice, and how far the Ark extended into the glacier they could not tell. If, however, on being uncovered, it turns out to be 300 cubits long, it will go hard with disbelievers.

On 9th August, 1947, Moscow Radio broadcast the reading of an article on the discovery of Noah's Ark on a glacier of Mount Ararat peak; but three months before, in May 1947, there appeared an article in a London magazine *The Modern Mystic and Monthly Science Review*, in which one, Vladimir Roskovitsky, said to be at present in the United States, told how he had been stationed as an air pilot at a Russian aerodrome at a very lonely spot 30 miles north-east of Mount Ararat. It was in the year 1916 of the First World War, just before the Russian Revolution of Kerensky put paid to the account and reign of the Romanoff Tsar.

Mr. Roskovitsky tells how, on a dry and hot day in August, he had been ordered to take his 'plane aloft with supercharger and booster, for a high altitude flight over Mount Ararat. He remembered that the mountains had not been climbed since 700 B.C., when pilgrims had gone there to scrape off tar or pitch from an old hulk of a very ancient ship, in order to get amulets to give good luck for crops and against too much rain. Lightning had struck and scared them off.

As a matter of fact, Mr. Roskovitsky is wrong about the ascent of Ararat; for it has been climbed many times since the far-off date he mentions.

He goes on:

On the east side of the snow-capped peak, the airman saw a blue lake that was frozen.

A colleague with him in the cockpit of the 'plane suddenly pointed downwards and Roskovitsky saw a queer erection like a wooden ship with stubbed masts. It lay at the end of the frozen lake where a stream disembogued in time of late spring thaw. They flew down to a few feet above the ice, and noted the immense size of the thing. It "was as long as a city block". A fourth part was under water—

ice, as it then was—and seemed grounded on the shore of the lake. One side near the front part had been dismantled, and off the other side, was "a great doorway", which was around 20 feet square. The door, apparently, had been double; for one side was missing. The ancient ship lay 14,000 feet up. This would, of course, mean in rarefied air, where breathing, as in the Andes, in South America, on the *paramo* at Tiahuanacu, would be attended with pain and difficulty.

Roskovitsky points out what is well known to explorers of Ararat, that, for nine months of the year, the spot is frozen. This prevents wood from rotting. Back at the base, the commandant reported to the Tsar's Government at Moscow and Petrograd, and an order came that soldiers be detailed to hack a road up into the Ararat range, and along cliffs and precipices to the lake of the Ark. It took them a month of hard labour to accomplish this pioneering work in which 150 men were engaged. The Ark was measured and photographed and the documents sent to Petrograd (now Leningrad).

It is characteristic of Russia, whether under the Tsars or the Soviets, that none of these documents have ever been released for western scientists to examine and study. Roskovitsky tells us that this strange ship contained hundreds of small rooms, and others of great size. The large chambers had a fence of great timbers across them, and the timber was 2 feet thick. It "looked as if meant for wild animal cages". Other rooms in the Ark were "lined with tiers of cages, with rows of tiny iron bars across the top. All was painted with a waxy pigment, as if to withstand prolonged damp or immersion. The work gave the impression that it had been done by artificers of an advanced civilization." The wood used seemed to be of the oleander or cypress family.

It will be remembered that old Noah's gopher wood has never been identified. Going out on the glacier of the lake, expeditions found on the peak above the ship remains of burnt timbers cut, apparently, from one side of the ship. It (the timber) had been used to make a small shrine or crude altar.

Now, going back to the earlier entrance into the Ark of the Turkish Commissioners, it may be said that a great earthquake—the region is volcanic and the slopes and altitudes of Ararat are strewn with lava, and plutonic rock such as the andesites and obsidian—had toppled down tremendous slides of rocks and earth, and *névé* (granular snow not compressed into ice and found at the head of glaciers) and had exposed the ancient hulk. This was in 1883, and the Turkish authorities had had to succour refugees from villages overwhelmed the avalanches from Mount Ararat.

An American missionary, Frederich Coan, tells in a book published privately at Claremont, California, in 1939, how a Nestorian archbishop, Nourri had, some years before, after three attempts, managed to scale Ararat and saw the old Ark wedged in the rocks and half-filled with ice and snow. He got inside and measured the Ark. He

Sea Serpent seen from English ship about 1850

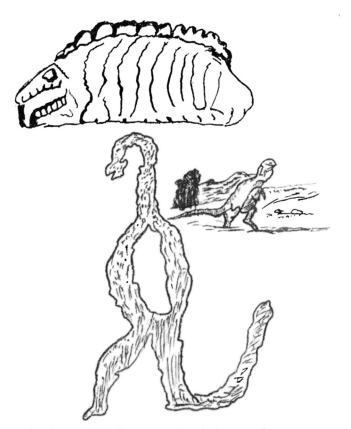

(*Top*) Oregon "Indian" prehistoric image of stegosaurus.
(*Bottom*) Prehistoric cliff petroglyph of tyrranosaurus
(Arizona). (*Inset*) Modern conception of same

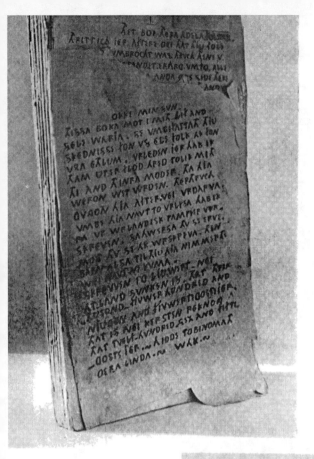

Oera Linda Boek manu-
script, with passage on
sinking of Atlan

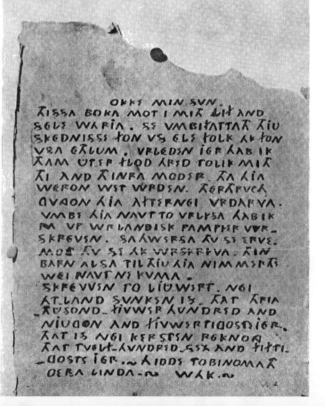

does not say if it had three stories, but says (very oddly!) it was exactly 300 cubits long, 50 cubits broad, and 30 cubits high (see Genesis, chap. 6). (Taking the Asiatic cubit at an average of 20 inches, these measurements would be 500 feet long, 83 feet broad, and 50 feet high, or about the average dimensions of a modern Transatlantic liner!) They certainly must have had some naval architects and big shipyards in those days, which might be 12,000 or 20,000 years ago, chronology being a matter impossible to determine accurately, on the fragmentary data we at present possess.

It seems that Nourri organized a company for the purpose of sending engineers and transport contractors to Mount Ararat, with a view to removing the Ark and taking it to be shown at the Chicago World's Fair. It does not speak well of the Chicago organizers that they jibbed at the proposition on the ground of expenses, risk and difficulty. Why, it would have paid its way one hundred times over and created such a furore all over the world that old Chicago would never have been forgotten as the last word in Yankee enterprise!

Here is a splendid chance for the British organizers of the Great World Fair, planned to be held on a site south of the Thames, London, in the 1950's, to ship this eye-popping exhibit from Ararat, with the doubtless benevolent assistance of the Government, in Angora. Clearly, it would have to be shipped out in sections; for no railroad or freight ship could transport this gigantic hulk as it stands. But of the enormous publicity value of this exhibit, and the financial profit that would ensure there can be no doubt—if Roskovitsky spoke the square-toed truth.

A rapid glance at this remote corner of the world shows the formidable nature of the task of the Sykes expedition.

Mount Ararat is located on the plateau of the Armenian Highlands, which are from 4,000 to 7,000 feet above sea level. Around the region lies the cradle of a very ancient civilization. Mount Ararat consists of two peaks, Great Ararat and Lesser Ararat. The height of Great Ararat is a little uncertain, since determinations made at different times say it is either 17,000 feet or 16,910 feet. Its two slopes cover a vast stretch of country, ranging over some 34 miles. Little Ararat is joined to Great Ararat by a *col*, or neck of rock which is variously given as 2·119 miles, or 2·3 miles high, and is called the Sardar-Belag-Sattel.

Down to about 4,500 feet the mountain is covered with perpetual snow, but it is said that it does now carry glaciers. The peak is visible 34 miles away at Erivan, and is about equally distant from the Black Sea, the Caspian and the Mediterranean. Ararat is isolated on all sides, and the peaks rise out of a massif of tumbled and volcanic ranges. Blocks of lava and banks of earth allow only a short belt of Alpine vegetation up to about 1¼ miles above sea level. There are cindery steppes and rock veins that have few water springs, so that the little Kurdish villages at the foot can grow very little.

Little Ararat is free from snow only in September and October. Glittering fields of unbroken *névé*, or compressed snow, cover both the north and west slopes of Ararat, and the landscape is bare, sterile and depressing. It reminds one of a lunar landscape strewn with volcanic andesites and obsidian.

Local traditions place the Garden of Eden in the valley of the river Aras, or Araxes, which runs to the east of the Ararat peaks and forms the frontier with the U.S.S.R. Noah's wife is said to have been buried at Marand, and at a village named Arghuri, close to a great chasm in the earth, legend has it that Noah, here linked with the Bacchus of old Greece and India, planted the first vineyard. Up to 1839, the local folk showed "Noah's vine", but in that year it was smashed flat by a fall of rock in a great earthquake.

Great Ararat is shaped like a dome, while little Ararat looks like a cone. The Armenian monks had a legend that Ararat was too holy for human feet ever to tread its summit; but that legend went west, when, in 1829, a German employed by the Russians, Dr. Johann Parrot, reached the top of the dome of ice of Great Ararat. The Armenians firmly believed that the remains of the Ark were, and are still on Ararat, but that God, to preserve it from destruction, forbade that anyone should ever come near the summit. The same pious belief is also held to-day, by a certain British religious Federation, who assert that the Ark will never be removed from the top of Ararat, because God hath forbidden it to man. But, it is not so much the action, or veto of the Deity as lack of enterprise, transport and finance that hitherto has kept the Ark *in situ* all these years. Also, oddly enough, the rulers of the Kremlin have done their best to keep all details and pictures of the Ark a secret from the West, since 1916, whether or no they have a desire to co-operate with God in this matter!

Why is this strange volcanic ridge called Ararat?

One theory is that Ararat is a phonetic variant of the name of the old Hindostan cradle of the white Aryan race, Aryavarta, which lay in north-west India, at the foot of the Himalayas. Ancient traditions also speak of a dim country called Airarat, to the south of the Caucasus, in the Armenian plains. Dr. Joseph Karst, the German savant, suggests that Aryavarta-Airarat was in the remote Northland, in the Moon Mountains, to the north and north-east of ancient Europe, where the waters of the Great Deluge broke when Greater Atlantis was submerged and sunk to perdition. That would link it with the old land of Hyperborei-Atlantis-Aeyre, which ranged from the region of Iceland far south to what is now Trinidad, West Indies. Here was what the ancients called the "Paradise of the North", whose genial climate and ideal surroundings were ruined and congealed in a terrible cataclysm of cosmic origin, which ushered in a reign of fog, ice and darkness and perpetual night for six months of the year.

No one knows whether the cause was by collision with some vast comet, or an asteroid which was part of the missing planet which

Bode's Law tells us once revolved in an orbit between Mars and Jupiter. It might have been in the appalling cataclysm of which the Chinese told the learned Jesuit missioner and historian, Martinius:

> At the beginning of the second heaven (this corresponds to what the old Aztec myths of world-destruction call a "sun"), the earth was shaken to its foundations. The sky sank lower towards the north. The sun, moon and stars changed their motions. The earth fell to pieces, and the waters in its bosom uprushed with violence and overflowed it. Man had rebelled against the high gods, and the system of the universe was all disordered. The planets altered their courses, and the grand harmony of the universe and nature was disturbed . . . The sky sank lower in the north . . .

What we do know, is that the Mountains of Ararat formed the old Highlands of the Assyrians, and that around Lake Van, in this region, there lived a mysterious race called the Ur-artu, or Ur-yaldu of the Bible. They seemed to have been linked with the mysterious Etruscans and with the Basques, both of whom were probably of the races of old Atlantis, subjected to and ruled by the great kings of this old empire of the west. The Basques called themselves the "Eus-*kaldu*-nu," or the "Euskal-*erri* (Ur)-nu" people. And it is singular that the Armenian name for Ararat: *Masis*, is a garbling of the old name for Ararat used by the Ur-artu—whom Herodotos called Alarodoi—and which was *Matzikki*, a place-name found *among the Basques* in old Iberian Spain, in the form of Mesketha, and meaning a finger or peak.

The name Ur-artu, once meaning the highlands of the Assyrians, became localized in the mountains of Ararat which lay in its centre. These people were neither Semites, nor Indo-Europeans. They appeared suddenly in the Near East, and apparently had come over the mountains from the west. They seem to have been at one time neighbours of the ancient Minoans of Knossos and Crete, and also to have lived in very brotherly relationship with the Etruscans. Like the Minoans, the Ur-artu stuck ornamented shields on the façades of their temples, as no other race but these two did. Again like the Etruscans, the Ur-artu took over another nation's alphabet. As we know, no scholar can read more than a few words of Etruscan; because, though the forms of their letters are Greco-Phœnician, the values are unknown. The Ur-artu adopted the Assyrian cuneiform though they were totally alien from this empire and had no Semitic blood in their veins. Indeed, for centuries, they were a thorn in the side of old Babylon and warred with the famous Queen Shammurat, or Semiramis.

Often, some clue to the mysteries of the origin of a race can be found in the name by which they call themselves. The Ur-artu called themselves the Chaldians, and their god was Chaldis. The name has a curious likeness to Caledonian, and as the Chaldians came from the west it may well be that they were a branch of the ancient Caledonian stock forced to flee from that region of Acheron, Hades, Charon and the Styx—all believed by Homer and the Greeks to be located in the north of the British Isles—in the dreadful day of the Great Flood and Cataclysm, when the genial continent of Atlan-Hyperborei-Aeyre was shattered to fragments and overwhelmed by the waters of the Arctic and Northern Atlantic. (Not for nothing was it that the stout Roman legionaries manning the walls of Agricola and Hadrian were scared to death of advancing into Caledonia. Superstition has weapons more powerful far than old Scottish steel or high modern explosive.)

Van was the old capital of the Urartu-Chaldians. It is on Lake Van, and this ancient race of skilled engineers, architects and soldiers. built a great aqueduct, more than 46 miles long, to bring sweet waters from the mountains, because the waters of Lake Van were "poisoned" with chemical impregnations. They built forts with a peculiar stepped turret projecting at one end. There is a model of one which an artist of theirs made, and which is now in the British Museum. They tamed a big bearded bison of a species long ago extinct. They had bronze vessels shaped like winged solar female divinities of a sort found elsewhere only in Etruria, and archaic Greece. They had a bronze snake which was an emblem of the great cataclysm that sank old Atlantis, the dragon Tiamat of the Deluge, and they used coloured glass and devised steel made from iron impregnated in mineral waters, which got them the name of Chalybes. They were the first people to make such a steel.

At last, the Armenians, coming over the mountains from the Caucasus, forced this race to retreat to high lands, but they never lost their warlike spirit. To-day, their descendants are found living in the mountains south of Trebizond, in Turkey. In a very much earlier day, these Urartu may have been ruled by a matriarchate, such as was well known among the people of Atlantis; for a gold medal shows an Urartuan goddess of fertility with a woman kneeling before her. There is some reason to suppose that remote ancestors of these mysterious Urartuans were among the people who assembled on the mountains or old Ararat to escape the rising waters of the Great Deluge, many thousands of years ago.

Now to come back to the ancient ship on Mount Ararat.

Nicholas of Damascus, or Damascenius, a historian who lived in the days of the Roman emperor Augustus Cæsar says that, on the mountain Baris, or Mingas, or Minyas,[1] many who fled from the Great

---

[1] Philological derivations have their risks and uncertainties. The savant Karst asserts that the name *Baris* is a variant of the older name of the "World Mountain" of Iran, called Haraberez, and is identical with Ararat. But in the old Scuthic, or Scythic dialect the word *Baris* means *ship*! It will be recalled that these barbarians overran old Persia, in the seventh century B.C., and vanished in the first century A.D., when it was supposed they became the ancestors of the Sarmatians, and hence of that other turbulent and troublemaking race known as the Poles.

Deluge were saved. On the top of Ararat, crowds of refugees from the plains watched the waters of the Great Deluge rising up the slopes of the mountains. An ancient man landed from a great ship, or ark, and the remains of the timbers of the ship were for a long time to be seen by wanderers. All round the summit terrified refugees were praying for a break in the flood and were watching in great fear the steadily rising height of the waters as the great waves lapped and sucked at the lower slopes of Ararat.

Damascenius says these refugees were there before the ark arrived, but he tells us that the ship-master was not Noah but Xisusthrus. I shall have a few words to say later, about old ship-master Noah, but it may be said that the old Jews in Babylon, and in old Egypt, took over and mixed up and garbled for purely nationalist reasons stories about the Great Cataclysm derived from far more ancient races. And this Noah is really a transmogrification of a sage, or Atlantean whose name is known from far Tahiti, in the Pacific, to the old land of Hyperborei-Atlantis. He was certainly *not* a Jew, at all, but a kingly scientist known by the names of Thoth, Taut, Tah, or Nowt, Set or Seth.[1]

Old traditions, ranging all over the globe, literally from old Europe, China and old India to Perú, Mexico, and the United States of America, make it very clear that there were more arks than one, and they were ships of gigantic size. Essentially, man alters very little in his manner of action or thought, and if, to-day, a great water cataclysm loomed, the ruling powers concerned with the salvation of the race would do much as was done by old Atlantis and her American colonies and empire: construct great ships and freight them with the finest biological and eugenic stocks in people, animals, plants and fruits, and a selection of archives, books, blue prints and specifications of great inventions and records of scientific discoveries or the more portable and valuable machines, which they judged to be of the greatest value and utility to the survivors who would re-people the world anew.

Old Father Noah's ark was only one of at least ten large ocean-going ships built in a day incredibly remote, whose very existence would be jeered at by the more crusted sort of historians and archæologists. Scraps of long lost Hellenic and Roman classic writers, often citing vanished Punic and Egyptian sources, joined to traditions and codices in old Toltec Mexico, Quiché Yucatan and American Indian traditions, lore and ritual in North America, make it crystal-clear that this Great Deluge was no mere Mesopotamian Flood. They show that it ranged from right across the Pacific to the shores of

---

[1] The Bardic songs of Wales speak of the return of King Arthur with seven companions from a voyage in a ship over a boundless ocean, in whose waves the rest of mankind had been submerged. Some folk contend that this semi-mythical hero was really an Atlantean, of the day when Brittia, Britannja, and Caledonia were closely related to old Atlan, or Aldland, sunk in a Great Cataclysm into the sea north of the Orkneys and west of Schoonland, or modern Scandinavia.

South, Central, and North and far North America, within what is now the Arctic circle, and passed eastwards across the south Atlantic to the proto-Mediterranean and the old Levant. Old Egypt escaped, so did old Africa, south of the Sahara, which was then an inland sea. It was global. Two great continents vanished—and they were lands that, in the previous thousands of years, had experienced at least three great cataclysms. They vanished like the cloud-wrack of a terrible dream. The pillared firmament was shaken to the very depths. Men were turned insane and paranoiac. Night was made hideous with the flames of human sacrifices. Old Eire, or Ireland, alone, remained a desert and uninhabited for 200 years as the White Book, or *Leabhar dhroma sneachta* records. Old Eire had been part of the great drowned land of Aeyre-Atlantis sunk in this very cataclysm. It seems to have been known as Banba. There is an old myth that the first person to set foot in Banba's "rugged land and shores before the world was drowned" was the Lady Cessar, or Cæsar, daughter of the Good Beatha. And be it remembered that the old Irish are the oldest branch of the Kelts and nearest to the root-stock. When Taut, or Thoth the Atlantean, garbled as Noah, by the Jew mythologists, was building his great ark-ship, he was asked by Beatha for an apartment, or cabin, in the ship to save him and his daughter from the approaching Danger. But Taut, or Nowt refused. Nowt or Naut was his other name and he certainly said "nowt" on that occasion, just as if he had been Mr. Molotov!

Men landed in these ark ships, not only on the shores of old Europe, or the mountains of Asia, but on the shores of North and South America. The land vomited flames and was foul with miasma of poisonous vapours and smokes and gases, and the beaches stank with rotting bodies of men and animals cast on them by terrific tidal waves, lashed by hurricanes and upheaved by tremors and quakes of submarine vulcanism. In North and South America, the refugees took to the shelter of tremendous tunnels, of mysterious origin, and, as the years passed, cannibalism raged in those ancient bores.

There is even a North American Indian story that a white woman came over the Great Waters from the east, either in some form of aeronautical transport, flying solus, or under her own power, by some sort of levitation with which it is said, the old Atlanteans were well acquainted. She landed on what are now the shores of eastern United States of America!

The great ark which landed on the top of Mount Ararat had for shipmaster, King Xisusthrus, or Xisuthrus. The Chusdim, or ancient Chaldæan story—and here again, we may have a race of probable *Caledonian* origin—has been fused by three writers: Syncellus, Eusebius and Josephus:

> Xisuthrus was the tenth in descent from the *protoplast*, the first created man. (This, of course, must be interpreted rationally, as the tenth of an early antediluvian dynasty.) His ark was an immense ship

for the accommodation of men and animals. He sent out birds from the ark, and some returned with feet bemired with mud. The third time they came back no more. Opening an aperture in the ark, he saw he was drifting towards a high mountain. He disembarked his wife, daughter and the pilot, and then built an altar to the gods, after kneeling in obeisance to the earth. He had orders to build the ship in the days before the Great Deluge came.

It was no galley or cockleshell of an old Mediterranean trireme. Xisusthrus's ark was five stadia long and two stadia broad. If we take the old Asiatic stadium as being equal to 485·1 feet, that ark was two and a half times as long as the liner *Queen Mary* of the Cunard-White Star line! It was also seven times her beam!

According to Alexander Polyhistor and Abydenus,[1] King Chronos, or *Time*, one of the early kings of Greater Atlantis, appeared in a dream to Xisusthrus and told him that, on the 15th of the month Dæsios, all the world would be destroyed by a great flood, and that he must write a history of all things and cache the records of ante-diluvian history in a vault in the city of the sun at Sipparah. He was also to build a great ship and freight her with himself, his friends and relatives, and selected animals, birds and plants, and then trust himself fearlessly to the deep. Berosus gives the incredible number of years during which these *ten* (Atlantean) Chaldæan kings reigned, from the first king Alorus, to the Great Deluge, as 462,000 years, or 120 *sari*; but it must be remembered that their years were not those of 365 days, but much nearer 260 days; since the Earth appeared then to have rotated in an orbit much nearer the sun, and close to Venus. More than one Central American myth, as well as totally unconnected traditions cited by the old Roman Varro, the historian, imply that the pre-cataclysmal Earth was much nearer the orbit of Venus than now, and that the years were naturally much shorter. Even so, it must be freely admitted that the more conventional histórian-chronologist, and the modern encyclopædic Wellsian writer, not to speak of the crusted archæologist will smile in their beards, or let rip most unaca-demic oaths and naughty words at being asked to agree that civilization existed on this earth for a period of 30,773 years prior to the foundation of old Babylon! None of these great luminaries will even *look* at evidence existing in rocks in Nicaragua, or in artifacts found deep in mines in California, suggesting that, even in Tertiary times, civilized races existed in old North and Central America, as well as in South America. However, old Father Time has a most objectionable habit of letting both scientists and historians know that the heresy of to-day becomes the dogma of to-morrow, and the derision of the day after that! He does not even spare the feelings and prejudices of museum

---

[1] It is curious that the followers of Zeordusht told Sir William Hamilton, about 1810 that the sacred books of the Behdins speak of a universal deluge called the Deluge of *Time*.

experts, or university archæologists, which, of course, is very pesky and irreverent of him.[1]

Xisusthrus, too, sent out birds from his ship-ark, as did the white culture heroes who landed in arks on the shores of what is now Oregon and Washington, United States of America. The old myth says that Xisusthrus, his wife and daughters and the unnamed pilot of the ark, were translated to the skies from the top of Ararat's peak. And those left on the ground heard a voice from aloft which said:

> Live the good life. Go back to Babylon and there dig ye up the buried records.

They obeyed, and rebuilt Babylon and founded cities and temples. A considerable part of this ark on Ararat remained in the time of Josephus (he died in A.D. 93); but Abydenus gives another turn to the story, in which Xisusthrus is made to escape from the ship while the folk of the country used the timbers of the ark as good-luck amulets[2] for the neck. Melo, cited by Eusebius, says that the man saved with his *sons* from the waters of the Deluge was afterwards driven away by the Armenians and retired into the mountains. Was it not Kinglake, in *Eothen*, who said that, in *his* day, in the old Levant, the degrees of spiritual depravity were in the order of Armenian, Greek and Jew? Zonar, in his Annals, asserts that the word Baris, the other name of the peak of Ararat, meant in Scythic, *ship*. As one has seen this does not square with the interpretation of Ararat-Haraberez (Iranian "World Mountain") by the German savant Karst (*Vide* page 404 *f.n. supra*).

I have already pointed out that in the museum of Istanbul there is, or used to be, a terra-cotta tablet. On this tablet, a scribe Ellit-Aya had copied from a very ancient lost record about the Deluge. It shows that, even in 2140 B.C., the Orient knew of the traditions of the Great Cataclysm. There were twelve books on the Great Deluge, one for each month. The Nineveh tablets of Assurbanipal in the British Museum *are at least* 1,540 *years later* than the terra-cotta tablet fragment! (*Vide* also chap. 8, page 391.)

[1] Let 'em all cheer up, and say with old Roman Cicero, that it is *most* impudent of the Babylonians, and those in the region of the Caucasus, to have pretended to observe the skies and the courses of the stars and to have preserved monuments that record these astronomical observations as extending back for 470,000 years! As Syncellus said in his *Old Egyptian Chronicle*—he was an old Byzantine historian and only "a few old fossils" to-day glance at his Latin: "There is a tablet called the 'Old Chronicle' among the Egyptians, and there are also the Hermaic books cited by Jamblichus as having been written one each year. I think Manetho was led astray by this Old Chronicle. It reckons thirty dynasties in one hundred and thirteen descents over an immense period of time, to wit, three myriads and 6,525 years, (36,525 years). And in the first year, appeared the long-eared rulers," (Mu-an?) "the Auritarum. They were the first series of the princes in old Egypt, and were followed by the second, the Mestræorum, and he begins the story of the Egyptians almost in this manner." True Eusebius says that the Egyptian year was a lunar month; but there are folk who refuse to believe that the ancient Egyptian priest-astronomers knew no better than this! They were too closely in touch with the migrants and refugees from old Atlantis, both before and after the Great Cataclysm, not to know the difference between a lunar month and a solar, or sidereal year.—AUTHOR.

[2] Jerome, Egyptian author of an ancient history of the Phœnicians, said the remains of *Argo*, the Ark, were on the mountains of Armenia.

Still another ark started out from the very ancient antediluvian city of Surippak, near the mouth of the Tigris, with the Chaldean Sitnapisti aboard. This ark grounded on the mountains of Nazir, 250 miles up the Tigris Valley and perhaps in the region of Lake Van. Exact chronology is impossible. One may refuse to agree with Polyhistor that from the time when Xisusthrus's ark grounded, to the age when the Medes conquered Babylon was 33,091 years! The *Oera Linda Boek* of the old Frisians would make it 1,597 years, and the Chinese Bamboo Annals give a date for the Great Deluge that would make the Mede conquest of Babylon happen only 1,074 years after the Great Cataclysm. Maybe, one can reconcile these conflicting dates in the probable fact that thousands of years separate the three great cataclysms that disrupted and sank Greater Atlantis and Lesser Atlantis, the latter associated with the seven islands of Proserpine or Proserpina and the great island of the Plato-Solon-Psonchis story, which is Poseidonis.

The Kings and sages of the antediluvian world, over which the shadow of Atlantis loomed large, engraved records of events and astronomical and astrological data upon stone pillars, Josephus says that a pillar of stone was still standing in his day, and that he had seen it. On it were recorded the revolutions and courses of the stars and planets, prior to the Great Deluge. There was a pillar of stone to withstand water, and one of brick to defy fire, since both of these elements, according to a traditional prediction by Adam,[1] were

---

[1] Adam figures in the Cortesian codex of old Mexico, along with Eve. They are seen sitting under a tree—the Tree of Life of the Osage Indians and the old Scandinavian eddas—and there are glyphs that denote human sacrifice. A serpent's head is seen near that of the woman. The serpent or dragon is the famous symbol of water cataclysm, or the Great Flood that destroyed the Paradise of the North, or Atlan-Aeyre-Hyperborei. We thus see what the old allegory of Genesis, so badly and naïvely garbled, means by the expulsion from Paradise. Moreover the Dragon of the old Mexican codices has thirteen small divisions, denoting days of the week, twenty of which made the sacred Mexican year. Again, we have a memory of the Hyperborean Paradise of the North, when the Earth revolved nearer the Sun, and *the year was one of* 260 *days, or* 20 *by* 13. Bustamente quotes an author of an old Mexican hieroglyphic manuscript which says the author had seen a very ancient chart on paper of coarse maguey leaves, in which was an orchard with a *sun* tree at whose foot twined a snake, and in the middle was the head and face of a woman. She bore the first child in the world and was called Otzomosco, or sweet pregnancy. Adam, in the Hindu *Pauranics*, was a great king of Atlantis who appointed seven vassal kings of Atlantis, one of whom was Mithra, the same Mithra of the Roman legionaries of Kipling's wall whose morning trumpets sang: "Rome is above the nations but thou art over all". It is Mithra's bull's blood bath which was so horribly transformed into the fountain of blood from Emmanuel's veins. After appointing the vassal princes, Adam withdrew into solitude, and renounced the world. Winchell, a nineteenth-century American professor lost his job at Vanderbilt University for asserting that Adam was *not* a white man! Eusebius de Salle said Adam was *red*, and Prichard held he was black or of black complexion, according to a very old and wide-spread tradition. The *Hagigah of the Talmud* says he was a giant who lost his stature and god-likeness. It will be remembered that, in old Atlantis, red, white and black races commingled, though it is probable that the rulers were white, though maybe, in the remote days of the earlier Atlantis, their skins were dark in complexion. It must also be remembered that old Hyperborei-Atlan-Aeyre was a great continent in a far warmer and more genial earth, when forests ranged right into the polar regions, and there was no frozen sea. Maybe it was the cold that changed the pigmentation of the skin. If we deem Adam a very early man, he may very well have been black. There is another aspect of this riddle of Adam the Atlantean, which may be

successively to destroy the world. It will be remembered that the "suns" of water and fire, ages in which cataclysms destroyed or would destroy the human race, figured in the Toltec and Aztec myths and painted codices in old Mexico.

Josephus gives the measurements of Noah's Ark of four storeys braced by cross-beams. It had a roof and firm walls, and, he says, came to rest on the Armenian mountains called by the Greeks "Apobaterion". "The remains are shown by the inhabitants to this day," he adds (*circa* A.D. 50). He tells us that the children of Seth—apparently giants of the kingdom of Thoth, or Taut of Atlantis—made a brick pillar and one of stone in which they engraved their discoveries. The one was a duplicate of the other, to guard against destruction. Josephus adds:

> Now, these pillars remain in the land of Siriad to this day . . . Noah quitted the land of Seth for fear that his family might be annihilated by the giants. Their span of life had been reduced to 120 years . . . and Jah turned dry land into sea to destroy the earth . . . The food of the antediluvians was fitted to maintain a long life, and they observed the stars over the period of the Great Year, that is 600 years. . . . . Ephorus and Nicolaus say that the antediluvians had a span of life of 1,000 years. (Remember that these were probably years of 260 days each.—AUTHOR.) As late as the days of Joshua, son of Nun, there were still giants of Hebron, who had bodies so large and faces so entirely different from other men, that they were surprising to the sight and terrible to the hearing. The bones of these giant men are still shown to this day.

Light on what happens in a Great Cataclysm which converts gods, to be euhemerized as great sage-kings, into twilight gods of underworlds and subterraneans and lords of Acheron and Styx, Hades and Hell, ruled over by Satan, Seth-Lucifer, is shown in the old Hindu

associated with the Panchæa of the Indian Ocean, an Atlantean island found by Evhemerus on a voyage he undertook by order of the Macedonian king, Cassandra, fourth century B.C. In the fourth century of our own era, the Chinese Buddhist monk, Fa-Hien (Kung of Wa-yang) was the first to light on the petroglyphs called Adam's footprints—5 feet long—on a peak in Ceylon, where Gautama is not known ever to have been. Prints of human feet in stone are, by the way, found all over South, Central and North America and are memorials of ancient culture heroes in black, who preceded the Great Cataclysm. (I know of some in a swamp in Nova Scotia.) Now, professors Haeckel and Peschel contended that early man made his appearance in a lost continent in the Indian Ocean, which they called Lemuria. What dim connection can we see between these pointers and the existence of a continent of the Indo-Pacific Ocean which was called Pan, and whose memories are seen in Panchæa, associated with Pan of Atlan, in the old Egyptian Punt, and in the Nip-pon or Y-pan-gui, a yellow-negroid race? Is the missing link found in the *trident* of Neptune, which curious weapon, as artifacts in old Californian graves show, was the weapon of an ancient Pacific sea power? And does the trident suggest a great war by the Dragon power of old Greater Atlantis upon a great sea power in the Indo-Pacific, which it conquered and whose emblem the trident it adopted? How comes it that Pan is still worshipped to-day, at the cattle fair at Killorglin, Eire, under the form of a goat enthroned on a platform to whom men and women dance and sing? They do it every August. What brings Pan pipes in *ancient* graves in Perú? Why would not the ancient Caledonians eat fish—there are South American tribes in the upper Amazon who share the same aversion? Was it because the fish is the symbol of a great war between the old Dragon power of imperial Atlantis and a great continent in the Pacific, or because the fish is the ancient symbol of a Great Flood?—AUTHOR.

theory of the *kalpas*. These are zodiacal periods of 36,020 years, wherein the Sun was deemed to have passed through the twelve signs of the Zodiac. "All things are reversed. North becomes South, and South, North. Gods become devils, and devils gods." Isaiah's Lucifer, or son of the morning, ruler of old Hyperborei-Atlan, who sat on the great mountain of the "Paradise of the North" and exalted his throne above the stars of God, descends into Hell, or Hades—that Hades which the ancient Greeks and Romans swore was in the *northern part of the British Isles*, land of ancient awe and mystery. Satan-Seth-Thoth is sunk into the watery abyss in the Great Cataclysm, and becomes confused and identified with the old Dragon of the Great Cataclysm. Or in other words, Greater Atlantis is called the Dragon of the Abyss and the Underworld. In another cycle, Lucifer may be again exalted to the stars, according to these ancient Aryo-Hindu myths!

According to the *Talmud*, it was the setting of the Pleiades which ushered in an era of terrible cold. Here, it may be recalled that this island-universe is known to have one star fewer than it had thousands of years ago. The onset of that cold and glaciation caused the great trek across the glaciers from the north to the shores of Central America. In Aztec Mexico, as in pagan Eire, the memory of the Pleiades' part in the Great Cataclysm was kept alive age by age. Ireland has the festival of relighting all fires in the *Samhuinn*. In old Mexico, on the mountains of Huizachtleatl, two leagues from Mexico City, the Aztec priests assembled on the summit when the seven stars of the Pleiades ascended the middle of the sky at the dawn of the winter solstice. All fires in both Ireland and old Mexico were then doused and relit. As late as 1830, the Irish walked round the sacred *bon*-fire, saying their prayers, while the young men and women indulged in day-dreams over the ashes.

The *Talmud* says that men could not endure the heat of *Kesil* (Sirius?) because of the excessive cold of the Pleiades. It is, again curious that the old Aztec symbol for the cold month was a hand (*titl*) pulling on a cord. They placed their *cold* hell in the North. *Titl* and *Kesil* seem to have a common root. The ancient Sabæo-Arabs called the constellation *Kesal*, which means to be asleep, numbed or cold. It seems likely that the predecessors of Ezra who held that the constellation called *Kesal* or *Kesil* were the seven stars of the Pleiades were right, rather than those who confused it with Sirius. Apparently, the ancients held that it was some cosmic association of Sirius[1] with

1 The Pehlavi texts of the Parsi fire-worshippers say that the Deluge came because the star Tistar (Sirius) was in Cancer, in the water sub-division called "Avrak". The water was pouring in on the same day when the destroyer rushed in and came again for mischief, in the direction of the west. Sirius rose about the same time as the stars of Cancer . . . "The water stood the height of man all over the earth, and noxious creatures, all killed by the rain, went into the great caves." The Zend Avesta tells how, before the Great Cataclysm, the world was warm and genial. But, at a meeting of gods and excellent mortals, Ahura Mazda predicted that snow flakes would fall thick on the high mountains and plains. The good shepherd, Yima was to make a great Vara, or square enclosure a mile wide on every side, make blazing red fires, and pen up in it the finest cattle, sheep, men, dogs,

the Pleiades that precipitated the Great Cataclysm, which disrupted and sank most of Hyperborei-Atlan, creating a cold hell of fog and icy darkness, during which the Ierne, or Ireland, and probably the British Isles of Scotland and England, or Brittia-Britanja-Caledonia, became a desert and uninhabited for two centuries. It is of this age of glaciation in the North that the old myths and books of the Quichés and the Popul-Vuh speak.

The Moslem Qu-ran, or Koran, says that old Noah planted an ebony tree and cut planks from it to make his great deluge ship, which is a not unlikely thing. We have a glimpse of some knowledge of physics and electro- or chemi-luminescence possessed by this old Atlantean Noah. The Qu-ran says he placed on the walls of the Ark *two luminous discs to make (or mark) day and night.* (This should be compared with the story of the unending light that shines from the walls of an ancient tower, or house, close to a dead Hy-Brazilian city in the jungle-forests of the fierce Suyas of the Matto Grosso, the savages by whom Colonel Fawcett may have been captured in 1926.)

Another curious glimpse is given in the Qu-ran:

> The hour draweth nigh . . . and the Moon is split asunder . . . and we opened the gates of heaven with water rushing down . . . and we bore him on the thing of planks and nails, sailing on beneath our eyes . . . when the water surged we bore you on it in a sailing ship.

While old Noah was making his great ship—and ancient myths said he had part of a respite of 120 years to do the shipbuilding job in—the giants, men of immense stature, gathered round the stocks and laughed and jeered:

> The deluge cannot harm us. We are too tall. Our feet are so monstrous in size we can close up the springs . . . But Jah heated the water and scalded their feet, and the flesh of their bodies.

South American tribes, on the western Amazon headwaters, speak of very ancient deluges of hot water that cascaded on the forests and mountains in the Great Cataclysm:

> As the waters rose, the giants hurled their children into the abyss. (*Rabbincial literature.*)

Was it to stay the flood, or put their children out of their misery?

The *Midrash-ha-Gadol* of the Rabbinical literature says that the giants told Noah that if a cataclysm of fire came on the world:

> We have a fire-animal called *Alitha*, which, when its name is spoken, will act as a spell against it. If water comes, we have sheets of iron to

women. Waters should flow in it by green banks and birds sing. "Make nine streets with houses and balconies for a thousand selected (eugenic) men and women in the middle part; and nine hundred more streets in other parts. Two of every kind of the finest fruits and trees, with the sweetest odours. Admit no humpbacks, no insane, none with decayed teeth, or leprosy, none impotent, no poverty, no lying, or meanness, or jealousy. None of the brands of mortals upon whom Angra Mainyu (Ahriman) hath set his seal. Seal up the Vara with thy golden ring. Make a door and window self-shining within. Here the men shall live for 150 years. When the great rain of Malkos ceaseth, the doors of the Vara shall open and men go forth to re-inhabit the earth."

cover the earth from waters rising from below. If the skies rain a deluge, we have a great *Akob*, or sponge. . . . Noah entered the ark when the water reached his knees and in full sight of the giants, in broad daylight. Jah assured him the giants would not stop up the abyss, nor the fruit in the ark mildew or lose colour . . . Noah was in the ark for a year, and he could not sleep and was also annoyed by the feral smell of the wild beasts. Those who entered the ark left it, no more and no fewer.

The *Sefar-ha-Yashar* adds that while Noah and the animals were in the ark, they were scared to death by hurricanes. Nothing, again, inherently unlikely in that!

Let us return to the question of the identity of the old man called Noah. Cosmas Indicopleustes, a merchant of Alexander, who travelled to Ceylon, India and Ethiopia, and became a monk *circa* A.D. 525, when he was suffering from indigestion and ophthalmia, said that Noah dwelt in the land of Atlantis, and when that continent sank, sailed in an ark-ship to the continent. What continent is not stated, but the tradition is a very ancient floating one, in the east. Floating, in more than one sense! It is evident, as already commented, that the Jews mis-appropriated Noah from, or in old Egypt and turned him into a Jew for their own national ends. He was known as Thoth, in Egypt, and given in *their* pantheon the head of an unknown monster. In the ancient empire of Atlantis in America, King Thoth, a man, not a god, was also known as Tah, Tauth, Taut, and Now, Naut, or Noe. He is called Noe, on a medal struck in the reign of Philip the Elder, at Apamea. The medal shows an ark on the water with a man and woman stepping out of it on to dry land, and two persons within. A raven perches on the roof, and a dove flutters with an olive branch. The medal has no connection with Hebraic myths, as in the Septuagint and the Old Testament.[1]

The name of Thoth ranges right round the world to Tahiti, in the South Seas! In the British Museum, there is a pectoral brought many years ago from Tahiti. It is very like one worn by Thoth of Egypt and old Hyperborei-Atlan. The suggestions are that in a far day the empire of old Atlantis extended to the Pacific, whether from the shores of America, or from the other Atlantean imperial colony of Panchæa in the Indian Ocean, and which had been founded by an Atlantean named Zeus, a man and a king (not a god) who led an expedition from pre-Minoan (?) Crete to Arabia, Iran, and the Indian Ocean.

In Tahiti, the old South Sea navigators and the missioners found great stepped pyramids of solid masonry, megalithic structures, and stone causeways, while in other islands there were solid structures of megalithic type, and, in one island, seen by Captain Cook, a very ancient circus, or amphitheatre, to which a curious causeway of coral

---

[1] Noah's ark in bronze was found, in 1886, in a very ancient stone circular tomb at Vetulonia, Etruria. It is said to be of the seventh century B.C., and shows signs of Phœnician workmanship. The animals in it are mostly domestic, with a rat shown gnawing a rope. A similar ancient ark was found in Sardinia.

led across a marsh. In the Hawaiian, or Sandwich Islands, it was noted that words, like the following, had European and Indo-European affinities—but, of course, the link, or common source, was Mu-an and Atlantean:

Kanaka, man (*cf.* with Sanscrit *Janaka*, to be born, and Anglo-Saxon, *cyn*); *La*, sun (*cf.* Ra, the sun: Egypt), *Vira*, the sun, in old Hy-Brazilian Atlantis, modern Portugal, and Perú, Sanscrit, *Laji*, to shine; *Maka*, face (*cf.* with Anglo-Saxon, *mug*); *Ma*, the moon (*cf.* with the most ancient word in the world, *Ma*, and *Mu*, the old motherland or drowned Pacific continent of Rutas-Mu, and with Sanscrit *Mah*, and Anglo-Saxon *Mona*).

These South Sea island pyramids[1] were associated with Tah, or Taut, or Thoth. Champollion, the late eighteenth century French Egyptologist, pointed out that Thoth was councillor to Pooh, the Moon. The old Hindus said that pyramids in India and Egypt were copies of the ancient mountain in the centre of the world, called Meru, whose root is linked with the *Mer* in America, and the ancient American race of the Meroes. They were the tomb of the son of the spirit of Heaven, Osiris, the Atlantean man, whose bones had been scattered over the face of the earth. It looks, therefore, as if, in a very far day, old Noah-Taut-Tah had ranged all over the world from the Pacific to Egypt, the Near East and Europe. Grasset de Saint Sauveur, who went on a voyage to the South Seas some time after that of Captain Cook, said:

The people of Tahiti, before the Europeans arrived, had priests, a religion of nature, immolated infants to the gods . . . (*N.B.* This is a trait derived from old Mu and found also in Central America where Mu had old colonies.—AUTHOR.) and had arts, commerce and navigation. They dress their hair in a way singularly like that of ancient Rome. They had 200 foot long houses and dressed for the table with speed and punctuality. Their canoes—different from those of other South Sea islands—had a mast with triangular sails . . . In war, they united many vessels to form a stage. They had names for all the stars, knew their rising and setting, had a 12-hour day and a 13-month year, measured by feet and counted by dozens. They had temples, but no islands. Their god was Toaheite.

Toaheite is a variant of the name Taut, or Thoth. Summing it all up, therefore, it looks as if old man Noah must have gone a devil of a long way before—if he did—he landed from his ark on a mountain top in some other world to the east!

Now, when the Great Flood poured out over Atlantis, a great leader named Merodach, who was an Atlantean, took refuge in an island called Soy. Where Soy was we do not know, but it was certainly a mere fragment of the Aldland, or Atlan remaining over after the Great Cataclysm, and it has also an odd, and perhaps, not entirely fortuitous

[1] One ancient eastern tradition is that the pyramid was a copy of the hill on which the Ark rested after the Great Flood. The sun came out after long ages of dark, cold and misery and wet, and a temple was built to him. It was the "Paradise of Eden, the garden of the gods". The old Hindu *Meru* consisted of eight diminishing towers, piled one on top of another, with stairways, and stepped. It was oriented to the four compass points.

resemblance to the name of Hoy, in the Orkneys, which was close to the sunken continent of Hyperborei-Atlan. In Soy, Merodach, with a band of refugees who numbered among them navigators, scientists, naval architects and engineers, supervised the construction of a very large ship. Aboard this ancient liner, he and the refugees sailed over the ocean to the Sahara, then an inland sea, across which they passed to the land of Egypt, which was then very much higher out of the water than it now is. Here, ancient traditions say they joined forces with former migrants from old Atlantis, who had built great pyramids for astronomical and astrological purposes. They used to meet in secret chambers within the Great Pyramid for astronomical and astrological study and the evolution of a wisdom-cult.

In a much later age, Merodach became transformed by the old Assyrians into the serpent-god, Marduk, who, in the Semitic myth, had a great battle with and dashed out the brains of Tiamat, the Dragon or serpent of chaos and water cataclysm. In the Assyrian Gallery of the British Museum, there is a wall plaque which shows Merodach, or Marduk, *armed with a double trident* from which rays lightning. I have already pointed out the possible significance of the trident of Neptune in relation to a dim Atlantean "Dragon" battle for world power with an ancient Pacific empire.

A later deluge took place in the age of Deucalion, bits of which myth are found incorporated in North and South American cataclysm traditions, ranging from the Orinoco to far Alaska! It is said to have happened in the later Bronze Age, perhaps when the seven islands of Prosperpine were submerged in the South Atlantic. His ark parallels that of Noah, but it grounded on the top of Parnassus. Says Apollodorus, in *Bibliotheca*:

> At the bidding of Zeus he (Deucalion) created men by throwing stones over his head. And the stones became men, and those which Pyrrha, his wife, threw, became women, and that is why the Greeks are called *laoi* (stones).

How far the old Parian chronicler was correct in dating Deucalion's deluge as happening in 1530 B.C. may be disputable. Local Athenian guides, in A.D. 200, used to show sightseers a hole in the ground, in the smaller precincts of the vast temple of Olympian Zeus, down which, they said, the water vanished after the deluge. The cleft was a cubit wide. Each year cakes and water were thrown down to feed the souls who perished in the deluge! But Lucian says this cleft was a former great chasm in the earth at Hieropolis, Syria, and that, in his day—Deucalion had built an altar and set up a temple, here—the chasm was much smaller. He goes on:

> I could see the hole . . . and twice a year, the priests, in the presence of people from Syria, Arabia and lands beyond the Euphrates, poured water from the sea down a cleft in the temple-floor and which was absorbed, in memory of the Deluge. It was Deucalion who started this festival. He sent out a dove from his ark on the waters.

There was also the story of an antediluvian named Nannakos, who lived for 300 years. Says Lucian in his *De Dea Syria*:

> Men, or his heirs, got tired of the old man, who had lived too long, said his friends. When they asked the oracle how long he would live, the reply was: "When he dies, all men will die with him!"[1]

Nannakos was said to have been an aged king in Phrygia who foresaw the coming of a great catastrophe, and who, says Suidas, gathered his people into sanctuaries to weep and pray. Lucian has a very curious passage on this old gentleman Nannakos:

> At the north gate of the great temple, there stood two tall columns or obelisks, 360 feet high, and up which twice a year a man climbed to stay seven days. Some say it signifies that men had ascended to mountain tops and tall trees to escape the deluge.

There was also the Great Deluge of Ogyges, when waves washed even over the snowy top of Parnassus. He was king of Eleusis, and Varro dates this catastrophe as in 2136 B.C. Ogyges is said to have founded Thebes (*not* the Egyptian Tabas, or Thebes), and connected with him are strange remains of megalithic type in the Copaic Lake, in central Bœotia. Here, dead cities are scattered in ruins, one being Gla, or La, or Goulas whose ancient name and history are unknown. Even legend and tradition are silent. It is a weird lost world of rocky hills, dead flats, crumbling forts, with gateways flanked with towers—they remind one of the ancient forts of the Urartu—ruins of a great palace, and all of massive masonry built to stand for ever and a day. It was such a dead city as the old Brazilian bandeiristas gazed on in the forests and mountains of Hy-Brazilian Atlantis, in the year A.D. 1745. Gla seems to have been erected by a people akin to the Mycenians, though with not quite the enormous size of the stones of Tiryns. Little pottery fragments and bits of furniture have been found, and all the signs are that the place was occupied for a very short time. There are signs of fire in the palace and the end seems to have been sudden and violent.

Sir James Frazer who visited the place, says:

> Everything bears the imprint of one plan and period. No trace of an earlier settlement, or a later one, is visible. Created at a blow, it would seem to have perished at a blow and never again inhabited. In silence and solitude, remote from all human haunts, its ancient grey walls look over a vast plain to distant mountains. The place is a mystery. *Was it the home of Ogyges and forsaken by him at the Deluge, when he retired to the higher and drier site, later known as Thebes?*

As we again see, Noah's ark was but one of the vast ships which

---

[1] There is a doubtless apocryphal story that someone consulted a Fabian oracle, or Socialist physician, as to the expectation of life of the ven. George Bernard Shaw, and that when the old gentleman heard of it, he said: "Let 'em all drown. I shall still go living on."

Macchipicchu Inca fortress, near Cuzco

Pan Pipe Indians (Andes): Pan-Atlan, lost Indian Ocean continent, had
a South American empire

Oera Linda Boek: Letters of the script of Frya, based on the solar wheel, and probably the origin of runes. Some Atlantean derivation seems indicated

Oera Linda Boek: (Line 1): Archaic "Tex" of Frya; (Line 2 and Line 1 end): Numerals including Zero, antedating Hindu-Arabian "metaphysical nought"; (Lines 3 to 6): Frya's Letters: u, ü, ê, e, i, j, y, b, p, t, th, d, f, v, r, n, ng, m, k, s, c, ks, gs

fled from a drowned or drowning continent, west to old America, east to Europe and Africa. There is, the reader may be surprised to hear, remarkable modern evidence for the presence on both European and ancient American soil *of remains of antediluvian ships*!

Giovanni Pontano, an Italian historian and statesman who died at Naples in A.D.1503, was one of many persons, who, in his day, on a mountain top high over the sea at Naples, saw, enclosed in the middle of a great boulder brought down by a hurricane, the remains of a great and ancient ship of antediluvian make. It was certainly no old Roman, or Carthaginian galley or trireme. The rock completely enclosed the old ship and it was evident that such a petrification must have taken thousands of years.

Another Italian, Alejandro Alejandro (1461–1525), says in one of his *incunabula,* titled *Dias Geniales*:

> In my day, as is well known, artificers cutting marble, found in the middle of the block, so extremely hard that it (the marble) could only with difficulty be broken open with pickaxes, a quantity of oil (*aceite*), as it might be in a vase, which was clear and limpid, and of excellent colour and odour. No one could say how the oil came to be enclosed within that block.

Again, in A.D. 1460, miners digging for metals in the mountains of the canton of Berne, in Switzerland, found, at a depth of 100 feet in the bowels of the earth, a most ancient wooden ship which must have perished untold ages before. It had carvings and was well-fashioned. By it lay masts, broken and eaten away with secular corrosion. There was *an anchor of iron*, and what gave the old Swiss miners a horrid turn was the sight in the timbers of *the bones and skulls of forty men.* Another contemporary account, in Latin, says that the ship had rotted shreds of what looked like sails of some woollen fibre adhering to her masts. Eye-witnesses told the story to old Baptista Fulgosa, Italian writer in forgotten Latin folios of many curious things in nature, read only by curious scholars of to-day.

I myself have seen in the mountains of the Savoie, not very far from Chambéry, France, huge iron and bronze rings fixed solidly into the rocks, and in places inaccessible to ordinary travellers. The local peasants assure one: "*Monsieur*, they go back to the days when the waters of the Great Deluge covered this land. Men with boats fastened them to these rings to moor them, while they climbed further above the reach of the swirling waters". One may believe it or not, of course. Also, in the mountains of the Voirons, close to the Swiss frontier in the French Haute Savoie, there is, on the Mont de Salève, about 1,500 feet up, what is locally called the Passe de Cheval. Here, engraved in a big block of stone, may be seen huge petroglyphs shaped like great hoof marks. They may be of Neolithic origin and linked with some cult of the white horse, associated with the old sacred groves of Germania and the Wilts downs of England, and ultimately going back to the hippo cults and horse-races of old Atlantis. But the peasants have quite other ideas about them:

V'la, monsieur, they were from the horse of a giant whom Noah could not get into the ark. When the Flood rose the monster animal leapt on to this rock, which was the highest part he could see. And as fast as the drowning people tried to clamber up, he up with his hooves and kicked 'em off till, he, too, was drowned.

So much for old Europe. Now let us look at old America. These antediluvian ships have been found by old Spanish miners at the time of the conquest. One was found in a mine in old Panama. It was a buried ship or galley of very ancient type. A Roman coin of Augustus Cæsar was also found in old Panama, and no explanations have ever been given of such finds, either here or in the United States of America. Then, about the year A.D. 1540, Spanish miners were running an adit into a *cerro* near Callao, Perú, on the hunt for silver or gold whose traces they thought they had detected. While throwing up the earth from a deep shaft they were startled to come on a ship of no fashion of their own day, but very ancient. It had borne over it the immense weight of the earth and rock and of the hill!

Have we here one of the craft in which the refugees fled to the shores of South America from the last cataclysm that sank the homeland of Mu?

In my next book in these series of ancient world mysteries I shall give some startling pictures of the last days of old Mu, and the terrible scenes on the shores of western South America, when they arrived, the air now lit, now shrouded in flames and palls of smoke and poisoned with gases, the light of the sun gone out, the beaches stinking with corpses of rotting men and animals, and monstrous-sized sea saurians, the land quaking like the sea, already itself raging under forces of vulcanism and typhoons and tidal waves, and of the life in the tunnels, after these Mu-ans had driven before them up into the highlands the old Ayars who obeyed the rule of a race of white kings far to the east in ancient Brazil!

At Cayatambo, in Perú, in the sixteenth century, there was found by Spanish miners, deep in a silver mine at the eighth stage of its depth, a nail or spike shaped like a cross and embedded in the body of a very hard rock, from which it had to be hacked out with another hard stone, clamped with a sharp point. The nail had been riveted to a piece of wood. It was about 6 inches long and the viceroy, Don Francisco de Toledo, who wanted it for his cabinet as a curio, was forestalled by an Augustinian monk who took it home to old Spain. The nail, it is said, was as free from rust as if it had only that day been placed in the shaft.

But old California is the land for startling antediluvian finds, followed closely in sheer mystery by the Ohio and the Middle West of the United States of America. In California, they include a skull of a man of apparently Tertiary age found 130 feet deep in a mine with *lava over it; six-toed giants:* a bronze cup filled with red paint; an image of a man of very archaic type with unknown letters on the sides of the carving; a mysterious causeway 18 feet under a desert; petroglyphs cut through iron scale in a wind-eroded cañon, depicting, from the life, *tyrannosaurus,* the most fearsome dinosaur, as done by some ancient artist who watched the monster; *an amazing human skull of giant size with a double row of teeth;* polished plummets, skillets, and granite tablets deep in old mines with signs of some antediluvian mining. All that has not been found, or at any rate reported so far, are the remains of an ancient ship.[1]

The old Toltec myth speaks of all the world drowning, except eight men who escaped in a house like an enclosed ark. They called it by the unwieldly name of "Tlapitlipetlocalli" and painted it on their rolls as a small boat with an awning on top, and eight heads peering out. In 1810 Baron Wilhelm von Humboldt found an old Mexican, or Aztec, painting depicting the old Mexican Noah, Coxcox or Pezpi, in the middle of a raging sea in a ship. A mountain rises above the waves and is crowned with a tree. All perished in the Great Deluge save Coxcox and his wife and family. From the mountain of Colhuacan, he sent out a vulture from the ark, which fed on rotting corpses and did not return. Only the humming bird came back with a leafy branch in its beak. There is the grim picture derived by the early missioner, Fray Andrés de Olmos from the old Mexicans. It is one of many years of cataclysm, in which we have a queer picture of Atlantean god-men from the land of Tullan, gathering round a great fire in a tunnel, and of one man who cast himself into the flames to have the honour of being made a sun:

> The chiefs peered round through the darkness and bet each other where the light would first appear. But all were wrong. They said: "Lo, he will rise there, or here, but when he rose in the east none had fixed on that point."

It is a vivid passage indicating the length of time these refugees spent in the endless dark of these ancient tunnels, and how they had lost their orientation entirely. Says the *Popul Vuh,* the Quiché Bible:

> Years had passed. Outside the earth was all dank and moist. The cold was great. The sun was not seen. Generations had lived and died,

[1] A truly amazing corroboration of the dentition of these antediluvian giants of ancient *America* is found in the *Hulin* section of the *Berakthoth,* or Babylonian *Talmud,* where it is said the giants, before the Great Deluge, *had numerous rows of teeth!* The old compilers of the *Hulin* can hardly be said to have heard of this Californian find! The *Hulin* tells us that these giants had feet 18 ells long, and ate one thousand oxen, horses, and camels each day. Even Barnum would have been hard put to it to maintain two of them in his wildest west show ever! We have the quaint passage telling us: "Noah saved Og, the giant, by giving him a place near the lattice door of the ark, through which Noah handed him food every day". Og had sworn to serve Noah and family for all time, so that Noah was not exactly moderate in the *quid* he expected for the *quo!* The Moslems say Og was a son of Noah's sister and survived Noah 1,500 years, till Moses killed him. Surely Moses, in the part of Jack the Giant-killer, will be new to most folk! But my friend, Comyns Beaumont, could tell them things about the *real* Moses which would surely upset a college of theological professors!—AUTHOR.

tongues were changed, and confused, ere the evaporated sea fell as rain, and the sun shone wanly thro' the blanket of dark and cold. The morning star rose and men and animals rose from the water courses and ravines and stood on the mountain tops . . The sun had as yet no heat . . . When the blazing sun first reappeared, after ages, men were afraid and hid in the forests and mountains and even on the water . . . Men left Tulan led by Tohi and set out to find the sun. The hardships were great. They sustained themselves on the mere smell of their staves. They went thro' many forests, crossed stern mountains and went along shingles, rubble and drifted sand, by the shores of the sea . . . Crossing seas of ice . . . And on a mountain called after the god Hacaritz, the sun came out, and they sang a hymn in memory of the men who nevermore would see the sun.

The Orinoco Indians on the upper waters near Encamarada, told old Frey Gili, the Franciscan missioner, that, in the Great Cataclysm, there arrived in a ship a white-bearded man who cut inscriptions on a high rock at Encamarada. The culture hero stayed a long time, put all things in order, and went away. "He returned to the other bank whence he had come. Perhaps you met him there?" naïvely enquired the Indian of the friar, as if the event had happened only yester-year! They also told the monk that they, too, had an ancient legend that woman was made from the ribs of man. It is odd that in old Mexico, Sahagun, the Spanish Missioner friar, was asked if *he* had met Quetzalcoatl, the white and bearded old culture hero in black, on the other bank, to which *he* had returned.

When the Prinz Maximilien zu Wied-Neuwied visited the land of the Mandan Indians, in Washington and Oregon, in 1834, he was told by a Mandan chief that a white-bearded man came to their ancestors in a great ship made with metal tools. He was the only man saved from the Great Deluge that covered the earth's surface, and he landed on a high mountain in the west. The old man from the ark-ship advised their ancestors, the Numungkake, to build a wooden tower on a hill, assuring them that the water would not reach higher than the point. They also say that the ark was built very large, and a part of the nation was saved in it, the rest perishing in the waters.

He was also told that, before that, the Numungkake lived in great tunnels below the ground—a story paralleled by the Apaches Indians, who say *their* remote ancestors came from a great fire island in the eastern ocean, where was a great port with an entrance of architectural masonry where ships had to be guided in by pilots. The Fire Dragon arose and made their ancestors flee from this island— which can be none other than the old Atlantean island of Pluto, mentioned by the lost and ancient Punic historian, Procles. The Apaches eventually reached the mountains of Tiahuanacu, where they were forced to take refuge in immense and ancient tunnels, through which they wandered *for years* carrying seeds and fruit plants.

The Mandans—who were mostly wiped out by smallpox, in 1830, the survivors being forcibly incorporated in the Redskin tribes of the Rickarees—added that the first men to emerge from these old American tunnels, were the *Histoppa*, or tattooed. They perished in the Deluge, having too soon emerged above ground to see how things were. The rest of the men stayed on below ground. Then one day, they saw a light shine over their heads. They sent out a mouse, who came back to say that the world above was uninhabited!

There are ancient North American traditions which actually assert that these mysterious tunnels were built or bored by an ancient race of *white men*, long since dead and who caused an ancient cataclysm!

The Mandans built a model of this ark,[1] and, each spring, danced round it in memory of the men saved from the Great Deluge. The *dance lasted for forty days* and the figure four, famed as the number associated with ancient solar relics, found in graves in Georgia and Florida, United States of America, as it was in old Perú, where the Inca emperor of the Sun claimed he ruled the four quarters of the world —played its part in this spring fête. They also said that a dove sent from the ark in the Deluge came back with a willow slip in her beak.[2]

The old Araucanian Indians of Chile had their traditions of an ark that grounded on the shores or mountains of old Chile in a great deluge. May we not, therefore, say that the solution of these riddles of the dim past of ancient and civilized man may ultimately have to be looked for not in old Europe or Asia, but in even older America, north and south?

The craft of the ship-builder and naval architect must be of incredible age. Miles Poindexter has pointed out how, thousands of years ago, the proto-Sumers invented sailing ships and carried out an extensive commerce in the Pacific and Indian Oceans in large ships with three and four masts. Their chiefs of Megalithic Age and culture were the *Ars*, and as the Mu-ans, fleeing from the great Pacific cataclysm that submerged the four great continental islands of Mu came into aggressive contact with the old *Ayars*, their South American, proto-Sumer descendants, old Sumer must be even more ancient as a world-power, with colonies in western South America, than Mr.

---

[1] I have been told of an aboriginal tribe in the mountains of Formosa, who keep a model of an ark in a mountain tarn, and dance round it in yearly rites.—AUTHOR.

[2] The Lewis and Clark expedition to Oregon in 1803–05, noted the blue eyes and silky hair of some of the Mandans, but heard nothing of these cataclysm traditions. Catlin, in 1832, wrote that the Mandans spoke fifty words of pure Welsh and one hundred and thirty words near-Welsh. They had circles of stones for their hearths in Welsh fashion, made Welsh blue beads, and navigated the Missouri in willow and raw hide coracles. Though the old Welsh Cwmry tradition is that two men escaped in an open vessel when all men were drowned, and that there were also two arks called Nwydd Nav and Neivion, and that on the ancient stone Gwyddon Ganheb all ârts and sciences of the world are engraved, I don't think this is concerned with the fact that two shiploads of Welsh were emigrated to America, in the reign of Edward I, by Prince Madoc. John Paul Marana, in the service of the Sultan of Turkey, *temp.* Charles II, of England wrote *The Turkish Spy* (London, 1734), in which he said that in British Canada lived the "Tuscoards" (Tuscarora Indians), and Doegs, who spoke Welsh and are believed to be descended from them. The name *Mandan* recalls the Welsh *madder* for red, and Catlin thought the Welsh called these Indians Mandan because of their red-dyed porcupine quills.—AUTHOR.

Poindexter thought. As early as 12000 B.C., these old Sumers had plank-built ships, and it is their description of the Ark that has been taken over by the Jews in *Genesis*. These old Sumers were linked with the ancient Anatolians, or forbears of the Toltecs, in deep-sea navigation. Their chiefs called themselves "Kings of the Sea".

The United States Admiral Rodman has described how the Tahitians —of whom I spoke earlier in this chapter—had inherited some of this very ancient lore of navigation in their use of a calabash, filled with water, with opposite holes so placed that, by sighting through them with the calabash placed level, they could get the altitude of the North Star, compared with that at Hawaii, which they knew.

An old Babylonian king, Nabonidus (*circa* 530 B.C.), when repairing the ancient sun temple at Sippara, found a clay cylinder, now in the British Museum, recording how an ancient Sumer, Naram Sin, son of Shar-Gena, had deposited it in those foundations in 5700 B.C. Eridu, at the head of the Persian Gulf, was the old Sumer sea port in 6000 B.C. It is now nearly 130 miles from the coast! These old Sumers called themselves rulers of the Four Quarters of the World, as did their Ayar white caste descendants in Incaic Perú. Menes, the first dynastic king of Egypt, with the old Sumer title of *Para* (Pharaoh, or father of the sun (?) is shown by Colonel Waddell to have been the rebel son of Sargon the Great of old Sumeria. It was this Menes who led an expedition to old Eire (Ireland) where he died from a bee sting, as is recorded on a badly-effaced hieroglyphic burial stone at Knock Many, or Hill of Menes. From old Sumer Iran, Ireland got the name of her *Mish* mountains and the trefoil Shamrock, a good luck and trinity symbol. The ancient Chinese, who also had large and ancient ships, also reached Ireland, thousands of years ago, and left those ancient Chinese seals, inscribed with hieroglyphs, which, when found in Irish river-beds, have so badly puzzled the archæologists.

Again, what about those mysterious Anuts—linked with the hairy Anus of North Japan—who, remote ages ago, had large ships, made great voyages east and west, and built those cyclopean enclosures with 12-foot thick walls, and the stone-faced canals on Ualan, Ponape and other western Pacific islands?

One may go farther back still. There are dim traditions in Greco-Phœnician myths about Saturn, son of the Ocean and ruler of Greater Atlantis who built a large ship and performed a remarkable ocean voyage in it. He is also said to have built a wonderful cave in the middle of the ocean, in which he and his wife and family took refuge in time of danger. The ancient Pauchs, or Phœnicians, had also the myth of the seven Cabiri, sons of the Sydyk, the Just Men, who are said to have built the first ship and voyaged over the ocean, after which they dedicated the relics to the god of the sea. (*Vide* Eusebius, in *Præparatio Evangelica*.)

Osiris, ancient king of the country, an Atlantean, husbandman, law-giver and inventor of wine—his other name is Bacchus—was forced to take refuge in an ark, or great ship, by the god of winds and the ocean, Typhon, or Typhoon, at the Great Deluge. The ship is called the *Argo*, or, in the similar myth of Iswara, in India, the *Argha*, or Ark. Typhon shut him in it by closing the top, and he entered that Ark on the 17th day of the month Aythyr. In the Noah story, in *Genesis*, we are told by the Jewish garblers that the fountains of the great deep broke up and the skies dissolved in a great deluge in the "second month, the 17*th day of the month*".

In the Greek myth, the mariners of the *Argonaut* send out a dove to observe the waters of the ocean, and act on her observation. Isis, Queen of Heaven, and the ancestress of the "Stella Maris" of the Roman Catholic Pontiff, was the receptacle of the hero-gods, sailing in a ship. This indicates that the ancient Atlantean-Hyperborean astronomers, centred *in the ancient British Isles* of old Avebury and Stanton Drew and Stonehenge, transferred to the skies the mystical notion of the solar system being an immense ship manned by seven planetary brothers, with the sun as pilot. Oldest China condenses this idea in a very ancient hieroglyph for *ship*: a boat, a mouth (*pilot*) and the number *eight*! (*Vide* pp. 419, 433.)

On the old Nile of Egypt, the Atlantean-Caledonian man, Osiris, transformed into a god, was annually sent afloat in the Argo (*Ark*), Theba, or Baris (*ship*). *Argo* was the first ship to reach proto-Hellenic Greece from Egypt, and Danaus was the pilot or shipmaster. Eratosthenes, in his *Catastrophe*, says that *Argo* was the first ship ever built, and the first to sail the ocean in ages long before the Great Cataclysm! Then, one has the old Goths in the *Eddas* who say that all the giants—and both Atlanteans and old Sumers were men of great stature and astonishing brain capacity, as skulls found in the old land of the proto-Sumers attest—were drowned in the Great Deluge, save one giant, who with his wife and family was saved in a ship and lived to propagate the next race of giants.

The Druids who probably took their mystical cults from the Chaldæans and the Magi, and whose red, high priest's hat the Roman Catholic Pontiff, or early Bishop of Rome, clapped on the pates of *his* cardinals, while himself taking over the triple tiara of the *pagan* Roman Pontiff Maximus, handed down traditions to the old Cwymric bards which tell how the gods sent on earth poison gases, or a wind whose every blast killed a man. (One may rationalize this as, perhaps, a cosmic catastrophe, or collision of the axis of the earth with a great comet, or a disintegrating lunar satellite, which caused great vulcanism with eruption of mephitic gases from craters.) Davis, in his *Mythology of British Druids*, says:

> The Patriarch, pure in mind, was shut up with a chosen band in an enclosure with a strong door. Here, the just ones were safe from injury. A tempest of fire arose and split the earth to the great deep. The lake Llion burst her bounds, the waves of the sea lifted themselves to the skies, on high round the borders of Britain. Rain fell in torrents. Water

covered the earth, washing away the impure into the chasms of the abyss. The lustration purified the polluted earth. The flood raised the Patriarch's ship on high from the ground, and bore it safe on the crest of the waves.

* * * * * *

The joint Anglo-American-Dutch expedition to seek for timbers of the ancient hulk on the summit of Mount Ararat, and clear up an ancient mystery, once for all, entered the troubled domain of high politics, in April and May, 1949. At that time, Moscow Radio and the U.S.S.R. official newspaper *Pravda*, put out a statement which affected to regard the whole affair as a veiled attempt on the part "of the Anglo-American military bloc to spy on the frontiers of the U.S.S.R.", from which the River Araxes separates Turkish Ararat and Russian Armenia. A glance at a map will show that the Ararat happens to occupy a sort of half-way house between the cis-Caspian U.S.S.R. and the valuable mineral deposits of the Black Sea and the Transjordan port of Akaba, adjoining the Gulf of Suez.

Since the Ankara Government of Turkey stands in deadly fear of her powerful Russian neighbour, who is believed to maintain a large army in battle formation on those borders, it is surmised that Ankara, for those reasons of security and high politics, declined to grant the necessary visas and permits to the expedition. Anyway, in certain London newspapers, in early June, 1949, there appeared a short news paragraph stating that "the proposed expedition to Mount Ararat has been ·cancelled, because the Ottoman Government would not grant the necessary permits. It is believed that Ankara was probably led to this decision by fear of trouble with the Soviet authorities."

On 17th June, 1949, an Associated Press message was cabled to London, stating:

Greensboro, North Carolina.—The search for Noah's Ark is going underground, for fear of Communist sabotage. Dr. A. J. Smith, leader of the American expedition to Ararat, says he will move to a secret assembly point for his ark-hunting expedition, because he thinks Soviet agents might try to wreck the plan.

The reader may be interested in certain other very curious ancient and modern references to this mysterious ship on Ararat, 14,000 feet up, in regions where rarefied air would render it very dangerous for folk who are not very physically fit or who may be troubled with our modern febrile age ailments of high or low blood pressure. An unknown writer called "Jerome the Egyptian", author of a lost work on the *History of the Phœnicians*—Apion, the Greek grammarian of the first century of our era, denied that this Jerome was in any way to be identified with Hieronymus Cardianus, the Alexandrian Greek general and historian who, about 240 B.C., was superintendent of the Dead Sea bed of asphalt—is said by Flavius Josephus and others to have made reference to this Ark on Ararat, as being still extant in his day. Joannes Zonaras, the Byzantine Greek historian and author of the *Kronikon*, who lived *circa* 1120 of our era, says that Noah sent out both a raven and a dove, in succession, from his ark-ship—a story or myth curiously parallelled by what is said in entirely independent myths of old Mexico and the pre-Columbian West Indies. He says the animals in the ark were "sacrificed to the god by Noah", on the top of the high mountain called "Excensum" by the Armenians, and that the remains of the timbers of the ark were to be seen on Ararat in his (Zonaras's) own day. The Midrash (Bereshith) adds that "Noah's grave is seen to this day in Armenia".

It is significant, too, that the meteorological phenomenon of the rainbow, as something hitherto unprecedented in the skies of our ancient Earth, is signalized in the *Book of Chilam Balam of Chumayel*, in which the old Mayan priests preserved the memory of the Great Cataclysm:

> And the rainbow appeared in the sky signifying that all below had been destroyed.

A curious Eastern tradition, said to be backed by "St. Ephrem", is that the body of Adam, who, in life, is said by the Koran to have been a "giant as tall as a palm tree", was, after his death, kept on the surface of the earth for many years, till a priest (Melchisedeck, said, in some quarters, to have been an Atlantean wise man, or priest) "buried it in the middle of the earth," or in a tunnel. Adam, whom Hindu lore says was a king of Greater or Old Atlantis, had said that his "redeemer and that of his posterity" would come from "the middle of the earth", which latter cryptic sentence may, or may not imply, a mysterious community of Elders, or Atlanteans who had gone underground at the time of the Great Cataclysm. And a certain "John Gregorie" says that Adam's body was subsequently embalmed and transmitted from father to son till it was placed by Noah "in the middle of the Ark".

One is further told that this singular position amidships in the Ark was chosen, because, owing to the tempest and commotion raging outside on the waters and over the doomed earth, no one could tell East from West! Adoration, therefore, of whatever gods or unknown God was or were worshipped by the mysterious Noah, took place in the centre of the great ship, which had a "sloping roof, but no helm, rudder, or sails"!

The Midrash and the Talmud identify old Noah with Bacchus; for they allege that the country where the Ark grounded was called "Rakschivan" (*Rak:* ship, or castle, and *schivan:* remaining fast, or drained off). Here, grew luxuriant wild vines, and, in modern times, the region became a "wine-land", for it was here that Noah first cultivated the vine.

The learned Latin father, Jerome (Eusebius Hieronymus Sophronius), born at Stridon, Dalmatia, in A.D. 346, died at Bethlehem in 420, has some interesting details in his *Liber de Sitie et Nominibus Locorum Hebraicorum*, which are here translated into English for the first time:

> . . . To-day, they say vestiges of the Ark of Noah still remain on the mountains of Ararat, and Jeremiah makes mention of those mountains in his vision against Babylon. Since the time when Noah sent forth from the Ark all the birds and animals into the land around and sacrificed beasts from the cages in his joy at being at last free of shipboard, the husbandmen of this region testify that some of the woods (timbers) of the ship still remain as monuments of the Great Deluge, as profane and secular histories all record . . . Berosus, the Chaldæan says: "This great ship rests near by a certain part of the mountains of the Carduenorum, in Armenia, and certain folk tear bitumen from it and carry it around . . . as purification by sacrifice, or to avert evil omens from themselves. Hieronymus (Jerome) the Egyptian has written a beautiful discourse of Phœnician antiquities, and he and Mnaseas and many others refer to the Ark. Nicholas Damascenius says it was on the Myniadis Mountain, called Beris, to which many fled for refuge, that the Ark grounded. Others floating in the ship arrived at that high mountain, and in all times and many ages the wood of the Ark was customarily shown, which, indeed, I suppose to be that which Moses, the law-giver, writes of in his books".

But this same Eusebius alleges that the Ark was not carried to the mountains of Ararat, "a region close to a plain where the Araxes flows, and which is incredibly fertile", but "to the highest mountains of the Taurus which hang over the Ararat country"

Thirteen centuries later, the Sieur Adam Olearius was in Armenia, and in a book titled *Les Voyages*, published at "Leide" (Leyden), in 1718, he says:

> Mount Ararat is called by the Armenians *Messina, Aghri* by the Persians, and *Subeilahn* by the Arabs. It is much higher than the Caucasus and it is easily the highest of all the mountains we saw in our voyage. Properly, it is only a great black rock with no verdure, and covered to the top with snow in summer and winter. Its prodigious height enables it to be seen 10 to fifteen leagues away, on the Caspian Sea. The Armenians and even the Persians believe there still rests on Ararat a part of the Ark, but that time has so hardened it that it seems petrified. When we were at Scamachie, a town of Media, we were shown in the church of the Armenians a cross as tall as a half-aune (ell) of a wood dark brown and very hard, that is said to be from the timbers of the Ark. Because they deem this a precious relic they envelop it in light crimson-red silk (*taffetas rouge cramoisie*). To-day, the mountain is inaccessible entirely, and because of the precipices that hem it in on all sides.

Jan Struys, the Hollander, who was captured and enslaved while he was travelling in the Near East, in or about A.D. 1670, was called on to heal of hernia a hermit who lived in a cell on Ararat. He undertook the operation with great reluctance, but, as even in those days, all Europeans were deemed in those lands to be possessed of magic powers of healing, exactly as was *el gran caballero*, the late R. B. Cunninghame Graham, made prisoner by a Berber chief in the Atlas of Mogreb-el-Aksa, in the late 1890's, Struys could not avoid the ordeal. Says he:

> When I took leave of the hermit he gave me a piece of wood very hard, of a dark red colour, with a cross and a silver chain which he wore at his neck, and also a stone which he told me he had taken from under the Ark, and this stone had gleams of sparkling ore (gold?) in it, but I lost it when the English captured a ship I was in.

The hermit gave him a "pedigree' with these relics:

> Datum in monte Ararat, die 22 Julii 1670 . . . The mountain of holy Ararat is about 35 miles high (*sic!*) . . . I have given him, the doctor who has successfully operated on me, a Cross, being of the wood of the real Ark of Noah, which I have cut out of a chamber of the said Ark with my own hands, I having been there personally myself. I have verbally demonstrated to the said John after what manner the said Ark is made. Besides this, I have given him a stone which, with my own hands, I have pulled from under the Ark, being a part of the rock, whereon it is supported. All this I testify to be true, and so true as I live in this *mea sancta eremetica habitatione de facto vivo.*
> *Dominicus Alexander Romanus.*

In the sixteenth century of our own age, other evidences of ancient and antediluvian catastrophes came to light. On the summit of a high mountain, the Stella, in Portugal, there is a lake near modern Coimbra, the ancient Herminius, which is in the east of the province of Alemtejo. In this lake, twelve leagues from the sea, are remains of the timbers of ships supposed to be antediluvian. An old French writer says: "The lake is very high up, and the people of the country swear that at such times as the Atlantic Ocean is agitated, the waters of this wonderful lake rise and foam in sympathy, and with great tumult of the waters. I am told there is, at this day (1738), a similar lake in the territory of Chiaves".

Eratosthenes, the librarian of Alexandria, who died 194 B.C., spoke of fragments of sea-going ships and oyster shells found in his day, far inland near the temple of Jupiter Ammon, in Libya. Also, the old Spanish geographer, Pomponius Mela, flourished A.D. 45, says that, far inland in Numidia, are other memorials of the Great Disaster, when the onrushing waters from the ocean of old Atlantis drowned the old lands of the Mediterranean or Middle Sea. These memorials were in the shape of old anchors fixed in rocks, and signs and vestiges that "here, far inland in Numidia, was once sea where now are barren and sandy plains". Ovid, too, speaks of ancient anchors of ships no one knows, found on the tops of the highest mountains. The old *Chinese Encyclopædia* says: "In Eastern Tartary you may see, going from the shores of the Eastern Sea towards Che-lu, sands where the Mongols say that in remote antiquity the waters of the

Deluge flooded the region now called the Sandy Sea". Strahlenberg, in his *Das Nord und Östliche Theil von Europa und Asien*, published at Stockholm, in 1730, says that in or about 1720, he saw "the whole lower hull of an ancient ship with a keel at Barabinsk, in Tartary, where is no ocean and 700 miles from the sea".

Nor may we forget that mysterious passage in the Irish version of Nennius, the *Leabhar Breathnach annso sis*. This strange story casts a ray into a deep abyss of the past and none to-day can say whence this old monkish historian, who lived in Brecknock or Radnor Forest, *circa* A.D. 796 derived this story. It is a reminder of the fact that, as the old Irish chronicles say, Ierne, or old Ireland remained a desert and uninhabited for 300 years after the Great Deluge. It is also a reminder of the remarkable science of the old Atlans. The old chronicle says the strange event happened in the "fourth age of the world, after the Scots came from Iberian Spain to Ireland:

> Three sons of a Spanish soldier came to Ireland with 30 ships, each of which contained 30 wives. And they held a port in Ireland, for many years, their ships being damaged by the seas. On their voyage back to Spain, there appeared to them in the middle of the sea a tower of glass (*turrim vitream*). The summit of this tower seemed covered with men, to whom they spoke, often, but had no answer. At length they determined to besiege this tower, and after a year's preparation, advanced towards it with the whole number of their ships, and all the women, one ship only excepted, which had been wrecked, and in which there were 30 men and 30 women. But when all had disembarked on the shore which surrounded the tower, the sea opened and swallowed them up . . .

The only comment I can make is that, in the ancient Irish stories of the voyages of Bran, Corra, and Mælduinn, whenever the word "glass" occurs, it is invariably associated with mysterious lost islands with Atlantean remains, such as "bridges of glass", "an isle of glass", "a great crystal tower with fringes of crystal", "ring forts with brazen ramparts, palisades and bridges over moats and wet fosses", "founts of hot and cold water", "islands of perpetual youth" to which wandering Irish Ulysses were drawn by fair women living without men, exactly as the Amazons of Poseidonis, of Atlantis, also of strange islands with a splendid race-course where white horses race quicker than the wind of the ocean! The reader will perhaps recall the earlier chapter of this book on Greater Atlantis, called Aeyre, pronounced exactly as is Eire, to-day, that stretched from the region of Iceland to modern Trinidad, West Indies, and was certainly known in the dim past to the old folk of Crom, the sun king of Ierne, or Ireland.

Auld Scotelan', too, has her memorials of the Great Deluge. Said a correspondent of a Newcastle-on-Tyne newspaper, writing from Edinburgh, on 25th May, 1726:

> We have an account from Airth, 18 miles from this city, near to the influx of the Carron, of a very rare piece of antiquity found on the south bank of the Forth, viz., a canoe of 36 feet long, 4 feet broad, in the

middle, and 4 feet 4 inches deep, also 4 inches thick in the sides. It is all of one piece of solid oak, sharp at the stem, and square at her stern. The river washing away the banks discovered a part of her. She was ordered to be dug up by Mr. Graham, judge-admiral and proprietor of the place. What was discovered of her was found to be above 15 feet under the ground. It is remarkable that she is finely polished, being perfectly smooth on the outside, and inside the wood is of an extraordinary hardness and not one knot in the whole.

Sir John Clerk says there lay above this ancient craft, strata of loam and clay, moss, sand and gravel. "This ancient boat was found not far from Arthur's Oven, or 'Templum Termini'."

Another very singular story is told in a manuscript note inserted in the copy of a dissertation on the antiquity of the Earth by the Reverend James Douglas, who read it at a meeting of the Royal Society, in London, on 12th May, 1785. I believe this is the first time that this curious story has appeared in a modern book. The volume containing this note belonged to the Reverend Vivyan Arundel of Exeter College, Oxon. It (the note) was signed "J.W.", and on paper with a watermark about 1790. J. W. says he was at Gibraltar when miners were blasting rocks to raise batteries about 50 feet above sea level. They found on the higher ground, near the Mole, the appearance of a human body which, "because the officer to whom notice of the find was sent was late in turning up, the miners impatiently blew up. The body was said to be 8½ *feet long*. Several of the pieces were taken up, and among them was a thigh bone with flesh, and, I think, an appearance of veins, all in a state of perfect petrifaction, as hard as marble itself, and in the solid part of the same stone was a sea-shell. The stalactitic matter indicates that the body was of very remote antiquity—*an antediluvian man*."

Lyell, in the nineteenth century, speaks of human remains brought from South America, and including a skull taken out of a sandstone rock "now overgrown with very large trees, near Santos, Brazil. The locality may have been an aboriginal cemetery which subsequently sank beneath the level of the sea and then was hove up again. The bones of pachyderms and an *extinct horse*, found in the alluvial there, *were of a more recent period*".

Does this human skull even *precede* the Great Cataclysm that sank or disrupted the great stone-walled cities of the Atlans of old Brazil? *Quien sabe?* All one can say is that here is another reminder that old America is a very ancient land in relation to the past history of our race.

It may be recalled that the famous French savant, Boucher de Perthes, brought a storm on his head when, in 1847, he announced that he had found in a quarry of Moulin-Quignon, near Abbeville, North France, silex axes which he said had been tools of antediluvian man. In March 1863, a worker found in the same quarry, close to where the silex axes had been found, a human tooth, then a bone.

Boucher de Perthes called up a colleague, and, in his presence, disinterred the half of a jaw of a race of men different from ours! All the archæologists could agree on was that the quarry workers, at least, had not been guilty of any fraud or spoof. The rest they left *sub judice!*

An amazing discovery was made, in 1577, near Reyden, in Switzerland, when, in a cave revealed by the fall of a very ancient decayed oak, there were found the bones of a giant man, 16 *feet tall!* The remains were sent to the senate of Luzern, and a well known physician of Basel, Felix Plater, reconstituted missing parts of the skeleton structure of the giant, which was then painted by an artist of Basel, Joannes Bock, and the remains were presented to the senate of Luzern. The figure of that giant is to-day found standing by the side of the coat of arms of the town of Luzern, and, no doubt, many an English visitor has remarked the fact. Admittedly, this giant of old Europe was a pigmy by the side of Adam, who the Moslems say was 60 feet tall and as large as a tall palm tree! Linnæus held the view that this old Atlan elder and his wife, were giants.

Some day, perhaps, in a saner age than that in which we now live or exist, in turmoil, fear and horror of what science may unloose on the so-called civilized nations in the way of devastating ray and atomic nuclear fissioning weapons, ever getting "better and better", one may hope that this ancient riddle of Ararat may be solved. Let us at least hope that the mystery may not be solved when forces of disintegration will be let loose in the region of this cloudland riddle of an ancient ship, 14,000 feet up, in a way strangely recalling that in which, *qua* Charles Lamb, the old Chinese mandarin learnt how to cook and roast his sucking pig!

AUTHOR'S NOTE

As this book goes to press, news cabled to London from Ankara, Turkey, states that the expedition led by Dr. Aaron Smith, of Greensborough, North Carolina, failed to find traces of the Ark, at 12,000 feet up. The western and northern slopes of Ararat were also explored without result; though, in summer 1948, Kurdish peasants reported to the Ottoman gendarmerie that the peasants had seen, high up on Ararat, revealed by the melting *névé* (hardened snow), an object like a big boat. Smith, said to be a former missionary in China, told me:

> We can't say if the Ark landed at a lower level; also it may have been completely buried by the débris of earthquakes, which are violent in this volcanic region. Again, it may exist on the north side of the mountain under ice and snow, and will be revealed at any time. Anyway, we have sure cleared the way for others, who may have better luck than ourselves.

Turks report finding other Ark ships. One was 12 days' walking time from Tokat, in central north Anatolia. It was said that three-quarters of it lay under earth, and the top was covered by trees and shrubs. "A thick black substance like tar seems to have preserved it."

Another Ark, or ancient hulk, was reported found at Mardin, near the Syrian frontier, and in the wild Judy Mountains. The finder said this No. 2 Ark was "well preserved, and inside it were three chambers, one of which was a small chapel or oratory". These Judy Mountains appear identical with the Gudi of the Koran, which says that there the Ark rested. Up to A.D. 655, there stood at Gudi, or Judy, in the south land of the Kurds, a convent said to have in it sacred fragments of the Ark. But Berosus, in the Chaldee story, places the "Apobaterion", or landing of the Ark, north-east of old Nineveh, or Mosul, in the ancient Gordyene range; in Hebrew, the "Qardu", or Kardi, or land of the Kurds. The old Franciscan monk, William of Rubruk, who passed under Ararat, on his way from Karakorum, in A.D. 1254, says the Ark rested on the higher of two peaks above the River Araxes. He called the mountain Masis, and said, in Latin: "Above Masis none ought to ascend, for it is the mother of the world. A pious monk has a piece of the Ark brought him by an angel, and it is still a holy relic in a church near the mountain."

The late Viscount James Bryce, who, on 11th September, 1876, found a piece of old timber, 4 feet long, far above the zone of vegetation on Ararat, but said he sighted no ship lying on or protruding from a glacier, points out the two peaks of Ararat are 7 miles apart, and that Persians called Ararat "Koh-i-Nuh", or Noah's Mountain. Apameia, or Celenæ, is another alleged resting-place of the Ark, while others make claims for the lofty peak of Argæus (Aghri Dagh, near Kaisariyeh, Anatolia).

It is the fact that the folk living round the mountain, as late as 1840, when a tremendous fall of rock wiped out the ancient vine stock, bearing grapes, and alleged to have been planted by Noah, never called the mountain Ararat.

One last word: I believe that the Noah *of Genesis* had no more existence than Sarah Gamp's friend's husband, Mr. 'Arris, or than old Sir John de Mandeville—who, too, cheerily said the Mountain of the Ark was 7 (*sic*) miles high and "could be seen in clere wedre", and rebuked folk who said that the Devil quitted the Ark when Noah said to him, *Benedicite*, and that they had "touched with their fyngres the place where the Feend quitted the Ark". Noah may probably be identified with Ma—*Nu*, of the old Hindu myth of the Great Deluge. All one can say, at this moment, is that the mystery still remains to be cleared up.

The United States expedition to Ararat seem to have had bad luck from the start. One is told that internal friction split the parties into sections. It looks as if their steps were dogged from Ankara to the base of the mountains. Some sinister individual stole their money. They were asked for $1,000 for the services of a guide, which is certainly, if true, an extortionate fee to exact. But, of course, the race, or the rulers of the Osmanli, as we have seen in the world wars, have proved unreliable "allies". On their way home from Turkey-in-Asia, other sinister individuals, suspected to be connected with a certain chief of espionnage, stole all the photographs they had taken. Whether this is so or not, or was attributable to their own carelessness, cannot be said, at the moment of writing; but that these photographs disappeared seems certain. Of course, to anyone who knows anything of treasure hunting, in the case of an expedition of this sort, just as one to Cocos Island, in North Pacific, or to some sunken galleon in the Caribbean waters, it will not be surprising that the cache, in the mountains of Ararat, still remains *perdu*.

The gods of hidden treasure, or archæological affairs of kindred sort, do not yield to the first comer. Often, prolonged searches and many disappointments attend the hunters. Ararat, just as many locations in the secret heart of old South America, ought rightly to be the quest of some well-endowed institution backed by the necessary official and diplomatic support. But in these austere days, with a world in fear and turmoil, it is hard to find (shall we say?), an enterprising newspaper owner, or publisher, who will back some modern H. M. Stanley to follow in the trail of the Livingstones of Ararat.

Who was this Noah of the Hebrew Bible?

Light is thrown on the mystery in the remarkable *Book of El Daoud*, which appears to be a document derived from some source in close contact with the later days of the doomed *Atlantis the Less*, the vast fragments left from the earlier cataclysms that sank the older and larger northern continents of Atlan-Aeyre and *Hypea*. Hypea was the northern Arctic, but very mild and warm continent of the far day when our Earth had an orbit much nearer the sun, and, as Mayan and Quiché sacred books import, completed the orbit in 260 days. Ages later old America had a very ancient American calendar, called the Venus Calendar, based on the known and observed fact of very ancient astronomers of another cycle (pre-Toltec) than ours, that our Earth went round the Sun eight times to the thirteen revolutions of Venus (a cataclysmic "perturbator"?):

Says *El Daoud*:

> Ma-Nu (Noah) and Pe-lu were selected to build two great ships of safety, and therein to embark their wives, sons and daughters, and a selection of the male and female animal life of the beautiful and friendly creatures of Atlantis. They had also to take with them certain seeds of fruit and corn that had reached a higher development in Atlan than in the other four continents. . . . In Atlan, the secret caverns of old Satanaku were filled with abominations created by his awful wickedness. The lowlands of Atlantis were thoroughly infected and infested with black magic, and the sacred heights were no longer needed for the Elders, or Dhuman-Adamics, who had scattered over the four other continents to instruct the folk there. It was the magic of yellow, red, and black rebels . . . By this time the power of levitation had waned, so that, as a rule, mankind required material facilities to cross the ocean. Atlan with its wonderful civilization was sunk . . . the like of it has never been on earth again to this day. . . . When the name of the Ineffable and Nameless One was spoken backward, a terrible quaking under the ocean sank Atlan, at the same period. Owing to the same cause, in other portions of the world, solid matter was thrown to the surface of the sea, forming those great islands now known as Australia and New Zealand. Virgin soil were they both, and not, as believed in later times, were they recovered portions of Lemuria and Atlan; for these were obliterated, lest their blight spread as a taint upon other portions of the Earth. Certain portions of Asia and Africa were affected by the Great Deluge, but not to any grievous extent, nor was there any loss of life thereby . . . Eight persons were in charge of each Ark-ship. . . .

However little it may be to the taste of some folk, one may be permitted to reiterate that, black as the land of Atlan had become, there was an inevitability about the Great Cataclysm. "Think not the doom of man reversed for *thee*," said our own Dr. Samuel Johnson. Or, as the Arabs say about the well of Kairouan, while Sidi Bu Ziballah from his warm dunghill shouts, in jocose tones, that all the Earth seems one vast and stercoraceous heap, and the "great red eye of day" touches the far shimmering skyline: "*Mektub*. What Allah hath willed, so shall it be. And thou canst not recall or blot out one line of it."

BIBLIOGRAPHY

ABYDENUS (4th century A.D.), fragments of lost histories of Cyprus, Arabia and Assyria.

ACADEMIE DES INSCRIPTIONS ET BELLES LETTRES: Comptes Rendus. Various Vols.

ADAIR, James. *History of American Nations* 1735–75).

ADAM BREMENSIS, *Historia, Gesta Hammaburgensis Ecclesia Pontificum ap-Pertz Monumenta.* (11th century writer).

AELIAN, Claudus. *Varia Historia* (A.D. 140).

ALCEDO, Antonio de. *Diccionaro geográfico-histórico de las Indias occidentales ó America.* (Madrid, 1786–89.)

ALCEDO Y HERRERA, Dionisio. Captain-General of Quito. Died A.D. 1777.

ALEJANDRO, Alejandro, *Dies Geniales.*

ALGEMEINE ENCYCLOPÆDIE (Winkler Prins), 1935.

ALIBRANDUS, Pontifex (Bremen), cited in Adam of Bremen's *Hamburg Chronicle* (*circa* A.D. 1067).

ANDAGOYA, Licenciado, *Relación de Conquista* (1541).

APACHES, oral traditions and ritual of.

APOLLODORUS (*floreat circa* 115 B.C.) *Bibliotheca.*

ARCHEOLOGIA BRAZILEIRA ARCHIVOS (Rio de Janeiro). Various volumes from Museu Nacional, Rio.

ARCHIVO GENERAL DE INDIAS (Sevilla). *Papeles per tenencientes d los Generales y Almirantes de Armados, años 1520–1624, y 1705–80.*

ARCHIVOS DE LA ACADEMIA DE HISTORIA (Madrid).

ARISTOTLE (384–322 B.C.). *Meteorologica.*

Pseudo-ARISTOTLE. *Aristotle Liber de Mirabilibus Ausculatationibus explicatus a Ioanne Beckmann.* (Edn.: Gottingæ, 1786.)

ARRIAN, or ARRIANUS (*flor.* A.D. 140), *Indica.*

ASIATIC RESEARCHES (Various volumes).

AUDIENCIAS (*Cartas* and Reports of, in *Archivo Gral de Indias,* relating to El Dorado and El Gran Paytite, sixteenth to early eighteenth century.) (Many of these reports are, for the first time, translated into English in this book.)

AUGUSTINE, ST. Latin citations in *De Civitate Dei* from lost Roman, Greek and other authors, relating to the Great Cataclysm, called the Deluge, and also referred to in Plato's dialogues from Solon and old Egyptian temple records at Sais and Heliopolis.

AUGUSTODUNENSIS, Honorius ("solitary" monk, *circa* A.D. 1125), *Summa Totius et Imagine Mundi* (Basileæ: 1544).

AVIENUS, Rufus Festus. *Ora Maritima.* (Early Phœnician and Carthaginian voyages into the Atlantic.)

AZTEC CODICES. *Chimalpopoca, Telleriano Remensis, Dresden, Mendoza and Mexicanus Vatican.*

BACH, Dr. Articulos, *Revista do Museo Paulista.*

BACH, Johann Nicolaus. *Solonis Atheniensis carminum quæ supersunt* (Ed. A.D. 1825).

BALDWIN, John Denison. *Ancient America* (1872).

BALLIVIAN. D.M.V., *Monumentos prehistoricos de Tiahúanacu* (La Paz: 1910).

BAMBOO ANNALS (ancient Chinese records found in grave, A.D. 279). Dr. James Legge's Chinese Classics (Hong Kong, 1865).

BANCROFT, H. H., *Native Races of the Pacific States.*

BANDELIER, H. F. Various works on pre-Columbian history of America.

BARAZA, FRAY CYPRIANO. *Relación Sumaria de la Vida . . . del U.P. Cypr. Baraza . . . muerto á manos de Barbaros en la Mission de los Moxos de la Provincia del Perú.* (Lima, *Imprenta Real de Josef de Cofriras,* 1704.) Very rare, black-letter vol. S. Americana.

BARLÆUS, Caspar, *In Brasilia rerum per octennum* (Clives: ex officina Tobiæ Silberling, 1658).

BEDE, The Venerable. *Historia Ecclesiastica.*

BELLORI, Jean Pierre (1615–96). Collector of old engravings and classic medallions and cameos, to court of Queen Christina of Sweden.

BENALCAZAR, Sebastian (de Moyano). Conquistadorian eye-witness of affairs in the Popayan, and Nueva Andalucia y Nueva Granada (modern Colombia. S.A.). (Died at Benalcaz. A man of action, he is not known to have left any MSS., or diaries.)

BENZONI, Geronimo (*floreat circa* 1550). *History of the New World.*

BERLIOUX, Prof. M.E.F. (of Lyon). *Les Atlantes* (1883).

BERREO, Antonio de. (*See* DE BERREO.)

BERTHELOT, Daniel, *Comptes Rendus de l'Académie des Inscriptions et Science* (Paris: 1886).

BLAS VALERA, Fray. Lost sixteenth-century MS. histories of Peruvian antiquities, citied in Fernando Montesinos's *Memorias Antigas y Politicas del Perú.* (Only one MS. known to exist, and is in J. B. Munoz's *collección,* Real Academia de la Historia, Madrid.)

BOAS, F. Report on N.W. Tribes of Dominion of Canada. '(Brit. Asscn. meeting at Bath, September 1888.)

BOCHART, Samuel, *Phaleg et Chanaan* (Caen: 1645 and 1651).

BOECK (German Hellenist). The Panathenæan Festival (ancient Athens) on Atlantean memories.

BOTURINI, Lorenzo Benaduci (Vide *Bustamente*), (1608-1740). Most of his valuable Span. MSS., and old Mexican painted records have been lost by neglect, in Mexico City. *Idea de una Historia.*

BRASSEUR DE BOURBOURG, Abbé Etienne-Charles. *Popul Vuh* (Quiche reprint with French translation); *Histoire des nations civilisés du Mexique et de l'Amérique centrale.* (Owner, in 1874, of very rare and valuable MSS. on obscure Central American races, Spanish and native writers.)

BRAZILIAN ARCHIVES (Museo Nacional, Rio de Janeiro, and Archivos Sao Paulo.

BUEHLER, Georg. *Grundriss der Indo-Arischen Philologie und der Altertümskünde.*

BUFFON, Comte Georges L. L. *Histoire Naturelle.*

BURTON, Sir Richard Francis. *Travels in the Brazilian Highlands* (1869).

BUSTAMENTE, Carlos Maria, *de Cronica, Mexicana Teoamoaxtli . . . redactado de un antiguo codice inedito del caballero Boturini* (1822) (Mexico).

CABEZA DE VACA, Alvaro Nuñez. *Deposition* before Notary re: Amazons of Paraguay, A.D. 1545.

CALMET, Dom Augustin. *Dissertorum Hebrorum Ritu Phonicio de Urbe West Capell* (*circa* A.D. 1710).

CAMARGO, Diego Muñoz. *Historia de Tlaxcala* (Mexico: 1892).

CARVAJAL, Fray Gaspar de. *Descubrimiento del Rio de las Amazonas según la Relación de Fr. G. de C.* (various sixteenth and early seventeenth century MSS.).

CASTELNAU (François L. de Laporte, Comte de). *Expédition dans les parties centrales de l'Amérique du Sud* (*Rio de Janeiro à Lima, Lima à Para* (1842–47), 6 tomes, Paris, 1850–61.

CATLIN, George (1796–1832), *Travels among the American Indians.*

CEDRENUS, Georgius. *Compendium historarium ab urbe condito ad Isaac Comnenum* (eleventh-century work).

CENSORINUS. *Liber de die Natali* (*circa* A.D. 238).

CHARLEVOIX, Père François Xavier de. *Histoire et description générale de la Nouvelle France* (1744).

CICERO, *De Divinatione.*

CIEZA DE LEON, Pedro. *La Crónica del Perú* (*circa* A.D. 1555).

CLAVIGERO, Francisco Javier, *Historia del Mexico* (1781); *Storia Antica del Messico* (Cesena, 1780).

COCHRANE, Captain Charles Stuart, R.N. *Journal of a Residence in Colómbia* (London, 1825).

COGULLUDO, Diego Lopez, *Historia de Yucathan* (Madrid: 1688).

COLETI, Giandomenico. *Dizionario storico-geografico dell'America Meridionale* (Venezia: 1771).

COLLIER, Jeremiah, A. M., *A Dictionary of Geography, History, Genealogy and Poetry* (London: 1705).

COLON, Fernando (son of Christopher Columbus), *Historia del Almirante Don Cristobal Colon.*

COLUMBUS, Christopher. *Viages.* (*Vide:* NAVARRETE, and PETER MARTYR DE ANGLIERA.)

CONGRÈS DES AMERICANISTES. Various reports and conferences in European capitals.

CORTESIAN CODEX (Mexico).

COSMOS INDICOPLEUSTES. *Topographia Christiana* (sixth century, A.D.).

CRANTOR. Philosopher of Soli, of First Academy of Platonists. References from Egyptian temple records, *re.* Atlantis.

CUERVO MARQUEZ, Carlos. *Prehistoria y viages* (Madrid: 1920).

CUNNINGHAM, Sir Alexander. *Corpus Inscriptionum Indicarum.*

CURTIN, Jeremiah. *Creation Myths of Primitive America.*

DA ROCHA PITTA, Sebastião. *Historia da America Portugueza* (Lisboa, 1880).

DARWIN, Charles. *Voyage of the Beagle.*

DA SYLVEIRA. Capitão Symão Estacio. *Relação Sumaria das Cosas do Maranhão* (Madrid (?), 1624. Very rare vol.).

DAVIS, Rev. Edward. *Mythology of the British Druids* (London, 1807).

DE ACOSTA, Fray José. *Historia natural y moral de las Indias.*

DE ACUÑA, Fray Cristobal. *New Discovery of the Great River of the Amazons* (Eng. trans. of the Madrid edn., 1641).

DE BERREO, Don Antonio. Letters to Carlos V. (in Archivo Gîal de Indias, Sevilla-Simancas).

DE BRY, Theodore. *Historia Americæ.* (Rhine edn., 1596, with fine "iconæ".

DE CARDENAS, Don Gabriel. Prologue to Garcilasso de la Vega's *Comentarios Reales de los Yncas* (Madrid, 1723).

DE CASTELNAU (F. Laporte), *Expédition dans les Parties Centrales de l'Amérique du Sud, par ordre du Gouvernement Français* (1843–47). (Paris: 1857.)

DE CHARENCEY (*Rivæ Americanæ*, 2e série, No. 2). Ages de Soleil.

DE ERCILLA, Alfonso (16th century), *La Araucana.*

DE GARCIA, Fray Pedro. *Origen de los Indiós del Nuevo Mundo* (Valencia, 1607).

DE GOMARA, Francisco Lopez (Capellan de la casa de Cortes), *Historia General de las Indias.*

DE GONGORA Y MARTINEZ, Don Manuel, *Antigüedades Prehistoricas* (Madrid: 1868).

DE GUSMAN, Don Nunno. Letters to Carlos, V., on the Mexican Amazons. (*Vide,* also, *Ramusio.*)

DE HERIARTE, Mauricio (Ouvidor-geral, Provedor-mor é auditor . . . pelo Governador Dom Pedro de Mello, 1662). *Descripção Estado do Maranhão* (Vienna: 1874).

DE HERRERA, Antonio. *Historia General de los Hechos de los Castellanos en las Islas de Tierra Firme del Mar Oceano.*

DE LA CONDAMINE, Charles Marie. *Voyage from the South Sea to Brazil and Guiana* (Paris, 1754).

DE LA MOTA PADILLA, El Licenciado, Don Matia, *Historia de la Conquista de la Provincia de la Nueva Galicia* (1742).

DE LAS CASAS, Fray Bartoloméo. *Historia General de las Indias.*

DE LEON, Don Juan Recio. *Breve Relación . . . de las Provincias de Tipuane Chunchos . . . y otras muchas . . . del grñde Rey del Paytite* (Madrid, 1626). (*Papeles Varios de Indias.* Lord Kingsborough's Library.)

De Llano Zapata, Don José Eusebio. *Memorias Historicas-Fisicas-Apologeticas de America Meridional.* (Lima, reprint of eighteenth-century edn., in Biblioteca Nacional del Perú, No. 388.)

De Magelhaes, General Conto. *O Selvagen: seus costumes, suas origems,* etc. (Rio de Janeiro, 1876.)

De Molina, Alonso. *Arte de la lengua mexicana y castellana, en casa de Pietro de Ocharte* (A.D. 1571).

De Montfaucon, Dom Bernard. *Livre de l'Antiquité* (Paris: 1724).

De Ordonez y Aguiar, Dom Ramon. MS. *Historia del cielo y la tierra . . . relación de los ritos y costumbres de los Culebras.* (Concg. Votan and the Phœnicians in Central America.)

De Ortiguera, Toribio. *Noticias y relación de Quito y del rio de las Amazonas.*

De Oviedo y Valdes, Capitán Gonzalo Fernandez. *Historia general y Natural des las Indias, Primer Conquista del Nuevo Mundo.*

De Ribeira, Don Hernando. Conquistador and follower of Cabeza de Vaca, in Paraguay, A.D. 1541. Testimony about the Amazon women.

De Rivero y Ustariz, Mariano. *Antigüedades Peruanos.*

De Sa Carvalho, J. R., translation by C. R. Enock of his *Brazilian Eldorado* (1938). For English readers this is an excellent account of the Matto Grosso.

De Sampaio, Xavier Ribeiro. *Diario da viagem no anno de 1774 e 1775* (Lisboa, 1826 edn.).

De San Vicente, or Vincente, Fray Marcelino. MS. *Relación de modo de decobrir el Dorado.*

De Vallencey. *Collectanea de Rebus Hibernicis.*

De Valenzuela, Francisco Ramirez (A.D. 1775), on the embalmed, Mexican double-headed eagle.

De Vedia, Don Enrique, cites Hernando Cortes' *Carta* to the Emperador Carlos V. (*History of the Primitive Indias*).

De Winton, Albert, extracts from manuscripts of, from São Paulo, to the author of this book.

De Zamora, Fray Alonso. *Historia de la Provincia de S. Antonio del Nuevo Reino de Granada, del Orden de Predicadores, compuesta por el M.R.P.M. F. Alonso de Zamora, su Provincial Qualificador del Santo Officio y Examinador Sinodal de su Arcobispado. Dedicada a la Milagrossa Imagem de N. Señora del Rosario que se venera en su Conuento de la Ciudad de Santa Fé.* (Barcelona, Em la Imprenta de Joseph Llopis, Año de 1701.)

Debeneditti, S., *L'Ancienne Civilisation des Barreales du N.W. Argentina* (1931).

Denis, Ferdinand. *Le Brésil (circa* 1830).

Diccionario Historico y Geographico e Ethnographico (Brazil). Various volumes. (Rio de Janeiro: 1922 *et seq.*)

Diodorus Siculus Works.

Do Couto, Frey Urbano, Manuscript on the Rio Xingú exploration in 18th century (archives in Rio de Janeiro).

Duran, Diego. *Historia de las Indias de la Nueva España* (Mexico: 1867).

ELLIT-AYA (*circa* 2140 B.C.), terra-cotta tablet of Deluge story.

"ENCICLOPEDIA UNIVERSAL ILLUSTRADA EUROPEO-AMERICANA" (Barcelona).

EUSEBIUS, Bishop of Cæsarea (A.D. 267–340). *Præparatio et Demonstratio Evangelica* (edition Vigerus, fo. 2 vols., Rothomagi, 1628).

EVHEMERUS (*circa* 300 B.C.), fragments of lost work, *Hiera Anagraphe*.

FAWCETT, Colonel P. H., D.S.O. References to lectures at Royal Geographical Society, London, and to letters.

FERGHIL, or VERGIL, or VIRGIL (Bischof Vergil von Salzburg). Irish monk who was threatened with excommunication for asserting the existence of the Antipodes, and of America!

FRAZER, Sir James, *Golden Bough*.

FULGOSA, Baptista. *Colectaneas* (15th century).

GAFFAREL, Professor Paul. *Etudes sur les rapports de l'Amérique et de l'Ancien continent avant Christophe Colomb* (Paris, 1869).

GANDAVO, Pero de Magalhães de (Peter Magellan). *Historia da provincia de Sancta Cruz.* (Very rare volume on the colonial history of Lusitanian Brazil, edition 1576.)

GARCIA, Frey Gregorio (de la orden de Predicadores), *Historia Ecclesiastica y Seglar de la Yndia Oriental y Occidental* (Bæca: 1620); *Origen de los Indiós del Nuevo Mundo e Indias Occidentales* (Madrid: 1729).

GARCILASSO (Lasso de le Vega, el Inca). *Comentarios Reales.* (Lima: 1918.)

GATTEFOSSE, R. M., *Les origines préhistoriques de l'Ecriture* (Lyon: 1925).

GERHARD, EDUARD. *Ueber die Kunst der Phönizer.*

GESENIUS, Guil. *Scripturæ Lingæque Phœniciæ monumenta quotquot supersunt* (Lipsiæ, 1837).

GOTTFRIED, J. L. *Newe Welt und Americanishe Historien* (edition 1631); *De Aanmerkenswaardigste Zee-en-Landreizen*, etc. (edition ·1727). The South American section is based on De Bry's *Historiæ Americæ* whose "iconæ" Gottfried reproduces.

GRAHAM, R. B. Cunninghame. *Gonzalez Jiminez de Quesada.*

GREGORY, Professor J. W. *Physical and Comparative Geography of South America* (1896). (Gregory was drowned, in an overset canoe, in 1932, while crossing the Pongo de Mainique rapids on the Rio Urubamba, Perú, when leading a geological expedition to settle the problem of the age when the Andes were upheaved from the bed of the Pacific.)

GRESSET DE SAINT SAUVEUR, *Encyclopedie des Voyages* (*circa* 1780).

GULLU Y RENTE, D. José, *Leyendas Americanas* (Madrid: 1856).

GUMILLA, Fray Joseph. *Histoire naturelle, civile, et géographique de l'Orénoque.* (Eidous's translation into French of the Spanish edition. Paris, 1848.)

HAKLUYT, Richard. *Principal Navigationes.*

HAMCONIUS, Martin, *Frisia seu de viris rebusque Frisiæ* (Frankekaræ, 1620).

HANNO. *Periplus* (Fifth century B.C.).

HARCOURT, Robert, *Travels* (1608).

HARRIS, John. *Moral History of the Spanish West Indies* (London, 1705).

HAUG——, *Landnámabok.*

HELIODORUS, *Æthiopicas.*

HERBORN, Nicolas, MS. Cod. No. 1374 (Trier: Stadtbibliothek).

HERMANN. Prof. Albert, *Unsere Ahnen und Atlantis* (Berlin, 1934), *Die Westländer in der Chineschen Kartographie* (Stockholm: 1922).

HERODOTUS. *Melpomena* and *History.*

HERRERA, Antonio (*see* DE HERRERA). *Historia General de los Hechos de los Castellanos en las islas i Tierra Firme del Mar Oceano.*

HOFFMANI, Joh. Jacobi, Lexicon Universale (Lugduni Batavorum: 1698).

HOLMBOË, M. C. A., *Traces de Buddhisme en Norvège* (Paris: 1852).

HOMER *Odyssey.*

HORNIUS, George. *De Originis Americanis* (Hague edition, 1652).

HRDLICKA, A., *Early man in South America.*

HULL, Professor. Geological works on South America.

HUMBOLDT, Baron Friedrich Alexander. *Ansichten von Natur* (3 Ausgabe); *Vue de·Cordillères et Monuments; Monuments and Ancient Inhabitants of America; Researches concerning the Ancient Inhabitants of America.*

HUNDERTPFUND, Rochus (18th century German Jesuit), mission on the Rio Xingú). (*Vide* MURR.)

ICAZBALCETA, J. G., *Colección de documentos para la Historia de Mexico.*

INDEX KEWENSIS.

IXTLILXOCHITL, Fernando de Alva Cortes. *Historia de los Chichimecs* (edition 1658 (?)).

JEFFERSON, Thos. (ex-President U.S.A.). *Notes on the State of Virginia* (1784).

"JENÆR LITERARZEITUNG" (1874).

JORDANES (JORNANDES). *Getica* (sixth century A.D.).

JOSEPH, F. L. (of Trinidad). *History of Trinidad* (1840, very rare volume).

JOSEPHUS, Flavius (*circa* A.D. 37 to *circa* A.D. 93). *Antiquities of the Jews.*

JUSTINUS, M, Junius, *Epitoma Historiarum Philippicarum Pompei Trogi.* (Trogus flourished 55 B.C. The original of his history was lost—some hint, by Justinus!)

JUVENAL. Roman satirist's reference to frog-worship and augury.

KALLISTHENES (pseudo), Coptic version (Abyssinian), and Josippon Gorionides' tenth century version of the Asiatic campaigns of Alexander the Great. (The genuine manuscript of Kallisthenes is lost, the Alexandrian manuscript of third century A.D. being spurious.)

KARST, Prof. Dr. Joseph. *Grundsteine zu einer Mitteländischen Asiatischen Urgeschichte* (*Leipzig*, 1928), and *Origines Mediterraneæ* (Heidelberg, 1931).

KATZER, Doktor Friedrich. *Grundzüge der Geologie des unteren Amazonas gebietes* (Leipzig, 1903).

KINGSBOROUGH, Viscount (Edward King). *Antiquities of Mexico* (1830–48). (He tries to prove a Jewish migration to Mexico; but it is no more convincing than the rumour that there are Irishmen suffering in Jerusalem, owing to Anglo-Saxon persecution.)

KIRCHER, Athanasius. *Œdipi Ægyptiaci Theatrum Hieroglyphicum.*

KOCH-GRUNBERG, Dr. Theodor, *Südamerikanischen Felszeichnungen. Zwei Jahren unter den Indianen* (Berlin: 1910).

KOESTER, H. *Travels in Brazil* (1816).

KRICKEBERG, Dr. W. Works on Central and S. America (Berliner Museum für Völkerkunde).

LERY, Jean de. *Histoire d'un voyage au Brésil en 1556–58.*

LESCARBOT, Marc. (French traveller to North America). *Histoire de la Nouvelle France* (1651).

LIPSIUS, Justin. *Dictionary.*

LOCH, Captain Erskine, D.S.O. (Letters to author of this book).

LORENZANO, Francisco. *Documentos Mexicanos.*

LUCIAN. *De Dea Syria.*

MAJOLUS, Dom Simon (Bishop of Moguntia), (Mainz). *Dies Caniculares,* 1613.

MARCELLINUS, Ammianus. *Historia Rerum Gestarum Libri XXXI* (Paris: 1680). (Only surviving book of 30 others, lost.)

MARCELLUS. *Tois Aithiopikos* (lost work cited by PROCLUS).

MARCOY, Paul (*pseudonym:* Saint-Cricq-Laurent). *Voyage à travers l'Amérique du Sud* (1869).

MARKHAM, Sir Clements. *Expedition into the Valley of the Amazons;* numerous works on Perú; and introductions to translations of Spanish-American chroniclers and historians, in the Hakluyt Society's series.

MARTINI, Fray Martin, or Martinius. *Historia Sinensis* (very rare volume).

MARTIUS, Professor von. *Zur Ethnographie Amerika's zumal Brazilien.*

MARTYR, Peter (PETER MARTYR DE ANGHIERA, or ANGLERIA). *De Orbe Novo* (edition 1526).

MASPERO, Gaston Camille (1846–1916). On Egyptian Hieroglyphs.

MAWE, John. *Viagem ao Interior do Brasil* (Lisboa, 1812).

MAXIMILIEN ZU WIED, Prinz. *Travels in the Interior of North America,* 1832–1834.

MEANS, Philip Ainsworth. Introduction to Fernando Montesinos's *Memorias Antigas Historiales del Perú.* (Means considerably underestimates the great antiquity of South American civilization.)

MENCIUS, or MONCIUS (MENG TSEU). Fourth century B.C. commentaries on Chinese history.

MENDEL, Tomas. *Relación* (1612).

Mexia, or Mejia, Pedro (end of fifteenth century A.D.). *Silva de Varia Lección.*

Mocquet, Jean. *Voyages* (editions 1645 and 1655). (A Rouen, chez Jacques Caillove, dans le Cour du Palais.)

Moke, H. J. *Histoire des Peuples Américains* (Bruxelles: 1847).

Molina, Avila. MS. *Tratado y Relación de las fabulas y ritos de los Ingas* (Madrid, *Archivos*).

Molina, Cristobal (*circa* 1550), *Cronica de la Conquista y Poblacion del Perú.*

Montessus de Ballore, F. de (capitaine d'artillerie française). *Military dept. report on San Salvador.*

Moreri, L. *Le Grand Dictionnaire Historique* (1740).

Motalinia, Toribia de Benevente, O. S. F. *Historia de los Indiós de Nueva España* (*circa* 1640).

Munter, Frederick. *Religion d. Karthäger* (1827).

Murr, Christoph Gottlieb von. *Reisen einiger Missionarien der Gesellschaft Jesu in Amerika,* and *Journal zur Kunstgeschichte.* Also *Neues Journal* (Nürnberg: 1775–99).

Museo Nacional (Rio de Janeiro). *Archeologia Brazileira Archivos.*

Museu Paraense. *Memorias de Historia natural e Ethnographicas* (various volumes).

Nau, E. *Histoire des Caciques d'Haïti* (Port-au-Prince).

Navarrete, Martin Fernandez. *Viajes de los Españoles.*

Nepos, Cornelius, Citations from lost books of.

Nieremberg, John Eusebius. *Historiæ Naturæ.*

Nuñez, H. B. Archæological works on Venezuela (Caracas, 1925).

Nuñez de la Vega, Fray Francisco. *Constituciones diœcesanas del obispade Chiapas* (Roma 1702). (Very rare volume not in British Museum, but of sections of which I have obtained photostats from the Bibliothèque Nationale (old French Royal Library), a few months before the Germans entered Paris, in 1940.)

Oakenfull, J. C. *Brazil, Past, Present and Future* (1919). A carefully written account of modern Brazil.

Odriezola, Manuel. *Documentos Literarios* (Lima: 1876).

Oera Linda Boek (Het). Latest translation into Dutch, with Frisian text opposite, by J. F. Overwijn (Enkhuizen, Holland: 1941).

Ordoñez Y Aguiar, Ramon de. MS. in Museo Nacional, Mexico City; *Historia del cielo y la tierra . . . y relación de las ritos y costumbres de los Culebras.*

Ortega Y Gasset, José. *Los Atlantides* (Madrid: 1924).

Ossendowski, Ferdinand. Works on West Africa and Asia.

PALAIS DU TROCADÉRO. Galérie Américaine du Musée d'Ethnographie. (Choix de pièces archéologiques, par E. T. Hamy, 1897).

PARIAN CHRONICLE. Marbles of Arundelian Collection, Oxford University, England.

PAULY, Antonio. *Ensayo de Etnografía Americana. Viajes y Exploraciones* (Buenos Aires: 1928).

PAUSANIAS. *Periegesis.*

PAUW, Cornelius de. *Recherches philosophiques sur les Américaines* 1768–70).

PELLIZA Y TOVAR, José. Cronista del Reino de Aragon, *Diversas Noticias Historiales.*

PEQUES, Abbé. *Histoire et phénomènes . . . des îles volcaniques de Santorin* (Paris: 1842).

PHILO JUDÆUS. *Of the Indestructibility of the World* (Paris: 1640).

PIEDRAHITA, Don Lucas Fernandez. *Historia General de la Conquista del Nuevo Reyno de Granada.*

PLATO. *Dialogues,* and *Scholiast ad Plat. Rep. (Politeian),* referring to memories of Atlantis.

PLINY (The Elder). *Historia Naturalis.*

PLUTARCH. *De Facie in orbe Lunæ.*

POCOCK, Roger. *Chorus to Adventurers.*

POINDEXTER, Miles. *Peruvian Pharaohs* (1938).

POLYBIUS. Fragments of lost works of, *re.* Amazons, Atlanteans and old Carthage.

POLYHISTOR, Alexander. *Antiquities of Babylon* and fragments of Berosus.

PROCLES (Carthaginian historian). Scholium on lost work of, cited by Boeck and Humboldt.

"POPUL VUH" (The Bible of the Quichés of old Yucatan).

POSIDONIUS. Lost book (fragments of), on Atlantis.

POSNANSKY, Professor Arturo. *Thesaurus ideographiarium americanarum* (in Spanish and German: Berlin, and La Paz, Bolivia, 1913). Also, *La Guia general ilustrada . . . de Tihuanacu é Islas del Sol y la Luna (Titicaca y Koaty.* La Paz, Bolivia: 1925).

PREUSS, Konrad Theodor. *Archäologische und ethnographische Forschungsreisen in Kolombien* (Zeitschrifte für Ethnologie. Berlin).

PROCLUS. *Commentary and Dissertation on the Timæus.*

PROCOPIUS. History, with references to expelled Hivites, Canaanites, or Phœnicians, and their colonies in North Africa.

PTOLEMY (Claudius). Second century A.D. *Geography.*

QU'RAN or KORAN. Passage on a disintegrating moon in Great Cataclysm.

RABBINICAL LITERATURE. *Midrash-ha-Gadol,* and *Sefar-ha-Yashar.*

RALEIGH, Sir Walter, *Discouerie of the Empire of Guiana*; also MSS. attributed to him, in the Sloan Collection.

RAMUSIO, Giovanni Battista. *Raccolta di Navigazione et Viaggi* (1550–63).

RANKING, John. *Historical Researches concerning Perú* (London, 1827).

RAWLINSON, Sir Henry Creswick. *Cuneiform Inscriptions in Central and Western Asia.*

REMESAL, Antonio de. *Historia de las provincias de Chiapa y Guatemala* (Madrid, 1619).

REVISTA TRIMENSAL DO INSTITUTO HISTORICO E GEOGRAPHICO BRAZILEIRO (Various volumes).

RIVÆ AMERICANÆ. *Traditions Américaines sur le Déluge.*

RIVERO, Mariano Eduardo (and VON TSCHUDI, John James). *Antigüedades Peruanas.*

ROBLEDO, Captain Jorge. *M.S. Relación de lo que sucedio al Magnefico señor capitan Jorge Robledo, en el descrubrimiento que hizo de las provincias de Antiochia.* (The time for the publication of this valuable MS., which is in the archives of the Academia Reale de Historia, Madrid, is considerably overdue, unless it is intended that it be left to *mañana!*)

RODRIGUES, J. Barbosa. *Muyrakyta e os Idolos symbolicos* (Rio de Janeiro: 1899).

RODRIGUEZ, Padre Manuel. *El Marañon y Amazonas* (Madrid: 1684) (Rodriguez was a member of the Compania de Iesus, and "procurador general de las provincia de Indias a la corte de Madrid").

ROOSEVELT, ex-President Theodore. *Trails through the Brazilian Wilderness.*

ROYAL IRISH ACADEMY, Proceedings (*art.* Westropp, Vol. 30).

RUDBECK, Prof. Olaf. *Atland eller Manheim* (Latin and Swedish), 1675–98.

SAHAGUN, Fray Bernardino. *Historia General de las Cosas de Nueva España* with Bustamente's Commentary on old Mexican antiquities.

SALCAMAYHU-PACHACUTI, Juan, Santa Cruz Yamqui. *Antiquities of Perú.*

SALLUST, C. S. Crispus. *Historiarum Fragmenta.*

SALVADOR, Fray. *El Dorado cartas* (letter-reports) to the Council of the Indies (*Archivo Gral*, Sevilla).

SARAVIA, Bravo. *Antigüedades del Perú.*

SARMIENTO, P. *Apology* for Padre Feijoo's *Theatre Critique* (on the South American Amazon women).

SAVILLE, Marshall Howard. Various archæological works and monographs, published under the auspices of the Museum of the American Indian, Heye Foundation.

SAYCE, Professor A. H. *Karian Language and Inscriptions* (1885).

SCALLON (the late) General Sir Robert Irvine, K.C.B., K.C.I.E. Letters to the author of this book on Arabo-Sabæan Inscriptions and old Indian antiquities.

SCHNIRDEL, Hulderike. *Travels in The Twentie Yeeres' Space, from 1534–54 in South America.*

SCHOMBURGHK, Sir Robert Herman. *Journals of Travels in Guiana and North Brazil.*

SCHREIBER, R. *Monumentos megalíticos y pictograficos en los altivalles del Provincia de Tucumán* (1928).

SCHUCHERT, Professor. *Geographical Review*, Vol. III, 1917.

SCHWENNHAGEN, Professor Ludovico. *Antiga Historia do Brazil, Imprensa oficial, Theresina*, 1928.

SCYLAX, Caryandenis (*flor.* 550 B.C., commissioned by Darius Hytaspes, King of Persia, to make discoveries in the East). *Periplus* (Amsterdam, 1639).

SENECA, L. Annæus (4? B.C.–A.D. 65). *Medea.*

SENECA, M. Annæus (The Rhetor, father of the above, 61 B.C.–A.D. 30). *Suasoriæ et Controversiæ.*

SHORT, John T. *North Americans of Antiquity* (1880).

SIMON, Frey Pedro. *Las Noticias Historiales de las Conquistas de Tierra firme en las Indias Occidentales* (Cuença, 1625).

SMITH, George (English Orientalist, A.D. 1840–76). The Story of the Akkadian Deluge, from the bricks of the cuneiform library at Nippur-Nineveh.

SMYTH, Lieutenant W., and Mr. F. Lowe. *Journey from Lima to Paraguay* (1835).

SOCIÉTE DES ANTIQUITÉS DU NORD (Kobenhavn). *Journals*, 1839–40.

SOLINUS. First century *Polyhistor.*

SOLON (The Athenian) (639?–559 B.C.). Lost Poem: *Atlantikos*, to which Plato, as a relation, had acccess for the Platonic dialogues *Timæus* and *Critias*. The poem was written somewhere between 570 and 560 B.C.

SOLORZANO-PEREIRA, Joannes de. *De Indiarum Jure* (Matriti (Madrid) 1639).

SOUTHEY, Robert (A.D. 1774–1843). *Commonplace Book; Travels in Brazil*; and *History of Brazil* (1817–22).

ST. JOHN, Molyneux. *Lord Dufferin's Travels through British Columbia, in 1876.*

SPANISH DOCUMENTS *re.* THE AMERICAS. (*See* ARCHIVO GRAL DE INDIAS.)

STEPHENS, J. Lloyd (American-English traveller, A.D. 1805–52). *Travels in Central America*, 1838–39.

STOEPEL, Dr. Karl Theodor. *Südamerikanische prähistorisch Tempel und Gottheiten Ergebnisse eigener ausgrabungen in Süd-Kolombien und Ecuador* (Heidelberg: 1912).

STRABO (Greek Geographer, 63 B.C.–post–A.D. 20). *Geography.*

STRAHLENBERG, Philip Johan. *Description of Northern and Eastern parts of Europe and Asia* (Siberia and Great Tartary) (1738).

SUFFRIDUS, Petrus (Leeuwarden, 1698). *De Frisonorum Antiquitate et Origini.*

SYNCELLUS, Georgius. *Cronographia* (antiquities of Egypt, Chaldæa, Africa, etc.) *Chronographia.*

SYRIANUS (teacher and master of PROCLUS, the Neo-Platonist of fifth century A.D.). Taught that Atlantis had actually existed.

TALMUD. *Yerushalmin and Berakthoth (Hulin).*

TELLO, J. C. *Antiguo Perú, primer epoca* (1929).

TE PITO TE HENUA (or Easter Island). Paymaster Wm. J. Thomson, U.S. Navy (Smithsonian Institution, Washington, D.C., 1891).

THEOPHRASTUS (Greek philosopher, who died *aged* 107, denouncing Nature and the gods for granting longevity to the crow and the stag! Born 395 ? B.C., died 288 ? B.C.). *History of Plants.*

THEOPOMPUS of CHIOS. Greek historian. (*flor.* 354 B.C.). Lost books cited by ÆLIANUS.

THEVET, André. *Les Singularités de la France Antarctique* (Paris, 1558). *Cosmographie Universelle.*

THOMSON, Paymaster W. J., U.S. Navy. (*See* TE PITO TE HENUA.)

TORQUEMADA, Fray Juan (Franciscan monk). *Monarquia Indiana* (edition 1723).

TSCHUDI, Dr. J. J. von. *Der Kechua Sprache.*

UHLE, Professor F. Max. Estudios Esmeraldenas (Quito: 1927).

ULLOA, Alfonso. *Historia de Colombo.*

UPHAGEN, Johann. *Parergon Historica.* (Dantzig: 1782.)

VALLANCEY. (*See* DE VALLANCEY.)

VARRO, M. Terentius (Roman scholar and writer, 116 B.C.–A.D. 27?). *De gente Populi Romani* (lost book cited by St. Augustine).

VELASCO, Fray Juan de. *Historia del reyno de Quito.*

VENEZUELA Documents (British Government: *Guiana Boundary Commission,* MSS. Dept., British Museum).

VERNEAU R. and RIVET, P. *Ethnographie ancienne de l'Ecuador* (Ministère de l'Instruction Publique, Paris, 1912.

VEYTIA. *Historia Antigua de Mexico.*

VIRGIL. (*See* FERGHIL.)

WALLACE, Alfred Russel (English naturalist, A.D. 1823–1913). *Notes of a Botanist on the Andes.*

WALLIS BUDGE, Sir E. *On the Sumerians.*

WHIPPLE, Lieutenant A. W. (U.S.). *Pacific R.R. Reports.*

WIRTH, Herman. *Die Ura Linda Kronik* (Berlin, 1934).

WORSAAE, J. J. A. *Nordens Forhistorie* (Kjöbenhaven, 1881).

XIMINEZ, Fray Francisco (Dominican missioner in Yucatan and Mexico). *Vocabulario del lengua Quiché.*

ZAMORA (*See* DE ZAMORA.)

ZAPATA. (*See* DE LLANO ZAPATA.)

ZARETE, Agustin de (Spanish Historian, A.D. 1492?–1560?). *Historia de la Conquista del Peru.*

ZONARAS, Johannes (Byzantium, twelfth century A.D.). *Annales.*

INDEX

Page numbers marked with an asterisk (*), or asterisks (**), refer to footnotes in the pages numbered. The affix *"Indiós"* denotes Central or South American tribes.

A

Aasland, 98*
Abasas, 389*
Abreu, Senhor Armando, 31
Abureñes (*Indiós*), 212, 215
Abyle, 143
Academy of Science (U.S.S.R.), 285
Accadia or Accadie, 282
Achaquara (*Indiós*), 225, 227
Acuña, Fray Cristobal de, 194, 215, 216
Adam, a black or red man, 409*; corpse of, 425; footprints of, 410*; a giant, 425, 430; King of Atlantis, 409*, 425; Toltecan, 409*
Adam of Bremen, 43
Adela, wife of Apol, 361-3, 367-9, 370, 389
Adenia (*Vide* "World's Deadliest Poison")
Ælianus, 113-15
Ænius Sylvius (Pope Pius II), 148
Æolians, 116, 397
Æpyornis, 274
Aerolites, 56
Aeronautics (Atlantis), 406 (*V.* also "Levitation")
Ague Tree, The, 343
Aguirre, Lopez de, 208, 209
Ahriman (Angra Mainyu), 412*
Ahura Mazda, 411*
Aikeambenanos, or Aikwambenanos, 185, 186, 187
Ainus, 422
Airarat, 402
Airships, 196, 259
Akaba, Gulf of, 424
Akkadians, 116
"Akob", 413
Alamanland, 371, 372
Alarcon, Capitan Fernando, 35
Alaska, 387
Albinism, fallacies of, 87-8
Alci, 387*
Aldega Muga, 368
Aldergamude, 370
Alejandro, Alejandro, 417
Alexander the Great, 366, 373*
Alfinger, Don Ambrosio de, 203-4
Algonquins, myths of, 41, 96
Alibrandus Pontifex, 395
Alitha (fire elemental), 412
Alpera, cave of, 13*, 270*
Alphabets, 34, 35, 139*; ancient N. Amer. tablets, 275

Altienza, Doña Iñez de, 208
Alton (petroglyphs of), 293
Amazons: Old World and the Americas, 24-91, 98*, 128 *et seq.*, 428; South America, 125 *et seq.;* treks of, 126 *et seq.;* 200, 212, 213, 219, 242, 253-4; statue of, 193; in Lake Titicaca, 147, 148, 149-52, 161, 165 *et seq.*, 181, 183, 184-87, 189-92; Central America, 140, 147, 154, 155, 157-60, 179, 179*; in West Indies, 152-54; Californian Amazons, 154-55; in Indian Ocean island, 149; African Amazons, 143, 144, 145; Amazon, or el Azoun, 143; Queen Myrina, 144-46; Amazon mounds, 143; of Dahomey, 145; in Egypt and Arabia, 145; Abyssinian, 148, 148*, 149, 161; in old Europe, 148*; South Sea gynæcocracies, 137; South Sea Amazons, 143; Classical Amazons, Moon cults of, 136; Queen Pentheselea, 136; old Karian kinship of, 138; Ægean Amazons, 138; degenerate male descendants of, 140; the Maza, or lunar cult of, 143; Queen Thalestris, 128; Asian Amazons, 128 *et seq.*, 133-37; Queen Hippolyta, 128, 134, 136; man-slayers (*Oior-pata*), 129; no Navigators, 129, 134-35; Scythian Amazons, 129, 132; racial strata of, 131-32; of Hebudes and the Loire, 132; the Nesides, 132; Caspian region Amazons, 133; Queens Martesia and Lampeto, 134; defeated by Theseus, 135; their weapons and double-axe, 135-36; decline and fall of, in Asia, 135; in modern Malayan hinterland, 137; in old Atlantis, 132; model of a South American Amazon township, 166, 166*, 170-1; unknown animals of, 171; Amazon axes and figurines, 193.
Amazon stones (*V.* "Green Stones")
Amazonas, or Marañon, Rio, 162-63; early Spanish navigation of, 244
Amber, 253
Ameghino, Florentino, 108, 304
Ammizaduga, King, 391
Amulets (U.S.S.R.), 285
Anatolia, 397, 422
Ancasmarca, 48, 49
Andes, age and cataclysms of, 37-41, 115, 258-59, 292, 293
Andiroba, 335
Andrieu, Jules, 378
Andromeda, 371*
Angli, The, 367*

Llanganati Highlands, 307
Lloyd George, Right Hon. David (Earl), 348
Loch Ness Monster, 331
Lockyer, Sir Norman, 384, 385
Lofoten Islands, 328
Lolos, mystery of the, 89
Lopez, General Don José Hilario, 15
Lost City of the Incas, 241 (V. also "Gran Paytiti")
Lost Worlds, 32, 106, 174, 293, 294, 321, 332, 333, 334, 356
Louis XIV, 351
Loup-garou, le (West Indian "liggaroo"), 65
Loys, Dr. de, 300
Lucan (M. Annæus Lucanus), 391*
Lucian, 415
Lucero, Fray Juan Lorenzo, 232, 235, 237, 238
Lucifer (King of Atlantis—Hyperborea), 411
Lull, Dr. R. L., 272
Lumholtz, Carl, 122
Lumkamakia, 370
Lunar Catastrophe, 113 (V. also "Moon")
Lunardi, Monseñor Federico, 15-9
Lund, Dr., 313, 314
Luzern, 430
Lyda, 387
Lynch, Dr. (Colonel) Arthur, 38, 38*

M

Ma, 139; Ama (fish goddess), 102
Macana, The, 252
Macara and Macaras, 12, 150
Macarona, 143
Macatoa, 206
Machimus, 115
Macrobius, 65*
Macusis (Indiós), 195-96
Madoc, Welsh prince, 421*
Madonnas (pagan American), 346*
Madre de Dios, Rio, 232
Maelstrom, 328
Magalhaens de Gandava (or Magalhães), Pero de, 255
Magdalena, Rio, 14, 16, 204
Magdalenian (Palæolithic) pictographs, 274, 288
Magic, 369*
Magy, or Magyars, 369, 369*, 370, 393
Mahatmas (necromancers), 341
Maidens' City, The, 368
Maize, 252-53
Makar, Macara, 139, 246*
Male and Female Islands, The, 149

Malthusianism and Mammoths, 286
Mammoths, 275, 279, 280, 285; meat of, at U.S.S.R. banquets, 285, 287, 288, 385, 393
Mammoth Cave, Kentucky, 288
Mams, The, 268
Manabi, 139*; monster of, 261, 308, 309
Manamavovos (Indiós), 237
Manchineel (mancinella or euphorbia), 335-37
Mandans, deluge cult of, 420-21, 421*
Manco Capac, 222
Manco Ccapac II, Inca, 239
Mandeville, Sir John, de, 266*, 432
Manetho of Sebennyta, 408*
Mandiocusyanas, 175
Maniacos (Indiós), 100
Manoa, Golden, The, 165, 199, 211, 217-19; Lago de, 242
Manoa (N. Perú), 219
Manta (Ecuador), 45, 261
Ma-Nu, 433
Mantis, praying, 355
Manusa y'akeneana, 186 (V. also "Ykami-abas")
Mapichi, Serra de, 217
Mapoyes (Indiós), 226
Maquereau, 139
Maracaibo, 150, 207
Marajó, Isla de, 307
Marañon, Rio, 23, 162-63, 189
Marawonne, 195
Marcellus, 70
Marduk, 415
Margarita, Isla de, 209, 210
Marihuana, or Marijuana, 345
Marine Biological Association, 290
Markham, Sir Clements, 241
Marquette, Père, 274
Marquez, Carlo Cuervo, 110
Marquires (Indiós), 253, 254
Mars, ancient N. Amer. sign of, 270
Marsaten, or Marsata, The, 376, 389, 390
Martinez, Juan, 210, 211, 219
Martyr, Peter (Anghierra), 152-53
Mas d'Azil, 109
Masis, 403, 431
Masks (ritual S. Amer.), 98
Massilia, 372
Mass Migrations of Indians (Brazil), 106, 175
Mastodons (of Mu), 265; of Bochicha, 268; N. Amer. 270, 275, 276, 279; domesticated and milked (?), 280, 280*, 285, 286; comparative dentition of, 286-88, 287, 287*, 288; compared with mammoth 288, 293*, 294, 313, 385
Maté, 334, 335
Matevil, 96
Matriarchates, 114, 137, 141, 261, 309, 362, 368, 387*, 404
Matto Grosso, 24, 27, 31, 37, 301

INDEX

INDEX

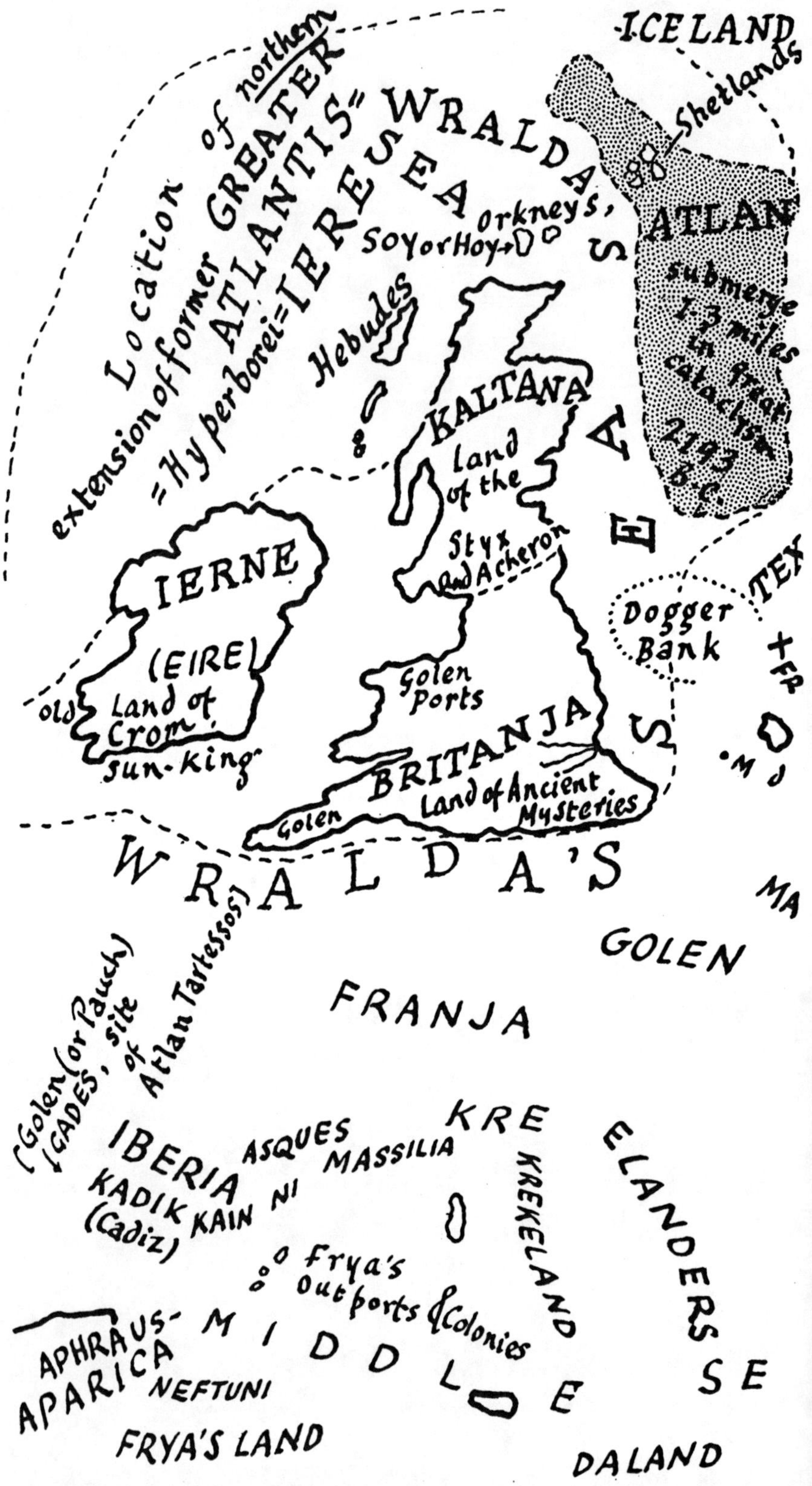

SKENLAND
(SCHOENLAND)
FINNS

Olaf
Rudbeck's
Atlantis

JUTLAND

"0"

BALTIC

Invasion of
MAGY AND
FINNS

ND

Flyland

staria

③

TUSSCHELAND
(TWISKLAND)

raburch
gburch
R
na

SAXONS

① Megalithic
cultures, early
Bronze & later
Stone ages

ITEN

② Hallstatt culture

③ Bell and Beaker
folk, stone and
bronze
ages

Inland Sea until
cataclysm forced
a passage to the
Middle Sea

Thynsburg of Nef-Tunis,
the Frisian

HARAOH'S LAND

COSIMO

COSIMO is a specialty publisher of books and publications that inspire, inform, and engage readers. Our mission is to offer unique books to niche audiences around the world.

COSIMO BOOKS publishes books and publications for innovative authors, nonprofit organizations, and businesses. COSIMO BOOKS specializes in bringing books back into print, publishing new books quickly and effectively, and making these publications available to readers around the world.

COSIMO CLASSICS offers a collection of distinctive titles by the great authors and thinkers throughout the ages. At COSIMO CLASSICS timeless works find new life as affordable books, covering a variety of subjects including: Business, Economics, History, Personal Development, Philosophy, Religion & Spirituality, and much more!

COSIMO REPORTS publishes public reports that affect your world, from global trends to the economy, and from health to geopolitics.

FOR MORE INFORMATION CONTACT US AT
INFO@COSIMOBOOKS.COM

❋ if you are a book lover interested in our current catalog of books

❋ if you represent a bookstore, book club, or anyone else interested in special discounts for bulk purchases

❋ if you are an author who wants to get published

❋ if you represent an organization or business seeking to publish books and other publications for your members, donors, or customers.

**COSIMO BOOKS ARE ALWAYS
AVAILABLE AT ONLINE BOOKSTORES**

**VISIT COSIMOBOOKS.COM
BE INSPIRED, BE INFORMED**

LaVergne, TN USA
14 April 2010
179247LV00003B/19/P